TENNIS

THE NEW YORK TIMES ENCYCLOPEDIA OF SPORTS

THE NEW YORK TIMES
ENCYCLOPEDIA OF SPORTS

VOLUME 6

TENNIS

EDITED BY
GENE BROWN
INTRODUCTION BY
FRANK LITSKY

ARNO PRESS
A NEW YORK TIMES COMPANY
NEW YORK 1979

GROLIER EDUCATIONAL CORPORATION
SHERMAN TURNPIKE, DANBURY, CT. 06816

Library of Congress Cataloging in Publication Data

Main entry under title:

Tennis.

(The New York times encyclopedia of sports; v. 6) Collection of articles reprinted from the New York times.
  Bibliography.
  Includes index.
  SUMMARY: Traces the history of tennis as presented in articles appearing in the "New York Times."
  1. Tennis. [1. Tennis] I. Brown, Gene. II. New York times.
III. Series: New York times encyclopedia of sports; v. 6.
GV565.N48 vol. 6 [GV995] 796s [796.34'2]   79-19940
ISBN 0-405-12632-8

Manufactured in the United States of America   SSH

Appendix © 1979, *The Encyclopedia Americana*.

The editors express special thanks to The Associated Press, United Press International, and Reuters for permission to include a number of dispatches originally distributed by those news services.

The New York Times Encyclopedia of Sports

Founding Editors: Herbert J. Cohen and Richard W. Lawall
Project Editors: Arleen Keylin and Suri Boiangiu
Editorial Assistant: Jonathan Cohen

Photographs on the following pages courtesy of UPI:
X, 9, 13, 67, 80, 88, 91, 99, 123, 136, 152, 155, 161, 168, 178,

CONTENTS

The modern game of tennis, invented a century ago as a country-club diversion, has grown into one of the world's major spectator and participant sports.

For most of its history, it has been an amateur sport, legally and philosophically if not always in actuality. Professional tennis attracted few athletes and often few spectators.

Interest in the game ballooned with the advent, in 1967, of open tennis—tournament competition open to professionals and amateurs alike. Prize money in 1979 totaled $12 million for the 100 Grand Prix tournaments worldwide for men and $5.5 million for the 38 tournaments for women. The world's two most important tournaments—the United States championships in New York City and the all-England championships at Wimbledon—each paid annual prize money exceeding $500,000.

In 1978, the leading money-winner among men was Bjorn Borg of Sweden. His tournament earnings were $691,886, and he made more than $1 million additional from endorsements, appearances, exhibitions and television commercials. The women's earnings leader in 1978 was Martina Navratilova, a Czechslovak expatriate living in the United States. Her tournament earnings for the year were $509,757.

Tennis as a participant sport grew tremendously in the 1970's, and indoor courts were built in all parts of the country. In the late 1970's, Americans were spending $1,250 million annually on racquets and $2,100 million on tennis balls.

Racquets are made of wood, aluminum or alloy, and they are strung under pressure with gut or nylon. The hollow ball is inflated rubber and is covered by felt.

The game is played by two or four people on a rectangular court 78 feet long and 27 feet wide. The court is divided by a net 3 feet high at the center and 3½ feet high at the sidelines. Originally, the court surface was grass, but in time grass courts became fewer because they were difficult and expensive to maintain and became worn after heavy use.

There are relatively few grass courts now outside England, Australia and the United States. Clay courts are prevalent on the European continent and in South America and most of the United States. California, a tennis haven, favors asphalt courts. Early indoor courts were usually made of wood, but newer indoor courts generally have artificial, plastic-like surfaces.

The idea of tennis is to hit the ball over the net into the court of the other player or players. It is the most popular of the net games, which include table tennis, badminton, court tennis, racquets, squash racquets, squash tennis, paddle tennis, paddleball and platform tennis.

The origins of tennis are obscure. A form of the game may have been played in Egypt, Greece or Rome. The name of the sport may come from the Greek, French or Arabic.

Writings from the 13th century show that tennis was played in France as *jeu de paume* (game of the hand). The ball was struck with the hand, years later with a glove, then a paddle and then a racquet. The game was played outdoors and then indoors.

The game was really court tennis (known in England as real tennis). It was played on a rectangular court with long walls, projections and a sloping roof with openings, all of which were in play. French and English kings played this game and built courts. The public liked the sport because it could bet on it, and betting became so prevalent and tumultuous that the sport almost died.

Court tennis eventually standardized the court at 110 feet long and 38 feet 8 inches wide, with concrete walls 30 feet high and a concrete floor. The game was introduced to the United States in the 17th or 18th century and was popular among the rich until the depression of the 1930's. Upkeep of courts became so expensive that most were abandoned, and only a few remain in use.

Modern tennis was invented in 1873 by Maj. Walter L. Wingfield, who introduced it at a lawn party in Wales. From court tennis, it borrowed the scoring system and the concept of ball, bat and net.

Wingfield called the game *Sphairistike*. He said a similar game was played in ancient Greece under that name, but that is probably incorrect. The name, in Greek, means "to play".

The first tennis court was narrower at the net than at the baseline. The net was 5 feet high, as in badminton. The game was played on a lawn and became known as lawn tennis, a designation that went out of style only in the mid 20th century.

The guests at Wingfield's party liked the new game, and one, a British Army officer, took racquets and balls to Bermuda. The next year, Mary Outerbridge, who lived in Staten Island, New York City, visited Bermuda. Shw saw tennis played there, liked it, learned the rules, obtained racquets and balls and took them home.

Her family laid out a tennis court on the edge of the cricket field at the Staten Island Cricket and Baseball club. Soon, the new sport spread to high society in New York, Philadelphia, Boston and Newport, R.I.

Rules were revised in England in 1875 and 1877. The All-England Club at Wimbledon, a London suburb, staged the first English championships in 1877. By 1879, the game had spread to California.

One drawback was the lack of uniform rules. To remedy that, E.H. Outerbridge, Mary's brother, invited Eastern tennis leaders to meet in 1881. The 34 clubs at the meeting formed the United States Lawn Tennis Association, still the governing body of American tennis although now known as the United States Tennis Association.

The USLTA adopted the English rules. It staged the first United States men's championships that year at Newport and the first women's championships in 1887 at the Philadelphia Cricket Club.

The national championships were eventually combined, and for 54 years they were played at the West Side Tennis Club in the Forest Hills section of New York City. In 1978, they were moved permanently to the new $9.5 million National Tennis Center in Flushing Meadow Park several miles from the Forest Hill courts.

The United States championships were played on grass until 1975. That year, many of the grass courts at the West Side Tennis Club were dug up and replaced by Har-Tru, a clay-like surface made from crushed rock. The new courts were slower than grass, which pleased European players.

In 1978, at the National Tennis Center, the championships were first played on courts of rubberized asphalt, a thin, rubberized coating atop cement. These courts were faster than clay but slower than grass or plain cement. Most American players preferred them to slower surfaces.

Tennis received wide international exposure in 1900 when Dwight F. Davis, a Harvard player, donated a cup for international team competition. Britain challenged the United States for the cup, and the Americans, with Davis on the team, won.

The trophy, the Davis Cup, became the most famous in tennis. Eventually, it was opened to competition among all nations, and eliminations are conducted almost year round. The cup has been won almost exclusively by the United States, Britain, France and Australia.

Perhaps the most famous of all tennis players was William Tatum Tilden 2d of Philadelphia. Big Bill Tilden did not win the United States championship until he was 27, but from 1920 to 1930 he won seven United States and three Wimbledon singles titles. He led the United States to eight consecutive Davis Cup titles from 1920 to 1927. He was tall, fast, haughty and dramatic. In 1931, he turned professional, and he was so durable that he played in a professional tournament at age 58.

Another American hero was Don Budge, a tall, angular redhead from Oakland, Calif. In 1937, he defeated Baron Gottfried Von Cramm of Germany in the Wimbledon final. Eighteen days later, they met on the same Wimbledon center court in the fifth and deciding match of the Davis Cup interzone final. Budge won in five sets in the most celebrated match in tennis history.

A year later, Budge became the first lawyer to win the Grand Slam, sweeping the Wimbledon, United States, French and Australian titles in one year. The only other man to achieve a Grand Slam was Rod Laver of Australia, who did it in 1962 as an amateur and 1969 as a professional. The only Grand Slam by a woman was the 1953 sweep by Maureen (Little Mo) Connolly of San Diego, Calif.

At age 14, Connolly became the youngest United States girls' champion (the age limit for that championship is 18). At 16, she became the second youngest women's champion. She had won three United States and three Wimbledon singles titles by the time a horseback riding accident ended her tennis career at 19.

The greatest woman player may have been Suzanne Lenglen of France, who had the grace of a ballerina and the temperament of a prima donna. Between 1919 and 1926, she won six singles, six doubles and three mixed doubles championships at Wimbledon.

In 1926, she played a celebrated match in Cannes, France, against Helen Wills, a 20-year-old Californian who had already won three United States titles. Interest was so great that scalpers sold 5-franc seats for 1,000 francs. Lenglen won. "There are other years," said Will, and there were. When she retired, she had won eight Wimbledon and seven United States singles championships.

The growth of professional football was accelerated when Charles C. (Cash and Carry) Pyle, the promoter, built a tour around Red Grange in 1925. In 1926, Pyle offered Lenglen $50,000 to turn professional and tour the United States playing matches. Lenglen accepted, and she toured with one other female and four male players, all of whom were paid. The tour was so successful that Lenglen received a $25,000 bonus, the five other players were paid $102,000 and Pyle made a profit of $80,000.

Other professional tours wre organized in later years. Bill Tilden was the star of the 1931 tour. Later groups included Don Budge, Jack Kramer, Pancho

Gonzales and Bobby Riggs, and after that such Australians as Rod Laver and Ken Rosewall.

The formula was to have the reigning amateur champion turn professional and play a coast-to-coast series against the winner of the most recent professional tour. Four or six players would play in one city on one night and drive hundreds of miles to play in another city the next night. Typically, one station wagon would carry most of the players and another would be occupied principally by the court carpeting, which would be laid over an arena floor.

Most tours made money, but the life was difficut, tiring and often dreary. And only a few players were involved. Other professionals gave lessons, but their earnings were never large.

Most tournament players remained amateurs. The good ones received travel and expense money from tournament directors, and the very good ones received additional money secretly and illegally.

Tournament directors made such under-the-table payments because several tournaments often sought the same players for the same weeks. So they often paid expense money to the players and then furnished room and board, or they provided additional travel money or extra train or airplane tickets. At the most, the best players made only a few hundred dollars per week.

The amateur concept, which worked when tennis was a rich man's sport, was crumbling. Amateurs officials fought to retain it mainly because they feared they would lose control of the sport to professional promoters.

In 1930, the United States and England proposed that professionals be allowed to play against amateurs, but 20 other nations voted them down. Belgium, one of those 20, said, "Tennis matches would become spectacles analogous to prize-fighting shows."

Pressure built in the 1960's to admit that tennis-playing amateurs were more professional than amateur. The big break came in 1967 when British leaders abolished the distinction between professionals and amateurs and said all players could play in the 1968 Wimbledon championships.

The International Lawn Tennis Federation threatened retaliation. But when the United States supported Britain and said it would leave the ILTF if necessary, the ILTF bowed and voted to accept the fact of open tennis—tournaments open to professionals and amateurs alike.

The ILTF created four classes of players—tournament professionals, teaching professionals, registered amateurs (who could win prize money) and amateurs. Eventually, the distinctions were consolidated into two classes of players—professionals and amateurs—but all players took part in the same tournaments. The only so-called amateurs on an international level were players from Eastern-bloc nations who were required to turn over their prize money to their national federations.

The era of open tennis began in April 1978 at Bournemouth, England. Attendance and gate receipts tripled, and open tournaments created excitement everywhere they were played. The first open Wimbledon was played that year, with Rod Laver winning. The first United States Open, played later that summer, was won by Arthur Ashe, an American amateur (later a professional).

Gradually, all of the world's major competition, including the Davis Cup, became fully open. The only important amateur competition in the United States now is played by colleges, and such modern stars as Jimmy Connors and John McEnroe have left college after a year or two to become full-time tournmanet professionals.

Prize money grew, but much more for men than women. A turning point came in 1970, when Jack Kramer, promoting the Pacific Southwest championships in Los Angeles, offered first prizes of $12,500 for men and $1,500 for women. Further, no woman would receive prize money unless she gained the quarterfinal round. When the women rebelled, the Philip Morris Company put up $5,000 for a rival women's tournament under the sponsorship of its Virginia Slims cigarette. Nine women, including Billie Jean King, signed $1 professional contracts and defied threats of suspension by the United States Lawn Tennis Association.

Virginia Slims soon sponsored an annual women's tour that grew through the years. In 1971, King became the first woman athlete in any sport to earn $100,000 in prize money in one year. And the outspoken Californian was a central figure in a circus-like promotion that gave new standing and public attention to women's tennis.

The provocateur was Bobby Riggs, once the world's best amateur player and then its best professional. He had become a golf and tennis hustler. He would play social tennis wearing an overcoat or carrying an umbrella or holding a dog or two on a leash or allowing chairs to be spotted on his side of the court, anything to stimulate bets.

In 1973, at age 55, he brashly announced that he could beat any female tennis player of any age. A match was made for Mother's Day against Margaret Smith Court of Australia, the world's top-ranked female player. Riggs walked onto the court, handed Smith a dozen roses, trounced her and won $12,500.

A $100,000 winner-take-all match was then arranged against King at the Houston Astrodome. ABC-TV showed the entire match live in prime time. A crowd of 30,492, the largest ever for tennis, watched from seats that cost up to $200 each. King routed Riggs in three straight sets and won the $100,000, but each player earned hundreds of thousands of dollars from ancillary rights and promotions. From then on, women's tennis moved toward equality.

—— Frank Litsky

CHAPTER 1

A SPORT FOR LADIES AND GENTLEMEN

Bill Tilden, generally thought to be the preeminent figure in tennis history, dominated men's tennis in the 1920's.

THE LOVERS OF LAWN-TENNIS.

A convention of delegates representing 35 lawn-tennis clubs, in different parts of the country, met last evening in the Fifth-Avenue Hotel and organized the United States Lawn-Tennis Club. It was the first convention of the kind ever held in this country. A constitution and by-laws were adopted, in which the annual dues were fixed at $5. The following officers were elected for the ensuing year: President—R. S. Oliver, of the Albany Lawn-Tennis Club; Vice-President—Samuel Campbell, of the Orange Lawn-Tennis Club; Secretary and Treas-

urer—Clarence M. Clark, of the Young America Cricket Club, of Philadelphia; Executive Committee—Dr. James Dwight, of the Beacon Park Athletic Club, Boston; George B Schofield Jr., of the Staten Island Cricket and Base-ball Club, and B. Mostyn, of the St. George's Club, Philadelphia. After the election of officers there was considerable discussion as to the kind of ball that should be used in matches and tournaments, and a number of delegates favored the English regulation ball, known as the Ayre's ball. The matter was finally left to the Executive Committee for decision. The rules of the All England Cricket and Lawn-Tennis Club for 1881, which have governed clubs in this country so far during the year, were adopted.

May 22, 1881

EVENTS OF A DAY IN THE FIELD OF SPORT

England Will Send a Team to Play for the Lawn Tennis Trophy.

MATCH MAY BE AT HOBOKEN

Probable Players on Both the English and American Single and Double Teams.

The last English mail brought welcome news for American lawn tennis players, for it contained an official notification to President Dwight of the United States National Lawn Tennis Association of the favorable result of a special meeting of the Council of the English Lawn Tennis Association, held in London, March 7.

As a result of the recent correspondence between President Dwight and Secretary Mewburn, a resolution was adopted by the British authorities officially recognizing the new Davis International Cup, and deciding to issue a challenge for a match to take place over here this season for the new trophy, providing a representative team can be secured to make the trip. A special committee was also appointed to arrange for the English players and settle all details of the match with the American officials.

The "deed of gift" attached to the new emblem requires that any challenge for it must be officially issued by the governing body of the challenging country, and requires that it must be received by May 1 to guarantee its acceptance. The teams are to be made up of two players in singles and one team in doubles on each side, so the visiting delegation may be made up of two, three, or four experts. The names of the challenging team and of the defenders must be declared two weeks before the date set for the first matches.

If no hitch upsets present plans, the Britishers will come over soon after the English championship meeting at Wimbledon, which ends about July 4. The visitors will have ten days or two weeks to rest, and then meet the American cracks, probably at Hoboken, beginning July 31. The Englishmen are expected to stay over for the American championship tournament at Newport, and may also play at Tuxedo after that.

E. H. Miles, Secretary of the Tuxedo Racquet Club, and also the amateur racquet and court tennis champion of England, is making special efforts to get up an international meeting at Tuxedo in September. He will play lawn tennis himself in the American tournaments this Summer, but he is hardly strong enough to be dangerous to the first-class American players.

It is impossible to tell yet who will come over to represent the English Association, but it is known that Dr. Eaves is now in South Africa with the Hospital Corps of the English army, and that Mahony, who was here twice before, is available again. An effort will be made to get the two famous Doherty brothers, for they hold the championship in doubles, while R. F. Doherty holds the single championship also. The younger brother has withdrawn from competition in singles now, because of poor health, but Mahony, E. D. Black, A. W. Gore, or S. H. Smith might be sent as the second man for singles.

All of the crack American players of last season will be available again, and Champion Whitman is practically sure of heading the American team, while Davis and Ward, the double champions, would surely be chosen for this event. For the second-string position in singles,

the choice will probably be between Larned, Davis and Wrenn, if he decides to play again this year.

Lawn tennis prospects for the coming season are already of the brightest, and the certainty of an international match this year makes it sure to be the greatest in the recent annals of the sport.

March 24, 1900

TENNIS CUP STAYS HERE

Englishmen Beaten in Deciding Matches at Longwood.

AMERICAN TEAM'S FAST PLAY

The Foreigners Altogether Were Puzzled by the Style Shown by Davis and Ward.

Special to The New York Times.

BOSTON, Aug. 9.—Dwight F. Davis and Holcombe Ward, American tennis champions in doubles, defeated the English pair, E. D. Black and H. R. Barrett, this evening in the International Tennis Tournament at Longwood in straight sets, 6-4, 6-4, 6-4. This was the third consecutive victory of the American team. Only two more matches remain to be played, though the tournament has already been won by the Americans. The Davis International Challenge Bowl will remain here another year, and the competition for it will again take place in this country next season. Although the match was decided in three sets, it was one of the prettiest and pluckiest tennis contests ever seen in this country. The Englishmen were in the end simply overwhelmed by a style of play with which they were entirely unfamiliar.

No one could have wished for a better exhibition of scientific all-round tennis. Both teams smashed and lobbed frequently, and the volleying at the net was often sensational. At least one lesson should be learned from the Englishmen's visit in regard to the conduct of a match. It is customary in England to play a short match without resting between sets, and never to take more than one or two, however long the struggle. Yesterday the Englishmen remained on the courts during the intervals, while the American players went indoors for a rub-down. But by agreement to-day no rests were to be taken until after the third set, and the rapidity of the matches added greatly to the interest of the contest.

Twice in the match Black and Barrett struck a pace equal to any part of their opponents' game. In the first set they took the first game with ease, and the third after a plucky struggle. The fifth was deuce, and went to the Englishmen, also, making the games 3-2 in their favor. Ward and Davis evened the score in the next by a long deuce game, the last of the match, and finished the set with a brilliant spurt of three straight games, each at fifteen. The second set was easier for the Americans. In the third, with the games 3-1 for Ward and Davis, the visitors put on tremendous speed, and won two out of three hard-fought deuce games, making the score three-all. The next to the last game of the match they won at love. In the course of the match Ward secured 14 earned points, Davis 25, Barret 7, and Black 19. Ward allowed his opponents 35 unearned points, Davis 30, Barrett 35, and Black 31. The summary of the match follows:

FIRST SET.

| Ward and Davis. | 2 | 4 | 3 | 4 | 3 | 10 | 2 | 4 | 4 | 4 | 40-6 |
| Black and Barrett | 4 | 0 | 5 | 0 | 5 | 8 | 4 | 1 | 1 | 1 | 29-4 |

SECOND SET.

| Ward and Davis. | 5 | 6 | 2 | 4 | 0 | 4 | 0 | 4 | 2 | 4 | 31-6 |
| Black and Barrett | 3 | 4 | 4 | 0 | 4 | 2 | 4 | 0 | 4 | 0 | 25-4 |

THIRD SET.

| Ward and Davis. | 4 | 4 | 0 | 4 | 3 | 5 | 5 | 4 | 0 | 4 | 33-6 |
| Black and Barrett | 2 | 2 | 4 | 2 | 5 | 3 | 7 | 2 | 4 | 1 | 32-4 |

Although the Englishmen have lost the cup for this year they are determined to win in the final matches in singles to-morrow. Gore will play Davis, while Black meets Champion Whitman. The sentiment here is that Whitman is almost a sure winner and that Davis has an even chance. Whether the Englishmen win or lose, they will make a great effort to retrieve themselves in the all-comers at Newport next week.

August 10, 1900

DOHERTY'S CHAMPIONSHIP

English Tennis Player Wins Challenge Match from Larned.

Took the Match and the American Title In Straight Sets—Englishman's Brilliant Play.

Special to The New York Times.

NEWPORT, R. I., Aug. 27.—H. L. Doherty, the tennis champion of Great Britain, to-day won the National championship in the singles of this country by defeating William A. Larned, the American holder and defender of the title, in straight sets by the score of 6—0, 6—3, 10—8. This is the first time that the American title and trophy have been won by a foreign player, and in addition to that it crowns the complete series of triumphs that the Britons have scored against the players of this country since their arrival.

To-day, for the first time in the history of lawn tennis, the champions of Great Britain and America met in a challenge match for the American championship.

The weather returned to its good behavior, and the day broke fair and warm. As an attraction the match overshadowed all the preceding ones, and there was a large attendance.

When the rivals appeared and began their preliminary working out, the interest reached a high pitch, and the tension was as severe in the gallery as it was among the players. Larned was at his best physically. His work of preparation had been hard and consistent, and he was just right. H. L. Doherty could not ask to be in better shape, his course of work through the all-comers being just enough to keep him right.

The players were very late in taking to the court, and it was long after 11 o'clock before they, with the linesmen and officials, pushed their way through the crowd and entered the inclosure. The reception accorded the men was warm.

Larned chose the initial service. He was very unsteady and lost the game at love, Doherty only earning 1 point. Then followed one of those sickening exhibitions of the American champion at his worst. He earned several points in the remainder of the set by the most brilliant sort of passing and placing, but he was so overcome by nervousness that he could not get the ball up and over the net. In consequence out of the 30 points that Doherty scored in this set he took 24 of that number on the American's nets and drives out of court. Such a thing as a love set was beyond all the calculations of the gallery, and they tried to cheer Larned on to better endeavor. With the playing of the second set, in which Larned only showed faint improvement, the gloom settled down over the vast gathering and they prepared to await the end which appeared to be inevitable.

Doherty all through the first and second sets had been sending the ball to Larned's back hand and scoring off his weak returns. At the beginning of the third set the resourceful little Englishman was forced to change his tactics. He was in that same marvelously steady stroke that has been the feature of all his contests. When he changed he began to send the ball at a speedy pace along the side lines of the opposing court, but in this he was not as successful as he had previously been in the other, for Larned varied his work from the base line to the net and was so good at passing that after Doherty had taken the lead at 5—3 Larned pulled up to deuce at 5—all by one of his most brilliant streaks of play. This caused the crowd to shout with glee at the prospect of Larned wining a set.

Probably no better tennis was ever played than that in the next two games. Larned emerged from a series of long-distance rallies with more confidence, and in the twelfth game he was superb, for Doherty was again four times within one stroke of taking the match, only to be turned back by the cleverly executed passes of the American.

At this stage the contest was of a highly spectacular nature, and several times the ball was kept in the air for a prolonged period, the point being earned by a pretty place or smash by the men. Fighting valiantly, the two players came up to eight-all on even terms. As the next was Doherty's service, Larned made a brave attempt to break through, but the Briton

made some sensational gets of balls that appeared to be beyond his reach, and took the vantage position at 9—8. Then the American champion wavered and was lost, for Doherty was keen to take advantage of the openings and errors of his opponent, and, hitting the ball with all his force, he soon had Larned in bad positions.

In this last game Larned's errors were the most costly, for he had the Briton almost out of breath, and had he been able to prolong the contest he might have won the set and possibly have saved the cup, for he was coming into his true form very fast.

Since coming to this country the Doherty brothers have won the Davis International Challenge Cup. At Longwood, Nahant, and Southampton, L. I., they also carried off the honors. They successfully defended their holding of the American doubles championship that they won last year from Ward and Davis, and to-day H. L. Doherty gains the title in the singles. This clean sweep of the American tennis courts has demonstrated their superiority over the players of this country.

When seen after the match Doherty said that it was not likely that they would return to this country next season, especially if there was a challenge received from this country for the Davis Cup, which he acknowledged had practically been promised and was assured. As these tournaments and the English National championship is played much earlier than those in this country, it might be possible that they would come over, but as the matter stood now he thought that he and his brother would default their holding of American titles and trophies next season. He said that he had but one regret, and that was that he had been unable to measure his skill against that of Malcolm D. Whitman.

August 28, 1903

ENGLAND LOSES CUP.

Australian Tennis Players Win Davis Trophy by 3 Matches to 2.

LONDON, July 23.—The Davis Cup, the coveted international lawn tennis trophy, has passed into the custody of Australia.

Norman E. Brookes and A. F. Wilding, Australasia, defeated the English defenders of the cup at Wimbledon to-day in three out of four single matches, as against one double and one single match to the credit of A. W. Gore and H. Roper Barrett, who represented the United Kingdom.

There was intense excitement among the spectators this afternoon when Gore, defeating Wilding, made the score two points all, but all hopes of the Englishmen retaining the trophy were quickly dispelled when Brookes and Barrett came together for the last play, the rubber game. The Australian had matters all his own way from the start, and never gave his opponent a look in. Summaries:

A. W. Gore, England, defeated A. F. Wilding, Australia, 3—6, 6—3, 7—5, 6—2.
Norman E. Brookes, Australian, defeated H. Roper Barrett, England, 6—2, 6—0, 6—3.

The victory of the Australian team for the Davis trophy will result in the Colonials taking the cup home unless it is decided to leave it in England to be competed for annually on the Wimbledon courts. If the trophy is taken to Australia another cup will be immediately offered in England and the United States specially invited to compete for it. There is a prospect of the Emperor of Germany offering an international tennis cup. King Edward is desirous of offering a suitable trophy for a world's tennis prize.

The Davis trophy was first competed for in 1900 on the Longwood courts, when M. D. Whitman, Dwight F. Davis, and Holcombe Ward defeated the English trio, A. W. Gore, H. Roper Barrett, and E. D. Black. The second series was held on the courts of the Crescent Athletic Club in 1902, which marked the first appearance of the famous Doherty brothers, who, with Dr. Plim, represented England. Larned replaced Davis on the American team, and the latter again won. The third challenging team was composed of the Doherty brothers, who defeated W. A. Larned and Robert D. Wrenn, and carried the trophy to England, where it remained until this year.

The following year the United States failed to challenge for the cup, but France and Austria sent teams, which were signally defeated by the English holders. The American followers of the game challenged in 1905 and W. A. Larned, Holcombe Ward, Beals C. Wright, and W. J. Clothier were selected to represent this country. The Americans defeated Belgium, France, and Australia on the way to the challenge round, but the Doherty brothers and S. H. Smith scored a straight line of victories.

Last year the American challenging team was composed of Holcombe Ward, Beals C. Wright, Raymond D. Little, and Kreigh Collins. Wright met with an accident, and Collins utterly failed to gain form. Wright and Little defeated the Australians three out of five matches and France defaulted. The Dohertys and Smith again successfully defended the cup, winning every match. This year the American team lost to Australia, while the representatives of the latter country defeated the Englishmen.

July 24, 1907

MISS HOTCHKISS TENNIS CHAMPION

California Girl Captures the Women's National Title at Philadelphia.

SHE ALSO WINS FOUR CUPS

PHILADELPHIA, June 26.—Capturing four cups, all emblematic of the highest honors in the lawn tennis world, Miss Hazel Hotchkiss of Berkeley, Cal., made a clean sweep to-day in the women's National tournament at the Philadelphia Cricket Club. She won the women's National singles championship, defeating in the challenge round Mrs. Barger-Wallace of New York; with Miss Rotch of Boston she won the women's doubles, and in partnership with Wallace F. Johnson of the University of Pennsylvania annexed the mixed doubles title. This is a record equaled not even by Miss May Sutton, the other California tennis wonder, who won only the singles championship. Miss Hotchkiss's victory over Mrs. Barger-Wallach was a hollow one, she allowing last year's champion six points in the first set and one game in two sets.

Miss Green and Miss Moyes, the Canadian champion, gave only two doubles against Miss Hotchkiss and Miss Rotch, while in the mixed doubles the Western girl participated in a still more striking victory, for her formidable opponents, Miss Louise Hammond of New York and Raymond D. Little, were beaten 6—2, 6—0.

In each case the victory was due to superior play, with no flukes to mar it, and the consensus of critical opinion is that Miss Hotchkiss is the greatest woman player ever seen here, with the possible exception of Miss Sutton. With a powerful backhand and forehand drive she is a lightning volleyer, and in overhead play is stronger than Miss Sutton who when the latter mader her only appearance in the East. Summary:

Singles.—Challenge Round—Miss Hazel Hotchkiss, California, (challenger,) beat Mrs. Barger-Wallach, New York, (holder,) 6—0, 6—1.
Women's Doubles.—Final Round—Miss Hotchkiss and Miss Rotch, Boston, beat Miss Green, Philadelphia, and Miss Moyes, Canada, 6—1, 6—1.
Mixed Doubles.—Final Round—Miss Hotchkiss and Wallace F. Johnson, University of Pennsylvania, beat Miss Louise Hammond, New York, and R. D. Little, New York, 6—2, 6—0.

June 27, 1909

CHAMPION LARNED RETAINS HIS TITLE

In Great Challenge Match Defender Downs Clothier in Five Hard Sets.

FIVE CLASSIC VICTORIES

Expensive Experiment Nearly Loses Match for Larned—Cross Court Work and Smashing Effective.

Special to The New York Times.

NEWPORT, R. I., Aug. 27.—William A. Larned to-day won his fifth holding of the American lawn tennis championship. In the challenge match of the twenty-ninth annual National championship tournament he defeated his challenger, William J. Clothier of Philadelphia, 3 sets to 2, by the scores 6—1, 6—2, 5—7, 1—6, 6—1. Yet with the full limit of five sets being played before the largest gallery that has ever assembled about the court of the Casino, there was relatively but few exciting moments in the competition. In the first two sets the champion smothered his challenger. In the third Clothier made a stand which brought out the most exciting tennis of the entire competition and scored the set. The fourth revealed the champion Larned in an experimental mood. He lost this set by faulty back court manoeuvring, and altogether it was slovenly tennis, far removed from championship form on the part of either of the participants.

Needing the fifth set to retain his title, Larned won it out of hand, although Clothier on the whole played up well, and so relieved it of being the walk-over that the fourth set had been.

The day was perfect for the sport when the champion began the service from the easterly court. Backing up his service with a neat attack, he maintained the lead by perfect crossing shots from close range, Clothier only scoring the fourth game. The last two Larned won at love. The second set found the two playing much the same tennis. Clothier was unable to hold his position, as Larned forced him wide of the court by placing to the sides and corners.

Clothier led off in the third set at 4—1 by spirited volleying. He was unsuccessful in checking Larned when the champion opened another wonderful volleying and smashing streak at the net which made it possible for Larned to win four games and take the lead at 5—4. On the tenth game Clothier made his stand. The volleyed rallies were splendid, and while Larned was here within two strokes of winning at 30—15 and 30—all, Clothier by his fine shots through Larned scored the game and the following two, taking the set in a brilliantly played finish. Apparently feeling himself secure, Larned played out the fourth set from his base line. His attempts at passing Clothier as he came up to the net failed, and altogether he lapsed into mediocrity, so that it was Clothier all the way through. Larned's net attack in the fifth and deciding game was superb. Nothing that Clothier could do could stop him.

Strangely enough, while all of the lines were covered there was no judging of foot faults on service, the one feature of the American game which has been adversely commented upon by visiting English players. Beyond this the work of the officials needs no comment.

Larned took the first set, 6—1. He played all around Clothier, who could not get past the champion. Of the bare ten points which Clothier scored during the set he earned but four, while Larned earned fifteen. The Philadelphian won his only game, the fourth, by clever placing. Larned appeared to be at the top of his game, while Clothier was far from his best form. The points:

Larned	5	4	4	1	4	4	4—26—6
Clothier	3	1	1	4	1	0	0—10—1

Clothier tried hard to dislodge Larned at the net in the second set, but could not drive the champion back, so that the challenger only scored four earned points in the set. Larned was very steady and scored seventeen places, while his smashing was unusually brilliant. The points:

Larned	4	4	3	4	2	7	4	4—32—6
Clothier	1	1	5	1	4	5	1	2—20—2

There was considerable surprise when Larned fell off in his game at the opening of the third set, and although he tied the score at the end of the tenth game, Clothier took the next two and the set, 7 to 5. Larned outplayed Clothier in the last two games, but the latter was lucky in getting away with some of his shots. The points:

Clothier	4	4	4	4	4	1	0	0	2	5	4	7—39—7
Larned	2	2	6	0	2	4	4	4	4	3	2	5—38—5

To the surprise of the gallery Larned stuck to his back court game in the fourth set, and inside of ten minutes, almost before it could be realized, Clothier had run out the set, and the match was two games all. The points:

Clothier	4	4	2	4	4	5	4—27—6
Larned	2	2	4	1	1	3	2—15—1

Then the real fight began. Larned came dashing in on the first ball returned in the fifth set, and once more intrenched himself close to the net. The first game quickly went to deuce, but Larned finally won it. Then he let up and allowed Clothier to make it one all. The champion won the remaining games. The points:

Larned	6	0	6	4	4	6	4—30—6
Clothier	4	4	4	2	1	4	2—21—1

With the inauguration of the National tennis championship tournament the first honors went to R. D. Sears. He held the title for seven successive years. In 1888 H. W. Slocum came to the front as a champion and won the title. After having retained it for two years he relinquished it. The honor went to O. S. Campbell in 1890, who held it until 1892. It went to R. D. Wrenn the following year. Wrenn was able to retain it for two years, and it went to F. H. Hovey in 1895.

In the two following years R. D. Wrenn again came into the limelight and won the title. In 1898, 1899, and 1900 Malcom D. Whitman was three times champion, and in the following two years the title went to W. A. Larned, the present titleholder. In 1903, 1904, 1905, and 1906 H. L. Dougherty, the English champion; H. Ward, B. C. Wright, and W. C. Clothier were the respective champions. W. A. Larned won the title again in 1907, and has held it up to the present time.

Boston has developed a number of champions—in fact more so than any other city—and quite a few of them have come from Harvard, Clothier's Alma Mater. Yale, Pennsylvania, and Princeton are also represented in the championship ranks by expert racquet wielders. In 1894 M. F. Goodby, an English player, became the runnerup to R. D. Wrenn.

Last year lawn tennis annals were enriched by the bracketing of the name of William A. Larned with that of Robert D. Wrenn as a four-time winner of the National championship in singles, still leaving the name of R. D. Sears, a sextuple winner, as the only racquet wielder to exceed this record.

Larned is an easy player and noted for the smoothness of his strokes, getting almost impossible returns with ease. Indeed, his ability makes his attack almost pitiless, and when at the top of his game it seems almost like a human being against an irresistible force.

Clothier, like Larned, is tall and possesses a wonderful amount of staying powers. During the season the Quaker City man has made a commendable showing, and, judging from the style of play he had shown during the tournament it was evident that he was a competent opponent to Larned.

The National champions and winners ofof the all-comers tournament follows:

Champion.	Winner All-Comers.
1881—R. D. Sears	R. D. Sears
1882—R. D. Sears	R. D. Sears
1883—R. D. Sears	R. D. Sears
1884—R. D. Sears	H. A. Taylor
1885—R. D. Sears	G. M. Brinley
1886—R. D. Sears	R. L. Beeckman
1887—R. D. Sears	H. W. Slocum, Jr.
1888—H. W. Slocum, Jr.	H. W. Slocum, Jr.
1889—H. W. Slocum, Jr.	Q. A. Shaw, Jr.
1890—O. S. Campbell	O. S. Campbell
1891—O. S. Campbell.	C. Hobart
1892—O. S. Campbell.	F. H. Hovey
1893—R. D. Wrenn	R. D. Wrenn
1894—R. D. Wrenn	M. F. Goodbody
1895—F. H. Hovey	F. H. Hovey
1896—R. D. Wrenn	R. D. Wrenn
1897—R. D. Wrenn	W. V. Eaves
1898—M. D. Whitman	M. D. Whitman
1899—M. D. Whitman	J. P. Paret
1900—M. D. Whitman	W. A. Larned
1901—W. A. Larned	W. A. Larned
1902—W. A. Larned	R. F. Doherty
1903—H. L. Doherty	H. L. Doherty
1904—H. Ward	H. Ward
1905—B. C. Wright	B. C. Wright
1906—W. J. Clothier	W. J. Clothier
1907—W. A. Larned	W. A. Larned
1908—W. A. Larned	B. C. Wright
1909—W. A. Larned	W. J. Clothier

August 28, 1909

TENNIS CHAMPION MUST PLAY THROUGH

Can No Longer Wait Until National Tournament Is Over to Defend His Title.

The National Lawn Tennis Association held its annual meeting at the Waldorf-Astoria yesterday afternoon and evening and made some important rules to govern the championship matches under their jurisdiction. Principal among the changes is that the old style of championship play by which a champion is permitted to await the finish of the National championship series and then engage in a special series with the winner shall be abolished. In the future the champion will be compelled to play through the entire tournament and take the same chances that all other contestants take.

Several attempts to bring about such a change have been made during the past few years, but enough opposition always developed to keep the old rule on the books. The resolution was introduced at yesterday's meeting by Lyle E. Mahan of the West Side Tennis Club, and his argument was based principally on the unfairness of the rule, which handicapped all contestants except the champion himself.

Robert D. Wrenn, prominent in tennis circles for years and the new President of the association, followed Mr. Mahan with a plea for such a change, and said that he had interviewed William A. Larned, the champion, previous to the latter's departure for Australia to engage in the international matches for the Davis Cup, and Larned had said at the time that he was perfectly satisfied with such a ruling if it was the pleasure of the association. This announcement brought into the fold practically all the opponents of the proposed change, and the motion, when put to a vote, was carried by an overwhelming majority. The count showed forty delegates favorable and only four opposed.

The Eastern preliminary double championships were awarded to the Longwood Cricket Club of Boston, Mass. The Southern preliminary singles and doubles went to Atlanta (Ga.) A. C. The Pittsburgh Athletic Association was the successful bidder for the clay court championships of the United States. The National ladies' singles and doubles and the National mixed singles and doubles, championships, were awarded to the Philadelphia Cricket Club. The Merion Cricket Club was successful in obtaining three events—the Pennsylvania State championship, the women's championship of Pennsylvania and the Eastern States, and the intercollegiate championship. The Seventh Regiment in this city again was awarded the indoor championships, including the National men's singles and doubles and the National women's singles and doubles. This award is for 1913, as the indoor championships for 1912 start at the armory to-day. The Western preliminary doubles and the Western doubles championships went to the Osawanna Club, Chicago, Ill.

An attempt to have the preliminary matches in the National tournament curtailed to best two in three instead of best three in five, as at present, met with failure. It was thought that by cutting the preliminaries up to the final sixteen men, it would not extend the tournament so long. The suggestion was downed on the principle that the preliminaries gave the players the best opportunity to show what was in them.

After a considerable discussion the old order of the National ranking, which gave individual standing to competitors in the National events, was declared obsolete, and a new ranking was introduced.

Individuals in the first ten will be rated numerically, and after that the competitors will be ranked in nine classes, according to their standing. Opinion was almost evenly divided on this score, and the contention was only won by the narrow margin of 71 to 68 votes.

A committee of five will be appointed by the President, (two of the committee, at least, being lawyers,) who will draw up a new Constitution and present it at the next meeting, in 1913.

Practically all of the 250 clubs affiliated with the Association were represented in person or by proxy at yesterday's meeting, which was the thirty-first annual gathering. One important change was made in the list of officers, due to the refusal of James Dwight of Boston to be a candidate for re-election to the office of President, which he had held for several years. Vice President Robert D. Wrenn was elected as Mr. Dwight's successor, and Henry W. Slocum of the Crescent A. C. succeeds Mr. Wrenn as Vice President. A. L. Hoskins of Philadelphia was re-elected Secretary and Richard Stevens of Hoboken was re-elected Treasurer. Dr. Sumner Hardy of San Francisco, S. F. Holterhoss of Cincinnati, and L. D. Scott of Atlanta were added to the Executive Committee.

Contrary to expectations there was considerable opposition shown to the selection of Newport for the National championships in singles and doubles. Roland

Hazard, a delegate from the Point Judith Country Club of Naragansett Pier, put in a strong plea for his club for the singles championship. He announced that the club was prepared to offer special prizes and would expect no help from the National Association in conducting the tournament. He also spoke of better facilities and the democracy of the place as strong reasons for a change. On the vote, however, Newport won, 30 to 15. Undaunted by this defeat, Mr. Hazard immediately put in another plea for the Point Judith Club as the place to hold the championship doubles. He again lost, but by a closer vote, 25 to 18. The Crescent A. C. was also a bidder for the championship doubles.

The association took a much needed step to curtail the list of entries in the

National Tournament by electing a committee which must pass on all prospective entrants and eliminate all who appear to have no chance. In past years many persons have entered the National championships who had little merit as tennis players, their reason for entering being simply for the sake of being identified as contenders for the championships. This has resulted in the tournament being long drawn out, while these entrants were being eliminated. The committee which is to consider all applications in the future will accept the entries of all who may have any chance for the title, but those of no merit will not be allowed to compete.

February 10, 1912

TENNIS PLAYERS CAN TAKE MONEY

Proposed Amendment to Limit Expenses Defeated at the National Association Meeting.

The administrative forces of the United States Lawn Tennis Association met with a setback yesterday at the thirty-second annual meeting of the association at the Hotel Martinique, when the delegates failed to pass the amateur rule, which was intended to prohibit players from accepting transportation or money for transportation, or board, lodging or other accommodations from any club, hotel or organization. The discussion was a heated one, and practically every delegate expressed an opinion on the subject, and the Western delegates led the opposition.

The supporters of the proposed amendment, led by H. W. Slocum, and LDyle D. Mahan, earnestly urged the delegates to accept the change as the only means of protecting the amateur status of the players. It was urged that the spirit of professionalism would eventually dominate the association. There was considerable misinterpretation of the rule, but the protracted discussion made it plain to all present The motion, which required a two-thirds vote of a total of 147 votes, was lost by 70 votes to 68.

The meeting, which was presided over by President Robert D. Wrenn of the National Association, barred from playing under the National Association rules and sanction players who are connected with the sale of tennis goods or with a firm manufacturing or selling tennis goods. This means either the elimination of several ranking players or necessitates the latter resigning the positions they now occupy.

What promised to be productive of a heated discussion was satisfactorily adjusted when the question of proxy voting was settled by permitting delegates to vote any number of proxies. This was considered a second victory for the West-

ern delegates, who were opposed to limiting the proxy votes.

The question of changing the constitution so as to give the right to vote as many proxies as one may desire was passed by a vote of 106 to 43. Two-thirds or 100 votes were necessary, and the discussion aroused heated sectional debate. The result was somewhat of a surprise, as it places the annual voting on the old footing

H. W. Slocum, Chairman of the Revision Committee, presented the report of the committee, and explained the work of the framers of the amendments, and emphasized the fact that the sole desire o' the committee was to preserve the best traditions of the sport. In introducing the resolution Mr. Slocum said in part: "I do not consider there have been serious breaches among our amateurs, but as time goes on the finger of suspicion may be pointed at our athletes just as it is done in other branches of sports that need not be mentioned.

"We think we have adopted what we think is to the best interests of the game. Our aim is entirely directed to the poor man as to what standard he shall adopt. It should be in keeping with the standard of other athletes of the world. The regulations are aimed to protect the poor man. We should say to him in plain terms there is a certain standard and there is a line beyond which you shall not go."

E. F. Torrey of the Yahmundaseers Club of Syracuse condemned the rule on the ground that it would work a hardship on players, especially young men who are encouraged in their tennis work, by being invited to be guests of the clubs where the tournaments are held, and to have their expenses paid during the tournament.

In presenting the objection of the California and other Western delegates, Harry Seymour, Chairman of the Tennis Committee of the Pittsburgh Athletic Association, pointed out that the passage of the amendment would mean the elimination of the matches between the North and South of California, and seriously interfere with the present arrangement, which enables the Pacific Coast to send first-class tennis representatives to the East to take part in the big Eastern tournament. He also said California owed its position in the tennis world through the hotel tennis tournaments. He read a letter from a prominent California player in which he stated that if Simon-pure amateurs were wanted it would practically eliminate young college players from the game, but what few players remained after the weeding-out process would be unquestioned amateurs.

February 15, 1913

M'LOUGHLIN LOSES CHALLENGE MATCH

A. F. Wilding's Great Playing Brings Him All-England Tennis Title Again.

By Marconi Transatlantic Wireless Telegraph to The New York Times.

LONDON, July 4.—"Yes, he was too good for me." That is the frank and candid way in which M. E. McLoughlin, the young American champion, explained his defeat by A. F. Wilding in the English lawn tennis championship at Wimbledon to-day, Wilding winning in straight sets of 8—6, 6—3, 10—8. Wilding surprised five out of every six persons who witnessed the match, and McLoughlin just as much as any one else. The American player in a conversation with THE NEW YORK TIMES correspondent after the match made no excuses for his failure.

"Perhaps," he said, "my backhand strokes were not as good as they ought to have been, but I played quite well, and you know why I lost just as well as I do."

Harold H. Hackett, Captain of the American Davis Cup team, whose chief purpose in visiting England is to endeavor to recover the Davis cup, was equally generous in his praise of Wilding. "It was just a case of one man being too good for the other," he said. He did not agree that McLoughlin did not serve as well as usual, though that is the general opinion.

It was a great match, and none in the history of the game ever aroused so much interest. Persons were waiting outside the gates soon after 9 o'clock in the morning, though play was not due to begin until 2:30 o'clock in the afternoon, and the ground filled up just as quickly as spectators could take up their position immediately they were admitted. At noon every seat not engaged was occupied two hours before the match began, and there was not even standing room around the court.

One American visitor offered $100 for two seats for himself and daughter, but he had to go away disappointed. James B. Duke's son and Ernest Lawford paid $10 for two $1 seats and thought themselves in luck to get them. Between 6,000 and 7,000 persons saw the match. and about the same number tried to see it but failed.

HOW WILDING WON.

Experience Aided the Holder to Retain the Tennis Title.

LONDON, England, July 4.—A. F. Wilding played the greatest game of his life to-day when he defeated Maurice E. McLoughlin for the English championship. The match from start to finish was of the heroic order, and while the American made many brilliant recoveries, he proved hardly a match for his older and more experienced opponent. He suffered, too, somewhat from ill luck, and his service was not up to his best, being as a rule much weaker than in the previous matches he had played since his arrival in England. His first service many times resulted in a fault. Wilding, on the other hand, was at the top of his form, and in order to win McLoughlin would have had to play his very best game.

When the two opponents faced each other at the start of the match, the great disparity between them was at once evident. Wilding is a grown, broad-shouldered man while McLoughlin looked more like a boy.

The New Zealander at first was much worried by the American's service, but as the match proceeded he became more accustomed to it, and, standing exactly at the back of the line, returned it with precision.

In the first set McLoughlin established a lead of two games to love by splendid baseline shots, but Wilding, winning his opponent's service, drew level at 2 all. Despite some double faults and a foot fault, McLoughlin gained a lead of 4 to 2 and 5 to 3, but he then netted a number of balls, allowing Wilding, who was driving and placing well, to equalise at 5 all. The New Zealander took the next game on his service after deuce had been called. Then the American retaliated with some magnificent short chops from the net. Some beautiful rallies were witnessed, but Wilding was passing the American frequently, and winning his own service, while he almost as easily took McLoughlin's.

McLoughlin appeared a little tired when the second set was called, while Wilding, who has the reputation of being able to play all day without turn-

ing a hair, was as fresh as ever. He took McLoughlin's service with comfort and after some brisk net play secured a lead of two games to love. The American had some bad luck in the course of a rally at the net in the third game, the ball hitting his body instead of his racket. After winning the third game off Wilding's service McLoughlin lost the fourth, his short rallies finding the net thrice in succession and Wilding serving strongly increased his lead to 4 to 1. The American then won his service, his two service balls entirely beating Wilding, but he could not maintain the spurt, and Wilding, making some fine passing drives, brought his lead to 5 to 2. After being love 30 in the next game McLoughlin made a fine recovery and looked as though he was going to win the set, but again his recovery did not last. The ninth game produced some fine bouts, and Wilding, after being twice within a point of winning, finally accomplished it with a net smash.

The third and last set, which was a hard and long one, opened with a protracted game which McLoughlin won on his service. The playing of both was of the highest order and each winning shot was received with rounds of applause. McLoughlin was now lobbing a lot and feeding his adversary's backhand. By these tactics he succeeded in winning the second game. He should have won the third also on his service after picking up from 15—40, but a double fault and a weak return into the net gave the game to Wilding, who was playing from the back line. The American throughout was very unlucky with his net services, the ball almost invariably falling off the net over the line. His service was not as telling as usual. He was rather overhitting the ball, and he suffered Wilding to gain a lead of four games to two. Even though he was losing the American maintained his imperturbability and showed no trace of nervousness. In the sixth game McLoughlin pulled up from 15 to 40 by two straight services and with two magnificent recoveries from apparently unplayable line drives took the game. He made another marvelous recovery in the eighth game, which he secured after Wilding was leading 40 to 15, making the score four all.

The next few games were full of interest. After a tremendous struggle deuce was called thrice. McLoughlin led by 5 games to 4, but Wilding equalized in his service. The next two games went with the service.

The American was leading at 40 to 15 in the thirteenth game when a double fault, followed by a netted ball, gave it to Wilding. The New Zealander was leading at seven games to six, and expected to win the set on his service, but after a heroic fight the American saved the set for the time being. Winning on his service, he got a lead of 8

to 7, but Wilding, showing no signs of fatigue, drew level, and then won two games in succession and the set.

The doubles championship was won by H. Roper Barrett and C. P. Dixon of Great Britain, the title holders, who beat Friedrich Wilhelm Rahe and Heinrich Kleinschroth of Germany, the challengers, by three sets to one, 6—2, 6—4, 4—6, 6—2.

The ladies' doubles champlonhip was won by Mrs. McNair and Miss D. P. Boothby, who beat Mrs. Sterry and Mrs. Lambert Chambers. The latter couple retired after the second set, owing to Mrs. Sterry straining one of her legs.

July 5, 1913

TENNIS RATING FOR WOMEN.

Committee Appointed to Select Players According to Season's Results.

Secretary George T. Adee of the Ranking Committee of the United States Lawn Tennis Association announced yesterday that for the first time in the history of the organization women players would receive a ranking this year. The announcement is in line with the policy of the National Association, which at its annual meeting last February referred the matter to the Ranking Committee to investigate, with power to act.

A committee of three prominent players, consisting of Mrs. Barger-Wallach of New York, Miss Louise Helen Adee of New York, and Mrs. Thomas C. Bundy, née May Sutton, the national woman champion of San Francisco, was appointed to gather the necessary data and make the selection of ranking players. It is not expected that more than twenty-five will receive official ranking for 1913.

Women's tournaments will not close in the East before Oct. 5, and no blanks will be sent out before that date. The players will be requested to fill in the dates and results of their matches for 1913. These will be passed upon by the Women's Committee, and finally approved by the Ranking Committee, which consists of Miles O. Charlock, Chairman; George T. Adee, Secretary, and Charles M. Bull, Jr.

September 17, 1913

ENGLAND MUST CHANGE HER TENNIS METHOD TO BEAT US

by P.. A. Vaile
Author of "Modern Lawn Tennis," &tc.

THE outstanding difference between English and American lawn tennis is that American lawn tennis is much more English than English lawn tennis.

I must explain this paradox.

The game now played in America, and, I may add, Australasia, is the genuine old English game with the addition of the chief development of modern lawn tennis, the American service. There is of course more volleying than there was in the days of yore, but the strokes and tactics of the game are substantially the same as they were fifteen years ago, with the single exception mentioned.

The game that is now played in England was introduced by the brothers R. F. and H. L. Doherty. It is unnecessary to say how successful they were. Until a few years before the lamented death of R. F. Doherty they had a wonderful series of successes, but their methods were entirely personal, and have resulted in placing England quite in the background of the lawn tennis world.

Recently a writer from America stated in an English sporting paper, as is undoubtedly the fact, that America has a much larger number of rising players than England. He went on to say that there was only one reason for this, namely, that the game is not encouraged at the public schools.

In this he was wrong. No doubt the ill-advised attitude of the English public schools and universities has much to do with the poor form of English lawn tennis players. These hoary, and in many cases benighted, institutions busy themselves greatly with cricket. They do all they can to foster England's national calamity—repression.

America's Gain in Tennis.

The universities give a half-blue for lawn tennis, the game of all games which encourages quick thought, dashing execution, keenness of eye and hand, and they glorify cricket, which as now played resembles nothing so

much as a Chinese play—which goes on forever; while the public schools, whose constant endeavor seems to be to turn out as many "machine-made" boys per annum as possible, absolutely bar lawn tennis.

I need not refer here to the large number of promising young players who are coming on in America, while England has not produced a champion, or a likely one, in ten years. In the same time Australasia, with an eighth of her population and the enormous handicap of distance, has found two—Norman Brookes and Anthony Wilding—who have between them held the singles championship on six occasions since 1907 and now hold the doubles championship.

Apart from the attitude of the authorities mentioned regarding the game so well encouraged in the United States, there is another reason for England's decadence in lawn tennis. This is a reason overlooked by the American critic, although it is of more importance to the game and has a worse effect on its progress in Eng-

land than the educational authorities' attitude. This reason is that the method of production of the strokes used by the present school of English players is utterly unsound, both from a mechanical and a lawn tennis point of view. There is not a single first-class player in the world who uses these strokes, nor is there one who uses them who shows any sign of being first class. I speak now, of course, of international form.

There is a fundamental rule in all athletic sports where a ball and a bat are used which demands that in order to get the best results the forearm and the shaft of the striking implement at the moment of impact shall be in one and the same straight line, and that this straight line being produced shall cross the point of impact. More clearly stated, it demands that the ball, the forearm, and the shaft or handle must be in a straight line.

Even when this rule is apparently violated, as, for instance, in the American service, the principle is maintained, for here, although there is an angle between the racket handle and the forearm looking at the player across the net the racket, the forearm, and the ball are in the same straight line as regards what I may call the plane of force.

The basic principle is well exemplified by the change that has taken place in the construction of the ball striking implements. Originally these were all crooked or curved. The cricket bat, lacrosse, the tennis racket, even the billiard cue, were all originally crooked. The first billiard cue was the ladies' bagatelle cue, which one sees even now occasionally.

The Essential Difference.

All these are now made so that the point of impact is in line with the shaft. The golf club and the real tennis racket still struggle against reason, but the Schenectady putter has done much to show golfers the defective construction of the golf club, and the other day I ordered for a real tennis player who has used a centre-shafted golf club with success six absolutely straight, real tennis rackets, probably the first ever made.

It may seem that I dwell overmuch on this point. It is almost impossible to do so. It strikes at the very foundation of the game. It constitutes the essential difference between English and American lawn tennis. The whole situation may be summed up in the statement that in this matter England is off the true game and that she will never come into her own again until she gets back to it.

In the American method the power goes down the one line; in the English method the power is diffused over a triangle formed by the forearm, a line through the racket handle, and an imaginary line from the elbow to the point of impact. Of course nobody would be silly enough to try to drive nails with a hammer that had a crooked handle but thousands of players of the present English school quite overlook the fact that the same laws govern both acts.

This defect is bad enough on the forehand, but it is infinitely worse on the backhand. The American backhand grip is a fine solid hold, giving the player plenty of power and a direct sweeping blow, one of the finest drives in the game. As a matter of fact I have never seen at Wimbledon a finer drive than T. R. Pell's backhand. It is a winning shot of the best class. Many players, in this stroke, place their thumb up the back of the handle, and a very fine stroke can be got in this manner. For ground strokes I nearly always do so.

The English backhand stroke now used is a particularly weak and effeminate stroke. In it the wrong part of the arm is presented to meet the shock of impact, while the objectionable angle referred to is much in evidence.

In the English forehand stroke there is such a waste of energy that the ladies have found themselves unable to follow the men's lead. They have thus retained the natural hold of the racket on the forehand, but have followed the men's bad example on the backhand. Mrs. Lambert Chambers, the woman champion of England, does not get any power into this stroke. Miss Sutton, (Mrs. Bundy,) however, plays a very fine backhand stroke of the genuine old English school. It would be a fine drive, but she cramps her finish somewhat by not allowing the forearm to turn

naturally, so that the thumb, instead of remaining below the handle as it is half way through the finish, at the end of the stroke, rides above the handle.

If the thumb is allowed to remain below, the arm becomes "locked" on the shoulder. If, however, the natural turn of the forearm is allowed full play, we get a fine natural finish.

There can be no question whatever that the method of production of the strokes of the game in America and the oversea dominions is superior to that of the so-called English school, and so long as it remains so American and Colonial lawn tennis has nothing to fear from the English.

Effects on the Game.

Having shown the different methods of producing the strokes, it will be interesting to consider what effects they have on the game. The American can reverse service and the ordinary reverse overhead service are two of the finest services in the world, but they are absolutely shut out of the game of any player who persists in retaining the English unchanged grip or any approximation thereto. This fact alone should be enough to condemn this hold.

The fact is that in modern lawn tennis, with its demand for a knowledge and mastery of spin of various sorts, a player must have his command in his wrist, or he is not playing the real game. The American has his lawn tennis in his wrist, the English player of today in his arm. That is the essential difference.

The American player makes the ball "talk" more than the English player does. He does all kinds of strange tricks with it. He makes it break and swerve and bound in all kinds of unexpected fashions. He keeps his opponent guessing all the time. He undoubtedly furnishes more amusement for the gallery, and in my opinion, for himself, which, after all, is one of the main points. Moreover, there can be no doubt, as I indicated in "Modern Lawn Tennis," that the whole science of the game is bound up in the knowledge of spin and what one can make the ball do by means of it.

It is, in my opinion, a certainty that if it comes to a battle between the English school and the American, the English school will not have a chance. I look upon the forthcoming Davis Cup tie as likely to mark a new era in the development of the game in England. It will probably show English players the kind of stuff that natural methods can produce, and it will tend to hasten the reintroduction in England of the genuine English game with the addition of the American service, which, taken together, now constitute the whole of modern lawn tennis.

July 26, 1914

MAURICE EVANS McLOUGHLIN
United States
Forest Hills, 1916

MODERN TENNIS IS HARD ON RACQUETS

Pell Not the Only "Smasher"— Bat "Doctors" Busy Keeping Strings in Tune.

T. R. Pell's recent boast that he is the world's champion smasher of tennis racquets, may have been made in the spirit of jest, but his claim to the title is not likely to go long unchallenged. His record of twenty-two racquets put out of commission in a season that is still young is undoubtedly a large number, yet it would be a mistake to suppose that Pell stands alone in his glory.

There are dozens of tournament players right here in New York who could at least run him a close second. Pell is not an exceptionally hard man on a racquet, but rather only one of an increasingly large class of players who find that tennis as it is played nowadays puts a strain on the racquet that cannot long be withstood.

When a man breaks a golf club it is a sign that he is either a beginner or an incurable "dub." In this game the more proficient a player becomes the more considerate he is of his sticks. In tennis the rule works just the other way. The novice and the player who plugs along year after year without getting anywhere hardly know what racquet trouble is. It is the tournament player, the crack, who punishes his bat.

Not that the old racquets were better made—ask any first-class stringer or racquet-maker and he will tell you otherwise. The modern racquet—that is, the racquet used by tournament players—is a much higher class product both as to workmanship and quality of wood and gut than the racquet of earlier days. It has undergone a process of refinement, so the makers say, that has shortened its life while making it a much more effective weapon in the hands of a skillful player—while it does last.

Church Another "Smasher."

Those employed in racquet making and stringing say that the real reason for the high rate of breakage is the development of the modern brand of high-speed tennis and the tendency on the part of tournament players to demand the lightest possible gut, strung to the tension of a violin string. The present-day tournament racquet is not built to last. The makers themselves admit it. So exacting are some of the younger players in the matter of the racquets they use that there is one expert in town now who does little else but keep them supplied with what they want. A shining example of the modern racquet smasher is George M. Church, the Princeton star, who demands only the lightest brand of gut—eighteen-gauge gut, it is called—and who uses a racquet strung almost to the breaking point. This gut is hardly heavier than shoe thread, and when drawn tight it imparts all kinds of "life" to the racquet. But it is not calculated to stand up under the wear and tear of a tournament. In fact, it has been estimated that a racquet such as Church uses begins to weaken after ten games, and is of little service after a few hard sets.

Church, naturally, keeps the racquet "doctor" busy. His record for breakage may not be so high as Pell's, but that may be partly due to luck and the fact that he always has another in reserve when the head of the racquet he happens to be using begins to show signs of "softening."

Slash Strings with Knife.

It is not an uncommon sight to see a player take out his knife and slash the strings of his racquet after a tournament match. The amateur, looking at those strings, might say they were in perfect condition, but that is only because he is not particular. The habit of playing with only the tightest-strung bat seemingly spoils a man for any other kind, and the moment the original spring of the gut is lost the player is no longer satisfied. So he cuts away the strings rather than take chances with a break or even with a slight shift of the strain that might tend to warp the frame.

The comparison of tournament racquet gut to violin strings is no exaggeration. In the case of a racquet such as Church uses it is absolutely necessary to draw the main strings—that is, the long ones in the centre of the head—equally taut. This is done by an expert stringer who has a highly sensitive musical ear. When he tightens one string he actually "tunes" the others up to the same musical key.

Pell is not so exacting in respect to the "tune," but demands a tight-strung racquet with gut slightly heavier than Church seeks. It has been said that Pell's famous backhand stroke has much to do with his heavy toll of racquets, and there is, no doubt, much truth in this. Pell has developed the backhand swing until it has become his most telling stroke, and no less an authority than Maurice McLoughlin has called Pell the greatest backhand player in the world. In making the stroke, Pell's forearm and wrist are held as rigid as iron; thus he puts terrifice strain on the racquet head.

"Cannon Ball" Disastrous.

McLoughlin himself is well up in the front rank of those who inflict heavy punishment on their racquets during a tournament. In his case, as might be expected, it is the service stroke that does the chief damage. When he is delivering the famous cannon ball serve the racquet in the hand of McLoughlin becomes a flail and the whole weight of his body is thrown into the stroke. In the East the Californian has a host of imitators, and, no doubt, some of the racquet makers' business may be attributed to his influence.

More than one veteran player has come to the conclusion that the rate of breakage is much higher than it should be, and there is a growing belief that the tendency to use only the tightest-strung racquets has gone too far. The more conservative followers of the sport contend that the ultra-tight racquet is not essential to a fast game, and in proof of this they point to Norman E. Brookes. In the Davis Cup matches last year the Australasian handled the most stinging shots McLoughlin could deliver and he used an old-fashioned square-headed bat with a ridiculously small handle—a racquet of the sort that most American players have relegated to the clubhouse walls as antique. His was a light racquet and not particularly tight strung. But if it in any way slackened the pace or kept Brookes from putting the full force into his strokes, neither McLoughlin nor any of the thousands who saw him play was able to discover it.

July 25, 1915

M'LOUGHLIN MAY NOT SEEK TENNIS TITLE

Business Likely to Keep Former Champion in West—Plans for All-Comers' Tournament.

While no official announcement has been made, it is believed in lawn tennis circles that the Championship Committee of the United States National Lawn Tennis Association favors an unrestricted entry list for the National All-Comers' Tournament next August at Forest Hills. There is a general feeling that the tournament should be all that its name implies, which means that the biggest entry list in the history of the tournament will be the result.

Last week Robert D. Wrenn, President of the National Association; George T. Adee, and Julian S. Myrick, with George S. Groesbeck, the civil engineer in charge of building the stands for the national championship, visited the Forest Hills courts. The details as to the arrangement of the field for the tournament were minutely discussed and provided for.

President Myrick of the West Side Tennis Club showed the officials of the National Association that the stands for the Davis Cup matches, which flanked the turf on the north and south, were 140 feet in length. In order to accommodate 7,000 spectators with seats on the stands the new plans call for a frontage of over 200 feet on the courts. Ample room will be provided so that spectators may walk about the field, which will be marked out for twenty-five playing courts. Only four or five of these courts will be marked between the stands, and on these courts the most important matches will be staged.

It is probable that the chief attraction of the national championship tournament will be missing this year. Maurice E. McLoughlin, the phenomenal Californian, is not likely to make the trip East this year. McLoughlin has notified the National Association that business affairs are likely to interfere with his competing for the championship. The absence of McLoughlin would mean a comparatively easy victory for R. Norris Williams, 2d, of Philadephia, the title holder. McLoughlin has taken life seriously, and realizes that he must settle down to business, which probably means that the tennis world will be deprived of one of the most brilliant stars that has brought honor to America.

April 25, 1915

JOHNSTON WEARS TENNIS CROWN

Young Californian Beats M. E. McLoughlin in Slashing Four-Set Match.

'COMET' STARTS OFF LIVELY

But ex-Champion Tires Perceptibly as Games Go Against Him at Forest Hills.

CARRY PLAYERS OFF COURT

Exciting Periods in Championship Final When New Champion Is Within Ace of Victory.

William M. Johnston inscribed his name upon the classic national tennis singles championship most impressively yesterday, using a forehand stroke that left no dispute as to his right to the title. The young player, who two seasons ago was hailed as the successor to Maurice E. McLoughlin, made good the prediction by the score of 1—6, 6—0, 7—5, 10—8, while thousands cheered the vanquished McLoughlin and the new holder of the highest honors of the American courts. It was a memorable battle and an inspiring scene at the climax on the field of the West Side Tennis Club, at Forest Hills, L. I., when the two men fighting for a sporting honor, and fighting with all that was in them, almost collapsed at the end and hoisted on the shoulders of their comrades with the cheers of the 7,000 spectators ringing in their ears, were carried from the field.

While the homage paid to Johnston for winning one of the greatest matches of the All Comers' tournament has ever known in its thirty-five years was sincere and true, still on all sides there was regret that McLoughlin, the hero, who overwhelmed Norman E. Brookes and the late Anthony F. Wilding in the great Davis Cup matches last year, should not have the permanent possession of the All Comers' Cup on which his name is twice inscribed.

It was not the same McLoughlin who stood in the court yesterday that overwhelmed the famous Australasians a year ago. Time had taken something from his game and as ever youth must be served; in this instance it fairly leaped to its reward. Except for the first set and the briefest of intervals thereafter Johnston was always the master of his mighty adversary. He knew the game of his opponent and, as in the ancient days when Greek met Greek, it was the dynamic power, resourcefulness, and stroke of Californian against Californian, with no quarter asked for nor given. Two months before the two had played for the Exposition championship at San Francisco, and at that time McLoughlin had carried the match and title after five of the hardest sets which the tournament produced. Then "The Comet" was on his old field of asphalt with the ball bounding high so that he could bring off his overhanders and where such a thing as ground strokes were unknown.

Probably never in all the years of the historic All Comers has a player displayed such phenomenal command of the ball with a forehand stroke. There were many competent judges present yesterday who declared that its equal was not to be found on the courts anywhere, and it is likely that a representative number of players, including R. Norris Williams, 2d, the playing through title holder who lost to it in the semi-final, Karl H. Behr and Harold H. Hackett, would willingly indorse the statement.

It was a stroke that stood the test, for no less than eight times in the fourth set was Johnston within a point of claiming the All Comers as his own when McLoughlin made thrilling stands as of old, and pushed the victory on a little further. When he moved up to the net in the ever-flashing rallies all of the power and certainty of Johnston's forehand came into action. Alert, with the eye of an eagle that saw every move and the flight of the ball as McLoughlin drove it at him with all his might, the younger player whipped the returns into the corners. He was like a cat on his feet, quick and sure, and never a false move. There were times when he nipped the best drives that the Comet sent over, and turned them back for passes. Repeatedly McLoughlin overhanded the ball for what to him seemed a certain ace, so that he relaxed and dropped his racquet to rest, as if the point was finished. Johnston made his recovery, however, and sending the ball back, found McLoughlin off his guard and so scored the point.

The cross volleys into the corners, the spots that had proved so profitable against Williams on the previous day, were the chief bit of manoeuvring that electrified the crowd. As Johnston played it, it was as irresistible as trying to check the march of time. He sent the ball into the left-hand corner of McLoughlin's court like a bolt of chain lightning. In order to play the ball with any success McLoughlin usually danced around it for a forehand shot, which put him wide of the court. Calmly stepping in to meet it, Johnston crossed with ever-increasing pace into the opposite corner. It was run, run, run for McLoughlin if he wanted the ball. He was on the defensive, and it was a position, as in all of his matches, in which he does not scintillate. So relentlessly was the younger player forcing the former champion and veteran that, even when he had glowing opportunities to make the point, McLoughlin put racquet to the ball too soon, and so piled up a total of 42 nets and 38 outs, as compared to 37 nets and 26 outs for his young rival. That was chiefly where the difference stood, for on actual earned points by placement Johnston only had a tally of 53 to 51 for the Comet.

McLoughlin in the first set played up to the net with his old abandon, smothering the returns so easily as to give no hint whatever as to what was to follow. Johnston probably took that first set to steady himself. He had it down to a hair breadth so that he rattled off seven games in a row to win the second set at love and the opening game of the third set. As he vainly tried to check the criss-cross rallies which inevitably trapped him McLoughlin seemed to feel that he was grimly fighting a hopeless fight. Johnston's drives and volleys were slitting the lines; he could not get the ball inside with any regularity, and when he tried to jam on speed he did not come anywhere near the court. There was not the same bite and the devastating pace to McLoughlin's service either. Johnston always handled the ball easily, so that only three service aces went down to the credit of "The Comet."

Leading at 5—4 on games in the fourth set, Johnston was three times within a stroke of the match; only to have the indomitable courage of McLoughlin flash to the fore as he smashed Johnston out of position and carried the games to 5—all. Leading at 7—6 on games, the same thing was repeated, while the crowd applauded as McLoughlin turned loose the whirlwind power of his volleys and Johnston worked miracles in the way of recoveries. It was repeated with variations until under the strain McLoughlin gave way. He had bellows to mend and failed to control his drives and short shots with anything like the certainty of Johnston, who made a sensational brace at 8—all. It was the spurt that saved the younger player as he forced the volleys to win the American title with a slashing drive straight down McLoughlin's forehand, the ball paralleling the line.

September 8, 1915

Molla Bjurstedt Mallory, became a major tennis player during World War I and remained dominant through the mid-1920's.

ANALYSIS OF THE PLAY OF MISS MOLLA BJURSTEDT, WOMEN'S NATIONAL TENNIS CHAMPION

Studies of Present American Champions

MISS BJURSTEDT'S GAME BASED ON SPEEDY DRIVE

Norway's Lawn Tennis Meteor, Who Holds Three American Titles, Also Places Wonderfully, But Serves and Kills Poorly.

In the world of lawn tennis, Miss Molla Bjurstedt has accomplished that for which others have often striven but which none has ever before attained.

She occupies a unique and envied place in the sphere of her athletic activity. Having spent less than a year and a half in this country, she is the holder of three women's national championships, a record that did not fall to the lot of even the redoubtable Mrs. May Sutton Bundy when she was at the height of her career. And more, this girl of Norway is the only foreigner to be chosen for the premier position by the ranking committee.

The last tennis year, aside from the national competitions, offered a ripe harvest of trophies to this new recruit, whose advent into the American tennis field has proved as much of a sensation as that of the native sons and daughters of California. "Success" appears to have been the first English word she

learned. She is the metropolitan champion, she won the Crescent Athletic Club invitation tournament, was first in the Pelham invitation, won the Middle States tournament, the Nyack tournament, the Tri-State, the Ohio State, and the Longwood, and this activity of lesser degree was crowned by her victories in the national events, the women's invitation at Forest Hills, the indoor at the Seventh Regiment, and the clay court at Pittsburgh. It is a record for the annals of tennis that will probably be unsurpassed for many years.

Was Not Preceded by Fame.

Miss Bjurstedt came to this country unheralded—almost unknown. In December, 1914, a short, sturdy girl stepped from a transatlantic liner to visit New York, and passed comparatively unknown into the confines of the big city. There was no applause for her then; she was just one of the

(PHOTO BY EDWIN LEVICK)

PHOTO © A.P.A.

(PHOTOS BY PAUL THOMPSON)

MRS. MOLLA BJURSTEDT MALLORY
United States
Gipsey Club (England), 1923

many—but in less than three months her name was known wherever tennis was played.

Highly interested in tennis in her own Norway, she naturally inclined to that pastime when she arrived here. Some of those with whom she became acquainted told her that there was an opportunity for her to enter in the women's national indoor championship, which was to be played at the Seventh Regiment Armory. She was probably the only one to have any faith in her chances of ultimate success in the event, and even her enthusiasm was undoubtedly dimmed by subsequent happenings. The American women, when practice play began for the tournament, did not take seriously this foreigner who had entered. The good players could not see the merit of her game. The result was that Miss Bjurstedt had to get her practice as best she might, playing against the lesser lights of the women's tennis world.

After her defeat of Mrs. William Lesher in straight sets. 6—1, 6—3, there was a change. Then the many as well as the few were ready to concede that the young lady, who came here breaking with her the title of champion of Norway, was really something more than an average player, and that it might have required real merit to win the honors in her home country. There began to be talk that Miss Marie Wagner, the then champion, who was in the lower half of the draw, might be called upon to face this Norse maiden in the finals.

As Miss Bjurstedt went through succeeding rounds with unvarying success, belief became certainty, and Miss Wagner and Miss Bjurstedt were the finalists for the national indoor championship. The result of that match was a triumph for Miss Bjurstedt, and it detracts from her honors no whit to say that 'Miss Wagner did not measure up to her accustomed playing ability. The champion of Norway won at 6—4, 6—4 by clearly outplacing her rival. This success started her on a path of wonderful accomplishment.

A Player, Not a Theorist.

If one were to ask Miss Bjurstedt how she plays tennis she would probably answer that it were better to seek the information from some one who had seen her play, rather than from herself. She is not a theorist on tennis, only a practical demonstrator of how to play the game so effectually that it is compara-

tively easy to win championships. She doesn't know how she does it, she just plays and plays because she likes the game. Liking the game has been a dominant factor in her success.

Not by any flight of imagination could one believe that Miss Bjurstedt was a form player. Radically she is not. It's a remarkable thing that this champion displays fault after fault, some of them glaring, and yet she is the champion. Those who make form their hobby and playing a side issue, could demonstrate at great length that Miss Bjurstedt should not be a champion. They could tell you that in many respects she is a weak player and substantiate the argument. There is only one solution, and this is that the Norse girl does so wonderfully well that which she does well at all that her strong points far outweigh the weak ones. She knows her own deficiencies in the game and is always playing to counteract their effect.

There is one outstanding feature of her play that is evident to even the untrained eye. That is her powerful forehand drive, and on this her whole game is based. It is not the usual stroke of the woman in tennis. It is the stroke rather of the man, the man from California, or the stroke that May Sutton Bundy used so effectually.

Molla Bjurstedt has mastered the stroke and she has become an adept, not only in making the drive, but in making it go to just the particular point that she wishes. She can play it to within an inch of the baseline and nick the corners as well as if the tennis ball followed a groove. Having played for twelve years on the open and covered courts of Norway, the champion has had ample opportunity to develop this drive to perfection, and it was this feature of her play that carried her through to the indoor championship of this country. She had no other asset of importance.

Has Now a Strong Backhand.

Realizing her inadequacies, she determined to develop her backhand, and this she has succeeded in doing until it is one of her valued strokes. After seeing her forehand drive there are those who call her backhand weak, but it is weak only by comparison. There is not the power that is developed with the forehand, but the stroke measures up to a high degree of excellence, better than that of almost any of the other players she will have to meet in

any of the championship events this year.

One feature of Miss Bjurstedt's play that makes her formidable is a natural agility. She can cover the court with the freedom and ease of a man. She seems to be everywhere at once and far outclasses the other women players in this particular. If there is something of the grace of the finished tennis player lacking, Miss Bjurstedt does not mind. Her one object is to get the ball back over the net and it is seldom that she loses on long rallies. To her opponents it seems that the ball is eternally popping back at them until at last they are passed or forced into an error.

Those who watched R. Lindley Murray in the recent indoor tournament at the Seventh Regiment were impressed with the manner in which he went after everything never conceding that he had been passed until the ball had actually passed out of play. It is characteristic of the California type of tennis and it must also be a characteristic of Norwegian tennis, for Miss Bjurstedt plays with the same degree of energy. Most women tennis players are prone to be somewhat lackadaisical, conceding the point without too much effort, if it looks to be out of range. But not so with the Norweigian. She tries for everything and many a point that would be scored against a less ambitious player is saved by her.

Probably one reason for this difference is the fact that Miss Bjurstedt has wonderful endurance. Apparently she is tireless in playing the game and she does not have to conserve her strength as some others have to do if they are to meet with any success. In any case endurance turns out to be a big asset in favor of the Norse girl. No one has ever seen her thoroughly exhausted after playing a hard match. Fatigue is one English word to which she has not been introduced.

Service Merely Puts Ball in Play.

After having recounted her good points, it may well be asked what are her weak points. First among them must be considered service. In this line Miss Bjurstedt is distinctly feminine. She has no service worth speaking of under that name. Service to her, instead of meaning a twist or a hard fast ball, is simply a method of beginning the play. The ball is almost lobbed over the net. There is little propelling force behind the racquet. Instead of the swift stroke far

above the head on the descending ball, Miss Bjurstedt almost pushes the ball away from her, rather than striking at it. It seems strange that a woman with such a terrific drive should be so weak in this point of the game. In playing the drive she does it as the Californians do, taking the ball as it rises instead of as it descends after the bound. The racquet for this stroke is never more than shoulder high, and seldom that.

But for the serve there must be a shoulder stroke and Miss Bjurstedt cannot swing the racquet with that motion. Hence she can't serve. A strong forearm is handled by a shoulder weakness, and her entire overhead game suffers. It may be for this reason that Miss Bjurstedt plays a deep court game, seldom making the run for the net to kill. She can't kill any more than she can serve. What she does do in the case of a short lob is to place it almost by laying her racquet against the ball, never driving down on it. And this is many times a successful mode of attack when she is at the net.

Miss Bjurstedt is not the best tennis strategist among women players, perhaps not quite so good as May Sutton Bundy, the only player of similar force with whom she may fairly be compared. However, strategy is a part of her game; she relies on outguessing her opponent and often does it successfully.

If one were to ask Miss Bjurstedt on what particular features of her game she most depends, she would probably say speed first—and the second point would be placement. Perfect in both of these elements, they make her the strongest player of the game among the women, with the possible exception of Mrs. Bundy, many times champion. These two met during this Winter in three matches played in California and Mrs. Bundy was strong enough to win two of them, while Miss Bjurstedt took the other. All were hard fought, closely contested events, and in a measure not conclusive as to the relative merit of the two. Mrs. Bundy, it is believed, will come East this Summer, and in that case the question of superiority will undoubtedly be settled conclusively.

It is generally true that natural ability is attributed to every champion, no matter what may be the line of athletic endeavor. Sometimes it is actually the case, and with reference to Miss Bjurstedt there seems to be little doubt. She has a natural aptitude for the game, believing in it not alone as a pastime, but as a health-giving exercise. She started playing in her native city of Christiania in 1903 as a member of the Christiania Lawn Tennis Club. At the start of her career she took a few lessons from a professional, thus getting the fundamentals of the game. A year later she played in her first tournament, and won. Every opportunity for play found her on a tennis court, and she determined that, as she liked the sport, she would apply herself to becoming a good player. From 1903 to 1915 she played regularly and won constantly. For ten years she was the champion of Norway. Then came the lure of greater conquest, and she visited the United States, with the success that has been recounted.

For tennis in her own country she has not a very high regard. There are few good players, according to her estimate; in fact, it is said that she could defeat most of the men. There was, however, one contestant in Norway who could give her a hard battle, and this was her younger sister, Valborg Bjurstedt. The two played together a great deal, and the younger girl displayed almost as high a degree of skill as Miss Molla Bjurstedt.

Within a few weeks the women's national indoor championship will be contested at the Seventh Regiment Armory, and Miss Bjurstedt will endeavor to claim anew the title which was the first which she won in this country. She will probably play in the other national events, but is not certain that her tournament competition will be as general as it was last season.

February 27, 1916

TILDEN NEW TITLEHOLDER.

Garland Defeated in Final of Clay Court Tourney.

CHICAGO, July 6.—William P. Tilden of Philadelphia defeated Charles S. Garland of Pittsburgh for the national clay court singles tennis championship here today, 6—4, 6—4, 4—6, 6—2.

In the men's doubles, Walter Hayes and Ralph Burdick of Chicago won in the final from Harold Garland, Pittsburgh, and Samuel Hardy, Chicago, 6—4, 6—2, 7—9, 6—2.

Miss Carrie Neely, Chicago, defeated Mrs. Adelaide Yeager, Los Angeles, in the final of the women's singles at 6—4, 6—2.

In the women's doubles Miss "Bobbie" Esch of Cleveland and Miss Dorothy Field of Chicago won in the final from Mrs. Yeager and Miss Neely, 6—4, 4—6, 6—4.

Tilden, in winning the championship, scored 131 points, while his opponent scored 129. The victor owed his title to his ability to vary his shots, according to the opponents he faced. In today's play, Tilden was not much bothered by a wrenched ankle, which came near costing him the semi-final round.

July 7, 1918

GREAT ADVANCE BY WOMEN AT THE NETS

Play of the Feminine Racquet Wielder Shows Improvement in Mixed Doubles.

The advance of women's tennis in America was strikingly illustrated by the high quality of play in last week's national tournament in Philadelphia, but the most significant strides were unquestionably revealed in the mixed doubles event. It has long been claimed that Americans cannot play good mixed doubles, one reason given being that the girls are not able to stand the pace of the American volleying game. In England a far higher standard has prevailed in mixed competition for some years.

There are two kinds of mixed doubles; the informal, week-end house-party type, and the stern, honest-to-goodness tournament play. In the former the men either hit consistently at one another, or pat easy ones to the girls, who shriek ecstatically whenever they make what is considered a good return. The latter, however, is relentless and purely business-like. Since it is one of the cardinal rules of doubles to play so far as possible at the weaker member of the opposing team, it is only natural that the girl should bear the brunt of the defensive work in any high-class mixed match. And since no chain is stronger than its weakest link, the power of a team usually depends upon the ability of its feminine member.

It is wrong to assume that a first-class male tennis player can score at will by simply slamming the ball at a girl. That may have been true years ago, but it by no means applies to such players as Mrs. George Wightman, Miss Eleanor Goss, Miss Marion Zinderstein, Miss Molla Bjurstedt, or Mrs. S. F. Weaver. These women ask no favors when they enter a mixed doubles tournament. They stand up close to the net and volley the hardest drives, and even when they are forced out of position in deep court they are quite capable of responding with deep lobs that have practically an offensive value. Moreover, they do not approve of poaching by their men partners. Certain shots are necessarily taken by the better volleyer, or the surer back-hand hitter, even on borrowed territory, and this applies to men's doubles as well as mixed. The deliberate sacrifice of position is bad tennis tactics at any time, and rightly resented by a partner of any ability whatever.

A player of the type of William T. Tilden is a poacher by instinct, and he flashes so many startling shots at crucial moments that his ranging propensities are readily forgiven. He has made a practice of playing men's doubles with very youthful partners, whom he can coach and command whenever necessary, and the system has proved remarkably successful. But it is astonishing how many mixed teams have proved winning combinations with practically a balance of power, good teamwork, mutual understanding, and an intelligent grasp of court tactics. Such a team is that of Mr. and Mrs. George W. Wightman, where there is no real weak spot, and where the woman knows as much tennis as almost any man in the game. Another well-balanced mixed team consists of Mrs. S. Fullerton Weaver and William Alex Campbell of the West Side Club, and it was unfortunate that this strong combination, winners of both the Pelham and the Ardsley invitation tournaments this season, could not take part in the national event.

When fully a dozen pairs of top-notch players appear as mixed doubles contenders, including such stars as Tilden, Vincent Richards, Craig Biddle, Wallace Johnson, and Irving Wright, as was the case last week at the Philadelphia Cricket Club, it is a sure sign that what was once a social pastime has developed into a real sport and that the experts of the racquet will henceforth look upon mixed doubles as something not merely to be politely tolerated, but as worthy of their best and most serious athletic efforts.

June 22, 1919

MLLE. LENGLEN VICTOR.

Wins Women's Tennis Singles Championship at Wimbledon.

WIMBLEDON, July 5, (by Associated Press.)—Suzanne Lenglen of France won the women's tennis singles international championship here today, by defeating Mrs. Lambert Chambers of England, 10—8, 4—6, 9—7.

Suzanne Lenglen, described as the "Little Lawn Tennis Wizard," is 20 years old, and came into the front rank of tennis players five years ago, when she won the world's hard court championship for women, defeating Mme. Golding. She also played as a partner with the famous Australian champion, A. F. Wilding, who was killed in action at the Dardanelles in 1915. For one so young she is said to use remarkable generalship, playing with a dash comparable to that of a masculine expert.

Mlle. Lenglen, whose approaching marriage adds a touch of romance to her present victory, developed her skill in the South of France. Small of stature, she is nimble and lithe, and frequently recovers a seemingly lost shot.

July 6, 1919

FOR KEEN UMPIRING IN TENNIS BATTLES

National Association of Referees Will Take Steps to Insure Care in Decisions.

THANKLESS PART TO PLAY

Importance of Matter, However, Is Felt by Authorities, and Clear Code Is Certain.

The National Umpires' Association has now been in existence for several years as an adjunct to the United States National Lawn Tennis Association, with Edward C. Conlin, most famous of tennis umpires, as Chairman. Starting as little more than a sub-committee, this important branch of the executive force has developed into an organization of real significance, including representatives of every club having membership in the U. S. N. L. T. A. With the interruptions of war no longer affecting tennis schedules, and with a majority of the leading tennis players of America already back in civilian life, the National Umpires' Association will this season have its first real opportunity to prove its value to the game by raising the standards of officiating in tournament play.

It is a recognized fact that no one likes to umpire a tennis match. It is a thankless job at best, with disgusted looks and inaudible remarks as its most likely reward. An umpire is rarely if ever infallible, and the chances are that the more conscientiously he tries to do his duty the more mistakes he will make, his popularity with the players entrusted to his care decreasing accordingly. Everybody is willing to criticise a player or even give a decision from the side lines, but ask him to sit up on the high chair and proclaim his opinions to all the world and see how quickly his judicial enthusiasm will vanish.

Foot-Fault a Crucial Point.

Particularly in such delicate matters as foot-faulting, illegal service, and the like is it difficult to get an impartial and courageous decision, even though the gallery may be exclaiming in unison over obvious infractions of the rules. How often has a tournament chairman tried to pick a foot-fault judge from an outspokenly critical crowd, only to find himself suddenly confronted by an excess of shyness and an incredible modesty as to personal qualifications. Aside from the unpleasantness of umpiring a match, it deprives the victim of the watching the play with an appreciative eye for even the rallies on his own court are wasted in the anxiety over close decision and the necessity of keeping an accurate score, a far more difficult proceeding than is generally realized.

The result of all these drawbacks is that the ordinary tournament umpiring is largely done by those whose chief qualification for the responsible position is good nature. Thus a player may easily go through the better part of a whole season under the eyes of lax and incompetent officials, only to have his attention called at a crucial point in an important match to a technical error which should have been corrected long before. The effect on his game can easily be imagined.

Miss Bjurstedt in Chair.

There are a few men in tennis who really seem to enjoy umpiring and who consequently do it exceedingly well. And there are others who are willing to sacrifice their time and convenience in a good cause. In such a spirit Miss Molla Bjurstedt recently umpired some of the matches in the girls' junior Metropolitan tournament, and how those youngsters appreciated having the national champion in the chair, even though the presence of the celebrity probably reduced the efficiency of the play of some of them by about thirty points to the game!

Tennis umpires in general are too much inclined to consider the opinions, real or fancied, of the players under their care. If a service is returned, for instance, they often let it go as good, although the receiver may have hit the ball merely for self-protection, being uncertain what the umpire might call it. The players themselves are quite undecided as to the truth of almost any really close decision, and it is only human nature to let the wish father the thought. Some altruistic sportsmen, such as Lindley Murray and Ichiya Kumagae, make a practice of calling all the close ones in their opponents favor, and these men need good umpiring to protect them against their own unselfishness.

Tournament play has reached a stage in America where the utmost care must be taken to preserve the absolute fairness of the game, with a complete absence of discrimination and an insistence upon the letter as well as the spirit of the rules. it is the purpose of the National Umpires' Association to uphold this standard as long as the national institution of lawn tennis continues to flourish.

June 1, 1919

WHY THE 'LOVE' IN TENNIS COUNTING?

Players Reviving Old Campaign Against Use of an Absurd Bit of Terminology.

Tennis players are beginning to revive an old campaign against the use of the word "love" to indicate "nothing" in the scoring system. They argue that this absurd bit of terminology has been the chief reason for the charge of effeminacy which for years has been held against tennis, and they are probably right. No excuse has ever been given for the utterly meaningless tennis terms except that they are as old as the game itself, which is considerable age, as athletic ages go.

Why should there be a tradition against the use of such simple and unmistakable expressions as "nothing," "nought" or "zero"? Why should games be scored fifteen points at a time up to thirty, then ten at a time up to fifty, assuming that the half-century is actually the limit implied by the count? Why should forty apiece be called "deuce"? (A fair question was asked at the New York State Tournament, naturally by a fair questioner, to this effect: "When they call 'deuce,' does it mean they ought to have won the point?")

There are answers to all of these queries and along with the present agitation in favor of "he-man tennis," a commendable spirit of curiosity and scholarly research is growing. The inherent manliness of what has now become the world's most popular game requires no special pleading. Those who find it a wishy-washy, namby-pamby affair are simply not playing tennis, and probably have never seen it played correctly. L. C. Wister, the old Princeton football star, who made the all-American team and later developed into a first-class tennis player, has gone on record as saying that a hard five-set match of singles takes far more out of him than the toughest football game he ever played in, and athletes in other "rough" lines have borne testimony to the same effect.

The Origin of "Love."

But what of the history of the tennis terms themselves? The toughest of the lot is the much derided "love" itself. It has always been used for the chubby, innocent cipher, and no one has ever been able to explain its origin. One possible and perhaps the best solution is offered by a foot-note in Singer's rare book on "Playing Cards," which states that there is an old Scotch word, "luff," meaning "nothing." Another word of similar sound and the same intention is said to be of Far Eastern

Suzanne Lenglen ruled center court at Wimbledon in the early 1920's. She won the title six times.

Helen Wills Moody first won the U.S. title in 1923 at the age of 17. Among her accomplishments were three straight U.S. titles and four consecutive victories at Wimbledon.

origin, and, as an old form of tennis unquestionably flourished in the Orient, this word may also have been the parent of "love."

As for "deuce," it is merely the equivalent of the French "deux," meaning that two points have to be won in succession to make the game. In an old scoring system, in which 45 followed 30, it was customary to call "a una" when 45 was reached, indicating one point more for game. But if this score were tied, the call would change to "a due," for in every game of racquets, from time immemorial it has been decreed that a tie within one point of game meant the necessity of winning two points in succession.

"Racquet's" Several Sources.

The important word "racquet' has been traced to various sources, the best etymology deriving it from the Dutch and Low German "racken," "to stretch," referring to the stretching of the strings, and appearing also in the "rack" upon which victims were stretched for torture. But there are two old Romance words, "rachette" and "rasquetta," meaning "the palm of the hand," and these may easily have been ancestors of "racquet." For tennis was ... ally played like hand-ball, the earliest strings being stretched between ... fingers, before progressing to a frame and handle of their own.

"Set" is easily enough explained as a group or collection of games, but with possible reference to the French "sept." as there were originally seven games in a set. "Vantage" is, of course, short for "advantage," with its old Italian and French parallels, "vantaggio" and "avauntage." "Volley"

comes directly from " a la volée," i.e., " on the fly."

Greek and Latin Equivalents.

The name "tennis" itself has many possible origins. The Greeks had a game known as "phennis," of which the Latin equivalent was "tenludium," or "the sport of tennis." Both were played by knocking a ball back and forth, and were probably precursors of the mediaeval French game. The Province of Tennois in France, where Paume, or handball, was exceedingly popular, may have given the modern tennis its name, although this may be a mere coincidence. There are those, also, who argue a derivation from "tenez," in the sense of "get ready," but this also seems far fetched.

Whatever the details of its history, tennis is surely one of the most ancient of all games, and it now seems destined to hold the affections of the world for all time. Chaucer and Shakespeare both referred to it, and France recorded the deeds of its famous players even earlier. Queen Elizabeth enjoyed watching her courtiers at play, but later the game fell into some disrepute because of the "gambling and cheating" attached to it. The real start of the modern game is attributed to a certain Major Wingfield, who in 1874 revived it in England under the weighty name of "Sphairistike," which was quickly abbreviated by its followers to "sticky." In 1875 the laws of lawn tennis were framed at Wimbledon, and now we have the Davis cup and Ichiya Kumagae, which is about enough statistics for those of us who are still struggling with "cases and decisions," "follow through" and "keep your eye on the ball."

July 27, 1919

TILDEN WINS TENNIS TITLE OF BRITAIN

Defeats Patterson in Challenge Round of Wimbledon Singles, 2—6, 6—3, 6—2, 6—4.

A VICTORY WELL EARNED

American's Game Called Soundest and Brainiest Ever Seen on English Courts.

U. S. TAKES DOUBLES, TOO

Garland and Williams Win Championship Match from Kingscote and Parke, 4—6, 6—4, 7—5, 6—2.

WIMBLEDON, England, July 3 (Associated Press).—William T. Tilden 2d of Philadelphia won the British lawn tennis championship in singles here today. Tilden defeated Gerald L. Patterson of Australia, the titleholder, in the challenge round, 2-6, 6-3, 6-2, 6-4.

The American's victory was conceded to have been well earned, his game being characterized by tennis experts as the soundest and brainiest tennis ever seen on English courts. The technique and cleverness he displayed, although probably beyond the comprehension of the average spectator in the finer points, were not lost upon seasoned tennis followers.

It was commented, along this line, that the American tennis experts seemed to have realized, when Patterson was in the United States last year, that he was decidedly vulnerable on the backhand, owing to his unorthodox method of twisting his arm so as to bring the forehand face of his racquet in use for backhand play, thereby locking his shoulder joints. This method usually collapses against an opponent who is keen enough to take advantage of the opening, and it did today.

Tilden in the first set opened with experiments all around the court and then settled down mercilessly to feeding his opponent's backhand, and, as the game progressed, Patterson got worse and worse under this method of attack.

Uses Famous Cut Stroke.

Tilden exploited his famous cut stroke to his opponent's backhand again and again in the last three sets, and Patterson was unable to get the spinning ball back over the net. He frequently hit into the bottom of the net. Then, when Patterson came up to the net, Tilden played a slower fast-dropping shot to his opponent's left hand. Almost invariably the ball was netted on the return.

These tactics were relentlessly exploited by Tilden, who showed Patterson, so far as the centre court crowds were concerned, in an entirely new rôle. Thousands of persons had believed he was unbeatable, only a few knowing he had a vulnerable joint in his armor.

In the first set Patterson led, 4-0, then 4—1 and 5—1, Patterson making a number of fine drives and serving magnificently. In the second set Tilden served first, taking the score to 2—0 and then 4—1. Patterson made it 3—5, and there was a protracted struggle for the ninth game, which Tilden finally won.

The third set went to 2 all, and then Tilden ran it out in the finest fashion. In the fourth set, after each man had alternately won, until Patterson led at 4—3, Tilden annexed three games in succession and won the set and match. The winner received a notable ovation.

Williams Star of Doubles.

C. S. Garland of Pittsburgh and Richard Norris Williams, 2d, of Boston won today's final in the British Tennis Doubles Championship from A. R. F. Kingscote and J. C. Parke of the British Davis Cup Team. The Americans took three of the four sets played. The scores were 4—6, 6—4, 7—5, 6—2.

It was a red-letter day for Williams. He was the directing brain and outstanding personality of the match. His opponents served upon his backhand until they found he always made brilliant returns down the center line. They then attacked his forehand only to find that the pace of his return often put the ball away. Williams's play generally was brilliant. In fast volleyed exchanges at the net he smashed finely and frequently sent over wining services which the Englishmen could not touch.

Garland did not start so well, but in the fourth set he played brilliantly. The features of his game were general all-round steadiness, great forehand driving and extraordinary quickness at the net. Sometimes he returned balls which it appeared impossible to get and scored on them.

Lycett's Spectacular Game.

Gerald L. Patterson of Australia and Mlle. Suzanne Lenglen of France defeated Randolph Lycett of Australia and Miss Elizabeth Ryan of California in the final of the mixed doubles. The winners took the match in straight sets, 7—5, 6—3.

It was the finest and most stubbornly contested mixed match ever seen in England, and according to some of the tennis experts, probably in the world. Lycett excels at this game, and although defeated, he was head and shoulders the best on the court, doing a five-sixths share of the work of his team. He killed overhead balls from every part of the court, and from the net position chased lobs which were over Miss Ryans head, retossed them to the base line and then got to the net again for the next return. His driving was magnificent, but Miss Ryans' work was slow.

Mlle Lenglen played wonderfully. She stood up to the hardest smashes at the net, sometimes scoring sensationally from them. Patterson served magnificently and in a masterly fashion killed overhead tosses, but the way Lycett retrieved many of his hardest overhead smashes never was equaled throughout the tournament. Today Lycett played a game which he never before had equaled for outstanding brilliancy.

It looked promising for a time for Lycett and Miss Ryan in the second set, when they carried the score to 3-1. Patterson and Mlle. Lenglen, however, then proceeded to win five games in succession for the set and the match. The set was marked throughout by the most sparkling plays.

The final in the ladies' doubles championship was won by Mlle. Lenglen and Miss Ryan. They beat Mrs. Lambert Chambers and Mrs. Larcombe in straight sets, 6—4, 6—0.

July 4, 1920

PROTECTING TENNIS COURTS

British Have Invented Cover That Guards Perfectly Against Rain.

Postponements because of rain have occurred in both the national doubles and national singles tennis tournaments this season and in both cases, more as a result of the soggy condition of the ground than because of an actual downpour at the scheduled time for the matches. Thus far no covering for the courts sufficiently protective to keep them ready for use, immediately after the rain has ceased, seems to have been devised in this country, but reports have reached here from England as to the effectiveness of a water proof cover used at the championship matches at Wimbledon this year. The use of such a protection, at least for the championship court, might well solve a difficult problem for the committees in charge of American tournaments.

The cover used at Wimbledon is constructed of specially waxed rot-proof canvas made up in two sections, each measuring 10 feet by 39 feet. Along the inner edges of the two sections and pocketed in the material are two steel hawsers terminated by shackles at either end. Each outside edge of the cover is secured by lashing to hooks cemented into the concrete bed in which the drainage is laid. For the purpose of uniting the two inner edges of the cover, wooden toggles and rope loops at intervals of about one yard are attached. To the centre of the cover is sewn a canvas storm flap to protect the join. This is fastened at its other edge to metal loops on the main cover.

At each end of the court are specially selected pitch pine masts, measuring 20 feet in height. These can be lowered laterally into the concrete trench. The masts are pivoted at the ground level, and the lower parts heavily weighted on the cantilever principle. When erected they are secured by wire stays, which are adjusted and pulled up to tension by screw dogs. From winches bolted to concrete beds at each end of court, steel hawsers (at the ends of which are hooks) are passed over the tops of the mast, the hooks being attached to the shackles already mentioned. The cover is then ready to be raised; two men working each winch are the only power required.

The drainage, constructed in concrete covered by an iron grill, runs down both sides of the court. These channels are joined up by means of drain pipes, running into a cesspool which is connected up with the main drainage.

This cover is said to be highly practical. It was invented by Edward Clive, who spent much time in experimenting and has since carried out various improvements, including the raising of the height at the centre. The All England Club is with its aid able to defy the weather. Within two minutes of heavy rain falling the whole of the centre court surface with its surrounds can be completely protected and rendered waterproof.

August 28, 1919

14

TILDEN CROWNED KING OF COURTS

Wins National Tennis Championship from Johnston in Five Spectacular Sets.

MATCH TENSELY DRAMATIC

Tragedy of the Air Casts Shadow Upon Bitterest Struggle in Game's History.

BOTH MEN REACH HEIGHTS

And Both Commit Unbelievable Errors—Sets Scored 6-1 1-6, 7-5, 5-7, 6-3—Officials Have Hard Day.

William T. Tilden, 2d, of Philadelphia, is the tennis champion of the United States and of the world in general. His victory over William M. Johnston, the former national title-holder, at the West Side Club, Forest Hills, yesterday afternoon, stamps him as not only the greatest of all living tennis players but, perhaps, the greatest of all time. It was a victory, however, completed only after five of the most terrific sets ever staged on a turf court, scored at 6—1, 1—6, 7—5, 5—7, 6—3. To what was probably the most dramatic scene in the history of lawn tennis was added the excitement of an airplane tragedy, in which Lieutenant J. M. Grier of the U. S. Navy and Sergeant Saxe of the army lost their lives in full view of the spectators, narrowly escaping a far more disastrous fall into the crowded stands themselves.

The minor events of the day resulted in victories for Vincent Richards in the junior singles, W. A. Campbell in the veterans' event, J.. L. Farquhar among the boys, the two Fred Andersons in the father and son doubles, and Harold Godshall and Richard Hinckley in the junior doubles.

The Tilden-Johnston struggle will go down on the records as the most astounding exhibition of tennis, the most nerve-racking battle that the courts have ever seen. It is not often that such a climax of competition lives up to every preliminary expectation. Yesterday, however, the wildest expectations were actually surpassed. Up to this time, the famous final of 1916, in which Richard Norris Williams, 2d., defeated Johnston for the championship, had been considered the apex of tennis history. But that great match faded into comparative insignificance yesterday.

Williams and Johnston played five sets of mechanically perfect tennis. Tilden and Johnston played five acts of incredible melodrama, with a thrill in every scene, with horrible errors leading suddenly to glorious achievements, with skill and courage and good and evil fortune inextricably mingled, and with a constant stimulus to cheers, groans and actual hysteria, so far as the spectators were concerned.

Conlin Maintains Control.

Those who had sympathies one way or the other, and this meant practically every one of the 10,000 or more in the crowd, when through more varieties of emotional reaction than the supposedly dignified and gentle game of lawn tennis could ever have been blamed for in the past. At times the mob spirit threatened to become unmanageable, as personal opinions were voiced from the stands in no uncertain terms. But Umpire E. C. Conlin kept a firm control of the proceedings throughout, and certainly no one was ever before given so difficult an assignment in the chair of arbitration. Rain, the airplane accident, a misunderstanding as to an important ruling, vitally affecting the result of the fourth set, and unusual frequency of close decisions by the linesmen all added to the umpire's troubles, but Conlin was not dismayed and finished his job in the same heroic spirit as was shown by the two men on the court.

To describe that amazing final to the most significant of all American tennis tournaments,' a tournament that unquestionably carried with it the world's championship, would require the superlative of all the adjectives that the journalism of the game has either used up or discarded in the past. It is enough to say that all future discussions of the Olympian heights of tennis will probably begin with the question, "Were you there when——?" and the answer will be either "You bet I was" or "Curses, no." For the proud possessors of the affirmative no amplification is necessary. For the sad negatives nothing can be done, for it will never happen again, at least not just that way.

Praise for the two contenders for the American championship of 1920 may be equally divided. There is plenty for both. Tilden's victory was a triumph of supertennis, a vindication of the game which the best judges have for some time considered invincible. But, if Tilden is the greatest tennis player that ever lived, Johnston is the gamest man that ever trod a court.

Conqueror's Wonderful Service.

Armed with his wonderful forehand drive, his aggressive volleys, and his stubborn determination never to say die, the former champion for five sets resisted a dazzling versatile game that theoretically should be rated at least 25 per cent. ahead of his own. The difference between the two men in the one detail of service is convincingly emphasized by the stroke analysis. Johnston did not serve a single ace in the entire match, and contributed more than his share of double faults. Tilden, on the other hand, had twenty technical aces to his credit, an average of four to a set, exclusive of the numerous occasions when an overwhelming service was miraculously returned by the courageous defender, only to lead to a sure score off the ground or on the volley.

It is by his service that the Tilden of yesterday will chiefly be remembered, for time and again it came to his rescue when all else had failed. But he had also a marvel of a backhand drive, a newly developed asset to his game, an offensive not a defensive stroke, and one which scored equally well across court or straight down the line. Johnston's backhand, except for its accuracy of placement, was largely a defensive weapon.

But, if the Californian had the worst of this comparison, he fared quite differently in the matter of volleying. Here he was distinctly Tilden's superior. Not only was he able to volley balls that would have knocked down an ordinary player, and to reach low, well-placed passing shots that could scarcely be seen in their flight, but he turned a majority of these extraordinary gets into actual factors in his attack, either scoring outright or forcing a defensive position which ultimately brought him the point. Tilden's volleying was too soft to finish the rallies, and depended too much on placement and undercutting for its success, whereas Johnston always picked the ball out of the air in a crisp, confident style that practically guaranteed results.

Overhead, also, Johnston was the better man yesterday, and he commanded a lob which proved exceedingly valuable in the pinches. But Tilden added a cruel chop to his terrific drives, and with the ability to mix up his ground-strokes thus he could afford to take fewer chances by the aerial route. Johnston nearly tripled the number of points earned by his opponent in volleying and smashing. On the other hand: Tilden almost doubled his rival's record of ground placements. In the percentage of errors and earned points in general they were practically even, the new champion finishing a far greater number of rallies one way or the other, and therefore deserving a vast amount of credit for his statistical showing.

In the last analysis, however, it was the edge on service that told the story, and it was this tremendous difference that made Johnston's fight such an astonishing one. He more than justified his reputation of being the world's greatest finalist, the greatest "money player" living, for the tennis that he offered yesterday would have annihilated any one but a Tilden, and a super Tilden, at that.

In the fourth set, with Tilden needing only two points for the match, Johnston returned a smash at his feet with such a ridiculously impossible shot that Tilden himself joined in the gasp of the spectators, and threw away the point in his amazement. Later in the same game, only one point intervened between the fighting defender and defeat, but he staved off the disaster, and eventually pulled out the set. In the final session he again saved a match point by a marvelously accurate placement off his backhand, and ultimately succumbed by barely missing the line in a desperate attempt to score.

Tilden Shows Courage.

As for Tilden, he also faced innumerable situations that called for more than ordinary courage, even with the advantage of his superior troke equipment. Twice in the rubber he lost his service..and had to accomplish the difficult task of breaking through in turn to save the match. When victory had seemed in his grasp in that fatal tenth game of the fourth set, only to vanish suddenly, it was peculiarly trying that rain should begin to fall immediately, ironically reminding him of what might have been, while the court was still dry. Added to this came a misunderstanding as to the replay of a point, which was given against him, followed by the interruption which made a new start necessary.

But if Tilden showed courage and a commendable control of his nerves in these situations the tennis that he exhibited in the opening set was something that stood on a pinnacle of supremacy, overwhelming in its magnificence, a unique display of matchless strength and skill that permitted no resistance, and took thought of nothing but its own perfection. That any one could hit a tennis ball so hard and so accurately against a national champion seemed utterly impossible, and it was not humanly possible for more than one set.

Tilden suffered an obvious letdown after that titanic exhibition of hitting, and after losing his service twice, deliberately threw away the second set, making no effort to return the last few shots. The third was the crucial test, and here Tilden came through triumphantly after having lost his service and retrieved the loss immediately, finishing with a decisive break in which he earned three of his four points. He had the fourth set and the match on his racquet, as stated above, but was foiled by Johnston's incredible get, and then lost the game on errors.

Rain Causes Interruption.

During the first rally of the next game, it began to rain, and the crowd instantly became a kaleidoscope of motion. Tilden looked inquiringly at Umpire Conlin, and evidently assuming that a let had been called, stopped playing. When they resumed, "Referee Adee awarded the point to Johnston, reversing Conlin's decision. They stopped at 30-all, and when they returned to the court, after the rain had ceased, Tilden served three double faults which directly lost him the set. Trailing at 40-0 on the final game, he brought off two forehand wallops off service that completely beat Johnston by sheer velocity, but netted in his attempt to deuce the score.

In the last set, Tilden had to break through Johnston's service three times to win. The match point finally came up on an error following a net-corder, from a half-volley, but Johnston saved it by poking the ball backhanded through an opening a few inches wide. A bad bound gave Tilden a service ace, and this time Johnston failed to save the situation, driving out after a great rally, for the set and match, 6—3.

It would be impossible to review the most important points and games in their regular order. Spectators will remember in particular some wonderful returns made by Tilden on the full run from far outside the court, with a slicing swing of the racquet, on one of which he fell flat, but won the point. They will recall how beautifully Johnston anticipated his opponent's movements from side to side as he volleyed close up, invariably picking the right spot for his finishing shot. Several lobs that landed right on the base-line will stand out for those who delight in finesse of placement, as will the remarkable accuracy of both men in the fifth set, when they were too weary to trust to speed alone, but persisted in aiming at the side-lines and generally succeeded in hitting them. But above all will remain in the memory that downward stab of Johnston's racquet as he returned a point-blank smash at his feet, and that amazing succession of service aces delivered by Tilden when he needed all his speed to win. It was a glorious victory.

The point score and stroke analysis tell the rest of the story:

FIRST SET.

Tilden	4 6 4 4 4 0 4—26—6
Johnston	1 4 2 2 2 4 1—16—1

STROKE ANALYSIS.

	O.	N.	V.	G.P.	S.A.	D.F.
Tilden	4	4	3	6	6	1
Johnston	5	5	5	2	0	1

SECOND SET.

Johnston	4 4 4 6 2 7 4—31—6
Tilden	1 1 1 4 4 5 1—17—1

STROKE ANALYSIS.

Johnston	6	4	7	7	0	2
Tilden	7	10	2	1	2	0

THIRD SET.

Tilden	4 2 4 0 6 4 1 6 6 0 5 4—42—7
Johnston	1 4 1 4 4 6 4 4 4 4 3 1—40—5

STROKE ANALYSIS.

Tilden	16	10	3	15	6	0
Johnston	14	4	7	7	0	0

FOURTH SET.

Johnston	3 4 7 5 1 4 1 1 1 8 11 4—50—7
Tilden	3 0 5 3 4 1 4 4 4 6 9 2—47—5

STROKE ANALYSIS.

Johnston	11	15	8	5	0	2
Tilden	13	20	2	12	5	4

FIFTH SET.

Tilden	0 5 4 2 1 4 4 4 7—31—6
Johnston	4 3 0 4 4 1 1 2 5—24—3

STROKE ANALYSIS.

Tilden	9	4	2	10	1	0
Johnston	6	9	5	7	0	2

RECAPITULATION.

	O.	N.	V.	GP.	SA.	DF.	Tot. Er.	Tot. End.
Tilden	39	48	12	44	20	5	102	76
Johnston	42	37	32	28	0	7	86	60

Results of Matches in Tennis Title Play at Forest Hills

All-Comers' Singles.

William T. Tilden, 2d, defeated William M. Johnston, 6—1, 1—6, 7—5, 5—7, 6—3.

Junior Singles.

Vincent Richards defeated W. W. Ingraham, 6—2, 6—4, 6—1.

Boys' Singles.

J. L. Farquhar defeated William Einsmann, 7—5, 6—1.

Veterans' Singles.

W. A. Campbell defeated R. N. Dana, 6—1, 1—6, 6—2.

Father and Son Doubles.

Fred G. Anderson and Fred C. Anderson defeated J. D. E. Jones and A. W. Jones, 3—6, 7—5, 6—4.

Junior Doubles.

Harold Godshall and Richard Hinckley defeated A. W. Jones and W. W. Ingraham, 4—6, 6—3, 4—6, 7—5, 6—4.

September 7, 1920

TRAINING FOR TENNIS CHAMPIONSHIP, AS TILDEN SEES IT

By WILLIAM L. CHENERY.

A CHAMPION is a sort of self-made king. He isn't elected like a poor President. On the contrary, on a really royal road the champion goes out and does the choosing. He decides to be king, and then discovers it to be necessary to fight a long list of men who also covet the regal job. In this way the modern athlete continues the tradition of the savage old chieftains, who were the first rulers of the race. If, for example, Babe Ruth had been born two or three thousand years ago he would have slammed himself into Valhalla, and in time his deeds would have been embalmed in German opera. It would then cost $5 instead of a $1.10 to see him.

That is the way it was with champions. Fancy what a place Jack Dempsey would have occupied when the strong and the swift were more than metaphorical kings. If Mr. Dempsey had happened to be traveling about Greece at the time that Messrs. Hector and Achilles were staging their well-known bout, Homer would have had to get out sporting extras to revise his story. But it is with another and a more recent and a strictly amateur champion that this story deals, and because it is not quite clear just what rôle he would have had in Valhalla or on Olympus, or even on the fields of Troy, it is easier to regard him in his native habitat, which is Philadelphia.

The great man of tennis is William T. Tilden, 2d. Champion of champions, king of them all is Tilden. The expert witnesses who testify daily in the sporting sections say that at his best there was never any equal to him. Tennis is an ancient game. It was talked about, if not played, when William Shakespeare listened and wrote. But so far as the records go nobody in all these centuries seems to have had more skill in driving the silly little ball made of rag and rubber around the court whereon the tennis king reigns. To become international and national champion William T. Tilden, 2d, confronted the world. One by one he conquered all aspirants in his field, and until another Summer brings fresh contests he is secure in the possession of his crown. It is no small honor he has won. International fame is his. Wherever tennis is played his name is known.

The retrospection of kings is often romantic, and so it happened that William T. Tilden was pursued to his tennis home, the Germantown Cricket Club of Philadelphia, for an interview. Those who have only seen the great tennis player in action would probably not recognize him in the repose of work-a-day habiliments. The tall, somewhat stooping, boyish-looking young man walking slowly across the cricket sward certainly did not resemble the tense, brilliant fighter of the Forest Hills court. When the international matches were being played in England an English paper announced that Tilden was only 20 years old. Actually he is 27, but the mistake might easily be made. He has at times the look of a boy.

How Tilden Trains.

In many ways he is a boy. There seem to be numerous infants and youngsters in the Tilden family and all centre around the Germantown Cricket

—Illustrated London News.

Tilden in Action.

Club. While the tournaments continue, the champion says it is quite impossible for him to settle down to his ordinary vocation, which is selling insurance, and consequently he amuses himself playing with his young kinsfolk. Even to the very young he is "Bill," and actually, despite the obvious reverence which young nephews and nieces accord him, the tennis champion and the children are on terms of equality. His present diversion seems in fact to be coaching "infant phenomena" in tennis. But a man does not fight as grimly as Tilden has fought and still retain untouched the face of youth. Tennis has taken its toll of the champion and its marks are left. Deep circles under the eyes and a habit of almost passionate concentration are the unsought accompaniments of the world championship. Tilden's nervous organization is keyed to a tremendous pitch. And yet when he was asked how he trained, without hesitancy he answered:

"I try to keep a normal mental attitude. I try to keep my mind right. The staleness of athletes, I think, is due to mental rather than to physical causes. Ty Cobb told me that he trained hard for six weeks and then broke training for a day to prevent staleness. After the interruption he goes back to strict system.

"I don't break training, but I try in various ways to keep my mental attitude balanced and normal. I stop playing for a day or two when it seems to be necessary, and I look for some diversion. A game of bridge, music or the theatre afford relief to me. The other night before playing against Bill Johnston I went to a friend's house and listened to a phonograph for two hours. My friend has interesting foreign records, which changed my state of mind. I went to bed about 11 and forgot all about tennis. The next morning when I awoke I felt quite ready for the match.

"I have not got any system of training except the system which attempts to keep things normal. I go to bed early, but not too early, not much before 11, and I sleep as late as I can. I think any drinking hurts the tennis game, and I find that for me very light smoking is best."

The tennis champion does smoke a few cigarettes, however, and his appetite—he counsels caution—is like that of a full back. On the day before he was scheduled to appear in the East-West match a thick steak, many potatoes and much corn were the objects of his luncheon desire. The human machine which moves at a championship pace seems to call for abundant fuel.

"I have been playing tennis," he continued, "since I was a little boy. I think that I won my first tournament when I was 7. I don't remember what it was, but the episode sticks. All through my boyhood, and, in fact, continuously, I have kept at the game.

"Behind the great skill of many men and women who win distinction in various lines there often lies the ambition and the struggles of some other member of the family. In literature and politics certainly a gifted youth frequently realizes the ambitions of a less talented relative. So it seems to have been with Tilden.

"I had an older brother, who has since died. He first got me to thinking about tennis. He was a good player, and he tried to make a good player out of me. I remember he used to say, 'Can't you swing on the ball?' I would try and try and he would teach me. All the training I had came from him. For the rest I worked out my own game.

"I am not a born tennis player. I am what you might call a hand-made tennis player. I have worked to learn tennis, and any other youngster who wants to work as hard can learn to play as good or a better game.

"All through my school and college days I played. Until I reached the university I played successfully. Then

I realized that the strokes and the system of play which were good enough for boys were not good enough for the larger competition. So I set about learning a better system. It took me about two full years to get it. I was 18 and 19 while this was going on and in the university. That is one of the reasons I slumped in tennis for the time.

"I practiced the system I finally learned by a process of elimination. Three things I watched—the stroke itself, the position of my feet and the distribution of the weight of my body. If my feet were placed correctly and my weight was properly distributed and still the ball did not respond, then I knew the stroke itself must be at fault, and so I worked on that. That was the way I learned the game. There were no coaches for college tennis and consequently the thing had to be worked out alone.

"I practice now as much as seems to be necessary. If I were to make a rule I should say three sets of tennis a day, four days in the week, would be a good average. But when getting ready for a match I train as much as is needed. You cannot tell how much that involves. The thing to do is to get your eye focused on the ball. That may come quickly or it may be slower. It may be desirable to play fifteen sets in one day and then to stop sharply for a day. It depends on your condition and on how quickly you respond."

Tilden is a nervous, wiry man. As with many who are successful in different ways, he absorbs energy from the crowd. His best game is played when excitement runs highest.

"I will be perfectly frank and honest," he said. "I love a crowd. In practice I am no good at all. Half of the kids I play with can beat me, mere children whom I coach, in practice. The excitement of a tournament inspires me and makes my game better."

Strength from the Crowd.

Tilden thinks he is "a hand-made tennis player," and he is doubtless wise in believing that the road to success lies in the preservation of a normal frame of mind and in the development of outside interests, and yet, after all, the crowd reaction is the test. To get energy and enthusiasm from the assembled throng is one of the most precious of gifts. Particularly it is the mark of orators and musicians. Lloyd George possesses it par excellence. He feels his crowds and returns to them the energies they have given. Dr. Anna Howard Shaw, the splendid suffragist leader, had the gift. It was wonderful to see her rise to the crowd. That trait most of all comes from the gods. Whether in tennis in music or in oratory the capacity to move to the level of the crowd's demands is as much a boon from nature as is the possession of Caruso's lyrical larynx.

William T. Tilden, 2d, lives, moves and has his being in the realm of tennis. Not only he thinks about his own game, but also he is interested in the national and international recognition of tennis. During the last ten years, in his judgment, a new era of tennis has appeared.

"The future of tennis is bright," he said. "This country ought to produce more good tennis players than any other nation. There are now hundreds and even thousands of boys between 12 and 18 years who play real tennis. This development is due to the system evolved by Julian S. Myrick, the system of junior play.

"By this system the youthful winners of various tennis championships finally get the chance to play in the national. That developed rivalry is the influence which has made for good tennis in this country. Where now other nations, Australia or England, have relatively

ew good junior players, we have very large numbers. They will become great players in the future.

"Thanks to this junior system and to the building of municipal courts tennis is becoming a truly national game. It is no longer a class game, thank God for that."

—London Sketch.
Champion's Great Reach.

Tennis and golf have in truth become national games during the last few years. It is a curious and significant development. Industrial civilization with its devastating ugliness seems to call for its compensations in sport. But for golf successful managers would find their success quite in-

tolerable, and without tennis the city-bred young and sturdy would discover the routine of industry not to be borne. The strength, the swiftness, the deftness, the surging energy which the human race needed before economic success compelled men and women to sit in dull offices seven hours daily must be used. Tennis is the channel through which these qualities are expressed. And so it happens naturally that the young Philadelphian whose unconquered skill with the racquet has given him international fame looks forward to the time when tennis has become the universal pastime of the nation.

The game has lifted him up. It has made his name familiar. As we sat on the veranda of the cricket club, visitors came and asked for tickets to the "Tilden game." It was not the East-West match, but the "Tilden game," a chance to observe their fellow-townsman in action, that they sought. Such unconscious recognition is a high reward. Tilden, however, wears his honors easily.

Praise for Johnston.

He is concerned about a fine technique, about sportsmanship and the general enjoyment of the game. The evolution of the game, the stroke which was originated by Lawford, and which by Clothier was developed into a low straight forehand drive, and which finally in the hands of men such as Tilden has become the modern drive of power and precision, is the thing which interests him. The motion of the ball over the strings, the subtle and almost unperceived direction taken, is the object of study.

Admiration for his fellows and in particular for the defeated national champion is frequently uttered.

"It is a great pleasure either to win or to lose to Bill Johnston," he said.

"I have done both an equal number of times. Each of us has won the same number of matches and I think the same number of sets. Johnston is a man whose perfect sportsmanship, absolute fairness and gameness make him a great credit to American tennis. I can only hope that I uphold the title as he has done."

Sincere admiration for his rivals and keen interest in the younger generation, these were the frequent subjects of his conversation. The number of his protégés seems large. For several he forsees great achievements, and, as for himself, he expects to keep on playing. "I have been a member of the Germantown Cricket Club since I was a little boy." he said. "Most of my playing has been done here. I am interested in seeing the youngsters develop now and in helping them. All of the tournament men owe much to others and in particular to the public which has made the great vogue of tennis possible by supporting it. I want to help the game."

Such is the conversation of the world's champion tennis player. But to see him, really it is necessary to picture the cousins and the aunts, the older and the young, the characteristic Americans' who take pride in the young king of tennis as before they were enthusiastic over the boy of seven who won his first match. To the aunts and cousins he gives his trophies, and in return they reward him in their kind. The normal life, the even balance on which a great game may be built, is in part doubtless their gift. The exchange is fair and interesting and it helps to explain the young man who has met the exactions of great tests and conquered. To the world they and Germantown have given a champion.

September 12, 1920

MLLE. LENGLEN WINS FROM MRS. MALLORY

French Star Defeats American Champion for World's Hard Court Tennis Title.

STEADINESS TURNS SCALES

Victor's Generalship Decides Final Match at St. Cloud— Scores Are 6-2, 6-3.

Copyright, 1921, by The New York Times Company.
By Wireless to THE NEW YORK TIMES.

PARIS, June 5.—On the hard courts of the St. Cloud Tennis Club Mrs. Molla Bjurstedt Mallory challenged Suzanne Lenglen today for the championship of the world. It was the first time that the young French girl has been seriously challenged since she grew up, but Mrs. Mallory, America's best woman player, was beaten in two straight sets, 6-2, 6-3.

Afterward when THE NEW YORK TIMES correspondent asked her what she thought of her opponent, Molla replied frankly. "She is just the steadiest player that ever was," said Mrs. Mallory. "She just sent back at me whatever I sent at her and waited for me to make a fault."

That is a true description of the game. Several times Mrs. Mallory was

outplayed. Almost, if not quite, as frequently, she outplayed her opponent. But she lost because while she gained many points Mlle. Lenglen rarely did lose one. The American's volley would end ignominiously in the net, while the French woman's never, or scarcely ever, failed to reach the other court.

"And her returns often enough were harder than the shots I sent up to her," Mrs. Mallory added, and this was true, too. This French girl who is so amazingly accurate can also hit as hard as most men who believe themselves to be of championship standard.

French Star Studies Rival.

Today's game was just as Mrs. Mallory has described it—a long psychological study. Suzanne has been watching the American champion all week and knew that if she left her alone Mrs. Mallory would defeat herself. Thus she began the first game. She let Mrs. Mallory go quietly for two or three shots across the net, then she began to hurry her, and the end was at once apparent. The American woman began to get rattled and her drives finished up in the net. At the fourth game the matter had become interesting. The score was 2—1 in favor of Mlle. Lenglen, and Mrs. Mallory made a tremendous effort to equalize. She won the first two points and the game went to deuce. Then Mlle. Lenglen won the advantage. With one of the finest returns of the game Mrs. Mallory equalized. But three times more she lost the advantage. The rallies were long and both women were playing with care as well as skill. In the end it was one of the few times the American woman really outplayed her rival. With two magnificent shots she got the lead and made the games 2 all.

It was, alas, her last effort. Suzanne gave her only one point in the next two games and the set ended in a crushing defeat. The next set was the same. In the third game the French girl's sandal began to give her trouble, and afterward she declared she was not playing her best because her feet were slipping inside her sandals. But from the viewpoint of the fans there was little to complain about. Wherever the ball went she went, too, and her returns never failed. Again and again Mrs. Mallory would find the net, giving a point to her opponent. But this young French woman, who when a girl was denied jam with her tea by her father unless her game met with his approval, never failed to make her point when it was humanly possible.

In the sixth game of the set Mrs. Mallory made a wonderful rally. She knew that nothing could save her, but decided to finish gamely. All the time she was playing against one of the most wonderful machines that have ever been created out of woman's body. And it is also a graceful machine. In build the two women, of whom Mlle. Lenglen is by some years the junior, are very different. The French woman is two to three inches taller and much more supple and nimble of limb. Often she had the American woman running from the end of the court after balls which she seemed to pick up without the least effort. Like Tilden among the men, she seems to be in an altogether different class from her contemporaries.

France Gets Lion's Share.

ST. CLOUD, France, June 5 (Associated Press).—The failure of Mrs. Molla Bjurstedt Mallory to defeat Mlle. Suzanne Lenglen in the women's singles of the world's hard court tennis championships, which closed here today, leaves the United States with only one championship out of five. Mlle. Lenglen won from Mrs. Mallory in straight sets, 6—2, 6—3, and France came out on top in both women's singles, women's doubles, mixed doubles and men's doubles.

The roll of honor now reads: Men's singles, William T. Tilden, America; women's singles, Mlle. Suzanne Lenglen, France; mixed doubles, Max Decugis and Mlle. Lenglen, France; women's doubles, Mlle. Lenglen and Mme. Golding, France; men's doubles, André Gobert and William H. Laurentz, France.

Mrs. Mallory's defeat by Mlle. Lenglen was a case of superior steadiness on the part of the winner coupled with her "soft" game, the French champion playing apparently under instructions and advice from close observers of Mrs. Mallory's play in previous games.

Mrs. Mallory fought hard.

"No woman in the world can beat Mrs. Mallory today," Tilden insidiously whispered into Mlle. Lenglen's ear just before she took the court, but Suzanne merely waved the champion away, saying: "America had its day yesterday; this is France's day."

Pair Will Meet Again.

Mlle. Lenglen just now is at the very acme of her game, but it is possible with a few more weeks' training that Mrs. Mallory will give her a closer contest when they met at Wimbledon. The somewhat strained feeling which seemed to exist between the two prior to today's match was smoothed out as Mlle. Lenglen hastened to the net after Mrs. Mallory netted the last ball. She reached over and shook the American warmly by the hand as the crowd cheered.

The match proved something of a disappointment on account of lack of dash in the play, Mlle. Lenglen absolutely refusing to take any chances at the net and playing safe all the way.

The difference in netted balls brought victory for Mlle. Lenglen. Mrs. Mallory netted thirty-two shots against nine for Mlle. Lenglen. Neither woman had a service ace. Mrs. Mallory outplaced Mlle. Lenglen, sixteen to ten, and had twenty-three outs to twenty-seven.

In the mixed doubles Mlle. Lenglen and Max Decugis won from Mme. Golding and W. H. Laurentz, 6—3, 6—2, after the Golding-Laurentz pair had defeated Mme Storms M. Washer of Belgium, 4—6, 6—4, 11—9, for the right to compete in the final.

In the finals for the men's doubles André Gobert and Laurentz won from Gerbault and Albarran, 6—4, 6—2, 6—8, 6—2. The experienced French team proved too much for their younger opponents.

Five hundred francs were offered today for seats to witness the Lenglen-Mallory match, and speculators who had obtained possession of many choice seats early in the week reaped a harvest. Never before in the history of tennis in France have such crowds witnessed the games, fully 5,000 persons being turned away.

June 6, 1921

TENNIS TITLE STAYS WITH FRENCH STAR

Mlle. Lenglen Defeats Miss Ryan in Wimbledon Challenge Round by 6-2, 6-0.

AN OVERWHELMING TRIUMPH

California Girl Is Outplayed in All Departments of Game—Tilden Beaten in Practice Match.

WIMBLEDON, England, July 1 (Associated Press).—Mlle. Suzanne Lenglen retained the British turf court women's singles tennis championship by defeating Miss Elizabeth Ryan of California in the challenge round here today. Mlle. Lenglen won in straight sets, 6—2, 6—0.

Miss Ryan started strongly and for a time it looked as if the match would be close. The stellar play of the remarkable little Frenchwoman, however, proved too much for the challenger as the match progressed and the result was never in doubt after the middle of the first set.

In this set Miss Ryan won the opening game, which went to deuce. Mlle. Lenglen won the second easily, but Miss Ryan took the third, which also went to deuce. Then the Frenchwoman, playing to her best form, ran out the set, winning five straight games. Miss Ryan seemed off her game toward the close of the set, frequently hitting too strongly, while Mlle. Lenglen made her well-placed service tell, while her backhand shots were admirable.

In the second set the champion demonstrated her superiority in all departments of the game. She hit consistently well on her back-hand and made few mistakes. She was in danger at no point, except in the third game, when the score went to deuce. The set lacked spectacular features.

Disappointing to Spectators.

The match was disappointing to the spectators, because of the comparative ease with which Mlle Lenglen defeated her opponent. The Californian appeared entirely out of form, repeatedly netting the ball or overshooting. Miss Ryan's ordinarily dangerous service failed to mystify Mlle. Lenglen, who, with brilliant backhand strokes, placed the ball easily out of the American's reach. Miss Ryan employed her usual chop shots, with occasional slashing drives. She was not fast enough, however, for the flashing Frenchwoman. Both players, for the most part, maintained positions at the baseline and made few excursions to the net.

An enormous crowd witnessed the matches, including Queen Mary, Princess Mary, former King Manuel of Portugal and many other notable persons.

The match in which Randolph Lycett and Max Woodnam opposed H. Roper Barrett of England and B. I. C. Norton of South Africa, in the semi-final of the men's doubles, was the best seen in the doubles in this tournament. Woosnam at times was unable to take care of his part of the court, but Lycett again and again scored with the most brilliant drives, covering his own and his partner's court, and the pair won by 8—6, 2—6, 6—3, 6—4. They will meet Arthur H. Lowe and Francis G. Lowe in the final round.

Zenzo Shimidzu, the Japanese star, in a practice match this afternoon defeated William T. Tilden 2d of Philadelphia, the world's singles champion, three sets out of four, 6—4, 6—2, 6—3, 5—7. Tennis experts who watched the match, however, said the scores should not be taken too seriously as indicating Tilden's condition.

July 2, 1921

TILDEN RETAINS HIS TENNIS TITLE

Defeats Norton in Challenge Round of British Turf Court Championship.

WAGES FINE UPHILL FIGHT

Beaten in First Two Sets, 4-6, 2-6, Then Wins Last Three, 6-1, 6-0, 7-5.

LYCETT-WOOSNAM VICTORS

Take Doubles Honors From Lowe Brothers, 6-3, 6-0, 7-5—Two Titles for Miss Ryan.

WIMBLEDON, July 2 (Associated Press).—William T. Tilden of Philadelphia, world's lawn tennis champion, successfully defended his title in the challenge round of the British turf court championships here today, defeating B. I. C. Norton, the South African star, in a five-set match, 4—6, 2—6, 6—1, 6—0, 7—5.

Tilden won the match by a superb uphill struggle. The contest was one of the closest and most sensational witnessed here in many a day. Beaten in the first two sets, he returned to form in the third, winning this and the fourth set by the scores of 6—1, 6—0.

In the fifth and deciding set the play was at first in Norton's favor, the South African leading, 3—2 and then 5—4. Tilden took it to deuce, however, and then captured the set and the match by winning the next two games.

Tilden by his victory retains the title he won at Wimbledon last year, when, by playing through the tournament and defeating Gerald Patterson of Australia in the challenge round, he captured not only the British championship but what is generally conceded to be the world's title.

The other titular honors now held by the Philadelphian are the American national championship and the world's hard court championship, which last he won this year in the matches at St. Cloud, France.

Mistakes Lose First Game.

Both Tilden and Norton received an ovation when they entered the courts. The American opened with a good service, but in the subsequent returns made mistakes and lost the first game. Then Norton double faulted and Tilden captured two games. Norton took the next game, the champion overhitting the line. The South African magnificently returned some of Tilden's "whiz-bang" services and led at 3—2. Norton, playing admirably, won his own service game, bringing the score to 4—2. Tilden netted chop strokes and double faulted, thus giving Norton the lead at 5—2. Tilden rallied, however, and ultimately reached 4—5, but Norton, playing brilliantly from the back court, again got a point when Tilden netted a half volley. Norton then won the set with a service ace.

Norton captured Tilden's first service game in the second set with splendid returning off the ground, with the champion netting or outing almost every time. Then Tilden endeavored to make an ace, but failed. Norton took the second game and the third. Tilden, in the main, beat himself, and the score went to 4—0 in Norton's favor. Tilden got the next service game with two "whiz-bangs" and hard driving. The next game was taken to 15 by the champion with grand driving. Norton in the seventh cross-volleyed some of Tilden's hardest drives and led, at 5—2. Tilden continued his numerous errors and lost the last game on Norton's service from love 40. Here Norton half-volleyed from the base line one of Tilden's hurricane drives and took the second set at 6—2.

In the third set Tilden got the first game on his service and then won Norton's service. Tilden in the next game thrice successively beat himself, but pulled the game out with four successive ace points. Tilden now was beating Norton finely all around the court, but the latter periodically brought out fine winners. Norton next captured his opponent's service game, but Tilden realized with a love game on drop shots, capturing the next game and the set, 6—1.

Tilden played the fourth set as if he meant it to be a one-man show. He sent over "whiz-bang" services and steadied himself beautifully. He played hurricane shots all around the court and captured a love set. In this set Norton never once appeared to be trying. He hit the ball in the wildest fashion, and Tilden took the set at 6—0.

Norton captured the first game in the fifth set, but Tilden evened the score and then took the lead at 2—1. Norton, however, drew level at 2-all and forged ahead at 3—2, with Tilden once more beating himself on easy shots. Norton got another point and led at 4—2, but ultimately, with the South African making most unaccountable mistakes, Tilden drew level at 4—4. Norton then went ahead to 5—4 with mediocre tennis. Norton twice got within a stroke of the match, but Tilden evened it at 5—5 after several deuce calls. Tilden then captured Norton's service game and led at 6—5. Two fine ace points gave the American 30-love, one being a cannon-ball ace. Tilden went to 40—15. The American netted the next ball, but served a whirlwind ace for the last point, winning the set, 7—5.

Lowe Brothers Lose.

Randolph Lycett and Max Woosnam, England, won the final match in the men's doubles of the British turf court lawn tennis championship tournament here today, defeating A. H. and F. G. Lowe, England, in straight sets, 6—3, 6—0, 7—5.

Woosnam and Lycett forced the Lowe brothers away from the baseline, where they are supreme, and sent them terrific smashes which the Lowes could not handle, and it was this style of play that carried the victors through.

In the first two sets the Lowe brothers were outclassed, but in the third set they staged a fine rally and took the lead at 5—4. Woosnam and Lycett, however, captured the next three games, thus winning the set and the championship.

The final match of the women's doubles in the British turf court tennis championship tournament was won here today by Mlle. Suzanne Lenglen, the French star, and Miss Elizabeth Ryan of California. They defeated Mrs. Beamish and Mrs. Peacock of England 6—1, 6—2.

Mlle. Lenglen and Miss Ryan showed far superior form to that of their opponents. They were always at the net attacking with vigorous volleying, and Mrs. Beamish and Mrs. Peacock, on the baseline, never had a chance.

In the final match for the All-England championship, Mr. Gilbert defeated F. M. B. Fisher 7—5, 4—6, 6—0.

Randolph Lycett of England and Miss Elizabeth Ryan of California defeated Max Woosnam and Miss F. M. Howkins of England in the final of the mixed doubles in the British turf court tennis championship 6—2, 6—1.

Lycett and Miss Ryan defeated their opponents with remarkable ease. The winners played a superb all-round game with hard driving and aggressive volleying, overpowering the British pair.

July 3, 1921

WOMEN'S NET TITLE FOR MRS. MALLORY

She Defeats Miss Browne at Forest Hills and Wins Singles Crown for Sixth Time.

SCORES ARE 4-6, 6-4, 6-2

Runner-Up Brilliant, but Fails to Overcome the Champion's Strong Baseline Play.

DOUBLES HONORS TO COAST

Miss Browne and Mrs. Williams Beat Miss Gilleaudeau and Mrs. Morris in Straight Sets.

Mrs. Molla Bjurstedt Mallory still occupies her unchallengable position at the top of the world of American women's tennisdom. The Norse girl won her sixth holding of the national title yesterday afternoon at the West Side Tennis Club in Forest Hills, when she defeated Miss Mary K. Browne of Santa Monica, Cal., holder of the championship from 1912 to 1914, in another of those spectacular battles which have distinguished Mrs. Mallory's progress all through the tournament to the final honors. Miss Browne won the first set, 6—4, and Mrs. Mallory the second and third sets, 6—4, 6—2. Mrs. Mallory's other championships in the national women's singles were won from 1915 to 1918, inclusively, and again in 1920.

The national laurels in doubles were captured by the California team, composed of Miss Browne and Mrs. Louise R. Williams. They defeated the metropolitan combination of Miss Helen Gilleaudeau and Mrs. L. Gouverneur Morris in the final round by scores of 6—3, 6—2. Miss Browne and Mrs. Williams thus become the successors of Mrs. Marion Zinderstein Jessup and Miss Eleanor Goss, who were prevented by Miss Goss's illness from playing through in defense of the title they had held since 1918.

The largest gallery of America's greatest week in women's tennis, since the match between Mrs. Mallory and Mlle. Lenglen, and numbering about the same as that one, between 7,000 and 8,000, had assembled when the champion and Miss Browne took the court, with Edward C. Conlin in the umpire's chair, which he has occupied in practically all of the important national matches of recent years. In their warming-up practice before the start of the match, both women seemed to be at the top of their form, and this indication was speedily borne out by their performance as soon as Mrs. Mallory started service in the opening game.

Champion Makes Errors.

Mrs. Mallory won this game with two running placements, after successive errors had made the points 30-all. The exchanges were brilliant from the very start. The rallies were often long, but never dull. Miss Browne held her dashing net attack in reserve in the introductory game, but carried it into effect with telling results in the next three, all of which she won for a lead of 3—1. In all three of these games Mrs. Mallory passed Miss Browne, with the latter playing up, in the first point, only to have the Californian persist in her aggressive tactics and force the champion into errors. Deuce was called twice in the third game and four times in the fourth before Miss Browne came through. Mrs. Mallory was netting the ball surprisingly often for her on shots to her forehand.

One of the sensations of Mrs. Mallory's tournament history was forthcoming in the fourth game of the opener, when she actually ran to the net in the effort to meet and defeat the Californian at the latter's own game. The attempt was not impressive, for the champion netted an easy volley for the final point of the game. On a previous foray to the net, in the same game, the champion volleyed back safely enough, but Miss Browne sent her return out of court. Following that game, and until late in the set, Mrs. Mallory returned to her baseline, where she is most at home.

Each won on service from the fifth to the eighth game and Miss Browne then held the lead at 5—3. Some of the most scintillating rallies of the match stirred rounds of applause and gasps of admiration in te seventh game, which Mrs. Mallory won after deuce had been called three times. Two net-corders were helpful to the champion, but she sent over two beautiful passing shots and her nets and outs missed the lines by inches only. Her forceful driving fairly battered down Miss Browne's magnificent volleying attack. But the Californian came back strongly in the eighth and tenth games .to take the set at 6—4, after the champion had won her service in the ninth game.

Miss Browne at Her Best.

The final game of the set revealed Miss Browne at her best. In forcefulness of driving and in the brilliancy of her volleying recoveries of Mrs. Mallory's hard drives Miss Browne's performance was masterful. A particularly striking rally occurred in the second exchange of the tenth game. Mrs Mallory was playing at the net and made two wonderful gets before she finally hit into the top of the net. Miss Browne followed with a volley for placement and yielded the succeeding point when Mrs. Mallory passed her cleanly. Mrs. Mallory then netted and drove the last ball out on an attempt to pass Miss Browne. She missed the line by an inch and lost the set, 6—4.

The first set showed Miss Browne clearly the superior in the variety of her strokes and in courtcraft. She utilized her volleying ability wisely. She did not rush to forecourt on any and all occasions, but bided her time until her forcing drives had prepared an opening. She knew too well Mrs. Mallory's ability to hit the lines on passing shots, given anything like a fair chance, to take unnecessary risks. When she did get to the net, Miss Browne played as only she among women can play, shining as much through her wonderful gets of cross-court drives as through her own finishing shots. Her backcourt manoeuvering was quite as sound as the champion's and she lobbed accurately to the baseline whenever she needed a few seconds' grace to recover position. Her court tactics were impeccable, and her execution of her shots matched them.

But in the second and third sets it was Mrs. Mallory who had the mastery by reason of her unparalleled steadiness of driving. She never missed except by narrow margins, and she applied so much power to her shots that only a player of Miss Browne's wonderful calibre could have met them at all successfully. She was never discouraged. One of the gamest and most courageous players in women's tennis, she allowed nothing to disturb her superb poise or to affect her grim determination to win. There was no variety to her tactics, but her ability to get the ball back and to control its flight with wizard-like delicacy, at the same time applying punishing speed to it, accomplished more than even the superbly finished courtcraft of Miss Browne could circumvent. Miss Browne employed the strokes and the tactics that could have beaten Mrs. Mallory, if anything could. But, seemingly, nothing in the world could have beaten the champion the way she was traveling in those last two sets.

Norse Girl Comes Back.

Miss Browne led at 2—1 and 3—2 in the second set, but Mrs. Mallory took the next three games for an unbeatable lead. Miss Browne broke through Mrs. Mallory's service in the ninth game, but lost the tenth on three outs, a net and a double fault, the set going to Mrs. Mallory at 6—4, a complete reversal of the opener. The seventh was the critical game of this session. Successive nets made the points 30—15 in Miss Browne's favor. Mrs. Mallory then hit the white of the baseline for a superb placement, but, on one of her rare excursions to forecourt, volleyed the next ball into the net. This made it 40—30 for Miss Browne, and she had her big chance to go into the lead at 4—3 with her own service up. But she sent the ball out of court three times running, and her opportunity evaporated.

The champion was never in serious danger in the third and rubber session. Miss Browne tried everything she knew to avert disaster, but could not. She mixed her shots and shanged her pace admirably. Her game was going as well as ever. But every resource she could summon to her aid was answered by the immovably steady driving of her opponent, who knows better than any other woman player how to profit by errors on the other side of the net. Those are sound, if not brilliant tactics of Mrs. Mallory's. They surely bring results. They might have defeated anybody else in the world yesterday among women players, just as they did Miss Browne.

Victor's Steadiness Counts.

Mrs. Mallory and Miss Browne divided the first two games of the rubber, Mrs. Mallory finishing the first with a beautiful forehand cross-court placement, and Miss Browne the second with a magnificent smash for a kill at the net. Then the champion took three straight games. Miss Browne made a fine effort to corral the fifth, but lost the decisive points by driving out and into the net off service. From that point on there was little doubt of the final outcome. The champion took two of the next three games and won the set at 6—2. Both did some remarkable getting in the final game, but Mrs. Mallory's steadiness forced the errors. Miss Browne volleyed beyond the sidelines for the point that gave Mrs. Mallory her renewed holding of the championship.

In gaining the title for a sixth time, Mrs. Mallory accomplished something that no other woman has ever done. Strictly speaking, it was her fifth championship, for the national tournament which she won in 1917 was dubbed a patriotic tournament, while having all the effect of a championship. She first won the title in 1915, succeeding Miss Browne, who had voluntarily retired after winning it the three preceding years. Miss Browne emerged from that retirement only to aid in the defense of the title against the invasion of Mlle. Lenglen, but in so doing accomplished one of the most remarkable comebacks in the history of the game.

When the last point of the match had been scored in her favor, Mrs. Mallory alarmed the galleries by stretching out on the turf, apparently in a state of collapse. But she was merely giving relief to tired nerves and soon walked off the court amid applause worthy of a splendidly won triumph. Miss Browne, who was the crowd's real idol, also awakened a young hurricane of applause as she walked to the clubhouse. After the match, Mrs. Mallory said that it was the hardest she had ever played, and that her opponent's change of pace and her skill in mixing long drives and tricky short cross-court drives with volleys left her uncertain until the last stroke as to whether she could win. It was in truth Miss Browne's splendid headwork that enabled her to make the wonderful showing she did against the greater strength and superior powers of endurance of her opponent.

The point score stroke analysis follows:

FIRST SET.

											Pts.	G.
Mrs. Mallory	4	2	4	6	4	2	7	1	4	2	36	4
Miss Browne	2	4	6	8	1	4	5	4	2	4	40	6

STROKE ANALYSIS.

	Nets.	Outs.	Placements.	Serv. Aces.	D'ble F's.
Mrs. Mallory	21	11	16	0	1
Miss Browne	9	11	7	0	0

SECOND SET.

											Pts.	G.
Mrs. Mallory	6	3	2	4	2	5	5	4	2	5	38	6
Miss Browne	4	5	4	0	4	3	3	1	4	3	31	4

STROKE ANALYSIS.

	Nets.	Outs.	Placements.	Serv. Aces.	D'ble F's.
Mrs. Mallory	17	8	10	0	0
Miss Browne	7	19	6	0	2

THIRD SET.

									Pts.	G.
Mrs. Mallory	4	3	4	4	6	1	6	5	33	6
Miss Browne	2	5	0	2	4	4	4	3	24	2

STROKE ANALYSIS.

	Nets.	Outs.	Placements.	Serv. Aces.	D'ble F's.
Mrs. Mallory	8	7	9	0	1
Miss Browne	6	18	8	0	0

RECAPITULATION.

	Nets.	Outs.	Pl.	S.A.	D.F.	E.P.	Ers.
Mrs. Mallory	46	26	35	0	2	35	74
Miss Browne	22	48	21	0	2	21	72

The final of the doubles was started as soon as Miss Browne had fairly recovered her breath after her exertions in the singles. Miss Browne and Mrs. Williams quickly established their superiority, despite some clever returns of Miss Gilleaudeau and Mrs. Morris. Mrs. Williams was a fitting mate for Miss Browne in hard and accurate volleying, and it was the attack of the Californians from fore court and their better teamwork that decided the issue so quickly and decisively in their favor. Both Californians received the benefit of numerous set-ups in the shape of soft returns which fairly invited kills.

August 21, 1921

TENNIS A MAJOR SPORT.

With seating accommodation for 20,000 spectators at Forest Hills for the Davis Cup Challenge round and with more than a dozen different countries represented in the preliminary trials, tennis is strengthening its claim to be ranked as a major sport. A few years ago the general public which is now thronging the courts of the West Side Tennis Club, as it will later in the month throng those of the Germantown Club, Philadelphia, would have scoffed at the thought of tennis being so regarded. The game has risen with striking rapidity.

In large measure the change of view has been due to the growing realization that tennis makes exhausting demands upon its exponents. It is due, also, to the extraordinary personal popularity gained by some of the leading players. As a game, of course, tennis requires speed and skill; it demands just as insistently generosity and good-fellowship. The combination as exemplified by such figures as TILDEN, JOHNSTON, BROOKS, WILDING and McLOUGHLIN has proved irresistible. The last named combined with his expertness that human factor, that indefinable " plus," which confers upon its possessor a unique appeal.

It is to these really first-rate players that tennis owes its transition from a purely class game to its present status of a national pastime.

When the two to three hours of continuous exertion demanded by a full five-set tennis match are compared with the short periods of a football game, with their regular rests between, and the purely intermittent activity of the baseball player, one is quite ready to accept Mr. TILDEN's statement that " tennis puts an athlete under the hardest physical, " mental and nervous strain of any " game played by mankind." Admissions to the same effect are on record by WISTER of Princeton and HARTE of Harvard, both All-American football players.

It is, however, in its international aspect that tennis has come surprisingly to the fore. The recent trip of the American players to Australia and New Zealand resulted in the right kind of an Anzac-American entente, while the prominence of Japan's representatives at Forest Hills is of the happiest augury. Waterloo may or may not have been won on the Eton playing fields, but far greater victories, victories for which diplomacy is striving, of international understanding, co-operation and friendliness, are and will be won in friendly contests like those at Forest Hills.

September 3, 1921

TILDEN RETAINS HIS NATIONAL NET TITLE

Champion Overwhelms Wallace F. Johnson in Straight Sets in Final Match.

SCORES ARE 6-1, 6-3, 6-1

Victor Piles Up 86 Points to His Opponent's 51—Richards Beats Davis in Exhibition.

Special to The New York Times.

PHILADELPHIA, Sept. 19.—William T. Tilden 2d had it on his mind today to show how completely and conclusively and quickly a national championship in lawn tennis could be won. Where, in 6dvance, it had been thought that he might be inclined to show leniency towards a fellow Philadelphian and, at the , ery least, allow him to win a set. Tilden showed himself merciless. Apparently there was just one thing that actuat2d him. He was the defending championship and he wished to renew his lease upon the title with as little œremony as possible. Accordingly, he accomplished the feat with neatness and dispatch in three straight sets, which were scored 6—1, 6—3, 6—1. He never gave Johnson a chance. To characterize the match in the vernacular, he smeared his opponent. He was so overwhelmingly superior to the chop stroke artist that no comparison was possible. The defeat was crushing. According to the evidence, the champion might have won in three love sets had he so elected.

Tilden Shows No Mercy.

It was apparent as soon as Tilden started service in the opening set that he meant business. He opened the game with an ace and finished it with an ace. In between he scored a place-

TILDEN'S SERVICE FASTEST IN GAME

Reaches 9 Feet 6 Inches in Air to Drive Ball Over Net on Straight Line.

Special to The New York Times.

PHILADELPHIA, Sept. 10.—That William T. Tilden, 2d, national tennis champion, who is defending his crown on his home club courts here at the Germantown Cricket Club, is the gifted possessor of the fastest service ever developed by any player in the history of the game is a fact that few followers of the sport would undertake to dispute. Not even the vividly remembered railroad service of Maurice McLoughlin, the California comet, could match Tilden's for velocity, and until Tilden assumed his reign McLoughlin's service has been a thing to write books about. Tilden is not landing his first ball in court of late as often as he was a year ago, but when he does connect correctly it still continues to rival a rifle shot in its pace.

McLoughlin's was a twist service, Tilden's is a straight service. McLoughlin's, like every other player's except Tilden's, described a curve in its flight. McLoughlin's was delivered with one leg off the ground, and the comet always followed it to the net. Tilden's first service is delivered with both feet on the ground and he never follows it in. The very force with which the ball is struck prevents an immediate dash to the net, leaving the server flat-footed. When the ball lands inside the lines it almost invariably hits a spot within a foot from the central corner of the service line. It never lands in the far corner. It answers the question as to the shortest distance between two points as accurately as any geometrical axiom.

In a discussion of the champion's speed

of service, the question arose as to the exact height at which Tilden must hit the ball to send it over the net and within his opponent's service line, keeping in mind the fact that the ball travels as nearly on a straight line as any implement propelled by human means could travel. The ball must clear a net three feet high a distance of 39 feet from the base line, and strike a point approximately 21 feet further along close to the service line on the other side of the net. To determine the point at which the ball was started on its travel thus becomes a problem in mathematics.

The accompanying diagram shows (a) the spot at the base line where Tilden is presumed to stand. The distance from (a) to (c), the opposite service line, is sixty feet and any of Tilden's first-ball service would be sure to travel within a negligible margin of that distance. The height of the net (d b) establishes the angle of the ball's travels and, obviously, the point (e) at the apex of the right-angled triangle is the point at which the ball was started.

Knowing the height of the net and the distance from the net to the service line, it is a simple matter to determine the distance from (d) to (c). The employment of a little multiplication and of square root does the trick. In the same way, when the dimensions of the large triangle from (a) to (c) and (e) to (c) have been worked out, the determination of the line (a)-(e) becomes easy.

As it works out, the answer is 9 feet 6 inches. This is of course an approximation, for no one service could be expected to duplicate another exactly in its points of departure and arrival, but, with that taken into consideration, Tilden must reach that enormous distance into the air in order to enable the ball, traveling in a straight line, to clear the net and land safely on the other side.

The feat sounds more difficult than it really is in the champion's case, for, of course, to Tilden's exceptional height and the long reach of his arm must be added most of the length of the racquet. But it is a powerful sweep and a unique one. It is more dangerous than any twist service, more difficult to handle, though it depends upon the element of speed alone.

The player accustomed to pposing Tilden knows exactly where the ball will probably land, but that avails him little. Familiarity with it makes it no easier to handle. It is almost as difficult to return and return safely as the cannon ball for which it has been nicknamed.

September 11, 1921

ment and made the fourth point on an cut by Johnson. He was putting everything he had in ball. Such severity of stroking might have beaten any man in the world. He followed by breaking through Johnson's service with equal ease and decisiveness. When Tilden decides that it is no time for nonsense and that he is out to win, it is the cue for the other man to stand from under. From his vast repertory of strokes the champion tried everything he had in this opening set. and everything he attempted went through successfully. Whether it was a chop or a slice, a volley or a smash, he could not miss the lines if he tried. He made every stroke tell. He took chances and got away with them. The greatest tennis player in the world was at his best and Johnson could not make the opposition look even interesting.

Tilden won the third game at love, with four placements in a row. His speed and his accuracy were dazzling. Then he broke through Johnson's service in another love game. The manner in which he asserted his unquestionable superiority was almost cruel. When he did not end the rally by his first shot, he placed the ball so well and gave it such speed that the next return was a set-up for him. Johnson forced the points to deuce in the fifth game, and just when it seemed as though he might have a chance, Tilden unleashed an extra burst of speed and it was all over.

Johnson Captures a Game.

Then the champion relaxed and allowed Johnson to take the next game on his service. He had been leading at 5—0 and could afford to ease up. But he finished out the set in the succeeding game with no formality whatever, earning one of his points on a volleying placement and taking the others on errors, into which Johnson was betrayed by the severity of the champion's forcing shots. Tilden made twenty-seven points to Johnson's eleven in this set and earned fifteen of the twenty-seven. His errors were one less than Johnson's. His superiority was overwhelming.

The same story was repeated in the second set. Johnson did not make a single earned point in either the first or the second session. Tilden did all the forcing and had all the winning shots. He dropped the first game on Johnson's service and then won three straight. After that the set was on ice for him. It was a romp. Johnson won the fifth and seventh games on his service, largely through Tilden's generosity. The champion had his winning lead and was content to rely upon his own service to maintain it to the end.

The entire match consumed only 42 minutes, and the third set was quickly over. Johnson won the fourth game in this set on service and that was all. He was overpowered by Tilden's superior pace. The only deuce games in the set were the one that Johnson won and the final one of the match. The champion's errors gave Johnson a chance at 30-all, with Tilden serving in this game. Then Tilden showed what he could do when he wanted to. He sent over three brilliant placements in a row, after Johnson had himself scored a placement to carry the points to deuce.

Tilden did it so easily that it looked like the simplest thing in the world. The final shot of the match passed Johnson as though he had been nitched to a lamppost. Superior pace told the tale. Tilden had it in serving, smashing and volleying, and he was better than Johnson in his ground strokes as well. Generally he prepared his openings so well with his superior speed that he could kill the ball on his second return. No more decisive victory has ever been scored in a national championship.

Scores 86 Points to 51.

Tilden scored 78 games to 5 in the three sets and 86 points to 51. His superiority is most strikingly classified in the department of placements. He had 28 to Johnson's 3, and he scored 5 service aces to Johnson's 1. Steady as Johnson is, he was outsteadied by the champion, who made 4 fewer outs, 1 less net and 1 double fault to 2.

At the conclusion of the championship final, which gave Tilden his second consecutive holding of the title, Vincent Richards and Willis E. Davis played an exhibition match, which the national junior champion won at 6—1, 6—3.

The point score and stroke analysis of the match follow:

FIRST SET.

					Pts.	G.
Tilden	4	4	4	5	2	4—27	6
Johnson	1	2	0	0	3	4	1—11	1

STROKE ANALYSIS.

	H.	O.	Pl.	SA.	DF.
Tilden	3	6	12	3	0
Johnson	3	8	0	0	1

SECOND SET.

								Pts.	G.
Tilden	2	4	4	4	3	4	1	5	4—31	6
Johnson	4	2	1	2	5	1	4	3	2—24	3

STROKE ANALYSIS.

	H.	O.	Pl.	SA.	DF.
Tilden	12	11	6	1	0
Johnson	11	8	0	0	1

THIRD SET.

							Pts.	G.
Tilden	4	4	4	3	4	5—28	6
Johnson	2	2	2	5	1	3—16	1

STROKE ANALYSIS.

	H.	O.	Pl.	SA.	DF.
Tilden	7	7	10	0	0
Johnson	11	7	3	1	0

RECAPITULATION.

	H.	O.	Pl.	SA.	DF.	EP.	E.
Tilden	24	22	28	5	1	28	47
Johnson	28	23	3	1	2	4	55

September 20, 1921

WIMBLEDON TO HAVE AN IDEAL STADIUM

Huge Tennis Structure Near Completion—A Possible Model for This Country.

What may turn out to be the model for the American lawn tennis stadium of the future is nearing completion at Wimbledon, England, and is expected to be in readiness for the opening of the annual British and so-called world's championships on June 26 next. The English Lawn Tennis Association, having been guaranteed the holding of these championships for some thirty years, has felt justified in erecting permanent stands. The building of similar stands in this country for the Davis Cup matches and the national championships has often been discussed, but, for reasons of uncertainty regarding the lease of their grounds or lack of sufficient funds or the want of a guarantee of permanent annual attractions, the clubs have not felt justified in the undertaking.

Nevertheless, there is general confidence that circumstances ultimately will make possible the erection of stands here seating 20,000 spectators or more, surrounding courts that will be used for the leading events of each season. With the West Side Club at Forest Hills, the Longwood Club in Boston and the Germantown Cricket Club in Philadelphia in line for Davis Cup or national championship tournaments every year, the need of such stadiums as that which is being constructed at Wimbledon is sure to become more and more apparent.

"The New Wimbledon" is described in interesting fashion in Country Life of London, by Bernard Darwin.

"By June 26, if all is well," says Mr. Darwin, "the New Wimbledon will be ready with some thirteen of its sixteen grass courts and its huge stand that will give to nearly fourteen thousand spectators a view of the centre court. That is a remarkable fact, if we remember that the work on the spot really began only last September."

An Imposing Structure.

"The New Wimbledon lies in a wonderfully pretty and peaceful spot close to the lake and the golf course of Wimbledon Park, with but a very few houses in sight. Once inside the grounds on our tour of inspection, we picked our way through the mud to the vast Roman theatre—of ferro-concrete—which is the grandstand. I do not think either pictures or statistics can quite convey how very big it is or what a tiny little grass plot the centre court looks in the midst of it. Already one begins to feel sorry for the champions who have to fight out their battles frowned down upon by that great circle of seats that rises heavenward tier upon tier. As to statistics, here are just a few that are sufficiently imposing. The area occupied by the theatre-stand is an inadequate word for it—is larger than that of the Albert Hall. If you go for a walk along the corridor, which runs the whole way around and from which open the numerous entrances to the seats, you will walk a quarter of a mile, all but a yard or two. The stand is a figure of twelve sides, four long and eight short. Its length over all from east to west is 278 feet, and from north to south 296 feet. All around are covered seats. There will be approximately 3,920 seats in the covered part of the stand and 475 in each of the uncovered stands on the east and west sides of the court, or nearly 10,000 in all. Behind the open stands and in the east and west gangways there will be room for about 3,000 and 4,000 people. At the southern end are the royal and committee boxes, the members, players and press stands.

"The centre court faces directly north and south, so that the players will not be troubled with a low sun in their eyes. The long axis of the stand is a few degrees west of true north, so that there will be no shadow on the grass portion of the court until quite late in the afternoon. The centre court must always, of course, be the chief attraction, but there will also be much good lawn tennis to be seen on the other grass courts, and there will be a fine general view of them to be obtained from the open back of the corridor.

Hard Courts Also Provided.

"The grass courts are, of course, those on which the work is now being most urgently pressed forward, but they do not make up the whole story of the New Wimbledon. There are to be ten hard courts as well, and one of these is to be a kind of centre court in miniature, with its own championship matches and very possibly the old stand moved from the old Wimbledon.

"Something should be said of the very elaborate laying of the grass courts, which has been done by the All England Club, with Commander Hillyard as the chief artist. To begin with, exceedingly thorough and careful draining has to be done, since the soil is heavy clay. There is, first of all, a herringbone system of three-inch agricultural drain pipes. Next comes a layer of from 6 to 8 inches of graded engine cinders. Over the cinders come 10 inches of fine loamy top-soil and, then, finally, the sacred turf itself.

"It is always a little sad to part with old friends, and the old Wimbledon has many pleasant associations; but of late years lawn tennis has grown so tremendously in popularity that the ordinary person's chance of seeing the big matches was almost negligible. Only those provident people who took seats months and months beforehand could see what is certainly one of the most thrilling and dramatic of all games from the spectator's point of view. The New Wimbledon will, at any rate, give 14,000 people a chance, and it is so attractive a spot that any tears shed over the passing of its predecessor should very soon be dried."

March 26, 1922

MLLE. LENGLEN WINS OVER MRS. MALLORY; SCORE IS 6-2, 6-0

French Expert Easily Retains Her World's Tennis Title at Wimbledon.

SHE WINS IN 35 MINUTES

Makes Quick Work of Match, Beating the American at Her Own Back-Court Tactics.

CROWD OF 14,000 ATTENDS

King and Queen Are Present, but Withdraw When Rain Comes— Patterson Defeats Anderson.

Copyright, 1922, by The New York Times Company.
Special Cable to THE NEW YORK TIMES.

LONDON, July 8.—Mlle. Suzanne Lenglen is still world's woman champion tennis player. She met Mrs. Molla Bjurstedt Mallory today at Wimbledon and defeated her by two sets to none. The games were 6—2, 6—0. Mrs. Mallory failed to score at all in the first game of the first set and from that moment on there was little doubt of the result. It was, in fact, a dull match. There was no marked difference in style between the two players to give it interest and the American champion failed to show the fire which won her victory over Mrs. Beamish yesterday. Mlle. Lenglen dominated the court in nearly every game and secured her title in thirty-five minutes of play.

There was an enormous crowd to see the match. Every reserved seat had been sold days ago and people began to gather at the gates at 7 o'clock in the morning in the hope of getting at least standing room. Thousands were turned away, disappointed. The King and Queen occupied the royal box, and among other distinguished visitors were the Earl of Balfour, Lord Desborough and Mrs. and Miss Lloyd George.

Unfortunately, rain came in the middle of the afternoon and kept on for an hour and three-quarters. It forced Gerald L. Patterson and James O. Anderson to suspend their thrilling contest in the semi-finals of the men's singles and lasted so long that the royalties and many other prominent guests gave up and went home in despair. So it was not until five minutes before 7 o'clock that Mlle. Lenglen and Mrs. Mallory appeared in the arena. The sun was just beginning to decline and threw shadows over the northwestern corner of the court. This made the light a little tricky, but, as the players changed ends every two games, it had small effect on the play.

Cheers from 14,000 Spectators.

Loud cheers from the Stadium in which about 14,000 persons were assembled greeted the players as they began to hit the ball about to limber up. Mlle. Lenglen won the toss and began service. After the fierceness of stroking to which the Patterson-Anderson match had accustomed the spectators, the style of play by the women seemed curiously mild.

The first game ended with Mlle. Lenglen putting the ball where Mrs. Mallory had to run to hit it and so drove it out. Mrs. Mallory also hit out of court as she took her service for the first time. Then Mlle. Lenglen beat Mrs. Mallory by a hard-hit ball just out of the latter's reach on her left hand. Forty-love was the score. By once more hitting Mrs. Mallory's service hard, Mlle. Lenglen took the next point and with it a love game.

The next game, however, was Mrs. Mallory's. She beat Mlle. Lenglen by putting two swift drives to her left side and then placing one to the other side of the court, and again by a fine stroke to Mlle. Lenglen's left. One of the best rallies of the match followed and for the first time Mrs. Mallory began to move up toward the net. From midcourt she put the ball in quick succession to the left and right of Mlle. Lenglen and then the French champion, as she tried to retaliate, drove out of bounds. Mlle. Lenglen managed to bring the score to 40—30, but a splendid shot by Mrs. Mallory straight past her opponent's right hand completely beat her and gave Mrs. Mallory the game.

French Star in Back Court.

Mlle. Lenglen captured the third game easily. She had adopted a baseline game and from the extreme ends of her court kept sending over hard shots which were generally inside the lines by inches. For a short time, when the score stood 15—love, Mrs. Mallory had the French champion running from side to side of the court, but this did not affect the sureness of Mlle. Lenglen's aim. She kept placing the ball in most difficult positions for Mrs. Mallory and won the game largely by hustling the American about.

Mrs. Mallory lost the first point of the fourth game by netting Mlle. Lenglen's return of service, but Mlle. Lenglen hit out on the next. Mrs. Mallory then gave away two points by netting and driving out. It seemed as though she would retrieve her position in the succeeding rally. Mlle. Lenglen tried placing the ball to the right and left of her opponent. Mrs. Mallory replied brilliantly and a series of sharp exchanges ensued with no marked advantage to either. Then Mrs. Mallory succumbed once more to the fatal attraction of the net. Mlle. Lenglen thus gathered in her third game to Mrs. Mallory's one.

However, the showing of the American began to revive the hopes of her supporters. As the next game opened, she treated Mlle. Lenglen to her own medicine and sent shots to either side of her. Mrs. Mallory hit Mlle. Lenglen's next service out, but as a new rally began, she made her way to mid-court and sent some long drives to the extreme corners that made Mlle. Lenglen distinctly unhappy. She tried to extricate herself by hitting straight down the line and went out. A series of rallies followed to Mrs. Mallory's advantage, but by hitting the net again she allowed the score to go to deuce.

An Opportunity Missed.

As Mlle. Lenglen then drove out of court, Mrs. Mallory should have finished the game at once. She had the chance on Mlle. Lenglen's curiously soft return. Mrs. Mallory smashed at it and hit the net. Mlle. Lenglen, however, was good to her rival and, by netting the next ball and outing another, threw away the game.

Each player hit out of court once as the sixth game started and the points soon went to 30-all. Then came some of the best hitting of the match, both driving diagonally across the full length of the court. Each took her returns squarely, but Mlle. Lenglen's superiority told in the end. She placed one too far over to the right for Mrs. Mallory's comfort. The latter reached it, but landed the ball in the net. Mrs. Mallory tried to regain her lost ground in a keen rally. Mlle. Lenglen moved gradually toward the net and sent over a lofty drop shot. Mrs. Mallory reached it and put it into the net.

The tale of the seventh game is soon told. Mlle. Lenglen served and Mrs. Mallory hit the first and fourth balls out and netted the other two. In the eighth game, the last of the first set, Mrs. Mallory pressed Mlle. Lenglen so hard that the French woman had to make one of her marvelous leaps to take a hot cross-court shot just over the net. Mrs. Mallory was fighting hard at this stage and made a splendid volleying rally. She could make no real headway, however, and lost the game and the set at 6–2.

Mlle. Lenglen received evidence of Mrs. Mallory's determination as the second set opened. The American did some fine placing, first to one side and then to the other, and forced her rival to hit out of court. In the next rally only the strength of Mlle. Lenglen's backhand strokes saved her and enabled her in the end to win the game, after deuce had been called twice.

The next game was just as keenly contested. Mlle. Lenglen showed less steadiness than at any other period of the match and, by hitting out and netting two or three of Mrs. Mallory's services, nearly threw away her advantage. In one thrilling exchange, Mrs. Mallory, at the net, put the ball just over. Mlle. Lenglen just managed to run in and play it, and the rally ended in a series of volleys at short range, in which Mlle. Lenglen was at last victor. The third game was remarkably even. The points were scored alternately till deuce was reached, and then Mrs. Mallory went to the net and volleyed a swift ball which Mlle. Lenglen barely managed to reach. The French girl drove her return to the baseline, however, and won the point. It was a disappointment that this game also went to Mlle. Lenglen, as she had by no means the better of it, and won it merely because Mrs. Mallory netted a ball which Mlle. Lenglen had only just been able to reach and return.

End Comes Quickly.

The end of the match now came swiftly. Mrs. Mallory got two points in the fourth game one of them through Mlle. Lenglen's trying a lofty drop shot and hitting out. But the fifth game went to Mlle. Lenglen as a love game. Mrs. Mallory won a point on service in the last game and then, after one fine rally, lost the set and match by netting the ball twice. She was fairly beaten. She had met an opponent who like herself relied on long drives down the court and counted little on service. She had won few of the rallies and had shown that she was neither as accurate nor as resourceful as the French champion. Again and again, after a series of exchanges the full length of the court, Mlle. Lenglen managed to put the ball just out of Mrs. Mallory's reach, and it was because she could not retaliate in kind that Mrs. Mallory had to confess herself vanquished.

Big Amphitheatre Packed.

WIMBLEDON, July 8 (Associated Press).—It was by playing like one inspired that Mlle. Suzanne Lenglen, the marvelous French girl and holder of the world's tennis championship for women, won swift and certain victory over the American champion, Mrs. Molla Bjurstedt Mallory, this afternoon. This was the event which the tennis world had awaited with the keenest interest ever since the match between these two rivals in the United States last year, which came to a sudden ending through the collapse of Mlle. Lenglen. Vast crowds packed every niche of the great centre court amphitheatre. The King and Queen of England were there; the Earl of Balfour, himself an ardent exponent of the game; former King Manuel of Portugal, many Lords and Ladies, and all the followers of tennis who could by reaching the scene of the battle early, by persuasion, coercion or other means, find their way to within sighting distance of the courts.

Notwithstanding that other contests promised royal sport, the Lenglen-Mallory match was the great magnet that attracted the thousands who waited for hours in the rain.

Outbursts of applause gave evidence of overwhelming partiality for the American woman finalist, but the French girl had many supporters, who grew in numbers as she showed her mastery of the sport. She carried herself with poise and confidence. If the nerves which had on prvious occasions assailed her at critical moments were still retained, there was no evidence of them. She played not only with confidence but with deliberation, and thus was able to find the weak spots in Mrs. Mallory's armor and take full advantage of them.

After the easy manner in which Mrs. Mallory had disposed of Mrs. Beamish yesterday in the semi-finals, it was expected that the American would make today's match a notable exhibition. It was thought that an anxious time was in store for Mlle. Lenglen, and that, even if ultimately Mrs. Mallory was beaten, the French champion would have full proof that she had been in a struggle. As it was, Mlle. Lenglen was the winner from start to finish.

The American Outclassed.

It is agreed that the American champion played excellent tennis and showed pluck and sportsmanship throughout. But, so far as the contest today was concerned, it is further agreed by the critics that she was outclassed. Her game would have disposed of any other of the speed of Mrs. Beamish, but with the French girl she did not succeed even in getting under way. The score hardly did her justice. In the second set she reached deuce in most of the games, but when it came to a critical moment Mlle. Lenglen was unbeatable. Her defense was impregnable, except to a clean winning stroke. She seldom netted or drove the ball out of bounds, so that her opponent was compelled always to take risks.

With remarkable generalship, Mlle. Lenglen controlled the positions of both players. She took no unnecessary risks, only thumping across hard shots when an ace point was required. After making a hole in her opponent's court, the French girl repeatedly sent over a drive which could not be reached. Sometimes Mrs. Mallory was brought to the net by a ball dropped over so close that she was unable to get back, then her opponent put across a clear winning pass.

At times Mrs. Mallory, too, made wonderful placements, occasionally putting the ball beyond reach, but she could not keep the pace long enough. She hit bravely throughout, but strategy told.

No Display of Nerves.

Those who expected some show of nerves on Suzanne's part, in view of her American experience, were disappointed, for there was never a moment when she lost her self-control in any sense, and she faced the critical gallery unflinchingly. On the other hand, Mrs. Mallory showed considerable nervousness at times and misjudged shots which ordinarily would have given her no trouble whatever.

The match was grimly businesslike, neither player evincing any emotion, annoyance or distress. When it ended with only two games to Mrs. Mallory's credit both smiled and shook hands over the net, while the applause from the multitude conveyed the onlookers' verdict that the better player had won.

Mrs. Mallory was the first to run up smilingly and shake hands with Mlle. Lenglen and congratulate her upon her victory, and the two stood chatting with the greatest apparent friendliness for a few seconds as they donned their sweaters after the match. Both received ovations as they left the court.

There was no attempt on the part of the spectators to shower personal congratulations on the winner. Among the first to greet her after she quit the court was Pat O'Hara Wood, her partner in the mixed doubles. Umpire Hillyard of the Wimbledon Club shook hands with both players.

Patterson's Victory Well Earned.

The victory of Gerald L. Patterson, the Australian star, over J. O. Anderson was a praiseworthy come-back in the face of an almost wholly Anderson gallery and after Patterson had lost two sets in the first three. Rain stopped the contest after each had won a set and they were 2—all in the third.

In the first set Patterson's hurricane service and swift volleying swept Anderson off his feet. It went to 5–0, Anderson being simply unable to intercept many of the swift services. Patterson also used effectively a chop-stroke with low bound to his opponent's backhand. Finally the set closed 6–1 in Patterson's favor.

In the second set Patterson foot-faulted several times and dropped two service games. Anderson then improved, becoming much steadier off the ground. Patterson netted a lot of cut shots, and Anderson won out on the ninth game.

The third set ran to sixteen games, Anderson again proving the victor. But from that on Patterson, with his whirlwind service and terrific volleying, overwhelmed his opponent and finished the match an easy victor. The scores were 6–1, 3–6, 7–9, 6–1, 6–3.

In the most spectacular men's doubles match of the Wimbledon tourney J. Washer, Belgium, and A. G. Watson, Ireland, defeated Henri Cochet and Jean Borotra of France, 8–6, 2–6, 6–2, 6–4.

July 9, 1922

MISS HELEN NEWINGTON WILLS
United States
Forest Hills, 1924

MRS. MALLORY WINS FROM MISS WILLS

Woman Tennis Champion Retains Her Title, Defeating Coast Girl by 6-3, 6-1.

DOUBLES FINAL THRILLING

California Player and Mrs. Jessup Capture Championship by Scores of 6-4, 7-9, 6-3.

Mrs. Molla Mallory is still queen of the American tennis court. She retained that title yesterday on the courts of the West Side Tennis Club at Forest Hills, L. I., by defeating Miss Helen Wills, of California. The scores of 6–3, 6–1 do not serve as true indication of the tenseness and interest of the contest. The match was a resumption of the age-old battle of youth against experience, of a coming star against a player who has reached the peak of her game.

The champion won, and youth again bowed to experience, but in defeat the 16-year-old girl from the Pacific coast did not disappoint her followers. She gave America's greatest player a real battle, and in the early stages of the match she presented a constant menace, and no one knew it better than "Marvelous Molla."

Neither was the day totally lost for the winsome Miss from California for, paired with Mrs. Marion Zinderstein Jessup, she won the national doubles title from Mrs. Mallory and Miss Sigourney by scores of 6–4, 7–9, 6–3.

There is no disparagement of the wonderful playing of Mrs. Mallory in saying that the girls' champion was the sensation of the day's play. Time and again, in both singles and doubles, she amazed the gallery of about 2,500 persons with the speed of her attack and her uncanny court generalship. Little wonder that the gallery cheered and cheered as she left the courts, smiling an unspoiled smile, which is no less good to see because it is rare.

Miss Wills a Serious Player.

Tennis is a serious proposition with Miss Wills and the fact is evident from her every move on the court. She seldom smiles or speaks and when she does it is only some essential word about the game. Although she was the cynosure of all eyes yesterday one felt that she was entirely oblivious to the fact. She played the game to the very limit of her ability and when Mrs. Mallory defeated her she had no excuses to offer.

In fact, before taking the court for the singles she said:

"I shall do my best, but I hardly expect to win," and though her best was not quite good enough to carry her into the championship it was good enough tennis to thrill all who saw the match.

Particularly in the first set did she threaten the titleholder. Her forcing drives to her opponent's base line had all the snap and speed of a powerful player and Mrs. Mallory found it impossible to handle these with her wonted effectiveness, but the champion's ability as a base-line player enabled her to get some sort of a return on most of these shots and in the end Miss Wills was frequently forced into costly errors.

She won the first game by breaking through Mrs. Mallory's service. The youngster started with a great placement on the opening point and the gallery voiced its approval. There followed three errors on Miss Wills's part and this brought Mrs. Mallory up to 40–15, but the Coast player rallied, forced Mrs. Mallory into a like number of errors and, after getting the vantage point, won the game by a smashing placement to the side line which Mrs. Mallory couldn't even get her racquet on.

Mrs. Mallory Evens Score.

Mrs. Mallory evened up the score on Miss Wills's service, the count in points being 4 and 2. Mrs. Mallory served a love game aided by wildness on the part of Miss Wills. The latter seemed a trifle nervous at this stage of the game, but if she was she soon got bravely over it. She won the following game on her service, but lost the next after it had reached deuce. Then, with Mrs. Mallory leading 3 to 2 in games, Miss Wills proved her gameness and her intent to give the Norse woman a real contest by pulling up on even terms again.

Mrs. Mallory won on her own service in the seventh. The next game was probably the most exciting of the match.

Miss Wills wavered slightly as the game began and the champion was soon leading at 40—30. Then Miss Wills brought the crowd to its feet by shooting a beautiful service ace past her opponent. There followed a series of long, tense rallies, Mrs. Mallory finally passing the younger player with a shot down the left-hand side of the court for the game point. With the score in games 5 to 3 against her, Miss Wills lost control of the ball temporarily and Mrs. Mallory went ahead to take the set at 6—3.

Although the Californian rallied gamely after Mrs. Mallory had won the first two games of the concluding set and captured the third game, that was all the brilliant playing of the title-holder would allow her. It was also apparent that her efforts in the opening set had told on Miss Wills, while Mrs. Mallory, as usual, was as fresh as when she first came on the court. Thus it was a comparatively easy matter for the champion to sweep through the remaining games to her seventh national title.

The point score and stroke analysis follow:

FIRST SET.

		Pts.	G.
Mrs. Mallory	3 4 4 1 6 1 4 6 4	33	6
Miss Wills	5 2 0 4 4 4 2 4 2	27	3

STROKE ANALYSIS.

	Outs.	Nets.	Pl.	Sa.	Df.
Mrs. Mallory	8	11	7	0	0
Miss Wills	17	8	7	1	1

SECOND SET.

		Pts.	G.
Mrs. Mallory	4 4 4 4 5 4 4	29	6
Miss Wills	0 1 6 0 3 1 2	13	1

STROKE ANALYSIS.

	Outs.	Nets.	Pl.	Sa.	Df.
Mrs. Mallory	5	2	9	0	0
Miss Wills	12	7	5	1	1

RECAPITULATION.

	Outs.	Nets.	Pls.	Sa.	Df.	Pts.	E.
Mrs. Mallory	13	13	16	0	0	16	26
Miss Wills	29	15	12	2	2	14	46

Doubles Match a Thriller.

The doubles match produced another thrilling contest and some of the best tennis of the tournament. Again it was Mrs. Mallory against Miss Wills, but this time a third star intervened and took an important place in the spotlight. This was Mrs. Marion Zinderstein Jessup of Wilmington, Del. The former Boston girl carried the burden of the battle for her team and it is largely due to her playing that the names of Jessup and Wills will go down in the records as the doubles champions of 1922, rather than those of Mallory and Sigourney.

As has been said Miss Wills was visibly weary after the strain and fast play of the singles and it was remarked that her playing in the doubles was unusually soft. Mrs. Jessup, on the other hand, has rarely shown to better advantage. She was erratic at times, but she rose to the occasion in the pinches and it was around her that the rally which won the title centred.

In the first set she and Miss Wills had a comparatively easy time, scoring 33 points to their opponents' 28 and winning at 6 games to 4. Then came the second set when the Jessup-Wills combination twice had the set and match point up only to lose it and finally have Mrs. Mallory and Miss Sigourney win at 9—7. Mrs. Jessup and Miss Wills directed much of their play at Miss Sigourney and it was in no small part due to the gradual improvement of the Boston girl that her team carried off that hard-fought second set.

After that set there was a ten-minute intermission and it was lucky for Miss Wills and Mrs. Jessup that it came just then, for the tide of battle had apparently set in against them and they needed time to pull themselves together. When the players took to the court again however, Mrs. Mallory and Miss Sigourney swept through the first three games and looked to be certain winners, only to have their opponents put on the finest kind of a rally and win six straight games and the match. Through it all the tennis was brilliant, the rallies long and hard-fought and the result pleasing, in that it brought a fair sharing of the spoils of the day.

The point score and stroke analysis follow:

FIRST SET.

		Pts.	G.
Wills-Jessup	1 4 4 1 4 5 6 0 4 4	33	6
Mallory-Sigourney	4 0 1 4 2 7 4 4 2 0	28	4

STROKE ANALYSIS.

	Outs.	Nets.	Pl.	S.A.	D.F
Wills	2	6	3	0	1
Jessup	8	7	9	0	1
Mallory	2	5	5	0	0
Sigourney	11	4	2	0	0

SECOND SET.

		Pts.	G.
Wills-Jessup—	4 1 4 1 2 5 4 4 5 5 4 8 0 4 0 5	51	7
Mallory-Sigourney—	1 4 2 4 4 3 2 6 3 7 0 5 4 1 4 7	57	9

STROKE ANALYSIS.

	Outs.	Nets.	Pl.	S.A.	D.F.
Wills	6	4	8	0	1
Jessup	10	23	10	0	0
Mallory	6	13	7	0	1
Sigourney	8	4	6	0	0

THIRD SET.

		Pts.	G.
Wills-Jessup	3 2 3 8 4 4 5 4 4	37	6
Mallory-Sigourney	5 4 5 6 2 1 8 1 2	29	3

STROKE ANALYSIS.

	Outs.	Nets.	Pl.	S.A.	D.F
Wills	3	0	2	0	0
Jessup	5	12	12	0	0
Mallory	4	8	5	0	0
Sigourney	7	4	4	0	0

RECAPITULATION.

	Outs.	Nets.	Pl.	S.A.	D.F.	Pts.	E.
Wills	11	10	13	0	2	13	23
Jessup	18	42	21	0	1	21	61
Mallory	12	26	17	0	1	17	30
Sigourney	26	12	12	0	0	12	38

August 20, 1922

TILDEN IS MONARCH OF TENNIS WORLD

Retains American Title by Defeating Johnston in Bitterly Contested Match.

BATTLE GOES FIVE SETS

Californian Takes First Two at 6-4, 6-3, Philadelphian Others at 6-2, 6-3, 6-4.

WINS THE BOWL OUTRIGHT

Champion Takes Permanent Possession by Third Successive Victory.

Special to The New York Times.

PHILADELPHIA, Sept. 16.—William T. Tilden, 2d, of Philadelphia, is still the lawn tennis monarch of the world. By defeating William M. Johnston of San Francisco at the Germantown Cricket Club, Manheim, this afternoon, in a bitterly-fought five-set match, he retained his title of American champion and, by virtue of having beaten Gerald L. Patterson of Australia, holder of the so-called world's championship, in the semi-finals, he can justly lay claim to the highest position the game affords. No loftier pinnacle could be scaled in all tennis than Tilden climbed today, when he downed his foremost rival by scores of 4—6, 3—6, 6—2, 6—3, 6—4.

This is the third successive year in which Tilden has won the American title and his victory today gives him permanent possession of the championship bowl which has been in competition since 1911. There are five names on the cup besides Tilden's. William A. Larned and Robert Lindley Murray each won it once and Maurice E. McLoughlin, Richard Norris Williams, 2d, and Johnston each had two legs on it.

The final of the Veteran's National singles was won by Dr. Philip B. Hawk, who defeated his fellow Philadelphian, Charles N. Beard, in two love sets. Hawk overwhelmed his opponent, winning in just thirty minutes. Hawk lost only one game in the entire tournament. This is the second year in succession in which he has captured the championship.

The championship final was witnessed by the biggest gallery ever assembled in Philadelphia for a tennis match. It numbered only 12,000, for the reason that no more than that number could crowd their way into the stands or find a lodging place elsewhere from which to watch the proceedings. Every seat was taken and the unreserved section was filled an hour before the time of starting. People were standing three and four deep in the rear of the unreserved stand and in the back rows of the reserved stands. Even the aisles had their quota, and the stand set apart for officials and press contained scores more of spectators than it was ever intended to hold. They even crowded the roof of it. Hundreds who came the last minute had to be turned away.

Johnston Receives Ovation.

It was one of the best behaved galleries of the year. Applause was bestowed discriminatingly and wholeheartedly. At some particularly brilliant rally, the gallery would fairly yell its appreciation. Possibly Johnston was the crowd's favorite, and when he walked off the court a beaten man the ovation accorded him was tremendous in volume and intensely moving in its sincerity. But it was a notably fair attitude that the gallery expressed all the time and Tilden also had his ovation. The champion was playing before a home crowd and he never for a moment lacked full appreciation of his brilliant play.

Tilden's victory was attributable to the fact that he had larger physical resources than Johnston to fall back upon when the crisis of the match came in the fourth set. The Philadelphian had laid down his plan of campaign with rare acumen. He knew and feared Johnston's skill as equal to his own, but he also knew that, in a long, hard, five-set match in which he was required to do a great amount of running, Johnston had not the physical strength to hold to his fastest pace. Accordingly, Tilden was entirely unworried when Johnston took the first two sets. He was playing a waiting game. He made sure of the third set and reserved his big effort for the fourth and fifth. He was gambling on Johnston's stamina and the event proved that he gambled wisely.

The break came in the fourth and fifth games of the fourth set. Up to that time Johnston had been playing the game of his life. He had won two of the first three sets by a clear-cut demonstration of super tennis. His forehand drive was mightier than Tilden's in the first two sessions and his backhand was as good as his forehand. Overhead he was at his best. Thus it was when he was leading two sets to one and with the games three-love in his favor in the fourth set.

If Johnston's strength had held out only ten minutes longer he would have been the 1922 champion. All he had to do was to maintain the pace of the first three games of the set. But he could not. His physical powers were not equal to the emergency.

Johnston's Game Collapses.

To Johnston's legion of supporters in the gallery the sudden collapse of his game was heartbreaking. The abruptness of the transition was astonishing. After the rest period of ten minutes Johnston started the fourth set as though he intended to make a runaway of it. He won the first game to Tilden's 15 and the second to 30. He was playing with dash and power and every ball that left his racquet traveled like a shot to the place he intended it to. His speed forced Tilden into errors and he pummeled the champion's backhand unmercifully. He finished the second game with a beautiful volley placement to Tilden's backhand. Johnston was crowding the net and getting away with it masterfully.

Then, on his own service, the Californian had a tought time winning the third game. Tilden had his back to the wall and was fighting with everything he knew. He was making unbelievable recoveries of shots that would have aced any other player in the world. Three times Tilden was within a point of the game, but each time Johston set grimly and doggedly to work and pulled himself out of the hole. His court covering was wonderful. Finally, he won the game by forcing Tilden to drive twice into the net.

This was where the turning point came. Johnston's frail body was beginning to rebel seriously at the heavy demands upon it. He resisted well in the fourth game, but Tilden won it after deuce had been called. Tilden was taking the net more and hitting more decisively as he saw Johnston weaken. He scored two brilliant passing shots in the fourth game, killed the ball after good position play in another rally, and finished it by forcing a net off service.

The beginning of the end was plainly discernible in the fifth game. Johnston's backhand was going to pieces. His returns were feeble and easily demolished by the champion, who was apparently as fresh as when he started. All the zip and power departed from the Californian's overhead shots. Given a set-up he could not put the ball away fast enough to keep Tilden from recovering it. From the fifth game on through the remainder of the set Johnston scored only six points. Tilden was quick to see the state his backhand was in, and he pounded it in every rally. Johnston responded with error after error.

It was little short of tragic to see the Californian so suddenly bereft of his strength when most he needed it. The championship had been only three games away. It was all but in his grasp when he had to watch it fade away through no faltering of will or spirit, but because the flesh was weak.

Almost tottering from exhaustion, Johnston struggled on through the fifth set, putting his heart into every rally and sticking to his task like the splendid fighter he is. The breaks were all against him, and two bad decisions by Linesman W. L. Robins were especially discouraging. Tilden drove the ball out in the opening game, but the linesman did not call it, and a long and exhausting rally ensued before Johnston finally took the point on a net by Tilden. Tilden won this game after deuce had been reached three times. The game was an additional drain upon the Californian's strength, but he won his service in the second game. This was a love game, and so, too, was the third, which Tilden won.

The point that gave Tilden the fourth game on Johnston's service was a heartbreaker. Tilden drove the ball in the final rally at least a foot beyond the base line, but the linesman was blind to the error, and the ball continued in play until Tilden scored a placement. Thus Tilden had a lead of 3—1, where Johnston should have had a chance of making it 2—all. Tilden's out was so manifest that the stands broke into righteous and vehement protest. The decision was inexcusable, and marred an otherwise wonderful afternoon's work by Umpire Clifford Black and his associate officials.

They divided the next two games, and Tilden was leading 4—2. Then Johnston broke through in a deuce game, only to lose his own service promptly thereafter. Making his last stand, Johnson again won Tilden's service in the ninth game, summoning the last vestiges of his energy to change the net and volley through for the winning placements. He strove gamely in the tenth game as well, but Tilden's hard hitting sent the points to 15—40 with the match point up. Johnston manoeuvred Tilden out of range in the next rally and killed the ball. The next point decided the championship. Tilden, on his second return, dynamited the ball straight down the side line for a clean passing shot off his forehand, and the match was over.

No summary of the match is complete without a tribute to Tilden's wonderful headwork in planning his part of the match as shrewdly as he did. He was fairly outplayed in the early stages, but was always biding his time, waiting for the right moment to strike, and when the time came he struck heavily. Tilden played magnificently in the fourth and fifth sets. Some of his gets, particularly backhand half-volleys, fairly made the spectators gasp their amazement.

Once he took the reins in hand, Tilden was attacking with every shot he sent across the net. His backhand slice worried Johnston greatly. The Californian seemed to have more trouble with it than with the champion's prodigious wallops off his forehand. When Tilden took the net in the final stages he fairly outplayed Johnston, great volleyer though the latter is. All through the match, in fact, Tilden made it extremely uncomfortable for his opponent at the net.

TENNIS FEDERATION BANS WORLD TITLES

Action Taken to Open Way for U. S. L. T. A. to Join International Body.

FIVE COUNTRIES ADMITTED

India's Application Deferred—Four National Championships Recognized—Pro. Title Created.

PARIS, March 16 (Associated Press).—The International Lawn Tennis Federation today formally abolished the present world championships, including those decided heretofore at the Wimbledon tournament in England, thus leaving the way open for the United States Lawn Tennis Association to become an active member of the federation.

It also recognized four national championships—those of England, France, the United States and Australia—and appointed a commission, in compliance with the American request, to organize a European zone for the Davis Cup competition.

The standard international rules, as drafted previously and approved yesterday by the Rules Board, were adopted by the federation. The question of entering the Olympic Games tennis events was left to the member nations for individual decision. No new regulations concerning amateur status were prescribed, but it was undertaken to create a world's professional championship, this word being used in the sense of a title and not of a tournament under the federation's auspices.

In explanation of this, it was stated that there was an evident necessity for the sanctioning of the professional title, to prevent appropriation of the championship by unqualified persons. In the future the title will be bestowed by the federation.

The commission appointed by the federation to arrange for the Davis Cup competition in the European zone, drawings for which were announced in the United States today, consists of A. M. Taylor and R. J. McNair, representing England, and E. R. Clarke of South Africa.

Five new countries were admitted to membership, namely, New Zealand, Canada, Poland, Jugoslavia and Argentina. India's application was deferred on the ground that that country has no constitution. Next year's meeting was set for March 22, in Paris.

March 17, 1923

In the second set Tilden won the first two games and Johnston then took two. They divided the two succeeding ones, and then Johnston won three in a row for the set. Tilden's errors off his backhand were costly in this session. Each played constantly to the other's left, and Johnston's control was the better.

Miraculous Shot by Tilden.

With breaks through service in the first and fifth games, Tilden had this his own way in the third set. The feature was a shot by Tilden in the seventh game. Johnston apparently had won the first point of this game as the result of a swift and widely angled overhead shot. It did not seem humanly possible that Tilden could touch the ball. Yet, with his back to the net, he made an incredible get on his backhand, and sent the ball back on a half volley across court to the side line. Johnston, not expecting a return, was out of position, and the shot aced him by a figurative mile. It was a miraculous shot, and the gallery rose to its collective feet to shout its admiration.

Johnston made a fine effort to retrieve the set in the eighth and final game, but his backhand drives wabbled under a strenuous attack, and Tilden cut loose with a cannonball service to finish the set with an ace. Then came the sudden shift of fortune already described.

In the match as a whole Tilden made 21 more earned points than Johnston and 5 more errors. He scored 4 more games and a total of 16 more points.

The point score and stroke analysis follow:

FIRST SET.

		Pts.G.
Tilden	5 0 4 4 2 2 4 0 4 2—27—4
Johnston	7 4 0 1 4 4 1 4 0 4—29—6

STROKE ANALYSIS.

	Nets.	Outs.	Pl.	SA.	DF.
Tilden	9	9	10	0	2
Johnston	6	10	8	1	0

SECOND SET.

| Tilden | 4 4 2 0 7 2 1 2 1—23—8 |
| Johnston | 0 1 4 4 5 4 4 4 4—30—6 |

STROKE ANALYSIS.

	Nets.	Outs.	Pl.	SA.	DF.
Tilden	8	12	6	1	2
Johnston	8	7	11	1	1

THIRD SET.

| Tilden | 4 5 1 4 4 1 4 6—29—6 |
| Johnston | 1 3 4 0 2 4 1—19—2 |

STROKE ANALYSIS.

	Nets.	Outs.	Pl.	SA.	DF.
Tilden	7	6	10	3	1
Johnston	5	8	5	0	2

FOURTH SET.

| Tilden | 1 2 6 5 4 4 4 4—34—6 |
| Johnston | 4 4 8 8 1 2 0 2 1—25—3 |

STROKE ANALYSIS.

	Nets.	Outs.	Pl.	SA.	DF.
Tilden	12	8	10	0	1
Johnston	15	9	7	0	0

FIFTH SET.

| Tilden | 7 0 4 4 4 2 5 4 2 4—36—6 |
| Johnston | 5 4 0 2 1 4 7 1 4 2—30—4 |

STROKE ANALYSIS.

	Nets.	Outs.	Pl.	SA.	DF.
Tilden	12	10	15	2	0
Johnston	14	5	5	0	0

RECAPITULATION.

	Nets.	Outs.	Pl.	SA.	DF.
Tilden	48	42	51	6	7
Johnston	49	39	42	2	4

Total games—Tilden, 25; Johnston, 21. Total earned points—Tilden, 189; Johnston, 138. Total earned points—Tilden, 57; Johnston, 138. Total errors—Tilden, 97; Johnston, 82. Time of match—1:50.

Umpire—R. Clifford Black. Net umpire—William S. Jamison. Foot fault judge—Albert J. Gibney. Service linesmen—T. Harry Martin and Percy S. Osborne. Base linesmen—Robert G. Kinsey and W. L. Robins. Side linesmen—Frank Zook, E. T. Hutchins, Harry S. Walsh and Albert J. Ostenforf. Centre service linesmen—Charles L. Frederick and Irving C. Wright.

September 17, 1922

LENGLEN AGAIN WINS WORLD TENNIS TITLE

Beats Miss McKane at Wimbledon, 6-2, 6-2, and Gains Crown for Fifth Time.

OUTGENERALS ENGLISH STAR

Drives Opponent From Net and Then Dominates Play From the Baseline.

U. S. DOUBLES TEAM LOSES

Mrs. Mallory and Richards Eliminated by 5-7, 6-3, 6-4—Hunter Meets Johnston Today.

WIMBLEDON, England, July 6 (Associated Press).—Suzanne Lenglen still is supreme among all the women tennis players of the world. With ease and certainty the French star defeated Miss Kathleen McKane the best of Britain's tennis playing women, this afternoon by the score of 6—2, 6—2, and so won, for the fifth successive season, the title of world's champion. It was the fifth meeting between this pair of stars, and, with one exception, it was the worst defeat Suzanne has administered to the lively British woman.

Mlle. Lenglen had the battle in hand from start to finish. Both players started carefully, seemingly with the intention of finding out what the tactics of the other would be, and the first game went to deuce three times. Suzanne soon found out that Miss McKane preferred the safer course of staying in the back court and trusting to deeper returns. So the French star, who can play well in any part of the court, adjusted herself to this style of battle and with her greatest accuracy and sureness in stroking had no difficulty in winning.

She took the first five games, then dropped two and then finished the set on her service.

Advances to Net.

Miss McKane is adept at volleying, and she decided to risk a few excursions to the net when the second set began. Her audacity was worth while, momentarily, giving her one of the first two games, but Suzanne soon drove her back into deeper court and took the net herself. For most of the time the French player also stayed on the back court and the struggle as a whole lacked thrills. It was merely a sure player exchanging blows until a weaker, uncertain opponent hit the ball inaccurately, driving it into the net or out of bounds.

The remainder of the day's program produced little that was exciting. For one thing, the weather, with the thermometer passing the hundred mark in the sun, was too hot for the European players whose game lacked the usual dash. Still it wasn't too hot to keep L. S. D. Deane and Mrs. Shepherd-Barron from beating the American pair, Vincent Richards and Mrs. Molla Mallory, who played a loose game. The score was 5—7, 6—3, 6—4.

Randolph Lycett and L. A. Godfrey of England entered the finals in the men's doubles by defeating Dr. A. H. Fyzee and L. S. D. Deane, Indian Davis Cup players, 8—6, 6—4, 6—3.

Win After Dull Match.

Mlle. Suzanne Lenglen and Miss Elizabeth Ryan entered the finals in the women's doubles by defeating Miss Kathleen McKane and Mrs. Lambert Chambers in a dull match the score of which was 6—1, 6—2. The victors will play the Misses Austin and Colyer in the finals. The youthful Misses Austin and Colyer advanced to the finals by defeating Mrs. Youle and Miss Rose 8—6, 6—4.

Tomorrow the tournament, which daily for a fortnight has drawn huge crowds to the courts, will come to an end. The chief event will be the tussle for the men's title between William M. Johnston of California and Francis T. Hunter of New Rochelle, N. Y. The other matches will be for the various doubles championships.

In the men's doubles, Eduardo Flaquer and Count de Gomar of Spain, will play Randolph Lycett and L. A. Godfree of England; in the women's doubles, Mlle. Lenglen and Miss Elizabeth Ryan will meet the Misses Austin and Colyer; in the mixed doubles, Lycett and Miss Ryan will play Deane and Mrs. Shepherd-Barron.

July 7, 1923

MISS WILLS WINS U. S. TENNIS TITLE

Mrs. Mallory Loses Crown to 17-Year-Old Girl at Forest Hills, 6-2, 6-1.

VICTOR ALWAYS AGGRESSIVE

Skillfully Manoeuvres for Position and Outgenerals Opponent From the Start.

ENGLISH CAPTURE DOUBLES

Miss McKane and Mrs. Covell Triumph Over Miss Goss and Mrs. Wightman Before 6,000 Fans.

The longest reign in the history of American women's lawn tennis was brought to an end in thirty-three minutes yesterday by a 17-year-old girl. Before a crowd of 6,000 at Forest Hills Miss Helen Wills of Berkeley, Cal., toppled Mrs. Molla Mallory off the throne which has stood impregnable before the assaults of the best players in the country for seven of the eight years since 1915.

The doubles title has gone across the seas for the first time in the history of the championship. In the final round Miss Kathleen McKane and Mrs. B. C. Covell of England defeated Miss Eleanor Goss of New York and Mrs. Hazel Hotchkiss Wightman of Boston, 2—6, 6—2, 6—1.

In 1919 the champion was defeated in the semi-finals by Miss Marion Zinderstein, now Mrs. J. B. Jessup, who fell before Mrs. Hazel Hotchkiss Wightman in the final. Mrs. Mallory's game that year was considerably below par as the result of an injury sustained when she fell downstairs. Yesterday's defeat, therefore, may be regarded as the first real dimming of Mrs. Mallory's star in the United States.

The victory of the California girl was one of the most crushing ever scored in a national championship. Only three games did she allow her opponent, winning at 6—2, 6—1. Not even the staunchest backers of Miss Wills looked for anything like this. They hardly dared hope that she could prevail by more than a narrow margin against the woman who had beaten the Western girl on every previous occasion in the last two years.

Quietly, in her characteristic manner, Miss Wills walked out to the courts with Mrs. Mallory, smiled into the champion's face as a dozen cameras clicked and then proceeded to make court history with one of the most devastating attacks ever launched at a titleholder.

Nothing like it has been seen in women's tennis in this country since the end of Mary Browne's reign in 1914, with the one exception of Mrs. Mallory's overpowering attack on Mlle. Lenglen at the West Side Club in 1921.

Seems Nervous at Start.

For just a few minutes the California girl hesitated, giving the impression of being nervous, as she began by hitting weakly into the net, but it needed only a few shots for her to find herself, to gain her composure, before the largest crowd that has witnessed a women's tennis match in the United States. Then she let loose the lightning of her strokes. Mrs. Mallory, playing at her best, from now to the end fought a losing battle that turned into a rout toward the finish. After winning Miss Wills's first two service games, the opening one at 7—5 and the second at love, the titleholder found herself facing a stone wall that catapulted her own strokes back at her with far more force than she had been able to apply.

In the four games that began with the fourth Mrs. Mallory got a single point. Of the sixteen points that the California girl scored in these four games five of them were earned on clean placements and almost all the others were won on forced errors off either her fast service or powerful forehand drives.

Miss Wills's court covering was as thorough as it seems humanly possible for any woman to reach. Gets of the most astonishing character were made, one after another, by the California girl, and so quick was she to anticipate, that even when Mrs. Mallory had worked her completely off the court she was always back into position for the champion's return.

It was this impenetrability of Miss Wills that made Mrs. Mallory realize the futility of her attack. Her sharply angled crossing shots to both the service court and baseline corners, usually certain point winners, were returned in the most brilliant fashion. Mrs. Mallory continued to fight with such lion-heartedness and fine sportsmanship that even those who were rabidly for Miss Wills were won and showed their appreciation in applause.

Miss Wills Mixes Pace.

But it was a losing fight. Never after the third game did the titleholder have a chance. Miss Wills never let down in either steadiness or pace. As the match progressed and the true wizardry of her game was brought out by Mrs. Mallory's heart-breaking fight, the stands were unable to restrain their emotion and broke into thunderous applause in the midst of rallies. Like an Amazon Miss Wills battled her way through the champion's defense, whipping her forehand drives across the net deep to the opposite baseline, then mixing pace and length to catch the other unprepared with soft volleys and chops just over the net. Try as hard as she could Mrs. Mallory was unable to anticipate soon enough and was forced continually into error-making when she was not aced.

The second set was the story of the first over again, with the exception that Miss Wills, in the full flush of success, started off strong and captured the opening game at love. Mrs. Mallory got the fourth at 5-3 and that was her last. Nothing that she could do could avail against the irresistible power of her young opponent's playing.

The final game was the most gripping of the match. Twelve points were scored, eight of them on placements. Trailing at 0—30 Miss Wills unleashed a trio of bullet drives that landed with marvelous precision in the base line corners for points. Mrs. Mallory got the advantage twice and then Miss Wills rose to her greatest heights by sending over two placements and winning the last point of Mrs. Mallory's volley into the net after both had come in to recover shots that hit the band at the top of the net.

When the last point was lost Mrs. Mallory ran to the net, her face in smiles, to congratulate Miss Wills. Still smiling she passed across the turf, amid the loud applause of the gallery, and ten minutes later, with her husband, Franklin I. Mallory, was enjoying the final round of the doubles championship.

After the sensational triumph of Miss Wills the doubles final held little interest, save for the presence of the English team on one side of the net. The spectators were as avowedly for Miss McKane and Mrs. Covell as they had been for Miss Wills in the singles. The English women were inclined to be erratic in the first set, particularly Miss McKane on her overhead shots. Miss Goss's strong service and volleying combined with Mrs. Wightman's severe and beautifully placed smashes were too much for their opponents and they won at 6—2.

Miss McKane and Mrs. Covell found themselves in the second set and maintained their fast pace through the third. Better team work, and greater steadiness, combined with a genius for finding the openings enabled them to take the two sets in as decisive fashion as their opponents had won the first. Mrs. Wightman and Miss Goss continued to play brilliant tennis but they were not as consistently good as the English pair, especially after deuce had been called and the most important points were at stake.

Miss Wills won the toss and began the service against Mrs. Mallory. She was plainly nervous and lost the first two points quickly on nets. Mrs. Mallory drove out and then led at 40—15 on her opponent's out.

Miss Wills pulled up to deuce on Mrs. Mallory's two nets off service. Mrs. Mallory won the game at 7—5 when Miss Wills hit into the net twice in succession. Miss Wills led at 30—0 on the other's errors in the second. Mrs. Mallory struck the ball low at the Californian's feet as she came forward and forced her into an error. Miss Wills took the next two points on errors and broke through to even the score at 1—all.

The champion broke through again in the third game at love on two placements, a net and a double fault. She outplaced Miss Wills and had her moving to make the most difficult returns. Miss Wills increased her pace in the third game and after a brilliant exchange took the first point on a placement. She took the second after running to all corners, aceing Mrs. Mallory at the baseline. She then won the next two points on errors and broke through to even the score at 2—all.

Miss Wills Takes Lead.

Miss Wills made her service effective in the fifth at 4—1 and went into the lead at 3—2. The crowd was applauding her wildly as she made the most beautiful gets and followed them to the forcing shots. The California star broke through again in the sixth at love and then took the seventh also without the loss of a point. Mrs. Mallory had won but one point in the last four games and the count was now 5—1 against her.

Miss Wills went into the lead at 30—15 in the eighth. Mrs. Mallory evened the score at 30—all and then went ahead. Miss Wills brought the score to deuce and then broke through for the set at 6—2 when Mrs. Mallory wilted before the strength of her attack and erred twice.

Miss Wills began the service again in the second set and won the opening game at love on a placement and three errors. Mrs. Mallory was falling off badly in control, and lost the second also at 5—3 on four errors and a beautiful crossing shot by Miss Wills, which passed the champion close to the net. Miss Wills won her third straight game at 4—2. Mrs. Mallory pulled up to 30—40 from 0—40, but drove out in the next rally.

Mrs. Mallory Scores.

Mrs. Mallory won her first game, the fourth, amid applause from the stands, after it had gone to deuce. A lapse from control by the California girl gave her the last points on outs. Miss Wills increased her lead to 4—1 in the fifth on a service ace, a net and two outs. The Western prodigy gave a magnificent exhibition of sharpshooting in the sixth, when she nicked the base line corners for three placement aces after trailing at 15—30. She broke through again in this game, after losing the advantage, by scoring three times in succession on placements. She then brought the match to an end by taking the seventh at 4—2 for the set at 6—1.

The point score and stroke analysis follow:

First Set.

POINT SCORE.

									G.	Pts.
Miss Wills	5	4	0	4	4	4	4	6	6	31
Mrs. Mallory	7	1	4	0	1	0	0	4	2	17

STROKE ANALYSIS.

	N	O	P	SA	DF
Miss Wills	5	5	10	0	1
Mrs. Mallory	11	10	6	0	0

Second Set.

POINT SCORE.

								G.	Pts.
Miss Wills	4	5	4	3	4	7	4	6	31
Mrs. Mallory	0	3	1	5	1	5	2	1	17

STROKE ANALYSIS.

	N	O	P	SA	DF
Miss Wills	5	8	10	1	0
Mrs. Mallory	12	8	4	0	0

Recapitulation.

	N	O	P	SA	DF
Miss Wills	10	13	20	1	1
Mrs. Mallory	23	18	10	0	0

	E	EP	TP	G	SETS
Miss Wills	24	21	62	12	2
Mrs. Mallory	41	10	34	3	0

Umpire—A. J. Gibney. Net umpire—A. Wallis Myers. Foot fault judge—A. J. Ostendorf. Linesmen—Frank Devitt, Benjamin F. Phillips, Rufus Davis, Ralph L. Boggs, R. D. Rickey, W. S. Jamison, Ed. Fisher, C. B. Winne, Clark Pool, Townsend Morgan.

AMERICANS CAPTURE DAVIS CUP DOUBLES

Tilden and Williams Triumph Over Anderson and Hawkes in Long Struggle.

TAKE FIRST SET AT 17-15

Lose Next Two, 11-13, 3-6, but Come From Behind to Win, 6-3, 6-2.

U. S. LEADS BY TWO TO ONE

Needs Only One Victory in Last Two Matches to Retain Trophy —10,000 at Stadium.

DAVIS CUP STANDING.

Team	Won.	Lost.
United States	2	1
Australia	1	2

TOMORROW'S SCHEDULE.

2:30 P. M.—Johnston vs. Hawkes.
3:30 P. M.—Tilden vs. Anderson

Staging a magnificent finish that will go down as one of the most sensational in Davis Cup history, William T. Tilden 2d and R. Norris Williams 2d, the United States doubles team, defeated James O. Anderson and John B. Hawkes of Australia yesterday in the third match of the international challenge round at the West Side Tennis Club, Forest Hills, L. I. A crowd of 10,000 speectators that had thrilled as Tilden and Williams captured the first set at the record-making score of 17-15 and then had seen the Australians take the next two sets, gave free reign to their emotions as the American pair rushed through the fourth and fifth sets in less than half the time it had taken to play the first. The final score was 17—15, 11—13, 3—6, 6—3, 6—2.

The exhibition by Tilden and Williams after the rest periods exceeds in sheer wizardry anything that has been seen in a doubles match in this country in many seasons. Anderson and Hawkes, in spite of the formidable character of their own play, were as helpless as trees in a storm before the lightning of the Americans.

It would be difficult to say which was the more magnificent in the victory, Tilden or Williams. Tilden, refreshed from the shower and rest following the third set, was a totally different player from what he had been in the second and third. No longer was he missing easy set-ups or dubbing over-head shots. Instead he was racing about the court as if inspired, bringing off marvelous gets and dazzling the stands with his daring drives and smashes made on the run. Williams, less steady than Tilden in these last two sets, was cheered again and again as he found the openings with his sharply sliced volleys that left Anderson standing in his tracks. It was nothing short of genius, the way in which the American captain angled his shots from the most difficult of positions and trapped his opponents.

First Set Goes to 32 Games.

In the first set Anderson made 44 errors to Hawkes's 16. In the second set the totals were 40 to 10. The Australian captain made 21 placements to his teammates' 3 in the first game and in the second, 14 to 5. Tilden was the guilty party on the American team in the first set, making 41 nets and outs and 7 double faults to Williams's 24 nets and outs and no double faults. One hour and thirty minutes were required to play the first set. Breaks were frequent, but both sides always evened up their score until the final break came in the thirty-first game. The second set required 53 minutes to play, although the Americans led at 5—4 in games and Tilden had the service in the tenth. The American team was several times within a point of breaking through in the seventeenth and nineteenth games, and the Australians in the twenty-second, but it was not until the twenty-fourth that the set was brought to an end.

The victory of the United States in the doubles gives the defending team the lead at 2 to 1 in the series. Tomorrow Johnston plays Hawkes at 2:30 and Tilden and Anderson follow. Victory in either of these two matches by an American will mean that the Davis Cup will stay in this country for another year. It is not regarded as likely that the Australians will take it with them to the Antipodes.

Two exhibitions followed the Davis Cup match. Vincent Richards of the United States team and Francis T. Hunter of New Rochelle defeated I. D. McInnis and Richard Schlesinger of the Australian team in doubles 6—3, 4—6, 6—2, and B. I. C. Norton of South Africa defeated Manuel Alonzo of Spain in singles, 6—3, 7—5.

Only six thousand spectators were in the stands when Anderson, Hawkes, Tilden and Williams came on the courts. A dozen cameras clicked as the four players warmed up. R. Clifford Black mounted the umpire's chair and play was called.

Anderson Starts Service.

Anderson began the service, winning his game at 6—4 on four errors by Tilden and service and placement aces by himself. Tilden started off on the second game by double faulting twice. The champion made up for these errors with two service aces and won the game at 6—4 on Anderson's errors. Hawkes won his game quickly at love on a placement by Anderson and three errors. The Americans evened the score at 2 all, after brilliant volleying, in the fourth, Tilden coming through with two placement aces. The first break in the set was made through Anderson in the fifth on the Australian captain's nets. Three times he was forced into errors by the Americans' returns off service at his feet.

The Antipodeans returned the favor in the sixth through Tilden on Williams's two errors and a double fault and a placement by Anderson off service. The Anzacs went into the lead in the seventh at 4—3, after trailing at 0—30 when Tilden erred twice and Anderson scored on a placement. Williams won his game at love on three errors and a placement. The Philadelphian was volleying brilliantly, making the most spectacular recoveries. In the ninth game, with the score at 30 all, Anderson hit Hawkes in the head with his first service ball as he stood close to the net. Hawkes was forced to retire for a few minutes while cold water was poured over his head. He returned to the court and the Australians won the game at 5—3, when Tilden drove out of court three times. Tilden gave the Anzacs all of their points in the game.

Tilden evened the score at 5 all by taking the tenth at love. Anderson won his own game in the eleventh when he sent across two placements in a row with the score at deuce. Williams evened the score again at 6 all when he and Tilden earned all four of their points in the twelfth. The Philadelphian scoring on a drive and service ace and Tilden on two placements. Game went on service in the next two games also. Hawkes winning the thieteenth at 4—2 on Tilden's errors and Anderson's placement, and Tilden taking the fourteenth at 4—1 on four errors, three of them by Anderson.

The Americans broke through Anderson in the fifteenth, two errors by Hawkes and Anderson costing them the game. The opportunity to take the set was lost when Williams tossed his service at love in the sixteenth. Williams netted twice and drove out of court once. The United States players were within a point of breaking through their opponents in the seventeenth when they led at 40—30 on Anderson's errors, but they fell off in control at this point and lost 4 of the next 5 points on errors. Tilden won the eighteenth at 4—2 and Hawkes took the nineteenth at love, thanks to the fine shooting of Anderson.

In the twentieth game the Americans led at 40—15. Tilden drove out and it was 40—30. In the next rally the Australians stood against the back stop while Williams shot the ball at them with overhead smashes. They kept lobbing back until Anderson found the op-

August 19, 1923

25

portunity to come up and shoot the ball through the two Americans like a streak. Anderson followed with two outs and the Americans won the game at 5—3.

Anderson scored on a placement and service ace in the twenty-first and took the game on the Americans' errors. Tilden evened the score at 11-all by duplicating Anderson's placement and service ace. The Americans then broke through Hawkes, earning three of their points, but the Anzacs again saved themselves by breaking through Williams on three errors and a placement. Hawkes was making marvelous gets in the next game, which the Australians won after the Americans had pulled up to deuce.

Tilden evened the score at 13-all in the twenty-sixth. Hawkes took the twenty-seventh at love on three earned points. The Australians were two times within a point of the set in the twenty-eighth, when they led at 40—15. A placement by Tilden and a net by Hawkes made the score deuce. Anderson netted and Williams shot across a service ace for the game amid thunderous applause and cheers from the stands. So brilliant was the play that the gallery was applauding in the midst of almost every rally.

Americans Win First Set.

Anderson won the twenty-ninth game. Tilden evened the score at 15-all by taking the thirtieth at love on three errors by Anderson and a placement by Tilden. Tilden and Williams broke through Hawkes in the thirty-first, after trailing at 15—40. Three errors in a row by the Anzacs spelled their doom. Williams came through with a placement ace for the game and then made his service effective in the thirty-second, scoring on a service ace for one of the crucial points. This gave the Americans the set at 17—15.

In the second set the play was of a much milder character. There were far fewer spectacular shots. The rallies were briefer and few games went to deuce. Anderson started the service and there was not a break until the ninth, when Anderson lost his service at 2—4.

The Americans pulled out the fourth game after trailing at 0—30, taking four points in a row on two outs and two placements. The fifth was the first deuce game, Tilden's two outs costing the Americans the game after Anderson had pulled up to deuce on a placement. Anderson's three outs in a row gave the Americans the sixth game. Every one of the Anzacs winning points were won on errors, although three of them were forced through by brilliant shooting. After evening the score at 4-all in the eighth, Tilden and Williams broke through Anderson in the ninth and with Tilden serving next it seemed a second set for the Americans, but after taking the first point the defending team dropped the next four, Williams netting twice and Tilden double-faulting and hitting outside. The score was now 5-all.

Close Play at Net.

Game followed service again for a long period. In the thirteenth game the ball struck the net-band four times in succession and fell over good to be picked up and sent back. Anderson ran in to take the fourth one and sent it back between the two Americans for a placement ace. Anderson's errors gave the other team the fourteenth game, making the score 7-all. Hawkes took the fifteenth at love on three errors and a placement. Anderson handed Williams the sixteenth on errors, after engaging the American pair in smashing exchanges from close quarters. Tilden and Williams were twice within a point of breaking through Anderson when they led at 40—15 in the seventeenth, but Tilden followed with an out and a net and Williams made two outs. Anderson's errors decided the eighteenth game in Tilden's favor.

In the nineteenth the Australians made a fine pull up from 0—40 to game. Williams fell off in accuracy and drove into the net three times in succession. Anderson got the advantage on a placement and, after Tilden had scored, shot across another drive for point. Williams's net gave the game to the Anzacs.

Hawkes was as steady as a rock up to this point. He had made only three outs and five nets in the set, a total of eight errors. While serving in this nineteenth game, Hawkes's first ball struck Anderson on the ear, making amends for the blow struck him in the first set.

The next two games were split. The Australians, leading at 11—10, were twice within a point of breaking through Tilden, and Anderson volleyed like a Titan to smash through the Americans defense, but he was not steady enough. His four nets and an out and a final net by Hawkes enabled the Americans to save themselves after some weak overhead work by Tilden.

Gallery Applauds Struggle.

The gallery showed its appreciation

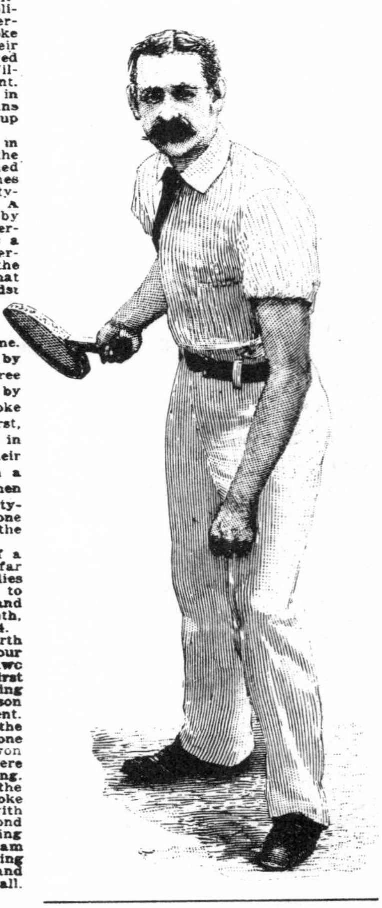

of the defending team's pull up when they changed courts.

The next two games were divided. Anderson and Hawkes, leading at 40-15, were within a point of the set. Williams's fine overhead work enabled the Americans to pull up to deuce. Hawkes's placement gave the others the advantage. Williams followed with a kill and went into the lead at advantage on Anderson's net. A placement by Hawkes and an out and a net by Williams' the last on a difficult shot, gave the game and set to Australia at 13—11.

In the third set the first break came earlier. The Australians, leading at 3—2, broke through Tilden in the sixth, Anderson bringing cheers from the stands with his four placements. Tilden and Williams pulled up to deuce from 15—40 on Hawkes's service in the seventh, but were unable to go any further. Anderson's placement and Tilden's out gave the crucial game to the Antipodeans. Williams won his game in convincing fashion, scoring on a service ace for the last point. Anderson brought the set to an end with a love game, duplicating Williams's feat of taking the last point on a service ace. The next to last point was a beautiful drop volley by Hawkes that trapped Tilden at the baseline after the champion had made a splendid get.

Tilden began the service in the fourth set. After making a double fault, he took the game by scoring on a service ace and a flashy drive. Anderson's vicious forehand shots gave him the second game at love. Williams won his game mainly on errors, and Hawkes took the fourth, making the games 2—all. A terrific smash off service and a double fault by Tilden gave the Australians a 30—0 lead in the next. Tilden pulled up to 30—all on a service ace and Hawkes's net off service, finally taking the game after Hawkes had scored between the two Americans.

Williams's drive between Anderson and Hawkes, giving the Americans the lead at 40—15, brought a wild cheer from the gallery. Anderson double-faulted and the first break was effected. The Americans led at 4—2.

The challengers broke through Williams in the seventh. Marvelous shots followed one after another in the eighth game. Williams's sliced volley and placement off service enabled the defending team to break through Hawkes to lead at 5—3. Tilden's two service aces gained the set for the United States at 6—3.

The gallery was almost in pandemonium. Inspired by their cheers, Tilden and Williams played magnificently and broke through Anderson in the first game, scoring on three placements in a row. Williams, sending the ball like a flash through the narrowest openings, caused the stands to rock with applause.

Continuing their good work, the Americans took the second game, earning three of their points on placements. Aroused by the way the tide had turned, Anderson smashed viciously overhead and scored on three successive placements. After Tilden had netted Hawkes's lob, Anderson found the opening again for the game. Tilden's smart drop volley and Williams's service ace gave the fourth to the Americans, and they now led at 3—1.

Anderson made it 3—2 when he flashed across a service ace in the fifth, after Williams had netted twice and driven out. The Philadelphian let down a bit in this game. Tilden started the sixth with a service ace and took the game on errors, making the score in games 4—2. Hawkes failed to lift Tilden's drive off his feet in the first rally of the seventh game. Williams followed with a service act. Hawkes netted another of Tilden's drives on the volley and the Americans broke through for a love game when Anderson volleyed out Williams's drive. Williams won the last game in quick fashion, bringing the match to an end after 2 hours and 42 minutes of actual play.

The point score and stroke analysis follow:

First Set.

POINT SCORE.

Tilden and Williams— Pts. G.
4 6 0 6 4 1 2 4 3 4 4 4 2 4 4 0 4 4 0
5 2 4 4 1 3 4 0 5 1 4 5 4—86 17

Anderson and Hawkes—
6 4 4 4 2 4 4 0 5 0 6 1 4 1 1 4 6 1 4
3 4 1 2 4 5 1 4 3 4 0 3 1—97 15

STROKE ANALYSIS.

	N.	O.	P.	SA.	DF.
Tilden	20	21	14	6	7
Williams	14	10	14	4	0
Anderson	25	18	21	3	1
Hawkes	8	7	3	0	1

Second Set.

POINT SCORE.

Tilden and Williams— Pts. G.
2 4 1 4 3 5 3 4 4 2 2 4 1 4 0 4 3 4 4
4 2 7 1 5—77 11

Anderson and Hawkes—
4 1 4 2 5 3 5 1 2 4 4 2 4 1 4 1 5 1 6
1 4 5 4 7—80 13

STROKE ANALYSIS.

	N.	O.	P.	SA.	DF.
Tilden	13	12	12	1	3
Williams	23	10	13	1	0
Anderson	22	17	14	0	1
Hawkes	6	4	5	0	0

Third Set.

POINT SCORE.

Tilden and Williams— Pts. G.
3 4 2 4 2 3 3 4 0—25 3

Anderson and Hawkes—
5 2 4 2 4 5 5 1 4—32 6

STROKE ANALYSIS.

	N.	O.	P.	SA.	DF.
Tilden	5	4	6	1	0
Williams	8	4	2	1	0
Anderson	4	5	4	2	0
Hawkes	2	4	5	0	0

Fourth Set.

POINT SCORE.

Tilden and Williams— Pts. G.
4 0 4 1 5 4 2 5 4—29 6

Anderson and Hawkes—
2 4 1 4 3 2 4 3 2—25 3

STROKE ANALYSIS.

	N.	O.	P.	SA.	DF.
Tilden	3	2	4	4	2
Williams	4	5	4	0	0
Anderson	7	3	7	1	1
Hawkes	4	2	1	0	0

Fifth Set.

POINT SCORE.

Tilden and Williams— Pts. G.
4 5 3 4 2 4 4 4—30 6

Anderson and Hawkes—
1 3 5 1 4 1 0 1—16 2

STROKE ANALYSIS.

	N.	O.	P.	SA.	DF.
Tilden	2	3	7	1	2
Williams	3	1	6	2	0
Anderson	4	4	6	1	0
Hawkes	5	1	0	0	0

RECAPITULATION.

	N.	O.	P.	SA.	DF.
Tilden	43	42	44	12	12
Williams	52	30	39	8	0
Anderson	62	47	51	7	3
Hawkes	25	18	13	0	-1

	E.	EP.	TP.	G.	Sets.
Tilden and Williams	179	108	259	43	3
Anderson and Hawkes	156	71	250	39	2

Umpires—R. Clifford Black. Net umpire—A. Wallis Myers. Foot fault judge—Albert J. Gibney. Linesmen—Harry T. Martin, W. S. Jamieson, Ben Dwight, Royal Richey, Howard Kinsey, B. M. Phillips, A. J. Ostendorff, Frank Devitt, Miles Charlock, H. C. Sherrard.

September 2, 1923

TILDEN AGAIN WINS U. S. TENNIS CROWN

Defeats Johnston In Straight Sets Before 12,000 Persons at Philadelphia.

SCORES ARE 6-4, 6-1, 6-4

Champion Captures Title for the Fourth Straight Time by Playing a Steady Game.

CALIFORNIAN IS ERRATIC

Lacks Judgment of Distance, Fails to Place Well and Shows Nervousness in Stroking.

Special to The New York Times.

PHILADELPHIA, Sept. 15.—William T. Tilden 2d of this city won the national lawn tennis championship this afternoon for the fourth consecutive year. It took only fifty-seven minutes for him to dispose of William M. Johnston of California in the final round of the tournament at the Germantown Cricket Club at 6—4, 6—1, 6—4. A gallery of 12,000 spectators, mindful of the wonderful struggle between the same two players last year, filled every available seat to witness one of the most disappointing finals played in the forty-two years' history of the championship.

Johnston was defeated before he went on the courts. He knew he was to face one of the greatest players the game has known just when that player was at the crest of form, and past experience told him that nothing less than his own very best could cope with such a genius. Except for a few sparse stretches, the Californian was far from being at his best. He was nervous and too cautious in his stroking, failed to time his shots accurately, and was woefully off on judgment of distance.

Even when his strokes were going right Johnston could not win the points. His best efforts were confounded by the masterly playing of Tilden, who turned back Johnston's finest strokes with daring passing shots made on the run. The champion showed greater speed and power in all the other rounds than he did in today's match, but his court covering and marvelous gets, which electrified the gallery again and again, surpassed anything seen here all week.

Tilden Returns Everything.

Nothing was too difficult for Tilden to return. From one corner to the other he raced with long strides, bringing off his fore and back hand drives while running at top speed and finding the opening in Johnston's court with astonishing control. Johnston, waiting at the net to finish off the return in the possibility that the other would be unable to get the ball back, stood in his tracks and realized the futility of trying to beat a player who could not be scored on. No matter how cleverly he manoeuvered for position, even with Tilden completely off the court, nothing less than a decisive smash or a sharply angled volley could escape the champion, and Johnston had few of either.

The effectiveness that the Californian displayed at close quarters in defeating Hunter on Friday was entirely missing today. In the three sets he did not earn more than five points from within the service court. This was due mainly to the fact that Tilden stopped his rushing attack dead at the very start by passing Johnston every time he dared to come up.

The Californian began his sallies forward in the second game, when he had the service. Four times in succession Tilden aced him; the first time off the backhand, the next two times on forehand crossing shots and the fourth time by sticking the ball at his feet. Cheers greeted the champion's last shot, which gave him the game at love after the most impressive exhibition of sharpshooting seen here all week.

Johnston learned his lesson in this game and thereafter was more cautious in exposing himself to the other's deadly fire. But when he found that he could not beat Tilden in a back-court game he was persuaded to throw caution to the wind and invade the dangerous territory. There almost invariably the same thing happened, Tilden could not be rushed.

Johnston's Morale Weakens.

All this told on Johnston's morale. He couldn't accomplish anything at the net, he couldn't handle Tilden's speed from the base line, he was tiring from continually running to get Tilden's shots of varied length and direction and he couldn't put the ball away for points even when he had the whole court before him.

Irritation at his continued dubbing of easy shots added to the mental hazards, and by the time the first set was over Johnston's last vestige of hope and confidence had vanished.

The first set had been closely contested although it was plainly evident where lay the superiority, but the second set displayed the drabbest tennis seen here all week. There was hardly a volley that won the applause of the stands. The 12,000 spectators sat silent as Johnston threw away point after point on errors. Tilden won the set at 6—1 with perhaps less exertion than has been used in winning any other set in a national title event. The point score was 26 to 14 and not a single one of Johnston's 14 was earned on a placement or service ace.

Tilden earned 5 of his 6 and had practically all of the other 21 handed to him. The third set was more evenly contested, but, except for the fourth game, when Johnston rose to his true height for the first and only time in the match, the tennis it furnished could hardly have been called interesting. It was due more to a let-down in control on Tilden's part than to aggressive playing by Johnston that the latter carried the score to 6—4.

Tilden Plays With Reserve.

Most of what has been said has been about Johnston for it was Johnston's deficiencies more than Tilden's brilliance that made the match so one-sided. Recognition has been made of how much those deficiencies were the result of Tilden's irresistible playing, and yet it cannot be said that the champion rose to his greatest flights. Any one who had seen him crash Manuel Alonso on Thursday and outplay the brilliant young Norton on Friday realized that Tilden was playing with plenty in reserve today. Only in spots did he show flashes of his lightning strokes. It was not with speed and power of stroking that he accomplished his purpose, but with clever placing and indefatigable court covering.

In such confusing fashion did he mix up his shots and change direction that Johnston was hurried in making most of his strokes and hardly had a moment's rest in the rallies. It was a drive to the rear corner, then one to the opposite corner, then a chop just over the net, then a stroke made with a flat racquet, another chop, a drive and so on until the rally was won or lost. And Johnston had wasted a lot of precious strength.

The champion's control was not of the best and, as Johnston, he was guilty of numerous error on shots that he should have made, but when he needed a point he went out and got it, regardless of how well Johnston played or how many yards of turf he had to cover.

In an exhibition doubles match that followed the playing of the final, R. Norris Williams 2d of this city, and Watson M. Washburn of New York, defeated Manuel Alonso of Spain and B. I. C. Norton of South Africa, 6—8, 6—0, 6—3. Rallies of the newest spectacular character were the order, Norton adding to the amusement of the stands with his antics and astonishing gets which excelled even those of Alonso.

Johnston and Tilden came on the courts at 2:30. Tilden twirled his racquet in the air and Johnston called the wrong side, the service going to the champion. Johnston broke through in the opening game at 5—3 on errors and Tilden took the second at love with four straight placements that caught Johnston at the net. The Californian had the advantage in the third on 3 nets and a double fault by Tilden, but he then drove into the net twice and lost the third straight point and game when Tilden sent the ball speeding down the side line off the back hand.

Fifth Goes to Deuce.

Tilden lost the range of the net in the fourth and dropped 4 points in a row. The fifth went to deuce three times. After the first time Tilden scored on a drop volley, Johnston on a kill; then Tilden sent over a service ace and, after hitting out, took the next two points and game on Johnston's nets. Tilden led at 40—0 on earned points in the sixth and then dropped five points in succession. Johnston made one of his few kills in the match in this game, putting the ball away from midcourt. The Californian won the seventh, also at 4—1, and Tilden ran out the next three for the set in quick fashion.

The second set was decided quickly at 6—1. Johnston defeated himself with his continual error making, dropping the last seven points in the set by hitting out or into the net. The Californian started the service in the third set. Tilden broke through at 4—2 with two passing shots and took the second game at 4—1 on two outs, a kill and a placement. Johnston looked like himself for the first time in breaking through for the fourth, after winning the third on service. He scored twice in succession on placements and a third time for the game after Tilden had netted a backhand shot. Johnston spoiled his good work in the fifth by hitting into the net four times, twice on volley shots. The last out was made on a brilliant drive that passed Tilden at the net and just missed the side line.

Fourteen points were required for a decision in the sixth, Tilden's passing shots giving him the game and a lead of 4—2. Game then followed service until Tilden had gained the necessary six to Johnston's four, each of the last four going at 4—2.

The point score and stroke analysis follow:

First Set.

POINT SCORE.

											Pts. G.
Tilden	3	4	6	0	7	3	1	4	4	4	—36—6
Johnston	5	0	4	4	5	5	4	2	2	1	—32—4

STROKE ANALYSIS.

	N	O	P	SA	DF
Tilden	12	13	16	1	1
Johnston	14	5	6	0	0

Second Set.

POINT SCORE.

								Pts. G.
Tilden	4	1	5	4	4	4	4	—26—6
Johnston	2	4	3	2	2	1	0	—14—1

STROKE ANALYSIS.

	N	O	P	SA	DF
Tilden	7	7	4	1	0
Johnston	14	6	0	0	1

Third Set.

POINT SCORE.

											Pts. G.
Tilden	4	4	1	2	4	8	2	4	2	4	—35—6
Johnston	2	1	4	4	2	6	4	2	4	2	—31—4

STROKE ANALYSIS.

	N	O	P	SA	DF
Tilden	13	10	10	1	0
Johnston	15	9	8	0	0

Recapitulation.

	N	O	P	SA	DF
Tilden	33	30	30	3	1
Johnston	43	20	14	0	1
	E	EP	TP	G	S
Tilden	63	53	97	18	3
Johnston	64	14	77	9	0

Umpire—R. Clifford Black. Net umpire—A. J. Gibney. Foot fault judge—C. N. Beard. Base linesmen—E. T. Hutchins and W. H. Sherrard. Service linesmen—T. Harry Martin and P. Osborne. Linesmen—L. J. Lunn, A. D. Baddy, Miles Charlock, H. Walsh, F. Zook and Irving Wright.

September 16, 1923

U. S. TENNIS PLAYERS SWEEP THE OLYMPICS

Take All Five First Places and Lead With 55 Points—France, Second, Has 28.

RICHARDS AND HUNTER WIN

Triumph Over Cochet-Brugnon of France in the Doubles, 4-6, 6-2, 6-3, 2-6, 6-3.

MRS. WIGHTMAN IS VICTOR

Pairs With Williams and Scores Over Mrs. Jessup and Richards in Mixed Doubles, 6-2, 6-3.

FINAL TENNIS POINT SCORE.

COLOMBES, France, July 21 (Associated Press).—The final point score in the Olympic tennis tourney follows:

United States	55	Italy	4
France	28	Holland	4
Great Britain	16	South Africa	3

COLOMBES, France, July 21 (Associated Press).—America's tennis stars tonight stood supreme among the world's best after this afternoon gaining two more triumphs, which gave them a clean sweep of all five Olympic championships.

The concluding victories were scored in the men's doubles by Vincent Richards and Francis T. Hunter, who beat the Frenchmen, Henri Cochet and Jacques Brugnon, in a stirring five-set struggle, and in the mixed doubles by R. Norris Williams 2d and Mrs. George Wightman, who easily defeated their compatriots, Vincent Richards and Mrs. Marion Z. Jessup, in straight sets. The score in the men's doubles was 4—6, 6—2, 6—3, 2—6, 6—3, and in the mixed doubles, 6—2, 6—3.

Bringing to a close the nine-day tournament, which was fought in torrid weather, at times under the handicap of unsatisfactory conditions, today's matches were witnessed by less than 1,000 persons. They proved an anticlimax after the sensational victories yesterday by Miss Helen Wills over Mlle. Emilienne Vlasto of France in the women's singles and by Vincent Richards over Henri Cochet of France in the men's singles, which clinched the team victory for the United States. Miss Wills and Mrs. Wightman having won the women's doubles the day previous.

The final triumph, however, added substantially to the score of the Americans, who finished with a total of 55 points, nearly double that of France, the nearest rival, which had 28 points. Great Britain took third place with 16 points, Italy and Holland gained 4 points each, and South Africa collected the remaining 3 points.

Three Hold Two Titles Each.

The two youngest American stars, Miss Wills and Richards, and Mrs. Wightman each emerged from the tournament with two titles. The national woman's champion gained the singles crown and shared the women's doubles title with Mrs. Wightman, who also won the mixed doubles title this afternoon. Richards won in the men's singles and men's doubles and, but for the heavy toll his triumph with Hunter exacted on his strength, might have scored a third victory in the mixed doubles with Mrs. Jessup.

This final, however, was quickly decided in favor of Williams and Mrs. Wightman, who were superior in strategy and stroking despite the fact that Williams was playing under the handicap of a bad ankle. Richards was obviously tired and Mrs. Jessup, who was unable to hold up her share of the burden, proved the weakest player of the quartet.

The Franco-American doubles final provided the afternoon's only thrills, but the match became tame when, after battling the Americans on even terms in the first four sets, Cochet and Brugnon wilted in the deciding sets while Richards and Hunter displayed the steadiest attack and best team work they had exhibited at any stage of the match.

Throughout the match, which sparkled with brilliant volleying, sensational gets and rapid-fire net exchanges, Richards and Cochet were the dominating figures on opposite sides of the net. Although he pulled himself together in the final set Hunter for the most part was erratic, repeatedly netting easy shots, while he and his team-mate frequently were caught flat-footed by Cochet's sharply angled drives which whistled through for placements.

Brugnon was the weak link on the French side of the net, his occasional flashes of brilliancy failing to offset his poor service and faulty returns while his partner rose to spectacular heights to keep his team in the running.

Richards Sets Fast Pace.

After a closely fought first set, in which the Frenchmen won through superior team work, the Americans quickly romped through the next two sets, with Richards leading in the dynamic attack. The fourth set saw the Frenchmen at their best. They smashed with far greater accuracy than their rivals and lobbed effectively, racing through the last four games in overwhelming fashion to square the match.

This rally, however, told on Cochet and Brugnon, for after a brief final stand in the fifth set they were easy victims of the fiery attack of the Americans. The recapitulation of the match shows that the French pair earned more points than their rivals, but also committed a great number of errors.

Third place in the men's doubles was decided in favor of France this afternoon when Jean Borotra and René Lacoste defeated Condon and Richardson of South Africa, 6—3, 10—8, 6—3.

The play-off for third place in the mixed doubles was scheduled for this afternoon, but owing to the injury suffered by the British woman star, Miss Kathleen McKane, when she fell Sunday, she and her partner, Mr. Gilbert, scratched, giving the Holland pair, Mme. Bouman and M. Timmer, a walk-over.

The point score of the men's doubles match follows:

FIRST SET.

											Pts.	G.
Richards-Hunter	7	4	3	2	0	4	1	4	0	1	—26	4
Cochet-Brugnon	5	1	5	4	4	2	4	2	4	4	—33	6

SECOND SET.

Richards-Hunter	4	4	3	4	4	4	4	4	—31	6
Cochet-Brugnon	2	2	5	1	6	2	0	2	—20	2

THIRD SET.

Richards-Hunter	4	8	2	1	4	4	4	4	4	—35	6
Cochet-Brugnon	2	6	4	4	1	1	6	0	1	—25	3

FOURTH SET.

Richards-Hunter	6	2	4	4	2	1	2	2	—23	2
Cochet-Brugnon	4	4	2	6	4	4	4	4	—32	6

FIFTH SET.

Richards-Hunter	4	4	2	3	5	4	6	2	4—34	6
Cochet-Brugnon	2	1	4	5	3	0	4	4	2—25	3

The point score of the mixed doubles match follows:

FIRST SET.

									Pts.	G.
Williams and Mrs. Wightman	4	4	4	5	1	4	5	4	—31	6
Richards and Mrs. Jessup	2	2	1	7	4	2	3	2	—23	2

SECOND SET.

Williams and Mrs. Wightman	4	9	0	2	4	3	4	4	4	—34	6
Richards and Mrs. Jessup	0	7	4	4	0	5	1	1	2	—[illegible]	3

July 22, 1924

MISS WILLS RETAINS HER NATIONAL TITLE

Beats Mrs. Mallory in Tennis Final at Forest Hills Before 8,000 by 6-1, 6-3.

IS SUPREME AT ALL TIMES

Tactical Skill Overwhelms Rival Second Straight Time in Championship Play.

ALSO VICTOR IN DOUBLES

Pairs With Mrs. Wightman and Conquers Miss Goss and Mrs. Jessup With Dazzling Attack, 6-4, 6-3.

AMERICA'S PREMIER DOUBLES TEAM
Wimbledon, 1924

Youth triumphant, in the person of Miss Helen Wills, the eighteen-year-old California girl, strode from the courts of the West Side Tennis Club at Forest Hills yesterday. The girl from the Golden West not only defended her national singles title, defeating Mrs. Molla Bjurstedt Mallory, 6-1, 6-3, before 8,000 persons, in the final, but, with Mrs. Hazel Hotchkiss Wightman, captured the national doubles championship.

The youthful victor had to face players who know the glory of reigning supreme. Mrs. Mallory has won the singles crown six times, while for the doubles title, Miss Wills and Mrs. Wightman were forced to meet Miss Eleanor Goss and Mrs. Marion Zinderstein Jessup, three times winners of the national title. But in both cases Miss Wills, fair of face and calm of countenance, was able to match her youth and vitality against experience, never letting up in the power of her strokes and sweeping through both finals in straight sets. The scores in the doubles were 6-4, 6-3.

It was the third time that Mrs. Mallory, the bronzed star from far away Norway, and Miss Wills, the fair performer from sunny California, have met in the final round of the championship tournament. In 1922 Miss Wills came out of the West, a mere child, with a faulty backhand, and fought her way to the final, but at that time she was no match for the Norsewoman and she failed in her attempt to take the cup.

Last year she came East again, vastly improved, and she overwhelmed Mrs. Mallory in straight sets with a burst of speed and a display of stroke that completely dazzled her opponent.

Yesterday she defended the championship with even finer tennis than she had shown to win it.

Californian is Cool.

Miss Wills played with characteristic calm to win her second national title, and she defended the championship quite as easily as she won it last year. Never for a moment was the outcome in doubt, as Mrs. Mallory lacked the confidence she displayed in the matches during the week which led to the final round. It was not until the very end that she took the aggressive, forcing her shots over the net with her powerful forehand and hammering relentlessly at her youthful opponent's backhand.

The last effort was made with all the Norse woman's waning stamina, and although it brought her two games, in a row, defeat was inevitable, and when Miss Wills finally determined to finish matters her opponent had little resistance left.

Although Miss Wills had only one service ace to her credit, her first ball was effective whenever it was inside, forcing errors on returns or making Mrs. Mallory play a defensive shot that was quickly put away. Miss Wills made comparatively few errors, being credited with thirty-eight, against fifteen earned points. The champion's greatest fault was overdriving the base line, but that was only to be expected considering the vigor with which she played. She had trouble also in making her shots travel at a low trajectory and for the most part she was satisfied to risk an out rather than the interference of the webbing.

Mrs. Mallory's service carried little pace and Miss Wills had no trouble making returns. Seldom was the loser able to pass the champion and she earned only five points in the two sets, the rest coming on her opponent's errors. But Mrs. Mallory's chief failing seemed to be a psychological one—a lack of confidence. She swept through her other opponents in easy fashion during the week, not losing a single set and never playing on the defensive at any time.

In Miss Wills, however, she evidently realized that she faced a finer player, one whose courage has never failed and whose calm demeanor never deserts her no matter how strenuous the going may be. She also realized that on the other side of the net was a racquet that commanded a variety of strokes and a player who could scurry over the court to cover a vast amount of territory. With such opposition it was no wonder that Mrs. Mallory lacked confidence.

Miss Wills Scores First.

Miss Wills started the service and ran through the first game in short order, using her powerful forehand drive and forcing Mrs. Mallory into numerous errors. Neither player traveled at a fast pace, but played with caution, evidently sizing up the opposition. Miss Wills ran her lead up to 2 love by breaking through on Mrs. Mallory's service in the second game, scoring once on a pretty placement down the side line and forcing her opponent into errors three times. Miss Wills started the next game with a service ace, but four errors in a row gave the chapter t[illegible] Mrs. Mallory. The young Californ[illegible] was using a little more pace and her [illegible]rehand was just missing her opponent's baseline.

She dropped back to a cautious style in the fourth and broke through Mrs. Mallory's service again, driving rapidly and relentlessly at the Norse woman's backhand and keeping her on the defensive throughout. Miss Wills ran out the next game on her own service, allowing her opponent only a single point, passing Mrs. Mallory once with a neat shot to her backhand corner, hitting in her first ball consistently and forcing netted returns.

At that point, with the score 1—4 against her, Mrs. Mallory cast caution to the winds and evidently decided to play with the power which she is known to possess. She increased the pace on her forehand drives and took the aggressive for the first time in the match. However, she did not have her usual accuracy, and two netted returns and two outs gave Miss Wills the game and the lead at 5—1.

Her failure to nick the lines on daring shots did not swerve Mrs. Mallory's determination to force the going, however, and she continued the fast pace in the next game, striving desperately to ward off the defeat which seemed imminent. But Miss Wills met drive for drive, scurried across the court to make seemingly impossible returns and fought back the attack with all the vigor of her youth and strong right arm. Five times the game went to deuce, first one having the advantage and then the other, but finally Miss Wills forced a bad return on her first ball and scored the winning point after a long rally in which Mrs. Mallory made beautiful gets in an attempt to prolong the set. Miss Wills, more confident with the first set to her credit, continued to play with speed and pace at the start of the second set.

She broke through Mrs. Mallory's serve hammering, at her opponent's backhand and twice scoring replacement aces to win the first game. She rushed the net and cross-courted Mrs. Mallory to take the deciding point in the second game. Twice more she passed her opponent with neatly angled drives to break through her opponent's service in the third. At this point the champion was using every stroke in her repertoire, conserving her energy and forcing the points to a quick conclusion. She fell into error making in the fourth, however, and Mrs. Mallory pulled up to 1—3, after the score had reached deuce twice.

Champion on Offensive.

Miss Wills, again attacking from close quarters, volleyed her way to victory in the fifth, allowing Mrs. Mallory only one point, when the Californian took the sixth on her own service, repeatedly getting in her first ball. She led at 5—1, and seemed to have the championship well in her grasp, but Mrs. Mallory, although outclassed in every department, still had her nerve and in the face of overwhelmingly odds, with the shadow of defeat ever lengthening across her path, she fought back in one last desperate effort to regain the laurels she lost to her youthful opponent in 1923. The Norse woman gathered all her strength for every drive and pulled up to 3—5 by taking the next two games in a row, but the effort cost her fatally in stamina, and when Miss Wills again attacked from the net in the ninth game Mrs. Mallory had little strength left to make returns of the high powered volleys and strong forehands that raked her court. Mrs. Mallory took the lead at 30—love, but after that she was through and Miss Wills gained her second leg on the silver trophy which represents the women's national championship.

Point Score and Analysis.

The point score and stroke analysis follow:

First Set.

POINT SCORE.

Miss Wills	4	4	1	4	4	4	9—30—6
Mrs. Mallory	0	2	4	2	1	1	7—17—1

STROKE ANALYSIS.

	S.A.	P.	O.	N.	D.F.	E.P.	E.
Miss Wills	1	5	8	5	1	6	14
Mrs. Mallory	0	3	11	13	0	3	27

Second Set.

POINT SCORE.

Miss Wills	5	4	4	4	4	4	1	3	4—33—6
Mrs. Mallory	3	1	2	6	1	2	4	5	2—26—3

STROKE ANALYSIS.

	S.A.	P.	O.	N.	D.F.	EP.	E.
Miss Wills	0	7	7	15	2	7	24
Mrs. Mallory	0	2	13	13	0	2	26

Recapitulation.

	S.A.	P.	O.	N.	D.F.
Miss Wills	1	12	15	20	3
Mrs. Mallory	0	5	24	26	0

	EP.	E.	Pts.	G.	Sets.
Miss Wills	15	38	63	12	2
Mrs. Mallory	5	50	43	4	0

Uphill Fight in Doubles.

After a short rest Miss Wills returned to the courts with Mrs. Wightman, to struggle for the doubles championship. First of all the Olympic title holders had to meet Miss Mary K. Browne and Mrs. S. Horace Dudley, a pair which has held the throne three times, in the semi-final round.

Miss Wills and Mrs. Wightman found themselves confronted with an uphill battle, as the former champions took a lead of 4—2 before the Olympic winners got their bearings. However, with Miss Wills sending her volleys to unguarded spots and Mrs. Wightman smashing ferociously from overhead the pair took the first set after a bitter struggle, 9—7, and ran out the second in short order, 6—1, to pass into the final round.,

The final match brought together four of the players who represented the United States in the Olympic Games. Miss Goss started the service and was plainly nervous, allowing herself to be caught in midcourt three times while her opponents scored placement aces. Miss Wills ran out the second game at love on her service, Miss Goss again making frequent errors, but the steady performance of her partner, who covered court brilliantly and made many splendid gets, tended to steady the team, and they ran out the next two games to even the count at 2 all.

The sensational work of Miss Wills at the net, where she volleyed at sharp angles, and of Mrs. Wightman, who smashed overhead with power and accuracy at every opportunity, was not to be denied, however, and theye again assumed the lead at 4—2. Games followed service for the next four games, but the break already had been made and the Olympic champions took the set at 6—4.

Carry Attack Forward.

Miss Wills and Mrs. Wightman continued to carry the attack to close quarters during the second set and they won the first two games in short order. The former national title holders took the third on Miss Goss's service, but Mrs. Wightman won the fourth after the score had gone to deuce. Mrs. Jessup, Miss Wills, Miss Goss and Mrs. Wightman followed with victories on their services, but in the ninth game the Olympic champions broke through on Mrs. Jessup, taking the set, 6—3, and adding the national title to their collection.

The point score follows

FIRST SET.

Miss Wills and Mrs. Wightman—										Pts.	G.
	4	4	0	4	4	4	2	4	1	4—31	6
Miss Goss and Mrs. Jessup—											
	1	0	4	6	2	2	4	0	4	1—24	4

SECOND SET.

Miss Dills and Mrs. Wightman—									Pts.	G.
	4	4	1	6	1	4	1	4	4—29	6
Miss Goss and Mrs. Jessup—										
	2	2	4	4	4	2	4	2	1—25	3

Th summaries:

Sngles, Final Round—Miss Helen Wills, California, defeated Mrs. Molla Bjurstedt Mallory, New York, 6—1, 6—3.

Doubles, Semi-final Round—Miss Helen Wills, California, and Mrs. Hazel Hotchkiss Wichtman, Boson, defeated Miss Mary K. Browne, California, and Mrs. S. Horace Dudley, California, 9—7, 6—1.

Final Round—Miss Wills and Mrs. Wightman defeated Miss Eleanor Goss, New York, and Mrs. Marion Zinderstein Jessup, Delaware, 6—4, 6—3.

August 17, 1924

TILDEN FOR 5TH YEAR IS TENNIS CHAMPION

Overwhelms Johnston in 58 Minutes in National Tournament Final, 6-1, 9-7, 6-2.

KEEPS RIVAL ON DEFENSIVE

Baffles Californian With Lightning Drives—Wins First Set in 12 Minutes.

For the fifth year in succession William T. Tilden 2d of Philadelphia won the national tennis championship yesterday when he defeated William Johnston of San Francisco in the final round of the all-comers tournament in the stadium of the West Side Tennis Club at Forest Hills. In so doing he equaled the record of consecutive victories established by William A. Larned, who won the title from 1907 through 1911, besides holding it in 1901 and 1902.

R. D. Sears, the first to hold the national championship, was supreme the seven years from 1881 through 1887, but there was little competition in those years and the winning of the title meant nothing of the struggle that was entailed during Larned's day and that must be made today, when the foremost players from the world over assemble to contend for the championship.

Tilden's victory over Johnston was his third in succession and his fourth in five years in the final of the championship. In 1919 Johnston defeated him in the title round. Each year since then Tilden has been the winner, vanquishing the Californian in the final in 1920, 1922, 1923 and this year and eliminating him in the fourth round in 1921. Wallace Johnson was his opponent in the final that year. Fifty-eight minutes were all that were required for Tilden to end the hopes of his rival yesterday and to demonstrate to the satisfaction of the 7,500 spectators that there is no player living, probably never has been one, worthy of his steel. As last year, Johnston did not get a set, yielding at 6—1, 9—7, 6—2.

As a matter of fact, it took only twelve minutes, not fifty-eight, for Tilden to make Johnston realize that his attempt to regain the crown he lost to the Philadelphian in 1920 was hopeless. In that short period the champion swept through the first set with a hurricane attack, taking the heart out of the Californian and ending any doubts which may have been entertained as to his ability to defeat the player who had annihilated Patterson in the semi-finals.

Greatest Tennis Ever Seen.

This first set will long furnish a basis of comparison for the play of the champion in the future. A former President of the United States Lawn Tennis Association, one who has been identified with the game for years, declared that Tilden's playing in this set was the greatest tennis he had ever seen, and this opinion was undoubtedly general.

Only the day before yesterday, in the semi-finals, Johnston had put up an exhibition against Patterson that had led to equally positive statements, so devastating had been his attack. Yesterday the Californian underwent the experience of his opponent of the day before. Like Patterson, he came to know the utter futility of trying to chain lightning.

The Tilden that Johnston met yesterday was not the Tilden who had played Richards or Alonso or Kinsey. Against these other opponents the champion had held something in reserve, rising to the heights only when the play was getting away from him or when stung by incidents of the play. It was a Tilden rampant who went on the court yesterday, deadly in earnest, with the zest for the fray and absolutely merciless. Johnston, in the six years that he has played Tilden, has never met him in so relentless a mood at the outset as Tilden was in yesterday.

Ordinarily Tilden takes matters easily at the outset and does not concern himself about winning until the play has gone to some lengths. Such was the case two years ago, when he did not buckle down to his best until Johnston had won the first two sets. It would be interesting to know why he deviated from his usual procedure yesterday. Perhaps he had been so impressed by Johnston's playing against Patterson that he felt that he could not afford to play carelessly for a moment. It was the general opinion that Johnston was far more dangerous than he was last year, and the Californian, himself, believed that he had a better chance to win than he had had since 1919.

Whatever may have been the reason, Tilden went into the match to win as quickly as possible. His strokes flashed through the opposite court with blinding speed, keeping Johnston at his baseline and wearing him out in exhausting exchanges from the baselines.

Holds Johnston on Baseline.

Tilden always got full length on his strokes, whereas after the ball had traveled across the net four or five times Johnston would gradually lose depth and pace, giving the champion the chance to come in to put the ball away in the corner. Although wilting under the strain of trying to hold off Tilden's ground strokes, Johnston realized that it would be suicidal to attempt to gain the net against such speed as this, and the first set was fought out almost entirely from back court.

Tilden's service weakened Johnston also. The champion put everything he had into his delivery, and, although he scored only seven aces outright in the match, he won numerous other points on Johnston's failure to return the ball accurately. The Californian disappointed his admirers greatly in this respect, for he had scored placements off Patterson's cannon-ball service constantly, and it had been expected that he would be able to do so against Tilden also.

The champion's second ball was a big thorn in Johnston's side, breaking too high and wide for him to do more than to get the tip of his racquet on it and send back a short return, which Tilden put away for a point. Neither his fore nor back hand returns measured up to his shots against the Australian. His forehand drive, one of the greatest the game has ever known, found the net constantly. When Johnston's forehand is not going right his whole game is off.

The main reason why it was not going right was because the Californian could not time his shots accurately nor take the ball shoulder high as he likes to. Tilden's drives were of so low a trajectory that when they struck the ground there was little rise to them and it was difficult for Johnston to get the ball over the net on an attacking shot. The Californian had to play as Tilden let him and not as he wanted to, as when he faced Patterson.

Gallery Applauds Players.

It was a pathetic disillusionment for the former national champion after rising to such heights in the semi-finals to be defeated so decisively. The gallery sympathized with him and from the start let it be known which player it wanted to win. But so magnificent was the play of Tilden that it compelled admiration and the applause for the champion at the end of rallies and while the players were changing courts was as prolonged for the champion as it was for his opponent. Particularly was this true in the concluding stages, when, with the stadium growing darker every moment, Tilden speeded up his play in order to bring the match to an end before rain should fall.

It was 3:54 when Albert J. Gibney of the Tennis Umpires' Association climbed into the umpire's chair, the photographers were cleared from the court and play began, with Tilden serving. An indication of what was to come was furnished at the very start when the champion took a love game on Johnston's four errors off service, three of his returns going into the net and one out of court. The Californian brought forth a cheer when he started off with a service ace in the second game.

Tilden had difficulty in handling his delivery and Johnston won the game by rushing in to take the ball after it had dropped from the top of the net and passing Tilden in his service court. Tilden's powerful drives that measured the full length of the court and Johnston's two errors off service gave the third game to the Philadelphian.

The fourth game found the champion giving the greatest exhibition of driving in the tournament. Four times in a row he stuck the ball in the corners, nicking the lines with placements of burning pace, two of them off service. Johnston was as helpless as an infant, compelled to stand in his tracks while his opponent put the ball where he pleased, never giving him a chance to get near it.

Champion Crowds Rival.

The champion continued in the same form in the fifth game and increased his lead to 5—1, scoring on two service aces. Johnston had not got a point in two games. The sixth game was bitterly fought, with Johnston trying in vain to handle Tilden's full length drives. After the ball had traveled over the net eight or ten times the Californian would weaken and lose length or would be forced into error making as Tilden crowded him with the ball.

Tilden broke through again at 6—4, the only deuce game in the set, and then brought the chapter to an end

when Johnston erred off service four times.

Tilden slackened his pace at the start of the second set. It looked as though he had winded himself a bit from his efforts in the first and was resting for a moment. He made four outs in succession in the opening game of the chapter and dropped the first two points in the second game. But with the score at 30—0 in Johnston's favor, Tilden increased his speed, scored on a line drive and took the game when Johnston made three nets in a row.

The last of the three was made on a volley shot when the Californian had the whole court before him.

It is not often that Johnston misses a volley, especially one as easy as was this one, and it was not often that he had the opportunity to get to the net safely again. Johnston stood up better in the driving exchanges in the third game and won it at 4—2. His three errors off service and a line drive by Tilden that passed him as he sought to close in evened the score at 2—all. Tilden broke through in the fifth game, scoring on a drive to the corner of the court, followed by another at a sharp angle that nicked the side line.

Johnston Breaks Through.

Johnston, for the first time in the match, broke through Tilden's service in the sixth, to the delight of the spectators, making a superb volley with Tilden off the court for one of the points and getting another on a double fault. The loss of his service game aroused the champion and he broke through again in the seventh. Twice Johnston sought to get to the net and twice Tilden passed him with smashes straight down the alley line. Both balls traveled in the same line. Once again did Johnston retaliate and break through Tilden in the eighth, scoring on a trap shot that caught Tilden in his back court, and getting another point on a double fault.

Johnston went into the lead by winning the ninth game on service when Tilden hit out of court three times and into the net once. Johnston fooled the champion with a change of pace, Tilden failing to get to the ball quickly enough. The Philadelphian always responded to such challenges and he proceeded to send over three blistering service aces that brought cheers from the gallery.

The next four games went on service, with Tilden winning his own on daring drives along the lines and Johnston earning his on trap shots and changes of pace. Tilden broke through in the fifteenth on two nets by Johnston, a line drive and a forehander across court that passed Johnston as he sought to close in. The score went to 30—all in the sixteenth. Tilden then sent over a service ace for the advantage and in the next rally worked Johnston off to one side and then volleyed the ball out of his reach for the final point of the set.

Johnston began the service again in the third set. Tilden returned it for errors and lost the game at 4—1. In the second game Johnston started off with a dazzling half volley that he lifted off his feet and sent across court for a placement. Tilden was as amazed at the shot as was the gallery and expressed his astonishment.

Johnston Stages a Rally.

Right after that the champion passed Johnston at the net and then took the game at 4—1. A pull-up enabled Johnston to win the third game at 5—3. This was his last one, Tilden taking five in a row, in which Johnston got only six points. The champion won the fourth at love on Johnston's easy errors, pulled up from 0—30 to take the fifth on Johnston's failure in using the chop stroke, and swept through the sixth.

Johnston was making less and less fight and the errors were coming rapidly. Tilden earned only one point in the seventh game, getting the others on Johnston's mistakes, and then, with many in the gallery leaving to escape the approaching rain, the champion speeded up his play and ended the game on service. Johnston questioned the linesman when Tilden's service was allowed to go for an ace on the third point. Tilden hit the ball purposely into the net and then sent over a cannon-ball service that Johnston was unable to do anything with for the match.

The point score and stroke analysis follow:

First Set.

POINT SCORE.

		Games.	Pts.
Tilden	4 2 4 4 4 6 4	6	28
Johnston	0 4 2 0 0 4 2	1	12

STROKE ANALYSIS.

	N.	O.	P.	S.A.	D.F.
Tilden	4	5	7	2	1
Johnston	15	4	1	1	0

Second Set.

POINT SCORE.

		Games.	Pts.
Tilden	1 4 2 4 5 2 4 1 2 4 1 5 0 1 4 4	9	47
Johnston	4 2 4 2 3 4 1 4 4 0 4 3 4 2 2 2	7	45

STROKE ANALYSIS.

	N.	O.	P.	S.A.	D.F.
Tilden	16	20	15	4	3
Johnston	14	14	6	0	0

Third Set.

POINT SCORE.

		Games.	Pts.
Tilden	1 4 3 4 4 4 4	6	28
Johnston	4 1 5 0 2 1 2	2	16

STROKE ANALYSIS.

	N.	O.	P.	S.A.	D.F.
Tilden	4	10	6	1	0
Johnston	12	9	2	0	0

Recapitulation.

	N.	O.	P.	S.A.	D.F.
Tilden	24	35	28	7	4
Johnston	41	27	9	1	0

	Errors.	Earned Points.	Total Points.	Games.	Sets.
Tilden	63	35	103	21	3
Johnston	68	10	73	19	0

Umpire—Albert J. Gibney. net. Umpire, Benjamin H. Dwight. Footfault Judge—R. Clifford Black. Service linesmen—William S. Jamison and T. Harry Martin. Base linesmen—Franklin H. Levitt and Miles S. Charlock. Side linesmen—Paul W. Gibbons, Harry Graff, Hallock C. Sherrard and C. B. Winne. Centre service linesmen—Benjamin M. Phillips and Irving C. Wright.

September 3, 1924

TENNIS WORLD AIMS AT STANDARD BALL

Prevalence of International Matches Proves Need of Greater Uniformity.

One of the results of the many international tennis matches of the past few years has been the growth of a worldwide movement to further standardize the ball. These matches have conclusively proved that players coming from a distance are frequently handicapped by a type of ball being used to which they are not accustomed. The difference in balls is not always due to their manufacture. Atmospheric conditions and other factors enter into the situation. The same ball will respond differently to certain strokes, or rebound differently from the same type of court situated in widely-separated countries. These are the problems which are being considered by committees from the various national tennis bodies and the manufacturers in various countries.

At a recent meeting of the council of the English Lawn Tennis Association, the ball, test committee, which has been carrying on an investigation, reported that a large number of tests had been made with twenty-five different makes of balls, all of which professed to comply with existing definitions of a lawn tennis ball which provide limits for its diameter, its weight and its bounce. The National Committee, in the course of its investigations, recorded the hardness of the ball, the inflation pressure, height of bounce after deflation, reduction in diameter after deflation, and the alteration in hardness of a ball in storage according to the length of time in storage.

Among their findings are statements to the effect that a soft ball will feel lighter on the racket than the harder ball; that with a given racket action it is possible to impart more spin to a soft ball than similar action will impart to a hard ball; that in base line driving the hard ball and the soft ball will each, after bouncing, come off the ground differently.

The council of the English Association, in accepting the committee's recommendations, voted to add a fourth requirement to the ball, which would define hardness or compression with a view to otbaining greater uniformity in performance. This addition to the rule would provide that a certain amount of pressure applied at each end of any diameter of the ball must compress it not more than a stated amount, nor less than another stated amount at an atmosphere of approximately 68 degrees Fahrenheit.

December 22, 1924

MLLE. LENGLEN WINS 6TH BRITISH TITLE

Beats Miss Fry, 6-2, 6-0, in Final at Wimbledon but Gets Only Two Love Games.

Copyright, 1925, by The New York Times Company. Special Cable to THE NEW YORK TIMES.

LONDON, July 3.—In a match that lasted just twenty-six minutes, Mlle. Suzanne Leglen of France defeated Miss Joan Fry, the 19-year-old English girl, in the final of the women's singles of the All-England lawn tennis championships at Wimbledon today, and won the title, 6—2, 6—0. In 1919 the French star first carried off the premier honors of England and she repeated that feat yearly until last season when she was taken ill in the final and had to leave the court, defaulting her match to Miss Kathleen McKane. By her victory today, she thus wins the crown for the sixth time.

Added interest attended the day's play through the sterling victory of the young Americans, Ray Casey of California, and John Hennessey of Indiana, in the men's doubles. They met Jacques Brugnon and Henri Cochet of France in a match that all the experts conceded to the Frenchmen, but they won by 7—5, 5—7, 9—7, 6—4, and gained the final where they will meet the champions, Rene Lacoste and Jean Borotra of France. This match, which is expected to prove one of the best, if not the best of the tourney, has been set over until Monday because Borotra has gained three finals and must be allowed time to rest between the struggles.

It was well known in advance of the engagement between Miss Fry and Mlle. Lenglen that the English girl stood little chance of more than extending the great French player, who now is at the very peak of her form. The English girl is a one-stroke player, but she is aggressive and extremely active and managed to take two games from Mlle. Lenglen. The latter was able to score only two love games on Miss Fry. Interest here is now centred chiefly in the showing Miss Fry will make against the American stars when she goes across to play in the Wightman Cup matches. Today, she was not frightened because she was pitted against the French ace, and she at once began attacking with precision. She made her rival run more than any of Mlle. Lenglen's other opponents have been able to and received great applause when she took the fifth and seventh games of the first set, but the outcome never was in doubt.

July 4, 1925

MISS WILLS RETAINS TWO TENNIS TITLES

Wins National Singles Final for Third Successive Year, Defeating Miss McKane.

SCORES ARE 3-6, 6-0, 6-2

Rallies Quickly After Losing First Set—Gains Championship Bowl Outright.

ALSO SCORES IN DOUBLES

With Miss Browne, She Beats Miss Ryan and Mrs. Bundy Before 7,000 at Forest Hills.

By ALLISON DANZIG.

For the third year in succession Miss Helen Wills won the national women's tennis title yesterday. Recovering from a slump that cost her the first set after she had gained a lead of 3—1, the 19-year-old Berkeley girl conquered Miss Kathleen McKane of England in the final round of the championship tournament at the West Side Tennis Club, Forest Hills. The score was 3—6, 6—0, 6—2. It was the fourth victory for Miss Wills over Miss McKane in their six meetings to date.

Twenty-five minutes were all that were required for Miss Wills to rush through the two last sets, during which time Miss McKane, faltering in control, got exactly the same number of points and two games. Having disposed of one rival, Miss Wills returned to the courts an hour later and, in her first meeting with Miss Elizabeth Ryan since she lost to the Californian at Seabright, retained the doubles championship with Miss Mary K. Browne of Santa Monica that she won with Mrs. Hazel Hotchkiss Wightman last season.

Miss Ryan, paired with Mrs. May Sutton Bundy, gave a brilliant performance at the net, but the speed of Miss Wills off the ground and Miss Browne's decisive smashes overhead were more than the opposing pair could cope with and after making a pull-up from 1—5 to 4—5 in the first set they yielded at 6—4, 6—3.

Referee Gibney Presents Cup.

Miss Wills's victory in the singles gave her permanent possession of the massive championship cup. It was a proud moment for the young girl from the Pacific Coast when Albert J. Gibney, referee of the tournament, who umpired the match in which Miss Wills defeated Mrs. Mallory for the title in 1923 and also was in the chair when she repeated her victory over the New York woman in the final last year, presented her with the handsome silver amphora, filled with a large bouquet of American beauty roses. Jones W. Mersereau, President of the United States Lawn Tennis Association, relieved the champion of her burden and, flanked by officials of the governing body, she posed smilingly for a dozen cameramen while the 7,000 spectators in the stadium applauded.

It was only four years ago that Miss Wills made her first appearance in the East, a young girl of 15 years with her hair in braids. Yet in that time she has accomplished what only three other players have been able to do in the thirty-eight years' history of the tournament. Mrs. Mallory, Miss Mary K. Browne before her, and Miss Hazel Hotchkiss, now Mrs. George W. Wightman, who reigned from 1909 through 1911, are the only other women who have succeeded in winning the championship three years in succession.

Only five players have taken a championship singles cup outright before Miss Wills. They were Miss Juliette Atkinson, who won the cup in competition from 1887 to 1898; Miss Elizabeth H. Moore, who took the second cup in 1905, and Miss Hotchkiss, Miss Browne and Mrs. Mallory, who holds two cups in her possession.

Miss Wills stands as the youngest player ever to accomplish this feat. May Sutton, now Mrs. Bundy, was slightly younger when she won the championship in 1904 than was Miss Wills in 1923, but the Berkeley girl is the youngest player to win the title for a third time. She will be 20 years old on Oct. 6.

The match yesterday between the champion and her English rival was one of the least interesting of the six in which they have met. It was an ideal day for tennis, and after the splendid performances of the two girls in the preceding rounds one of the most brilliant and bitterly fought matches in the history of women's tennis was expected.

Miss McKane, however, never reached the heights that she did against Mrs. Mallory, except for an occasional clever bit of work at the net, and after the first set gave the impression of being tired and lacking in the will to win. She did not seek close quarters nearly so often as she did against Miss Ryan and Mrs. Mallory and when she did go forward her strokes were lacking in the crispness and finality that have been associated with her volleying game.

Champion's Play Lapses.

Miss Wills, at the outset, was rampant. Keenly on edge and keeping right on top of the ball every moment, the champion raised the gallery to a high pitch of enthusiasm as she drove the ball to the corners with tremendous, sweeping strokes, getting the sharpest angles on them. Miss McKane could make no headway against the furious attack of the other and she seldom made any attempt to brave the fire from her opponent's racquet and go to the net. Then, when it appeared the California girl was going to walk away with the match, Miss Wills for some unknown reason, softened in her stroking and lapsed into constant error making.

Five games in a row she allowed to slip away from her, in four of which she held substantial leads. Miss McKane took full advantage of the other's slump and brought her volleying into play. It was easy for her to get to the net now and indeed she was drawn there whether she wanted to go forward or not, for Miss Wills made the mistake of shortening length on her strokes, pulling her opponent up.

Then the American girl found herself in hot water and resorted to lobbing. She failed to get sufficient depth on her lobs and Miss McKane handled them safely until she had worked Miss Wills off to the side, when she angled the ball to the opposite side for a placement.

The champion lost the sixth game after leading at 40—15; the seventh, after leading at 40—30; the eighth, after the score had stood at 30—0 in her favor and the ninth after leading at 30—15. With the score at 30—40 against her, Miss Wills double faulted for the final point.

The start of the second set found Miss Wills playing as she had at the outset. Once again she was running her opponent ragged with blistering drives to the far corners and her service accurately placed and carrying great pace, gave Miss McKane the greatest difficulty. Against such speed as this the invader found it impossible to stroke with control and she constantly drove out of court. A number of times these errors were to be attributed to the fact that she was thinking more about getting to the net behind her drive than she was about the drive itself and the ball hit far outside the baseline. Miss Wills eased up a bit as she found that she had the situation in hand and took the set at love in eleven minutes.

In the final set Miss Will's lobbing played a big part in her victory. Miss McKane went to the net from the start, but the effort was usually in vain, for Miss Wills sent the ball over her head in a parabola, to land almost invariably on the baseline or within inches of it. The English girl never lost heart when Mrs. Mallory passed her persistently down the line or across court, but these lobs did not give her a chance to get at the ball and she became discouraged.

She won the first game with two placements, one of them an overhead shot from the net. Miss Wills won the second at 4—1 with the aid of her service and broke through in the third at the same score, passing Miss McKane and forcing her into erring on a volley shot. The English girl broke through in the fourth and tied the score at 2-all, forcing Miss Wills out of position to score on two soft volley shots. This was the last game she got.

Finishes With a Rush.

Miss Wills, lobbing and driving alternately, outmanoeuvred and outsteadied her opponent and took four games in a row with the loss of only three points. In the final game the champion's service was at its best, and with the score at 40—0 she aroused the gallery to a high pitch as she fought with almost tigerish fury for the last point, raking Miss McKane's court with a series of burning drives off the forehand and backhand. The English girl made a heroic effort to save herself, and after three remarkable gets missed the side line by an inch on a daring backhand drive.

The record of the meetings between Miss Wills and Miss McKane follows: Miss Wills defeated Miss McKane in 1923 in the Wightman Cup matches at 6—2, 7—5, and in the national championship at 2—6, 6—2, 7—5. In 1924 Miss McKane defeated the American in the Wightman Cup matches abroad at 6—2, 6—2, and at Wimbledon in the final at 4—6, 6—4, 6—4. In the Wightman Cup matches this year Miss Wills won at 6—1, 1—6, 9—7.

The point score and stroke analysis of the singles final follows:

First Set.

POINT SCORE.

									Total Pts.	G.
Miss Wills	1	4	4	4	2	4	5	2	2—28	8
Miss McKane	4	1	1	2	4	6	5	4	4—31	6

STROKE ANALYSIS.

	N.	O.	P.	S.A.	D.F.
Miss Wills	10	13	9	1	1
Miss McKane	5	11	7	0	0

Second Set.

POINT SCORE.

						Total Pts.	G.
Miss Wills	6	4	4	4	4	4—28	6
Miss McKane	4	1	2	2	2	0—11	0

STROKE ANALYSIS.

	N.	O.	P.	S.A.	D.F.
Miss Wills	3	6	1	1	1
Miss McKane	11	12	2	0	1

Third Set.

POINT SCORE.

								Total Pts.	G.
Miss Wills	2	4	4	1	4	4	4	4—27	6
Miss McKane	4	1	1	4	1	1	2	0—14	2

STROKE ANALYSIS.

	N.	O.	P.	S.A.	D.F.
Miss Wills	2	8	8	2	0
Miss McKane	4	11	6	0	2

Recapitulation.

	N.	O.	P.	S.A.	D.F.
Miss Wills	14	25	18	4	2
Miss McKane	20	34	15	0	3
	E.	E.P.	T.P.	G.	Sets.
Miss Wills	41	22	79	15	2
Miss McKane	37	15	56	8	1

Umpire—Benjamin Dwight. Net umpire—A. L. Hoskins. Service linesmen—Fred Pond and Miles Charlock. Centre service linesmen—G. W. Dunscombe and S. Wallis Merriken. Side linesmen—C. Stewart, Fred Letson, Harold Swain and Schuyler Van Bloem. Base linesmen—C. Snow and C. E. Winne. Foot fault judge—Thomas Trask.

Time of match—45 minutes.

The point score and stroke analysis of the doubles final follows:

First Set.

POINT SCORE.

										Total Pts.	G.
Miss Wills and Miss Browne—	6	2	4	4	4	4	4	2	3	7—39	6
Miss Ryan and Mrs. Bundy—	4	4	1	2	1	2	6	4	4	5—33	4

STROKE ANALYSIS.

	N.	O.	P.	S.A.	D.F.
Miss Wills	8	7	5	1	1
Miss Browne	5	7	16	0	0
Miss Ryan	4	2	2	0	1
Mrs. Bundy	6	4	3	0	0
Mrs. Bundy	2	1	2	0	1

Second Set.

POINT SCORE.

									Total Pts.	G.
Miss Wills and Miss Browne—	4	6	3	3	5	8	5	4	4—42	6
Miss Ryan and Mrs. Bundy—	0	8	5	5	3	6	8	6	0—30	3

STROKE ANALYSIS.

	N.	O.	P.	S.A.	D.F.
Miss Wills	2	5	10	2	0
Miss Browne	5	8	12	0	1
Miss Ryan	7	7	7	0	0

Recapitulation.

	N.	O.	P.	S.A.	D.F.
Miss Wills	10	12	15	3	1
Miss Browne	10	15	28	0	1
Miss Ryan	11	9	9	0	1
Mrs. Bundy	8	5	5	0	1
	E.	E.P.	T.P.	G.	Sets.
Miss Wills and Miss Browne—	49	46	81	12	2
Miss Ryan and Mrs. Bundy—	35	14	63	7	0

Umpire—Rufus Davis. Net umpire—Henry Graef. Service linesmen—Miles Charlock and Fred Pond. Centre service linesmen—W. D. Bourne and O. Bostwick. Base linesmen—R. C. James and J. W. Anderson. Side linesmen—Frank Sheridan, G. Anderson, E. R. McEvery and C. S. Hall. Foot fault judge—Beals C. Wright.

Time of match—45 minutes.

August 25, 1925

TILDEN WINS TITLE SIXTH YEAR IN ROW

Beats Johnston After Bitter Struggle on Forest Hills Court, 4-6, 11-9, 6-3, 4-6, 6-3.

14,000 PACK THE STADIUM

See Tennis Champion Rise to His Greatest Heights When Pressed the Hardest.

COAST STAR FORCES FIGHT

Carries Attack to Rival and Stirs Gallery to Thunderous Applause With Many Brilliant Shots.

By ALLISON DANZIG.

A new mark in modern American tennis was set yesterday when William T. Tilden 2d won the national championship for the sixth successive year and captured his second challenge trophy outright. Playing before a gallery of 14,000 wild and enthusiastic spectators who filled the stadium at the West Side Tennis Club to capacity, the Philadelphian defeated William Johnston in a thrilling five-set match that required two hours and ten minutes of play. The score was 4—6, 11—9, 6—3, 4—6, 6—3.

Not since 1922 has Johnston made such a great fight against the champion as he did yesterday, nor has any match of the six in which they have met in the final of the championship are used a gallary to more thunderous applause then reverberated through the concrete enclosure almost continuously during this struggle. Johnston's well-wishers were there in thousands and Tilden's were too, and between them they made the welkin ring as it has not rung all season at Forest Hills.

Forgetting these two crushing defeats at the hands of Tilden in 1923 and last year, Johnston went out on the courts and fought with all the blistering pace and deadlines that characterized his grade in 1915 when he conquered Maurice McLaughlin and Dick Williams to win the title for the first time.

Carries Attack to Tilden.

Volleying flawlessly with punching strokes and whipping his mighty forehand across the net at a low altitude, the Californian carried the attack to his opponent with such impetuousness that for the first and second sets Tilden had to call upon all his brilliancy as a shot-maker to stay on even terms with him. Taking the first set by breaking through in the tenth game, Johnston never faltered in the second chapter until in the eighteenth game he stood at set point.

At this stage the gallery was in a state of such excitement that it could hardly control itself. Every shot was followed with breathless interest, every winning stroke of Johnston's threw the spectators almost into a state of frenzy. It was the same keyed-up gallery, ready to break into pandemonium at any moment that saw Johnston take the two first sets from Tilden in the 1922 final.

Three times Johnston stood within a single stroke of taking this set, but nervousness and the inability to control his shots in the critical moments cost him the game, one of the longest in the match, and Tilden took the next two games for the set. This failure to rise to the occasion in a moment of great opportunity characterized Johnston's play for the rest of the match. He wasted a lead of 3—1 in the third set and after breaking through Tilden's service to lead at 2—1 in the final set he allowed a lead of 40—15 to slip away in the fourth game, and instead of his going ahead at 3—1 the score became 2—all. These lapses on the Californian's part caused a great deal of anguish to his thousands of admirers.

An indication of how close the match was is furnished in the point score. Only two points separated them in the totals. Tilden having 191 to 189 for Johnston. Johnston made 147 errors to Tilden's 140, while the Californian scored five more earned points than did the other, 49 to 44.

Victory Sets Modern Record.

The victory of Tilden, gained over a field that included the outstanding players of the world, enabled him to surpass the mark of five consecutive triumphs of William A. Larned, a mark that has stood since 1911. Richard D. Sears, in the days when tennis was in its infancy and competition was confined practically entirely to players in the East, won the title the seven first years it was played for, from 1881 through 1887. But his achievement is not to be compared with Tilden's. For four years he stood out until the challenge round, while Tilden has played through every tournament and has demonstrated his superiority over players from all quarters of the globe, as well as all sections of the United States.

Winning the American title during the time the Philadelphian has held sway has amounted practically to earning the world's championship, a test of such physical proportions alone as to make the tournaments of the early Newport days, with their small fields and their matches decided by the best two out of three sets, pale into almost child's play by comparison.

Even Larned, meeting a much stiffer brand of opposition, was not required to play through, for it was not until later that the challenge round was abandoned. Larned won the title in all seven times, but Hugh L. Doherty of England, the only foreign player to capture our title, took the crown from him in 1903 after he had won it the two years preceding, and it was not until 1907 that he began his five-year reign.

Tilden's triumph yesterday was perhaps the most notable of his six. Almost throughout the season the champion has been encountering difficulties, and the desperate straits in which he found himself in the Davis Cup matches against Lacoste and Borotra of France raised serious doubts as to his invincibility, maintained so unquestionably for five years. At last, it seemed, the world's recognized greatest player was slipping.

Strain Tells on Champion.

Never before had Tilden's physical condition, one of the biggest factors in his undisputed reign, been so sorely tried as it was against Lacoste, and the near collapse of the Philadelphian in that match seemed to point toward the disintegration of one of the greatest fighting machines in the history of the game.

Entering the tournament for the first time since he won the title with disturbing questions being raised on all sides by players and critics alike, Tilden answered them by appearing in each match in the pink of physical condition and playing with all the mastery and sureness that has characterized his game since 1920. Against Richards, in his first real test, he was the great shot maker of old, striding the court like a colossus, and yesterday he was equally his old self. He missed more shots than he has been known to in the past, but that characteristic faculty for rising to unassailable heights when under stress, so pronounced in his five-set match with Shimizu in 1921 and in his 1922 struggle with Johnston, was no less evident yesterday.

It can be said that, regardless of the closeness of the match, in spite of Johnston's rushing start there was never much real fear entertained as to Tilden's ability to come through in the end. He was in danger, but with his great backhand shots working in such beautiful fashion and his legs carrying him in untiring fashion across the turf with giant strides it was realized that the champion was at the peak of form and condition and that Johnston faced a herculean task.

If Tilden ever entertained any doubts as to his ability to win his face never showed it. He was the personification of confidence, cool, calculating, with the brain of the tennis master, smiling in enjoyment of the play even when it was going against him.

Johnston in Serious Mood.

Johnston was of a more serious mood. He knew the task he had cut out for him, even when he was carrying Tilden before him, and throughout the two hours and ten minutes that the match lasted he played with a concentration and absorption in his work that contrasted sharply with Tilden's lighter mood.

Bitter experience had taught Johnston that Tilden is never more dangerous, never more to be feared, than when he is in the hole. He could look back to that match in 1922 when he had Tilden 3—0 in the fourth set and victory seemed at hand, a victory that would have given him his third leg on the challenge trophy and permanent possession of it. Instead of winning he saw his hopes go up in the smoke of a rampant champion's burning placements, and the cup passed out of competition into Tilden's hands.

The knowledge of the champion's great rallying powers, which he showed in defeating Lacoste after being four times within a point of defeat in the third set, must have been a disturbing element to Johnston and caused him to slump at so many critical moments. It is by such narrow margins as this, the ability to come through in a pinch, that many matches are decided, and while Johnston's faltering cannot, perhaps, be said to have cost him the match, it did prevent him from gaining a lead of 20 in sets.

The psychological advantage of such a lead, putting the burden of a rally upon Tilden, would have been inestimable to one so mentally strung as was Johnston, particularly when he appreciated the fact that Tilden had defeated him every year in the championship since 1919, when the Californian gained his only victory over the champion.

No finer day could have been asked for a championship final than was yesterday. Following upon a week of unfavorable weather, the warmth of the sun and the clear sky came as a relief. As early as 1 o'clock the crowd began to assemble. Train after train unloaded its burden of humanity at Forest Hills and an hour before play started the streets were swarming with eager fans and were clogged with motor cars.

Seats Fill Rapidly.

Lines half a block long formed at the numerous ticket windows and when Tilden and Johnston came on the courts only a few seats were vacant. These were taken rapidly and shortly after the match got under way many were standing on the top tier while others sat in the aisles.

Johnston and Tilden faced the usual array of cameras and after a short practice session Umpire Benjamin H. Dwight, Chairman of the National Tennis Umpires' Association, sent the two rivals away on the battle of the year.

Johnston started the service and won the opening game at love as Tilden hit the first three balls served into the net or out of court. The champion gained a lead of 40-0 in the second but Johnston pulled up to deuce with the aid of a lob placement. Tilden then won the game with a service ace.

Johnston began to go to the net in the third, only to be passed down the line and forced into a volley error on his second advance. Tilden broke through and then lost his own game after a series of long driving volleys. Johnston was adding pace to his strokes right along and stirred the gallery as he pasted the ball to the corners, keeping Tilden on the run. He won the third game with two volleys, one a backhand shot that was cheered.

Johnston Breaks Through Again.

The Californian broke through again in the sixth game when Tilden failed on a kill and double faulted. The champion retaliated in the seventh as Johnston lapsed in control. He tied the score at 4—all when Johnston, after leading at 40—15, returned service four times in a row for errors. Johnston ran through the ninth game at love, scoring the final point on a short drive across court. He then set himself to break through in the tenth. Driving with murderous power and forcing Tilden wide of the court, he gained a lead of 40—15.

Standing within a point of losing the set, Tilden pulled up to deuce on Johnston's two errors. A double fault gave Johnston the advantage, and in a stirring driving duel Johnston drove deep to Tilden's back court, forcing him to hit out of court. The roar that went up from the gallery as the umpire called the first set for Johnston must have been heard in Times Square.

Service was of little value in the second set. In no less than ten of the first fourteen games service was broken through. Johnston won the first game and broke through in the second on Tilden's errors after trailing at 15—40. His outs cost him his own game in the third after he had scored on a beautiful overhead shot from deep court. Break followed break until Tilden won the eighth on service and tied the score.

Tilden broke through in the ninth and was twice within a point of the set in the tenth. Johnston finally won the game after a number of close decisions that aroused the gallery. A drop volley by Johnston, following a great recovery by Tilden, gave the Californian the advantage and Tilden double faulted.

Johnston rushed through the eleventh with two service aces and was twice within two points of the set in the twelfth, only to falter and err on easy shots. The next four games went quickly on errors.

The eighteenth game furnished the tensest moments of the match. In one furious volley after another the two men assailed each other with powerful drives. Tilden mixed up his pace and length when he found Johnston's defense could not be broken down by speed. With the score at deuce, Tilden sent up a lob which went out, giving Johnston set point.

Tilden Scores Service Ace.

A service ace by the champion saved him and "brought the house down." Twice more the Californian stood within a stroke of the set, but his errors cost him his advantage, and Tilden brought the game to an end with a backhand volley after 18 points had been disputed. Johnston seemed disheartened by his failure to come through and dropped the next two games quickly.

The third set found the Californian beginning to show signs of stress. Neither of the two played at top speed, and Tilden, after dropping three games in a row on errors, took five straight. Johnston was hitting into the net constantly toward the end, finding it impossible to get the ball above the barrier.

After the rest period Johnston came out refreshed and let loose with burning speed. He won the first game at 6—4 and broke through in the second with four placements, two of them marvelous low backhand volleys that were wildly applauded. He led at 40—0 in the third but inability to handle Tilden's service cost him the game. He held his lead to the end, and after Tilden had won the ninth game with a great exhibition of driving off the backhand, Johnston pulled up from 15—40 to take the tenth for the set. This was the signal for the gallery to break into a frenzied burst of cheering.

Tilden steeled himself as the final set started and two blistering drives, one passing Johnston at the net, gave him the first game. Johnston, covering court in admirable fashion, took the second and third, volleying with deadliness after forcing Tilden wide of the court. A backhand volley gave him a lead of 40-15 in the fourth and then he slumped, making four errors on simple shots in succession.

Coast Star Continues to Err.

Johnston continued to err in the fifth game and the gallery sensed that his chance was gone. He won the sixth on Tilden's three outs and the champion took the next three games for the set and match, keeping Johnston on the run and sticking the ball through the narrowest openings.

With the score at 40—15 in the final game, Tilden paused to measure the service line carefully and then put across a cannonball service ace. Johnston had failed again but he had made a magnificent fight and Tilden put his arm around Johnston's shoulder to show how much he sympathized with him and appreciated his game but futile effort.

In the forty-four years that the national championship has been held since 1881, there being no play in 1917, only sixteen players have succeeded in winning the title. They are Richard D. Sears, Henry W. Slocum, Oliver S. Campbell, Robert D. Wrenn, Frederick H. Hovey, Malcolm D. Whitman, William A. Larned, Hugh L. Doherty, Holcombe Ward, Beals C. Wright, William J. Clothier, Maurice E. McLoughlin, R. Norris Williams 2d, William Johnston, R. Lindley Murray and William T. Tilden.

Sears and Larned each won the championship seven times. Tilden has won it six times. Whenn was titleholder four times, Campbell three times, Whitman three times, Slocum, McLoughlin, Williams and Johnston each won it twice, while the six others each won it once. Of the sixteen champions all are living except Doherty.

The point score and stroke analysis:

First Set.

POINT SCORE.

	Games	Total
Tilden	0 6 4 2 0 2 4 5 0 3—4	26
Johnston	4 4 1 4 4 4 2 3 4 5—6	35

STROKE ANALYSIS.

	N.	O.	P.	SA.	DF.
Tilden	10	14	2	2	2
Johnston	10	12	9	0	0

Second Set.

POINT SCORE.

	Games	Total
Tilden—	0 3 5 2 4 0 4 4 4 6 1 5 4 2 1 4 1 1 0 4 4—11	68
Johnston—	4 5 3 4 2 4 0 2 2 8 4 3 1 4 4 1 4 8 2 2— 9	67

STROKE ANALYSIS.

	N.	O.	P.	SA.	DF.
Tilden	17	31	11	4	2
Johnston	25	27	14	3	1

Third Set.

POINT SCORE.

	Games	Total
Tilden	4 0 1 3 4 4 4 4 4—6	28
Johnston	2 4 4 5 1 1 1 1 1—3	20

STROKE ANALYSIS.

	N.	O.	P.	SA.	DF.
Tilden	11	6	6	2	2
Johnston	14	6	1	0	0

Fourth Set.

POINT SCORE.

	Games	Total
Tilden	4 3 5 0 5 5 6 3 4 4—4	39
Johnston	6 5 3 4 3 7 4 5 2 6—6	45

STROKE ANALYSIS.

	N.	O.	P.	SA.	DF.
Tilden	13	18	10	0	0
Johnston	12	16	12	2	1

Fifth Set.

POINT SCORE.

	Games	Total
Tilden	4 1 2 5 4 2 4 4 4—6	30
Johnston	1 4 4 3 2 4 2 0 2—3	22

STROKE ANALYSIS.

	N.	O.	P.	SA.	DF.
Tilden	6	8	5	2	0
Johnston	14	9	8	0	0

RECAPITULATION.

	N.	O.	P.	SA.	DF.
Tilden	57	77	34	10	6
Johnston	75	70	44	5	2
	E.	**EP.**	**TP.**	**G.**	**Sets.**
Tilden	140	44	191	31	3
Johnston	147	49	189	27	2

Umpire—Benjamin H. Dwight. Net Umpire—Rufus Davis. Service Linesmen—Irving Wright and Harry Martin. Center Service Linesman—Paul W. Gibbons. Side Linesmen—Miles Charlock, Fred Pond, Benjamin Phillips and G. E. Dunscombe. Base Linesmen—Charles A. Anderson and Commander W. S. Anderson. Foot Fault Judge—Albert J. Gidney. Time of match—2:02.

September 20, 1925

LENGLEN IS WINNER OVER HELEN WILLS IN FURIOUS BATTLE

French Tennis Star Exhausted After 6-3, 8-6 Victory Over American Girl.

BAD RULING UPSETS LATTER

Probably Cost Her Set—Discouraged, She Lets Down From Brilliant Play.

GREAT OVATION TO VICTOR

She Is Buried Under Roses Before Throng—Faints After Doubles Triumph.

By FERDINAND TUOHY.

Special Cable to THE NEW YORK TIMES

CANNES, Feb. 16.—Some spectacles will remain forever, even in a newspaper man's mind. Such a one was that of Suzanne Lenglen, lying on a bed on the sixth floor of the Carlton Hotel here at noon today, directly after her grueling victory over Helen Wills, 6–3, 8–6, in a simple game of tennis, yet a game which made continents stand still, and was the most important sporting event of modern times exclusively in the hands of the fair sex.

A few minutes before I had left her enthroned in a flowery bower in the middle of the tennis court, like a Broadway favorite after a successful first night.

From a balcony high above the Mediterranean, I next glimpsed her being swept along a side street by a frantically cheering mob.

Then she lay before me in complete whiteness of coat and skirt, capped by her vivid, crimson face.

Quiet While Furore Rages.

Only Mme. Lenglen moved about the room, arranging gifts of dolls and flowers above the furore still arising from the street, as I asked Suzanne how she had won, and waited while she gasped back to breath and then broke into a torrent of French, openly, perhaps challengingly, as if to say "Now, for God's sake, will you English nd Americans leave me alone for a moment and accept my supremacy, however much it may be getting boresome!"

In fact, I believe she said something very like that, though her first frantic thoughts were for her stricken father at Nice, while I fought with time to capture every notion, opinion, thought and reaction from the victor of Europe. Nor was Suzanne silent. She rebelled against being forced to play, maintained the champion's right to do what she pleases pleaded for tennis goodwill, explained away her indifferent display by her private worry and the public din during the match, developed praise for her rival, though somewhat grudgingly, and concluded on the defiant note that she, Suzanne, intended to improve "malgre tout" and to remain enthroned for many years more, with her racquet as her sceptre.

Gives Grudging Praise to Helen.

With difficulty I dragged from the prostrate girl such grim, little verbal bouquets as "Helen showed more intelligence than I imagined. She has style and production of strokes. She will improve."

Yet none of this—not even Helen's splendid drives and placings—worried Suzanne, according to Suzanne. A little more magnanimity might have issued from that white couch and its palpitating burden, and with little damage to the truth of the day, as most of those present saw it.

"Elle se defende, la petite," said a French spectator of our amazing courtside champion.

"What a game Helen is putting up!" echoed the serried Anglo-American brigade. "She'll have her yet."

Suzanne might have beckoned to the rising star more fervently without in any way weakening her own puissant case, since today she, too, played like a champion.

For many games in the memorable second set she fell steadily behind, yet she overhauled the challenger, to win fresher than Helen, and this afternoon the French girl gave one of the pluckiest performances ever seen on a tennis court when she was carried in a collapsing state to victory with Vlasto in the women's doubles over Helen Wills and Contostavos.

She is to leave here later with her mother in an automobile for Nice. She is absolutely all in and is cancelling tonight's celebration held here in her honor.

Helen Exceeds Expectations.

As for the match itself it is already passing into history after one acre, for one hour, had given almost the greatest sporting story of history. The pointage was: First set Helen 17 points, Suzanne 31. Second set, Helen 46, Suzanne 52. In the whole match Helen hit 32 outs and Suzanne 30 while each player double faulted only once each in the match.

As Morpurgo said afterward, Lenglen played far below her form which was confirmed by Suzanne herself saying that she never got a solitary one of her famous shots home—though for that surely, Helen was in some measure responsible.

Helen made her admirers, who are legion, fairly roar with joy as she more than exceeded expectations, playing well within herself, and remaining permanently on the offensive almost throughout the long drawnout second set. The crashed drives with masculine strength and more than masculine precision home along the side and baselines, causing the panting Suzanne to scurry hither and thither as she certainly had never scurried before.

Struggle a Thrilling One.

And Suzanne's incessant, weak returns! How some other day Helen, more experienced, may profit by them with the net crashes entirely absent in this day's battle virtually fought out on the baseline!

Though, perhaps, all honors were even—Helen, for playing so magnificently, Suzanne for so doggedly defending her empire.

"There are other years," ventured Helen, almost imperceptibly. "I play in the singles at Nice. Helen can come there if she likes," throws out Suzanne.

But how thrilling it is to see femininity linked in such a struggle as today's. Suzanne, exquisitely garbed in pink and white, purring her usual approval to admiration as she skipped about the courts cotton clad Helen following behind with her strange,

AN INTERNATIONAL MIXED DOUBLES TEAM

catlike tread as if saying, "I really am quite a modest little girl, much too modest for all this."

Since 8 in the morning the entire social register of the Riviera, flanked by a goodly slice of the Almanac de Gothar and Debrett, had been fighting their way to the Carlton courts in one long procession of automobiles stretching out along the Nice and Monte Carlo road.

And for three hours we sat there in the bleachers, 4,000 strong, just as when we were waiting for Dempsey and Carpentier, laughing hysterically at each trivial incident—as when chic women trod the skyline transparently on the rooftops or when the gendarmes engaged in arboreal pursuits in trying to compel the young locals to descend from the branches of trees.

Then each celebrity would be hailed on

Point Score, Stroke Analysis, Of Great Contest at Cannes

First Set.

POINT SCORE.

Mlle. Lenglen...4 2 3 4 4 4 1 4 5—31—6	
Miss Wills.......0 4 5 0 0 2 4 1 3—19—3	

STROKE ANALYSIS.

	A.	P.	N.	O.	DF.	EP.	E.
Mlle. Lenglen........	0	5	3	11	0	5	14
Miss Wills	0	5	14	12	0	5	26

Second Set.

POINT SCORE.

Mlle. Lenglen—	
0 5 2 2 4 4 5 4 4 4 3 6 5—53—8	
Miss Wills—	
4 3 4 4 1 1 7 2 6 0 2 5 4 2—46—6	

STROKE ANALYSIS.

	A.	P.	N.	O.	DF.	EP.	E.
Mlle. Lenglen	2	12	10	19	1	14	30
Miss Wills	0	16	17	20	1	16	38

Recapitulation.

	A.	P.	N.	O.	DF.	EP.	E.	TP.
Mlle. Lenglen ..2	17	13	30	1	19	44	83	
Miss Wills 0	21	31	32	1	21	64	65	

his entry as at a first night, and pretentious jokes would be cracked among the building of stands which went on beneath us until Suzanne sent her first service over.

Turmoil While the Struggle Raged.

At that moment one surely never beheld such a vivid rainbow effect beneath a blazing sun as was afforded by hundreds of the smartest women of Europe all assembled in their Helen and Suzanne frocks specially ordered for the occasion.

Once the game began we ceased to behave. Within we applauded each punch or, rather, stroke while the rally

still proceeded, cheering frantically when Helen excelled, while without, demos got a little of his own back in the presence of a thousand strong company of locals, rooting through the uplifted draping for Suzanne and France. From hotel windows and roofs hundreds of yards away little figures signaled their participation in the contest by waving handkerchiefs and flags at each point.

Repeatedly poor, susceptible Suzanne implored for calm, only for the turmoil to break out anew, sending her almost down in defeat before the outwardly unperturbed but inwardly quivering little poker face.

Then when the battle was at the tensest moment came the errors of linesmen, giving three outs against Miss Wills, all of which were in, and ending in letting Suzanne think she had won the match before she actually had. As events turned out Helen proceeded to win two more games before the end. Upon this, of course, the dukes and movie men invaded the court one and all and the limp and gasping Suzanne was held up in the midst of masses of floral offerings, a complete Tetrazzini of tennis, while hundreds of movie men and still men snapped or reeled her for you. Meanwhile the lone little California girl hung practically unsung in the background, not thinking she was wanted.

So ended this epic for the present. To be resumed at a later date when it may be hoped that in addition to acclaiming so obviously and joyously a coming champion we may spare a turn of applause for her who showed us today that she knows how to fight gamely.

As Helen says: "It is always like this; when the public have had a champion for many years they want to see her beaten."

Helen must have studied philosophy in addition to art. Nor would the future going be less difficult if Suzanne, perhaps, took a course in the same school.

Caution Dominates Play.

CANNES, France, Feb. 16 (P).—Suzanne Lenglen remains undisputed tennis champion of the world by virtue of her victory today over Helen Wills after one of the most dramatic matches in the history of tennis, ending with both very near collapse.

Both seemed conscious of the responsibility resting on them, and for once the emotions of the California girl were not entirely held in check. Care and caution dominated the play, which during the greater part of the time was from the baseline. But as the fight became more bitter more driving power was put into the strokes, and when finally Mlle. Lenglen had achieved victory she threw her racquet in the air and leaped for very joy.

Surrounded with flowers and showered with congratulations from many of the great of the world, an ovation was given Suzanne such as perhaps she had never experienced in her career. The reaction made the tears flow down her face as friends gathered about her but the cheers of the multitude soon brought back the smile of the victor.

"I told you you would have to congratulate me," she said to one who had previously expressed some doubt as to her ability to win.

Helen Wills, with youth in her favor, took her defeat philosophically. "There will be other tennis matches; other years are coming," was all she would say.

Decision Costs Helen Set.

The California girl took the lead in the first set, as had been hoped by her supporters, and the score stood 2—1 at the end of the third game. But the French champion, playing with old-time skill and finesse, evened matters in the fourth, and won also the fifth and sixth. Helen took the next game, but Suzanne finished the set with careful placements.

The second set was most dramatic. Miss Wills started by winning her service game at love. She took the next after deuce had been called, and then the third.

Suzanne began to cough, placed a hand over her heart and stepped to the sidelines, where she took a long draught of cognac with water.

Spurred by the stimulant, the French girl won the next three games, evening the count. Miss Wills took the seventh, another deuce game.

The French girl evened it again, and then Helen made it 5—4, needing only one game to take the set. She had run the score up to 40—15 in this game when, with one point to go for the set, an unaccountable decision by the linesman completely upset her.

Suzanne's return struck several inches outside the line, spectators in the stands were firmly convinced, and Helen herself made no attempt to strike at it. Nevertheless it was allowed as a point for Mlle. Lenglen by the linesman, Cyril Tolley, the former British amateur golf champion, who is also a tennis enthusiast.

Miss Wills changed over to receive Suzanne's service, thinking she had won her own, when she was called back.

"What did you call that? she asked Mr. Tolley, showing emotion for the first time.

"Inside," Tolley replied.

Helen threw up both hands in a gesture of despair, while thousands of spectators at her end of the court shouted: "Out!"

From then on the American girl put up a spiritless fight and allowed Mlle. Lenglen to take the initiative. She went down, 6 to 5, and then tied the

set at 6-all, but, although she brought the last two games to deuce, the old spirit was missing.

Upon her arrival from Nice Mlle. Lenglen was nearly mobbed by her admirers, and had the greatest difficulty in making her way through the crowds, which were larger outside the courts than in the stands. The roofs of neighboring houses were burdened so heavily with spectators that they might be expected to crash in at any moment. Periscopes were utilized by men standing outside the high fences to get a view of the play.

The match was contested under the most trying circumstances ever beheld in tennis. Fully 2,000 spectators from the most varied outside vantage points imaginable kept up a running fire, cheering, talking and commenting, to the intense annoyance of Suzanne, who spoke to the crowd after the manner of a Queen addressing her subjects, ordering them to remain silent. When her orders were ignored she pleaded, "Please be quiet."

Women Faint In Crush.

There was nearly a riot when the gates to the courts opened two hours before the match. Several women, who had stood in line all night, fainted.

One section of the stand was occupied by members of various royal families, including former King Manual of Portugal, Grand Duke Michael of Russia, Prince George of Greece, the Rajah of Pudukota and others.

Two hours after Suzanne and Helen met in the singles combat they again faced one another, but this time attended by their respective partners, Didi Vlasto and Henriette Contoslavos. Again Mlle. Lenglen was victorious, playing until her utter collapse. She with her partner won to the score of 6—4, 8—6.

The California girl, however, dominated the doubles courts and showed much better tennis than any of the others; she had had her injured knee dressed in the interval and opened up a terrific attack, always directed at Suzanne.

Mlle. Lenglen gave signs of her approaching collapse in the middle of the second set. She and Mlle. Vlasto centred their attack upon Mlle. Contoslavos, leaving Helen standing on her side of the court. Every time the ball came near the American girl, however, it was killed for an irretrievable point.

She was cheered as she left the court and surrounded by fans, in strange contrast to her lonely exit after her singles match with Suzanne.

Mlle. Lenglen fainted after the doubles match and had to be assisted off the court. Miss Wills, without a look at Suzanne, shook hands with Mlle. Vlasto and then walked off.

February 17, 1926

Mlle. Lenglen Continues to Defy Defeat by Best of U. S. Players

French Star's Triumph Over Versatile Game of Miss Browne in Paris Explodes More Theories on Chances of Her Being Defeated by an American.

By ALLISON DANZIG.

In 1921, when word was received that Suzanne Lenglen was coming to the United States, there was considerable speculation as to what American player would be the worthiest opponent for the French champion. Mrs. Molla Mallory was the title holder that year and had been since 1915, with the exception of the year 1919.

Miss Helen Wills had hardly been heard of at that time. That was the year in which she made her first appearance in the East, a girl of 15, with a reputation already gained on the Pacific Coast. Mlle. Lenglen was then established as the world's greatest woman player, with three victories to her credit in the English championship.

The decisiveness with which the French girl had beaten Mrs. Mallory in their meetings abroad did not augur for the success of the American champion on her home courts, and in spite of the fact that she was the national title holder there were many who were inclined to favor another as America's first hope to turn back the invader.

Their choice was Miss Mary K. Browne of Santa Monica, Cal.

Whether or not it was because of the coming of Mlle. Lenglen is not known, but in 1921 Miss Browne made her come-back to the East with Mrs. May Sutton Bundy. Not since 1914 had the California girl played in a national championship, although she had met Mrs. Mallory in a series of matches for the benefit of the Red Cross during the war period. After winning the title for three years in a row Miss Browne had dropped out of the Eastern competition.

The fact that Miss Browne had won the greater number of the benefit matches with Mrs. Mallory was one reason why she was favored over the latter as the worthier opponent for Mlle. Lenglen, but it was only a minor reason. The disastrous experiences of the American champion against the French girl on foreign courts also weighed against Mrs. Mallory, but there was a still bigger reason for the leaning toward Miss Browne.

Miss Browne stood out in 1921 as the leading exponent of the masculine style of play in the women's ranks. Marion Zinderstein Jessup, who had beaten Mrs. Mallory in the 1919 championship, and Miss Eleanor Goss were also adept at this style, but for general all around excellence, experience and knowledge of tactics, Miss Browne stood out pre-eminent.

Mrs. Mallory, from the beginning of her career in America in 1915, had been a one-stroke player, and as she had won the title repeatedly with that stroke she had confined her efforts toward making it more and more powerful. No player in the world had a stronger forehand drive than the American champion in 1921. This single weapon, together with her almost inexhaustible stamina, her lion-hearted courage and her indomitable will to win, kept her at the top year after year.

But Mrs. Mallory lacked a volleying game. She was not versed in the finesse and subtlety of the change of pace. There was not the variety to her game that Miss Browne had—and it was agreed that this lack of variety stood as an insurmountable obstacle in the way of her defeating Suzanne Lenglen.

The French champion from girlhood had built up her game by playing tennis as men play it, and with men. It was her father's idea that to rise above the other players of her sex Mlle. Lenglen must not merely master the knack of driving a ball hard and with control, which was the only essential of the game as then played by the leading English women, but that she must be taught the tennis methods of the men. And so, upon the foundation of this idea, began the training

which was to make Mlle. Lenglen the most versatile woman player the game has known—a woman who could not only drive off the forehand and backhand, but could volley and smash with the deadly effect of a man, who was master of all the niceties of stroke variety, and who thus was able to win her points with a minimum of effort through the use of a tactical scheme rather than sheer power alone.

Miss Browne was regarded as the one player in this country who had the equipment to battle Mlle. Lenglen at her own game. Mrs. Hazel Hotchkiss Wightman, perhaps the greatest woman court strategist the game has known in the United States, might have been nominated at the crest of her career, but in 1921 Mrs. Wightman had given up singles championship play.

But it turned out that Miss Browne did not have a chance to face Mlle. Lenglen in 1921. Mrs. Mallory stood in the way of a meeting between them and Mlle. Lenglen defaulted to the American champion in the second round after losing the opening set. Mrs. Mallory went on to win the title again, defeating Miss Browne in the final. But in spite of the defeat of Miss Browne, who gave the title holder the stiffest battle she encountered in the tournament, taking a set from her, there were many who still held to the belief that the California girl was the player best suited to cope with Mlle. Lenglen's style of play.

Last week, almost five years later, Mlle. Lenglen and Miss Browne met on the courts of France. The American girl got one game. It may be that Miss Browne has gone back a great deal since 1921, for last year she suffered repeated defeats, yet her victory over Mrs. Kathleen McKane Godfree a few days before meeting Mlle. Lenglen seems to indicate differently.

Contrasting the great bid for victory made by Miss Wills at Cannes against the French girl with the showing made by Miss Browne, who is still regarded as a better court strategist and more versatile player than Miss Wills, it seems that all the theories of 1921 were merely theories. The other deduction to be made is that Mlle. Lenglen is so transcendent a player that all theorizing on how to defeat her is futile.

June 15, 1926

THE INCOMPARABLE SUZANNE.

The most spectacular woman tennis player, six times holder of the singles championship, has dropped out of the Wimbledon tournament. Suzanne Lenglen retires from it because of ill health. Her surrender to physical necessity was quietly made, without heroics in keeping with her flashing, dramatic temperament. A woman of great natural nervous energy, she achieved by her magnificent playing a pre-eminence that she sometimes presumed upon for spurts of anger and hauteur that caused astonishment and gave offense. She was often criticized for being erratic and too inconsiderate of the interests of true sport, but her supremacy in the game, as well as her personal eccentricities, made her the target for more comment of all kinds than any other woman player.

Particularly in this country resentment was felt because she retired from the contest with Mrs. Mallory after losing the first set. For her present withdrawal, however, there is no cause for suspecting reasons other than those she gives. Her playing recently had been almost flawless, and she had little to fear from her opponents. She started for the courts, but was suffering too much pain to play. Pleading by her partner may yet induce her to go into the doubles, but she has taken herself definitely out of the singles race. However, if she never strokes another ball, she could retire with the certainty that she has set a high mark for other women players to shoot at. Her whimsical idiosyncrasies they need not emulate.

June 29, 1926

MRS. MALLORY WINS BACK TENNIS CROWN

Thrills Gallery of 3,000 as She Conquers Miss Ryan in Sensational Title Final.

TRIUMPHS BY 4-6, 6-4, 9-7

Former Champion Trailing, 0-4, in the Last Set When She Smashes Way Through.

TIES MARK WITH 7TH TITLE

Crowd Cheers Frantically as She Regains Laurels She Lost to Miss Wills in 1923.

By ALLISON DANZIG.

The sceptre in American women's tennis returned to Mrs. Molla Mallory yesterday. Time turned back at Forest Hills as the New York woman, holder for six years of the title, fought her way to a stunning victory over Miss Elizabeth Ryan of California to regain the crown which she lost to Miss Helen Wills in 1923 and to tie the record for all time of the number of championships won by a single player, either man or woman.

In all the thirty-nine years of the women's national championship there has probably never been a more sensational victory scored in a final round than Mrs. Mallory's yesterday.

Trailing at 0—4 in the final set, in which she was within a single stroke of defeat in the fourteenth game, the New York woman threw the 3,000 spectators in the Stadium into a frenzy of delight as she fought her way through four games in a row with a savageness of stroking that crushed all opposition.

Miss Ryan Wilts Before Attack.

Miss Ryan, clearly the favorite from the start up to this point, wilted be-

fore the devastating attack, which completely broke up her volleying game. She fought desperately through seven more games to hold off Mrs. Mallory's penetrating forcing shots, and then, amid screams of joy from the whole gallery, Mrs. Mallory brought the play to a climax by breaking through service and winning her own game for the match. The score was 4—6, 6—4, 9—7.

It is not often that a tennis gathering runs the gamut of emotions that those 3,000 spectators experienced yesterday. There were moments when the suspense was so terrific that it set hearts to ponding wildly as the match hung in the balance on a single stroke.

Because Mrs. Mallory's cause was almost unanimously regarded as hopeless, the onlookers broke into applause at her every winning shot, cheered her on excitedly as she fought her way to victory in the second set, and then the safety valve was blown off as she staged her rally in the final chapter. The stadium fairly rocked as Mrs. Mallory won the last point, and of all those 3,000 people none was so unrestrainedly exuberant as the champion.

Mrs. Mallory Shows Her Joy.

Mrs. Mallory danced with joy, throwing her racquet into the air, waving to the cheering stands and unrestrainedly giving vent to her glee. One would have thought, as she received the championship cup from Jones W. Mersereau, President of the United States Lawn Tennis Association, that Mrs. Mallory was experiencing a new thrill.

Certainly she showed greater happiness than she did over any of her victories in the past. And well she might. Looked upon as having passed the prime of her career and given little consideration as a championship contender, the New York woman showed that the same courageous fighting spirit and iron will to win that kept her at the top for seven years and that enabled her to triumph over Mlle. Lenglen at Forest Hills in 1921, are still as strong as ever within her.

What other woman player has ever come so hopelessly from behind to win a championship final? William Tilden, with all his great fifth-set rallies, could have done no better.

By winning the championship yesterday for the seventh time Mrs. Mallory equaled the record of victories scored by Richard D. Sears and William A. Larned, both of whom captured the men's title the same number of years, and of Mrs. Lambert Chambers, champion at Wimbledon seven times.

Mlle. Lenglen has won at Wimbledon six times, while Tilden has captured the American title six times. Mrs. Mallory's other victories were scored in 1915, 1916, 1918, 1920, 1921 and 1922.

Won Honors Eight Years.

In addition she also won the patriotic tournament of 1917, so that she has held the honors eight years in all, one more than any other player has ever held either the American or English crown.

Frustrated in her effort for the singles crown, Miss Ryan came back on the courts later to win the doubles championship with Miss Eleanor Goss. In the final round they defeated Miss Mary K. Browne and Mrs. Charlotte Hosmer Chapin, 3—6, 6—4, 12—10.

The final set of this match was a repetition of the singles final, except that Miss Ryan, after having her lead cut down, finally managed to prevail.

Trailing at 0—3 and again at 2—5 and 0—40, Miss Browne and Mrs. Chapin rallied to launch a furious attack from the net that carried them to 5—all.

Then began a desperate struggle in which service was broken through repeatedly and in which all four players performed valiantly in rallies of exciting give and take at the net.

Miss Browne and Mrs. Chapin both brought off any number of remarkable recoveries, but they were finally forced to yield before the sustained power of Miss Goss's driving and overhead smashes and Miss Ryan's clever placements.

In an exhibition match doubles which preceded the doubles finals, Miss Penelope Anderson and Henri Cochet of France and Miss Martha Bayard and Jacques Brugnon of France divided two sets. The former team won the first at 6—1 and lost the second at 7—5.

The singles final was remarkable for the closeness of the play. In both the first and second sets neither player ever held a commanding lead, and only in the first four games of the final chapter was the play one-sided. The point score and stroke analysis show how closely the two women were matched.

Miss Ryan won one more point than Mrs. Mallory, 112 to 111, while the champion gained two more games, 19 to 17. Mrs. Mallory made eight more errors and seven more earned points than Miss Ryan.

It was the magnificent sharp-shooting of Mrs. Mallory that decided the issue. The champion needed only to fall behind to become rampant, and she was never so deadly in her stroking as she was in overcoming the 4—0 lead of Miss Ryan in the final set, a lead that had been gained in hardly more than six minutes on Mrs. Mallory's inexcusable errors.

In the next four games Mrs. Mallory scored nine placements to win 16 points, and in this last set she made 17 to 9 for Miss Ryan. This remarkable accuracy and keenness of Mrs. Mallory for penetrating the openings completely broke up Miss Ryan's net attack. During the last twelve games the Californian scored only one winning volley shot, which speaks for itself.

Not only did Miss Ryan's short-court game become a total loss, but her chopped drives to deep territory made no impression whatever upon Mrs. Mallory in the late stages, contrasting with their effect earlier in the match, when they induced error-making repeatedly.

Mrs. Mallory Supreme.

Mrs. Mallory did not seem to know how to make an error any longer. Everything that came over the net was sent back like a bolt to open territory, keeping Miss Ryan on the run until she was badly tired and fell off in control.

Mrs. Mallory, to add the last straw, completely smothered her opponent's drop shots, crafty trap strokes, which Miss Ryan made with such delicate finesse to catch Mrs. Mallory flat-footed in her back court in the two first sets, were now retrieved by a fleet-footed, keenly alert opponent every time and returned with winning shots.

Mrs. Mallory had the advantage of what might be called the "breaks" in the concluding stages, winning a number of points when the ball hit the top of the net fence and rolled the right way for her. But, on the other hand, she was the victim of a number of what seemed doubtful decisions, one of which cost her a point in the twelfth game that put Miss Ryan within two points of the match.

Mrs. Mallory showed her fine sportsmanship by refusing to question the decision and silenced the crowd, which objected to the decision, with a wave of her arm.

In the fourteenth game Miss Ryan was at match point, but her errors in returning service—a weakness she showed throughout the match—cost her her opportunity.

Crucial Struggle Begins.

Mrs. Mallory pulled out the game, and then there began a desperate struggle in the fifteenth.

Miss Ryan gained a 30—0 lead in this game. Mrs. Mallory pulled up to 30—all and then scored on a fluke return of service, the ball just getting over the net.

Miss Ryan brought the score to deuce. Fighting desperately to get to the net, she found her efforts wasted when Mrs. Mallory scored on a net-cord placement. The deciding break was made.

In the final game, Miss Ryan showed her championship fibre, trailing at 0—40, and with defeat only a point away she fought Mrs. Mallory through the next four rallies and gained the advantage point.

Here her control waned as Mrs. Mallory pounded her base corners and the champion took the next two points on errors for the match.

The point score and stroke analysis of the final match between Miss Ryan and Mrs. Mallory follows:

First Set.

POINT SCORE.

Mrs. Mallory	1	4	4	4	1	4	4	0	5	1—4	28
Miss Ryan	4	1	6	6	4	2	1	4	3	4—6	35

STROKE ANALYSIS.

	N.	O.	P.	SA.	DF.
Mrs. Mallory	14	7	7	0	2
Miss Ryan	9	8	12	0	4

Second Set.

POINT SCORE.

Mrs. Mallory	2	4	2	4	1	6	5	1	4	4—6	33
Miss Ryan	4	0	4	2	4	4	3	4	2	2—4	29

STROKE ANALYSIS.

	N.	O.	P.	SA.	DF.
Mrs. Mallory	16	6	13	0	0
Miss Ryan	11	8	7	0	1

Third Set.

POINT SCORE.

Mrs. Mallory	1	2	2	1	4	4	4	4	1	4	1	4	1	7	5	5—7	50
Miss Ryan	4	4	4	4	2	2	0	2	4	1	4	2	4	5	3	3—9	48

STROKE ANALYSIS.

	N.	O.	P.	SA.	DF.
Mrs. Mallory	19	14	17	0	4
Miss Ryan	16	15	9	2	2

Recapitulation.

	N.	O.	P.	SA.	DF.	E.	EP.	TP.	G.	S.
Mrs. Mallory	49	27	37	0	6	82	37	111	19	2
Miss Ryan	36	31	28	2	7	74	30	112	17	1

Umpire—Ben Dwight. Net Umpire—T. T. Mattman. Service linesmen—Frank Danielsen and Schuyler Vanbloem. Centre service linesmen—S. Wallis Merrihew and J. W. Anderson. Side linesmen—Fred Letson, E. R. Carter, Norman Andrieni and Stephen Tilton. Base linesmen—Alder B. Stewart and C. G. James. Foot fault judge—Beals C. Wright.

Time of match—1:10.

August 24, 1926

TILDEN VANQUISHED; HIS SIX-YEAR REIGN IN U. S. TENNIS ENDS

Champion Put Out of National Play by Cochet of France, 6-8, 6-1, 6-3, 1-6, 8-6.

FIGHTS FIERCELY TO END

Ignores Hurt Knee, Striving in Vain to Save Day With One of His Famous Rallies.

TWO OTHER FRENCHMEN WIN

Richards Lone U. S. Survivor as Johnston Bows to Borotra and Williams to Lacoste.

By ALLISON DANZIG.

The six-year reign of William Tilden over tennisdom came to an end yesterday, William Johnston also went down to defeat and France placed three men in the semi-finals of the national championship at the West Side Tennis Club, Forest Hills. Six years of American supremacy on the courts crumpled under a French attack that eliminated three of America's Big Four, leaving Vincent Richards as the only hope of the United States to keep the title from going overseas.

Tilden, the invincible, the player whose magic with a racquet has confounded the greatest players of the world and made America supreme in tennis, at last has relinquished his sceptre.

The tall, gaunt Tilden, who has stood challenging all comers, at last has toppled after reigning so absolutely for six years that he had come to be regarded as the most powerful potentate in amateur sports, immune to defeat in national championship play and capable of rising superior to any crisis through the sheer wizardry of his strokes.

Even the injury to his knee that paved the way for his defeat by René Lacoste last Saturday, his first in Davis Cup singles, had been looked upon as a negligible consideration, so supreme was the confidence in Tilden's mastery. But it was that injury that undermined the champion's great playing strength, as Henri Cochet of France fought his way to victory in five sets at 6—8, 6—1, 6—3, 1—6, 8—6.

Falls With Colors Flying.

If ever a champion went down with colors flying William Tilden was that champion yesterday. Fighting from behind all the way during the two hours that the match lasted, the Philadelphian won the hearts of the 8,000 spectators in the stadium as he never won them in victory. He gave himself unsparingly and with reckless disregard for his underpinning in his vain effort to withstand the demoralizing steadiness and craftily placed shots of his opponent.

The climax of the match, the point at which the gallery broke into its wildest demonstrations, was during the final set when Tilden, trailing at 1—4, rallied to volley Cochet dizzy with one of the most sensational exhibitions he ever gave at the net and pull up to 4-all. Every winning shot of the American was greeted with roars of applause and with each successive game in the series of three hearts became lighter with hope for an American victory.

When Tilden won the eighth game there were few who believed that the catastrophe would occur. The champion, it was agreed, was still the old champion, capable of lifting his game in an emergency to unassailable heights. But after leading at 40—15 on Cochet's service in the ninth game, Tilden had reached the end of his rope. The player whose last-minute pull-ups had brought him out of the jaws of defeat so many times in the past finally met his master.

Cochet, playing with the coolness of a veteran of twice his years and absorbing the champion's cannonball service and lightning drives with machinelike steadiness, confounded the American's most desperate efforts and checkmated his every thrust with counter-strokes of craft. Tilden's service enabled him to go into the lead at 6—5, and then the débâcle came as the invader crushed all opposition in the next three games, in which Tilden got only four points.

Let full justice be done Cochet, the player who achieved what had been looked upon as the impossible. Fairness to Tilden necessitated consideration of the bearing his physical condition had upon the match, but fairness to the young Frenchman also calls for due acknowledgment of the fact that

Tilden, even with the fullest support of his legs, would have been extended to the limit to prevail over Cochet, and still might well have failed.

Cochet Amazes Onlookers.

Those who last saw Cochet in this country in 1922 were unable to comprehend how he could have beaten Richards abroad twice this year, but satisfactory explanation was furnished yesterday. No French player that ever came to the United States has given a more masterly exhibition than did Cochet against the champion. There was a confidence about this young player that those who have watched him in action abroad looked upon as a foreboding sign. Cochet was at his best for the first time in this country, and went about his task as though he never had any doubt about the outcome.

This 24-year-old youth was coolness personified. In the face of Tilden's most devastating swipes he maintained the even tenor of his way, assimilating speed as though he were brought up on it and eternally getting the ball back as steadily as the patter of rain. Lacoste had come to be regarded as the most mechanically perfect player in **tennis, but Cochet could have given him spades and a couple of racquets yesterday.**

At the end of a rally in the seventh game of the third set Major A. P. Simmonds, the umpire, called out "advantage Lacoste." Cochet stopped in his act of serving and looked quizzically at the official, who raised his hat, amid the laughter of the spectators, to apologize for his mistake. But the mistake was easy enough to understand. Major Simmonds, like many another person there, must have been under the delusion this machine-like youth was Lacoste.

But Cochet was more than a machine. There was a tennis brain directing this mechanically perfect player's shots that left Tilden at his wits' end in trying to fathom its workings. It was not Cochet's strokes that were so irresistible, but the craftiness with which they were deployed.

Off the ground the Frenchman was outclassed in speed and depth, for, as regards pace, his strokes for the most part were hardly more than defensive returns, crossing the net at high altitude and bounding high off the turf to afford Tilden the opportunity to get set for his pasting returns. Playing safe against Tilden's blistering shots, Cochet awaited his opportunities to let loose with a forcing stroke—opportunities which made himself by the changing direction and varying length he employed. Once he had the champion wide of the court and on the run, then Cochet's shots sought a lower level and deeper territory and usually in the American's backhand corner.

If his ground strokes were lacking in severity, Cochet's volleys were the last word in finality. Any time that the Frenchman came to the net he was a dangerous figure, deadly overhead and sure on the straight volley. As a rule, Tilden can dislodge any opponent who entrenches himself at the net, but he was always worried yesterday when Cochet bearded his forcing shots. Because Cochet is so deft a volleyer and handles his racquet like an artist at close quarters, the champion knew that he must put the ball out of his reach or directly on top of his feet to stump him, and he could not hit the bull's-eye. Lobbing was out of the question, for Cochet handled everything overhead with unfailing precision.

Against an opponent of this calibre, who was a stonewall in his back court and a catapult at close quarters, Tilden never had a moment's peace of mind, except in the fourth set, when he carried all before him by the sheer fury of his attack. The champion appreciated from the very start the size of the task facing him, for Cochet against Hunter had given h[illegible]ling of what to expect, and for the first time in the tournament the gallery saw an aroused Tilden in the very first game—a Tilden who hit out with bludgeon strokes off the ground, capitalized his cannonball service for its full worth, jockeyed with all his cunning for positional advantages and who exploited his volleying game as few have seen him exploit it in all the years that he has held the title.

It is doubtful whether many appreciated how magnificent a volleyer Tilden can be until this match, so seldom has he felt it necessary to seek close grips with his opponents.

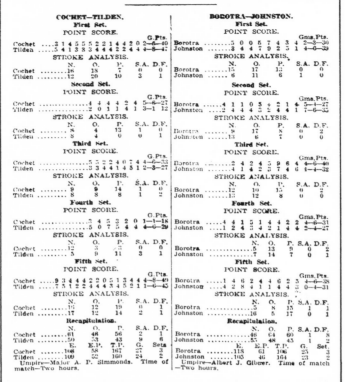

Point Score and Stroke Analyses Show How Tilden and Johnston Met Defeat

COCHET—TILDEN.

First Set.

POINT SCORE.

		G.Pts.
Cochet	3 1 4 5 5 5 2 2 1 4 4 2 0	2—6—40
Tilden	5 4 1 3 3 3 4 4 4 2 2 4 4	4—8—47

STROKE ANALYSIS.

	N.	O.	P.	S.A.	D.F.
Cochet	16	18	7	0	0
Tilden	12	20	10	3	1

Second Set.

POINT SCORE.

		G.Pts.
Cochet	4 4 4 4 2 4	5—6—27
Tilden	2 0 1 1 4 1	3—1 12

STROKE ANALYSIS.

	N.	O.	P.	S.A.	D.F.
Cochet	8	4	13	1	0
Tilden	8	4	0	0	1

Third Set.

POINT SCORE.

		G.Pts.
Cochet	5 5 2 2 4 0 7 4	4—6—33
Tilden	3 3 4 4 1 4 5 1	2—3—27

STROKE ANALYSIS.

	N.	O.	P.	S.A.	D.F.
Cochet	9	9	14	1	0
Tilden	8	8	8	1	2

Fourth Set.

POINT SCORE.

		G.Pts.
Cochet	3 4 5 3 2 0	1—1—18
Tilden	5 0 7 5 4 4	4—6—29

STROKE ANALYSIS.

	N.	O.	P.	S.A.	D.F.
Cochet	12	3	3	0	0
Tilden	5	9	11	3	1

Fifth Set.

POINT SCORE.

		G.Pts.
Cochet	9 3 4 4 4 2 2 0 5 1 3 4 4	4—8—49
Tilden	7 5 1 2 2 4 4 4 3 4 5 2 1	1—6—45

STROKE ANALYSIS.

	N.	O.	P.	S.A.	D.F.
Cochet	16	12	19	0	1
Tilden	17	12	14	2	1

Recapitulation.

	N.	O.	P.	S.A.	D.F.
Cochet	61	48	56	2	1
Tilden	50	53	43	9	6

	E.	E.P.	T.P.	G.	Sets
Cochet	108	58	167	27	3
Tilden	109	52	160	24	2

Umpire—Major A. P. Simmonds. Time of match—Two hours.

BOROTRA—JOHNSTON.

First Set.

POINT SCORE.

		Gms.Pts.
Borotra	5 0 0 5 7 4 3 4	2—3—30
Johnston	3 4 4 7 9 2 5 1	4—6—39

STROKE ANALYSIS.

	N.	O.	P.	S.A.	D.F.
Borotra	15	17	13	0	0
Johnston	6	11	6	1	0

Second Set.

POINT SCORE.

		Gms.Pts.
Borotra	4 1 1 0 5 4 2 1 4	5—4—27
Johnston	2 4 4 4 3 2 4 4 1	7—6—35

STROKE ANALYSIS.

	N.	O.	P.	S.A.	D.F.
Borotra	9	17	8	0	2
Johnston	13	6	7	0	0

Third Set.

POINT SCORE.

		Gms.Pts.
Borotra	2 4 2 4 5 9 6 4	4—6—40
Johnston	4 1 4 2 3 7 4 6	4—4—32

STROKE ANALYSIS.

	N.	O.	P.	S.A.	D.F.
Borotra	12	10	15	0	2
Johnston	13	12	8	0	0

Fourth Set.

POINT SCORE.

		Gms.Pts.
Borotra	4 4 1 5 1 4 4 2 2	4—6—31
Johnston	1 2 4 3 4 2 1 4 4	2—4—27

STROKE ANALYSIS.

	N.	O.	P.	S.A.	D.F.
Borotra	5	13	9	0	2
Johnston	7	14	7	0	1

Fifth Set.

POINT SCORE.

		Gms.Pts.
Borotra	1 4 6 2 4 4 6 2 5	4—6—38
Johnston	4 2 8 4 1 1 4 4 3	0—4—31

STROKE ANALYSIS.

	N.	O.	P.	S.A.	D.F.
Borotra	5	8	15	1	1
Johnston	16	5	17	0	1

Recapitulation.

	N.	O.	P.	S.A.	D.F.
Borotra	46	64	60	1	8
Johnston	55	48	45	1	2

	E.	E.P.	T.P.	G.	Set.
Borotra	118	61	106	25	3
Johnston	105	46	164	23	2

Umpire—Albert J. Gibrer. Time of match—Two hours.

was a reason for his change in tactics yesterday, a change which he adopted on Wednesday also. The strain of plugging up the gaps in his back court called for greater demands upon his knee than the work of holding his position at the net, and for that reason Tilden the driver and chopper became a volleyer.

And what a volleyer the champion was! Even Richards at his best could not have performed more sensationally than did the champion as he twisted and stooped and went through every sort of evolution in bringing off low drop volleys off his feet and smashes in the air.

Frenchman Remains Calm.

There were times, particularly in the fourth set and during the champion's rally in the final chapter when it seemed that human resistance to this sort of shot-making was futile, but Cochet was never worried and in due time put in his oar to take the play away from the champion with shot-making at the net that evoked almost equally thunderous applause. Everything that the champion did well Cochet did also, **and he was able to do it over a longer period than** Tilden, rising to irresistible heights in the final stages when Tilden was making the last desperate stand of a champion who felt his crown slipping away from him.

So totally absorbed were the officials, as well as the spectators, in this match that all thought of the other contests was forgotten until the last point was played, and as a result the play in the three other matches got away to a late start. Two hours after Tilden walked off the courts a beaten man, Johnston also passed out of the play in five sets, the victim of Jean Borotra.

Borotra, who had never before taken even a set from the Californian and who was subdued in three sets in the Davis Cup challenge round last week, blasted the hopes of Johnston just when it seemed that, with Tilden out of the competition, he had a real chance to break through and regain the title which he held in 1915 and 1919. The score was 3—6, 4—6, 6—3, 6—4, 6—4.

Williams Also Falls.

Long before the Basque had finished his rally, which carried him to victory from the almost hopeless position of 0—2 in sets, René Lacoste had disposed of Dick Williams, captain of the Davis Cup team and No. 4 in the American ranking, at 6—0, 6—3, 8—6, and Richards had eliminated Jacques Brugnon, at 6—2, 6—1, 6—2.

Thus, for the second time this year, the situation developed in which the United States found itself with only one representative left in the semi-finals of a national tennis championship. Last February Tilden and Richards bowed to Borotra and Lacoste, respectively, in the indoor play at the Seventh Regiment Armory, while Brugnon also gained a bracket in the semi-finals, leaving John Van Ryn, a Princeton undergraduate, as America's last entry. The title went to Lacoste and unless Richards reaches his most inspired heights France is likely to carry off the turf court crown also.

There is deep confidence in Richards, however. The New York youth has been playing the best tennis of all the Americans since his return from abroad, and while he did not show to advantage yesterday against Brugnon it may be expected that he will rise to the occasion this afternoon and play in his best form against Borotra while Lacoste and Cochet are having it out in the other semi-final. Lacoste is favored to win over Cochet, though the latter, if he plays in the same form that he showed yesterday, will have an equal chance of winning.

Gallery Is Stunned.

The triumph of Borotra over Johnston was as unexpected as was the defeat of Tilden, but the gallery, dazed by the downfall of the champion, failed to show any great reaction to the upset. Anything was possible after Cochet's victory. Johnston has lost many a heart-breaking match during the six years that he has tried to break up the monopoly Tilden has held on the title, but yesterday's was in a way the most distressing one of all.

Leading at 2—0 in sets, the Californian looked to be a certain winner, and at last it appeared he would have the opportunity to test his strength against Richards in championship play. As he has always beaten Richards in a three-out-of-five-set match, there was reason for him to look forward with confidence to a match with the New York youth, and then would come his big opportunity to regain the crown.

But for the seventh successive year **Johnston's dream went up in smoke—the smoke of Borotra's lightning drives** and darting volleys, and America's second ranking player passed out of the play along with the world's first.

It was Borotra's volleying that decided the match. The spectacular Basque, unable to collect his forces in the first two sets in the face of the Californian's destructive forehand drives, took to the air in the third set, and out of the air, as he leaped for his volleys and overhead kills, came the shots from his racquet that put the quietus upon Johnston.

The pace set by the Basque in the three last sets at times carried Johnston off his feet. Never for a minute did Borotra cease going to the net and everything that came within his reach there was doomed to destruction. There were times when he faltered in control and volleyed into the net as Johnston gauged his openings accurately, but in general Borotra was irresistible up forward.

Johnston's control in the later stages of the match was not at its best, and his forehand drive found the net with irritating persistency, costing him precious points at times when he had the advantage in position. **In the final set the Californian made a tremendous fight for the third game, winning it at 8—6 with a marvelous exhibition of volleying, and when he continued his** deadly work at close quarters in the fourth to lead at 3—1 it seemed that Borotra's rally was to be in vain.

Basque Never Loses Smile.

But the Basque, never discouraged and smiling his appreciation of his opponent's shot-making, came back to take the play away from Johnston at the net and ran through three games in a row, earning 7 of his 14 points on placements. This brilliant display of pyrotechnics by the Basque stung Johnston into dynamic action in the eighth and he broke through on three placements to tie the score at 4 all.

That was his last game, though he led at 30—0 in the ninth. Borotra pulled up on even terms on the Californian's errors, lashed out from the net to break through at 5—3 and the play came to an end in the tenth as Johnston's control lapsed in the face of his opponent's ruthless stroking from the net.

The other two matches were tame in comparison to the big two. Williams had one of his erratic days and, except at the start of the second set and in the late stages of the final chapter, practically defeated himself on errors. The Philadelphian redeemed himself in the last set when he pulled up from 2—5 to 5—all, averting defeat four times in the process by the margin of a single stroke and bringing off such bewildering cross-court volleys and drives that Lacoste, for all his steadiness, was helpless. There was nothing the French youth could do when he could not get his racquet on the ball.

In the thirteenth game Williams made another of his pull-ups from 15—40 to deuce and there seemed a good prospect of his winning the set, but he lapsed into his erring ways and dropped the game and Lacoste relentlessly mowed down all opposition in the fourteenth to bring the play to a close.

Brugnon appeared to be tired in his match with Richards, showing the effects of his strenuous match with Dr. George King on Wednesday. Had he been fresher he would have had an excellent opportunity for winning at least a set, for Richards was none too keen himself. The New York youth, realizing that he had nothing to fear, was not taking matters any more seriously than was necessary, conserving his energies for the bigger test today against Borotra. Whenever he needed points he made them, either with beautiful volleys or clean passing shots, and there was no reason to become alarmed over his sluggishness.

Third Set Bitterly Fought.

There was no indication from the way in which the play started in the match between Tilden and Cochet of the startling outcome it was to have. The champion, showing a keenness that he had not manifested in his previous matches, was a rampant figure from the start, and as he bombarded Cochet's back court with murderous swipes that were measured to the inch it seemed that the French youth was up against greater power than he could withstand. His soft returns were set-ups for the American and his control was wavering, and in short order Tilden took the first two games, getting all of his points on errors.

Beginning with the third game Cochet began to find himself, and soon the thought behind his strokes was revealed as he started Tilden on the long run that was to continue to the end of the match. Four games in succession went to the invader, games which Til-

den tried his best to win but in vain, as Cochet outguessed him and caught him off balance with confusing changes of direction. Finding the going too rough from back court, Tilden launched a volleying attack and swept through three games to lead at 5—4, bringing off sensational low volleys that were unapproachable.

Now it was Cochet's turn to go to the front again as Tilden faltered in control in the lengthy driving rallies, and then the champion, trailing at 5—6, went forward to hew out his points at the net, taking three games in a row for the set.

The second set found Tilden in a slump. He lost something of his aggressiveness and errors marred his stroking repeatedly. Cochet, on the other hand, was adding pressure to his play with each game and was beginning to reveal the genius of his volley attack. After falling behind at 0—4, Tilden made little effort, preferring to let the set go. Tilden did not make a single placement in this set.

The third set marked the beginning of the real struggle. Tilden brought all of his cunning and resources to bear, and every game in this set was fought for with the most dogged determination. Cochet took the first two games after they had gone to deuce. Tilden tied the score at 2—all and at 3—all, and then developed a bewildering struggle in the seventh game, which went to 7—5 before Cochet was able to pull it out with a remarkable soft shot down the line off a kill by the champion. He broke through in the eighth on Tilden's errors and outplaced the champion in the ninth for the set.

After the rest period the champion returned to the court to let loose an avalanche of service aces, cannonball drives and volleys that had Cochet reeling. The French youth simply had to wait until the champion's attack had spent itself and then took command again in the final chapter. He won the opening game, 9—7, after a desperate combat that found both

players scoring on electrifying strokes, broke through in the fourth to lead at 3—1 on volleys and increased it to 4—1.

Here it was that Tilden staged his rally that carried him to 4—all and ultimately to 6—5, after which Cochet went to the front, taking the last games with three placements in a row as Tilden rushed madly about the court trying to plug up the gaps that Cochet opened with his consummate placing.

The summaries:

Fourth Round.

Henri Cochet defeated William T. Tilden 2d, 6—8, 6—1, 1—6, 8—6.
Rene Lacoste defeated R. Norris Williams 2d, 6—0, 6—3, 8—6.
Vincent Richards defeated Jacques Brugnon, 6—2, 6—1, 6—2.
Jean Borotra defeated William Johnston, 3—6, 4—6, 6—3, 6—4, 6—4.

September 17, 1926

LACOSTE VANQUISHES TILDEN IN FIVE SETS

7,500 Jam St. Cloud Courts to See French Ace Win Grueling Match, 6-4, 4-6, 5-7, 6-3, 11-9.

DISPLAYS GREAT COURAGE

Plays On In Third Set Despite Painful Attack of Cramps Caused by Fall.

TILDEN'S TENNIS ERRATIC

He Falls Twice In Final Set After Coming Within Point of Taking International Title.

ST. CLOUD, France, June 5.—Rene Lacoste is the hero of France and her international tennis champion tonight after an amazing, fighting victory over William T. Tilden at the Woodland courts today.

Although featured by bursts of almost unbelievable plays by both players, the match was an endurance contest rather than a battle of skill. The match went to five sets, two of them lasting to deuce. There was more than three and a half hours of play with interminable volleys, particularly in the first three engagements, enduring many times as many as forty or fifty returns. Lacoste won by 6—4, 4—6, 5—7, 6—3, 11—9. Lacoste's glorious success against odds such as a tennis star seldom overcome, came when he had been almost carried off the court with cramps after the painful third encounter and after Tilden in the last set had twice thrown away the match point by unexplainable errors.

Lacoste Overcomes Odds.

Lacoste repeatedly clawed himself away from what seemed sure defeat, winning numerous games in which Tilden led by 40—15 and, by will power and returns

that overcame a lagging physique, he pulled his cramped muscles into play that won him point after point.

Tilden's game was one to baffle tennis experts and the 7,500 persons who jammed the grand stands to overflowing so that many climbed in trees and hundreds made the long taxi trip to St. Cloud only to be turned away. At times Tilden showed form execution and headwork such as could not be rivalled by any performances of this great player in his best days.

Nothing ever has been seen in France to equal three serves made by the American in the tenth game of the last set. Smarting with resentment against Umpire Alan Muhr, American sportsman, who two games before had, for the third time, committed the unheard-of atrocity of calling his service bad on account of a footfault, Tilden delivered three serves which should live in tennis statistics. Calling upon Muhr to watch his footwork as he stepped up to serve, Tilden smashed a sizzler over which Lacoste by a miracle shot back to lose on a placement by Tilden.

Service Baffles Lacoste.

Tilden's next three serves were three of a kind. They were the kind which no player, however agile or however gifted, could hope to return except by downright luck. Squarely placed inside, these scorching serves seemed to burn the court where they struck, while Lacoste's racquet swung madly, too late by a second, and Tilden took a love game.

Coupled with this masterly exhibition, which was almost duplicated in some other flashes of play, Tilden repeatedly lost his service and perpetrated the offense, bewildering on the part of a player of his great calibre, by a serving a double fault to lose the match.

Most sport writers and experts who witnessed this contest, great in many respects, will agree, I think, that Tilden lost through the grave error of adopting Lacoste's own style of play and attempting to match steadiness with steadiness, forgetting his own unequalled manner of mixing his returns with every conceivable variation and failing to take advantage of Lacoste's bad leg by making him run to all sides of the court.

If Tilden had pursued this style from the outset, one might have been led to infer the generosity of these tactics and there may have been some induced to believe he was overconfident of victory. But none who heard Tilden's reproaches to the umpire or saw some of his nasty looks at doubtful decisions could maintain he, for one moment, intended throwing the match away.

Strain of Match Great.

From this aspect the almost mixed

RENE LACOSTE
France
Forest Hills, 1924

personalities which caused Tilden to play like Lacoste and Lacoste in moments to play almost like Tilden as well as the breathless closeness of the score made the last set a contest played under a strain of almost unexampled excitement. The crowd, making an effort to refrain from demonstrations, received expostulations over and over from the umpire when it could not contain sentiments and gasped and exploded in shouts of admiration in the midst of volleys.

When Lacoste had taken the victory, the French fans dashed down out of the stands and raised their nearly exhausted idol to their shoulders, carrying him in triumph to the training quarters, where his second massage of the match was administered before he left the grounds.

The contest was featured by the amusing character and display of the two stars' actions, both appearing in sweaters and playing in them two sets, while Lacoste discarded his famous long-peaked white cap for a tan one of the same design. Tilden, as usual, gave vent to frequent comments on

the plays, exclaiming, "Gee!" when he missed a stroke to the mirth of the French galleries, who bellowed for a translation.

This attitude later turned to grim silence and Lacoste's good-natured calm became an admirable nerve struggle against agonizing twinges from a besetting leg cramp.

Lacoste's Backhand Deadly.

The first two sets were featured by endless rallies, Lacoste's accurate backhand cut working wicked execution which won the first set. But in the second, Tilden turned the tables. Remarkably few points were scored on placements in these sets, one or the other losing after exhausting exchanges on nets or outs.

The point score, in the commencement of the next set, shows rallies of eight, ten, twenty-two, sixteen, thirty-one and forty-two returns by both players. The strokes were largely forehand and backhand drives, varied with Lacoste's swift-sailing drops over the net and Tilden's vicious cuts and smashes.

The fourth game at this rate of play lasted twelve minutes, when the score went to 2—all. In the next game, Muhr called the first footfault, which Tilden accepted, demanding with a certain grace, "Which foot, Muhr?"

The score went to 4—3 in Tilden's favor when Lacoste, in attempting to dive under Tilden's placement in front, slid down in heap and came up limping. In the next play it was evident that the French player's leg was refusing to obey and the cramp grew steadily worse. Tilden won this game, but Lacoste, hobbling rapidly about, succeeded in capturing the next one.

Lacoste Tries Net.

Tilden took another game with Lacoste trying to play the net but, on account of his leg, failing to bring down Tilden's lobs. By painful efforts, Lacoste deuced the set at 5—all, but going down again on the court he was obliged to cling to the net post for over a minute before being able to attempt walking.

Tilden shot many errors but took the next two games and the French hopes grew dim as Lacoste, supported by friends, was assisted from the court for a ten minute intermission, his blanched face distorted with suffering. A massage in this interval worked wonders for the Frenchman, who came back walking briskly. He appeared for the first time in many years bareheaded on the court. He soon drew a laugh from the crowd however, when, after losing a game he ran to the side lines and came running back to play wearing a hat and under it the expression of one who had accomplished a clever bit of strategy.

The games alternated until 3—all, when Lacoste took a sudden spurt and evened the count at two sets each amid an enormous demonstration from the galleries.

Even then there was not the slightest inkling of Lacoste's approaching victory. Not one in twenty present would have hazarded any wealth on the Frenchman's chances, but as the final set went on and ran to deuce, the atmosphere on the court was one of bustling tenseness. Every play seemed endless.

Frenchman Wins Game.

The score went to 3 all. Then Lacoste won a game and the cheers of the crowd. Tilden took the eighth game, Lacoste the ninth, and at this point Tilden, with his four-service love game, reached the summits of execution. Tilden also captured another game and with the score 6—5 in the American's favor Tilden drove out again and again to lose points. Lacoste again took the lead at 7—6 and Tilden evened the score.

A slight sprinkle of rain started during the next game and it began to look as if the match might be stopped, as was the first attempt to play the Borotra - Lacoste vs. Tilden - Hunter match.

Lacoste's cramp was beginning to show again as the score reached 8—7 in Tilden's favor, but two remarkable placements and two equally admirable returns of Tilden's placements helped him make the standing 8 all. Tilden took another game and in the next led 40—15 only to lose after twice failing on advantage to take the match point. Rain was drizzling during the last two games, but not sufficiently to cause either player to slip.

Tilden Seems Weary.

Tilden seemed fagged and drove wildly, while the grandstand whooped. Still there were who deemed Tilden finished. He won the opening point with a neat placement which Lacoste duplicated on the second play. Lacoste smashed Tilden's easy ball and led 30—15. Tilden then put over one of his serves that can't be touched and made it 30 all, but on the next volley netted on the second exchange. With the score 30—40 America's greatest living tennis player stood up and served a double fault.

Miss Kea Bouman of Holland captured the women's singles title from Mrs. Peacock of South Africa, triumphing over science with youth in two straight sets, 6—2, 6—4.

June 6, 1927

MISS WILLS SWEEPS TO WIMBLEDON TITLE

Tennis Crown Comes Here First Time in 20 Years When She Beats Señorita de Alvarez.

WINS IN TWO SETS, 6-2, 6-4

Trails at 3-4 in Second, but Quickly Gains Upper Hand With Scorching Drives.

COCHET TAKES 5-SET FINAL

Borotra Seven Times at Match Point, but Loses—Tilden and Hunter Advance In Doubles.

WIMBLEDON, England, July 2.—Miss Helen Wills won her first Wimbledon championship here this afternoon and captured the famous tennis trophy for America for the first time in twenty years. Mrs. May Sutton Bundy of California having been the last American winner. Miss Wills defeated Señorita Elia de Alvarez of Spain in the final today, 6—2, 6—4. She set a pace that was too hot for her rival and although she gained a lead of 4—3 in the second set, the American rallied to take command again.

Henri Cochet of France won the men's singles championship after a five-set struggle with his compatriot, Jean Borotra. The latter stood at match point seven times, five times in one game when he was ahead at 5—3 in the fourth set, but each time the cup of victory was dashed from his lips by the calm and calculating Cochet, who now must be ranked as the world's greatest five-set player, a title that once was held only by William T. Tilden.

Miss Wills's match with Señorita de Alvarez was much closer than the score implies. As a display of sparkling strokes, directed by shrewd tactics, the match has never been excelled in the women's championship final at Wimbledon. The American, who had been wasting no time in sharpening her strokes in her previous matches, started the first set at concert pitch. She secured a big initial advantage and won the set without serious opposition.

Second Set Is Different.

The second set, however, told a very different tale. Steadying down, while losing none of her brilliance, Señorita de Alvarez began to make an even fight of the match. While Miss Wills was hitting the ball harder, Señorita de Alvarez was hitting it sooner and thus for a time she more than discounted the Californian's pace.

Scoring many points with her acutely angled backhand placements, the señorita recovered after being two games down and secured a 4—3 lead. There seemed no reason why she shouldn't maintain this winning streak and take the set, but it proved to be an issue of stamina rather than of strokes. There was a stirring rally in the eighth game as long as a Summer's day and after it had gone against her Señorita de Alvarez found herself in the twilight of her physical resources.

Miss Wills then swept through the next two games and won the match without further difficulty. She had played the match, with the exception of the first half of the first set, at her best controlled but highest speed, forcing the Spanish girl into error-making. These tactics probably were the soundest she could have adopted, for her rival, when she can get to the net, is doubly dangerous.

The California girl began the match as though her object was to sweep the señorita off her feet before she could get going. She went quickly into a lead of 3—0, taking a love game on her service and another against her rival's. Then Señorita de Alvarez began to find her feet and her strokes. She won the fourth game and had several chances to take the fifth, but became unsteady at the critical moments.

Takes the Sixth Game.

She took the sixth, mainly through dropping a series of short backhand placements within three yards of the net. Miss Wills, however, captured the next game with the aid of two service aces and won the set with some assistance from the net cord shots that favored her.

The first game of the second set went to deuce four times. Scoring a service ace, however, Miss Wills won it after making Señorita de Alvarez run all over the court. In the next game, the Señorita would make as many as five brilliant strokes in a rally, only to lose it by one wild swing. Her opponent secured a 2—0 lead with her service to follow, but at this juncture the Spanish girl suddenly came to life and by well-angled placements broke through Miss Wills's service.

For a sequence of two games the American became somewhat unsteady and the señorita, employing brilliant strokes in conjunction with some very sound tactics, evened the count at 2 all. The next game was close, but Miss Wills just won it. Señorita de Alvarez again tied the score on a series of beautiful placements which ended the long rallies.

Miss Wills trailed in the next game at 15—40, with the señorita serving, but she pulled up to deuce. After deuce had been called four more times, the señorita, employing some well-angled backhand placements, took the lead at 4—3.

Long Rally Thrills Stands.

There was great excitement as the next game began. Its chief feature was the tremendous rally, in which the ball crossed the net thirty times. At its close both girls leaned exhausted on their racquets, but Miss Wills, having won it and the game, recovered sooner. Then she easily won her service, the Spanish girl still being out of breath, and reached match point. Then the señorita hit out of court, uttered a long "Oh!"

and knocked the ball high in the air before rushing to the net to congratulate the victor.

The Cochet vs. Borotra match, won by the former at 4—6, 4—6, 6—3, 6—4, 7—5, was expected to be another of those finest volleying encounters into which the French final at Wimbledon almost invariably resolves itself. It was, but with a difference. In many respects it closely resembled the five-set Cochet-Tilden struggle, but again there was a difference.

Tilden's sudden collapse, when he was within a point of the match and still in the full tide of his strength was a mystery. Borotra gained some of his advantages at match point in the fifth set when he was almost at the end of his physical resources. Cochet having pushed him closely from the first and being much fresher at the last.

Cochet's eleventh hour victory, however, was a tribute not only to his stamina but to his strategy and his unconquerable will to win. In that five feet five inches of rugged manhood lies enough bulldog determination for ten tennis players. To have five match points called against you in one game and to win that game and to have seven match points called against you in a match and still win is no mean feat.

Cochet Sets His Jaw.

Cochet, with his jaw set, balanced himself coolly on the knife edge of defeat seven times. Borotra pronounced the sentence of death. Seven times Cochet stood on the scaffold with the noose around his neck, but he elected to die fighting if he had to die and in the end it was Borotra who perished.

Borotra played a volleying game from the start. Once at the net he couldn't be passed, whereas he was able to pass Cochet by cleverly jabbing his strokes through the narrow openings. In the second set it was the same story.

In the third Cochet gained a lead of 3—1, but Borotra evened the count. The Lyons star then rallied and took the set. It was Borotra, who gained a 3—1 lead in the next set, but he couldn't hold it, Cochet evening the match at two sets all.

The memorable final set began in the same fashion. The Basque, who had braced himself for his last effort, led at 2—1, 3—1, and finally at 5—2. He gained his first match point in the next game, but lost it, and then began that epic game which decided the match.

Borotra Gains the Lead.

Borotra, serving, went ahead but was pulled back to deuce. It was evident that he could win in fore court, but not in the back, and it was important for him to win as soon as possible in view of his state of fatigue. The crowd got quite out of hand while Cochet coolly juggled

with fate. Several times the umpire cautioned the crowd not to applaud during the rallies and Cochet himself held up an admonitory hand.

Finally the little man's stubborn refusal to accept defeat was rewarded. He saved the game, and every one, including Borotra, knew the match was over. He patted Cochet on the back as they crossed over and the latter quickly swept to victory.

William Tilden and Francis Hunter gained the final in the men's doubles after a close battle with Randolph Lycett and his brother-in-law, H. W. Austin. The score was 6–0, 10–8, 6–4. After the Americans won the first set, the match resolved itself into a struggle between Tilden and Lycett.

Lycett, once reckoned as one of the best doubles players in the world, still is deserving of that appellation. He won game after game single-handed. In fact, he had to because the support he received from Austin sometimes was negligible and always uncertain. Hunter was none too brilliant, but Tilden played his usual spectacular and effective game in the back court and at the net and it was mainly due to his efforts that America avoided the loss of the middle set.

Brugnon and Cochet Win.

The French pair of Cochet and Jacques Brugnon, winner of the championship last year, became the other finalist by conquering Louis Raymond and J. Condon of South Africa, 6–1, 6–2, 7–5. In this match, too, there was a set in danger, but it was the third one rather than the second. The South Africans had gained a lead of 5–2, but they could not hold it when the champions opened up with their full array of screaming drives, volleys and smashes. The French pair gave an exhibition of doubles play for which brilliance and cooperation seldom has been surpassed.

In the women's doubles this afternoon, Mrs. Kitty McKane Godfree and Miss Betty Nuthall triumphed over Miss Joan Fry and Miss Peggy Saunders, 3–6, 6–2, 6–1, and gained the semi-finals where they will oppose Miss Wills and Miss Elizabeth Ryan on Monday, the Americans already having reached that round. Whichever wins will face Miss Bobbie Heinie and Mrs. J. Peacock for the title as the South Africans now are in the final.

Hunter and Miss Ryan are paired with Mr. and Mrs. Lycett in the quarter final of the mixed doubles and are considered to have an excellent chance of ultimately winning the title. In fact, the chances of the Americans in the men's doubles and the women's doubles also are looked upon as very good and it might be that the United States will carry off four of the five championships.

The summaries:

Men's Singles, final round—Henri Cochet, France, defeated Jean Borotra, France, 4–6, 4–6, 6–3, 6–4, 7–5.
Women's Singles, final round—Miss Helen Wills, United States, defeated Senorita Elia de Alvarez, Spain, 6–2, 6–4.
Mixed Doubles, third round—D. M. Greig and Mrs. M. Watson, England, defeated S. W. Standring and Miss E. Phayre, England, 6–1, 6–1; J. Condon and Mrs. J. Peacock, South Africa, defeated Jacques Brugnon and Miss E. L. Colyer, France and England, 6–4, 3–6, 6–3.
Fourth Round—Greig and Mrs. Watson defeated Baron von Kehrling and Miss Ellen Bennett, Hungary and England, 7–5, 6–4.
Men's Doubles, semi-final round—William T. Tilden and Francis T. Hunter, United States, defeated Randolph Lycett and H. W. Austin, England, 6–0, 10–8, 6–4; Brugnon and Cochet, France, defeated Louis Raymond and J. Condon, South Africa, 6–1, 6–2, 7–5.

Point Score for Women's Final.

WIMBLEDON, England, July 2 (P).—The point score of the final match in the women's singles in the Wimbledon lawn tennis tournament between Miss Helen Wills and Senorita Elia de Alvarez follows:

FIRST SET.

Miss Wills	4	4	4	2	5	3	4	4—30—6
Senorita de Alvarez	2	2	1	4	3	5	1	2—20—2

SECOND SET.

Miss Wills	9	4	3	2	4	1	6	4	4	4—41—6
Senorita de Alvarez	7	2	5	4	2	4	8	1	0	2—35—4

MISS WILLS REGAINS U. S. TENNIS CROWN

Beats Miss Nuthall of England at Forest Hills by Score of 6-1, 6-4.

12 MINUTES FOR FIRST SET

English Girl Rallies in Second, but Finally Bows to Victor's Smashing Attack.

BOTH DRIVE FEROCIOUSLY

16-Year-Old Girl Captivates Crowd With Blistering Speed — Mrs. McKane and Miss Harvey Win.

By ALLISON DANZIG

The scepter of power in American tennis, which illness compelled her to relinquish last August after a reign of three years, returned to Miss Helen Wills yesterday, and today, with the Wimbledon crown also in her possession and victories over every prominent amateur of the United States, England and continental Europe to her credit, the 21-year-old Berkeley girl holds sway as the unrivalled empress of the courts. Only Mlle. Suzanne Lenglen challenges her position as world's champion, and as the French girl is outside the pale of amateur tennis the American is left without further world's to conquer.

The last obstacle in the path of Miss Wills's ascent to the tennis Olympus was removed yesterday when, in the final round of the women's national championship, the Berkeley girl defeated 16-year-old Betty Nuthall of England, 6–1, 6–4, in the greatest exhibition of destructive hitting power that has been put on by two women in the forty years' history of the tournament.

A gallery of 6,000 spectators, gathered in the stadium of the West Side Tennis Club at Forest Hills to see this first meeting between the two most celebrated players of the amateur ranks, sat enthralled at the savageness of the struggle, which was maintained at so furious a tempo as to make even most men's tennis seem tame by comparison.

Plays Her Greatest Tennis.

They saw Miss Wills, playing by far the most magnificent tennis she has ever shown in the championship, let loose with an attack of such withering pace and deadly accuracy as to make a mockery of Miss Nuthall's efforts to hold her off, in spite of the fact that the ball was coming from the English girl's racquet, too, like a bolt of lightning.

In the space of twelve short minutes they saw the American pound her way to victory in the first set with the loss of only twelve points, and then they saw Miss Nuthall, cool, diagnosing, little court general that she is, soften her game at strategic moments to throw a hitch into Miss Wills's machine-like attack, break through her service twice and extend her nearer to the breaking point than any other player has extended her this season.

There were moments in that second set, particularly when Miss Nuthall

led at 30-0 in the second game, with the score at 1-all, and again when she pulled up from 1-4 to 3-4 with the loss of only two points, when the prospect was far from remote that the English girl might carry the play to three sets.

With each game Miss Nuthall was becoming more and more dangerous as she mixed up her attack with traps and lobs that had Miss Wills fighting on the defensive, and if only she could reduce her errors to a minimum in the face of Miss Wills's continual hammering at her backhand, the gallery, whose heart was with the younger player, felt that there was hope for her.

Miss Wills on the Attack.

But Miss Wills, whose game had softened both from sheer weariness after her annihilating bombardment in the first set and because of the fact that the ball was coming back softer and at varying length and bounding higher than she likes to take it, sensed the seriousness of the situation and again turned on the full power of her pulverizing forehand.

The scepter that she wields is a scepter of temporal power, crushing in its brutal finality both the spirit and physical resistance. Miss Nuthall's spirit was never crushed, but those overpowering drives of Miss Wills, skimming across the net the full length of the court, were more

than flesh and blood could withstand, and the courageous fight of the 16-year-old girl against the inevitable came to an end in the tenth game.

Later in the afternoon, Miss Nuthall returned to the court with Miss Joan Fry to make her second bid for an American title in the all-English final of the doubles against Mrs. Kathleen McKane Godfree and Miss Ermyntrude Harvey. Once again she went down in defeat but not until she and Miss Fry, finding themselves in the second set with the score stood 4–1 against them, aroused the gallery to a frenzy of delight as they took seven games in a row in spectacular fashion to win the second chapter and gain a lead of 2–0 in the final set.

At this point, Mrs. McKane, who has no superior as a doubles player, and Miss Harvey aroused themselves from their slump and played such beautiful doubles as to win over the gallery in spite of itself as they carried the attack to their younger opponents and made evident the weakness in their defense.

Tie the Count at 2-All.

Tying the score at 2-all, they went ahead at 4—3, and after Miss Nuthall and Miss Fry had drawn level at 4-all, thanks to the splendid volleying of the latter and Miss Nuthall's gleaming drives, Mrs. Godfree won her game on service and Miss Fry was broken through in the tenth game, bringing the play to an end at

Times Wide World Photo.
Miss Wills (Left) Being Congratulated by Miss Nuthall After Yesterday's Match.

6—1, 4—6, 6—4. This was the second time that Mrs. Godfree has won the American doubles title, her first victory being gained in 1923 with Mrs. B. C. Covell.

Albert J. Gibney, the hard-working referee of the tournament, to whom much credit is due for his fine management of the championship under the most trying weather conditions, and Louis B. Dailey, President of the Eastern Lawn Tennis Association and Treasurer of the National L. T. A., presented the cups to the winners and runners-up in the two events, along with their felicitations and bouquets of American Beauty roses, while the gallery also paid its tribute to both the winners and losers, and especially to Miss Nuthall, who has captivated the American tennis public as have few other players.

During the interval granted Miss Nuthall for rest between the singles and the doubles match an exhibition of mixed doubles was put on which the spectators found almost as entertaining in stretches as either of the championship events. With Manuel Alonso on the court, paired with Miss Kea Bouman of Holland, the element of the spectacular was always provided, for there is no more sensational retriever than is the Spanish internationalist, who outdid himself yesterday in going back to the stadium wall for lobs.

Miss Gwynneth Sterry of England and Clarence J. Griffin of California were their opponents, and, although Miss Sterry's service and volleying were of brilliant character and Griffin's soft shots were always placed with a foxiness that kept their opponents guessing, Miss Bouman and Alonso had the more finishing shots. The first set went to the latter pair at 6—3, and the play was called to a halt when the score stood 4—1 in their favor in the second set.

Duel in Singles Final.

The final of the singles was, for the first set, almost entirely a duel between two of the greatest forehands ever developed in women's tennis. In the second set, by which time Miss Wills had gained a wholesome respect for her younger opponent's forehand, the issue resolved itself into a question of which player's backhand could stand up under pressure the better, and they were two marvelous backhands.

Of volleying there was almost none. Miss Wills made a winning volley for the first point of the match and a losing one, as well as her last, in the same game, while Miss Nuthall's first and only excursion to the net was made in the sixth game, when she brought the score to deuce with as sound a volley as the tournament witnessed.

From the moment Umpire Benjamin H. Dwight called "play" the two girls assailed each other hammer and tongs with drives that fairly burned up the turf. The very first rally gave the gallery an inkling of what to expect, as the ball crossed the net a half dozen times like spray from a machine gun.

Miss Wills was a pitiless foeman, seeking to kill with every shot as she clouted the ball with tremendous swipes that skimmed the net and crowded Miss Nuthall on the base-line. It took a stout heart and a hand of steel to stand up against this kind of pounding, and, though Miss Nuthall was never daunted and replied with savage drives in kind, she could not maintain control when the ball was coming back on top of her to cramp and hurry her stroke.

Gets a Fast Start.

In eight minutes Miss Wills had ruthlessly hammered out the five first games with the loss of only six points, and the gallery, sympathizing with her younger opponent, could see no hope for her. One might as well try singlehanded to "take" a machine gun nest as to resist an attack of such blinding speed and power.

In the sixth game, with the score 15—40 against her, Miss Nuthall brought a roar of delight from the stands as she returned one of Miss Wills's forcing shots with a lightning placement, followed it up with her lone volley of the match, won the next point on Miss Wills's failure to return service and then captured the game with a beautiful backhand shot down the line that was softened to catch her opponent off guard.

This last shot gave Miss Nuthall her cue in the second set after Miss Wills had won the seventh game for the first set. The second game of the second set found the English girl beginning to mix up her attack consistently and, for the first time, Miss Wills was put squarely on the defensive and at a loss to know where to expect the ball.

Instead of trading paceful drives with Miss Wills, on which the latter thrived, Miss Nuthall softened her strokes, sought a higher trajectory to get a higher bound (not to play safe) and changed the length on her shots with almost every other shot. Miss Wills could not maintain the momentum of her attack against this kind of opposition, and her own shots softened and sought a higher level. Then developed the duel of backhands, with the American directing almost every return to the left of Miss Nuthall in the long rallies.

The English girl's backhand served her marvelously in these endurance tests, but generally it was she who finally yielded the point on an error under constant pressure, and Miss Wills forged a head to a lead of 4—1. Now it was that Miss Nuthall assumed command to completely spike Miss Wills's attack with the shifting direction and provoking softness of her returns. The American could not paste the ball when it was bounding shoulder high, and she had to scramble to get her racquet on it, and she appeared to be somewhat at a loss as Miss Nuthall took the two next games.

But in the eighth game Miss Nuthall had a lapse in control, and her errors made the score 5—3. Two blistering forehand drives put her in the running again as she won the ninth, and it was felt that if Miss Wills did not win the tenth on service almost anything might happen. The Berkeley girl showed her championship fiber by rising to the occasion, and there was no withstanding her as she raked the opposing court to force Miss Nuthall into errors and brought the match to a close.

August 31, 1927

TILDEN AND JOHNSTON BEATEN AS FRANCE WINS THE DAVIS CUP

Final Score Is 3 Matches to 2, Lacoste and Cochet Triumphing in Singles.

LACOSTE CONQUERS TILDEN

Wins Great Duel, 6-3, 4-6, 6-3, 6-2—Cochet Defeats Johnston, 6-4, 4-6, 6-2, 6-4.

BATTLES THRILL 15,000

Frenzied Crowd Forgets Tennis Etiquette as French Score Their First Victory in Classic.

By ALLISON DANZIG.

Special to The New York Times.

PHILADELPHIA, Sept. 10. — The tennis empire takes its way eastward across the Atlantic. The longest reign in the history of the Davis Cup came to an end today and a new circle began, as France's invaders won the two final matches in the challenge round to capture the series with the United States at three matches to two at the Germantown Cricket Club and won the cup for the first time in the twenty-two times that the historic trophy has been competed for since 1900.

Thus ends the dominion of the English-speaking world in these international classics, which heretofore had been won only by the United States, Great Britain and Australia. Seven of America's ten victories have been gained since 1920, when the cup was brought back from the Antipodes; Australia has won it six times and Great Britain five.

France, to celebrate its first triumph, which marks the culmination of three successive years of effort in the challenge round and which was witnessed by the French Ambassador, Paul Claudel, will place the massive silver bowl and tray in the Louvre for keeping until it shall have been yielded to another nation.

Conquerors Are Conquered.

The same two players who went to Australia to lift the cup in 1920 and who have been the mainstay of its defense ever since, were the same two players who fought so gallantly but in vain today to extend America's tenure to another year, but the ravages of time had taken their toll and youth, in the person of Rene Lacoste and Henri Cochet, earned the day.

To Cochet, the player who ended William Tilden's six-year reign as national champion last September and who triumphed over the Philadelphian again in the final at Wimbledon last July, fell the honor of winning the match that clinched the victory for France when he defeated William Johnston in four sets at 6—4, 4—6, 6—2, 6—4.

However, it is to Rene Lacoste, the phlegmatic, sad-visaged young Parisian, on whom France should bestow the double palm, the Croix de Guerre and the Red Badge of the Legion of Honor, for it was his victory over William Tilden in the first of the two singles matches today that really decided the series.

Tilden Apparently Invincible.

With the United States leading at two matches to one and Tilden playing in apparently invincible form, all signs pointed toward another American victory when the Philadelphian and his twenty-three-year-old opponent went on the courts.

But the same machine-like defense maintained inexorably against the most terrific pressure which proved the undoing of Tilden in the challenge round last year, and again at St. Cloud in June, once more stood adamant against the thirty-four-year-old veteran's shafts of lightning until the American had shot his bolt and his physical powers disintegrated.

By the middle of the third set Tilden's racquet, the racquet that had once been the symbol of the most autocratic power that ever held sway on the courts, had become a harmless bit of wood and string in the hands of a physically exhausted giant

and Lacoste relentlessly went forward to victory at 6—3, 4—6, 6—3, 6—2.

Nothing that the stage has to offer can equal in drama the scene that was enacted on the hallowed Germantown turf.

A crowd of 15,000 tennis fans stormed the gates, hundreds of whom were turned back. Also, so great was the throng that got inside that the two sections of the grand stand, the bleachers and the extra stands all proved inadequate to hold them. Hundreds sat in the aisles, stood on chairs and sat on the ground, and when Johnston and Cochet went on the court there was a mad rush for seats on the adjoining court that swept a score of police guards aside.

Gallery Partisan One.

It was a thoroughly partisan gallery that looked down upon the play, a gallery that came scenting an

American victory and which, when Tilden had been defeated and all hope had been abandoned, was so carried away by Johnston's great bid for victory over Cochet that it broke all bounds of tennis etiquette and cheered madly both the American's winning shots and Cochet's mistakes.

In the fourth set of the match, when Johnston, hitting into a streak of magnificent tennis that had Cochet reeling before his attack, pulled up from 2–5 to 4–5 and 0–30 on the French youth's service, the stands were in continuous uproar. In vain Umpire Paul Gibbons pleaded with them to remain quiet while the ball was in play. He might as well have tried to turn back the tide. Cheers, shrieks and storms of applause went up to the skies as they begged Little Bill to come on.

And who could blame them? Wasn't Johnston making one of the gamest fights to save the cup that has been seen in the long history of the match? Johnston the "has been" and the "hollow shell" as they called him after his crushing defeat by La Coste on Thursday, was playing like one possessed, ripping the turf apart with his murderous forehand volleying as no one has seen him rally in years, and battering the harried Cochet from pillar to post.

It would have been a strange gallery that could have controlled its mad excitement under the circumstances, and so the place became a seething furnace of human exhortations as the little Californian fought his way to within two points of tying the score at 5—all in the fourth set.

Little Bill Falters.

But at this critical point, with Cochet erring miserably and looking toward Captain Pierre Gillou in bewilderment, plainly at a loss how to regain command, Johnston faltered. Over-anxiousness or perhaps nervousness that was partly the result of the uproar, interrupted the fluency of his stroking, the magic punch went out of his racquet and after he had been passed at the net he drove his backhand over the line, passed the line by an inch on a high volley and after a long rally his forehand found the net.

The match was over, the cup had been won for France and Cochet, in an ecstasy of happiness, threw his racquet thirty feet high into the air as he ran forward to throw his arms around his recent adversary. At the same moment Captain Gillou and Lacoste, their faces beaming with delight, walked out on the court to shower Cochet with congratulations, and the genial Borotra joined in the celebration.

For the next half hour the court swarmed with players, officials, spectators and photographers who insisted on taking pictures of all the members of the two teams, the officials and every one else who had any pretensions to being a tennis celebrity. The massive cup and tray were brought out. Ambassador Claudel entered into the ceremonies and President Jones A. Mersereau of the United States Lawn Tennis Association made the presentation speech as the prize was turned over to Captain Gillou.

Mme. Cochet, the wife of the 26-year-old youth from Lyons who had brought such glory to the valor of French tennis, was so overcome with happiness that she burst into tears and was still weeping a half hour after the play was over. It was an occasion that will remain forever in the memory of those who saw it, this first victory of France in the play for the cup that Secretary of War Dwight F. Davis offered in competition in 1900.

Lesson to Be Learned.

That it will be only the first of more victories to come for France is the lesson that is to be gained from the results of today's play. Tilden and Johnston have apparently seen their best days. Both are capable of playing as good tennis as ever they did in their lives, and this they both did today, but only for a certain number of sets. No longer is it possible for them to maintain the pace through a five-set match. While their physical powers endure they are as formidable as ever, but, unhappily for America's lost supremacy, the years have taken their toll of them and they must make way for the younger blood of France's masters of the court.

Tilden, victor over Crochet on Thursday and in the doubles with Frank Hunter over Jean Borotra and Jacques Brugnon, undertook more than was within physical capacity when he sought to bring victory practically single-handed to America today. It would have been the greatest triumph of the Philadelphian's long and glorious career on the courts had he been able to crown his three days of play with a victory that would have retained the cup for the United States. But almost from the outset the gallery had a premonition of what was to come.

Lacoste a Stone Wall.

Lacoste, driving with uncanny steadiness that characterizes his game at its best, was a stone wall against which the American wasted his strength in one long rally after another. Instinctively one felt that Tilden could not last against such pitiless efficiency, and it became apparent that he was going to have to pay dearly for every point he won. His only hope was to take every chance, hit for the lines with the smallest possible margin of safety and go to the net.

Tilden came to that understanding immediately himself, for he hit out for the base line almost from the start. His range was badly off in the first set, his drives overreaching the chalk strip by feet, and in spite of the fact that he was serving magnificently and volleying well his errors were far too numerous for him to make any headway against the flawless strokes of Lacoste.

Tilden was taking all the chances, hitting the harder and lower over the net, but always the ball kept coming back, and at good length, and the points were to Lacoste.

Lacoste did not make a single earned point in the opening set, Tilden contributing all 28 of them on errors. Four of them came in the fourth game, when the only break through service was made by Lacoste.

Tilden Seeks the Net.

The second set found Tilden tightening in control, in spite of the fact that he was still taking chances with his lengths, and he now sought the net at every opportunity when he had the service. But the strain was telling on him, and, after he had broken through in the second game and won the third with three beautiful placements, one of them a kill to lead at 3–0, he contented himself with holding his own service inviolate. Any shot that he had to scramble for he allowed to go unchallenged, particularly drop shots, and Lacoste won two service games at love, scoring 7 placements out of 8 points.

The crucial game of the set was the seventh. Lacoste gained a 40—0 lead on Tilden's service, and ordinarily the American would have made no effort to save the game, but he realized that if he lost his service it might mean the loss of the set and he went to the net for two beautiful volleys that were cheered wildly.

Lacoste's steadiness deserted him in this game and Tilden finally pulled it out at 7–5. The effort, however, told on him, and he lost the next two games. Lacoste pulling up from 15—40 to break through in the ninth, after Tilden had twice been at set point.

It looked serious indeed for Tilden now, for he was tiring badly and did not have the energy left to go to the net. The gallery was on tenterhooks when Lacoste began serving in the tenth. A placement off service and Lacoste's out gave Tilden a 30—0 lead and he carried it to 40—15 with a great kill from deep court. Lacoste pulled up to deuce on two errors, twice more saving the set by a point, but here he made one of his few unworthy errors in the match flubbing a set up shot near the net. That gave Tilden the advantage point and he took the set with a passing shot that was cheered to the echo.

Point Scores of the Final Tennis Matches Which France Won to Capture Davis Cup

LACOSTE VS. TILDEN.

First Set.

POINT SCORE.

										Pts.	G.
Lacoste	4	0	4	4	5	1	4	1	5	—28	6
Tilden	2	4	0	2	3	4	0	4	3	—22	3

STROKE ANALYSIS.

	N.	O.	P.	S.A.	D.F.
Lacoste	4	6	0	0	1
Tilden	11	17	5	6	0

Second Set.

POINT SCORE.

										Pts.	G.
Lacoste	2	2	1	4	1	4	5	6	5	3—33	4
Tilden	4	4	4	0	4	0	7	4	3	5—35	6

STROKE ANALYSIS.

	N.	O.	P.	S.A.	D.F.
Lacoste	6	13	13	0	1
Tilden	10	10	12	3	0

Third Set.

POINT SCORE.

										Pts.	G.
Lacoste	2	6	2	4	2	4	4	4	4	6—32	6
Tilden	4	4	4	0	4	1	1	1	0	3—19	3

STROKE ANALYSIS.

	N.	O.	P.	S.A.	D.F.
Lacoste	5	5	2	1	0
Tilden	17	10	9	0	2

Fourth Set.

POINT SCORE.

								Pts.	G.
Lacoste	4	4	3	4	4	2	4	4—29	6
Tilden	1	1	5	2	0	4	0	2—15	2

STROKE ANALYSIS.

	N.	O.	P.	S.A.	D.F.
Lacoste	4	4	6	0	0
Tilden	6	15	7	0	2

RECAPITULATION.

	N.	O.	P.	S.A.	D.F.
Lacoste	19	28	21	1	2
Tilden	44	52	33	9	4

	E.	E.P.	T.P.	G.	Sets.
Lacoste	49	22	122	21	3
Tilden	100	42	91	14	1

Umpire—Benjamin H. Dwight. Net umpire—Paul W. Gibbons. Footprint judge—L. Richards. Service linesmen—T. H. Martin and Irving C. Wright. Centre service linesmen—A. T. Batty and K. Snyder. Side linesmen—Harry Walsh, Wilbur Jamison, Franklin Devitt and H. White. Base linesmen—H. Hothersall and Frank Donnelson. Time of match—1:13

COCHET VS. JOHNSTON.

First Set.

POINT SCORE.

										Pts.	G.
Cochet	1	5	0	3	4	4	5	4	1	4—31	6
Johnston	4	3	4	5	0	2	3	0	4	2—27	4

STROKE ANALYSIS.

	N.	O.	P.	S.A.	D.F.
Cochet	7	12	5	0	0
Johnston	12	13	7	1	1

Second Set.

POINT SCORE.

										Pts.	G.
Cochet	4	2	5	1	1	4	1	0	4	2—24	4
Johnston	0	4	3	4	4	2	4	4	1	4—30	6

STROKE ANALYSIS.

	N.	O.	P.	S.A.	D.F.
Cochet	8	10	9	0	1
Johnston	4	8	11	0	3

Third Set.

POINT SCORE.

								Pts.	G.
Cochet	5	4	4	4	2	2	4	7—32	6
Johnston	3	1	1	0	4	4	0	5—18	2

STROKE ANALYSIS.

	N.	O.	P.	S.A.	D.F.
Cochet	4	8	12	0	0
Johnston	14	6	6	0	0

Fourth Set.

POINT SCORE.

										Pts.	G.
Cochet	4	4	4	6	2	5	8	8	0	4—45	6
Johnston	2	0	6	4	4	3	6	10	4	2—41	4

STROKE ANALYSIS.

	N.	O.	P.	S.A.	D.F.
Cochet	10	13	15	0	2
Johnston	15	14	16	0	1

Recapitulation.

	N.	O.	P.	S.A.	D.F.
Cochet	29	43	41	0	3
Johnston	45	41	40	1	5

	E.	E.P.	T.P.	G.	Sets.
Cochet	75	41	132	22	3
Johnston	91	41	116	16	1

Umpire—Paul W. Gibbons. Net umpire—A. P. Hawes. Footprint judge—Wilbur Jamison. Service linesmen—H. L. Richards, P. S. Osborne. Centre service linesmen—L. Colfelt, W. F. Kirkpatrick. Side linesmen—Harry Walsh, A. L. Burtis, W. R. C. Evans and F. H. Devitt. Base linesmen—Frank Donnelson and F. Zook.

Time of match—1:26.

American Pulls Up Even.

With the sets one all, there was more hope for Tilden, but one still had the feeling that the advantage lay with Lacoste as the fresher and more physically enduring of the two. Tilden had had no opportunity to spare himself as he did in the match with Cochet, when he coasted in the second set. He had to work just as hard in the second set against Lacoste as in the first, and that boded ill for him.

Both players relaxed at the start of the third chapter and games went on service to 3-all. Tilden's aggressiveness asserted itself in the fifth, when he scored on two blazing forehand drives across court and a gem of a volley. But this was the beginning of the end for him. His strength was exhausted and he had not enough left in reserve to control his shots.

Lacoste took the next four games with the loss of only four points and the gallery sat silent and depressed by the careless errors from Tilden's racquet. The American was too weary and spent to do more than lift his racquet.

The rest period did Tilden no good. Ten minutes of grace meant nothing to the veteran of 34 years. He had already given everything he had. He got only two points in the first two games of the fourth set, though he rallied to pull up from 0-40 and win the third game with two marvelous volleys.

Tilden was too far gone to make good a lead of 30—0 in the fourth. Lacoste got eight points in a row on errors and one volley, and, after Tilden had made a last gallant effort in the sixth, to win it with two blasting drives, Lacoste won the seventh at love, and two beautiful cross-court drives gave him the eighth for the set and match.

A perfect baseline defense that turned back everything with flawless precision had spiked the attack of the most spectacular player in the game. Tilden for all his virtuosity and daring had found that he did not have enough finishing shots to make any impression against a stone wall that catapulted back his most murderous smashes, and he realized the futility of opposition. Lacoste had robbed him of his confidence and will to win as well as his stamina.

The stroke analysis tells the story graphically. Tilden, while he scored 33 placements and 9 service aces to Lacoste's 21 and 1, made 100 errors to the others 49. Lacosta was never more the machine.

After the defeat of Tilden the gallery resigned itself to the loss of the cup. Johnston, after his overwhelming defeat by Lacoste on Thursday, was looked upon as hardly more than a sacrifice offering for Cochet. It can be appreciated then what were the feelings of the thousands in the stands when the little Californian started out after Cochet with a savageness that took the French youth by surprise. In the twinkling of an eye Johnston had won the first game at 4—1 and rushed into a lead of 4—0 in the second, whipping his forehand through the court like a bullet.

The crowd was in a turmoil. Cheer after cheer went up and every one asked his neighbor if this could be the same Johnston who couldn't get the ball over the net against Lacoste.

Johnston Makes Misplays.

At this point five errors in a row from Johnston's bat brought forth groans of disappointment but they changed to cheers again when he won the third at love and broke through at 5–3 to lead at 3–1. Cochet was slow to find himself against the hard hitting of Johnston and his few excursions to the net resulted in errors.

Beginning with the fourth game, however, the situation took on a different complexion. Cochet as cool as ice and always master of himself, now steadied in control, added pressure to his stroke and began to make the ingenious shots that stamp him as the greatest artist of the courts. Johnston could not put the ball away. His errors began to mount, and Cochet took five of the six next games for the set.

Again the question presented itself as to how long Johnston could sustain his powerful driving. But to the surprise of every one the little Californian came back stronger in the second set than he was in the first.

Battle on Even Terms.

Cochet was not as steady as he usually is at the start of this set, and Johnston stayed on even terms to 3 all, both players losing their service games twice. In the seventh game the Californian electrified the gallery with four placements, two of them volley shots, and two more blasting drives carried him into a 5–3 lead. Johnston's volleying now was so perfect as he lifted the ball from his feet on the hardest shots, and he was forcing his openings so relentlessly with his cannonball forehand, that Cochet, in spite of his miraculous recoveries, could not hold him off.

The stands were giving the Cali-

fornian ovation after ovation, and hope sprang anew for an American victory. Johnston faltered for a brief period and lost the match game on errors, but the tenth found him sailing along again and Cochet, driven from corner to corner, finally yielded the set after a sensational duel at the net, where Johnston brought off three superb low volleys in succession.

The pace was more than Johnston could stand, however, and he fell into a slump in the third set. His forehand found the net repeatedly, his backhand was vulnerable to Cochet's spinning drives to the corner. The French youth was stroking in his most inspired fashion, making the most impossible shots for placements. With the score 4–0 against him Johnston aroused the gallery by taking the two next games with his aggressive driving and volleying, but his errors cost him the seventh, and Cochet broke through in the eighth after a long struggle in spite of Johnston's spectacular volleying and overhead smashing.

Johnston Rallies Again.

It was inconceivable now that Johnston could pull out the match against the more youthful and brilliant young Frenchman. But again the California veteran surprised everyone by volleying with the score 2–0 against him in the fourth set

and playing his best tennis of the match. From this point on the gallery was stunned to the depths, at one moment exalting as Johnston scored on a murderous forehand or biting volley, at the next moment despairing as he made a costly error.

Both players were giving everything they had in the most bitterly fought volleys, and there were any number of close decisions on the lines that brought cries of protest from the stands when they went against Johnston.

Three times Johnston was at game point and he could not put over the necessary winning shot. As a consequence he was always behind, though he had a chance to tie the score at 2 all and 3 all, when Cochet after winning the second deuce game in succession, broke through at 8–6 in the seventh, in which Johnston led at 40–30, all hope was given up. Johnston was behind at 2–5 and Cochet had run him ragged in the seventh passing him five times as Johnston sought to get to the net.

Gallery Goes Wild.

But at this point came the American's rally that set the gallery wild. Four smoking drives enabled him to break through in the eighth at 10–8 after Cochet had twice been at match point. The loss of that game had a disturbing effect upon the French

youth, while Johnston, spurred on by his escape from defeat, as well as by the frenzied cheers of the spectators, pressed the attack in the ninth, pasting every ball on the nose, crowding the net to volley in sensational fashion and giving Cochet no rest. When he won the game at love the crowd cheered wildly. Cochet was a badly worried youth. His control was gone, as well as his confidence, and he was like a rudderless ship before the storm.

The suspense was terrific at the tenth game. Cochet, overanxious, popped the ball into the net. Again he netted the ball in the next rally and the stands were in bedlam, cheering his errors. But, with the score 0–40 against him, the young invader took a grip on himself and passed Johnston as he closed in.

Johnston's backhand drive overhit the line by an inch, making the score 30–all, and when the Californian put a high volley out of court by a hair a big groan went up from the stands, which protested that the volley had hit the line. Cochet was now at match point again. He served, Johnston returned the ball safely, it crossed and recrossed the net as the gallery hung breathlessly on every stroke, and then Johnston's drive landed in the net and the match was over. Cochet had won the Davis Cup for Fraance.

September 11, 1927

LACOSTE DEFEATS TILDEN IN 3 SETS TO KEEP U. S. TITLE

Gallery of 14,000 Sees Youth Conquer Age in Titanic Tennis Struggle, 11-9, 6-3, 11-9.

CUP AGAIN GOES TO FRANCE

First Time in the 46 Years of Play an Invader Has Scored Twice.

TILDEN FIGHTS GALLANTLY

Leads 3-1 in Second Set and 5-2 in Third, but Stamina Falls as Rival Presses on to Victory.

By ALLISON DANZIG.

For the first time in the forty-six years' history of the tournament, the national tennis championship was won by a foreign player a second time yesterday when Jean Rene Lacoste of France retained the title which he succeeded to last year after the six-year reign of William T. Tilden 2d of Philadelphia had been brought to an end by Henri Cochet, another Frenchman.

In one of the greatest struggles that ever brought the championship to a conclusion, the 23-year-old Parisian triumphed over Tilden in

Times Wide World Photo.

René Lacoste,
With National Singles Tennis Championship Cup Which He Retained Yesterday by Beating William T. Tilden.

three sets, frustrating the hopes of the American of equaling the record of seven victories established by Richard D. Sears, and marking the first time that Tilden has failed to win a set from Lacoste in their many meetings on turf courts. The score was 11–9, 6–3, 11–9.

Close to two hours, an hour and fifty-three minutes to be exact, was required for a decision in this titanic struggle between the player who formerly stood as the invincible monarch of the courts and the youth who has succeeded to his position. Many a five-set match has been finished in far less time than that, but no five-set struggle that Tilden has lost or saved with one of his dramatic climbs to unassailable heights under stress has surpassed yesterday's harrowing battle between age and youth in the desperateness of the conflict and its appeal to the emotions, or in the magnificent quality of the play.

Stadium Is Packed.

A gallery of 14,000 spectators, a gallery that packed the Forest Hills stadium to the last seat and that stood at the top of the last tier and in every other available space, looked down upon this terrific struggle, and at the end it knew that it had been privileged to see one of the most ennobling fights a former champion ever made to regain his crown.

Tilden, in the years of his most ruthless sway, was never a more majestic figure, never played more upon the heart-strings of a gallery than he did yesterday as he gave the last ounce of his superb physique to break through a defense that was as enduring as rock, and failed; failed in spite of the fact that he was three times at set point in the first chapter, in spite of the fact that he led at 3–1 in the second set, and once again in spite of the fact that he held the commanding lead of 5–2 in the third set and was twice within a stroke of taking this chapter.

He failed because youth stood in the balance against him—youth in the person of an untiring sphinx that was as deadly as fate in the uncanny perfection of his control, who assimilated the giant Tilden's most murderous swipes and cannon-ball serves as though they were mere pat balls and who made such incredible saves as to have broken the spirit of nine men out of ten.

But the spirit of Tilden was one thing that never broke. Long before the end of the match, yes, by the end of that agonizing first set which had the gallery cheering Tilden madly and beseeching him to put over the one vital stroke that was lacking, those marvelous legs of the Philadelphian were slowing up.

By the second set the fires of his wrathful forehanders were slumbering, and the third set found him a drooping figure, his head slunk forward, so utterly exhausted that not even the pitchers of ice water that he doused over himself could stimulate his frayed nerves, which must have ached painfully.

Gallery Is for Tilden.

It was a spectacle to have won the heart of the most partisan French protagonist, the sight of this giant of the courts, once the mightiest of the mighty, flogging on his tired body in the unequal battle between youth and age. If there were any French partisans present, they did not make themselves known. One and all those 14,000 spectators were heart and soul for Tilden as he made his heroic fight to prevent the last of the world's biggest tennis crowns go the way of all crowns.

If they cheered him in the first set, if they raised the roof when he gained his lead of 3–1 in the second chapter and again when he slashed his way ahead at 5–2 in the third, the din was nothing compared to the ovation Tilden received when, later on in the final chapter, the Philadelphian came back like a man from the grave to save himself from defeat twice by a single point in the fourteenth game. That game was one of the most agonizing a tennis gallery ever sat through as a shell of a man staved off the inevitable by a classic exhibition of fighting entirely on nerve.

The gallery, hopelessly in the despond as the machine-like Lacoste pulled up from 2–5 to 5-all and then to 7–6, took one despairing look at the drooping figure of Tilden as Lacoste began to serve, and resigned itself to seeing the end. In spite of the fact that the American steeled himself and sent the ball back like rifle fire, he could make no impression against a youth who dug his chops out of the ground and made the most heart-breaking gets of his cannonball drives.

So Lacoste reached 40–30, one point away from victory. The suspense was terrific as the next rally began and when Tilden pulled up to deuce on Lacoste's out, a sigh of relief went up. But the next moment Lacoste was again at match point as Tilden failed to return his rally safely.

Tilden Gets the Game.

Again the French youth netted at the crucial point and the game went on and on until finally, after deuce had been called the fifth time, Lacoste drove out and Tilden whipped home a lightning drive down the line for the game.

How they cheered Tilden! And when he went on to win the fifteenth game at 4–1, with his cannonball service, to lead at 8–7, the crowd was fairly wild with delight. Visions arose again of victory for him, at least in this set, but they speedily vanished when Lacoste won the next two games, breaking through in the seventeenth as Tilden lost all control.

Once more the American aroused the gallery to a wild pitch when he broke through for a love game with two placements, but that was the end. Dead on his feet, Tilden fought Lacoste tooth and nail in the nineteenth, which finally went to the younger player at 8–6, as he scored on three placements in a row, and then, utterly at the end of his rope, he yielded quickly in the twentieth through his errors, to bring the match to an end.

It was a match, the like of which will not be seen again soon. As an exposition of the utmost daring and brilliancy of shot-making and equally of the perfect stage to which the defense can be developed, it has had few equals in the history of tennis.

On the one side of the net stood the perfect tactician and most ruthless attacker the game probably has ever seen, master of every shot and skilled in the necromancy of spin. On the other side was the player who has reduced the defense to a mathematical science; who has done more than that, who has developed his dedefense to the state when it becomes an offense, subconscious in its working but none the less effective in the pressure it brings to bear as the ball is sent back deeper and deeper and into more and more remote territory.

Both exponents of the attack and the defense were at their best yesterday, and the reaction of the gallery at the end was that it had seen the best that tennis can offer. As one of the spectators remarked, everything else will seem stale after this match. He had seen the zenith.

The defensive player won, but in no small measure it was because youth was on his side. As perfect as was Lacoste's defense, Tilden still might well have prevailed through the sheer magnificence of his stroking had not fatigue set in and robbed him of the strength to control his shots.

In the first set, when Tilden led at 7–6 and 40-love on his own service, it was his errors that robbed him of his big chance. His cannon ball service failed him at this critical point, though it was only by a hair that he failed to put over an ace for the set, and when Tilden cannot put over an ace in a pinch he is usually tired.

Plan of Match Upset.

Had the American put over that one point for which the gallery begged there is no telling who would have won the match. With the first set in the bag he could have loafed through the second and saved himself entirely for the third. Instead he had to keep going in the second, and while he switched from a driving to a chopping game that did not take so much out of him, still the strain was too much for him.

The day has passed when Tilden can maintain a burning pace for two full sets. He knows that as well as the next man, and so he plans his campaign to go "all out" in the first, coast in the second and come back strong in the third, relying upon the rest period to regenerate the dynamo for the fourth.

Had he won the first and relaxed in the second, it is hardly conceivable that he could have failed to make good his 5–2 lead in the third, which would have given him a 2–1 lead to work on after the intermission, with the psychological advantage on his side.

However, even had Tilden won the first set, it may be presuming too much to concede that he would have gone on to victory in the third. After all, this 23-year-old Lacoste is a wonder, a miracle-worker, and he might have stopped even a rampant Tilden at 5–2.

There are moments when Lacoste has had bad spells, when he is human, if to err is human, but those moments are rarer than an American victory over France. When he is in the hole and sets himself to the task, such moments are practically non-existent. You can drive away at him all the day long, mix chops, slices, drives and volleys in a mad melange, run him to the corners until he is dizzy and always you get nothing for your pains but the chance to hit the ball again. It always comes back like no champion ever does.

The gallery, as partisan as it was, as whole-heartedly as it favored Tilden, could not help but be carried away by the incredible feats of Lacoste. Unmindful of the cheers for his opponent, playing a lone hand, the youthful invader concentrated upon his work and kept the ball in play—kept it in play when Tilden was sending his terrific service straight at him, kept it in play when he had to scramble to the far corners of the court for a blistering drive to his back-hand, and kept it in play when the American was loading his shots with such heavy spin that a spoon would have been needed by any other player to dig it out of the turf.

A defense so impregnable as that, a defense which confounded all of Tilden's ingenuity as he brought all of his artifices to bear, along with his devastating speed and power, should have undermined the morale of any opponent. That Tilden stuck to his guns and fought on as he has seldom fought before, in spite of the fact that he was on his last legs, while his adversary was flitting nimbly about the court on his toes, is to the American's glory.

In victory Tilden was never more magnificent a figure that he was yesterday in defeat, and Lacoste, in his years of triumph, was never greater than he was in the victory at Forest Hills.

Jean Borotra, Lacoste's team-mate, who seldom before has been heard to extol the merits of his compatriots, could only shake his head at the end. "If René keeps on playing tennis like that," he said, "how is any one ever going to beat him?"

With the French and American championships both in his possession and victories to his credit over both Tilden and Johnston in the Davis Cup challenge round, the 23-year-old Parisian stands as the unchallenged monarch of the courts, the pride of France and her hope for a continuation of her sweeping success in the future.

All the honors belong to her. She has the Davis Cup. Cochet has the Wimbledon championship and Lacoste has the French and the American indoor and outdoor championship. What else is there to say, except that the season is over, and the French will all be back in the United States again after the Davis Cup challenge round matches in Paris in July?

The point score and stroke analysis of the final of the national championship singles follows:

First Set.

POINT SCORE.

Lacoste—

	G.	Pts.
4 2 4 3 0 6 4 0 4 1 5 1 1 5 5 2 4 7 4 4—	11	66

Tilden—

	G.	Pts.
0 4 2 5 4 4 0 4 0 4 3 4 1 3 3 4 1 9 2 1—	9	61

STROKE ANALYSIS.

	N.	O.	P.	SA.	DF.
Lacoste	14	22	8	1	0
Tilden	30	26	21	4	1

Second Set.

		G.	Pts.
Lacoste	4 0 2 4 4 4 4 5 4—	6	31
Tilden	1 4 4 6 1 0 1 3 1—	3	21

STROKE ANALYSIS.

	N.	O.	P.	SA.	DF.
Lacoste	5	7	7	1	0
Tilden	13	10	7	2	0

Third Set.

POINT SCORE

Lacoste—

	G.	Pts.
1 1 5 2 2 4 1 4 6 4 0 4 7 7 2 4 4 0 8 4—	11	70

Tilden—

	G.	Pts.
4 4 3 4 4 1 4 0 4 2 4 0 5 9 4 2 1 4 6 1—	9	66

STROKE ANALYSIS.

	N.	O.	P.	SA.	DF.
Lacoste	17	25	17	0	1
Tilden	23	28	20	3	2

Recapitulation.

	N.	O.	P.	SA	DF.
Lacoste	36	54	32	2	1
Tilden	66	64	48	9	3

	E.	EP.	TP.	G.	Sets.
Lacoste	91	34	167	28	3
Tilden	133	57	148	21	0

Umpire—Benjamin H. Dwight. Net umpire—Rufus Davis. Foot fault judge—Benjamin M. Phillips. Service linesmen—Irving C. Wright and H. L. Richards. Centre service linesmen—W. L. Creevy and H. T. Mattice. Side linesmen—C. E. Hall, William Jamison, N. G. Andreini and O. M. Bostwick. Base linesmen—Charles A. Anderson and Frank G. Danielson.

Time of match—1:53.

September 18, 1927

RICHARDS CAPTURES PRO TENNIS CROWN

Becomes First U. S. Champion by Beating Kinsey in Straight Sets, 11-9, 6-4, 6-3.

$1,000 TO TITLEHOLDER

Also Gains Leg on Longue Vue Trophy — Wood and Heston Eliminated in Semi-Finals.

Fifteen hundred tennis enthusiasts turned out at the Notlek courts yesterday afternoon to see Vincent Richards win the first United States professional tennis championship, gain a first leg on the Longue Vue trophy, which was donated by R. A. Gusheey, and take away the $1,000 check which went with the title.

Richards defeated Howard Kinsey in straight sets, 11–9, 6–4, 6–3, to gain the first pro tennis title ever

contended for in this country.

The former Davis Cup star was spotty in his play and took some time to get accustomed to Kinsey's speedy cut strokes. When he was pressed, though, Richards seldom failed to get across the necessary points. His overhead and volleying game, generally his best point getter, was faulty in the first half of the play, and on many occasions he smashed the ball out of bounds when he had easy kills. In the last half, however, he showed all of the greatness he displayed two years ago as an amateur.

With the score 3—all in the first set, Kinsey broke through Richards's service and then captured his own to lead, 5—3, but the New York star rallied to even the count. Each won on service until the score stood at 9—all, when Richards rushed through to take the set.

The Californian began the second set much the same as the first, remaining in the backcourt, but changed his tactics slightly. He continually hammered Richards's backhand, and when he reeled off four consecutive games there seemed little doubt that he would even the match.

Richards, however, began to hammer the lines with all of his old daring and to force the play at the net. He took the fifth game on his service and came from behind 40-love on the sixth to win. With the score at deuce in the next game, he served across two service aces to make it 3—4. Kinsey then changed his racquet, but this did not stem the tide, for Richards swept through the next three games to triumph.

The New Yorker went into the third set with a lead of 2—1 and captured the fourth game on Kinsey's service when the Californian doublefaulted on the final point.

The next four games were divided, each man taking his serevice, Richards winning the ninth and set, 6—3.

The Davis Cup star gained the final by defeating Charles Wood in the morning, 6—0, 6—1, 6—2. He ran off ten consecutive games before the Fairview player gleaned one.

Kinsey disposed of Paul Heston, the Washington star, in the semifinals, 6—0, 6—4, 6—3. The California player received $700 for placing second, while Wood and Heston each received $100.

September 26, 1927

Tilden's Glare Held Responsible for Defeat Of Attempt to Ban Frowning at Officials

By The Associated Press.

CHICAGO, Feb. 14.—The American privilege of glaring at the officials, whether it be in baseball, boxing or tennis, was saved to the tennis players of the land, it was learned today, by Big Bill Tilden when this right was on trial at the United States Lawn Tennis Association meeting here last Saturday.

Advocates of the English code offered a regulation forbidding the players' glaring at the officials. Tilden rose with some choice remarks and some very impressive glaring, and the rule against "dirty looks" was voted down.

The most successful tennis match in this section in many years was the Tilden-Hunter exhibition against Lott and Hennessey Saturday night, drawing gate receipts of more than $6,000, it has just been announced. This paid for the canvas court and other indoor equipment and left a profit for the Chicago Tennis Association, which at once began plans for featuring other exhibitions by National stars.

February 15, 1928

Times Wide World Photo.

Miss Helen Wills receiving trophy from Walter Merrill Hall after retaining national tennis title by defeating Miss Jacobs.

MISS WILLS RETAINS NATIONAL NET CROWN

Conquers Miss Jacobs, 6-2, 6-1, and Wins Championship for the Fifth Time.

ALSO TAKES DOUBLES TITLE

Paired With Mrs. Wightman She Defeats Miss Cross-Mrs. Harper, 6-2, 6-2.

ENDS BRILLIANT CAMPAIGN

Champion Triumphed at Auteuil, Wimbledon and Forest Hills Without Loss of a Set.

By ALLISON DANZIG.

The most devastating power ever applied to a tennis ball by a woman, the power that was described as revolutionizing at Wimbledon, carried Miss Helen Wills, twenty-three-year-old Berkeley (Cal.) girl, to her fifth national championship yesterday, bringing to a close the campaign that has seen her win the premier laurels of tennis at Auteuil, Wimbledon and Forest Hills without the loss of a set in three months of play.

In the final round of the forty-first annual championship tournament, before a gallery of 4,000 spectators in the stadium of the West Side Tennis Club, Miss Wills defeated Miss Helen Jacobs of Santa Barbara, Cal., in thirty-three minutes at 6—2, 6—1, thereby taking her place as the only woman with the exception of Mrs. Molla Mallory of New York to win the title five times.

Mrs. Mallory captured the crown seven times and, in addition, won the patriotic tournament in 1917, which amounted to a championship, although it was not so officially designated. Mrs. Hazel Hotchkiss Wightman and Miss Elizabeth Moore come next to Miss Wills with four victories each.

Second Leg on Trophy.

Miss Wills's triumph yesterday, which was made a double one when she and Mrs. Wightman defeated Miss Edith Cross and Mrs. Lawrence Harper of California for the doubles championship, 6—2, 6—2, gave her a second leg on the singles challenge trophy. The present trophy was offered in competition in 1926, after the California girl had retired the previous one the year before.

Mrs. Mallory, whose reign was brought to an end in 1923 by Miss Wills, scored the first leg on the new cup in 1926. That year Miss Wills was unable to defend her title owing to her weakened condition following her operation for appendicitis. Miss Wills scored her first leg on the cup last year.

In addition to establishing a second claim on the challenge cup, Miss Wills also added a mammoth silver vase to her collection of prizes with yesterday's victory. Walter Merrill Hall, President of the West Side Tennis Club, presented her with the trophy, filled with American Beauty roses, while a score of cameras, talking motion picture machines and regular motion picture machines registered the scene, with a radio furnishing music from an airplane invisible behind a cloud.

The airplane, talking movies and other cameras were representative of the modern era of mechanical progress and in Miss Wills was personified the no less remarkable development of women's tennis. Here, before the eyes of the multitude, was the player whose annihilating speed has held the capitals of the game aghast and has more closely approximated the destructiveness of the masculine players' strokes than that of any other woman in the history of tennis.

Ablest Players Repulsed.

The ablest players of the world have gone up against that speed in the French, English and American championships, the Wightman Cup matches and in invitation tournaments. The best that any of them could do against it was to win three games in a set and five in a match, until Miss Wills met Mrs. Charlotte Hosmer Chapin of Springfield, Mass., in the fourth round of the play at Forest Hills.

Mrs. Chapin won six games from the champion and came within a point of reaching 5—all in the second set, the nearest that any player has come to putting a serious complexion on any of Miss Wills's matches since she dropped the opening set of her first engagement at Wimbledon in 1927 to Miss Gwynneth Sterry of England.

For just a few minutes in yesterday's match the gauntlet was thrown down to Miss Wills in a manner to excite the gallery to a pitch of almost frenzied applause and to arouse the hope that here, in the attractive nineteen-year-old Miss Jacobs, her invincible namesake had at last found an adversary capable of putting her mettle to the supreme test. This was in the third and fourth games of the opening set, when Miss Jacobs, producing a forehand drive incomparably superior in its pace and the cleanness of contact between ball and racquet to anything that she had shown in the past, scored one magnificent placement after another to take two games in a row and tie the score at 2—all.

Tastes Her Own Medicine.

One may well imagine the sensations of the spectators upon seeing Miss Wills, accustomed to burying her opponents under an avalanche of drives, tasting a sample of her own medicine. The reaction was all the more startling because of the fact that the champion had started out on her usual procession, taking the first two games in hardly sixty seconds with the loss of only one point.

It was with the score at 15—40 against her in the third game that Miss Jacobs suddenly came out of the coma that habitually seizes upon Miss Wills's opponents and galvanized the silent gallery into a cheering, sympathizing rooting section that found itself looking down upon a stirring battle royal instead of a slaughter.

Hitting a blistering forehand drive straight down the line to Miss Wills's backhand corner and judiciously varying to a short cross-court stroke that the champion could not even approach, Miss Jacobs had the gathering wild as she took four points in a row to win the game, the last point coming on a masterly short chop stroke that trapped her opponent at the base line.

The cheers that greeted Miss Jacobs as she changed court were mild compared to the ovation the young challenger received when she pulled out of the very same hole, 15—40, to win the fourth.

Errors Aid Miss Jacobs.

Miss Wills's errors in returning service had contributed to her loss of the third game. It was entirely Miss Jacobs's magnificent shot-making that won the next game. She produced four stunning drives, three of them making the chalk fly along the side line and the other, a cross-court return of service, costing Miss Wills her own game.

With the score at 2—all Miss Jacobs continued to outplay the champion to 30—15 in the fifth game, and the air was electric with suspense and excitement. If Miss Wills was worried she succeeded in masking her feelings, but from the way in which she bent over her racquet, tensely awaiting service and concentrated on her task, the champion must have had as clear an understanding of the serious possibilities of the situation as did the gallery.

But those possibilities never materialized. At this nerve-wracking juncture Miss Jacobs suddenly cracked, lost all control, and the play reverted to almost the one-sided character it had assumed in the first two games. Miss Wills won twelve points in a row, all of them save one on her opponent's errors, took four games in a row with the loss of only three points, including the two that Miss Jacobs held at 30—15, and increased her string of games to nine before her opponent got another, the sixth of the second set.

Miss Jacobs made a better fight in the second set than the score indicates, losing three games after deuce had been called, including the last, which Miss Wills won from 15—40. But in spite of the fact that she was hitting aggressively and making Miss Wills do plenty of running after volleys and drives of alternating length, all doubt as to the outcome ended with that first set. The challenger could not control the ball, and her 49 errors, as contrasted with Miss Wills's 19, tell the story.

Backhand Is at Fault.

It was Miss Jacobs's backhand that was most grievously at fault—her backhand which is ordinarily her best stroke and big point winner. It was her forehand which served her best yesterday, although in the second set it betrayed her no less than did her backhand, as she persistently put the ball yards beyond the lines.

A partial explanation for these errors of Miss Jacobs is to be found in the relentless pressure of Miss Wills's attack. The champion was not hitting with quite the same drastic speed that she had used in her previous matches, particularly on her forehand, but she was applying an even, almost invariable amount of power with each successive stroke, and the cumulative effect was to wear down her opponent and destroy her timing and accuracy.

Miss Jacobs was driven unmercifully from one side of the court to another to hold off those inexorable forcing shots to the far corners, and she used up additional energy in going to the net, where she performed brilliantly at times but finally broke down badly and missed one set-up volley after another.

Miss Wills did not go to the net a single time. She can volley as well as Miss Jacobs, if not better, but she put her sole reliance in those battering ground strokes which have spelled the doom of the best players in the world, and they were sufficient.

Chooses Lesser Evil.

It was her backhand which did the most damaging work. Miss Jacobs wisely refrained from putting the ball on the champion's forehand, but it was merely a case of choosing the lesser evil. Miss Wills's backhand, if not the greatest in the women's ranks, is good enough to beat any forehand, and from the fifth game of the first set on to the end her backhand driving was something to marvel at in the pacefulness of the shot and the perfection of her control, regardless of the level from which it was made.

Miss Jacobs's backhand at its best was equally to be admired, but it did not stand up under pounding as did the champion's. Perhaps, had the challenger remained as daring as she had been in the first set, she would have achieved some additional measure of success, but instead of hitting for the lines she became more cautious and played the ball through the centre of the court, with the result that Miss Wills did not have to scramble as widely to make her strokes as did the other.

The stroke analysis shows a remarkable similarity for the two sets. Miss Wills made six placements in each chapter and seven outs in each, while Miss Jacobs made seven placements in each and nineteen outs in the first and eighteen in the second.

The doubles match was expected to develop into a close struggle, but Miss Cross and Mrs. Harper did not have their strokes under control and largely defeated themselves on errors.

Miss Wills Is Brilliant.

Miss Wills was brilliant both in her driving and at the net, while Mrs. Wightman featured with her deadly smashing. Their opponents made the mistake of chopping to Mrs. Wightman, who has one of the most accurate overhead strokes of any player in tennis.

Between the singles and doubles finals an exhibition was put on between Miss Sarah Palfrey of Boston and Miss Evelyn Parsons of California and Miss Marjorie Gladman of California and Miss Marie Fenesterer of Englewood, N. J. The former youngsters, playing beautiful tennis, won the first set at 6-0 and were leading at 3-1 in the second when a halt was called to the proceedings.

The point score and stroke analysis of the singles final follow:

First Set.

POINT SCORE.

									G.	Pts.
Miss Wills	4	4	3	4	4	4	4	4	6	31
Miss Jacobs	0	1	5	6	2	0	0	1	2	15

STROKE ANALYSIS.

	N.	O.	PL.	SA.	DF.
Miss Wills	1	7	6	1	0
Miss Jacobs	4	19	7	0	1

Second Set.

POINT SCORE.

								G.	Pts.
Miss Wills	5	4	4	4	5	2	7	6	31
Miss Jacobs	3	2	0	1	3	4	5	1	18

STROKE ANALYSIS.

	N.	O.	PL.	SA.	DF.
Miss Wills	4	7	6	0	0
Miss Jacobs	5	18	7	0	2

Recapitulation.

	N.	O.	PL.	SA.	DF.
Miss Wills	5	14	12	1	0
Miss Jacobs	9	37	14	0	3

	E.	EP.	TP.	G.	Sets.
Miss Wills	19	13	62	12	2
Miss Jacobs	49	14	5	5	1

Umpire—Rufus Davis. Net Umpire—C. S. Hall. Foot Fault Judge—Benjamin N. Phillips. Service Linesmen—Frank Danielson and F. Lamb. Centre Service Linesmen—Ralph L. Baggs and S. Wallis Merrihew. Side Linesmen—J. W. Anderson, U. S. Johnston, N. G. Andreini and G. Dunscombe. Base Linesmen—E. R. Carter and Fred M. Letson.

Time of game—33 minutes.

August 28, 1928

WIMBLEDON CROWN KEPT BY MISS WILLS

U. S. Champion Beats Miss Jacobs, Fellow-Californian, 6-1, 6-2, in Tennis Final.

LOSER FIGHTS GALLANTLY

But Miss Wills Plays at Top Form to Capture Title for 3d Successive Year.

Special Cable to THE NEW YORK TIMES.

WIMBLEDON, England, July 5.—Miss Helen Wills sailed through to her third successive Wimbledon championship today when she defeated Miss Helen Jacobs, 6-1, 6-2, in England's first all-American tennis final.

Miss Wills did it with such ease and such cool certainty that the match became a mere walk-over. The two sets were over in forty minutes. The younger Berkeley (Cal.) girl often made gallant attempts to reach the champion's swift drives, but she was never able to meet Miss Wills's game.

Not once was the imperturbable Miss Wills in danger of losing her crown. She did not have to exert herself, although there were times when Miss Jacobs's well-placed volleys close to the side lines made the champion run. Miss Wills was not always as accurate as she can be, nor did her strokes come hurtling across the net with the bullet-like speed she can often give them. She hit out of the court and into the net occasionally and was responsible for at least half of Miss Jacobs's points. But in every emergency she was unconquerable. Playing close to the base line, she maintained a rock-bound defense while her raking back-hand drives had her opponent at her mercy.

Times Wide World Photo.

MISS HELEN WILLS, VICTOR IN WIMBLEDON FINAL.

Miss Jacobs Fights Till End.

As for Miss Jacobs, she revealed a dependable backhand. She seemed to be overanxious to dispose of easy balls, with the result that she sent them flying out of court time and again. In the last game of each set, however, Miss Jacobs went down fighting stubbornly. With the score 1-5 against her in the first set she saved herself with six points before she gave in. Repeatedly games went to deuce and Miss Wills's advantage, but Miss Jacobs doggedly went for far-off shots and won the points. After a long rally from baseline to baseline, however, Miss Wills would put an end to the matter by rushing to the net and crashing a swift cross-court volley far out of her opponent's reach.

In the second set the match point was reached with Miss Jacobs serving and the score 30-40 against her. Again the younger Californian saved herself by a powerful forehand smash which Miss Wills could only hit into the net. But the end was bound to come. Miss Wills won the match when Miss Jacobs sent a volley yards behind the baseline. The champion did not seem happy in defeating her sister Californian. As soon as the match was over, however, she smiled and ran forward to shake hands with Miss Jacobs.

July 6, 1929

MISS WILLS VICTOR; RETAINS HER TITLE

Repulses Challenge of Mrs. Watson, 6-4, 6-2, and Carries Off Sixth National Crown.

WINS THE CUP OUTRIGHT

Triumph Over English Star Gives Californian Second Trophy at Forest Hills.

DOUBLES FINAL TO BRITISH

Mrs. Watson-Mrs. Michell Beat Compatriots, Mrs. Covell-Mrs. Shepherd-Barron, 2-6, 6-3, 6-4.

By ALLISON DANZIG.

The omnipotent racquet that has swept the courts of America and Europe for three years without the loss of a set, completed its execution in the women's tennis championship yesterday to carry Miss Helen Wills to her sixth victory in the national singles, gain her second challenge cup outright and complete a second trinity of triumphs at Auteuil, Wimbledon and Forest Hills.

In the final round of the annual tournament at the West Side Tennis Club the 23-year-old Berkeley, Cal., girl turned back the spirited challenge of Mrs. Phoebe Watson of England, the only serious opposition she encountered in six rounds of play, to win by the margin of 6-4, 6-2.

With this victory Miss Wills completed the most impressive march that has been staged through a championship tournament since Mlle. Suzanne Lenglen spread-eagled the field at Wimbledon in 1925 with the loss of only five games. The American girl did not quite equal that performance, for she dropped eight games in all. The fact that Mrs. Watson took six of the eight is evidence enough of the quality of the tennis that the champion faced yesterday.

Victor Put on Mettle.

The 9,000 spectators who thronged to the stadium of the West Side Club to see Miss Wills gain a victory that was looked upon as inevitable and also to witness the triumph of the Wimbledon champions, Mrs. Watson and Mrs. L. R. C. Michell, over Mrs. B. C. Covell and Mrs. Dorothy Shepherd-Barron at 2–6, 6—3, 6—4 in the final of the doubles, were privileged to see the Californian put on her mettle for the first time all week. They were not privileged, however, to look upon a characteristic exhibition of Miss Wills's hitting power for the reason that the starch was taken out of the champion's ordinarily jolting drives by a stunning forehand that was consistently excelling hers in length and pace.

It may seem incomprehensible to those who watched Miss Wills mow down her opponents in the previous rounds that her drive could play second fiddle to another's, but that was what it was doing for the most part yesterday. It was not speed that won the match for the champion, but superior control and great-er lasting power.

Knocking the cover off a ball that rises high well within the baseline to invite punishment is one thing, but it is an entirely different proposition to maltreat a ball that comes skimming over the net with the velocity of a bullet, that reaches out for the last inch of length and whose constantly changing direction compelled Miss Wills to do more scrambling than she had done all week. That was the kind of ball that Mrs. Watson was hitting all through the match, except for the periods when she was forced to relax from the strenuousness of her exertions, and the gallery was fairly in a frenzy of delight with the way in which she was standing up to the champion in the furious back-court onslaughts.

Scores Fifteen Placements.

The stroke analysis shows at a glance how Mrs. Watson was lacing the ball and how Miss Wills was winning her points. In the two sets the English woman scored fifteen placements to Miss Wills's six, probably the first time in years that any one has won more earned points than has the American champion, but Mrs. Watson gave away 63 points on nets and outs to her opponent's 37. These errors, together with Miss Wills's effective service, which was a big comfort to her, lost and won the match.

Fatigue was responsible for a great many of those errors by Mrs. Watson—fatigue that set in as a result of the physical effort called for in the making of her terrific forehanders and in standing up against the forcing shots of Miss Wills—but they were also to be attributed to the fact that the English woman was taking much greater chances than her opponent and playing continually for the lines.

It is not often that any one has succeeded in forcing Miss Wills to assume a defensive rôle so squarely as Mrs. Watson did yesterday. For the greater part of the opening set and at times in the second the champion was doing no more than putting the ball in play, and it was an effort to do even that.

Sends Up High Returns.

With the ball coming back like lead into her backhand corner, Miss Wills could do little more than send up soft high returns that enabled her to recover position. It repeatedly happened that Mrs. Watson, after getting in a damaging blow that had the other fighting desperately to save herself, lost the point through her daring efforts to make a kill, while Miss Wills hung on and waited for the error.

It must not be thought, though, that the champion was playing merely a passive role. She was hitting out at times with terrific swipes and forcing her opponent into error-making, but she wasn't getting the consistent length or pace on her strokes that did the other. Whereas Miss Wills was waiting until she could get set squarely before letting loose with her heaviest ammunition, Mrs. Watson was belaboring the ball with every ounce of power she commanded from start to finish.

How wholesome a respect Miss Wills had for the other's forehand was shown by her efforts to keep the ball on Mrs. Watson's backhand, though she discovered that the English woman could be just as dangerous off the left wing. What she lacked in pace there she made up in length and direction. But it was no easy task to keep the ball away from Mrs. Watson's forehand. With the ball coming back in such unexpected quarters as Mrs. Watson shifted from straight line drives to short cross court returns that were beautifully angled, the American had to be satisfied to make any kind of shot that would get over the net.

Wrests the Opening Set.

It required only twenty-one minutes for Miss Wills to take twelve successive games from Mrs. Molla Mallory on Friday, but she was that long in wresting the opening set from Mrs. Watson. The English woman threw down the gauntlet from the very outset and by the third game the gallery had a thorough understanding that there were to be no more parades for Miss Wills in this tournament.

The first two games were won in orthodox fashion, Mrs. Watson pounding her opponent's backhand to win the first at 30 and Miss Wills's service accounting for the second at 15. In the third game the cheering began with a vengeance as Mrs. Watson gained a 30-0 lead. She lost the game after it had gone to deuce, but Miss Wills had to expend plenty of energy to win it, as Mrs. Watson pulled her to the net with changes of length and sent her scurrying to the back corners with admirable generalship.

The fourth game was a thriller. Sixteen points were required for a decision and throughout these desperately fought rallies Mrs. Watson was hitting the harder and deeper and making her opponent do most of the running. When the English woman finally broke through, it was the first time any one had succeeded in winning a game from Miss Wills on her service in the tournament and the gallery vented its appreciation in lusty fashion.

Concern Is Apparent.

The score was now 2 all and already Mrs. Watson had won one more game than any other player in the tournament had taken from the champion. That Miss Wills was becoming concerned was plainly apparent from the seriousness of her expression and she had more reason to be when Mrs. Watson pulled out the fifth game from 0—30.

Miss Wills was hitting a soft, high ball all the way in this game and she couldn't very well do anything else, for Mrs. Watson was giving her no chance to get set for her strokes, pulling her to the corners and drawing her up to the service court with shortened length.

So clearly was Mrs. Watson holding her own up to this time that there seemed to be a strong possibility of Miss Wills losing her first set in three years. Certainly she couldn't continue to remain on the defensive and beat Mrs. Watson. The champion realized the necessity for drastic measures and the sixth game found her going along in invincible fashion.

A service ace was followed by a stinging forehand drive, and Mrs. Watson's error made the score 40—0. At this point the gallery looked on in amazement as Mrs. Watson outsteadied her opponent to take the next three points and draw up to deuce. But Miss Wills rose to the occasion and saved the game and then went on to win the next two with the loss of only one point.

Mrs. Watson was in a slump now, losing control and softening in her stroking, and gave Miss Wills seven of her eight points on errors. But in the next game she let loose again with her marvelous line drives to keep Miss Wills on the defensive and pull up to 4—5.

Fails to Sustain Pace.

The English woman, however, was unable to sustain the pace she set in this game and Miss Wills, hitting out in her best fashion and serving beautifully, took four points in a row to win the set. Mrs. Watson made one more placement than Miss Wills in the set, but the champion's three service aces and eight less errors gave her a margin of ten points.

With the end of this set it was realized that Mrs. Watson's chances of victory were now almost negligible. While she had the strokes and the tactics to extend the champion to the limit the physical equation was against her and it was now a question of how much longer her stamina would hold out. Already she was beginning to play in streaks and even if she won the second set it seemed unlikely that she would have anything left in reserve for a third.

The start of the second set showed how much the first had taken out of her. Mrs. Watson offered little opposition as Miss Wills took the first two games at 15 each, almost entirely on trivial errors. With the third game Mrs. Watson got her second wind and once more the gallery looked on delightedly as she whaled the ball relentlessly through another 16-point game that saw Miss Wills hitting hard but yet not as hard nor as low or as deep as her opponent.

The effort of winning this game weakened Mrs. Watson and she lost the next three points. After she had pulled up to 30—40 her game collapsed and Miss Wills, now confident of the outcome but still playing carefully and with a cool head, went to 5—1.

Makes Courageous Effort.

Mrs. Watson made one more courageous effort to stave off the inevitable. With the score 40—0 against her and Miss Wills only a point away from the match, the English woman put over two placements and finally pulled out the game, to bring a storm of cheers from the stands. But in the next game Miss Wills quickly gained a lead of 40—15, and after Mrs. Watson had averted defeat at the fourth point, the champion drove hard to her opponent's backhand and Mrs. Watson's return found the net to end the match.

With that last point Miss Wills had completed another year of sweeping success and the women's tennis season had come to an end. Samuel H. Collom, president of the United States Lawn Tennis Association, presented the three-year challenge trophy, filled with American Beauty roses, to the champion, while a score of cameramen hastened to record the scene. Miss Wills also received a second trophy, given to each year's winner, and Mrs. Watson was presented with the runner-up cup, amid an enthusiastic demonstration from the gallery.

Following the singles match Miss Betty Nuthall and H. W. Austin of England paired against Miss Wills and Frank Shields in a mixed doubles exhibition which was called with the score at 8-all in the first set in order to make way for the final of the women's doubles. Prior to the singles, Shields had beaten Austin in one set of singles, 6—4.

Mrs. Watson was still feeling the effects of her match with Miss Wills when she went on the court for the doubles. In the morning she and Mrs. Michell had finished their semi-final match with Miss Nuthall and Miss Helen Jacobs, which they won after a long struggle at 9—11, 6—3, 6—4.

Mrs. Watson's inability to hold up her end of the play put her side in the hole from the start, and it was not until they had lost the first set at 6—2 that Mrs. Watson began to tighten in control and to force the openings for Mrs. Michell at the net. Mrs. Covell and Mrs. Shepherd-Barron, with a more mobile formation than their countrywomen, gained a 4—2 lead in the final set and it looked as though they were going to reverse the result of the final of the Wimbledon doubles.

But with defeat imminent, Mrs. Watson and Mrs. Michell staged a rally that carried them through four successive games. Mrs. Michell was stowing away everything in sight at the net, but the burden of the play was put upon her partner, and Mrs. Watson's plucky stand and brilliant driving saved the day.

The point score and stroke analysis of the singles final follow:

First Set.

POINT SCORE.

											Pts.	G.
Miss Wills	2	4	5	7	2	5	4	4	2	4	39	6
Mrs. Watson	4	1	3	9	4	3	0	1	4	0	29	4

STROKE ANALYSIS.

	N.	O.	P.	SA.	DF.
Miss Wills	15	8	5	3	0
Mrs. Watson	16	15	6	0	0

Second Set.

POINT SCORE.

									Pts.	G.
Miss Wills	4	4	7	4	4	4	4	4	35	6
Mrs. Watson	1	1	9	2	2	2	6	2	25	2

STROKE ANALYSIS.

	N.	O.	P.	SA.	DF.
Miss Wills	3	11	1	1	2
Mrs. Watson	12	29	9	0	1

Recapitulation.

	N.	O.	P.	SA.	DF.
Miss Wills	18	19	6	4	2
Mrs. Watson	28	35	15	0	1

	E.	E.P.	T.P.	G.	Sets.
Miss Wills	39	10	74	12	2
Mrs. Watson	64	15	54	6	0

Umpire—Rufus Davis. Net umpire—Mel Kann. Foot fault judge—Beals C. Wright. Service linesmen—H. L. Mattice and Frank Danielson. Centre service linesmen—Edward E. Jenkins and S. Wallis Merrihew. Side linesmen—W. S. Creevy, Norman Andreim, Frank Sheridan and Captain Walter Anderson. Base linesmen—Oveido Bostwick and C. G. James. Time of match—40 minutes.

THE SUMMARIES.

Singles.

FINAL ROUND.

Miss Helen Wills defeated Mrs. Phoebe Watson, 6—4, 6—2.

Doubles.

SEMI-FINAL ROUND.

Mrs. Watson and Mrs. L. R. C. Michell defeated Miss Betty Nuthall and Miss Helen Jacobs, 9—11, 6—3, 6—4.

FINAL ROUND.

Mrs. Watson and Mrs. Michell defeated Mrs. E. C. Covell and Mrs. Dorothy Shepherd-Barron, 2—6, 6—3, 6—4.

August 25, 1929

TILDEN WINS TITLE FOR SEVENTH TIME

Beats Hunter in 5 Sets for National Tennis Crown—Ties Mark of Sears, Larned.

OVERCOMES 2-1 SET LEAD

Triumphs Over His Doubles Partner by 3-6, 6-3, 4-6, 6-2, 6-4 at Forest Hills.

9,000 SEE THE FINAL MATCH

Charest of Washington Turns Erck Aaoue of Dallas, 4-6, 6-2, 6-1, for Veterans' Title.

By ALLISON DANZIG.

The dominion of William Tilden over American tennis was re-establish by title as well as in fact yesterday. Three years after his reign was brought to an end by an interlude of French triumph, the 36-year-old Philadelphia veteran captured the national championship for the seventh time, thereby equaling the record held jointly by Richard D. Sears and William A. Larned, and assuring himself of being ranked first in American tennis for the tenth consecutive time.

A gallery of 9,000 at the stadium of the West Side Tennis Club at Forest Hills witnessed the restoration of the crown as Tilden defeated Francis T. Hunter of New Rochelle in the final round of the forty-eighth annual tournament.

The match went to five sets, with Tilden trailing 2 to 1, but there was never any question as to the ultimate reckoning, and the final two chapters found the once invincible monarch of the courts electrifying the gallery as of yore with a withering onslaught of drives and service aces that brooked no opposition. The score was 3-6, 6-3, 4-6, 6-2, 6-4.

It was a happy Tilden who ran forward to the net to greet his beaten doubles partner while the cheers of the thousands paid tribute to a champion who had come back. Hunter, downhearted for the moment over his failure for the second successive year in the final of the championship, found his smile again and threw his arm around Tilden's shoulder as they posed before a battery of cameras while President Samuel H. Collom of the United States Lawn Tennis Association presented the champion with the challenge trophy. On that trophy René Lacoste of France holds two legs, gained in 1926 and 1927, while Henri Cochet of France was the winner last year, when he beat Hunter in five sets.

Staying Powers Still Great.

In defeating Hunter in the fifth set twenty-four hours after he had been carried to the maximum number of sets by John Doeg in a struggle of two hours and a half, Tilden showed that for all his years his staying powers are still as great as those of the younger generation of players. In both matches the champion produced his greatest tennis in the last two chapters, when nothing less than his best was called for. The ability to rise to unassailable heights under stress, that confounded his opponents in the days of his world supremacy, was again in evidence in both of these struggles.

In the last meeting between Tilden and Hunter, in the Eastern championship at Rye, Tilden was the winner in three sets against a passive Hunter. It was a different Hunter yesterday, a Hunter fired with ambition to climb the last rung up the tennis ladder.

The opening set found the rugged New Rochelle internationalist laying down a barrage upon Tilden's back court that had the Philadelphian running to cover up. Tilden's control was none too good at this stage and it was largely his service that was keeping him on even terms until the ninth came, when Hunter, hitting powerfully to the corners, effected the lone break in the set. How erratic Tilden was playing in this chapter is shown by the fact that he made 27 errors to Hunter's 17.

Tilden Tightens in Control.

The second set saw Tilden tighten in control and add pressure to his strokes while his footwork was speeded up until he was retrieving everything in sight. Hunter stood firm in the face of this assault, but gradually was forced to give ground as Tilden broke through in a long deuce game to gain a 3-0 lead. Try as he would, Hunter could not regain that lost ground and he was soon shaking his head, realizing the magnitude of his task against an aroused Tilden, who covered court unflaggingly and whose backhand half volleys from the base line were repeatedly converting apparent winners for Hunter into points for himself.

After winning this set, however, to draw level, Tilden patently slackened pace in the third set and Hunter, hitting furiously, gained a 4-0 lead with the loss of only five points. It seemed that Tilden was going to concede the set, but instead he now braced and launched a rally that took him to 4—5. With his service to come, it looked as though he was going to square the score, but Hunter checked this rally with a bombardment that exacted four errors from Tilden's racquet, and Tilden left the court trailing, 2 sets to 1.

The onslaught that was looked for from the champion when he returned from the showers was immediately forthcoming. Hunter took the opening game of the fourth set on service and then Tilden set sail.

Five games in a row fell to him, only one of them going to deuce, and not until he had gained set point at 40—15 in the seventh was Hunter able to stem the tide. In this set Tilden scored 11 placements to Hunter's 2.

The final chapter saw Hunter in his most dangerous mood and both men playing their best tennis of the match. Two 2-all games went on service and then Tilden, mixing up his length and pace craftily, broke through in the fifth game, after which he won the sixth for a 4—2 lead.

That lead was sufficient to settle any doubts as to the outcome of the match. Hunter was playing like a man possessed in the seventh, and he had Tilden running as he won the ninth to make the score 5—4, but the champion, playing coolly and with every confidence, finished matters in the tenth.

Hunter made two ruthless returns of service, but Tilden's great recoveries put them to nought, and with the score at 30-0 the champion put over a service ace and followed with another service that Hunter drove out of court, bringing the match to an end.

Tilden, George Lott and a number of the other high-ranking players left last night for Detroit, where today they will take part in a series of exhibition matches at the Detroit Tennis Club.

The point score and stroke analysis follow:

First Set.
POINT SCORE.

											Pts. G.
Tilden	...3	5	1	4	0	4	2	2		2—27—3	
Hunter	...5	3	4	2	4	2	4	4		4—32—6	

STROKE ANALYSIS.

	N.	O.	P.	SA.	DF.
Tilden	16	11	5	1	0
Hunter	8	9	4	1	0

Second Set.
POINT SCORE.

										Pts. G.
Tilden	...4	7	3	4	1	4	4		4—36—6	
Hunter	...1	5	5	5	2	4	2	6	2—32—3	

STROKE ANALYSIS.

	N.	O.	P.	SA.	DF.
Tilden	14	11	11	3	1
Hunter	7	15	6	0	2

Third Set.
POINT SCORE.

										Pts. G.
Tilden	...2	1	1	1	4	7	0	4	1—25—4	
Hunter	...4	4	4	4	1	5	4	0	1—31—6	

STROKE ANALYSIS.

	N.	O.	P.	SA.	DF.
Tilden	11	8	9	1	2
Hunter	7	6	9	1	2

Fourth Set.
POINT SCORE.

									Pts. G.
Tilden	...0	4	4	4	5	4	5	4—30—6	
Hunter	...4	2	0	2	3	0	7	1—19—2	

STROKE ANALYSIS.

	N.	O.	P.	SA.	DF.
Tilden	7	9	11	3	0
Hunter	10	5	2	1	1

Fifth Set.
POINT SCORE.

										Pts. G.
Tilden	...1	4	2	4	4	4	1	4	2—30—6	
Hunter	...4	0	4	0	1	2	4	1	4	0—20—4

STROKE ANALYSIS.

	N.	O.	P.	SA.	DF.
Tilden	5	8	6	5	1
Hunter	9	9	5	1	1

Recapitulation.

	N.	O.	P.	SA.	DF.
Tilden	53	47	42	13	4
Hunter	41	44	26	4	6

	E.	EP.	TP.	G.	Sets
Tilden	104	55	146	25	3
Hunter	91	30	134	21	2

Umpire—Rufus Davis. Net umpire—Benjamin H. Dwight. Foot fault judge—Benjamin Phillips. Service linesmen—Theodore Mattmann and Frank Danielson. Centre service linesmen—Harold Swain and Paul Harding. Side linesmen—C. G. James, H. L. Richards, H. G. Andrieni and George Abbott. Base linesmen—Fred L. Pond and Harry Mattice. Time of match—1:39.

September 15, 1929

MOSS EXPLAINS BAN ON NEGROES IN TENNIS

Barring of Two Entrants in Junior Title Event in Line With U. S. L. T. A. Policy, He Says

The exclusion of two young negro players from the national junior indoor tennis championships is in line with a policy of the United States Lawn Tennis Association, executive secretary Edward B. Moss announced yesterday through The Associated Press, replying to a letter of protest from the National Association for the Advancement of Colored People.

Moss's communication follows:

"Answering your letter of Dec. 24, the policy of the United States Lawn Tennis Association has been to decline the entry of colored players in our championships.

"In pursuing this policy we make no reflection upon the colored race, but we believe that as a practical matter, the present method of separate associations for the administration of the affairs and championships of colored and white players should be continued."

The players in question were Reginald Weir of the City College of New York and Gerald L. Norman Jr., captain of the Flushing High School tennis team.

December 28, 1929

Tilden Receiving the Cup After Winning the Title at Forest Hills.
Left to Right—Hunter, Tilden and Samuel H. Collom, President of the United States Lawn Tennis Association.

Times Wide World Photo.

COCHET WINS TITLE; MRS. MOODY VICTOR

Tilden Falls Before Rival's Brilliant Play in the French Hard Court Final.

LOSER IN GALLANT FIGHT

Takes First Set Before 10,000 at Auteuil, but Loses by 3-6, 8-6, 6-3, 6-1.

MISS JACOBS IS DEFEATED

Mrs. Moody Triumphs Easily by 6-2, 6-1, Over California Challenger to Retain Crown.

By The Associated Press.

AUTEUIL, France, June 1.—Henri Cochet of France carried off the men's singles title and Mrs. Helen Wills Moody of the United States retained the women's singles crown in the French hard-court tourney today.

Big Bill Tilden, fighting a gallant but vain battle against the little Frenchman's racquet wizardry, was beaten by Cochet, 3—6, 8—6, 6—3, 6—1, in the final, while Miss Helen Jacobs of Berkeley, Cal., lost in straight sets to Mrs. Moody, 6—2, 6—1.

The predominant emotion among the 10,000 spectators who witnessed the clash between the two girls from California seemed to be one of surprise that any one should have the sheer audacity to think of challenging Mrs. Moody's right to the crown.

Great as Cochet was in victory Tilden was magnificent in defeat. Seven times champion of America and for years the world's leading player, he lost not because he played poor tennis but because the standard of excellence reached by Cochet has seldom been equaled, certainly never surpassed in the history of the sport.

Overshadows Those of Past.

Many veterans of the tennis epics of the past thirty years, who speak of Norman Brookes, the Dohertys, Maurice McLoughlin, Wilding and Lacoste, almost with reverence, thought that Cochet's display of fireworks today overshadowed anything shown by those giants of the past. As his unsuccessful adversary of today once said, "He is the genius of tennis."

Cochet started the first set with his usual conchalance, but Tilden also appeared unimpressed by the importance of the match. The American lost his service and Cochet ran into a lead of 3—1. Here Tilden rallied to play such tennis as he never had shown in France and ran out five games for the set. He had such wonderful timing and was getting such length and speed to his drives that Cochet, playing lazily, was overwhelmed.

Tilden appeared to have a cut on the ball in the second set that Cochet never before had faced, and the little Frenchman began to show signs of worry. Suddenly, however, he appeared to solve the problem of Tilden's bouncing strokes from a heavy top spin and ran three games to

lead, 6—5. Then Tilden carried his service and games were 6—all. Then came the break in the match when a crowd of self-appointed linesmen in the stands howled, booed and whistled at what they judged bad decisions. Tilden halted momentarily, waiting for the noise to abate. He was visibly nervous when he resumed play and Cochet broke through his service, captured the set at 8—6, and squared the match.

Tilden Changes Style.

Beginning the third set, Tilden changed his style, starting a fierce driving campaign and playing especially to Cochet's backhand, but the Frenchman always seemed to be on top of the ball, and he was returning Tilden's famous cannonball service, in use for the first time in the match, with extreme rapidity. Taking the ball on the rise, he broke through Tilden twice to lead, 5—1. Tilden's last stand occurred here and by a superhuman effort he won two

games to bring the score to 5—3. This spurt left him tired and unable to reach Cochet's slow, tantalizing trapshots just over the net and he dropped the set, 6—3.

As they began the fourth set Tilden was the only man out of the 10,000 present who did not know he was a beaten player. Cochet had reached the peak of his game. Several times Tilden shook his head despairingly as he watched Cochet's lightning, sharp-angled strokes sail just out of his reach. He managed to win only the third game on his own service, his rival running out the last four games with the same apparent unstraining of mind or muscle.

After the match Cochet said: "Tilden played the best game he ever played against me in the last three years. But I am beginning to know his style."

"That was the best I know how to play," Tilden said.

Commits Three Double Faults.

The women's final lacked the thrills of the Cochet-Tilden match There was only one department of the game in which Miss Jacobs held Mrs. Moody fairly even and that was in service. Miss Jacobs's service is just about as powerful as Mrs. Moody's, but not quite so accurate. Miss Jacobs committed three double faults in the first set and two in the second.

The challenger tried chop strokes in the second set, but the champion, playing perfect mechanical tennis, won the first five games and only when the unruly spectators again booed and hissed a lineman's decision calling one of Miss Jacobs's services bad which the crowd thought good, did Mrs. Moody relax, allowing Miss Jacobs to take the sixth game.

June 2, 1930

MRS. MOODY VICTOR IN WIMBLEDON FINAL

Captures Fourth Title in Row by Defeating Miss Ryan, 6-2, 6-2, Before 15,000.

PRIME MINISTER ATTENDS

U. S. Doubles Teams Win and Bring About All-American Men's, Women's Finals.

ALLISON-VAN RYN ADVANCE

Beat Gregory-Collins and Will Meet Lott-Doeg, Who Turn Back Cochet-Brugnon

By FERDINAND KUHN Jr.

Special Cable to THE NEW YORK TIMES

WIMBLEDON, England, July 4. For the fourth year in succession Mrs. Helen Wills Moody has won the women's singles championship at Wimbledon.

Mrs. Moody won the crown today by beating another Californian, Miss Elizabeth Ryan, 6—2, 6—2, before 15,000 on a Fourth of July which marked the most overwhelming triumph American tennis stars have ever gained over foreign rivals. As a result of today's matches the four greatest prizes in tennis are bound to go to Americans for the first time in the history of the international game.

Such a rout for players of other nations by Americans has never been known at Wimbledon since the dim, far-off days when tennis was still young. It is doubtful, in fact, if a similar situation has ever been known in any great sporting competition. Near the end of the tournament, in which 128 stars from twenty-three nations were

Times Wide World Photo.

RETAINS WOMEN'S SINGLE CROWN AT WIMBLEDON.

Mrs. Helen Wills Moody, Who Defeated Miss Elizabeth Ryan in Final, in Action at English Championship Tourney.

---

entered, Americans stand supreme in men's singles, women's singles, men's doubles and women's doubles. That such a record should have been set on this Fourth of July made it a memorable holiday for the hundreds of Americans who flocked to Wimbledon to see tennis history made.

Begin the American Sweep.

The American sweep began today when George Lott and John Doeg defeated the ex-champions, Henri Cochet and Jacques Brugnon, 8—6, 3—6, 6—3, 6—1, and eliminated the last survivors of the French dynasty which has ruled the courts for the past six years. It continued when Wilmer Allison and John Van Ryn, the present champions, extinguished the last British hope by defeating J. Colin Gregory and Ian G. Collins,

4—6, 7—5, 6—3, 6—3. On Monday on the centre court Allison and Van Ryn will meet Lott and Doeg for the title that comes closer than any other to being the doubles championship of the world.

On the No. 1 Court Miss Edith Cross and Miss Sarah Palfrey continued the American procession by defeating the British doubles team of Miss B. Feltham and Miss Mary Heeley, 8—6, 6—2. Tomorrow they will play for the championship against the team of Mrs. Moody and Miss Ryan which had already reached the final round. The biggest prize of all will be contested for tomorrow by William T. Tilden and Allison—Tilden having defeated Jean Borotra on Wednesday and Allison having toppled Cochet from his champion's throne earlier in the week.

The only crumb of consolation left for the rest of the world is a share in the mixed doubles championship in which Miss Ryan still survives to represent America and in which many of the best American stars did not enter. The final will bring Jack Crawford of Australia and Miss Ryan face to face with the German team of Daniel Prenn and Fräulein H. Krahwinckel on the centre court tomorrow.

Miss Ryan Is Applauded.

So astonishing was the collective record of the Americans as it unfolded itself on the electric scoreboard, that even the Mrs. Moody-Miss Ryan final was overshadowed. It was never anything like a fight, although no one could help applauding the woman who played at Wimbledon as far back as 1912 and who, after surviving the stiffest kind of competition, was challenging for the tennis championship.

Miss Ryan came on the court grinning and flashing her teeth, and acting as if she were quite happy, regardless of the outcome. She hadn't long to wait for the defeat which was apparent in the first few games and became overwhelming before the swift two-set match was over. All her craftiness and cunning were unavailing against Mrs. Moody, who showed once more she is a peerless champion without any rival in sight who can wrest the laurels from her.

No amount of mixing up of shots was of the slightest use against Mrs. Moody, who had things all her own way. Miss Ryan was seldom allowed to settle down, and only once in a while was she able to do as she planned. Her only effective trick against the champion was a tantalizing drop shot which hopped over the net and then fell almost dead while Mrs. Moody had to rush from the baseline to retrieve it. Those were shots, however, that even Borotra or Allison couldn't have saved and at match point Mrs. Moody—with a sense of humor nobody expected of her—quietly gave Miss Ryan a dose of her own medicine by sending over a brilliant drop shot herself.

Drives to the Corners.

For most of the match she stood almost motionless in the centre of the baseline driving far and deep to the corners with monotonous regularity, while Miss Ryan kept running in an endless and fruitless chase.

Miss Ryan's drop shots captured Mrs. Moody's first service, but the champion quickly got into her unbeatable stride. Miss Ryan had one chance in the fourth game, with only one point needed for the game, but hit out at the net with Mrs. Moody at her mercy. Miss Ryan won the next game, getting Mrs. Moody's powerful service back with those same deceptive, gentle shots, but that was all she could do. In the second set Miss Ryan started weakly, losing a love game. In the next game Miss Ryan again enticed Mrs. Moody to the net and passed her with brilliant shots, but the champion quickly regained the lead and held it. The later games went to deuce, but Miss Ryan now was foot faulting and Mrs. Moody was driving with power that increased with every game. It would be interesting to watch her in a three or four-set match against some one of her own calibre. Only in one game was the champion weak—in the sixth when her backhand was not up to the mark. In the others she was incomparable and took the last two without ever being pressed.

No Challenger in Sight.

So Mrs. Moody is still Queen of Wimbledon—a queen more commanding, more majestic than ever before. Nobody has come across the horizon from Europe or America to challenge her. Miss Helen Jacobs, hitherto America's best next to Mrs. Moody, failed this year, and as she grows older she is not likely to be any better as a match for Mrs. Moody.

Mrs. Phoebe Watson, who gave Mrs. Moody a short-lived fright in the Wightman Cup matches, is not strong enough to defeat her. The only revelation of the tournament has been Fraulein Cecilie Aussem of Germany, who, under Tilden's astute coaching, is developing into a real challenger with a varied and accurate game. But she hasn't yet Mrs. Moody's physical power and stamina—she was all but worn out at the end of her match with Miss Ryan just before her dramatic collapse- and without it all Tilden's coaching will do her little good.

Mrs. Moody herself cannot be expected to continue tennis forever. More than any one else, she has been scanning the Wimbledon field for some worthy challenger who can take her place, but in this respect, at least, she has been disappointed. She must remain champion for a year at least and probably much longer.

Americans Break Through.

The doubles battle between Lott and Doeg and the French team of Cochet and Brugnon was a battle of services which seesawed without a break until the thirteenth game of the first set, when the Americans broke through for the first time. Lott was the mainstay of the American pair, whether guarding the baseline or the net. Never in any of his singles matches has he seemed to have such a long reach as today, while his smashes were so terrific that they never allowed any reply. Doeg's service won valuable points for the Americans, but he poached incessantly on Lott's territory.

As for the French, Cochet was back in his old form—more fiery than he has been this year and certainly in better fighting trim than when Allison defeated him. His work at the net was deadly, but his teammate, Brugnon, was ineffective with his overhead play. At one time the ball was lobbed to Brugnon six times in succession, in a nice easy position for a smash, and each time Brugnon merely got it back tamely. It was left to Cochet in the end to make the kill, which he did with such terrific force that the ball bounced high into the crowded stands.

In the other doubles match it was again a battle of services, but this time Allison and Van Ryn were playing with perfect teamwork, while the British team of Gregory and Collins did not always agree on their next move. Gregory often was far from the place he should have been in, and roamed far into his partner's court for balls that did not belong to him. Just as last year, when they won the championship, Allison and Van Ryn knew and trusted each other in every shot and never failed. It did not matter who was at the net and who was serving- both were great on attack and defense as well.

After today's performances the odds ought to be on Allison and Van Ryn against Lott and Doeg. The match originally was scheduled for tomorrow, but as Allison is playing Tilden in the singles, it was agreed to postpone his doubles struggle until Monday.

Celebrities Are Present.

Prime Minister Ramsay MacDonald was among the array of celebrities who watched the American Fourth of July triumphs from the royal box today. Wearing an informal brown lounge suit, the Premier arrived early and kept busy throughout the afternoon greeting royalty and other notables arriving for the matches. Princess Helena Victoria, King George's sister, was the first to come and sat next to the Premier. Then came ex-King Manoel of Portugal with ex-Queen Amalie and after them the President-elect of Brazil, Dr. Julio Prestes, with his entourage. Admiral Lord Jellicoe, Lord d'Abernon, former Ambassador to Germany, and Lord Brentford, formerly Home Secretary in the Baldwin Cabinet, also witnessed the American victories.

July 5, 1930

William T. Tilden.

TILDEN WINS TITLE BY BEATING ALLISON IN WIMBLEDON FINAL

King and Queen Among 20,000 Who See Veteran Regain Crown He Held Nine Years Ago.

SCORE IS 6-3, 9-7, 6-4

Victor's Powerful Service Important Factor in Match With Fellow-American.

MRS. MOODY-MISS RYAN WIN

Conquer Miss Palfrey-Miss Cross, 6-2, 9-7, in Final — Miss Ryan-Crawford Take Mixed Doubles.

By FERDINAND KUHN Jr.
Special Cable to THE NEW YORK TIMES.

WIMBLEDON, England. July 5.— After nine long years, William T. Tilden again reached the topmost heights of tennis today.

At the age of 37 Tilden regained the Wimbledon singles championship by defeating the 25-year-old Wilmer Allison in straight sets, 6—3, 9—7, 6—4. Thus a complete cycle of nine years has turned and the tall Philadelphian is again monarch of the courts as he was in 1921.

Allison was serving when the match was decided and truly enough it was all over when the young Texan hit out in returning one of Tilden's lobs. From the 20,000 in the stands a shout went up and in the royal box King George, Queen Mary and Prince George smiled and applauded as Allison ran to the net to greet the new champion. Tilden was grinning, for he had done the trick which all experts had said couldn't be done. His long, uphill fight was over and it had ended in a complete triumph.

Plays With Relentless Precision.

This was no fading Tilden who shattered Allison's hopes today. It was the Tilden of five, six or seven years ago—the champion whose blasting cannonball service and uncanny control of all sorts of strokes made him the dominating figure in world tennis for so many years. He defeated Allison with the relentless precision of a tennis master who would allow no interference from upstarts

Wilmer Allison.

Acme Photo.

—even from a teammate. Allison never had a chance except when Tilden—like the luckless Henri Cochet—threw at least two valuable games to the young Texan with the intention of saving his greatest efforts for later in the match.

The new women's doubles champions also were crowned at Wimbledon today when Mrs. Helen Wills Moody and Miss Elizabeth Ryan defeated Miss Edith Cross and Miss Sarah Palfrey, 6—2, 9—7. Later in the afternoon Miss Ryan won a share in a second championship by capturing the mixed doubles title with Jack Crawford of Australia from the German team of Fraulein H. Krahwinckel and Daniel Prenn, 6—1, 6—3.

The last of the championships will be decided on Monday when Allison and John Van Ryn defend their doubles title against John Doeg and George Lott, the United States doubles champions. That will be only a little family party between friends, but it will finish the most memorable series of tennis triumphs that United States stars ever have won on foreign courts.

Tilden's Come-back Crowns Record.

Never in the history of Wimbledon has one nation dominated so completely as the United States has this year, and that the record should be crowned by Tilden's come-back makes it one that other generations of tennis stars will remember when they come to struggle for Wimbledon's prizes.

Hardly had Tilden and Allison walked on to the centre court for their history-making match when there was a commotion in the crowd. Queen Mary, in a gown of salmon pink with flowers and a trimmed toque to match, was entering the royal box, followed by the King, who was wearing a light gray suit

with a gray derby hat. Every one in the crowd stood up and a wave of cheers for the royal family crashed across the court while Allison, on the base line, and Tilden, near the net, stood at rigid attention facing the King and Queen.

The ceremonies, however, had no effect on Tilden for he started like a whirlwind, attacking Allison's service. In the first game he was lucky with two net-cord shots, while Allison double-faulted once to help him. Tilden's service in the next game was terrifying and although Allison stood up to it manfully, he couldn't stem the onslaught. Tilden was steaming over his most tremendous serves and driving so hard from deep court that all Allison could do was to try to slow down the pace.

Allison Forced to Retreat.

When Allison tried to storm the net Tilden passed him, forcing him to retreat to the baseline where it was safer. The Texan won the third and fifth games on his own service, but Tilden went ahead at 4-2.

Tilden was keeping such marvelous length to his shots that he had little to fear from Allison except when he tried drop shots, and the Texan smashed them back out of his reach. The first set was Tilden's easily by 6—3, and even so Tilden had given at least one game away.

The second set was a protracted seesaw duel which went with service until the sixteenth game, when Tilden broke through. Tilden's service was so terrific that Allison was able to make only five points against it throughout the set. Allison's service often rivaled Tilden's, and there were times when it sizzled past the tall Philadelphian and made him look helpless. Tilden may have been waiting for a break, but his opponent was so good that it took sixteen games until the break came.

Tilden had a chance in the eighth game, but lost it by hitting an easy passing shot into the net. In the tenth game Tilden, who had been beaming with good humor throughout the match, suddenly was roused to anger by a dubious decision of a linesman and unleashed a bombardment of cannonball drives. Allison was equal to it and evened the score at 6—all, passing Tilden at the end with a sparkling little drop-shot duel at the net.

Allison Is Upset.

The score reached 8—7 in favor of Tilden, who made a heroic effort to win the sixteenth game against service. Three superb passing shots helped him, but even so Allison brought the score to deuce four times. At a crucial moment, with Allison at advantage and needing only a point to tie at 8—all, he foot-faulted. That upset him and he double-faulted, making it Tilden's advantage. Allison then sent over a difficult backhand volley which shot past the sidelines and the long, spectacular set was over.

By now Allison had scarcely hope left, but he never wilted, although he must have been tiring under the assault. The last set started like the previous one—a duel of services—but after the score had been at 2-all, Tilden pulled up to 4—2 and extinguished Allison's last hope of winning the set. Tilden could have won more decisively except for his old fault of trying a burst of magnificence. He was careless in the seventh game and lost his own service, making it 4—3. He captured Allison's service for 5—3, and now was ready for his own service which would end the match in a blaze of glory.

But Tilden was fooled. Leaping off the ground close to the net, Allison killed Tilden's most beautiful drives and altogether made a hodgepodge of Tilden's magnificent serves. So the match ended on Allison's service, not on Tilden's, and it ended without the last spectacular shots which Tilden had hoped for.

July 6, 1930

BAN ON OPEN TENNIS IS LIKELY TO STAY

Belgian, Opposition's Leader, Fears Matches Would Become Analogous to Boxing Shows.

20 NATIONS FIGHT PROJECT

American and British Proposal Would Kill Amateur Tennis, Federation Is Warned.

PARIS, April 3 (Æ).—Despite agitation not much hope is held out for any future lifting of the International Tennis Federations ban on open tournaments. The United States and England alone voted in favor of allowing amateurs to compete with professionals at the federation assembly, which overwhelmingly rejected the American proposal.

The twenty nations recorded in opposition are Germany, Argentina, Australia, Belgium, Brazil, Canada, Chile, Spain, France, Holland, Hungary, India, Italy, Monaco, New Zealand, Poland, South Africa, Switzerland, Yugoslavia and Czechoslovakia.

France was conspicuous in opposition, but the actual fight against the American proposal was led by Chevalier Paul De Borman, president of the Belgian Tennis Federation. The Belgian president, former Davis Cup player himself, argued that if the motion were put through, "tennis matches would become spectacles analogous to prize-fighting shows."

M. De Borman thought and said that the work of tennis professionals should be confined to teaching the game to amateurs. To permit open tennis tournaments would sound the death knell of amateur tennis, he asserted.

For the French, M. Pierre Gillou, captain of the French Davis Cup team, confined himself to endorsing the views of Chevalier De Borman.

The delegates of Australia and New Zealand, although previously instructed to vote for open championships, refrained from voting as a result of the Chevalier's address.

April 4, 1930

TILDEN WINS TITLE, DEPOSING RICHARDS

Gives Superb Exhibition Before 4,000 at Forest Hills in U. S. Professional Net Final.

ROUTS RIVAL, 7-5, 6-2, 6-1

Loser's 4-2 Margin in First Set Soon Effaced by Veteran's Forceful Drives.

By ALLISON DANZIG.

Four thousand spectators, looking down from the stadium of the West Side Tennis Club at Forest Hills yesterday, sat in on one of the transcendent exhibitions of American tennis history as William T. Tilden 2d of Philadelphia wrested the national professional championship from Vincent Richards.

Nothing less than awe-inspiring would suitably classify the paralyzing onslaught which the 38-year-old master of the courts turned loose on his former rival of the amateur ranks, to administer the most crushing defeat Richards has ever sustained at his hands in championship play.

In one minute less than an hour, Tilden's electrifying drives, ferreting out the openings in a torrential stream, in conjunction with his cyclonic service, had exacted their toll and established him beyond any doubt as the monarch of all the professional realm. The score was 7—5, 6—2, 6—1.

ACTION DURING DOUBLES FINAL AT PROFESSIONAL TOURNEY AND THE NEW SINGLES CHAMPION.

Times Wide World Photo.

Richards and Kinsey (Background) Playing Tilden and Hunter at Forest Hills.

For a brief period in the first set there was the prospect of a tremendous struggle, such a struggle as was witnessed on the Forest Hills turf a year ago when Richards and Karel Kozeluh of Czechoslovakia met in the final.

Richards Gains Early Lead.

The defending champion, making a surprisingly strong stand from the back of the court, where his ground strokes actually were superior to his opponent's, and making capital of his service and an occasional volley, broke through in the first game and took a lead of 4—2.

To this point it was a real match and the gallery, dividing its plaudits equally between the two players, prepared itself for another of those desperate turf court battles such as Tilden and Richards waged in 1926. And then Tilden, like a thoroughbred that has lagged at the post and settled into his stride, began to come up.

Tilden started to put on greater pressure and almost in the twinkling of an eye, the battle-scarred Davis Cup veteran found the range, rid himself of the errors that had been cropping up in his play and with confidence in his control, collected his forces to turn on as devastating and demoralizing a barrage of drives as a Forest Hills gallery ever witnessed.

There may have been a time when a man applied a lawn-tennis racquet to a ball with better control, shrewder calculation and more implacably than Tilden did in the second and third sets, but no one at Forest Hills yesterday would believe it.

Performance Nearly Perfect.

Here, in truth, was a performance that approached absolute perfection, a performance that Tilden seldom has equaled.

No player in the world, not even Cochet, could conceivably have stood up successfully against the tennis Tilden played in these two sets, though that does not mean that the Philadelphian yesterday would necessarily have beaten the French master, who a few years ago at Wimbledon overcame Tilden's lead of two sets and 5—1 in the third chapter.

The one shot that raised havoc with Richards more than any other was a cross-court forehand drive that came over the net with meteoric speed to nail the baseline corner. Preparatory to that shot, Tilden pulled his opponent out of position with a sharply angled drive or a twisting service to his backhand and then, like clockwork, came that heart-breaking finishing shot to the other side that was yards beyond approach.

But, as damaging as was Tilden's forehand, his backhand was almost equally as big a factor and the most spectacular of his winning shots were made from the left side, often on the dead run.

Richards Volleys Superbly.

The New York youth volleyed superbly and had the gallery cheering frantically, but his opportunities for these winning thrusts became fewer and fewer as the match progressed.

In the third set Richards fell and twisted a muscle of his leg, but gamely resumed play, after Tilden had rushed to his aid, and Richards was cheered wildly by the sympathetic gallery as he won the game, his last in the match.

After a short rest period, Tilden and Richards returned to the courts to engage each other again in the final of the doubles. In a spectacular drawn-out struggle, filled with brilliant rallies, Richards and Howard Kinsey of California successfully defended their crown by defeating Tilden and Francis T. Hunter of New Rochelle, 7—9, 7—5, 3—6, 6—4, 6—3.

George Agutter, president of the Professional Lawn Tennis Association, presented the cups to the winners and also the huge Golden Jubilee Medals, which were donated by Julian S. Myrick, chairman of the Golden Jubilee committee of the United States Lawn Tennis Association.

July 13, 1931

Times Wide World Photo.

William T. Tilden 2d After his Victory Over Vincent Richards.

SEVENTH U. S. TITLE WON BY MRS. MOODY

Coast Star Beats Mrs. Whittingstall, 6-4, 6-1, in Tennis Final at Forest Hills.

MATCH OVER IN 35 MINUTES

Victor Completes Fourth Year of Competition Without Loss of Set in Singles.

4,000 WITNESS THE EVENT

Thrilled by English Girl's Valiant Efforts at Start—Doubles Final on Card Today.

By ALLISON DANZIG.

The tennis champion without a crown assumed the royal purple again yesterday to restore the women's national title to the United States and reestablish her invincibility after a year's absence from the championship.

In the final round of the forty-fourth annual tournament at the West Side Tennis Club, Forest Hills, before a gallery that was held down to 4,000 spectators by the unfavorable weather, Mrs. Helen Wills Moody of California conclusively defeated Mrs. Eileen Bennett Whittingstall of England at 6—4, 6—1, to capture the championship for the seventh time and complete her fourth year of competition without the loss of a set in singles.

Miss Betty Nuthall of England, whom Mrs. Whittingstall eliminated in the semi-finals, was the 1930 winner.

Technically, with her triumph yesterday, which gave her her first leg on the new cup put up last year, Mrs. Moody equaled the record held by Mrs. Molla Mallory of New York for the number of American singles championship victories.

But Mrs. Mallory stands in the records as winning eight national tournaments, and although one of them, that of 1917, is listed as a patriotic tournament and not a championship, the field was of championship class and by general disposition Mrs. Moody must yet win the crown again to duplicate the achievement of Mrs. Mallory.

Doubles Final on Card Today.

The final of the doubles will be played this afternoon at 3:30. The contestants will be Miss Nuthall and Mrs. Whittingstall and Miss Jacobs and Miss Dorothy Round of England. As an added attraction, Mrs. Moody will appear in an exhibition match, either in singles against Manuel Alonso of Spain or in mixed doubles.

Final-day tickets which admitted to yesterday's play will also be honored today, while the price of admission has been set at $1.25.

To fill out the program yesterday an exhibition of mixed doubles was put on in which Miss Nuthall and Clarence J. (Peck) Griffin of California, former national doubles champion with William Johnston,

Times Wide World Photo.

PRESENTATION OF THE CHAMPIONSHIP TROPHY AT FOREST HILLS.
Mrs. Eileen Bennett Whittingstall, Mrs. Helen Wills Moody and Louis J. Carruthers, President of the United States Lawn Tennis Association.

opposed Miss Jacobs and Alonso. The former pair won the first two sets at 6—2 each and Miss Jacobs and Alonso won the third, 6—1.

The championship singles final failed to bring out the pulsating struggle that had been anticipated and within thirty-five minutes after Rufus Davis had called "play" from the umpire's chair the match was over.

As a matter of fact, Mrs. Moody's work had been accomplished once she had fought off the stirring challenge of Mrs. Whittingstall in the first set, a challenge that saw the slender British girl, trailing at 0—3, play magnificent tennis to win the next three games with the loss of only two points and stir the gallery to almost a frenzy of enthusiasm.

Mrs. Moody on Defensive.

During these three games, in the last two of which Mrs. Whittingstall won six successive points with five placements and a service ace, the gauntlet was thrown down to the invincible Californian in such masterful fashion that there appeared to be every prospect of a tremendous battle in which Mrs. Moody might have to yield the first set she has lost since Miss Gwynneth Sterry of England wrested the opening chapter

from her at Wimbledon in 1927.

Mrs. Whittingstall, far from being the oppressed and quiescent victim of the Californian's dreadnaught forehanders, was whole-heartedly the aggressor, carrying the attack to her opponent with so much speed and weight behind her drives and getting such depth and angles on them that Mrs. Moody was put squarely on the defensive.

When Mrs. Whittingstall won her third game in a row to square the score at 3—all the crowd fairly roared its delight. There was no mistaking where its sympathy lay and the sight of any one outplaying Mrs. Moody was so novel as to captivate any gathering.

But with that one great effort, an effort that probably would have put her in the lead at 4—2 had it not been for a questionable decision on the service line in the third game, Mrs. Whittingstall was finished. She managed to win her next service game in the eighth to make the score 4—all, but after that she had nothing left in reserve except her nerve.

Loser's Hard Fight Recalled.

Mrs. Whittingstall, without being unfair to Mrs. Moody or minimizing the splendid tennis and courage the champion showed, was beaten before

she went on the court. Her conquests of Miss Nuthall and Miss Jacobs on successive days were Pyrrhic victories that left her in possession of the field, but with her physical forces decimated.

Two bitterly fought three-set matches on successive days were too much for her slight physique, and in the final set yesterday she had neither the strength nor the control to stand up against Mrs. Moody's withering service and flawless drives.

The English girl, as badly spent as she was, never gave up the fight and collected her waning forces repeatedly to seek her fortune at the net. But it was obvious soon after she had won her last game of the match, the second of the final set, that she understood the fate that awaited her at the hands of her unerring, resourceful opponent, whose stamina had hardly been tapped and whose game gathered momentum as Mrs. Whittingstall's lost acceleration.

Mrs. Moody showed in this match, as she did throughout the championship, that she still has all of her old speed, though she does not use it as consistently as formerly, and in addition a variety and resourcefulness that were lacking to her game heretofore.

Her passing shots were seldom better attuned to penetrate the narrowest opening than they were in this match and their effectiveness did much to undermine the confidence of her opponent.

Carruthers Presents Cups.

Louis J. Carruthers, president of the United States Lawn Tennis Association, presented the cups to Mrs. Moody and Mrs. Whittingstall while a score of cameras registered the scene. The championship cup, filled with American Beauty roses, was turned over to Mrs. Moody, who has already won two of them outright and expects to compete long enough to retire the present one, if successful.

Mrs. Moody will not go to Boston for the national mixed doubles, but will return to California, having ended her season in the East for 1931 except for her exhibition match today.

The point socre and stroke analysis of the match follow:

First Set. POINT SCORE.					G.Pts.
Mrs. Moody ....4 4 6 0 1 1 4 2 4 5—6—31					
Mrs. Whittingstall .1 1 4 4 4 4 0 4 1 3—4—25					

STROKE ANALYSIS.	N.	O.	PL.	SA.	DF.
Mrs. Moody 9	9	7	3	1	
Mrs. Whittingstall 7	11	6	1	3	

Second Set. POINT SCORE.					G.Pts.
Mrs. Moody ....4 3 4 5 4 4 4—6—28					
Mrs. Whittingstall ......1 5 1 3 1 2 1—1—14					

STROKE ANALYSIS.	N.	O.	PL.	SA.	DF.
Mrs. Moody 5	3	6	1	1	
Mrs. Whittingstall 7	12	3	2	3	

Recapitulation.	N.	O.	PL.	SA.	DF.
Mrs. Moody 14	12	13	4	2	
Mrs. Whittingstall 14	23	9	3	5	

	E.	EP.	TP.	G.	S.
Mrs. Moody 28	17	59	12	2	
Mrs. Whittingstall 42	12	40	5	0	

Umpire—Rufus Davis. Time of match—35 minutes.

August 24, 1931

Senorita de Alvarez Creates a Sensation At Wimbledon, Playing in Short Trousers

By The Associated Press.

WIMBLEDON, England, June 23. —Señorita Lili de Alvarez set tongues to wagging and eyes popping when she appeared on the famous centre court today to play Bunny Austin's sister, Mrs. R. Lycett, in a tennis garb of her own creation featuring short trousers.

Old ladies gasped and old gentlemen gurgled as the comely Spanish player pranced about in preliminary practice in her "divided skirt" of cream crêpe de chine, topped by a close-fitting bodice.

What the outcome of Señorita de Alvarez's revolutionary gesture in tennis court fashions would be caused much speculation. Most of the tennis experts, turned stylists for the moment, were of the opinion the innovation in dress would be short-lived. Most of them agreed the costume, despite the freedom of movement it gave, was not very becoming.

June 24, 1931

FRANCE DEFEATS U.S. TO KEEP DAVIS CUP

Series Is Clinched, 3-2, When Borotra Halts Allison, 1-6, 3-6, 6-4, 6-2, 7-5.

12,000 WATCH THE PLAY

Great Excitement Prevails as the Tense Duel Comes to a Close.

VINES VANQUISHES COCHET

U. S. Star Rallies After Losing First Two Sets, Scoring by 4-6, 0-6, 7-5, 8-6, 6-2.

By HERBERT L. MATTHEWS.
Wireless to THE NEW YORK TIMES.

PARIS, July 31.—France, by a score of 3 to 2, today retained the Davis Cup for the sixth consecutive year as Jean Borotra defeated Wilmer Allison of the United States, while Ellsworth Vines turned back Henri Cochet, giving the challengers their second point.

Both matches went five sets. The score of the Borotra-Allison match was 1—6, 3—6, 6—4. 6—2, 7—5. Vines won from Cochet by 4—6, 0—6, 7—5, 8—6, 6—2.

The Borotra-Allison match ended amid excitement unparalleled in Davis Cup Play. A shot which made tennis history came with Allison leading in games at 5—4, advantage out, on Borotra's service in the fifth set.

Borotra's first serve hit the net. His second, delivered softly, fell, according to Allison's certain belief, beyond the service line. Allison, thinking he had won the match, made no effort to hit the ball in, but batted it idly far out of his opponent's court.

Takes Heart Out of Allison.

It took him several seconds to realize the lineman had not called "faute," and when he did comprehend, he almost literally collapsed. All the heart went out of him and he hit everything out or into the net, except one point, after that.

The majority of newspaper men, including Frenchmen, who were well placed in the press section, consider the linesman's decision wrong.

There is no questioning the decision, of course, but it promises to be one of the most discussed events in modern tennis. At best, it was doubtful, and it is considered by all a great pity that Allison, who was the first American since Bill Tilden to more than hold his own in a Davis Cup final, should be deprived of the credit and glory of playing a chief part in bringing the cup back to the United States.

Had Vines lost, it simply would have been a case of depriving Allison of an undecisive point, but Vines's well-merited victory over Cochet at best made the incident all the more regrettable.

Borotra Deserving of Credit.

None here desires to take any credit from Borotra, who came back after losing the first two sets to outplay the fast-tiring Allison, who had had two exhausting days in the doubles yesterday and the opening singles on Friday.

Allison outclassed the Basque by a wide margin in the first two sets. He had fine pace and depth and kept Borotra on the run all the time.

In the third set Allison began to crack, showing the effects of three days of hard play. Borotra began rushing the net with his old effectiveness and after exchanging services to 3-all, broke through Allison's, won his own and, after losing the next, ran out the set.

Borotra, who is famous for his remarkable recuperative powers after a short rest, came back after the ten-minute interval playing at his best. Allison kept even for four games, then lost four straight.

Crowd in Continuous Uproar.

The final set had the crowd in a continuous uproar. The tenseness and excitement of the 12,000 spectators led to demonstrations of booing and hissing hitherto considered unbelievable at Roland Garros Stadium.

Borotra was performing the miracle of getting better as the match progressed despite his fatigue. When he broke through Allison's serve to begin, and won his own, the crowd went frantic.

YESTERDAY'S DAVIS CUP WINNERS.

Ellsworth Vines.

Jean Borotra.

Times Wide World Photo.

The psychology of coming from behind to the plaudits of the crowd was all in favor of Borotra, and the Texan showed he had the stuff of a great player in him by coming right back to win three straight, taking the lead.

On Borotra's serve came the first of several tense incidents. After the game had been deuced three times the same linesman who later was to make the famous decision permitted a ball to be called good which Borotra himself was so sure was out that he deliberately threw the next point away while the crowd booed and hissed him.

Basque Trails by 2—4.

The Basque lost that game and was trailing by 2—4. Then each lost his service, giving Allison a 5-3 lead. Allison, serving, got a 40-15 lead, which meant he needed two points for the match, but he lost both and the game.

It was the next game in which the decision came. Borotra permitted his opponent to come up from 0—40 to deuce. Then, for the third time, he stopped to change his shoes, while the crowd roared disapproval. He hit the next ball out and it was in that charged atmosphere that the decision against Allison was rendered.

Since the cup was lost, the Vines-Cochet match became a mere exhibition, but it would be a great mistake to think that Cochet let down. He had never lost a Davis Cup match before and was never even carried to five sets.

Moreover, he played as well today as he ever did, but Vines was better and finally showed the Parisians the sort of tennis of which he was capable. He did not do so, however, until he seemed hopelessly outclassed, as Cochet ran away with the first set and took the second at love. When trailing at 0—4, Vines, under orders, threw the next two games, for which he was soundly booed by the crowd.

Vines was not rattled and he started making Cochet run in the third. The Frenchman, who, like Allison, played all three days, began to tire.

It takes a great deal to make Cochet tire, but Vines had found his game and thenceforth clearly outplayed his opponent. It was courageous, intelligent tennis, and was a far cry from his previous poor showing here.

August 1, 1932

VINES DEFEATS LOTT IN FOUR-SET BATTLE

19-Year-Old Californian Wins by 7-9, 6-3, 9-7, 7-5 in National Tennis Final.

THRILLS CROWD OF 10,000

New Champion Stages Spectacular Rallies to Take Third and Fourth Sets.

PLAY LIKENED TO TILDEN'S

Victor Shows Irresistible Power in Prevailing Over Masterful Game of Chicagoan.

By ALLISON DANZIG.

The men's national tennis championship returned to California last night in the custody of one of the youngest players to win the title in the fifty-one years of its history.

In the final round of the Golden Jubilee tournament, before a gallery of 10,000 spectators in the stadium of the West Side Tennis Club, Forest Hills, H. Ellsworth Vines Jr., 19-year-old Pasadena stripling, defeated George M. Lott Jr. of Chicago at 7—9, 6—3, 9—7, 7—5.

Vines thus established himself as twentieth in the line of American champions. He succeeds John Hope Doeg of Newark, N. J., formerly of Santa Monica, Cal., as the title-holder.

Not since William Johnston came out of the West almost twenty years ago has the Pacific Coast sent so transcendently gifted an emissary in quest of the game's highest honors as came into this richly merited heritage yesterday. Here, beyond doubt, is a player of majestic stature and talents surpassing those of any other amateur on the American horizon, a player who is the nearest approach to another Tilden the game has produced in ten years in this country.

Lott Praises Conqueror.

No greater tribute could have been paid to the surpassing brilliance of his play than was offered last night when Lott, with magnificent sportsmanship, declared: "I have no regrets losing to a player like Vines. I played the best tennis I know how to play, but you can't beat the kind of tennis Vines played."

Lott spoke not only like a chevalier but truly. The likeable, unaffected Chicago youth indeed played his best tennis, the best, certainly, he was ever put forth in the championship, and nothing short of a Tildenesque performance would have sufficed to turn him back in this excruciatingly close match with its tremendously spectacular finish.

Who else but a Tilden or a Cochet could have denied the Lott of yesterday the third set, in which he led at 5—3, and later at 5—4 and 30—0?

Times Wide World Photo.

H. Ellsworth Vines Jr., Louis J. Carruthers, President of the United States Lawn Tennis Association, and George M. Lott Jr.

Could even Tilden have equaled the rapacity of the solemn, almost lackadaisical Californian in pulling up from 2—5 and 15—40 in the final set with one of the most sensational exhibitions of machine-gun shooting ever witnessed at Forest Hills?

Employs Smashing Game.

Those were the questions that some were asking at the West Side Tennis Club last night. Heretical though it sounds to any one who has looked upon the feats of Tilden during the past decade, it is indicative of the depths to which yesterday's gallery was stirred by the entrancing, almost phenomenal succession of wrathful drives and overhead smashes that were catapulted from the racquet of the lanky, dour-visaged young Pasadenan.

Lott, playing almost errorless tennis, mixing his spin and length in masterful fashion, volleying as few others can volley and fighting himself out of untenable positions with a courage and resourcefulness that won him repeated ovations, found that nothing he could do could avail against such sublime shot-making as this.

There never has been a time when the Chicago youth fought with more unwavering tenacity or with intenser concentration, never a time when he was more fertile in his devices or more intriguing in the variety and shading of his strokes, than in this match. If ever he wanted to win a match in his life, this was the one, with its championship title and its manifold rewards.

Lott's Fight Wins Gallery.

The gallery, unmistakable in its sympathy for Vines, was so won over by the lion-hearted efforts of the Chicagoan that in the closing stages it was cheering him fully as lustily as it was his opponent, and as Lott changed courts after he had lost his service in the eleventh game of the final set he received the greatest ovation of the day.

It was an ovation for a man fighting against hopeless odds, who was heroically using all the human agencies at his command against an opponent whose weapons could do the almost super-human.

It mattered not that it was a losing fight, all that mattered was that Lott was fighting might and main and giving everything he had to the very last, and the satisfaction he derived from that great effort was his reward, a reward sweeter than the fruits of many of his victories.

Taking the whole match in retrospect, Lott played consistently the better tennis. From start to finish his was a championship performance in which his game was sustained on a high plane without a single bad slump.

Vines Plays in Streaks.

Vines, for most of the two hours and seventeen minutes of battle, played in streaks. One minute holding the gallery spell-bound with the withering fire of his racquet, the next minute he was in the doldrums, wasting opportunities in prodigal fashion as he did in the first set, in which he led at 5—4 and 40—0 and then proceeded to waste three set-points, ultimately to yield the chapter.

The Californian's saving grace was his ability to lift his game when he stood with his back to the wall and reach heights which Lott found impossible to scale: Time and again Vines pulled himself out of the hole to confound Lott, and generally it was his service that extricated him from his danger, though as a general thing Lott's twist service was as effective as the Californian's faster delivery and in the first set was a distinctly bigger asset.

Indeed, it seemed that Vines needed the incentive of rising to an emergency to show his true wares. For when he held a lead he could fall into the most lamentable slumps and give his admirers a nightmare with his almost endless errors, most of them made on the forehand.

Not all of these errors were inexcusable, for Lott's alternate use of the chop and the drive, with their changing spin and speed, was calculated to have a disturbing effect upon his opponent's control, but there were many mistakes Vines made when the ball invited punishment and the shot presented no difficulties.

Offset Errors With Placements.

The stroke analysis offers a helpful commentary in visualizing the kind of tennis Vines was playing. In the four sets he made 130 errors, to Lott's 99, but to offset these he is credited with 70 placements, to the Chicagoan's 24. In every set he made more than twice as many placements as did Lott, and he lost the first set in spite of the fact that he scored outright 21 times to Lott's 8 aside from the service aces.

Vines's seven double faults in this opening chapter were pretty near a record for a championship final. To those who had seen the Californian's electrifying delivery against Frederick Perry the day before, it was incomprehensible that it could have fallen off so badly in twenty-four hours.

Starting with the second chapter,

Point Score, Stroke Analysis Of Final in Title Tennis

FIRST SET.

Point Score.

				G. Pts.
Vines	.4 1 4 5 4 3 3 4 4 4 4 1 9 1 2 2			2—7—55
Lott	..1 4 2 7 1 5 5 2 2 6 0 4 7 4 4 4			4—9—58

Stroke Analysis.

	N.	O.	Pl.	SA.	DF.
Vines	.21	19	21	3	7
Lott	.14	17	8	2	0

SECOND SET.

Point Score.

				G. Pts.
Vines	.7 2 4 3 4 2 4 4			5—6—35
Lott	.5 4 0 5 2 4 0 2			3—3—25

Stroke Analysis.

	N.	O.	Pl.	SA.	DF.
Vines	.10	6	14	1	1
Lott	.11	8	6	1	1

THIRD SET.

Point Score.

				G. Pts.
Vines	.2 4 1 4 0 4 2 3 5 4 2 4 1 4 5			4—9—49
Lott	.4 2 4 4 1 4 5 3 2 4 1 4 0 3			6—7—43

Stroke Analysis.

	N.	O.	Pl.	SA.	DF.
Vines	.17	18	17	2	1
Lott	.12	15	5	1	0

FOURTH SET.

Point Score.

				G. Pts.
Vines	.1 1 4 4 0 1 3 5 4 4 6			4—7—37
Lott	.4 4 1 2 4 4 5 3 1 2 4			1—5—35

Stroke Analysis.

	N.	O.	Pl.	SA.	DF.
Vines	.18	9	18	1	3
Lott	.12	6	5	0	0

RECAPITULATION.

	N.	O.	Pl.	SA.	DF.
Vines	.66	52	70	7	12
Lott	.49	49	24	6	1

	E.	EP.	TP.	G.	S.
Vines	.130	77	176	29	3
Lott	.99	30	106	24	1

OFFICIALS OF MATCH.

Umpire—Rufus Davis, chairman of the Tennis Umpires Association. Net umpire—W. Scott Johnston. Foot-fault judge—Benjamin Phillips. Service linesmen—William Jameson and H. L. Richards. Centre service linesmen—Rex Morford and Gerald P. Lumsden. Side linesmen—C. G. James, H. T. Mattice, H. Le Bair and John T. (Terry) McGovern. Base linesmen—H. S. McMorris and W. A. Creevy. Time of match—2.17.

Vines's service was much more effective and, as has been noted, came to his aid at critical junctures repeatedly, but in general it was not the terrifying weapon it was against Perry, lacking in the paralyzing speed which he has at his command, and Lott in the early stages was returning it successfully, as he had returned Doeg's the day before.

Twice Beaten by Lott.

The victory of the Californian was the first he has scored over Lott in three meetings this year. The Chicagoan defeated him at New Orleans on clay late in the Winter and at Southampton won by default when Vines was seized with indigestion with the score at two sets each.

On the strength of those two decisions, Lott went into yesterday's match with high confidence and those who had been watching his splendid play all week in the championship rated him the formidable opponent he proved to be.

That he lost was not owing to any deficiency, mental or physical, on his part. He played beautiful tennis, heady tennis, such tennis as was calculated to make trouble for any player on the courts, but he was simply up against an opponent who, when he had no other alternative, could play such tennis as a Tilden plays.

The match, while it was marked by periods when the errors greatly exceeded the earned points, as when Vines contributed 18 of Lott's 19 points in the first six games of the fourth set on errors, was a worthy final to the jubilee tournament of the United States Lawn Tennis Association.

It was notable for the few decisions which were challenged on the lines, which came as a relief after the transpirings in the Vines-Perry match, and the quality of the play, if not always of the highest order, at times was as magnificent as anything seen at Forest Hills in years.

In the last two sets in particular, there were rallies that had the gallery looking on entranced, as one dazzling shot followed another from every sector of the court and Vine's demolishing overhead shots, angled every time to the lines, regardless of the depth from which they were made, alone were almost worth the price of admission.

It remained for the last fifteen minutes of play to bring out the greatest tennis of the day, if not the greatest that has been seen at Forest Hills since Tilden's match with Rene Lacoste in the 1927 final, with the exception of his performance against Vincent Richards last July.

The rampant Vines that the gallery saw during this period as he pulled out the set from 2—5 and 15—40 was the Vines who has been winning almost everything in sight all season and the Vines whom the custodians of America's Davis Cup destinies visualize as the youth to lead henceforth in the struggle for the reclamation of the international trophy.

Many see in him the coming champion of the world, with Perry of England as his only real rival in Europe aside from the veteran Henri Cochet of France.

The slim young Californian's victory yesterday was in the nature of a birthday present, for on the twenty-eighth of this month he will attain his twentieth year. When he left last night on the long journey to the Pacific Coast he carried also with him, in addition to the championship cup, the national clay court crown, the Longwood Bowl, Seabright and Newport cups and numerous trophies won in doubles with Keith Gledhill of Santa Barbara, who was the first to greet him yesterday as he walked off the court to speak into the microphone.

Vines plans to return to the University of Southern California for his sophomore year and will be available for the 1932 Davis Cup team "if called."

September 13, 1931

Seven-Year Campaign for U. S. Tennis Title Ends Successfully for Miss Jacobs

MISS JACOBS VICTOR IN U. S. TENNIS FINAL

Overwhelms Miss Babcock at Forest Hills, 6-2, 6-2—Match Lasts 31 Minutes.

SUCCEEDS AFTER 7 YEARS

23-Year-Old Berkeley Star Finally Rewarded With Crown Mrs. Moody Relinquished.

By ALLISON DANZIG.

After seven years of campaigning, Miss Helen Jacobs finally has been rewarded with the highest prize in American women's tennis.

In one of the shortest final-round matches on record in the national championship, the 23-year-old Berkeley (Cal.) girl defeated Miss Carolyn Babcock of Los Angeles by the crushing margin of 6—2, 6—2 yesterday to succeed Mrs. Helen Wills Moody as the titleholder.

Mrs. Moody, seven times winner of the crown, did not participate in the tournament, remaining abroad after carrying off the French and British championships.

2,500 Witness Final.

There have been more one-sided victories scored in a national final than was Miss Jacobs's, but probably never has a gallery been more genuinely disappointed than were the 2,500 spectators who sat in the stadium of the West Side Tennis Club at Forest Hills and saw the 20-year-old conqueror of Mrs. Lawrence Harper and Miss Joan Ridley throw away points with such prodigality that the match was over thirty-one minutes after Rufus Davis had called "play" from the umpire's chair.

But decisively beaten though she was, Miss Babcock had no cause to be humiliated. The path to the championship throne is a long and thorny one. That she should have fought her way to the final in her second championship tournament is a distinction of which any one might well be proud.

Miss Babcock has only to refer to the career of Miss Jacobs to assuage her disappointment. Hailed as a coming champion when she won the national girls' title in 1924 and 1925, the Berkeley girl competed in the women's tournament in 1925 and was put out in the second round by Miss Penelope Anderson. From that time on it was Miss Jacobs's unhappy experience to be overshadowed by the greatness of Helen Wills.

Reached Final in 1928.

In 1928, Miss Jacobs reached the championship final, only to be overwhelmed by Miss Wills at 6—2, 6—1, and then came perhaps her bitterest experience of all in 1930, when, with Miss Wills remaining out of the tournament, the Berkeley girl was stricken ill abroad and was unable to take advantage of her opportunity of gaining the title.

After winning both of her Wightman Cup singles matches last year, Miss Jacobs underwent the disappointment of being put out of the national singles by Mrs. Eileen Bennett Whittingstall of England in the quarter-finals, but with admirable fortitude, she went abroad this Summer, won one of her Wightman Cup matches, finished a runner-up to Mrs. Moody at Wimbledon and now, seven years after she first played for the national crown and five after she made her début as a Wightman Cup player, she has finally reached her goal.

In her triumphant march to the throne, Miss Jacobs, in succession, defeated Miss Virginia Rice of Boston, Mrs. Frederick McBride (the former Miss Penelope Anderson) of New York, Mrs. John Van Ryn of East Orange, Mrs. Elsie Goldsack Pittman of England and Miss Babcock.

PRESENTATION OF CUPS TO WINNER AND RUNNER-UP IN TITLE TENNIS.

Times Wide World Photo.

Dr. Philip B. Hawk, President of West Side Tennis Club; Miss Carolyn Babcock, Miss Helen Jacobs, Louis Carruthers, President of U. S. L. T. A., and Samuel Hardy, Referee.

Aided by Rival's Errors.

The Berkeley girl's victory yesterday was gained with almost less effort than any of her others in the championship. That was owing not only to the mistakes of her young opponent, who made 52 errors to Miss Jacobs's 23, but also to the fact that the champion studiously abstained from giving her opponent the opportunity to make the dangerous cross court shots which were the undoing of Mrs. Harper and Miss Ridley.

In her first service game, the Los Angeles girl demonstrated how dangerous she could be at the net when she took Miss Jacobs's hard drive on the run and volleyed it back across court on the backhand with a finality that brought a roar from the stands.

Another volley of the same kind enabled her to pull out the fourth game to square the score at 2-all, and up to this point there appeared to be every prospect of a close, bitterly fought match.

When Miss Babcock pulled from 0—40 to 30—40 in the fifth game with two piercing drives that forced the Berkeley girl's volleys to go awry, the seriousness of Miss Jacobs's expression became more pronounced.

Breaking Point Near.

But the breaking point in Miss Babcock's game was only a point away and after she had missed an overhead smash in the succeeding rally to fall behind at 2—3, her opponent definitely took command.

Miss Jacobs won the next two games at 15 each, entirely on errors, with Miss Babcock returning service faultily three successive times in the seventh, and the Berkeley girl pulled up from 30—40 to break through again in the eighth for the set.

Miss Jacobs had now won four games in a row and when she added a fifth at love at the start of the second set, with three first services that Miss Babcock was unable to handle, the stands had an inkling that the match was won and lost.

Miss Babcock revived the hopes of her adherents as she shook off her nervousness and hit out boldly to follow her forcing shots to the net and even the score at 1-all, but Miss Jacobs, in answer to this challenge, did heavy execution with her marvelous backhand to go ahead at 2—1.

The fourth game saw Miss Babcock lapse into another slump, to drop her service on four trivial errors, and the end seemed at hand. But now came a last rally by the Los Angeles girl.

Returning service beautifully and playing the ball high to her opponent's backhand, she broke through Miss Jacobs for the first time in the match, but the rally was short-lived. Miss Babcock became timid in her hitting, found it impossible to sustain her control and got only two more points in the match, losing the sixth and eighth games at love and the seventh at 30.

Miss Jacobs's success did not end with her victory in the singles. After Berkeley Bell had defeated Manuel Alonso in an exhibition at 10—8, 6—4, the champion went back on the court with Miss Sarah Palfrey of Boston and won the doubles championship by defeating Mrs. Marjorie Morrill Painter of Boston and Miss Alice Marble of San Francisco, 8—6, 6—1.

The point score and stroke analysis of the singles match follow:

FIRST SET.

Point Score.

									G.	Pts.
Miss Jacobs	4	1	4	3	4	4	4	5	6	29
Miss Babcock	1	4	1	5	2	1	1	3	2	18

Stroke Analysis.

	N.	O.	P.	S.A.	D.F.
Miss Jacobs	7	5	3	0	1
Miss Babcock	12	13	5	0	1

SECOND SET.

Point Score.

									G.	Pts.
Miss Jacobs	4	3	4	4	3	4	4	4	6	30
Miss Babcock	0	5	2	1	5	0	2	0	2	15

Stroke Analysis.

	N.	O.	P.	S.A.	D.F.
Miss Jacobs	4	6	4	0	0
Miss Babcock	16	8	5	0	2

RECAPITULATION.

	N.	O.	P.	S.A.	D.F.
Miss Jacobs	11	11	7	0	1
Miss Babcock	28	21	10	0	3

	E.	E.P.	T.P.	G.	Sets.
Miss Jacobs	23	7	59	12	2
Miss Babcock	52	10	33	4	0

Umpire—Rufus Davis. Time of match—31 minutes.

August 22, 1932

VINES ROUTS COCHET IN U. S. TENNIS FINAL AND RETAINS TITLE

Remorseless Attack of Coast Star Subdues French Ace by 6-4, 6-4, 6-4.

14,880 ACCLAIM VICTOR

Capacity Throng at Forest Hills Thrilled by Champion's Superb Triumph.

MATCH OVER IN AN HOUR

Loser Defeats Allison in Fifth Set of Their Postponed Semi-Final Encounter, 7-5.

By ALLISON DANZIG.

The largest crowd to witness a tennis match in this country since 1927 saw the world's most celebrated amateur hammered down yesterday by the most appalling speed generated by a racquet since William Tilden was at the zenith of his career.

It was the hand of Ellsworth Vines that propelled the racquet and before the torrential stream of withering drives that came from it all the sagacity, the finesse and the powers of divination of Henri Cochet were utterly unavailing.

Filling the stadium of the West Side Tennis Club to the capacity of its seating and standing room, 14,880 looked on spellbound as the towering 20-year-old youth from Pasadena, Cal., blighted the game of the most gifted artist of the courts with his electrifying drives and service and successfully consummated his defense of his national championship.

Not even the satisfaction of a set was allowed Cochet, nor was a lead of 4—2, such as he manufactured in the opening chapter, sufficient to exact any concession from his rampant young rival.

Victor Finds His Speed.

Then it was, at this disadvantageous point, that Vines shook off the same obsession for error-making that had almost cost him his semi-final match with Clifford Sutter on Friday and let loose with an avalanche of wrathful strokes that had the crowd roaring in a frenzy of delight to the end of the contest.

The end came exactly one hour after Rufus Davis had called "play" from the umpire's chair. The score was 6—4, 6—4, 6—4, and never, after that opening advantage, did the French ace threaten again or appear to have more than the slimmest chance of winning.

The player who has ruled the courts from 1928 on, whose invincibility has kept the Davis Cup in France since he helped to wrest it from the United States in 1927 and whose stature in tennis has been almost commensurate with Tilden's, so great has been the fear in which his delicately attuned game is held, has met his master in the serious-visaged young Californian armed with the hammer of Thor.

Play Dazzles the Gallery.

The gallery could scarcely believe its eyes, so baffled was Cochet by the relentless onslaught that was beating down upon his court, but then it was difficult to believe that any one could hit a ball with the frightful speed with which Vines was raking the lines.

Cochet stated that never before in his years of experience, not even excepting his matches with Tilden, had he faced so hard a barrage as the American champion sent at him, and he made that statement to a linesman directly after he had narrowly escaped being hit in the head by a cyclonic service ace that traveled so fast it was almost impossible to see the ball.

The defeat of the French master did not come as a startling surprise, for Vines had vanquished him in the Davis Cup challenge round on sand courts last July and was figured to stand a better chance on the faster turf courts of Forest Hills, where his speed would be enhanced rather than minimized.

But that the American champion should win in three sets was more than probably any one in the great assemblage had bargained on, particularly after Vines's alarming showing in the semi-final.

Cochet generally was rated an even favorite and there were some who estimated him a 3-to-2 choice after his impressive victory over Wilmer Allison of Austin, Texas. He defeated Allison, 7—5, yesterday morning in the deciding set of their semi-final match, which was interrupted by darkness Friday evening with the score standing 2 sets-all.

Davis Cup Play Recalled.

The fact that Vines had beaten him in Paris was not taken seriously by these backers of the French champion, who argued that the Davis Cup match was played after the series had been clinched for France and that Cochet was indifferent to its outcome.

Vines's triumph yesterday leaves no ground for any such disparagement as his 5-set victory in Paris elicited. No one who sat in the stadium and saw the conscientious effort that Cochet made to quell the tempest of the American's attack can question reasonably that the French champion was keen to win the title—much keener than some of the private reports from abroad had led one to believe earlier in the week.

It was a thoroughly earned victory that the California youth gained and it stamps him more than ever as the logical successor to the mantle of Cochet, inherited from Tilden, and lifts American hopes to a new high for the reclamation of the Davis Cup in 1933. It also climaxed the most successful season that a player of this country has enjoyed in many years.

In addition to carrying off the championship trophy and thus becoming the first player to win the title two years running since Tilden scored his sixth successive victory in 1925, Vines also captured the championship at Wimbledon; annexed the national doubles with Keith Gledhill; gained the first victory scored over Cochet in Davis Cup singles play since the trophy left this country, and won the Newport singles, the only grass court tournament in which he competed in the United States this season.

Reminder of Tilden Victories.

His double victory in the English and American championships marks him as the first American to accomplish this feat in more than a decade, Tilden being the last to win both crowns before him.

The champion left with Gledhill for home last night at 6:30, half an hour after Cochet had boarded a liner for France, and will stop over in Detroit today for exhibition matches. He will compete in the Pacific Southwest championships at Los Angeles and on Oct. 6 will sail with Gledhill, Allison and John Van Ryn for a five months' tour of Honolulu, Australia, Tasmania and New Zealand, returning March 1.

It was a great day of tennis that was provided at Forest Hills yesterday and it was a great crowd that turned out for it. Lured by the prospect of a meeting between the two most renowned amateurs of the day, the first match between them to be staged in this country, and also by the ideal weather, the tennis populace of the metropolitan area stormed the Long Island capital of the game in numbers such had not been seen there since Tilden played René Lacoste in the 1927 final.

As early as 11 o'clock there were 1,300 on hand to see the finish of the match between Cochet and Allison, and when the final got under way there were close to 13,000 in the huge concrete enclosure. Before the first set was over, the late arrivals had filled every remaining vacant seat, hundreds were seated in the aisles and hundreds more stood in the portal entrances and at the top of the stadium. In addition, 2,000 were unable to get into the stadium.

All Vantage Places Filled.

P. Schuyler Van Bloem, chairman of the championship committee of the West Side Tennis Club, estimated that there were 13,500 persons seated in the stands, 800 more standing or sitting in the aisles and 580 accommodated in the marquee, the rendezvous of officials, players, club members and guests.

If it was not the largest crowd ever to see a tennis match in this country, it was the equal of any other and it stood as a testimonial to the tremendous magnetism that the names of Cochet and Vines hold for the sporting world.

One other championship final was decided during the day. Clarence M. Charest, one-armed player from Washington and titleholder in 1929, regained the veterans' national crown by defeating Frederick C. Baggs, the defender, 7—5, 6—4.

As an added and concluding attraction, an exhibition doubles contest was put on, in which George M. Lott Jr. of Chicago and Sidney B. Wood

Jr. of New York won the first two sets from Gregory Mangin of Newark and Berkeley Bell of Austin, Texas, 6—3, 9—7, and lost the third, 6—4.

Gallery at a High Pitch.

The 1,500 early comers who turned out for the finish of the match between Cochet and Allison witnessed some of the most dazzling tennis furnished in the entire tournament. With both men laboring under a big strain as they faced the necessity of producing their best forthwith, the play was a bit ragged at the outset, but by the second game the quality improved and the issue was joined in a fashion to stir the gallery to an excited pitch.

Cochet's keenness to win was extremely pronounced. Vigilantly on guard every second and his nervous tension manifesting itself in his request to have the typewriters and telegraph instruments in the press box silenced, the French champion paid his opponent the compliment of playing his best tennis, as though the fate of the Davis Cup hung in the balance.

There were some who figured that Cochet was under a handicap in the final because of his expenditure of energy in the morning. Had the championship round been a grueling test of endurance, this contention would have been plausible, but since the set with Allison lasted hardly more than half an hour and the final only an hour, the French champion was on the court in all for no more than the normal duration of a championship match.

The master from Europe showed no particular signs of fatigue against Vines. While he did a considerable amount of running, there were many shots from Vines's racquet which he made no effort to retrieve.

It would have been as useless as to chase rainbows, for the American's drives came so low over the net, pitched so fast from the turf, from which they picked up additional pace, and were directed with such utter contempt for safety methods toward the lines that the ball was irredeemably beyond interception before Cochet could move out of his tracks.

The point scores and stroke analyses:

COCHET VS. ALLISON.

FIFTH SET.

Point Score.

													Pts.	G.
Cochet	1	8	0	4	5	4	4	5	3	4	4	4	46	7
Allison	4	6	4	2	7	2	1	7	5	1	2	2	43	5

Stroke Analysis.

	N.	O.	P.	SA.	DF.
Cochet	20	13	13	2	1
Allison	15	14	8	1	2

Umpire—Ben Dwight. Time of set—33 minutes.

VINES VS. COCHET.

FIRST SET.

Point Score.

											Pts.	G.
Vines	4	0	1	4	1	3	4	6	4	4	31	6
Cochet	2	4	4	0	4	5	2	4	1	2	28	4

Stroke Analysis.

	N.	O.	P.	SA.	DF.
Vines	14	9	9	2	3
Cochet	13	5	2	6	2

SECOND SET.

Point Score.

											Pts.	G.
Vines	2	5	0	4	2	4	7	5	2	4	35	6
Cochet	4	3	4	0	4	2	5	3	4	0	29	4

Stroke Analysis.

	N.	O.	P.	SA.	DF.
Vines	19	8	15	1	0
Cochet	13	6	2	0	0

THIRD SET.

Point Score.

											Pts.	G.
Vines	4	5	1	4	0	2	4	4	2	4	30	6
Cochet	2	3	4	1	4	4	2	2	4	1	27	4

Stroke Analysis.

	N.	O.	P.	SA.	DF.
Vines	14	8	8	3	1
Cochet	9	10	4	0	0

RECAPITULATION.

	N.	O.	P.	SA.	DF.	E.	EP.	TP.	G.	Sets
Vines	47	25	32	6	4	76	35	96	18	3
Cochet	35	21	8	0	2	58	8	84	12	0

Umpire—Rufus Davis. Time of match—One hour.

September 11, 1932

BRITAIN CAPTURES DAVIS CUP BY 3-2

Perry Beats Merlin of France by 4-6, 8-6, 6-2, 7-5 to Decide Tennis Series.

LAST TRIUMPH IN 1912

By LANSING WARREN.

Wireless to THE NEW YORK TIMES.

PARIS, July 30.—Great Britain gained possession of the Davis Cup today, but only by the narrowest of margins, defeating France by three matches to two.

The losers, who held that greatest of tennis trophies for the last six years, did not surrender it without a superb effort, intensely spectacular in its moving heroism.

It had been said by all the experts that France could not win without a miracle. The miracle almost happened in the Roland Garros Stadium at Auteuil today.

First Henri Cochet tied the challenge-round score at 2—all with a glorious uphill victory over H. W. (Bunny) Austin by 5—7, 6—4, 4—6, 6—4, 6—4. Then his much-underestimated team-mate, André Merlin, playing in his first Davis Cup competition, won himself lasting fame in the annals of tennis.

If his was not the greatest tennis ever seen, it certainly was one of the finest exhibitions of nerve and downright grit that has ever been witnessed in a challenge round.

Merlin lost by 4—6, 8—6, 6—2, 7—5 to Fred Perry of England, as had been predicted, but not in the style which every one expected. This factor and the excitement of Cochet's previous astonishing victory perhaps made Merlin's performance seem all the more remarkable.

Breathless Enthusiasm Prevails.

At any rate, all circumstances considered, breathless enthusiasm and tension ran so high during today's play that it was impossible to be unaffected by it.

During the first two sets of Merlin's fight against Perry to save the cup for France the crowd could not refrain from cheering, applauding and even laughing at Perry's uncontrollable confusion as the young Frenchman scored point after point in masterly fashion.

Merlin entered the court a young boy for whom every one felt sorry. There probably was not a person present who would have cared to risk a dime on his chances. After Merlin's performance in the match with Perry there are very few who would be willing to assert that Jean Borotra would have done any better.

Merlin was allowed to give full play today to his natural style of smashing, driving and hitting. From start to finish he kept Perry in constant danger of committing the unforgivable act of blowing up and losing the cup for Great Britain.

Perry Faces the Facts.

Perry had a very difficult game to play. Though he lost his head in the beginning when he found himself outplayed by such an unsuspected adversary, he saved himself by facing the facts. He realized that he must play this match not as against a young junior making a desperate, boyish bid for reputation, but in the same way he would play against Cochet, Ellsworth Vines or Jack Crawford if he meant to win.

Before Perry fully realized this, he had lost the first set and Merlin had run twice to set point in the second set. The British player had the crowd shouting, roaring, laughing and screaming against him and was unnerved. Merlin thrived upon the plaudits and upon the opportunity to display his points in tennis.

Perry was first amused, then irritated and finally completely rattled. He deserves great credit for recovering his composure in such hostile circumstances and playing the splendid game he did when every point he scored brought groans from the gallery.

The French crowd cannot be blamed for its partiality. There is something infectious in Merlin's demeanor and assurance. In addition, the pure beauty of many of his strokes inspired an irresistible impulse to cheer his scoring even in those who had come hoping Great Britain would win.

Constantly on the Alert.

Perry wasn't insensible to it himself. This, in a psychological way, might account for his state of mind, although the Britisher soon saw he could not afford to give away any points. Merlin's carriage, his erect, springy step, his alertness and constant leg activity and the sureness of his every muscular movement demanded admiration, despite its cocky aspect in one so young and new to championship play.

Merlin acted with perfect calm and sportsmanship, even undertaking to calm the outraged howls from the grand stands at the umpire's close decisions. He pleaded for silence and sportsmanlike behavior with the self-assurance of a Cochet. The spectators responded to him as they did to Cochet.

Merlin started with a rush and won in quick succession the first six points. The crowd laughed and applauded, thinking it a joke but still believing Perry would directly take command and put things in order. Merlin triumphantly went to 5 to 2, however, winning long rallies by finely delivered net shots and driving Perry back again and again by perfectly gauged lobs. The crowd became frantic with excitement.

Perry sent over many a seemingly winning shot, but Merlin, by superhuman exertion:, recovered them. Once when Perry shot a lob over his head Merlin, after swinging for it and missing it, dug down court faster than the ball and was ready for it when it landed. He did not drop a single point without making the utmost endeavor to save it.

Spectators Applaud Madly.

Perry shot over many good drives and sm[illegible] shots, but Merlin recovered them, a[illegible] the match went on into long [illegible]es and deuce games Merlin was [illegible]ing ahead. When he took that first set the crowd, already almost delirious with joy over Cochet's success and Merlin's brilliant shots, went simply mad applauding.

The second set started like a repetition of the first, and Merlin gained a 3-1 lead. Perry braced, but only to allow Merlin to take the lead again at 5—4. In the next game, on Perry's service, twice Merlin reached set point and Perry just saved himself and the game.

Perry then won the following game, but Merlin again equaled the score. Then Merlin cracked and Perry captured the set, 8—6, recovering his nerve at the same time. Perry's success moderated the cheering and allowed him to quiet his nerves. He won the third set always against the strong opposition of the tiring Merlin, who had been exceeding his powers.

After the rest period, Perry started straight for victory, but when he led by 4—1 Merlin made a determined rally. By the most astonishingly nervy efforts he managed to tie the score. He received ovation after ovation and much advice from René Lacoste between games. Perry was on the verge of a case of nerves again.

Forced to Utmost Efforts.

This set also was deuced, and Merlin drove Perry to his utmost efforts even up to the last stroke which gave the cup to Great Britain for the first time since 1912.

Even then the crowd could not feel disheartened because Merlin had made such a splendid fight, and it had the grace to cheer Perry, which it couldn't do after Friday's defeats.

Cochet's victory over Austin was hardly less exciting and certainly produced finer tennis. It demonstrated, however, that while Cochet is still a magnificent player, he has lost the precision in execution that never used to fail him. The match was full of complexities owing to the science and headwork on both sides. Austin had the advantage almost throughout the match because of his superior execution.

In the ninth game of the fifth set Cochet came from behind and forged ahead to his fighting victory. Many games ran to deuce and especially in the early stages there were long exchanges and wily moves and countermoves. Cochet later forced the pace and found Austin his equal in speed.

The last part of the match was played with both men tiring visibly, but Cochet's triumph was only by a hair's breadth after Austin had once pulled up from match point. The victory was scored by the last-minute determination of a veteran player to give everything to win.

Keyed to a High Pitch.

Cochet rarely shows emotion, but he was wildly excited and giving his best at the finish. Keyed to a high pitch, he performed some of his old time feats in the way of hitting. The crowd cheered him madly when he scored the final point and Martin Plaa, the professional trainer, threw his arms about him and kissed him.

The Davis Cup, one of the few highly prized pieces of silver left in this inflated monetary world, now goes to England. It does not look safe there even from possible French invasion. France, which lost an opportunity to tie the American record of seven successive Davis Cup victories, could not have lost in a more thrilling manner.

The United States and Australia will have a healthy rival in France in the fight to enter the challenge round next year. Young players such as Merlin are coming along, the Borotra-Brugnon combination is still playing doubles in a way rivaled only by George Lott and John Van Ryn, and Cochet is still capable of amazing feats.

July 31, 1933

AMERICAN WIGHTMAN CUP TEAM, DONOR OF TROPHY AND OFFICIALS AT FOREST HILLS.

Times Wide World Photo.

Louis J. Carruthers, Member of Cup Committee; Miss Alice Marble, Mrs. John Van Ryn, Miss Helen Jacobs, Mrs. George W. Wightman, Who Gave Cup; Miss Sarah Palfrey, Miss Carolin Babcock and Julian S. Myrick, Chairman of Cup Committee.

U. S. WOMEN ANNEX WIGHTMAN CUP, 4-3, FOR 3D YEAR IN ROW

Miss Jacobs Clinches Series With British by Downing Miss Scriven in 3 Sets.

GAME RALLY BY LOSERS

Invading Tennis Stars Make Strong Fight After Trailing by 3-0 Margin.

MISS ROUND IS A WINNER

Registers Triumph Over Miss Palfrey—Miss Nuthall Scores— Mrs. Moody on Sidelines.

By ALLISON DANZIG.

Standing off a dangerous rally by the British, the crippled United States Wightman Cup team won the women's international tennis trophy for the third year in a row at Forest Hills yesterday. The final score was 4—3.

The home forces triumphed despite the absence of Mrs. Helen Wills Moody and the fact that they were further handicapped by the inability of Miss Alice Marble to play in the singles.

To Miss Helen Jacobs of Berkeley, Cal., the national champion, fell the honor and the herculean task of clinching the victory for America after Miss Sarah Palfrey and Miss Carolin Babcock had failed in their substitute rôles to stem the oncoming rush of the aroused English players.

With a gallery of 5,000 spectators looking on in suspense, Miss Jacobs herself appeared to be tottering on the precipice of defeat.

Miss Margaret (Peggy) Scriven led her at 5—3 in the deciding set of the final singles match. So skilfully had the hard-hitting, left-handed British lass broken up the American's game that it seemed almost certain that she, too, should be engulfed in the uprising of John Bull's courageous daughters.

Onlookers Not Optimistic.

Victory for Miss Scriven would completely erase the 3-0 lead that the defending team had piled up on the opening day. There was hardly a person in the West Side Tennis Club Stadium who entertained the remotest hope that this victory could be denied the plucky English girl with her awkward, flail-like forehand.

But with the score at 30—all in the ninth game and Miss Scriven only 2 points away from winning, Miss Jacobs showed her championship mettle with an exhibition of fortitude and resourcefulness under stress that has seldom been equaled in these international team matches.

No less than four times the American stood within two strokes of defeat, once in this ninth game and three times more in the tenth.

But valiantly as Miss Scriven fought to get those 2 points, cleverly as she alternated in the use of hard, jolting drives and soft, high floaters to her opponent's backhand, she could never get any closer to victory.

Runs Through Four Games.

Hanging on grimly, meeting her rival at her own pat-ball tactics and taking to the net when necessary, the game California girl stirred the intensely worked-up gallery to a frenzy of delight by running through four successive games to win the tense struggle. The score was 5—7, 6—2, 7—5.

A great sigh of relief went up from the stands as Miss Scriven's last drive overreached the base line. It meant the end of a day of suspense.

Also it meant the seventh victory for the United States in the eleven times that the cup has been played for and, in addition, it marked the first time in the history of the competition that either country has won the trophy three years running.

At the outset of the afternoon's proceedings scarcely any one conceded the invading forces the barest chance of salvaging the series. But when Miss Babcock, playing her first Wightman Cup match, went down before the cannonading drives of Miss Betty Nuthall at 1—6, 6—1, 6—3, the feeling of security did not run so high.

Replaces Miss Marble.

The Los Angeles girl was substituting for Miss Marble, who had played herself to exhaustion at East Hampton and was not in the condition to assume the burden of a singles assignment.

Next Miss Palfrey and Miss Dorothy Round went on the court. Here was the match that the gallery had been waiting for. Miss Palfrey had completely won over the stands with the magnificent manner in which she had filled in for the injured Mrs. Moody against Miss Scriven on Friday. The ovation that was tendered her as she appeared on the centre turf testified to the popularity of her victory.

Here was the 20-year-old girl again to undertake the task of defeating the player who had wrested a set from Mrs. Moody at Wimbledon this year. The stadium probably would have held a considerable larger number of spectators had Mrs. Moody been able to assume her allotted part in the play and face her dangerous rival at Wimbledon. But next to this, there is probably no other match that the gallery would have relished more than the meeting between Miss Palfrey and Miss Round.

Battle Provides Thrills.

They were not disappointed, except in the score. Miss Round, a vastly improved player over the one who lost to Miss Jacobs on Friday, won at 6—4, 10—8, but only after a thrilling battle between classic stylists.

Beaten though she was, Miss Palfrey lost nothing in lustre. The fidelity and acumen with which she stood up under the punishing forehand of her opponent to pull up from 3—5 to 6—5 stamped her as distinctly a player worthy of her international spurs.

So stirring was the struggle between Miss Round and Miss Palfrey that one forgot about the team issue hanging in the balance in the

Point Scores of Cup Matches

MISS NUTHALL VS. MISS BABCOCK.

First Set.

POINT SCORE.

								G.Pts.
Miss Nuthall	1	1	8	3	3	4	1	1—21
Miss Babcock	4	4	10	5	5	1	4	—6—33

STROKE ANALYSIS.

	N.	O.	P.	SA.	DF.
Miss Nuthall	6	18	2	0	4
Miss Babcock	8	10	3	2	1

Second Set.

POINT SCORE.

							G.Pts.
Miss Nuthall	4	6	5	4	4	1	5—6—.5
Miss Babcock	0	4	3	0	2	4	3—1—16

STROKE ANALYSIS.

	N.	O.	P.	SA.	DF.
Miss Nuthall	3	8	6	1	1
Miss Babcock	5	17	4	0	0

Third Set.

POINT SCORE.

									G.Pts.
Miss Nuthall	4	4	2	4	4	4	4	1	4—6—31
Miss Babcock	0	6	4	2	2	1	1	4	0—3—29

STROKE ANALYSIS.

	N.	O.	P.	SA.	DF.
Miss Nuthall	6	10	10	0	1
Miss Babcock	10	11	3	0	0

Recapitulation.

	N.	O.	P.	SA.	DF.
Miss Nuthall	15	36	18	1	6
Miss Babcock	23	38	10	2	1
	E.	EP.	TP.	G.	Sets.
Miss Nuthall	57	19	81	13	2
Miss Babcock	62	12	69	10	1

Miss Babcock started service.

Umpire—Harry T. Mattice. Time of match—57 minutes.

MISS ROUND VS. MISS PALFREY.

First Set.

POINT SCORE.

										G.Pts.
Miss Round	4	1	2	8	4	0	3	4	4	5—6 35
Miss Palfrey	2	4	4	6	2	4	5	2	1	3—4 33

STROKE ANALYSIS.

	N.	O.	P.	S.A.	D.F.
Miss Round	10	16	6	0	1
Miss Palfrey	12	16	6	0	1

Second Set.

POINT SCORE.

Miss Round— G.Pts.
1 4 4 4 2 4 4 4 3 0 2 4 8 2 4 2 5 6—10 63
Miss Palfrey—
4 2 6 2 4 1 2 2 5 4 4 0 6 4 1 4 3 4— 8 58

STROKE ANALYSIS.

	N.	O.	P.	S.A.	D.F.
Miss Round	20	16	18	1	1
Miss Palfrey	21	22	21	0	1

Recapitulation.

	N.	O.	P.	S.A.	D.F.
Miss Round	30	32	24	1	2
Miss Palfrey	33	38	27	0	2
	E.	E.P.	T.P.	G.	Sets.
Miss Round	64	25	98	16	2
Miss Palfrey	73	27	91	12	0

Miss Round started service.

Umpire—Benjamin H. Dwight. Time of match—1:05.

MISS JACOBS VS. MISS SCRIVEN.

First Set.

POINT SCORE.

Miss Jacobs— G.Pts.
3 4 4 4 3 4 4 1 2 2 2 1—5—34
Miss Scriven—
5 1 0 2 5 1 0 4 4 4 4 4—7—34

STROKE ANALYSIS.

	N.	O.	P.	SA.	DF.
Miss Jacobs	11	10	6	4	0
Miss Scriven	10	14	13	0	0

Second Set.

POINT SCORE.

								G.Pts.
Miss Jacobs	4	5	0	4	4	0	4	4—6—25
Miss Scriven	2	3	4	2	1	4	0	1—2—17

STROKE ANALYSIS.

	N.	O.	P.	SA.	DF.
Miss Jacobs	10	5	6	0	1
Miss Scriven	8	11	1	0	0

Third Set.

POINT SCORE.

G.Pts.
Miss Jacobs—
4 1 1 3 4 6 3 1 4 5 4 4—7—40
Miss Scriven—
0 4 4 5 1 4 5 4 2 3 2 0—5—34

STROKE ANALYSIS.

	N.	O.	P.	SA.	DF.
Miss Jacobs	8	15	4	1	1
Miss Scriven	15	19	10	0	1

Recapitulation.

	N.	O.	P.	SA.	DF.
Miss Jacobs	29	30	16	5	2
Miss Scriven	33	44	24	0	1
	E.	EP.	TP.	G.	Sets.
Miss Jacobs	61	21	90	18	2
Miss Scriven	78	24	85	14	1

Miss Jacobs started service.

Umpire—J. Shaw. Time of match—1:17.

enthusiasm and excitement occasioned by the brilliant passages of strokes.

But once the two players had left the enclosure the stands were faced with the reality of the team score, which was taking on a different complexion in alarming fashion.

The United States was now leading by the bare margin of 3 to 2, with two more matches to be played. With Mrs. Moody out of the picture and Miss Marble's condition anything but reassuring, it was evident that little hope could be held out for an American victory in the doubles. The die must be cast in the singles match between Miss Jacobs and Miss Scriven.

Miss Jacobs Falters.

It can be imagined, then, what were the sensations of the crowd as Miss Jacobs, after establishing the commanding lead of 5–2 in the opening set, frittered away her opportunity and yielded five games in a row.

The tension was eased somewhat as the American champion equalized by taking the second chapter, but Miss Scriven adopted different tactics after the rest period and they succeeded in alarming fashion.

Abjuring the rapacious speed with which she had been belaboring the ball for every bit of length of the court and concentrating on undermining the American's backhand with soft, high-bounding returns, Miss Scriven went to the front at 3–1. Miss Jacobs was not only faltering badly on the left but her chop was functioning poorly and she could not get to the net, so deadly were her opponent's passing shots.

The American managed to pull up to 3-all as her service came to her rescue and Miss Scriven wasted golden opportunities after opening up glaring gaps in Miss Jacobs's court with her clever tactics. But the English girl braced, reduced her errors to a minimum in almost interminable rallies and went ahead to 5—3.

Changes Her Tactics.

The match seemed as good as lost now to the United States and with it the cup. But Miss Jacobs, keeping stout heart when all about her were becoming faint-hearted, changed her tactics too and won a great strategic victory.

Miss Scriven, with victory apparently in her grasp, made the mistake of switching back to her hard-driving game, while Miss Jacobs resorted to safety measures. The former lost the ninth game through her errors, as she forced to make the kill, and her concentration and confidence were shaken badly.

With the tenth game she went back to the soft-ball style of play, but her control was shaken and Miss Jacobs outsteadied her in the painfully long exchanges from back court.

Not only was the American the steadier now, but she fenced the more skillfully for position and asserted her attacking shots when she had exacted her opening.

When the American pulled out the eleventh game from 0—30 it was obvious that Miss Scriven had lost a magnificent battle. Shaken badly and unable to steady her hand, she not only yielded four straight points from 30—0 but dropped her own service at love in the tenth.

Thus was the Wightman Cup won and lost for 1933 in what must be set down as the most dramatic series in the eleven years' history of this splendid competition.

British Take Doubles.

As was anticipated, the British won the concluding doubles, in which Miss Nuthall and Miss Freda James defeated Miss Marble and Mrs. John Van Ryn, the former Marjorie Gladman, 7—5, 6—2.

There is a possibility that had Miss Jacobs been beaten by Miss Scriven, the United States might still have won the cup, for Mrs. Moody was on hand, prepared to come to the aid of the defense should the verdict rest upon the seventh match. The celebrated Californian appeared in a marquee box attired in her tennis costume.

Julian S. Myrick, chairman of the Wightman Cup Committee of the United States Lawn Tennis Association, and Mrs. George W. Wightman, the acting team captain, had strongly urged Mrs. Moody against playing under any circumstances.

The world's premier player was satisfied to remain out should the United States win one of the three singles yesterday but she insisted upon playing in the event that the issue was to be settled with the final doubles.

Happily for Mrs. Moody's health, it was not necessary for her to take to the courts. The condition of her strained back had improved with a day of rest, but her friends and counselors were opposed to her running the risk of bringing on complications by playing in the series.

Although forced out of the international matches for the first time since 1926, when she underwent an operation for appendicitis, Mrs. Moody plans to compete in the national singles starting at Forest Hills Aug. 14. Until that week, then, will be deferred the prospect of another meeting between her and Miss Round.

The showing of the British girl yesterday put an entirely different complexion on this anticipated meeting. After her disappointing performance against Miss Jacobs on Friday it was difficult to conceive how she could make any headway at all against so savage a barrage as Mrs. Moody lays down upon the court.

But against Miss Palfrey, Miss Round showed her true mettle, with her backhand standing forth as worthy of the steel of the Wimbledon champion. Indeed, she was hardly to be recognized as the same player at all.

Where on Friday she had been nervous and lacking in confidence and patchy in her hitting, yesterday Miss Round attacked boldly and masterfully from both sides and played her cards so coolly and headily that the Boston girl's diversified offense was unavailing against her.

Miss Palfrey was every bit the player she was against Miss Scriven and her generalship was no less consummate, but her weapons were not quite equal to standing up under the terrific pressure that Miss Round maintained.

Not only Miss Round, but every member of the visiting team played tennis of a superior grade in the closing session. The change in the weather undoubtedly accounted in large part for their movement.

It was a perfect day for tennis, with a warm sun overhead and fast, dry turf under foot, and the quality of the play was uniformly of a high standard throughout the afternoon. All three of the singles matches developed into tense struggles that had the gallery wrought up to a high pitch.

The fluctuating turns of fortune in each battle, together with the fierceness with which these young women gave their all in the effort to save the day for their country, made the session a memorable one in Wightman Cup annals.

August 6, 1933

MISS JACOBS WINS WHEN MRS. MOODY DEFAULTS IN 3D SET

8,000 at Final of U. S. Tennis See 'Queen of Courts' Come to End of Long Reign.

SAYS PAIN WEAKENED HER

By ALLISON DANZIG.

Mrs. Helen Wills Moody no longer rules the courts.

The reign of the world's pre-eminent woman tennis player, the most absolute in the annals of the game, came to an end at Forest Hills yesterday under dramatic circumstances that have been paralleled only once in the forty-six-year history of the national championship.

With the score standing 3—0 against her in the third set of her punishing final-round match with Miss Helen Jacobs, the defending titleholder, Mrs. Moody walked over to the umpire's chair and informed him that she was unable to play any longer.

The crowd of 8,000 spectators, thrilled by the magnificent play of Miss Jacobs and tingling with the expectancy of seeing Mrs. Moody beaten for the first time on any court since 1926, had little inkling of the nature of Mrs. Moody's remarks.

Incident in 1921 Recalled.

It was not until the celebrated Californian took up her blue sweater and Miss Jacobs rushed to her to plead that she continue, that the gallery sensed the significance of her action.

Mrs. Moody defaulted under physical distress, just as Mlle. Suzanne Lenglen had defaulted to Mrs. Molla Mallory in the second set of their second-round championship match at Forest Hills in 1921.

Exhausted by the terrific struggle that had been waged in a fourteen-game first set and feeling that she was on the point of fainting from the pain in her injured back, Mrs. Moody retired from the court and Miss Jacobs, amid the wild acclaim of the spectators, was declared the winner by 8—6, 3—6, 3—0 and default.

Mrs. Moody's Statement.

The following statement was given out by Mrs. Moody following the match:

In the third set of my singles match I felt as if I were going to faint because of pain in my back and hip and a complete numbness of my right leg.

The match was long and by defaulting I do not wish to detract from the excellence of Miss Jacobs's play.

I feel that I have spoiled the finish of the national championship, and wish that I had followed the advice of my doctor and returned to California. I still feel that I did right in withdrawing because I felt that I was on the verge of a collapse on the court.

Retains Her Title.

Thus came to a conclusion the most exciting women's tournament in years, with Mrs. Moody beaten for the first time in the championship since 1922 and Miss Jacobs established the titleholder for the second successive year. It was not, however, the end of the day's dramatic developments.

After it had been announced that Mrs. Moody would be unable to appear with Miss Elizabeth Ryan for the final round of the doubles against Miss Betty Nuthall and Miss Freda James of England, who won the title by default, an exhibition match was put on. Miss Alice Marble of San Francisco substituted for Mrs. Moody as Miss Ryan's partner against the British team.

With the score standing at 4-all in the second set of the exhibition after the American pair had won the first set at 6—4, Miss Nuthall hit an overhead smash. The ball, traveling too fast for Miss Marble to get out of the way or to guard herself, struck the California girl in the eye.

Suffers Painful Injury.

Miss Marble fell to the ground and there was great concern in the stands as officials and players rushed to her aid. After a few minutes, Rufus Davis, the umpire, announced that Miss Marble had suffered a painful injury and that Miss Nuthall and Miss James again had won by default.

It was a day such as will not soon be forgotten by those who sat in the stadium of the West Side Tennis Club. The officials of the club and of the United States Lawn Tennis Association, harried by the record-breaking postponements brought on by rain, almost sighed with relief to have the tournament finally over with, a week later than scheduled.

When Mrs. Moody lost a set last Sunday to Miss Nuthall, the first she has yielded in this country since 1926, there was enough excitement to have made this tournament stand out indelibly.

But it was nothing compared to the stir created yesterday by the defeat of the player who had stood invincibly against the best in the world since 1927.

It was likened to the defeat of William Tilden in the men's championship at Forest Hills by Henri Cochet of France in 1926.

In spite of the fact that it was known Mrs. Moody was not in the condition to show the full strength of her hand, it was difficult to believe that the player who had held such absolute sway could have met her master.

Miss Jacobs had never been able to make the slightest headway against her, and even the defending champion's victory over Miss Round in the semi-finals of Miss Round by Friday failed to shake the faith in Mrs. Moody's capacity to come through to the title.

Indeed, the general feeling was that Mrs. Moody's chances of victory in the final were improved by the elimination of Miss Round by Miss Jacobs. That furnishes an indication of how little it was thought the former champion had to fear from her California rival.

Mrs. Moody Not at Best.

The stunning reversal that came about is to be explained on two scores. First, it would be a misrepresentation to say that Mrs. Moody was at her best.

To any one who has watched the great Californian in action in the past it was obvious from the outset that she was not hitting with anything like her accustomed severity. The speed that had subdued her opponents and left them with a feeling of hopelessness even before they went on the court simply was not at Mrs. Moody's command yesterday.

There was plenty of length to her shots and for the first two sets she was giving herself unstintingly in the desperate work of plugging up the gaps in her court before Miss Jacobs's inexorable forcing shots. But so far as her offense was concerned, Mrs. Moody was not to be recognized as the player of former years. In the final set her defense, too, folded up as she came to the end of her physical resources.

Having made allowances for the shortcomings in Mrs. Moody's preparedness for so strenuous an ordeal, it is now to be set down that these shortcomings were accentuated by the brilliance of Miss Jacobs's play.

More Dangerous Foe.

The Berkeley girl whom Mrs. Moody faced yesterday was a far more dangerous opponent than she had been in any of their previous encounters.

Uncertain with her forehand, erratic at the net and lacking in confidence all through the season, Miss Jacobs was almost ignored from the start of the championship.

There was some question, too, of whether she had the stamina to undergo the rigors of championship match play, for at Seabright she had fainted at her hotel and had been on the verge of a collapse after being defeated by Miss Sarah Palfrey in the final.

But against Mrs. Moody, Miss Jacobs was a great player, fighting with the heart of a champion. If she was in distress from her exertions, she never showed it until the second set, when Mrs. Moody's use of the drop-shot compelled her to do a tremendous amount of running.

Against Miss Round, it was Miss Jacobs's forehand chop that carried the day. Yesterday that chop was again tremendously important, remarkable for its uniform deep length and its accuracy.

But the Berkeley girl had other telling weapons also. Her service was a big help, pulling her out of holes repeatedly in the bitterly fought first set, and her volleying and overhead smashing were the most vivid seen in the tournament.

Mrs. Moody's lack of length on her lobs was partly responsible for the deadliness of Miss Jacobs's overhead hitting. But even on the deeper tosses, the champion handled the difficult shots well and her volley was seldom to be denied.

Hard Battle Forecast.

At the very start of the match it was apparent that Mrs. Moody had a battle on her hands. Miss Jacobs was hardly missing a thing from the back of the court and she was playing the ball so deep and changing direction with such fine judgment that Mrs. Moody was seldom given the chance to get set for her stroke.

Under pressure at her base line and forced to scramble for almost every ball that came over, Mrs. Moody had no alternative but to throw herself into the struggle without regard for her weakened back.

Almost every rally was prolonged and the fur fairly flew without a let-up in that prolonged opening set.

Miss Jacobs was not only getting fully as good length on her chop and her backhand as was her opponent but she was hitting the more crisply of the two. The lack of her usual drastic pace was plainly noticeable in Mrs. Moody's drives, and Miss Jacobs, instead of being hurried, had the time to get into position and time her shots with precision.

Not only was the defending champion holding her own from the back of the court but the depth of her drives opened the way for safe advances to the net. There

STARS BEFORE NATIONAL CHAMPIONSHIP FINAL YESTERDAY.

Times Wide World Photo.

Holcombe Ward, Vice President of the United States Lawn Tennis Association; Miss Helen Jacobs and Mrs. Helen Wills Moody.

she was seldom to be denied, for Mrs. Moody's lobs were too short and Miss Jacobs hammered them down into the corners time and again.

The struggle was so even in this set that it was impossible to foretell the winner, though it was obvious enough that Mrs. Moody's lasting powers were to be tested to the limit. Miss Jacobs went into a 3-1 lead and Mrs. Moody got back on even terms at 3-all.

Games Follow Service.

From that point on games followed service until Miss Jacobs, after being denied at set-point in the tenth game, broke through in the fourteenth. In three games in this set Mrs. Moody had a commanding lead only to dissipate them or rather to yield to the power of Miss Jacobs's service.

In the opening game Mrs. Moody was ahead at 40—15. In the ninth game she held a 40—0 advantage, and Miss Jacobs also pulled out the eleventh after being down 0—30.

The regularity with which Miss Jacobs extricated herself from difficulties must have had a disturbing effect upon her opponent.

Miss Jacobs was rising to brilliant heights in making these pull-ups, but Mrs. Moody's inability to lunge for services that she might have returned also ruined her opportunities.

When the former champion finally weakened and yielded the last two games of the set on errors, it was thought that she had done her best for the day and that she would be at the mercy of her opponent in the second set. But in this chapter Mrs. Moody, far from being resigned to defeat, changed her tactics and the tide turned.

Instead of hitting for length as she had been doing in the first set, Mrs. Moody now resorted to drop shots, alternately playing the ball short and deep.

Miss Jacobs was now put on the defensive and was kept on the run between her baseline and the net in pursuit of trap shots and lobs.

The strain told on the champion, particularly after the tremendous amount of energy she had used up in the first chapter, and Mrs. Moody quickly went ahead at 3-0.

It was thought that Miss Jacobs would allow the set to go, having dropped her service twice. But the champion got her second wind and came back to tie the score at 3-all.

Mrs. Moody was resorting to drop shots perhaps too frequently now and Miss Jacobs, on the watch for them, was not caught out of position behind her baseline.

But after drawing level, Miss Jacobs was sorely fatigued and was able to offer little opposition, even against her tiring opponent. Mrs. Moody took the next three games to square the match and when the players left the court for a ten-minute intermission it appeared to be either's match.

End Soon in Sight.

But the first game of the final set was all that was needed to reveal that Mrs. Moody's chances of carrying the day were remote. Two double faults from her racquet gave the gallery an inkling of her weakened condition, and when Miss Jacobs, hitting with confidence and great severity, took the second game from 0—30 the end was in sight.

On the last point of this game Mrs. Moody had an easy shot on her forehand and when she feebly put the ball into the bottom of the net there was not the slightest doubt of her helplessness.

In the third game she made two weak efforts to get to the net, but each time Miss Jacobs passed her magnificently, once from the forehand and once from the backhand, and the last shot of the match was a forehand drive by Mrs. Moody that overreached the line.

Trailing at 0—3 on two service breaks, Mrs. Moody's defeat was now seen to be a matter of only a few more minutes. It came sooner than any one expected, for the former champion defaulted at this point.

It was unfortunate that Miss Jacobs had to be denied the satisfaction of winning the match in the only manner that a player finds satisfactory, and there can be no question that she would have won it with her racquet had the play gone on to its logical conclusion.

Views Are Varying.

There were some who thought that Mrs. Moody might have continued, if only to go through the motions of playing, but on the other hand the fact must be faced that Mrs. Moody was running the risk of injuring herself permanently by going on in her weakened condition and with her back injury.

Perhaps it would have been for the best if she had followed her

doctor's orders during the Wightman Cup matches and given up tennis for the year. At any rate, she had the courage to undertake to play through the tournament, and as keen as is the regret that the match had to come to such an ending, it is tempered by the thought of what might have been the consequences had Mrs. Moody seen the third set through to an end.

After rushing out through one of the rear underground portals of the stadium, Miss Jacobs came back on the court to receive the championship trophy.

The tumultuous cheering with which she was greeted testified to the gallery's appreciation of her superb performance and must have wiped out any disappointment she felt over the untimely end of the match.

Miss Jacobs had received Mrs. Moody's decision with sympathy and the finest sportsmanship and her manner of conducting herself added to the popularity of her victory.

Holcombe Ward, vice president of the United States Lawn Tennis Association, acting in behalf of Harry S. Knox, the president, who lives on the Pacific coast, presented the yearly trophy to Miss Jacobs and also the perpetual trophy, filled with American Beauty roses.

Mrs. Moody will not go to Brookline for the national mixed doubles. She probably will leave for California shortly.

Unbeaten in Event since 1922.

Not since the first year in which she competed for the women's title had Mrs. Moody met defeat in the championship. That was in 1922, when she was runner-up to Mrs. Mallory.

In 1923, Mrs. Moody—then Helen Wills—wrested the title from the latter, retained it in 1924 and 1925 and allowed it to go undefended in 1926, after undergoing an operation for appendicitis in Europe.

In 1927 Mrs. Moody came back to regain the crown and has won it every year since, with the exception of 1930 and 1932, when she did not participate in the championship.

With seven victories to her credit, she was expected yesterday to equal the record of eight triumphs set by Mrs. Mallory.

The player whom Miss Jacobs frustrated yesterday had not lost a set here or abroad from 1927 until Miss Round took the second chapter from her at Wimbledon this year.

She had not lost a set in our championship since the 1925 final, when she was carried into three sets by Miss Kathleen McKane and the last time she had been defeated was at Rye in August, 1926. Mrs. Mallory that year vanquished her in three sets in the semi-finals of the New York State championship at the Westchester-Biltmore Country Club, a week after Miss Ryan had defeated her in the final at Seabright in two sets.

In all those six years of Mrs. Moody's invincibility from 1927 on, Miss Jacobs had never succeeded in taking a set from her. Their first big meeting came in 1927 when Miss Jacobs, competing in the championship for the first time, reached the semi-finals and there lost to Mrs. Moody at 6—0, 6—2.

Scored in Straight Sets.

The following year they met in the final of our championship, and again Mrs. Moody won by the decisive margin of 6—2, 6—1. In 1929 they faced each other in the final at Wimbledon, and the verdict was 6—1, 6—2.

In 1931, Mrs. Moody scored her most crushing victory of all, defeat-

ing Miss Jacobs in love sets in the final at Seabright. In their last previous match, Mrs. Moody won the Wimbledon championship by defeating her California rival in the concluding round, 6—3, 6—1.

The overwhelming margin of Mrs. Moody's supremacy in all of these meetings was responsible in large part for the fact that she was established so strong a favorite yesterday. Even if she were not physically at her peak, it was figured that her weapons were sufficient to encompass the downfall of the Berkeley girl again.

The point score and stroke analysis of the match between Mrs. Moody and Miss Jacobs follow:

FIRST SET.

Point Score.

		Pts.	G.
Miss Jacobs	5 2 4 4 1 0 4 2 6 3 4 1 4 4	44.	8
Mrs. Moody	3 4 2 2 4 4 0 4 4 5 2 4 2 2	42.	6

Stroke Analysis.

	N.	O.	Pl.	SA.DF.
Miss Jacobs	18	19	9	2 1
Mrs. Moody	15	16	3	1 1

SECOND SET.

Point Score.

		Pts.	G.
Miss Jacobs	3 1 0 5 4 5 4 2 2	26.	3
Mrs. Moody	5 4 4 3 0 3 6 4 4	33.	6

Stroke Analysis.

	N.	O.	Pl.	SA.DF.
Miss Jacobs	5	17	5	1 3
Mrs. Moody	9	9	8	0 1

THIRD SET.

Point Score.

		Pts.	G.
Miss Jacobs	4 4 4	12.	3
Mrs. Moody	2 2 1	5.	0

Stroke Analysis.

	N.	O.	Pl.	SA.DF.
Miss Jacobs	2	3	3	0 0
Mrs. Moody	1	6	0	0 2

RECAPITULATION.

	N.	O.	Pl.	SA.DF.
Miss Jacobs	25	39	17	3 4
Mrs. Moody	25	31	11	1 5

	E.	EP.	TP.	G.Sets.
Miss Jacobs	64	20	82	14 2
Mrs. Moody	61	12	80	12 1

Miss Jacobs served first.
Umpire—Benjamin H. Dwight. Time of match—1:02.

August 27, 1933

PERRY TURNS BACK CRAWFORD IN FINAL

Rallies Brilliantly to Down Australian Ace for Tennis Title of U. S.

11,000 SEE THE MATCH

First Briton to Win Crown in 30 Years Scores by 6-3, 11-13, 4-6, 6-0, 6-1.

By ALLISON DANZIG.

For the first time in thirty years, the United States tennis championship has been won by a player from the British Isles.

Frederick J. Perry, England's Davis Cup hero of the year, carried off the crown at Forest Hills yesterday by overcoming Jack Crawford of Australia in five sets. The score was 6—3, 11—13, 4—6, 6—0, 6—1.

Of all the year's many disappointments, none was perhaps more bitter to the vanquished than was the defeat of Crawford. Champion of England, France and his own country, he saw his quest of a "grand slam" frustrated.

Leading by two sets to one and apparently holding his opponent in check, Crawford, the player who had come to be regarded as the invincible iron man of the courts,

Mrs. Moody's Tennis Record.

1921—Won girls' national singles championship.

1922—Won girls' national singles championship.

1923—Won women's national singles championship; member of American Wightman Cup team.

1924—Won women's national singles championship; won women's doubles championship with Mrs. George W. Wightman; won national mixed doubles championship with Vincent Richards; won Olympic singles championship; won Olympic doubles championship with Mrs. Wightman; lost in Wimbledon singles championship in final round, but won doubles title with Mrs. Wightman; member of American Wightman Cup team.

1925—Won women's national singles championship; won women's national doubles championship with Miss Mary K. Browne; member of American Wightman Cup team.

1926—Won singles and doubles matches in international tennis match with France at Paris. Did not compete in nationals or Wightman Cup play.

1927—Won women's national singles championship; won Wimbledon singles championship; member of Wightman Cup team.

1928—Won women's national singles championship; won national doubles championship with Mrs. Wightman; won national mixed doubles with John B. Hawkes of Australia; won Wimbledon singles championship; member of Wightman Cup team.

1929—Won women's national singles championship; won Wimbledon singles championship; member of Wightman Cup team.

1930—Won Wimbledon singles championship; member of Wightman Cup team. Did not compete in nationals.

1931—Won women's national singles championship; member of Wightman Cup team.

1932—Won Wimbledon singles championship; member of Wightman Cup team. Did not compete in nationals.

1933—Won Wimbledon singles championship; member of Wightman Cup team, but did not play.

came back after the rest period to run into an avalanche of blistering drives that had him reeling on the defensive.

Look On in Amazement.

The gallery of 11,000 spectators that turned out for this all-foreign final looked on in amazement at the almost incredible turn the play had taken. But it was not nearly as dazed as was Crawford.

Listless, faltering in his movements and obviously in physical distress, the Australian was utterly at the mercy of his opponent as the latter swept through a love set in thirteen minutes. In fifteen minutes more the match ended with Crawford on the verge of collapse. The giant of the courts had been hammered into a mere shell of himself and for all of his gameness could win only one of the last thirteen games of the match.

Two hours and eight minutes after Benjamin H. Dwight had called play from the umpire's chair, Perry joyfully threw his racquet high into the air, hurdled the net into the arms of his almost tottering opponent and stood acclaimed as the champion of the United States.

Collapse Is Inexplicable.

As inexplicable as was the collapse of Crawford, who ruled the general favorite to win, too much praise cannot be given Perry for his victory. He is the first Briton to gain the championship final since Hugh L. Doherty, who won in 1903.

The Australian manifestly was in bad shape physically in the last two sets and said that he felt himself in a daze at the end of the third chapter. The tremendous toll taken of his strength in warding off Perry's strokes was largely responsible, even though he had appeared to be in distress in his other matches.

Admittedly, the British youth would never have had such a procession at the end had Crawford not been in such poor condition. Even when the Australian was in the plentitude of his powers, however, it was all he could do to hold his swift-moving and sharp-hitting opponent on even terms.

Crawford went into this match with the most vaunted ground strokes in amateur tennis and with a backhand that was thought to have no equal in its steadfastness. Perry proved differently, at least for this day.

Concentrates on Backhand.

With magnificent disdain, the dynamic British ace set about from the start to reduce his opponent's strongest citadel. It was the concentration of his attack upon Crawford's backhand that forced the Australian to yield the first set.

Crawford actually found it necessary at times to leave his baseline and go to the net, so untenable was his back court in the face of the other's forcing drives.

So much depth did Perry have on his shots, so everlastingly was he making the chalk fly on the corners, that the Australian was desperately pressed to keep the ball in play with his more tempered and less daring strokes.

This same situation obtained in the bitterly prolonged second set, which lasted an hour and two minutes, and it was not until the twenty-third game of this chapter that Crawford ever held any kind of a lead in the match after winning the opening game on service.

Perry led at 3—1 in this set, and at that stage Crawford's backers were shaking their heads in despair, wondering whether he was to have even the satisfaction of winning a set.

Times Wide World Photo.

PRESENTATION OF TROPHY AT FOREST HILLS.
Fred Perry Receiving Prize From Holcombe Ward, Vice President of the United States Lawn Tennis Association, While Jack Crawford Looks On.

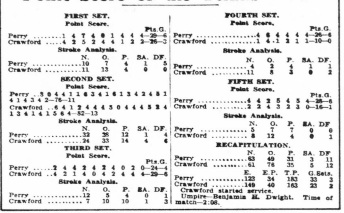

Point Score of the Tennis Final

FIRST SET.
Point Score.

		Pts.G.
Perry	1 4 7 4 0 1 4 4	4—29—6
Crawford	4 2 5 2 4 4 1 2	2—26—3

Stroke Analysis.

	N.	O.	P.	SA.	DF.
Perry	10	7	4	1	5
Crawford	11	13	4	0	0

SECOND SET.
Point Score.

| Perry ..... | 3 0 4 4 1 1 6 3 4 1 6 1 3 4 2 4 5 1 |
| 4 1 4 3 4 2—7 6—11 |
| Crawford .. | 6 4 1 2 4 4 4 5 0 4 4 4 5 2 4 |
| 1 3 4 1 4 1 5 6 4—8 2—13 |

Stroke Analysis.

	N.	O.	P.	SA.	DF.
Perry	32	38	12	1	9
Crawford	24	33	14	4	6

THIRD SET.
Point Score.

		Pts.G.
Perry	2 4 4 2 4 2 4 0 2	0—24—4
Crawford ..	4 2 1 4 4 2 4 4	4—29—6

Stroke Analysis.

	N.	O.	P.	SA.	DF.
Perry	12	5	4	0	1
Crawford	7	10	10	1	3

FOURTH SET.
Point Score.

		Pts.G.
Perry	4 6 4 4 4	4—26—6
Crawford	1 4 .1 2 1	1—10—0

Stroke Analysis.

	N.	O.	P.	SA.	DF.
Perry	4	2	4	1	1
Crawford	11	8	3	0	2

FIFTH SET.
Point Score.

		Pts.G.
Perry	4 4 2 5 4 5	4—28—6
Crawford	2 2 4 3 2 3	0—16—1

Stroke Analysis.

	N.	O.	P.	SA.	DF.
Perry	5	7	7	0	0
Crawford	8	12	4	0	1

RECAPITULATION.

	N.	O.	P.	SA.	DF.
Perry	63	49	31	3	11
Crawford	61	76	35	5	12

	E.	E.P.	T.P.	G.Sets.
Perry	123	34	183	33	3
Crawford	149	40	163	23	2

Crawford started service.
Umpire—Benjamin H. Dwight. Time of match—2:08.

Perry Slackens the Pace.

Toward the end of this almost interminable set, Perry began to slacken pace just a bit, relieving the terrific pressure that Crawford had found himself under unceasingly from the outset. This gave the Australian the chance to assert himself and to take command. So dismally did his service fail him, as it did almost throughout the match, and so uneven was his control off the ground that Crawford repeatedly passed up opportunities.

It was not until he had lost his own service twice in a row, double faulting at game point each time, after first breaking through Perry's, that Crawford salvaged the set.

A remarkable recovery of a lob, one of the most phenomenal feats of the tournament, saved the twenty-third game for him. Perry, who could not get over the shock, double faulted and was broken through.

It was felt that the player who won this set would win the match, and that feeling became more pronounced as the third chapter got under way. Crawford was continuing to double fault, but his ground strokes were now functioning beautifully.

His backhand was cutting a wide swath through Perry's court, and the English ace was now the one who was pressed to hold his ground, though he was giving little, until the very end.

With the score 30—40 against him in the ninth game, Perry allowed Crawford's return of service to go uncontested directly in front of him, thinking that the ball was out.

That mistake in judgment cost him his service game and appeared to have a disturbing effect upon his concentration, as Crawford took the next game at love for the set.

As the players left the court, all signs seemed to point to victory for the Australian. It was thought that Perry had shot his bolt and that he was becoming a little discouraged over the increasing adamancy of Crawford's defense and the stiffening pressure of his attack.

Then came the greatest shock of the tournament. Perry returned fired with ambition and with more vitality than he had showed at the outset, while Crawford was almost passive. He must have realized as early as this that he did not have enough left in reserve to carry on

to victory.

Perry Serves Brilliantly.

Serving like a streak, Perry won the first game of the fourth set at 15 and then came the rout. Three nets by Perry gave Crawford a 40-15 lead and after that he was almost blown off the court. His two double faults enabled Perry to pull out the second game and he took the next four with the loss of only five points.

Crawford was making little effort toward the end of this set and it was figured that he was saving himself for the fifth. So it was, but he had little to save. He yielded the second game on service after leading at 40—30, revived the hopes of his adherents as he broke through in the third and then came the final straw.

The fourth game was productive of some of the most magnificent shot-making of the match. Crawford went ahead at 40—30, but the effort drained the last bit of his reserve.

Crawford's three outs gave Perry the game, and from then on to the end Crawford was reeling groggily before the lightning smashes of Perry that almost tore the racquet from the Australian's hand in his baseline corners.

Play in a Gale.

Considering the fact that a strong gale was blowing down upon the court and often raising havoc with the timing of the strokes, the match brought out a remarkably fine grade of tennis worthy of the lustre of the two combatants.

Crawford did not play quite as good grade of tennis as he did against Sidney Wood and his service was lamentably at fault most of the time. But it should be remembered that he was facing an antagonist who was hitting with stabbing speed and depth to crowd the Australian's stroke.

Frankie Parker, young American star, defeated Vivian McGrath, youthful Australian famous for his two-handed backhand shot, in an exhibition match. The score was 6—0, 3—6, 7—5.

September 11, 1933

Perry Downs Crawford in Straight Sets, Capturing Australian Net Championship

By The Associated Press.

SYDNEY, Australia, Jan. 27.—Frederick J. Perry, star of the English Davis Cup team and United States singles champion, today furthered his claim to world tennis honors as he defeated Jack Crawford in straight sets in the final of the Australian championship.

Playing a dashing, faultless game, Perry won at 6–3, 7–5, 6–1. He also won the doubles title yesterday with his cup team-mate, G. P. Hughes.

It was the fourth meeting between the world's two ranking amateur players and the third victory for Perry. The Australian's only triumph came in an Australian-English series a few weeks ago.

It was in the Australian tournament last year that Crawford started a victory string which carried him to within one set of a "grand slam" in world tennis and it was

his conqueror of yesterday, Perry, who stopped him then.

After taking the Australian title last year Crawford won the French and then the Wimbledon crown and led Perry two sets to one in the United States final, only to wilt before the aggressive play of the Englishman. He lost the next two sets and the match.

With Ellsworth Vines and Henri Cochet now in the professional ranks, Perry ranks as the No. 1 amateur of the world, with a chance of winning the fourfold honors Crawford just missed in 1933.

Since England holds the Davis Cup and will play only in the challenge round late in July, Perry will be in a position to play his best in the French and Wimbledon championships and still have sufficient time to rest before defending the international trophy.

January 28, 1934

Henry W. (Bunny) Austin.   Times Wide World Photo.

VICTORY OF PERRY KEEPS DAVIS CUP

England's Ace Halts Shields, 6-4, 4-6, 6-2, 15-13, in Thriller at Wimbledon.

WOOD BEATEN BY AUSTIN

By FERDINAND KUHN Jr.
Special Cable to THE NEW YORK TIMES.

WIMBLEDON, England, July 31.—The quest that has taken American tennis teams across the Atlantic for seven long years ended in another failure on Wimbledon's historic centre court today.

Beneath a pitiless sun a crowd of 16,000 saw the English team win both singles matches from the Americans and keep the Davis Cup on this side of the ocean for another year. It was the first time in twenty-one years that the cup has been won on English soil. The final score in matches was four to one.

Frank Shields lost the deciding match to Fred Perry, but only after a titanic struggle that will live a long time in tennis history. Fighting with magnificent courage and not losing until he was at the point of exhaustion, Shields took the British champion to twenty-eight games in the final set before going out. The score was 6—4, 4—6, 6—2, 15—13.

Makes the Cup Secure.

Perry's victory made the cup secure for England, for two other matches out of five in the challenge round had been won on Saturday. Later today it was easy for Henry W. (Bunny) Austin to defeat Sidney B. Wood Jr. in a kind of an exhibition match, 6—4, 4—6, 9—6, 8—6, 6—3.

Then Princess Helena Victoria, the King's cousin, presented the gleaming silver bowl to Roper Barrett, non-playing captain of the British team, and thousands went home happy. Many of them did not fail to notice the Union Jack flying above the Stars and Stripes on the flagpole of the All England Club.

England—for so many years the world's underdog in international

sports—was sitting on top of the world.

The Americans' defeat today was not unexpected for they had been pushed into a desperate position by their two defeats Saturday. Perry's victory especially had been almost a foregone conclusion, but only those who knew Shields were prepared for the tremendous fight which the New York boy put up right to the bitter end.

Both Are Near Exhaustion.

Many times Shields seemed to have that agonizing fourth set within his grasp and he had Perry so exhausted that anything might have happened in a fifth. The set finally ended after an hour and one-quarter after both players were so tired that they seemed incapable of finding the stroke to finish it. It might have lasted until darkness fell and still those two might have gone on fighting.

Twice Perry got to the match point in the final game and twice Shields snatched it away from him. In the end Perry was the more exhausted of the two.

"That last set has taken twenty years off my life," said Perry as he walked off the court.

He struggled to the dressing room and there slumped down upon a bench almost too dazed to say a word.

Faces Many Obstacles.

Shields's performance was all the more wonderful because of the obstacles against him. He must have foot-faulted twenty times during the match. Toward the end calls from the foot-fault judge were so incessant that Shields seldom got to the net after his serve until the ball actually was being returned to him.

What effect it had upon his game one could only guess, but he never gave a word or gesture of complaint. Right to the end he behaved like a gallant sportsman and the crowd cheered him for it as he left the court.

Shields was such a great-hearted fighter today that somehow he could rise above the mistakes in his game. He wasn't playing badly; he was far better than he was on Saturday against Austin. His backhand was less unreliable than usual and one could feel the great effort he was making to control the ball.

But Perry had all the strokes with which to dictate the game and that meant for most of the match

that Shields was on the defensive. Naturally Perry attacked Shields's backhand relentlessly.

Forces American to Lose.

Again and again he would drive down to Shields's backhand corner until the American hit down or out to lose a rally. Shields invariably lobbed when he saw his man racing in and it was then that Perry collared many a point by beautiful smashing shots.

Perry's low, long drives were often a delight to watch. His passing shots were ready on forehand or backhand. If anything was wrong with his game today it was overcautiousness.

With a lead of three-love in the first set, Perry promised a quick ending, but it turned out to be a hard set for him. A curious thing about the match was the number of times that Perry came within a point of winning a game only to lose it and be forced to struggle through several deuces. But Shields's service had no terrors today and when Shields lost his service the first set was over.

Shields was steadier in the second set, which he won after some fine volleying. There were glaring weaknesses in Perry's strokes now, and the English champion seemed to be worrying about them. In the third set Shields was completely outclassed. No matter how hard he tried to volley he was almost always passed by Perry's glorious forehand drive across court. It seemed that the fourth set would go the same way when Perry rolled up a lead of 3—1.

But then Perry showed his overcautiousness again and gave Shields a chance to fight back. He lost his service to let Shields jump into a lead of 5—4. He won the next game with a fine smash to the baseline, making it 5-all. Now the match was locked into a grim, deathlike struggle, from which it seemed neither player could escape before nightfall.

The Pendulum Swings.

First one and then the other won

the advantage, but neither was able to conclude the set. Both were so tired it didn't matter much who was serving. Games went against service with monotonous regularity. There were many terrible strokes, but both were fighting their hardest—Shields not only fighting Perry but the foot-fault judge, whose barking "Fault!" would have got on the nerves of almost any other player.

Toward the end Perry was always in the lead and Shields had to find service aces to save himself. He began slipping and falling in leaping for Perry's passing shots, and finally Perry was within a stroke of the match on Shields's service.

Then came two match points which Shields saved and at last a beautiful passing shot which was too much for Shields as he ran in, full of courage, to volley.

With the cup lost to America, Wood appeared during the next match as if he didn't mind being beaten by Austin. There were times when he made Austin play his best, especially when he sent two glorious backhand strokes skimming the full length of the court, as he did during his great match against Jack Crawford last week.

In places the match was better tennis than what had gone before, but the tension and the glory of fight were missing.

WIMBLEDON, England, July 31 (P).—The point score of the Perry-Shields match follows:

First Set.

		G.Pts.
Perry 6 4 4 0 4 1 4 2 7	4—6	36
Shields 4 1 1 4 6 4 2 4 5	2—4	33

(Perry served first.)

Second Set.

| Perry ....1 0 4 4 4 1 2 1 5 | 2—4 | 24 |
| Shields ....4 4 2 2 1 4 4 4 3 | 4—6 | 32 |

Third Set.

| Perry ....4 4 6 2 4 1 4 4 | 6 | 29 |
| Shields ....1 2 4 4 2 4 1 1 | 2 | 19 |

Fourth Set.

Perry 4 3 4 4 4 1 4 2 6 5 0 4		
2 4 2 4 4 2 4 0 0 4 4 1 4 2 4	7—15	90
Shields 1 5 0 0 6 4 1 4 8 4 4 1		
4 2 4 2 1 4 0 4 4 1 1 4 1 4 0	5—13	79

August 1, 1934

U.S. TENNIS BODY VOTES 8-WEEK RULE

Decides to Limit Time During Which Amateur Players May Receive Expenses.

BUT WAIVER IS POSSIBLE

National Singles for Men and Women to Be Held Together on 'Wimbledon' Basis.

By The Associated Press.

CINCINNATI, Feb. 9.—The United States Lawn Tennis Association late today ratified allegiance to the controversial eight-week rule and at the same time adopted a means by which the rule may be waived.

It accepted the rule, promulgated by the International Tennis Federation, as its executive committee urged. At the same time it approved, though not without dispute, what the committee offered as a "clarifying rider."

The rule says amateur players may not accept expenses for more than eight weeks in any one year, including time spent traveling from one tournament to another. The "clarifying rider" exempts participants in national and sectional tournaments if they are certified by their sectional associations as "official representatives" of such sections. In such cases traveling time does not count.

Moves With Dispatch.

But for a flurry over the eight-week rule the meeting moved with dispatch and harmony.

The association decided to put on a "Wimbledon" basis the national singles for both men and women. Both tournaments were awarded to the West Side Tennis Club of Forest Hills, L. I., for the period Aug. 29 to Sept. 6. It will be the first time the events have been held together.

The U. S. L. T. A. backed its president, W. Merrill Hall of New York, in rejecting a suggestion of Czechoslovakia that amateurs be permitted to accept money for appearing in tennis action-films. Great Britain had supported the proposal. Hall turned the suggestion down, declaring it an "encroachment upon the amateur spirit" which "would only be the first of a series" of similar demands.

It awarded the intercollegiate championships to Northwestern University for June 24-29, the national clay court tournament to Chicago June 17-22, the public parks championships to New Orleans Aug. 19-24, announced tentative dates for the men's and women's doubles championships, at the Longwood Tennis Club, Boston, as Aug. 17 or 19, and awarded the junior and boys' singles and doubles to Culver, Ind., Aug. 12-17 and the girls' championships to the Merion C. C., Philadelphia, opening Sept. 2.

It was decided to hold the 1936 Winter meeting—with no date set—in Philadelphia.

Adoption of the eight-week rule

and its qualifying resolution, drawn to meet objections voiced previously by the Western Lawn Tennis Association, proved the high spot of the meeting, but the major issue surprisingly found objection coming as much from the East as from the West.

William Rowland, Philadelphia, former member of the U. S. L. T. A. executive committee, said he viewed enforcement as devolving upon a "rule-breaking committee" and asked, amid laughter, if "the rule-breaking committee" would be "prepared to provide bail for amateurs who might side-step the rule."

Ray Jones, Louisville, Ky., saw the rule as "a distinct threat" to many tournaments, citing that "people won't patronize a tournament with a lot of local players" participating.

Rowland drew from Hall the admission that "no similar exception had been made in other countries," and added "it is foolish to adopt a rule and at the same time adopt a plan of action by which you don't expect to enforce it."

"We don't need to put ourselves in the position of being a deputy sheriff for the International Tennis Federation." he declared.

The qualifying resolution places administration of the rule on a committee, empowered to make exceptions of any player "provided * * * that * * * to come within the exception so granted (he) must first be designated as the official representative in such champion-

ship by his sectional association."

Award of the intercollegiate championships to Northwestern University was interpreted by many as a distinct turn in favor of clay court competition. A bid to conduct the matches at the Merion Cricket Club, Philadelphia, extended by Paul W. Gibbons, Philadelphia, was ruled informally as out of order and was not pressed.

A report of Lawrence A. Baker of Washington, D. C., treasurer, indicated the U. S. L. T. A. profited some $8,600 through tournament play last year—"Not much," he observed, "but considerable when you remember the nature of the times."

February 10, 1935

MRS. MOODY VANQUISHES MISS JACOBS, 6-3, 3-6, 7-5, BY STAGING GREAT RALLY

DUEL THRILLS 19,000

Victor Sweeps Through 5 Games in Row to End Final at Wimbledon.

TITLE IS HER SEVENTH

Come-Back Campaign After 2-Year Absence From Courts Climaxed by Triumph.

ALLISON-VAN RYN BEATEN

Bow to Crawford-Quist in Five Sets—Misses Stammers and James Score.

By FERDINAND KUHN JR.
Special Cable to THE NEW YORK TIMES.

WIMBLEDON, England, July 6.—Mrs. Helen Wills Moody's dream of winning another Wimbledon championship came true on the centre court today, but only after such a dramatic uphill struggle as she has not had to fight in many years.

Mrs. Moody just managed to defeat her old rival, Miss Helen Jacobs, after winning the first set, losing the second, and trailing, 2 games to 5, in the third. Once Miss Jacobs reached match point and before that Mrs. Moody had thrown up her hands as if everything were

over and she could do no more.

Suddenly, to the utter amazement of the crowd of 19,000, she summoned up all the power and all the courage of her greatest days as champion. She put more sting into her strokes, she began to run for points instead of playing wearily from the baseline, and before long she had reeled off five straight games and gained a great triumph. The score was 6-3, 3-6, 7-5.

Still Queen of Courts.

Thus Mrs. Moody became the Wimbledon champion for the seventh time—a record equaled only by Mrs. Lambert Chambers in the days before the war. She is not as great as she once was; she is not as quick getting to the ball and shows signs of tiring more easily. Yet Mrs. Moody proved today that she is still the queen of the courts, able to defeat the best challengers the world can send against her.

As for Miss Jacobs, today's defeat came as a bitter disappointment after so many years of trying. Four times she has reached the Wimbledon final and four times she has failed to crown her career with the championship, losing thrice to Mrs. Moody. Never once has she beaten Mrs. Moody in a match that went its full length. Today Miss Jacobs made the supreme effort of her life and the crowd was hoping that she would get her greatest wish at last. But Mrs. Moody was still too good for her.

Both Players Cheered.

A roar of cheers went up from the packed stands as Miss Jacobs hit out after the last long rally. They were cheers of sympathy for the girl who had had victory snatched from her grasp and cheers of admiration for Mrs. Moody, so cool, so perfectly poised in every crisis. This time Mrs. Moody's poker face was one vast smile as she walked off the court. She was so excited that she kissed Sir Herbert Wilberforce, secretary of the All-England Tennis Club, who came on the court to greet her.

"What a match!" she said to him. "I never ought to have had it."

Other championships were decided today, but they were only incidental. The Australian team of Jack Crawford and Adrian Quist won the men's doubles title after a slashing five-set struggle with Wilmer Allison and John Van Ryn of the United States, who were hoping to win their third Wimbledon championship. The score was 6-3, 5-7, 6-2, 5-7, 7-5. Miss Katherine Stammers and Miss Freda James of Great Britain won the women's doubles title from Mrs. René Mathieu of France and Mrs. Hilda Krahwinkel Sperling of Germany, 6-1, 6-4.

The mixed doubles honors went to Miss Dorothy Round and Fred Perry of Great Britain, who defeated Mr. and Mrs. H. C. Hopman of Australia, 7-5, 4-6, 6-3.

But as the crowd streamed home long past the dinner hour, it was talking only of the women's singles and of Mrs. Moody's comeback from the very edge of defeat. It was a match that will be talked about long after the day's doubles and most of the other matches at Wimbledon this year have been forgotten.

From the beginning it was clear Miss Jacobs was determined to get even with Mrs. Moody for all the disappointments of the past six years. From start to finish there was a grim expression on her face as if she were thinking to herself: "I'm going to beat her this time." —as if she felt her hour had struck.

She ran for every point as she has never run before. She puffed with the effort she was making, but she never let her weariness slow up her game. She showed it only in her backhand, which faltered as her endurance ebbed.

Concentrates on Strokes.

Mrs. Moody, on the other hand, seemed determined just to concentrate on every stroke and play it as well as she could. If she was thinking of her seventh championship or of proving her come-back to the whole world, after an absence from the courts of almost two years, she did not show it, even when things were going against her.

She began as usual by standing calmly on the baseline, keeping Miss Jacobs on the run with a stream of perfect drives to one side of the court and then to the other. Miss Jacobs retaliated by keeping her fellow Californian on the run and moved up from 0-3 to 3-all. But Miss Jacobs could not keep the ball in the court at crucial moments, whereas all the time and Mrs. Moody won the next three games for the set.

At the start of the second set Miss Jacobs got her backhand under control, while Mrs. Moody was showing unmistakable signs of weariness.

Miss Jacobs was volleying, smashing and making winning points when they seemed impossible. In the ninth game, with Miss Jacobs leading at 5—3, Mrs. Moody decided to come to the net, but it was too late. Miss Jacobs held her service and captured the set amid a roar of approval from the crowd that was backing her almost for the first time in her experience at Wimbledon.

Leans on Her Racquet.

Things were not going well for Mrs. Moody. Between every game she leaned on her racquet as if her back were troubling her again, and when she walked to her position the usual springiness of her step was gone. Miss Jacobs did not make matters easier by playing to her far backhand corner.

From 2—all in the third set, Miss Jacobs began to forge ahead with superb volleys which left Mrs. Moody helpless. She led by 3—2 and then by 4—2, finishing the sixth game with a ferocious serve that knocked the racket from Mrs. Moody's hand.

Now Mrs. Moody had her back to the wall and drove harder and harder to force a surrender. The seventh game went to deuce four times until Mrs. Moody lost it by missing an easy smash which should have been hers. With a smile on her face, she threw up her hands as if to tell the crowd this was the end.

Yet Mrs. Moody held on grimly. After fierce exchanges and long rallies, Miss Jacobs got to match point in the ninth game with a fine smash, but missed the crucial point by putting an easy smash into the net. Then she volleyed out and Mrs. Moody was saved.

Miss Jacobs's backhand now showed the effect of long strain, while Mrs. Moody was putting all her strength and skill into her forehand drives and running and leaping for the ball. In desperation, Miss Jacobs made two brave volleys in the eleventh game, but hit out and this brought Mrs. Moody into the lead for the first time in the set, 6—5.

By now Miss Jacobs was so dazed she forgot she was serving and had to be reminded by the umpire. She started with two heroic services, but they were all she could do. After the twelfth game had swung to deuce three times, Miss Jacobs hit three successive shots out. The match was over after an hour and forty minutes of grueling play.

Allison Is Erratic.

In the men's doubles match Allison was erratic and in the first set especially he failed to support his partner as he should have done. But in the second set the Americans began to show the teamwork which brought them two Wimbledon championships and the Australians found it almost impossible to pass them at the net.

The teams were so evenly matched that every game went to deuce a half dozen or more times. Finally the Americans found a loophole in Quist's service and captured the set, making the score 1—all.

Quist was everywhere in the third set, leaping, smashing and volleying with deadly effect. The set was over quickly, but the Americans' teamwork again tightened in the fourth and they managed to find chinks in the Australians' armor. In the fifth all games went to deuce until, with the score 5—all and advantage, Crawford scored with a dazzling shot down the centre which neither of the Americans could touch.

Quist lost two match points in the twelfth game, but the third time he did not miss his chance and Australia won its first men's doubles championship in the history of Wimbledon.

Answers Her Critics.

WIMBLEDON, England, July 6 (AP).—Mrs. Helen Wills Moody's victory today supplied all the vindication she ever will need for the incident in the American championship final of 1933 when, suffering from a back injury, she walked off the court in the third set with Miss Helen Jacobs leading, 3—0. She was accused then of quitting, of depriving Miss Jacobs of a chance for a clean-cut, undisputed victory. Today, however, she gave a conclusive rebuff to any one who ever questioned her fighting heart. Mrs. Moody's victory came as a surprise to that cross-section of expert tennis opinion that could not believe the San Francisco veteran could remain out of competition for almost two years and then came back to regain her old dominance of women's tennis.

Mrs. Moody, beginning her comeback campaign only a little more than a month ago, won her first tournament, the St. George's Hill competition, but ran into what seemed at the time to be a stunning setback when she was trounced by Miss Katherine Stammers, British southpaw, in the semi-final round of the Kent championship.

In the fourth round of the Wimbledon tournament Mrs. Moody narrowly escaped elimination at the hands of an unknown, Miss Emma Ceskova of Czechoslovakia, but rallied from a bad case of nerves to win, 3—6, 6—4, 6—2. Until today that was the only set she lost during the tournament.

The triumph marked the third time Mrs. Moody has scored over Miss Jacobs in the Wimbledon final. She won in 1929 and again in 1932 from the Berkeley girl, who holds the American title. Mrs. Moody reached the final at Wimbledon in her first appearance here in 1924, but was beaten on that occasion by Miss Kitty McKane of England.

She began her string of British championship victories in 1927, beating Miss Elia de Alvarez of Spain. She repeated against the same opponent in 1928, defeated Miss Jacobs in 1929, Miss Elizabeth Ryan in 1930, Miss Jacobs again in 1932 and Miss Dorothy Round of England in 1933.

The Point Score.

By The Associated Press.

FIRST SET.

Point Score.

		Pts.	G.
Mrs. Moody	.....4 4 4 2 0 0 10 4 4—	32	6
Miss Jacobs	.....2 2 1 4 4 4 8 2 2—	29	3

Stroke Analysis.

	N.	O.	P.	S.A.	D.F.
Mrs. Moody	11	9	5	2	0
Miss Jacobs	10	15	8	1	0

SECOND SET.

Point Score.

		Pts.	G.
Mrs. Moody	......5 2 1 6 1 4 3 0 0—	22	3
Miss Jacobs	......3 4 4 4 4 0 5 4 4—	32	6

Stroke Analysis.

	N.	O.	P.	S.A.	D.F.
Mrs. Moody	12	12	4	0	0
Miss Jacobs	7	11	6	2	1

THIRD SET.

Point Score.

		Pts.	G.
Mrs. Moody	.5 0 3 4 2 2 4 4 7 4 5 7—	47	7
Miss Jacobs	.3 4 5 0 4 4 6 2 5 2 3 5—	43	5

Stroke Analysis.

	N.	O.	P.	S.A.	D.F.
Mrs. Moody	18	16	15	1	1
Miss Jacobs	13	18	7	1	0

RECAPITULATION.

	N.	O.	P.	S.A.	D.F.
Mrs. Moody	41	37	24	3	1
Miss Jacobs	30	44	21	4	1

	E.	E.P.	T.P.	G.	Sets.
Mrs. Moody	79	27	101	16	2
Miss Jacobs	75	25	104	14	1

July 7, 1935

Modern Wimbledon Record Created by Perry in Taking Three Straight Titles

PERRY WINS EASILY FROM VON CRAMM

Sweeps Through British Final, 6-1, 6-1, 6-0, as German Injures Thigh Muscle.

FANS UNAWARE OF MISHAP

Crowd of 18,000 Learns of It After Match — Allison and Van Ryn Bow in Doubles.

By W. F. LEYSMITH
Special Cable to THE NEW YORK TIMES.

WIMBLEDON, England, July 3 —Something was wrong with Baron Gottfried von Cramm today, but what?

For forty-four minutes that tightly packed, mystified center court gallery waited almost in silence while Fred Perry, after winning an electrifying first game that ran to 24 points, raced through straight sets at 6—1, 6—1, 6—0 to his third successive all-England singles championship against an opponent who scarcely moved a foot in the last chapter for a ball that didn't come straight at him.

The crowd rose to its feet for the first time to cheer Perry as he shook hands across the net — the first tennis star to win here three years in a row since the challenge round was abolished in 1922.

Then the officials hurried to the court and surrounded the pale German. In a moment the umpire called for silence.

"Baron von Cramm," the umpire said, "strained a muscle in a thigh in his first service of the match today, and he is sorry he could not play better."

"Play On," His Reply

But for an occasional, almost imperceptible, limp the German had hidden his injury from the crowd and from his opponent. Puzzled himself early in the second set at the weakening of his opposition, Perry had run to the net and made inquiry, only to be met with a smile and a gesture of "Play on."

Perry seemed as dejected and disappointed as the crowd, many of whom waited on line since 7 o'clock the night before to witness what was expected to be the hardest-fought final in the history of the Wimbledon tournaments. It was all over in the first game. Thereafter von Cramm had no more of a chance against Perry's murderous forehand drive than a school boy.

"There was only one game for me," the German said in his dressing room. "I am sorrier for Perry and the crowd than I am for myself."

It certainly was not von Cramm's lucky day. On his way to the grounds he missed an automobile crash by inches.

Admires German's Pluck

Perry was full of admiration for the way von Cramm fought on when he must have been suffering intense pain.

"Von Cramm beat me in Paris a month ago and naturally I wanted another chance," he said.

Miss Helen Jacobs, who meets Mrs. Hilda Krahwinkel Sperling in the women's singles final tomorrow, reached her second title round today when, in partnership with Mrs. Sarah Palfrey Fabyan, she beat Miss Joan Ingram and Mrs. Phyllis Mudford King. Miss Jacobs dominated the game, and with Mrs. Fabyan also volleying well, the Britons as often as not found their shots cut off at the net. The score was 6—4, 6—3.

Tomorrow the American pair will meet the defenders of the title, Miss Kay Stammers and Miss Freda James, who today gained a surprisingly easy victory over Miss Dorothy Andrus and Mrs. Sylvia Henrotin, 6—0, 6—4. The American-French team never found its touch until the English pair had the first set and a lead of 5—1 in the second. Then Mrs. Andrus and Mrs. Henrotin won three games in a row, but that was as far as they got.

Budge's Team Scores

Donald Budge and Mrs. Fabyan entered the mixed doubles final, defeating Camille Malfroy of New Zealand and Mrs. Sperling, now a resident of Denmark, by 6—4, 6—3. Both Americans were severe volleyers and kept Mrs. Sperling on the basline, and this one-forward, one-back formation was the losing team's undoing.

Wilmer Allison and John Van Ryn, who had received an unexpected "life" through the retirement of the German doubles team, von Cramm and Heiner Henkel, got the center court crowd delirious with excitement before they lost by

7—5, 6—4, 3—6, 11—9 to the British Davis Cup pair, Charles Tuckey and Pat Hughes.

At first it looked as if Tuckey, with his vicious forehand drive down the sidelines, and Hughes, smashing down the center, would run away until, in the third set, the Americans came back with all their old fire to make a match of it. Tuckey hits every shot hard; Hughes mixes his with spinners, yet it was the Americans' service that upset them.

Britons Break Through

Van Ryn lost his service at 5-all in the first set and Allison at four games all in the second, which in each case was enough to give the Britons the set. Both are capable of serving cannonballs.

Then came the Americans' brilliant challenge. They both rushed to the net and for a while had Tuckey, the burly Army champion, gasping for breath as he raced back and forth along the baseline. The Americans' volleying, too, was tremendous.

Allison, whose right wrist still was strapped, threw every ounce of energy into the attack that brought every spectator to his feet. Allison saved shot after shot and scored two winners while on his knees, amid such noise and cheering as is seldom heard at Wimbledon.

Twice the British missed a match point, or rather, the Americans saved it. Once, in the fifteenth game, and again in the eighteenth, when, with the Britons leading at 9—8, Van Ryn sent down three unplayable smashes to even the score. Finally there was a badly hit smash from Allison to give the British another chance and Hughes saw that it wasn't missed.

Tomorrow Hughes and Tuckey will meet Charles Hare and Fred Wilde, victors today over Jean Borotra and Jacques Brugnon, in an all-British final. Lycett and Godfree were the last Britons to win the doubles here, in 1923, and actually Lycett was Australian born.

THE POINT SCORE

FIRST SET

								Pts.	G.
Perry	13	2	5	4	4	4	4—36		6
Von Cramm	11	4	3	1	2	2	1—24		1

SECOND SET

Perry	0	5	4	4	4	4	4—25		6
Von Cramm	4	3	2	2	2	1	1—15		1

THIRD SET

Perry	4	4	4	5	6	5—28			6
Von Cramm	1	2	2	3	4	3—15			0

RECAPITULATION

	A.	Pl.	O.	N.D.F.
Perry	9	22	17	16 2
Von Cramm	2	17	27	30 1

	E.	E.P.	T.P.	G. Sets.
Perry	35	31	89	18 3
Von Cramm	58	19	54	2 0

July 4, 1936

ALICE MARBLE UPSETS HELEN JACOBS; PERRY TRIUMPHS

13,000 AT NET FINALS

Miss Marble Ends 4-Year Reign of Miss Jacobs— Wins, 4-6, 6-3, 6-2.

PERRY SETS NEW RECORD

Becomes First Overseas Player to Take U. S. Title 3 Times In Beating Budge.

BRITON CLOSE TO DEFEAT

Scores, 2-6, 6-2, 8-6, 1-6, 10-8, After Rival Is Twice Two Points From Victory.

By ALLISON DANZIG

The four-year reign of Miss Helen Jacobs as national tennis champion was brought to an end by Miss Alice Marble at Forest Hills yesterday, and Frederick Perry of Great Britain averted defeat by two points against Donald Budge to set an all-time record in winning his third American crown.

With a crowd of 13,000 spectators cheering her on from the stadium of the West Side Tennis Club, the blonde, beautifully proportioned girl from San Francisco and Palm Springs capped her comeback campaign following a two years' absence by defeating Miss Jacobs after it had appeared that the titleholder was the master of the court.

The score was 4—6, 6—3, 6—2, and Miss Marble's performance in the final set was one of the finest exhibitions of virtuosity and politic generalship the tournament has seen in years.

Miss Jacobs Is Balked

The wild excitement occasioned by the downfall of the defending champion, which balked Miss Jacobs in her effort to establish a new record of five consecutive victories in the championship, was a mere murmur, however, compared with the Niagara of the roar that was heard later in the afternoon as Budge threatened to lower the colors of the world's champion.

Leading by 5—3 in the fifth set of an almost interminable match that had been interrupted twice by rain and which was played for the most part in poor light with a highly keyed-up, moving crowd as the disturbing background to the flight of the ball, Budge tightened up at the critical juncture and blew his chance against a rampant Perry.

Once in the tenth game and again in the sixteenth, the red-haired youth from Oakland was only two points away from the greatest victory of his career, but on both occasions he was found wanting.

Acclaimed by the Crowd

Two hours and forty-five minutes after Benjamin H. Dwight had got the match under way, Perry left the court the winner at 2—6, 6—2, 8—6, 1—6, 10—8, acclaimed as the first player from overseas in history to carry off our title three times.

It was a particularly sweet victory for the British champion, though for the greater part of the fourth set he appeared to be indifferent to the outcome, for it reestablished him on the pinnacle in America after his defeat by Wilmer Allison last year, when he suffered a bad fall in the opening set.

For Budge, it was a heart-breaking experience after he had come so close to victory, but though beaten, the stalwart Californian with the murderous backhand proved definitely that he belongs among the great players of the world in his third season of championship competition.

Considering the conditions under which the match was played, he kept his concentration beautifully, far better than did Perry, who appeared to be distracted and annoyed by the wild enthusiasm of the crowd's devotion to his opponent's cause and so completely lost his touch and aggressiveness after his masterful performance in the third set as to leave the gallery mystified.

Crowd Never Discouraged

It was regrettable that rain should have intervened for the first time in the ten days of the championship to mar the prize match of the men's tournament. But in spite of the interruptions from the intermittent showers, which never discouraged the intrepid, enthusiastic crowd, some of the finest tennis Forest Hills has witnessed in years was on display.

Times Wide World Photo.

FREDERICK PERRY AFTER VICTORY YESTERDAY

Don Budge swept all of the major tournaments in 1938. He took the Australian, French, British and U.S. titles—a tennis grand slam.

The third set was a magnificent battle in which the rare excellence of Perry's ground strokes stood forth radiantly, and the final set brought forth some of the greatest shot making of the season as the game but wilting Budge gave his last ounce of energy in the vain effort to stay the firm, skilled hand and masterful divination of the British champion.

So worked up was the gallery over the men's final that it almost forgot about the triumph of Miss Marble until Walter Merrill Hall, president of the United States Lawn Tennis Association, presented the championship trophies. But during the course of her ascension to the throne, the California girl could hardly have been more royally acclaimed.

Whether or not it was because the crowd, psychologically, is against the champion in sport, there was no mistaking that the great majority of the 13,000 spectators' sympathies were with Miss Marble. Considering the fact that Miss Jacobs was wearing a bandage on her injured thumb, which she was quick to disclaim as contributing to her defeat, one might have expected it to be otherwise.

Threatens to End Career

On the other hand, there was the consideration that the challenger was making her return to the championship after overcoming an illness that at one time threatened to end her career on the courts. Two years ago Miss Marble was looked upon as the player of destiny in American women's tennis, born to wear the purple through the finest endowment of strokes and physical attributes of any player in the game.

Then, in the Spring of 1934, as the third ranking player of the country, Miss Marble went abroad as a member of the Wightman Cup squad and during a match in Roland Garros Stadium in Paris against Mrs. Sylvia Henrotin she was stricken ill and collapsed.

That was the last seen or heard of the San Francisco girl in tennis until last year, when she took up her racquet again on the Pacific Coast.

Under the coaching of Miss Eleanor Tennant of Palm Springs, a former first-ten ranking player, Miss Marble launched her comeback and made a radical alteration in her forehand, changing to the Eastern grip. Convinced that she was ready to return to championship play in the East after she had beaten Miss Carolin Babcock and other ranking players of California, she reappeared in the East this Summer.

The same masculine elements that had marked her game in 1933 were in evidence again, particularly the strength of her service and her command at the net. She won the Longwood Bowl tournament and the Seabright Bowl and then was beaten by Mrs. Henrotin at Rye in the Eastern championships. After that she went to the final at Essex and was beaten by Miss Jacobs in three sets.

Opinion Is Conflicting

When the national championship got under way there was conflicting opinion as to Miss Marble's chances.

As masterful as had been her game for the most part, at times she had played a very inferior grade of tennis.

At her best, it was admitted that the Palm Springs girl was the equal if not the superior of any of

Presentation of Trophy at Forest Hills

Associated Press Photo.

Walter Merrill Hall, president of the United States Lawn Tennis Association, giving prize to Miss Alice Marble after her victory in the national championship final, while Miss Helen Jacobs looks on.

Point Scores of Tennis Finals

Men's Final

PERRY VS. BUDGE

FIRST SET
Point Score

					Pts. G.
Perry	2 1 5 1 2 0 4				5—20—2
Budge	4 4 3 4 4 4 2				7—32—6

Stroke Analysis

	N.	O.	PL.	SA.	DF.
Perry	11	13	4	1	0
Budge	8	7	5	3	0

SECOND SET
Point Score

					Pts. G.
Perry	4 5 6 1 7 4 4				4—35—6
Budge	0 7 4 4 5 1 1				1—23—2

Stroke Analysis

	N.	O.	PL.	SA.	DF.
Perry	3	11	6	4	0
Budge	11	12	7	2	2

THIRD SET
Point Score

					Pts. G.
Perry	7 1 4 8 3 2 4 0 4 0 4 2 4				—47—8
Budge	5 4 1 6 5 4 2 4 2 4 1 4 0 1				—43—6

Stroke Analysis

	N.	O.	PL.	SA.	DF.
Perry	17	11	9	3	1
Budge	17	13	3	0	0

FOURTH SET
Point Score

					Pts. G.
Perry	3 0 6 1 3 4				1—18—1
Budge	5 4 4 4 5 6				4—32—6

Stroke Analysis

	N.	O.	PL.	SA.	DF.
Perry	11	4	1	4	0
Budge	6	7	8	1	0

FIFTH SET
Point Score

					Pts. G.
Perry	3 4 0 4 1 4 4 3 4 5 4 0 2 4 4 5 5 4				—60—10
Budge	5 2 4 2 4 6 1 5 1 3 2 4 4 1 6 3 3 1				—57—8

Stroke Analysis

	N.	O.	PL.	SA.	DF.
Perry	19	21	20	3	1
Budge	19	17	15	1	1

RECAPITULATION

	N.	O.	PL.	SA.	DF.
Perry	61	64	43	12	6
Budge	62	60	48	8	3

	E.	EP.	TP.	G.	Sets.
Perry	131	55	180	27	3
Budge	125	56	187	28	2

Umpire—Benjamin H. Dwight. Time of match (actual playing time)—2 hours.

Women's Final

MISS MARBLE VS. MISS JACOBS

FIRST SET
Point Score

					Pts. G.
Miss Marble	4 5 1 7 3 0 2 5 1				2—30	4
Miss Jacobs	2 3 4 5 5 4 4 3 4				4—38	6

Stroke Analysis

	N.	O.	PL.	S.A.	D.F.
Miss Marble	13	21	9	2	1
Miss Jacobs	6	13	1	2	0

SECOND SET
Point Score

					Pts. G.
Miss Marble	4 1 4 4 4 2 4				6—33	6
Miss Jacobs	6 4 2 1 0 1 4				2—24	3

Stroke Analysis

	N.	O.	PL.	S.A.	D.F.
Miss Marble	3	15	11	0	1
Miss Jacobs	7	15	5	0	0

THIRD SET
Point Score

					Pts. G.
Miss Marble	4 4 4 4 5 2 4				4—31	6
Miss Jacobs	1 1 2 0 7 4 0				1—16	2

Stroke Analysis

	N.	O.	PL.	S.A.	D.F.
Miss Marble	8	4	0	0	0
Miss Jacobs	3	20	4	0	0

RECAPITULATION

	N.	O.	Pl.	S.A.	D.F.
Miss Marble	24	4	28	2	2
Miss Jacobs	16	4	10	2	0

	E.	F.P.	T.P.	G.	Sets.
Miss Marble	66	30	94	16	2
Miss Jacobs	64	12	78	11	1

Umpire—Louis Shaw. Time of match—1:07.

Veterans' Final

BIDWELL VS. BASSFORD

FIRST SET
Point Score

					Pts. G.
Bidwell	4 4 5 4 4 4 2 1				4—32—6
Bassford	1 2 3 1 6 2 4 4				2—25—3

SECOND SET
Point Score

					Pts. G.
Bidwell	5 4 4 2 4 4 4				4—31—6
Bassford	7 1 2 4 2 2 1				1—20—2

her rivals, but it was a moot question as to whether she had consolidated her game sufficiently to stand up against an opponent of the strength of Miss Jacobs. Her play at Forest Hills up to the final was not particularly outstanding, and after Miss Jacobs's thoroughly convincing performance in defeating Miss Katherine Stammers it was doubted whether Miss Marble could reverse the result of their meeting at Essex.

But Miss Marble saved her best tennis for the supreme day and was so much better than she had been in any other match of the season as to confound critical opinion. Miss Jacobs was not the same player she was against Miss Stammers, particularly in the final set, when her whole game collapsed feebly.

But Miss Jacobs's collapse was brought on by the pressure of a jolting, shifting attack that ran her unmercifully and exposed the inadequacy of either her chop or her topped forehand to stand against the flat, beautifully fluent drive of Miss Marble. It was not until Miss Marble appeared to be on the road to defeat that she played her finest tennis, after she had slumped and lost command of the first set and fallen behind at 0—2 in the second.

The superiority of the challenger's weapons was established at the outset, when she went ahead at 3—1. Miss Marble was hitting so deeply and serving so strongly that Miss Jacobs was desperately pressed to keep the ball in play. Neither her forehand chop nor backhand drive could withstand the pressure as she was kept running into the corners.

The crowd was unable to contain its delight over Miss Marble's play and she was squarely in command of the situation when, suddenly, her control deserted her and Miss Jacobs, fighting courageously, found the tide turning in her favor. Beginning with the sixth game, Miss Marble broke badly and the champion, getting everything back and lobbing effectively, took the set and went ahead at 2—0 in the second.

Miss Marble's chances of winning at this stage seemed slim indeed. But starting with the third game, she concentrated on Miss Jacobs's backhand, began to interpolate drop shots and from there on to the end of the match had the champion hopelessly on the defensive.

Miss Jacobs found it impossible to maintain position against her opponent's changes of length and direction. The pressure on her backhand was too much for her and she could not get to the drop shots which Miss Marble was bringing off.

Overhead Game Weak

Miss Marble was the master both with her ground strokes and with her volleys and smashes, which were bringing roars from the crowd. The champion sought to meet the issue at the net, but her overhead hitting was weak. She never knew where to expect the attack, was caught on the wrong foot repeatedly and her whole game broke down.

After the rest period, the play became even more one-sided, with Miss Marble giving an exhibition of targetry from the forehand that had the crowd cheering.

Miss Jacobs's chop was utterly inadequate, and she lost the first four games, winning only four points. Then Miss Jacobs, fighting valiantly, rallied. She pulled out the fifth game after Miss Marble had been within a point of a 5-0 lead, and then won the sixth on her service as her opponent's control wavered.

The crowd was now cheering on the champion for her game stand and one wondered whether Mrs. Molla Mallory's rally of 1926, when she was down 0—4 in the third set to Miss Elizabeth Ryan, was to be repeated. But Miss Marble now lifted her game, broke down Miss Jacobs's backhand defense to win the seventh game at love and then broke through at 15 in the eighth as Miss Jacobs's control failed under pressure.

Sets a Furious Pace

The Budge-Perry match started with the American at the peak of his game and setting so furious a pace as to keep the British champion on the defensive all the way. Budge's service was scorching in its speed and from both the forehand and backhand he was nailing the ball into the corners.

The cheers for the American's play subsided in the second set as Perry launched a counter-attack and put on pressure that took some of the starch out of his opponent's strokes. The British ace was serving the better of the two now and returning Budge's service regularly.

Budge's control broke under the pace and depth of Perry's drives and after the score had reached 2-all dropped the next four games. There was a half hour suspension after the seventh game, owing to the rain.

The third set was the best in the match in the high quality of the tennis on both sides. Budge's backhand and serve were off at the start and he fell behind at 1—3, but then he rallied and a magnificent battle developed.

Budge's backhand was now lashing the ball into Perry's backhand corner and opening the court for his drop volleys and cross-court punching volleys. So much better was his service that he won two

games in succession at love.

Baseline Is Untenable

Perry was hard pressed to stay on even terms, falling behind at 0—30 in the ninth, but then the champion hit into his best streak of the match. He was so irresistible from the back of the court that Budge found his own baseline untenable and was forced into volley errors when he came in. Perry won the thirteenth game at love with two service aces and broke through in the fourteenth at fifteen.

The champion looked like a champion indeed at this stage and when the players left the court for the rest period it seemed the match would end in the fourth set. Perry came out strong for the first game of the fourth chapter, but after leading at 40—30 and losing the game with a double fault, he suddenly slowed down perceptibly and lost his dash and aggressiveness.

Rain came up again and also the wind and the British ace slumped badly. At times he seemed to be totally unconcerned about his mounting errors or the outcome of the match, playing carelessly and making no effort to get to the net. Budge, attacking impetuously and letting nothing disturb his concen-

tration, staged a procession as Perry double-faulted four times and hit ball after ball into the net, particularly from his backhand. Then came the final set, which saw the gallery stage its noisiest demonstrations of the day.

Perry continued to remain in his back court and could do no better than stay on even terms, with Budge hitting so fiercely from both the forehand and backhand and serving so well.

Then the American broke through in the sixth game with a deadly smash and a backhand passing shot, and the stadium was in an uproar.

The cheers changed to groans when Budge slumped and lost his service in the seventh and then back to cheers as he broke through again in the eighth on Perry's errors.

It looked like Budge's match as he set himself to serve, with the score 5—3 in his favor, but the Californian broke under the strain, played badly and lost the game with a double fault. In the next game he pulled up from 15—40 to deuce, two points removed from victory, but then he tightened and gave Perry a set-up at the net and

then hit out of court.

The battle fluctuated from there on until Budge was two points away from winning again in the sixteenth. Then Perry, serving irresistibly and going to the net for a smash, pulled out of the hole, and that was the end of Budge's hopes.

Weary from his constant running to the net and into the corners for Perry's fastidiously correct drives, the game American was at Perry's mercy and the aroused British champion showed none. Four beautiful drives from Perry's racquet, two of them passing shots, cost the groggy Budge his service game and the champion ended the match with a service ace in the eighteenth.

For the third year in succession Raymond B. Bidwell of Boston won the national veterans' tennis championship, gaining permanent possession of the Challenge Trophy, which was presented to him by Dr. S. Ellsworth Davenport 2d.

In the final round the strong, unusually active Bostonian defeated Henry Bassford of Larchmont, N. Y., 6—3, 6—2. Bassford won the title in 1928 and 1930.

September 13, 1936

Budge Routs von Cramm in Final

SMASHING VICTORY GIVES BUDGE TITLE

Wins by 6-3, 6-4, 6-2 From von Cramm—He and Mako Top Germans in 5 Sets

HOPES FOR DAVIS CUP SOAR

U. S. Tennis Star and Rival Presented to Queen Mary After Wimbledon Match

Wireless to THE NEW YORK TIMES.

WIMBLEDON, England, July 2.— American domination of world tennis was re-established today when Donald Budge overwhelmed Baron Gottfried von Cramm of Germany to take the singles championship in the all-England tournament and then, with the aid of Gene Mako, won a thrilling five-set victory over von Cramm and Heinrich Henkel to enter the final of doubles.

Few in the vast crowd that watched those eight glorious sets will ever forget they were present when America's newest tennis genius entered into his inheritance at 21. Unless he accepts tempting offers to turn professional, there will be no one in sight to challenge his sovereignty for many years.

Tonight it appeared as certain as anything can be in tennis that Budge and Mako will have no difficulty in taking the doubles championship tomorrow from last year's titleholders, George P. Hughes and C. R. D. Tuckey of Great Britain. The champions were not impressive in their semi-final triumph over Ladislaus Hecht and Roderich Menzel, the Czech team. And although they do not play especially well to-

Times Wide World Radiophoto.

JUST AFTER FINAL AT WIMBLEDON YESTERDAY
Baron Gottfried von Cramm congratulating Don Budge after the United States star had defeated the German in straight sets.

gether, their individual prowess gives Budge and Miss Alice Marble a good chance to annex the mixed doubles title from Mrs. Rene Mathieu and Yvon Petra of France.

May Accomplish the Maximum

But it isn't so much Budge's chance to make tennis history by winning the maximum of three out of five championships here as the effect on America's drive to recapture the Davis Cup after all these years that Budge's two matches had today.

The singles victory, scored by 6—3, 6—4, 6—2, naturally caused no surprise to those who watched the way Budge mowed down his opponents with the loss of only one set. But the completeness of his victory, the more impressive after his nervous start, which enabled von Cramm to take a 3-1 lead, astounded all who saw it.

More thrilling and more important as far as the Davis Cup is concerned was the way Budge and Mako pulled themselves together to sweep through the team they undoubtedly will meet in the interzone finals.

The doubles score was 4—6, 4—6, 6—2, 6—4, 6—3. Yet the critics who had picked von Cramm and Henkel on the basis of the latter's supposed superiority over Mako seemed infallible seers at the end of the first two sets. Mako barely was able to get his racquet on either von Cramm's or Henkel's ripping serves. Budge's forehand, which had troubled him in the early stages of his championship match, was not working well and the Germans took the two sets in exactly forty minutes.

Mako Rallies Team-Mate

Much of the credit for the way the Americans came back must be given to Mako, despite what the critics said. Almost to the very end he was an easy mark for the opposition's serves, but they began to come over with less disconcerting speed. And he kept the flag flying with his fine net play until his more powerful partner at last found the range and made the combination as unbeatable as he had been individually earlier in the day.

The elimination of Mrs. Dorothy Andrus, the American, and Mrs. Sylvia Henrotin of France by Mrs. Phyllis Mudford King and Miss Joan Pittman, the English team, 6—3, 6—4, means that the United States, after the elimination of Miss Marble and Miss Helen Jacobs, will not be represented in either women's singles or doubles. But America has glory enough for one Wimbledon.

However, for a time, things looked distinctly unpromising for the United States when Budge, after leading, 40—30, on his opening service, drove out, then lost 2 points at the net for the game. The German took his own service at 15. Budge having his greatest difficulty with both von Cramm's sizzling first and "spinner" deliveries.

Budge then took his own service, but when von Cramm annexed his own at love for a lead of 3—1 in games there were fears that the veteran who beat the Californian in the Wimbledon semi-finals in 1935 might repeat the victory.

Cup Match Recalled

But it was written that the match instead should follow the lines of Budge's triumph over the German in their Davis Cup meeting also in 1935. The redhead took a game which had appeared flawless against lesser men and pounded it to pieces, running out the set with five straight games.

A footfault called on von Cramm in the fifth game may have served to slow down not only the cannon-ball service he has learned from Bill Tilden but his game in general. But the way Budge dominated the court, particularly after he regained control of those short, sharply angled cross-court shots behind which he glides so smoothly to the net, is sufficient explanation of the result.

There was an interval in the match when the two players bowed low to salute Queen Mary, an inveterate Wimbledon fan, on her arrival in the royal box. Then Budge resumed his drive to the championship. He took the first two games, and although von Cramm rallied to hold his own service, the American took the next for a 3-1 lead.

But Budge's game was not yet functioning on all twelve cylinders and von Cramm made his final drive. His service again became effective and he took advantage of Budge's attack of errors to break service at love and draw even at 3—3 and finally go ahead at 4—3. This was his last stand in the set. Despite a double fault Budge took his own service then, after several magnificent rallies, broke von Cramm's for a 5-4 lead. He won the set game at love.

Budge swept on, breaking his opponent's opening service in the third set. Then came the redhead's one and only attack of carelessness, the last souvenir of the tennis immaturity he is putting behind him. He was leading in the next game, 40—0, but allowed von Cramm to creep up, one point after another to deuce. Then Budge took two advantages but the German fought back to deuce each time, once aided by a net cord which made an already good drop shot unplayable. Von Cramm finally got his own advantage and took the game.

It was to be one of the two games he got in that set. Budge, with his service and every department of his game working to perfection, took the next four for a 5-1 lead, but not without a good fight for the sixth game.

German Not Through

Von Cramm was not quite finished. He took his own service at 15. At 40—15 in the eighth game Budge had two match points but von Cramm fought back to deuce and won three successive advantages.

Budge's passing shots each time, however, held him in check and on the third match point the American drove squarely to von Cramm's back-hand corner. The Baron, barely getting his racquet on the ball, drove it into the stands—a vain effort which seemed to symbolize the crushing nature of his defeat.

Standing room along the sides of the center court had been filled ever since the grounds were opened at noon, but there were more thousands came. They were not interested in any except Budge's matches, and when they realized their places were gone they strolled about the grounds for hours until it was time for him and Mako to take on the Germans. Then they quickly filled the few gaps resulting from the departure of those who were on the point of collapse from standing.

From the very first game it seemed as if the Americans were doomed to failure. Both von Cramm's and Henkel's services were so powerful that Budge had the greatest difficulties getting them past the net man and Mako must have failed to return at least 50 per cent of the services to him in the first set.

Break in Ninth Game

Yet both Americans were going strong on their own service and it was clear that one break through service would decide. It came in the ninth game. Von Cramm then took his service and the first set was gone. It was as simple as that, although in the eighth the Americans worked up Henkel's service from 40—0 to win two advantages which they couldn't convert into a game.

The second set started badly indeed, Budge dropping his service and Henkel taking his. But Mako held his own to keep the team in the running.

In the fourth game on von Cramm's service, the Germans were leading, 40—30, and Budge thought a sizzler had aced him. Instead it was called a fault. The Americans made it their advantage and took the game despite Mako's wild drive, which tipped Henkel's hand.

But von Cramm and Henkel continued with their most effective services and all-round play to take the next three games. Budge took his service to reduce their lead but Henkel annexed the set game at love.

There was every reason to believe the Americans were beaten and this impression was deepened when Mako trailed on his opening service in the third set at 15—40. But there, with their backs against the wall, Budge and his partner retreated no further. They brought the score to deuce, fought off a German advantage and took the game on two of Mako's most resplendent smashes.

Although Budge was in difficulties in the next game at 0—30, he went on to take it; then Henkel's service was broken for a 3-1 lead.

So swiftly had the fortunes of war changed that the Germans may be pardoned for their bewilderment. Their services began to lose their zip, and although von Cramm held his service, the Americans took the next two games for the set.

Games went with service in the fourth until in the eighth chapter Henkel again lost his to yield a 5-3 lead to the Americans. Mako dropped his service at love, the Germans taking the net with force and decision, but von Cramm's was broken for the tying set.

In the fifth Henkel finally won

Wimbledon Point Score

By The Associated Press.

FIRST SET
Point Score

											Pts.G.
Budge	3	1	5	0	5	5	4	4			4—31—6
Von Cramm	..5	4	3	4	3	3	2	2			2—28—3

Stroke Analysis

	SA.	P.	N.	O.	DF.
Budge	0	8	9	9	0
Von Cramm	0	10	10	13	0

SECOND SET
Point Score

										Pts.G.
Budge	4	4	3	4	2	0	1	4	5	4—31—6
Von Cramm.2	2	5	1	4	4	4	1	3	1—27—4

his service after Budge had taken his for an opening lead. Trailing, 0—30, on Henkel's delivery, the Americans fought their way to 30—30, then took the advantage on a dazzling exchange of volleys which found all four within the forecourt trading shots, none of which was allowed to touch the turf.

Budge and Mako failed to convert their advantage into a game; four times over Mako, only to be turned back by Budge. Then the Americans got the advantage, but Henkel's fast service left Budge flatfooted. It was Henkel's advantage, but Budge sent a spinner across the court that Henkel volleyed into the net. And so the points see-sawed until finally Henkel pulled out the game.

Monotony Finally Broken

Games now went with service until, with the Americans leading at 4—3, there came a break that decided the match. For five games the receivers of service made no more than two points in each game and it had seemed as if this might go on indefinitely.

But von Cramm got himself into difficulties at 15—40, and although Mako lobbed short, permitting Henkel to make an easy kill, Gene dropped a perfect lob at the next point for the game.

With a 5-3 lead in games on Budge's service, the Americans were down at 15—30, but Henkel drove out to make it 30—all. At the end of a short rally von Cramm drove out, preparing the way for match point, and Budge's service to Henkel in the forehand corner left the German standing there while the crowd broke out into cheers.

At the end of their singles match Budge and von Cramm had been called to the royal box to be presented to the Queen Mother.

After it was all over Budge denied reports that he would become a professional, saying, "I'm going to defend my title next year—I guess I'll remain an amateur for years and years and years."

Stroke Analysis

	SA.	P.	N.	O.	DF.
Budge	0	6	7	9	2
Von Cramm......0	9	11	13	1

THIRD SET
Point Score

									Pts.G.
Budge	4	5	4	6	4	8	1	8—40—6
Von Cramm	...2	7	1	4	0	6	4	6—30—2

Stroke Analysis

	SA.	P.	N.	O.	DF.
Budge	2	20	8	7	1
Von Cramm	...0	15	7	11	0

July 3, 1937

Budge Puts Americans in Davis Cup Challenge Round by Defeating von Cramm

U.S. TENNIS TEAM TOPS GERMANY, 3-2

Budge's Fine Rally Halts von Cramm, 6-8, 5-7, 6-4, 6-2, 8-6, at Wimbledon

TENSE FIGHT IN LAST SET

Don Erases Rival's 4-1 Lead —Henkel First Halts Grant to Tie Interzone Final

By THOMAS J. HAMILTON JR.
Wireless to THE NEW YORK TIMES.

WIMBLEDON, England, July 20.—Donald Budge defeated Baron Gottfried von Cramm today, 6—8, 5—7, 6—4, 6—2, 8—6, in a match which will be forever memorable in every land where lawn tennis is played. In doing so, the California redhead not only brought the United States within striking distance of the Davis Cup, for ten long years in alien hands, but vindicated his fighting ability inherited from his Scottish ancestors.

His victory was all the more striking because every one, with the possible exception of a few of the most rabid German supporters of von Cramm, had been sure Budge would win without the slightest difficulty. Bryan M. (Bitsy) Grant of Atlanta lost to Heiner Henkel as expected, 7—5, 2—6, 6—3, 6—4, but connoisseurs of tennis merely murmured among themselves that this was a good thing, because with the score 2—2 in the interzone finals between the United States and Germany von Cramm would be encouraged to play the game of his life and so would succeed in giving at least enough competition to produce an interesting match.

To the surprise and amazement of all von Cramm proceeded to produce tennis that was unbelievable, coming from a player who had been the weaker member of the German doubles team yesterday.

Pate Has Anxious Time

When the German captured the first two sets, Walter Pate, non-playing American captain, from his chair in the shadow of the umpire's stand, merely ordered himself some tea. But when Budge, after coming back in Frank Merriwell style to take the third and fourth sets and even the match, trailed at 1—4 in the final set, then indeed things looked black.

Pate wrung his hands—and so did a small but voluble band of Americans who sought to match the enthusiasm of a larger number of Germans and von Cramm's English supporters.

But Budge was equal to the emergency. He took the next three games and with the score in matches 2—all, in sets 2—2 and in games 4—4, it seemed time for

somebody to cry: "Hold, enough."

However, six more games followed, each packed with thrills such as scarcely another sport can produce, before Budge in the fourteenth converted his fifth match point with a forehand placement to von Cramm's backhand, which the game German knew it was hopeless to try for.

America's 3-2 conquest, accounted for by Budge's two singles triumphs and his doubles victory with Mako, settled all controversy concerning Pate's choice of Grant over Frank Parker, who had beaten Henkel in the Wimbledon quarter-finals, for the No. 2 singles berth. Had Pate done so and Parker repeated his victory, at least one of the Americans present would not have been scared out of at least ten years of his mortal existence.

Challenge Round Opens Saturday

But, as it was, the United States did win and there is every prospect of an American victory over Great Britain in the challenge round beginning Saturday. If so much had not depended on the outcome, perhaps the two gallant sportsmen who contested the deciding match would not have climbed the heights they are capable of scaling and did scale.

"I chose Grant," Pate said afterward, "because after watching him practice for two weeks after Wim-

bledon I was convinced Bitsy had a better chance against Henkel because of his greater experience."

Parker was the first to congratulate Pate after they had reached the clubhouse of the All-England Club and, with Grant heartbroken over his two defeats, one can leave it at that, along with Pate's summing up of those fifty-eight games between Budge and von Cramm: "I couldn't stand another such two hours."

"How did Budge have such a narrow escape in a match with a player to whom he had lost at Wimbledon in 1935 but had defeated in the interzone Davis Cup finals the same year and again at Wimbledon in the finals only a few weeks ago?" is a query to which there are several answers.

Pate, for instance, pointed out that Budge's shoulder was rather sore from his and Mako's doubles match with von Cramm and Henkel yesterday. But the simplest answer is perhaps the best. Von Cramm was playing inspired tennis, especially in the first two sets, and Budge, though slightly off his game, had the fighting heart which enabled him to come back despite his troubles.

Von Cramm Wins Toss

From the very start, it was evident that Von Cramm was a far different player from yesterday. Winning the toss, he took his open-

ing service at love and although Budge held his it seemed obvious he would have his work cut out for him.

Budge's ground strokes and his service both were giving him trouble, while his volleying lacked decision. Also he showed a curious lethargy which caused him to fail to try for Von Cramm's drop shots and other hard ones that he usually gobbles up.

Later, even another fault developed. On crucial points Budge was misjudging shots, many of which were well within reach and which disconcertingly halted their course on the baseline.

All this may sound as though Von Cramm merely was lucky to force Budge to five sets. Quite to the contrary. His fast service was as fast as Budge's and his "kicker" was forcing Budge to sprint beyond the sidelines on the advantage court. His favorite strategy—manoeuvring for position until he could drive into Budge's backhand corner, then rushing to the net and volleying out of reach of Budge's forehand—came off time and time again.

But with his game gradually catching hold, Budge fought up from 40—0 to two advantages in the fifth only to lose the game on Von Cramm's service ace. Games went with service until the ninth when Budge converted his fifth advantage and broke through to lead 5—4. With a chance for the set, however, Budge missed two easy forehands to drop his service at love.

The next three games went with service. Two service aces placed Budge out of danger in the twelfth, but he yielded the fourteenth and the set.

Budge came back in the second set, working up to advantage in the opening game, but von Cramm held fast. The Californian was in difficulties in the sixth when trailing, 15-40, but he also held, and the set went with service until the twelfth game.

Von Cramm still was a most formidable opponent, but with Budge leading, 40 love, it seemed this might go on indefinitely. Instead, von Cramm took the next four points for advantage and set point with bold net play and passing shots which cost Budge heavily the few times he ventured to the net. Von Cramm missed a volley to deuce the game but converted his next advantage for the set on a volley which Budge, misjudging, allowed to light squarely on the left sideline.

Budge Begins Rally

In the third set it was now or never for Budge. Throwing off his lethargy, he attacked with a forcing backhand to the opposite corner to break von Cramm's service in the opening game and hold his own for a 2-0 lead.

Budge had an advantage in the third but failed to handle a drop shot, and von Cramm took the game on a service ace. Then he broke Budge's service at love to draw even.

Budge had lost his service on ground strokes, but in the fifth the situation was reversed, Budge breaking through von Cramm at love. He then took his own service at love for a 4-2 lead.

This, as it turned out, was good enough, von Cramm failing to break through. Budge now was only one

The Point Scores

By The Associated Press.

BUDGE vs. VON CRAMM

FIRST SET

		Pts.G.
Budge ......041454249024 02—41	6
von Cramm...424170427441 44—48	8

SECOND SET

		Pts.G.
Budge ....44242724114 34—40	5
von Cramm.......60424541414 6—41	7

THIRD SET

		Pts.G.
Budge ....443044 2440—29	6
von Cramm........125400 4240—22	4

FOURTH SET

		Pts.G.
Budge ....4444 0414—25	6
von Cramm........0221 4141—15	2

FIFTH SET

		Pts.G.
Budge .....2412044654 04410—50	8
von Cramm..414440147 1400 8—42	6

RECAPITULATION

	A.	P.	N.	O.	DF.
Budge	8	49	50	53	4
von Cramm	8	53	59	65	4

HENKEL vs. GRANT

FIRST SET

		Pts.G.
Henkel ....444064162044—39	7
Grant ....10244148 4411—34	5

SECOND SET

		Pts.G.
Henkel ....2514244 1—23	2
Grant ....47464114—31	6

THIRD SET

		Pts.G.
Henkel ....41545412 5—31	6
Grant ....04323414 3—24	3

FOURTH SET

		Pts.G.
Henkel ....5 1015 150455—41	6
Grant ....7 843434033—39	4

RECAPITULATION

	A.	P.	N.	O.	DF.
Henkel	10	36	46	48	1
Grant	0	33	31	56	1

set down and it did not take him long to even the score in sets.

Don annexed the first four games of the fourth in five minutes with the loss of only five points. Von Cramm held his next two services, but it was Budge's set handily.

Even during his comeback in the third and fourth sets, Budge got into trouble occasionally, so it seemed his chances of taking the fifth and final one depended upon his ability to hold his own services until von Cramm weakened.

German Breaks Through

The first three games went with service, but in the fourth von Cramm took the best Budge could produce on the rise, rushed to the net and held it to break through. With a 3—1 lead, von Cramm then took own service at love as his supporters went wild.

For the first time a look of anxiety crossed Budge's face, although Pate, who had been coaching him, before he offered Budge a towel as the players changed courts used the towel on himself first. He really needed it more.

Aided perhaps by the fact that his less robust opponent was beginning to lose the benefits of the rest interval after the third set, Budge now threw caution to the winds, rushing to the net behind each return of von Cramm's now weakening service. Helped by a net cord, Budge broke through von Cramm at love, then took his own service at 15 to square the set and match.

This run of three games seemed to promise that the suspense would soon be over. Instead it was just beginning.

Von Cramm led, 40-15, in the next game, but, aided by a double default, Budge fought up to an advantage. Quick to realize his danger, the German drew on his nerves of steel, deuced the game with magnificent volleying, fought off another Budge advantage and went on to capture the game with service ace.

Budge held his service without difficulty to deuce the set, but von

Cramm took his own in the eleventh at love. With it again his turn to take the net Budge squared the match by winning his delivery at love.

Six all! And now the two final games were at hand, although few realized it.

Obviously weakening, the German dropped his service at love but called on his last resources to meet the threat of Budge's service at the net. It was almost the von Cramm of the first two sets who so determinedly was volleying to make it 30-all, but he drove out the next point and Budge had match point in his grasp.

Still von Cramm fought on. After a long rally he scored a placement to Budge's forehand to deuce the game. Then he got two advantages at the net. Each time Budge held, but there were heads shaking over the psychological effect if he should drop this game after all his valiant efforts.

Now Budge got another advantage with a zipping service which von Cramm netted, but lost it on von Cramm's brave placement to the American's forehand. Budge smashed for another, only to smash an easy one into the net, smashed again but drove out from his backhand.

German's Charge Fails

But now von Cramm, white with

the strain, ended a long rally with an out. After a brief rally the German again charged the net and lost all save honor when he left his backhand open and Budge did not let that opportunity go by.

Budge's triumph meant so much because of the failure of Grant's scarcely less valiant fight to gain an American victory beforehand. The Atlantan's spurt in the first set just fell short and, although he took the second handily, Henkel broke service at crucial moments for the third and fourth.

With Henkel flashing net play similar to his work in the doubles yesterday, Grant was lucky to get one game of the first six in the opening set. Then, soft-balling Henkel as he does American opponents, he took four straight to deuce the set. But Henkel returned to the net to put shots well out of reach of his diminutive opponent in the next two games with the loss of only two points for the set.

Grant, fighting back valiantly, took five straight games in the second set and squared the match.

In the third set, Henkel was beginning to solve Grant's game. Instead of trying to drive, he chopped hard, concentrating on placements. A three-game run helped him to take the set, but this seemed no cause for too much worry.

Bitsy Returns in Shorts

Returning after the interval in shorts, instead of the flannels he had worn previously, Grant got into trouble immediately. He trailed at love—40, but finally held his service.

Scrambling for gets which other players would be reluctant even to try for, Grant then proceeded to produce the best tennis he has played this season in England. He had four advantages on Henkel's service, but the German finally held his delivery. Although Grant threatened again in both the fourth and sixth games, he still could not break through.

It was clear as the set progressed and Grant's threats to break Henkel weakened that the moment Bitsy lost his own service he would be finished. Perhaps over-conscious of this, Grant tried to play safe in the ninth and Henkel broke his service at love.

Not relenting, Henkel advanced to 40—15. Although Grant bravely fought off two set points to deuce the score, Henkel got another advantage on a placement too far away for Grant to reach, then put over a serve too hot for Grant to handle.

July 21, 1937

Wimbledon Title Retained by Budge

BUDGE TOPS AUSTIN IN FINAL, 6-1, 6-0, 6-3

U. S. Ace Is Invincible as He Takes Only 66 Minutes for Defense of English Title

20,000 SEE HIM SCORE

Never Played Better,' Don Says—American Sweep at Tennis Possible Today

By THOMAS J. HAMILTON

Wireless to THE NEW YORK TIMES.

WIMBLEDON, England, July 1.— Playing with precision and power that would not be denied, Don Budge today made doubly sure of his place among the immortals of tennis with a crushing victory over Henry W. (Bunny) Austin which gave the American the Wimbledon singles championship for the second year in succession.

The score of 6—1, 6—0, 6—3 was overwhelming but Budge's superiority was still more overwhelming. The three sets required only sixty-

six minutes to play, and Budge, who had won fourteen games in a row, might have made it two love sets instead of one but for a slight lapse of concentration in the closing stages.

At it was, he allowed the Englishman only four games. In 1932 Ellsworth Vines defeated this same unfortunate Austin in straight sets with the loss of only ten games. Last year, in winning the title for the first time, Budge allowed Baron Gottfried von Cramm only nine.

Master of All Amateurs

But today will ever be memorable in the career of Budge, not because of comparative scores, but because it demonstrated he had attained his full stature in the game of which he is now the undisputed master— at least in amateur tennis.

Once he had conquered his early raggedness, which permitted Austin to hold his opening service for his only tally in the first set, Budge had every shot in his great collection working at its best.

Asked by this correspondent tonight to explain how it happened, Budge smiled and said, "It was just one of those things."

"I was right—I never played better," he continued before going on to praise Austin for carrying on throughout the tournament despite the strain of becoming a father for the first time.

Actually Austin, despite the arrival of his daughter and his 31 years, today played one of the best games of his career. Except for an unwise tendency to go to the net when the situation did not justify it—certainly not against Budge— Austin produced the same orthodox

game that for years has kept him tantalizingly close to the heights.

Austin Sticks to Task

Even against a champion like Budge playing in today's form Austin never despaired. The moment Budge weakened Austin was quick as a flash to seize his opportunity— it was thus that he got his game in the first set and three in the third— and when Budge was content to stay on the baseline Austin most of the time held his own and occasionally even won a point with an untouchable placement.

Most of Austin's points, however, came from Budge's errors—which is by no means a contradiction of Budge's statement that he was "right" today. For he had to lose points now and then because there were so few winners from Austin that most of the games would otherwise have been decided at love.

Yet Austin started strongly. There was a most prolonged struggle over the first game, for Budge's first service was not functioning correctly and in unanswerable fashion. And since Budge took a certain amount of time to find his length, Austin held his own service at love. But then Budge found his game and never looked back. It wasn't anything like blowing his opponent off the court, but a calm, cool application of irresistible pressure. A couple of times in the fourth game Austin, willing to try anything, hastened to the net only to despair at the passing shots that he could not get near.

Englishman Rallies

The first set thus went calmly and the second rapidly, although Austin managed to lead at 40—15 in the fifth game and even win an advantage after Budge had drawn level.

Now the spectacle was growing unbelievable for Austin, giving his best, like the plucky fighter that he is, was producing wonder shots that only elicited still greater shots in reply. Drop shots that other players would not have attempted drew Budge in from deep in the backcourt and he put them away. Passed at the net, caught on the wrong foot on the baseline, it was all one—he gained in strength and precision as the games raced on.

Still without a sign of faltering, Budge went on through the first half of the third set, although Austin led at 40—15 in the third game. By this time it was obvious Budge was trying to close out the match with a run of seventeen games, which would have made history indeed, and the gallery applauded Austin every time he managed to save a point.

At this point the weather, which had been threatening throughout the match, produced a cold drizzle, and since it was obvious that the tournament officials hoped the match could be concluded without postponement, Budge redoubled his efforts to finish his opponent.

Budge's Service Broken

Austin, rising to the challenge, fought on all the harder and with his drives making up in precision their inferiority in power to Budge's swooping backhand, he broke Budge's service in the fourth.

A shout went up from every side of the center court stands in tribute to this effort and swelled to a roar as Austin, redoubling his efforts, took the next game at 15 and Budge was leading by only 3—2.

The American came back to take the sixth at love, but Austin captured the next before a real downpour of rain forced the authorities to order an interval.

When they returned, Budge quickly annexed the eighth game, then, after falling in the ninth, proceeded to contradict the habits of ordinary mortals by taking the next three points for a 15—40 lead. A short rally and Budge missed his first match point, then another, and Austin put his forehand in the net to decide the match and the championship.

After such a glorious victory Budge could not resist the attendants who beleaguered him to get his signature on the balls used in this historic match. Then, while Austin, in token of his defeat, laughingly held an armful of Budge's rackets, the champion spoke in the rain to a British television audience.

Eden in Royal Box

From these activities Budge and Austin were summoned to the royal box, where the Californian received the congratulations of Queen Mary and the Duke and Duchess of Kent. Sitting in the back row, unnoticed by the crowd, was Anthony Eden, who has been playing tennis mainly since he left the Foreign Office.

After such a triumph everything else today was anticlimax. But tomorrow not only will bring another meeting between those rivals of long standing, Mrs. Helen Wills Moody and Miss Helen Jacobs in the women's singles final but the possibility of a clean sweep of the championships for the United States promises to be at least more dramatic.

The all-American final in women's singles makes certain that the United States will hold both major championships. The men's doubles, next most important branch of the tournament, finds Budge and Gene Mako defending their title in the final against Henner Henkel and Georg von Metaxa of Germany, who were victors over Franz Kukuljevic and Josip Pallada of Yugoslavia to-

day, 7—5, 6—2, 6—4.

By defeating Mrs. Bobbie Heine Miller and Miss Margaret Morphew, South African team, 7—5, 6—4, Mrs. Sarah Palfrey Fabyan and Miss Alice Marble of the United States won their way to the final of women's doubles, where they will meet Mme. René Mathieu of France and Miss Adeline (Billy) Yorke of England.

Budge and Miss Marble Gain

The victory of Budge and Miss Marble over R. A. Shayes and Miss Joan Saunders of England, 6—4, 6—2, put another American team in the last round of mixed doubles against the half-American side of Henkel and Mrs. Fabyan.

As if this were not enough, the United States today came close to putting three out of four players in the final of women's doubles as well, since Mme. Mathieu and Miss Yorke had a hard fight before they eliminated Mrs. Dorothy Andrus and Mme. Sylvia Henrotin, 3—6, 6—3, 6—4.

But, of course, all other considerations pale in comparison with the drama of the latest contest between Mrs. Moody and Miss Jacobs after their historic match here for the championship three years ago. He is bold indeed who would venture to prophesy the outcome. But there is no question one of the greatest crowds ever assembled at Wimbledon will be packing every

inch of space around the center court.

THE POINT SCORE
BUDGE VS. AUSTIN

First Set								Pts.	G.
Budge	9	0	4	6	4	7	4—34		6
Austin	7	4	2	4	1	5	2—25		1

Second Set									
Budge	5	4	5	4	8	4—30			6
Austin	3	1	3	2	6	1—16			0

Third Set									
Budge	5	4	7	4	1	4	2	4—35	6
Austin	3	2	5	6	4	0	4	1 2—27	3

Stroke Analysis					
	SA.	P.	N.	O.	DF.
Budge	6	40	24	23	3
Austin	1	17	24	28	1
	E.	E.P.	T.P.	G.	Sets.
Budge	50	46	99	18	3
Austin	53	18	68	4	0

July 2, 1938

DON BUDGE'S RECORD

J. Donald Budge of California now stands as the first player in history to win in the same year all four of the world's major tennis titles—the Australian, French, British and American. It is his ironic destiny to be playing so well that he makes the tournaments in which he participates uninteresting. Since Von Cramm has been at least temporarily removed from the amateur

ranks, there is now no one in those ranks consistently capable of extending him. He seems to play tennis on another level altogether than that of his best opponents, and when he is only on even terms, as he was with Gene Mako in the second set of Saturday's final match, many of the spectators conclude merely that he is purposely throwing away points. When he is in full stride human opposition

seems hopeless. Whether Perry or Vines could stop him in his present form is the foremost question that fans now seriously debate, and thousands yearn for an open tournament, so that Budge would not have to turn professional for them to get that question answered.

September 26, 1938

BUDGE AND MISS MARBLE CAPTURE U.S. TENNIS FINALS

MAKO TAKES A SET

But Bows, 6-3, 6-8, 6-2, 6-1—Budge Wins 4th Main Title in Year

FEAT SETS A PRECEDENT

Miss Marble Disposes of Miss Wynne in 22 Minutes, 6-0, 6-3, Before 12,000

By ALLISON DANZIG

The book was closed yesterday on the greatest record of success ever compiled by a lawn tennis player in one season of national and international championship competition.

J. Donald Budge of Oakland, Calif., stood as the first player in history to win all four of the world's major tennis titles in the same year when he defeated Gene Mako of Los Angeles in the Forest Hills Stadium in the final round of the national championship. The

score was 6—3, 6—8, 6—2, 6—1.

The triumph of the 23-year-old red-headed giant, which followed upon the overwhelming victory of Miss Alice Marble of Beverly Hills, Calif., over Miss Nancye Wynne of Australia at 6—0, 6—3, in the shortest women's final on record, completed a campaign of unparalleled achievement on three continents.

Compared With Jones's Slam

No one before him has held at one and the same time the American, British, French and Australian crowns, all of which have fallen in 1938 to the rapacity of Budge's fifteen-ounce racquet for a grand slam that invites comparison with the accomplishment of Bobby Jones in golf.

In this respect, at least, Budge takes precedence over William Tilden, the Frenchmen, Henri Cochet and René Lacoste; Ellsworth Vines, Wilmer Allison, Fred Perry, the Briton, and all the other great modern champions. Jack Crawford of Australia came closest to winning four major crowns when, in 1933, he won three of the titles and led Perry, two sets to one, in the American final.

To complete Budge's record of conquest for the year: He led the United States to victory in the defense of the Davis Cup against Australia at Germantown. He won the British and American doubles and

mixed doubles and gained permanent possession of the mammoth Newport Casino Challenge Cup.

Farewell to Forest Hills?

He leaves Forest Hills behind him, possibly for the last time, and heads for the Pacific Southwest championships at Los Angeles with the satisfaction of having won every singles match of consequence in which he started and of establishing a mark that promises to stand for many years. Here, truly, is one of the great competitors of sport and one of the most genuine sportsmen to grace the game.

A gallery of 12,000 looked on under a stinging sun as Budge made history. That the stadium was not filled to capacity was probably attributable to the conviction that the outcome of his meeting with his doubles partner was foreordained. Despite the amazingly fine tennis Mako had produced to concoct the defeat of John Bromwich in the semi-finals, few, if any, conceded the stalwart, blond Los Angeles youth the slightest chance of staying the all-conquering march of the Oakland terror.

But if any had the notion that this was to be a Damon and Pythias act, they were speedily disillusioned. True, the play was animated by friendly manifestations across the net whose contagion was communicated to the gallery, particularly in

The Point Scores

BUDGE VS. MAKO

FIRST GAME
FIRST SET

					G.	Pts.
Budge	.....4 0 6 5 4 4 0 1 4—6					28
Mako	.....0 4 4 3 0 2 4 4 2—3					23

Stroke Analysis

	N.	O.	P.	SA.	DF.
Budge	8	11	14	1	1
Mako	6	7	3	0	0

SECOND SET
Point Score

					G.	Pts.
Budge	.1 4 0 4 5 5 4 1 0 1 2 4 3—2—6					36
Mako	..4 2 4 1 3 3 1 4 4 4 4 1 5 4—8					44

Stroke Analysis

	N.	O.	P.	SA.	DF.
Budge	8	20	13	2	3
Mako	12	8	12	1	1

THIRD SET
Point Score

					G.	Pts.
Budge	.....6 4 4 3 5 6 0 4—6					34
M'ko	.....4 1 1 3 3 8 4 1—2					25

Stroke Analysis

	N.	O.	P.	SA.	DF.
Budge	11	8	13	5	1
Mako	6	10	5	0	0

FOURTH SET
Point Score

					G.	Pts.
Budge	.....4 6 0 4 6 4 4—6					28
Mako	.....1 4 4 0 4 1 2—1					16

Stroke Analysis

	N.	O.	P.	SA.	DF.
Budge	4	9	10	2	0
Mako	9	4	3	0	3

RECAPITULATION

	N.	O.	P.	SA.	DF.
Budge	31	48	50	10	5
Mako	33	29	23	1	4

	E.	EP.	TP.	G.	Sets.
Budge	84	60	126	24	3
Mako	66	24	108	14	1

Umpire—Benjamin H. Dwight. Time of match—1:18. Budge started service.

MISS MARBLE VS. MISS WYNNE
FIRST SET
Point Score

		Pts.	G.
Miss Marble	.....4 4 4 4 5 4—25		6
Miss Wynne	.....0 2 1 1 3 1—8		0

Stroke Analysis

	N.	O.	P.	SA.	DF.
Miss Marble	1	3	5	1	1
Miss Wynne	5	13	2	1	1

SECOND SET
Point Score

		Pts.	G.
Miss Marble	.....4 1 5 4 2 4 4 2 4—30		6
Miss Wynne	.....1 4 3 0 4 1 0 4 1—18		3

Stroke Analysis

	N.	O.	P.	SA.	DF.
Miss Marble	4	5	7	0	4
Miss Wynne	11	11	4	1	1

RECAPITULATION

	N.	O.	P.	SA.	DF.
Miss Marble	5	8	12	1	5
Miss Wynne	16	24	6	2	2

	E.	EP.	TP.	G.	Sets.
Miss Marble	18	13	55	12	2
Miss Wynne	12	8	26	3	0

Umpire—Louis W. Shaw, Bayonne, N. J. Time of match—22 minutes. Miss Marble started service.

the third set, when the crowd was roaring with mirth as the doubles champions trapped each other repeatedly with drop shots.

Speed Marks Match

But there was no holding back on either side and there was no trace of amiability in the scorching forehand drives with which Mako caught Budge in faulty position inside the baseline or the murderous backhand and volcanic service which Budge turned loose.

If Mako had the satisfaction of being the only player in the tournament to wrest a set from the champion, it was not because Budge willed it that way. The circumstances under which it was won might have given rise to skepticism as to the validity of the achievement, for it was salvaged from a 2-5 deficit after Mako had slumped badly in the face of Budge's pitilessly raking bombardment.

Possibly at this point Budge, in the security of his commanding lead, may have relented and elected to relax the pressure of his cannonading on his helpless opponent, but if he proposed to go further than yield a game or two, his subsequent distress as his strokes got out of hand was a first class bit

of acting, and he never pretended to thespian honors.

It would be considerably less than justice not to accord Mako that full measure of praise he deserves for the brilliant tennis he put forth in winning six of the next seven games. His flat forehand was striking like lightning. His backhand slice stood up unwaveringly from any angle. He used the lob and drop shot with his usual aplomb and success and his control was so steadfast that Budge got precious little he did not earn.

The champion, struggling to regain his concentration and accuracy after getting only 3 points in three games, found his touch had deserted him. Nothing would work right for him and his footwork became faulty as he was caught out of position or hit from his heels, while his smash failed glaringly.

It was a worried-looking Budge who stared at Mako's beautiful back-hand drive that went passing by him for a final point of the set as the gallery cheered tumultuously.

With the start of the third set, command of the match reverted to the champion, and he was never seriously challenged again. Possibly Mako was content with taking that set, but whether he was or not, there was not much he could have done to stay the fate that speedily engulfed him.

Budge turned loose a tornado of controlled speed such as had been visited upon no other opponent in the tournament, with his service making the chalk fly on the lines, and Mako found that neither his drop shots nor lobs, nor blistering forehand drives could avail against

the sharpshooting that scored 30 earned points for the champion in the last two sets.

When the match ended, Mako received an ovation from the gallery for a performance which, in conjunction with his victories over Bromwich, Franjo Puncec of Yugoslavia and Frank Kovacs, should earn him a high place in the 1938 rankings and possibly serious consideration from the Davis Cup committee in 1939.

Miss Marble's victory over Miss Wynne, restoring her to the championship throne she occupied in 1936, was achieved with one of the most ruthless attacks ever launched by a woman at Forest Hills.

In the almost incredible time of twenty-two minutes the blond Californian had accomplished her task and was walking to the marquee to pose for a score of cameras as she received the cup from President Holcombe Ward of the U. S. L. T. A. after bestowing a kiss upon Umpire Louis W Shaw.

It took just seven minutes for Miss Marble to run out the opening set, in which she allowed her opponent only 8 points. Play started at a terrific pace and it was sustained at that clip to the end. There were no long rallies. Both players were hitting uncompromisingly, throwing caution to the winds, and Miss Wynne, unable to get her strokes under control, was stampeded into summary defeat, as she was in the final at Essex.

Miss Marble has seldom, if ever, had her whole battery of weapons so obedient to her dictates. From both the forehand and the backhand she was hitting with killing

pace and length, with her forehand serving her better probably than on any other occasion of her career.

Her service was so strong and deep that Miss Wynne could do little with it, and her volleys, on the few occasions she went forward, were the last word. The Californian's speed of foot was equal to that of her strokes, and from start to finish she flew around the court, attacking unmercifully in a remarkable exhibition of sustained power under almost perfect control.

Miss Wynne, swept off her feet and unable to get her own powerful weapons in hand as she was hurried into faulty timing and execution, made no effort to slow down the pace of the match. Had she changed her methods, she might have broken up the deadly precision of Miss Marble's attack, but the only type of game she knows is the one Miss Marble plays, and so she hastened the end with her mounting streak of over-hit balls.

Henry H. Bassford of Hartsdale is the new veterans' champion. In the final round he defeated Armand L. Bruneau of Brooklyn, 8—6, 4—6, 6—4.

Bruneau led at 4—2 in the first set and 3—1 in the third, and he punished Bassford severely with his drop shots and remarkably accurate lobs, but the Brooklyn veteran's backhand failed to stand up when opportunity called, and Bassford, playing his best tennis when behind, pulled out of the hole each time, to win after Bruneau had stood him off at match point four times.

September 25, 1938

ALICE MARBLE WIMBLEDON VICTOR

FIVE TITLES TO U. S.

Miss Marble Stars in Sweep, Routing Miss Stammers, 6-2, 6-0

PRAISED BY QUEEN MARY

By T. J. HAMILTON
Wireless to THE NEW YORK TIMES.

WIMBLEDON, England, July 8.—All five Wimbledon championships were again in the possession of the United States tonight after a wind-swept and rainy afternoon in the all-England tennis tournament, which will long be remembered for the sustained brilliance of Miss Alice Marble's defeat of Miss Kay Stammers for the women's singles title.

The score of 6—2, 6—0 scarcely revealed the overwhelming superiority of Miss Marble, the San Francisco girl, who was unsuccessful in

After Wimbledon Final Yesterday

Times Wide World Radiophoto

Miss Alice Marble and Miss Kay Stammers shaking hands across the net following the American champion's victory.

her bids for the title here in 1937 and last year.

After the match, which caused critics here to speak of her as being in the class with the late Suzanne Lenglen and Mrs. Helen Wills Moody when they were at their greatest, Miss Marble and Miss Stammers were summoned to the royal box, where the American girl was congratulated by Queen Mary and the United States Ambassador, Joseph P. Kennedy, on her success. Miss Marble bowed deep as her Majesty shook her hand, while the English girl curtsied.

Hare and Wilde Beaten

Two more triumphs in the doubles finals came to her later in the day after Bobby Riggs and Elwood Cooke defeated Charles Hare and Frank Wilde of England for the men's doubles championship, 6—3, 3—6, 6—3, 9—7. She and Mrs. Sarah Palfrey Fabyan retained their women's doubles title with a 6-1, 6-0 victory over Miss Helen Jacobs of Berkeley, Calif., and Miss Billy Yorke of England, and Miss Marble, who with Don Budge won the mixed doubles the last two years, teamed with Riggs in a 9-7, 6-1 triumph over Wilde and Mrs. Nina Brown.

With Riggs's triumph over his compatriot, Cooke, yesterday for the men's singles title, the United States thus repeated its clean sweep of last year, when Budge was the undisputed master.

This was to be an "open" Wimbledon, but even so the United States swept the boards, for Don McNeill, who came to grief after his victory over Riggs in the French championships, helped things along by capturing the men's consolations here (the all-England plate) by defeating J. Van Den Eynde of Belgium, 8—6, 6—2.

Seldom in the annals of Wimbledon has a woman player demonstrated such a combination of overwhelming power and varied attack as Miss Marble brought into play against Miss Stammers. In its way, her victory was perhaps even more impressive than her rout of Mme. Hilda Krahwinkel Sperling of Denmark in the semi-finals.

A Formidable Opponent

For Miss Stammers, as she proved in her own semi-final victory over Mrs. Fabyan, when she is playing at her best is a formidable opponent. A left-hander, she had an advantage in handling Miss Marble's kicking service, and her forehand, sweeping across the court to her opponent's backhand corner, is an effective forcing shot against most women players. Had Miss Marble showed the least bit of raggedness, Miss Stammers would have been ready to pounce on the chance.

But against Miss Marble playing as she was today, Miss Stammers tried everything to no avail. There is no absolute standard of form to provide a comparison, but it would seem that Miss Stammers was playing as well as she did against Mrs. Fabyan. That was not good enough today.

There is nothing to be done against a player who, after being

passed in midcourt by a lovely drive down the sidelines, runs back and replies with a perfect dropshot off the backhand. That was just one instance of the type of thing Miss Marble was doing all afternoon, and Miss Stammers, who never before had got into the Wimbledon semi-finals, simply was unfortunate in her opponent.

Even when her forehand was working well, it encountered the stone wall of Miss Marble's defense, and the American girl's cunning change of pace seldom gave Miss Stammers a chance to get set for her drives. Miss Stammers's most effective shot turned out to be a sharply angled one cross-court, but Miss Marble's length was so well controlled that she rarely got a chance to use it.

Nevertheless, Miss Stammers, who is going to the United States with the British Wightman Cup team, possibly to meet Miss Marble again, had no reason to be ashamed of her valiant fight. Her defeat was not quite a rout, although from the very start, when Miss Marble took a 2-0 lead, the result was certain. Miss Marble lost her service in the third game—the gallery applauded her sportsmanship when, believing she had put off Miss Stammers by dropping a ball while a rally was going on, she appealed unsuccessfully to the umpire to have the point played over—but got back her margin of lead with unanswerable volleying and was never pressed thereafter.

The gallery, which packed every seat and inch of standing room around the center court, kept applauding whenever Miss Stammers gave them an opportunity. But there were not many such occasions and game after game slipped past.

Pressure Kept On

The first set was gone with the loss of only one more game and Miss Marble, never relaxing her pressure, went steadily on. Miss Stammers, however, was fighting doggedly and lost only one game at love in the second set.

But it was not until the final game, when Miss Marble was leading with the score love—40 against service, that Miss Stammers managed to make a stand. Then, as the gallery roared, the English girl put everything she had into a series of fine drives, which fought off three set points and brought her to deuce. But she drove out the next point and after a long rally it was all over.

The victory of Riggs and Cooke, who succeed Budge and Gene Mako as men's doubles champions, over Hare and Wilde largely turned on the question of whether they would tire themselves out after their terribly hard fight of yesterday for the singles title. Cooke had played raggedly in the semi-finals of mixed doubles earlier in the afternoon—he and Mrs. Fabyan had lost to Wilde and Mrs. Brown, 6—3, 7—5—but as it turned out, he was by far the best player of the match.

Play was ragged throughout, but the Americans had no difficulty capturing the first set and took a brief lead in the second. But then the English pair took a spurt and, breaking Riggs's service, annexed the set; both Cooke and Riggs were tiring, although still high in spirits.

Then, however, while Riggs continued his losing shots, Cooke sprang into the breach. He was aided in the fight by the fact that Wilde became more and more erratic while Hare, perhaps because he mistrusted his injured arm, seldom put away his smashes at the

net for winners. Time after time, instead of making a certain point with an angled volley, he sent the ball zooming straight down the court. The replies from Riggs and Cooke, particularly the latter, often were clean winners.

Thus aided, Cooke and Riggs took the third set, and without much difficulty. The fourth set was

Wimbledon Champions

Men's Singles—Bobby Riggs, Chicago.
Women's Singles—Miss Alice Marble, San Francisco.
Men's Doubles—Riggs and Elwood Cooke, Portland, Ore.
Women's Doubles—Miss Marble and Mrs. Sarah Palfrey Fabyan, Cambridge, Mass.
Mixed Doubles—Riggs and Miss Marble.

close—the Englishmen were volleying effectively down the center—but when the Americans got a 7-6 lead on Cooke's service, it seemed their troubles were over. They got within a point of winning the match when one of the strangest episodes for first-class tennis robbed the encounter of its seriousness.

Not only did Cooke double-fault on a match point but he and Riggs —more often Riggs—lost four more successive points for the match and finally dropped the game to make it 7—7.

A fifth set promised trouble for the Americans, but they managed to spare themselves the ordeal by taking the next two games at love. Both Miss Jacobs and Miss Yorke seemed to sense the hopelessness of their match with Miss Marble and Mrs. Fabyan, who volleyed unanswerably whenever a rally was otherwise in doubt. Miss Yorke was

a weak partner for Miss Jacobs, but in any case, it was no contest.

In the mixed doubles Wilde played much better in the early stages and again when, after he and Mrs. Brown trailed at 5—3, they came up to make a long fight for the first set. Once it was lost, however, Riggs and Miss Marble, despite all the matches they had played in the last couple of days, put on pressure and this Wimbledon was over.

Wins In 25 Minutes

WIMBLEDON, England, July 8 (P).—It took Miss Alice Marble just twenty-five minutes to win the all-England women's singles title, and in doing so she helped lead the American array of tennis players to one of the greatest triumphs in international sport.

Miss Marble became the first woman to hold three American and three Wimbledon titles at the same time. The San Francisco girl is going to Ireland to play next week before sailing for New York on the Champlain on July 19.

THE POINT SCORE

MISS MARBLE VS. MISS STAMMERS
First Set

									Pts.	G.
Miss Marble...	7	4	4	5	4	1	4		—33	6
Miss Stammers.	5	0	6	3	0	4	2	2	—22	2

Miss Marble started serving.

Second Set

Miss Marble.........	4	5	4	4	5	—26	6
Miss Stammers......	2	3	0	2	1	3	—11	0

Miss Marble started serving.

STROKE ANALYSIS
RECAPITULATION

	N.	O.	P.	SA.	DF.
Miss Marble........	11	12	18	0	0
Miss Stammers.....	18	22	10	0	1
	E.	EP.	TP.	G.	Sets.
Miss Marble........	23	18	59	12	2
Miss Stammers.....	41	10	33	2	0

July 9, 1939

Sweep of Final Matches Against U.S. Wins Davis Cup for Australia, 3 to 2

BROMWICH VICTORY LIFTS NET TROPHY

He Routs Parker, 6-0, 6-3, 6-1, After Quist Beats Riggs, 6-1, 6-4, 3-6, 3-6, 6-4

RALLY IS UNPRECEDENTED

By ALLISON DANZIG
Special to THE NEW YORK TIMES.

HAVERFORD, Pa., Sept. 4.—The clock turned back to 1914 today as an Australian tennis team won the Davis Cup preparatory to heading home to join the colors.

In a rally without precedent in the long history of the challenge round, the players from Down

Under completed their sweep of the last three matches in the series with the United States at the Merion Cricket Club today to reclaim the Davis Cup for Australia for the first time since 1919.

With the United States leading by 2 matches to 1 by virtue of its victories in the opening singles, Adrian Quist overcame Robert Riggs in a beautifully fought endurance contest, 6—1, 6—4, 3—6, 3—6, 6—4, and John Bromwich summarily squelched America's fading hopes with a crushing victory over Frank Parker, 6—0, 6—3, 6—1.

These two triumphs, in conjunction with their victory in the doubles yesterday, gave the Australians the verdict by 3 to 2, marking the first time since the cup was put in competition in 1900 that a team had lost the first two matches in the challenge round and still managed to win.

Ward Makes Presentation

While President Holcombe Ward of the United States Lawn Tennis Association was turning the Davis Cup over to the victors in the presentation ceremonies on the courts, a cablegram was placed in the hands of Sir Norman Brookes, instructing Captain Harry Hopman and his team to return home by the first available boat. Twenty-five years ago, Sir Norman received similar instructions to report for war duty after he and Anthony Wilding had won the cup from the United States at Forest Hills.

At first it was reported that the team would leave tonight for Los Angeles to sail on the 13th for the Antipodes, but later this evening it developed that there is still a chance that Quist, Bromwich, Hopman and Jack Crawford may compete in our national championships, beginning at Forest Hills on Thursday.

It seems that Sir Norman, president of the Australian Association, has two reservations on the S. S. Monterey of the Matson Line, sailing from Los Angeles on the 13th, and that he wishes to turn them over to the team, deferring his departure until his two daughters arrive here from England to join him and Lady Brookes in sailing on the Mariposa on Oct. 10.

Will Phone to Australia

Captain Hopman, however, is unwilling to split up the team, stating that it won the cup as a team and will return as a team. He plans to call the Australian Association tomorrow from New York and ask that the men be allowed to play at Forest Hills and sail on the Mariposa. Sir Norman is understood to be making efforts to obtain two additional reservations on the Monterey so that the four players can leave together next week.

At any rate, the Davis Cup will leave these shores in the near future on a 10,000-mile trip, and it may be years before it will be seen again here. There will be no further competition until the new world war is over (there was a four-year lapse after the 1914 matches) and even should hostilities be brought to an early conclusion, it is going to be all the more difficult to beat the Australians on their own courts, which are considerably faster than American turf.

As the winning players gathered around the cup, which apparently every one but themselves had thought was sure to remain here after the opening day's matches, they were as happy as a lot of schoolboys. The fact that all of them might be carrying guns within a few months did not enter into their thoughts for the moment. That scrap could wait for a little while. All that counted at this time was that they had redeemed themselves magnificently, coming from far behind to achieve the victory which they had been favored to gain originally by odds of 3 to 1.

Crowd Acclaims Triumph

The triumph was whole-heartedly acclaimed by the crowd of 7,500, despite its keen disappointment over America's loss of the cup. How much the spectators wanted the trophy to stay here was evidenced in the enthusiasm with which they cheered Riggs as he came back brilliantly after losing ten successive games in the first two sets, and his defeat, after he appeared to have the tiring Quist at his mercy at the start of the fifth set, left them depressed and fearing the worst.

Their fears were quickly realized, for it was soon perceived that Parker, with his totally inadequate and incessantly attacked forehand, was no match for Bromwich, who took the first seven games, lost the next three and then won ten more in succession before yielding the only other one that Parker got.

In winning today, Quist and Bromwich, particularly the former, vindicated the judgment of those who had visualized them as such dangerous threats before the series started. They were so much better than they had been on the opening day that there was no comparison. The greater speed of the turf, dried out by two additional days of sun, probably had something to do with it, and Sir Norman had predicted that in the role of underdogs they would play better tennis than they did when they were the big favorites.

Quist expressed the belief after his match that he had played the best tennis he has ever produced in this country and vouchsafed that his lack of a stiff test in months preparatory to his meeting with Parker on Saturday had been responsible for his faulty play on that occasion. Today, the 26-year-old Australian had his ground strokes functioning beautifully, and it was the strength of his drives, especially his powerful, flat forehand that enabled him to turn the tables on Riggs, who defeated him in the opening match of last year's challenge round series.

Takes Ten Games in Row

The gallery could scarcely credit its eyes as Quist ran ten games in succession after losing the first one of the match on his service. Riggs had turned in such a masterful performance against Bromwich that the crowd had complete confidence in his ability to clinch the cup, but here he was being played to a standstill.

Against the Australian's fast, deep drives the American was hitting raggedly from both sides. He could not generate any pace, he was short of length and he was not volleying well, chiefly for the reason that his approaching shots were not giving him adequate protection against so sharp a hitter as Quist.

Quist got better and better and his superiority stood out particularly in the return of service. He was keeping his service high on Riggs's backhand and the American did not like it, and Riggs was not putting Quist's backhand under the pressure that did Parker.

In the second set Riggs called on his drop shots in the effort to break up Quist's drives, but neither they nor his lobs availed. The Australian continued to pound the ball back deep and get to the net for winning volleys and smashes and Riggs continued to volley badly or to find himself passed.

The play was getting closer now, with long deuce games the rule, but Riggs could not break up Quist's procession until the score stood 4—0. In the next game Quist reached 40—15 on two passing shots and a double fault, and here the tide turned. The pace of the bitterly fought games finally began to tell on the Australian and his errors enabled the other to salvage the game.

Riggs now forged ahead, fighting with might and main and getting more speed and length on his shots as the opposition weakened. The crowd cheered him on and it seemed that he might save the set as he went to 3—4. But Quist, conserving his energies for his service, saved the vitally important eighth game from 15—30 to stay ahead at 5—3.

When Riggs won the ninth quickly with his service the gallery was prepared to see him get on even terms, for Quist was plainly fading. But the Australian had saved himself in the ninth again for his service, and after Captain Hopman had administered to him, he went out and took the tenth game at love for the set, Riggs presenting him with the first two points on weak returns of service that brought groans from the worked-up gallery.

The match was decided here in this second set. Riggs came back to win the third after some of the most sensational play of the match. At first Quist appeared ready to concede it. Then, at 0—2, he changed his mind as he perceived that Riggs was tiring too and presenting him with point after point on bad mistakes, and shortly they were going at it hammer and tongs again until Quist finally broke from fatigue.

After the rest period Riggs played his finest tennis of the match to break down Quist's resistance. The American had all his confidence now. He was timing his shots perfectly and his drop volleys were working like a charm as he carefully opened the court, while his marvelous backhand lobs were keeping the other back.

Returns to the Fight

Quist looked like a very tired man as he lost the last four games of the set, with Riggs going along like a whirlwind, and when the American took the first game of the last set from 0—30 with two volleys and a smash the crowd was sure that the cup was safe. But Quist had far more in reserve than any one suspected. He now came back into the fight with the same kind of tennis he had shown at the start.

Riggs, taken back by the strength of the resistance, was forced on the defensive. His volleying touch deserted him. His lobs lost the necessary length and Quist's deadly forehand, which Riggs insisted on attacking, passed him beautifully time and again.

Quist took five games in a row. Here Riggs braced and staged a rally that had the crowd in an agony of suspense and excitement. Fighting magnificently, Riggs pulled up to 4—5, saving a match point in the bitterly contested ninth game of 16 points, but Quist put everything he had into the tenth, attacked irresistibly at the net and with his service, and the match ended as Riggs's return of service overreached the base line.

A Keen Disappointment

The match between Parker and Bromwich was an anticlimax despite the fact that it was the deciding one. After his victory over Quist, Parker's performance today was a keen disappointment and his forehand never before has looked so utterly inadequate. Bromwich hit nine out of every ten balls to the forehand and it was by everlastingly adhering to this plan that he won by his crushing margin.

The tennis was totally uninteresting to watch. At first the gallery started chuckling as the two players stood at their baselines and exchanged 30, 40 or even 50 drives, with hardly a volley, the first game lasting six minutes. But after a set of that, it had had enough, and some of the crowd began to leave.

Parker caused a flurry as he took three games in a row from 0—1 in the second set to lead, 3—1, attacking brilliantly at the net and smashing more decisively. But from then on he was at Bromwich's mercy, whether he stayed back or went forward. He could not keep the ball away from the Australian's double-handed drive, and no matter to which side he played it or how high he sought to keep it, it always came back. Bromwich won the next ten games with the loss of eleven points, dropped the next one, and then ended the hopelessly uneven match.

Davis Cup Point Scores

QUIST VS. RIGGS

FIRST SET

Point Score

							Pts.	G.
Quist	4	4	4	5	6	4	5—32	6
Riggs	6	0	2	3	4	1	3—19	1

Stroke Analysis

	N.	O.	P.	SA.	DF.
Quist	4	4	10	0	0
Riggs	11	11	11	0	0

SECOND SET

Point Score

										Pts.	G.
Quist	6	4	6	7	3	2	1	4	1	4—38	6
Riggs	4	0	4	5	5	4	4	2	4	0—32	4

Stroke Analysis

	N.	O.	P.	SA.	DF.
Quist	8	9	11	0	0
Riggs	10	15	14	1	2

THIRD SET

Point Score

									Pts.	G.
Quist	0	1	4	4	3	4	3	3	1—23	3
Riggs	4	4	2	0	5	1	5	5	4—30	6

Stroke Analysis

	N.	O.	P.	SA.	DF.
Quist	7	13	10	0	0
Riggs	5	8	10	0	0

FOURTH SET

Point Score

									Pts.	G.
Quist	4	1	4	1	4	1	0	4	1—20	3
Riggs	2	4	2	4	1	4	4	6	4—31	6

Stroke Analysis

	N.	O.	P.	SA.	DF.
Quist	7	10	12	0	1
Riggs	4	4	12	1	0

FIFTH SET

Point Score

										Pts.	G.
Quist	2	4	4	5	5	4	2	2	7	4—39	6
Riggs	4	2	0	3	3	0	4	4	9	1—30	4

Stroke Analysis

	N.	O.	P.	SA.	DF.
Quist	12	8	15	0	0
Riggs	9	15	9	1	0

RECAPITULATION

	N.	O.	P.	SA.	DF.
Quist	38	44	58	0	1
Riggs	39	53	56	3	2

	E.	EP.	TP.	G.	Sets.
Quist	83	58	152	24	3
Riggs	94	59	142	21	2

Quist started service.

Umpire—Paul W. Gibbons. Time of match—2:06.

BROMWICH VS. PARKER

FIRST SET

Point Score

							Pts.	G.
Bromwich	9	4	7	5	4	4	—33	6
Parker	7	1	5	3	1	2	—19	0

Stroke Analysis

	N.	O.	P.	SA.	DF.
Bromwich	1	12	9	0	0
Parker	6	17	6	0	1

SECOND SET

Point Score

									Pts.	G.
Bromwich	4	0	2	2	4	4	4	4	4—28	6
Parker	1	4	4	4	1	1	2	0	2—19	3

Stroke Analysis

	N.	O.	P.	SA.	DF.
Bromwich	4	7	12	0	1
Parker	3	13	7	0	0

THIRD SET

Point Score

							Pts.	G.
Bromwich	5	4	4	4	4	2	6—29	6
Parker	3	2	0	0	0	4	4—13	1

Stroke Analysis

	N.	O.	P.	SA.	DF.
Bromwich	5	4	11	0	0
Parker	4	14	4	0	0

RECAPITULATION

	N.	O.	P.	SA.	DF.
Bromwich	10	23	32	0	1
Parker	13	44	17	0	1

	E.	EP.	TP.	G.	Sets.
Bromwich	34	32	90	18	3
Parker	58	17	51	4	0

Bromwich started service.

Umpire—Benjamin H. Dwight. Time of match—1:16.

September 5, 1939

Riggs and Kovacs Sign for Tour As Tennis Pros With Budge, Perry

Alexis Thompson to Book 80 Matches in U. S. and Canada for Stars—First Appearance Is Slated in Garden on Dec. 26

By ROSCOE McGOWEN

Two more top-ranking tennis players deserted the amateur game to become professionals yesterday. Bobby Riggs, national singles champion, and Frank Kovacs, holder of the indoor title, have signed contracts to appear in a series of eighty matches throughout the United States and Canada.

Announcement of these signings, along with those of Don Budge, former world professional singles and doubles titleholder, and Fred Perry, present possessor of those two titles, was made yesterday by Alexis Thompson, owner of the Philadelphia Eagles of the National Football League and head of the East-West Sporting Club, Inc., of 9 Rockefeller Plaza, New York City.

This quartet of tennis aces, Thompson said, will open the campaign in Madison Square Garden on the night of Friday, Dec. 26, when Budge and Kovacs and Riggs and Perry will meet in singles, while the doubles on the same program will pit Budge and Perry, "the world's greatest professionals," against Riggs and Kovacs, "1941's leading amateurs."

Atlantic City on Schedule

The only definite following date, according to Harry M. Thayer, business manager for Thompson, will be in Philadelphia on Dec. 30. "But," he said, "the boys probably, almost definitely, will appear in Atlantic City on New Year's Day."

Contemplated stops on the tour, according to Thayer, include Boston, Providence, Washington, Baltimore, Hershey, Pa.; Pittsburgh, Youngstown, Ohio; Chicago, Minneapolis, Milwaukee, Detroit, three Canadian cities—Hamilton, Toronto and Montreal—Syracuse, Rochester, Buffalo, Cleveland, Akron, Toledo, Indianapolis, Cincinnati and Louisville.

Perhaps the outstanding feature of Thompson's promotion is the percentage arrangement on which the four players will be paid. Heretofore players who have turned pro have worked under an arrangement whereby each was paid the same amount for all appearances, win or lose.

Thompson has signed his four stars on a stipulation that the No. 1 player of the tour will receive 36 per cent of the players' share; the No. 2 man, 28 per cent; the No. 3 player, 21 per cent, and the No. 4 player, 15 per cent.

Results to Decide Shares

"Thus," explained Thompson, "the amount any player realizes from the tour will depend upon how well he plays. The No. 1 player should receive between $40,000 and $45,000, while the fellow who finishes fourth on the tour will draw from $10,000 to $15,000 less."

Thompson has guaranteed the four players that their total share of the tour's receipts will not be less than $100,000. In addition, Thompson personally has guaranteed a cash bonus each night for the doubles winners—an amount which he did not reveal.

Only two of the players—Budge and Riggs — were present yesterday at Toots Shor's restaurant where Thompson made the announcement.

November 27, 1941

Miss Betz Upsets Miss Brough in Three-Set Women's National Tennis Final

LOS ANGELES GIRL VICTOR, 4-6, 6-1, 6-4

Miss Betz Reverses Result of 2 Previous Matches to Beat Miss Brough for Title

---

MULLOY AND TALBERT WIN

Halt Schroeder-Wood in U. S. Doubles Final at Forest Hills, 9-7, 7-5, 6-1

By ALLISON DANZIG

The player who had conquered every rival and won every major women's tennis tournament on grass this season met her Waterloo yesterday in the final of the national championship at Forest Hills.

Miss Pauline Betz of Los Angeles and Rollins College is the new champion.

A fighter who stands up to adversity as have few other women players, the blond Californian ended the long winning streak of Miss Louise Brough of Beverly Hills, Calif., in a beautifully fought match as 8,000 looked on in the stadium of the West Side Tennis Club. The score was 4—6, 6—1, 6—4.

A year ago Miss Betz lost the championship final to Mrs. Sarah Palfrey Cooke after defeating her

Miss Pauline Betz leaping over the net to greet her opponent, Miss Louise Brough, after the national championship final, in which the former triumphed in three sets.
Associated Press

in two previous meetings. Yesterday it was her good fortune to turn the tables on the 19-year-old Miss Brough, who had beaten her in the finals at Rye and Manchester.

Miss Brough did not play quite so well at Forest Hills as she had elsewhere. Miss Mary Arnold carried her to three sets and so did Miss Helen Bernhard whom she had overwhelmed at East Hampton.

Against Miss Betz, Miss Brough played like Alice Marble for a good part of the first set and at times in the third, but she paid the penalty for her extreme youth and lack of experience in failing to assert her hand boldly against an opponent who attacked at every opportunity.

A Splendid Net Player

Miss Brough has the best service and one of the finest backhands and is the most accomplished net player in the women's ranks. She is fast around the court, too, but she hung back too much and allowed her hitting to become tentative.

Miss Betz played her best tennis of the year. She has an extremely strong backhand and seldom has it served her so well, across court or straight. Her forehand, the vulnerable point of her game, stood up remarkably well, excelling her backhand at times in its pace and length.

From both sides Miss Betz was whaling the ball. She was tearing around the court with her usual abandon and taking heavy falls. She was rushing into the volleying position at every chance and her lobs were a particularly strong factor.

Probably it was Miss Betz's lobs that discouraged her rival from going to the net. They were not always of good length, but Miss Brough became chary of them and was not nearly so effective overhead as she usually is, putting even the short ones into the net.

In the opening set Miss Betz led at 3—1 and then lost the next four games, three of them at 6—4. In the second set Miss Betz lost her opening service and then ran six games in a row. Miss Brough was letting her rival take over the attack almost entirely and her control crumpled against Miss Betz's sweeping drives.

Deciding Set a Thriller

The third set was a stirring battle. Miss Betz's ground strokes were at their best and she was doing most of the volleying. Failure to take advantage of openings cost her important points, but she kept attacking regardless, while Miss Brough alternately played aggressive and defensive tennis.

Miss Betz broke through for a 3-2 lead with her volleys, lost her service and then effected the deciding break in the seventh. The match ended with Miss Brough hitting into the alley.

Lieutenant Gardnar Mulloy of the Jacksonville Naval Air Station and William Talbert of Cincinnati were crowned the new men's doubles champions. In the final they defeated Ted Schroeder of Glendale, Calif., and Sidney B. Wood Jr. of New York, 9—7, 7—5, 6—1.

In service, return of service and in their volleying and smashing, Mulloy and Talbert maintained a high efficiency. Wood failed to back up his service at the net and the deciding breaks were made through him in the first and second sets. Schroeder cracked in the third, when the play turned into a rout.

The mixed doubles semi-final between Miss Betz and Pancho Segura and Mrs. Patricia Canning Todd and Alejo Russell provoked the greatest demonstration of the day. Mrs. Todd and Russell won, 4—6, 7—5, 6—3. In the other semi-final Miss Brough and Schroeder defeated Miss Margaret Osborne and Tom Brown of California, 6—1, 7—9, 6—2.

September 7, 1942

Schroeder Defeats Parker in Stirring 5-Set Match for National Tennis Title

10,000 FANS THRILL TO GREAT NET FINAL

Schroeder Topples Parker in Forest Hills Stadium, 8-6, 7-5, 3-6, 4-6, 6-2

MISS BROUGH WINS TWICE

Takes Women's Doubles With Miss Osborne and Mixed Title With Schroeder

By ALLISON DANZIG

In one of the most enthralling matches the tournament ever has provided Frederick R. (Ted) Schroeder Jr. of Glendale, Calif., volleyed down the superb resistance of Frank Parker of Hollywood, Calif., yesterday to win the men's national amateur tennis championship at Forest Hills.

For two and a half hours two wiry, tight-lipped antagonists fought tooth-and-nail, each inspiring the other to reach increasing heights of brilliance in a match that was all attack or counter-attack.

Ten thousand spectators looked down from the stadium of the West Side Tennis Club upon this fluctuating match and made the welkin ring with the stormiest, most partisan cheering heard there in years. When the verdict finally was reached at 8—6, 7—5, 3—6, 4—6, 6—2 in favor of the 21-year-old Schroeder, who will report to Annapolis on Friday in the V-7 Division of the Naval Reserve, the crowd roared its appreciation of one of the great finals of tennis.

Miss Betty Gunn of Montana, Schroeder's fiancée, ran out from the marquee to throw her arms around the new champion, to whom she is to be married when he has received his commission.

Parker Gets Ovation

For the 27-year-old Parker, an unsuccessful contender for the championship since he was the boy wonder of the courts, there was the ovation that goes to a fighter game to the core who never gives up nor slackens his effort in the face of the most discouraging vicissitudes.

Denied the first set after leading by 4-2, as well as the second, in which he established the huge advantage of 5—2 and deuce on his

Miss Margaret Osborne and Miss Louise Brough with their trophies after they beat Miss Pauline Betz and Miss Doris Hart to take doubles.
The New York Times

own service, Parker won over the crowd with the dazzling tennis he produced when his plight seemed hopeless.

Schroeder, a fighter who refuses to let up or give an inch without a contest, had to yield to the deadly targetry of his rival's volley and forcing shots in the third set. The play was taken away from Schroeder again after he had led at 3—2 and 40—15 on his service in the fourth, as Parker harried him unmercifully.

Another player might have weakened in the face of so violent a resurgence, but not Schroeder. Now it was the turn of the lithe, sinewy youth from Glendale to show the steel in his fiber.

Volleys Turn Tide

In the fifth set he tore after Parker full blast with his dynamic volleying attack. Behind his whiplash service and his return of service Schroeder rushed to close quarters, from where his smoking forehand cross-court volleys, his biting backhand volleys, his adroit block volleys and his reverberating smashes overwhelmed resistance.

Parker fought with all his cunning and skill to stem the onslaught, but it was beyond his power. Though he got only two games the fight was much closer, and had not Parker's straight backhand passing shots failed by inches time and again Schroeder would

not have taken five games in a row, three of them going to deuce.

Leading at 5—1, Schroeder went to 40—0. Here Parker made a magnificent rally and stood off three match points. Again Schroeder reached 40—0 in the eighth game, and twice more Parker turned him back at match point.

The crowd was ready to tear down the stadium if Parker pulled out this game, too, but Schroeder served, went to the net and brought the fight to an end with a cross-court forehand volley.

Parker Leads in Points

Parker won more points than Schroeder, 180 to 177. Schroeder had 88 earned points to Parker's 55 and 125 errors to 89.

Schroeder captured ten successive games that went to deuce-six of seven in the first set, all three in the second and the first in the third. Parker then took the next five that went to deuce, three in the third and both in the fourth.

Early in the afternoon Miss Louise Brough of Beverly Hills, who had been beaten in the singles final by Miss Pauline Betz of Los Angeles on Sunday, teamed with Miss Margaret Osborne of San Francisco to win the women's doubles crown. Miss Brough and Miss Osborne lost the first set and were down, 3—5, in the second before they went on to victory over Miss Betz and Miss Doris Hart of Miami,

2—6, 7—5, 6—0.

In the closing match, with darkness settling upon the stadium, Mrs. Patricia Canning Todd of Jackson Heights and Alejo Russell of Argentina had the crowd roaring without let-up as they challenged Miss Brough and Schroeder in three exciting sets. However, the Californians won, 3—6, 6—1, 6—4, each of them thus carrying off two titles.

Before the mixed doubles final, thirty members of the American Women's Voluntary Services, which shared in the proceeds of the championships, paraded in the stadium. With the post band from Mitchel Field providing the music, they passed in review before their national president, Mrs. Alice McLean.

Lieutenant Henry Kelleher, speaking for Colonel Douglas Johnson, praised the contribution of the A. W. V. S. to the war effort. President Alrick H. Man of the West Side Tennis Club and P. Schuyler Van Bloem, general chairman of the tournament committee, also spoke and Conrad Thibault sang the national anthem.

September 8, 1942

MRS. COOKE HALTS MISS BETZ IN FINAL

Bostonian Regains U. S. Tennis Crown With 3-6, 8-6, 6-4 Victory in Tense Match

---

RIVAL'S 3-YEAR REIGN ENDS

Talbert Again Tops Segura to Gain Last Round at Forest Hills, 7-5, 6-3, 6-4

By ALLISON DANZIG

The three-year reign of Miss Pauline Betz of Los Angeles as Women's National Tennis Champion ended in the Forest Hills Stadium yesterday. Back on the throne again sits Mrs. Sarah Palfrey Cooke of Boston, titleholder in 1941 and the only player from the East to win the crown since Mrs. Mallory's seventh triumph in 1926.

In a beautifully fought final that had the 10,000 spectators in a state of almost breathless excitement, with the outcome in doubt to the last stroke, Mrs. Cooke rose to her most shining moments when her fortunes seemed to be ebbing fast, to snatch victory from a valiant rival, through the sheer brilliance and enterprise of her attack. The score was 3—6, 8—6, 6—4.

William F. Talbert of Wilmington, Del., invincible all season, faltered under a savage opening onslaught from Francisco (Pancho) Segura in the semi-finals of the men's singles, but rallied from 1—4 to assert his supremacy once again over his rival from Ecuador, 7—5, 6—3, 6—4.

Talbert will face Sgt. Frank Parker of the Army Air Forces for the championship today, as he did a year ago. Parker won in four sets on that occasion. He will face a more dangerous Talbert this time and sentiment appears to lean slightly in favor of the 1944 runner-up.

Talbert was on the court for nearly two hours in the final of the men's doubles. With Lieut. Gardnar Mulloy, USNR, his partner in winning the 1942 championship, he stood off the challenge of Air Cadet Robert Falkenburg and S1/C Jack Tuero without reaching a decision. The match was called because of darkness with the score 10—all in the third set. Mulloy and Talbert won the first, 12—10, and lost the second, 10—8.

Talbert left the court limping slightly from a pulled muscle and because of the fact that he still has a semi-final mixed doubles match to play this championship will not be concluded until tomorrow. The men's and women's doubles finals will be held today along with the men's singles and one semi-final of the mixed.

The doubles match concluded one of the most interesting days of tennis Forest Hills has provided in recent years. The crowd was the largest to gather in the stadium since 1942.

Ceremonies for V-J Day

Before Mrs. Cooke and Miss Betz went on the court there was a short ceremony in observance of V-J Day. After the playing of the National Anthem, P. Schuyler Van Bloem, president of the West Side Tennis Club, expressed the nation's gratitude for the successful conclusion of the war. Then, with the crowd standing, Lieut. (j. g.) R. Frank Crawley, Navy chaplain, led in prayer.

The women's singles final was the stirring fight that had been anticipated. Mrs. Cooke had beaten Miss Betz at Rye and in the national clay court championship, as well as in the 1941 final at Forest Hills, and figured to be the blonde Californian's most dangerous rival, even though Mrs. Cooke has been out of competition almost entirely since her triumph of four years ago.

Mrs. Cooke won because she had the better game and because she played it up to the hilt when anything short of her best would have been inadequate in the final stages. Miss Betz has a fine backhand, a courage that never wavers and more speed around the court than any rival in the top flight.

All of these assets, however, were not enough. Mrs. Cooke had the better forehand and was more effective in the forecourt, particularly overhead. There was purpose and calculation in her every stroke and she had the weapons to profit by the openings her strategy effected.

Mrs. Cooke at Her Best

With all her attributes, Mrs. Cooke had to play the finest tennis she had shown in years to overcome Miss Betz's magnificent resistance when the latter led, 4—3, in the final set, with service following. The new champion's performance was almost perfection in the last three games. Her ground strokes were infallible and she hit so deep and at such angles that she had her rival running frantically to keep on the ball.

The spectators obviously were for the little player from New England. They had looked on silently as she lost five games in a row after leading, 3—1, in the first set. They had cheered her on as she went ahead at 5—2 in the second and had exulted when she stopped Miss Betz's rally to square the match.

In the fluctuating final set, they almost gave up hope for Mrs. Cooke at 3—4 and then roared forth encouragement as she launched her unbeatable rally to run the defending champion ragged and keep her under merciless pressure from every quarter. At 15—40 in the final game, match point, a breathless silence fell upon the scene and then cheers split the air as Miss Betz's volley went out of court to mark the crowning of a new champion.

The stroke analysis reveals how extremely close was the play. Miss Cooke made 63 errors to her rival's 62 and 39 earned points to 44.

In the men's semi-final Segura started like a ball of fire and hit with such jolting speed that Talbert found himself outplayed until the score stood 4-1 against him. Segura was returning service like a shot and, surprisingly, beating Talbert from the back of the court in the lengthy backhand duels.

Talbert was missing far more often than is his wont, both off the ground and with his volley, and he was not getting his first service into play. It seemed that nothing could stop Segura from taking the set, but Talbert settled down and as he found his control and length Segura fell off in accuracy under the pressure and the American eventually had the situation under control.

The set ended on an unhappy note as Talbert scored on the baseball and whistles and cries of protest against the decision filled the air.

After that set Segura was never so effective again. He slumped badly in the second, but rallied in the third. He reached brilliant heights in this final chapter, to win volumes of applause with his game fight, but Talbert had his game in hand and the superiority of his backhand and service pulled him out on top after the score had gone to 4-all.

THE SUMMARIES

MEN'S SINGLES
Semi-Final Round—William F. Talbert defeated Francisco Segura, 7—5, 6—3, 6—4.

WOMEN'S SINGLES
Final—Mrs. Sarah Palfrey Cooke defeated Miss Pauline Betz, 3—6, 8—6, 6—4.

September 3, 1945

THE CHAMPION AND RUNNER-UP IN TITLE TENNIS

Mrs. Sarah Palfrey Cooke and Miss Pauline Betz

The New York Times

Louise Brough took 3 consecutive Wimbledon titles (1948-50) and won the U.S. championship in 1947.

Richard (Pancho) Gonzalez won the U.S. amateur title in 1948 and 1949. Most of his career, however, was spent on the pro tour, playing one-night stands that drew relatively little newspaper coverage. It is tempting to speculate as to how he might have done had the era of open tennis come during his prime.

PARKER CONQUERS TALBERT IN FINAL

Keeps U. S. Tennis Title With 14-12, 6-1, 6-2 Victory in Forest Hills Stadium

---

LEG INJURY HAMPERS RIVAL

But Wilmington Player Takes Doubles Championships With Mulloy and Miss Osborne

By ALLISON DANZIG

Sgt. Frank Parker's 9,000-mile flight from Guam to defend his national amateur tennis championship had its happy landing yesterday.

A gathering of 13,500, filling the Forest Hills Stadium for the first time since pre-war days, acclaimed the lithe, perfectly conditioned noncom from the Army Air Forces as he ended the long winning streak of William F. Talbert of Wilmington, Del., in the final of the sixty-fourth annual tournament.

One magnificent set lasting 1 hour 6 minutes settled the issue in this return meeting of last year's finalists. Talbert, invincible throughout the season, entered the one match he had dreamed of winning with a lame leg and when he finally lost that ordeal of twenty-six games, after standing at set point in the twentieth and leading by 12—11 and 30—0, his hopes were sunk and the end came quickly, at 14—12, 6—1, 6—2.

The great crowd that poured into the West Side Tennis Club Stadium will not soon forget the enthralling fight that Talbert made despite the trick fate had dealt him in a knee injury. Equally memorable was the accuracy of the inscrutable Parker, playing in his first tournament of the year in the East, in standing up to the violence of Talbert's service and ground strokes and all but breaking his rival's heart with the deadly targetry of his straight backhand passing shots.

Talbert Not At His Best

Parker's performance was so completely up to his standard of well-nigh perfect control of the ball and he was so game a fighter that to raise any doubt about his victory seems unworthy. At the same time, in fairness to Talbert, who had won ten successive tournaments this year, it must be said that he was in no condition to do himself full justice.

His tennis in the first set was amazingly fine but his limp was only too apparent. He was laboring under a handicap in his volleying and when he had to change direction or run wide for the ball.

Talbert had pulled a tendon in his left knee in the third set of his semi-final with Francisco Segura on Sunday. It was not until he aggravated it in the men's doubles match which followed, that his injury became noticeable and it was not until yesterday morning that it was realized how lame he was.

Talbert has seldom played so brilliantly as he did in the long opening set. His volleying was adversely affected and there were times when he allowed balls to go unchallenged, but in general he was attacking with speed, length and daring and serving magnificently.

Talbert was the aggressor almost throughout that first set. He did virtually all the volleying, Parker going forward hardly more than half a dozen times, and he was hitting for the winner regularly.

Parker, however, had so much depth on his shots and kept on so much pressure from the back court that his defense amounted to attack. Whenever Talbert went to the net Parker sighted for the lines and his aim was so true that it was courting disaster to go forward unless the court was wide open.

Long Driving Rallies

The driving exchanges were superb. For the most part they fought it out from the backhand, but occasionally they switched to the forehand and there were rallies in which the ball crossed the net thirty times or more.

In the opening set Talbert earned 41 points, 8 on service aces, to Parkers 22, of which 2 were on service. The errors told the story, as they usually do in Parker's victories. He made only 36 in the 26 games to Talbert's 63.

Parker won the second set in eighteen minutes and the third in seventeen. In the last two sets Parker made a total of only thirteen errors, to Talbert's thirty-five.

In winning the championship for the second year in a row, Parker did not lose a set. He will leave for Guam on Wednesday.

Talbert later had the satisfaction of carrying off two titles. With Lieut. Gardnar Mulloy, USNR, he won the men's doubles, repeating their triumph of 1942, and with Miss Margaret Osborne of San Francisco captured the mixed doubles cups for the third year in a row to earn outright possession.

In the men's doubles final, Talbert and Mulloy defeated Air Cadet Robert Falkenburg and S/1c Jack Tuero, 12—10, 8—10, 12—10, 6—2. The match was resumed at 10-all in the third set, where it had been interrupted by darkness on Sunday.

Talbert and Miss Osborne defeated Miss Doris Hart and Falkenburg in the mixed doubles final, 6—4, 6—4.

Miss Osborne and Miss Drough tied a record by winning the women's doubles for the fourth year in a row. They beat Miss Pauline Betz and Miss Hart in the final.

September 4, 1945

Kramer Turns Back Tom Brown in Straight Sets to Annex U.S. Tennis Crown

14,000 SEE FINAL END AT 9-7, 6-3, 6-0

Kramer Halts the Advance of Tom Brown and Carries Off National Tennis Title

---

MISS BETZ WINS, 11-9, 6-3

By ALLISON DANZIG

John Kramer had his rendezvous with his manifest destiny yesterday.

The 25-year-old Californian at last sits on the national tennis throne which was ticketed for his future occupancy from the time he first came East as a junior.

The victim of successive vicissitudes that upset the timetable of his elevation, the tall, sandy-haired ex-lieutenant of the United States Coast Guard toppled the meteoric new pretender to the crown, Tom Brown of San Francisco, in a manner to establish him as one of the real masters of the all-court attack

Miss Pauline Betz returning the ball to Miss Doris Hart in match at Forest Hills yesterday

Associated Press

to win the championship, 9-7, 6-3, 6-0.

With 14,000 spectators looking down from the packed embankments of the Forest Hills Stadium, Kramer slugged it out with the bombarding Brown in one long, blazing set. When the decision finally went against the 23-year-old Army veteran, after he had saved four set points in a thrilling tenth game and broken through service for a 7-6 lead, the conqueror of Frank Parker and Gardnar Mulloy had shot his bolt of lightning.

Master of the Court

From then on Kramer was indisputably the master of the court, so sound and faithful to the tenets of orthodoxy and keeping on such grinding pressure with his lethal service, return of service and volleys that the lacerating drives of Brown were reduced to impotency in the final set.

Rushing ahead at 3—0 in the second set, Kramer fought off Brown's last outburst of sensational hitting in the ninth game. Four times again the youth from San Francisco saved set point, amid roaring cheers, and twice he held advantage, a stroke away from an equalizing break.

When he lost the game and the set, Brown must have known beyond question that he had met his master. Any lingering doubts that he may have had were speedily resolved as the cool, poised youth on the other side of the net kept his backhand under implacable pressure with a withering onslaught of forcing shots that broke down resistance and opened wide the court for flying cross-court volleys.

In sixteen minutes Kramer swept through the final set at love, with his every high-voltage stroke functioning faultlessly in carrying out an attack as impeccably correct in its conception as it was sound in execution.

Winning Streak Ends

An hour and eleven minutes after Umpire Harold Lebair had called "play," including the time-out taken to quiet the boos and uproarious protests on decisions in the explosive opening set, Brown had come to the end of his meteoric winning streak and Kramer was seated on the throne of the mighty.

The crowd that turned out for the men's final and to see Miss Pauline Betz of Los Angeles come from behind with reckless courage under punishment to defeat Miss Doris Hart of Miami, 11—9, 6—3, for her fourth women's crown, filled the stadium to the last seat. There were 15,000 present on Saturday, but the tournament officials closed the gate early yesterday to prevent overcrowding, and many were turned away.

The successive sell-outs marked the first time the stadium has been filled to capacity two days running. A record for gross receipts was set also. They were estimated at $125,000, and the paid attendance at 75,000.

A record was established, too, for a women's championship final in the length of the opening set, which required twenty games and fifty-six minutes of play for a decision.

That Miss Betz won the set is a testimonial to as unconquerable a competitive spirit as the championship has known. It was also attributable to the collapse of Miss Hart's backhand after she

had led at 5—2, with her own service coming up, and had punished the champion severely with the variety and forcefulness of her manuevers.

A Storm of Protest

The deciding break came in the twentieth game and it brought forth a storm of protest from the crowd. Leading at 30—15, Miss Hart served. Her first service looked to have over-reached the line and when Miss Betz knocked the ball back down the middle of the court the Florida girl made no effort to return it, thinking the serve faulty. The linesmen, however, signalled that the serve was good and the umpire, Louis Shaw, called the score "30-all."

A roar of indignation went up, but the decision stood. Miss Hart won the next point for 40—30 and then erred three times in succession to lose the game and the set.

Whether she was upset by the decision or was feeling the effects of the long, wearing fight, Miss Hart was never so effective again.

Miss Betz succeeds Mrs. Sarah Palfrey Cooke as the titleholder.

Mrs. Cooke, who did not defend, defeated the Californian in the final last year and in 1941. Miss Betz won in 1942, 1943 and 1944.

Miss Margaret Osborne of San Francisco and William Talbert of Wilmington, Del., retained the mixed doubles championship. In the final they defeated Miss Louise Brough and Robert Kimbrell of Los Angeles, 6—3, 6—4.

September 9, 1946

AT MEETING TO FORM WORLD PRO TENNIS LEAGUE

Left to right, seated: Welby Van Horn, Vincent Richards, who was named commissioner, and Bobby Riggs. Standing: Jack March and Wayne Sabin. The session was held at the Waldorf-Astoria yesterday.
Associated Press

Pro Tennis Leaders Set Up World League, Name Vincent Richards as Commissioner

By ALLISON DANZIG

Professional tennis now has a commissioner, as in baseball and football.

Vincent Richards, winner of many of the games' highest honors, has been named overlord of a new organization known as the World Professional Tennis League. Announcement of Richards' appointment was made yesterday at a Waldorf-Astoria luncheon by Tony Owen of Hollywood, Calif., the president of the league.

The purposes of the new association, as outlined by Owen and Richards, are to organize professional tennis on a solid foundation and guide its policy and management. Tournaments will be booked and supervised throughout the country and also abroad. Eventually, it is planned that the league shall embrace such organizations as the Professional Lawn Tennis Association and the Professional Players Association if the membership of these groups eelct to affiliate with the

league.

The first event to be sponsored by the league will be the $10,000 professional tournament starting tomorrow at the Philadelphia arena. The players participating will include Robert L. Riggs, Donald Budge, Frank Kovacs, Fred Perry, Welby Van Horn, Wayne Sabin, George Lott, John Nogrady and Jack Jossi.

"We plan to operate, said Owen, "as a service organization for the players. Our aim is not only to promote the interests of the men at the top but to see that the players of the lower flight benefit financially to a greater extent than they have in the past. Our eventual goal is to put every player under contract and guarantee him a living wage.

Richards, member of United States Davis Cup teams, winner of the national doubles championship repeatedly and also of the Olympic title, said he had taken the office of commissioner for one year with-

out compensation to help put professional tennis on a strong footing. The league offers the chance, he said, for the professional side of the game to put its house in order and stand before the public as entirely worthy of its trust and confidence. A big step was taken in this direction, he pointed out, in the negotiation of a five-year contract in 1946 for the holding of the national championship at Forest Hills.

Others to speak at the luncheon were Renville McMann, president of the West Side Tennis Club; Samuel B. Hardy, former Davis Cup team captain; Riggs and Arthur Flynn.

The officers of the league, in addition to president Owen, are William P. Jacobs, vice president, and Robert L. Harman, secretary. Serving on the board of directors are L. B. Icely, Hardy and P. Schuyler Van Bloem, tournament director at the West Side Tennis Club, Forest Hills. Organization headquarters are at 500 Fifth Avenue and Beverly Hills, Calif.

March 16, 1947

MISS BROUGH WINS THREE NET CROWNS IN ENGLISH EVENT

Beats Miss Hart and Takes Women's Doubles and Mixed Doubles at Wimbledon

MULLOY AND BROWN LOSE

By HERBERT L. MATTHEWS
Special to THE NEW YORK TIMES.

LONDON, July 3—Miss Louise Brough, American woman's champion, climbed to the pinnacle of the tennis world today by winning three championships at Wimbledon —singles, women's doubles and the mixed doubles.

Of all the great women players in Wimbledon's long and illustrious history only two have been able to win the triple crown. They were Miss Alice Marble of the United States and the late Suzanne Lenglen of France. Mlle. Lenglen won it thrice.

It was a great day for that awkward, unbelievable Australian, John Bromwich too because he teamed with Miss Brough to retain the mixed doubles title they won last year and earlier he paired with his young brilliant compatriot, Frank Sedgman, to beat the Americans Gardnar Mulloy and Tom Brown for the men's doubles championship.

For Miss Hart it was a hard and unlucky day, for she played three times and lost three times. She deserved a better fate because of all the women players she has the most polished and easiest style. The way she fought back every time from defeat to near victory showed she had plenty of gameness.

Lacks the Extra Punch

Somehow she just lacks the extra punch and that was what cost her the match with Miss Brough, which began the day. Wimbledon was turning them away this afternoon. This has been the best attended tournament in the All England club's history — and it possibly saw the worst tennis on the whole.

Old timers sighed for the good old days when players like Bill Tilden Henri Cochet, Fred Perry, Helen Wills and Suzanne Lenglen came to Wimbledon. There were no such players this year although there were some very good ones. It takes very good players to perform a feat such as Miss Brough's today.

Miss Hart, who lost by 6—3,

VICTOR IN ENGLAND

Miss Louise Brough
The New York Times

3—6, looked better when they began their match. She got off to a two-love start but Miss Brough began putting on more pressure and with the score three to one against her, took five straight games. She goes for everything and can retrieve impossible shots.

Miss Hart seemed rattled in the crucial eighth game when she was serving with the score three to four. A double fault and three shots into the net cooked her goose because Miss Brough went on to win her own serve next.

Breaks Through Again

Miss Brough broke through Miss Hart's service again in the third game of the second set. Miss Hart still was netting them and hitting them out. But with the score one to three and love-forty Miss Hart rallied to win her service and then break through to make it even at 3—3.

They went on winning their services until the count was 5—5. Neither was playing up to her form, perhaps because of anxiety. When Miss Hart lost her service in the eleventh game it looked like the end, particularly when Miss Brough went on to make it match point at 40—15. That was where Miss Hart showed what a fine match player she is. She fought up to deuce, then staved off another match point with a beautiful angle shot to the corner and finally won to make it 6—6.

It was great playing, but she threw her chance away, losing her own service through errors. Miss Brough was out to kill on her next service and again made it 40—15. She hit the first match point out but the next one shot into an unreachable corner and the match was over.

The men's doubles, won by the Australians at 5—7, 7—5, 7—5, 9—7, followed. It provided the worst tennis of the day and it was a toss-up as to who would win. The trouble was that Brown was a way off his game. Mulloy must often have felt that he was playing

three men. That young American giant has everything it takes.

Had Brown come anywhere near his level, the Americans would have swept the Australians off the court in three straight sets. As it was, they won the first and were leading 5—2 in the third set and 5—3 in the fourth only to lose the match. In the fourth set they threw away no fewer than seven set points. They really beat themselves.

Sedgman was brilliant if very erratic, but, as it happened, his brilliance came at the right times. Bromwich, looking and acting weary from his long losing match with Falkenburg yesterday, was his customary steady canny intelligent self. He is one of those players who looks easy to beat but he nearly always wins.

Few Good Rallies

The story of today's match lay simply in the innumerable times Brown hit into the net or out of court. It was dull and dreary playing on the whole, with few rallies worth watching.

The Americans started the third set as if they meant to steam roller the Australians. They made it

three love, then 4—1, then 5—2, and then they lost five straight games.

It was the first break through of Mulloy's service that proved crucial. The Americans were leading at 5-3 and thirty love. Then Brown netted three in a row. The next shot was the easiest kind of a floater for Mulloy but he dribbled it into the net.

It annoyed him enough to take a spare ball and lob it over the royal box and grandstand into the far beyond. There was good reason to despair because that was the last chance.

History repeated itself in the fourth and last set. The Americans got out to a 5-3 lead with Mulloy serving and they even got to forty love. The Aussies fought back to deuce on some fine playing and then Brown hit an easy one out and netted the next one to lose the game.

More opportunities came later with Sedgman serving and the Americans leading at 7—6 and love forty and again they threw their opportunities away.

July 4, 1948

Gonzales, Mrs. du Pont Capture U.S. Tennis Singles Titles

20-YEAR-OLD STAR DEFEATS STURGESS

Gonzales Victor Over South African Stylist in the Final Round, 6-2, 6-3, 14-12

LOUISE BROUGH IS UPSET

Winner in 1947 Loses Crown to Mrs. duPont in Stirring Contest, 4-6, 6-4, 15-13

By ALLISON DANZIG

The rankest outsider of modern times sits on the tennis throne today.

Unknown in the East until he made his first appearance on turf a year ago, Richard (Pancho) Gonzales, stalwart, 20-year-old Californian from Los Angeles with the thundering service and the touch of a master in his volley, won the amateur championship of the United States yesterday in one of the most exciting finishes the tournament has known.

With darkness settling upon the stadium of the West Side Tennis Club in Forest Hills and the referee, Dr. S. Ellsworth Davenport 2d, prepared to call a postponement if a decision was not reached

forthwith in the almost interminable third set, Gonzales leaped for the kill that had twice escaped him by a single stroke in his final-round match with Eric Sturgess of South Africa.

Amid the cheers of the 11,000 spectators who had taken successive drenchings during the long afternoon's showers but stayed to the last in complete disregard of discomfort and the fading light, the strong young Californian steeled himself for the victory that must be now or possibly never, and gained it at the twelfth hour.

With the score 13—12 in Gonzales' favor in the third set, the Californian, who had been helpless to make any headway against Sturgess' service since he had twice stood at match point in the twelfth game, tore for the net, where he had given so dazzling a display all afternoon. Two unbeatable volleys, one a delicately turned drop shot, carried him to 40—15, once again a stroke removed from victory.

Dead Game Antagonist

The gallery screamed from the excitement and tension, and then a big "shush" spread through the stands. In absolute silence Sturgess, a dead game antagonist who had grown stronger and stronger through this nerve-wracking last set, toed the line to serve. The ball came back; they were in a rally, with the crowd hanging on every stroke, and then came the shot that turned the place into a bedlam.

From his fine, if erratic, backhand, Gonzales whipped the ball like a bullet straight down. Sturgess, rushing in desperately, was caught a step short of position. His half-volley hardly got off the ground, to land in the net, and the seventeenth ranking player of the country and the last American seeded in the draw sat on the throne occupied by Jack Kramer for the past two years. The score of the match was 6—2, 6—3, 14—12.

The victory of the young Californian, whose record for the season had been lacking in any distinction except for a triumph over Gardnar Mulloy at Southampton and victories over Frank Parker and Jaroslav Drobny of Czechoslovakia in making his way to the final round of the championship, followed upon another exciting finish to the women's tournament.

In the longest final match on record since 1898 in the days when women played for the best of five sets, Mrs. William duPont of Wilmington, Del., the former Margaret Osborne, wrested the title from Miss Louise Brough of Beverly Hills, Calif., winner this year of the Wimbledon title. Escaping defeat by a stroke in the same twelfth game of the third set in which Sturgess had staved off disaster, Mrs. duPont finally crowned her years of effort by effecting the lone break in the record-breaking set to win the match at 4—6, 6—4, 15—13.

On Court Two Hours

It was not until almost three hours after Louis Shaw had called "play" from the umpire's chair that the forty-eight-game match ended. Actually, Mrs. duPont and Miss Brough were on the court two hours. Twice play had to be suspended as rain intervened, first at 4—3 in Mrs. duPont's favor in the second set and again at 2-all in the third.

The gallery, keeping its seats when the first shower broke early in the second set, was caught by the heavy downpour that followed and, with the portal exits clogged, was thoroughly soaked as tarpaulin covers were pulled over the court. It was too wet to care very much about seeking cover when the next downfall interrupted play again.

Owing to the interruptions and the seemingly endless length of the third set of the women's final, during which the crowd showed its impatience to have the men's final get under way, the match between Gonzales and Sturgess had to be played in fading light and encircling gloom from the start and almost in darkness for the last fifteen minutes.

It was rather unfortunate for the fine sportsman from South Africa that he had to take the Californian's scorching service in such light, though he handled it very well when he had any chance at all, and Gonzales, whose court deportment is equally to be commended, commented upon this advantage in his remarks over the loud speaker after President Lawrence Baker of the U. S. Lawn Tennis Association had presented the championship to him.

Since any further play was out of the question when the men's singles ended, the mixed doubles championship could not be brought to a conclusion. The unfinished semi-final match will be put on at 2:30 this afternoon and the final round will follow. It was announced that holders of tenth-day ticket stubs would be admitted free of charge and for others the admission fee would be $1.20.

Gonzales, one of the youngest players to win the championship, established himself in the forefront of the candidates for the 1949 American Davis Cup team with his victory over Sturgess, if he had not done that in defeating Parker and Drobny.

His performance yesterday was not the equal of the tennis that has been played in the stadium by other champions, but it answered a number of questions in a manner much to his credit, and, considering his limited experience on grass and the fact that prior to 1947 he had been denied full opportunity of competing in California tournaments for a number of years, it is extraordinary that his game should have arrived at such maturity as he showed in the championship.

Against Drobny, the superbly built youth from Los Angeles had demonstrated one of the very strongest services in the game and his skill as a volleyer, as well as his ability to stay in a bitter fight and prevail in the face of discouraging vicissitudes.

Yesterday, against one of the real stylists of tennis, whose main strength is the classic game of a developing attack carefully prepared from the back of the court and carried forward with discretion and diplomacy, Gonzales showed that he has the ground strokes required of a player who aspires to reach the first class.

Ground strokes did not count for too much in the Drobny match except on the return of service. It was all service and volley, and the rallies were of short duration. Yesterday, there was a different kind of match.

It was a match fought chiefly from the back of the court. The volley was important and it was the stroke that won for Gonzales, but his service in the first two sets was not the battering assault weapon it had been against the player from Czechoslovakia, and he could not have got in so many winning shots from the court had his ground strokes not provided the proper approach to give him safe access.

It was thought that the Californian would have to serve at his best to win against so genuinely sound an opponent and so clever a strategist as Sturgess. After the effort he had expended with his delivery against Parker and Drobny there was some doubt as to whether it would be as formidable yesterday.

It turned out that his service was not that strong, nevertheless Gonzales demonstrated his superiority in the first two sets and had the staying powers and the ability to lift his service in the third when Sturgess was playing his best tennis of the match and threatening more and more after escaping disaster in the twelfth game.

Sturgess did not quite come up to expectations yesterday until the late stages. Whether it was the poor light or the drabness of the weather, his ground strokes were not under the control he had shown all week and he was not as secure in his volleying. His backhand disappointed in particular and suffered by comparison with Gonzales' as the rivals concentrated in attacking the offside.

Point Scores of the Title Matches

GONZALES VS. STURGESS

FIRST SET

Point Score

	Point Score — Pts.	G.
Gonzales	4 4 3 4 4 2 6 6—33	6
Sturgess	1 1 3 0 2 4 4 4—21	2

Stroke Analysis

	N.	O.	PL.	SA.	DF.
Gonzales	9	6	10	2	1
Sturgess	9	12	4	1	0

SECOND SET

Point Score

	Point Score — Pts.	G.
Gonzales	1 7 2 8 4 4 1 6 4—37	6
Sturgess	4 5 4 6 1 0 4 4 1—29	3

Stroke Analysis

	N.	O.	PL.	SA.	DF.
Gonzales	10	7	12	1	0
Sturgess	15	9	12	0	0

THIRD SET

Point Score

	Point Score — Pts.	G.
Gonzales	4 1 7 6 2 4 2 0 4 1 4 5 4 2 4 0 5 0 9 3 4 1 4 0 4 4—84	14
Sturgess	0 4 5 4 4 2 4 4 1 4 0 7 1 4 1 4 3 4 7 5 0 4 1 4 1 1—79	12

Stroke Analysis

	N.	O.	PL.	SA.	DF.
Gonzales	25	30	29	13	1
Sturgess	18	20	21	2	4

RECAPITULATION

	N.	O.	PL.	SA.	DF.
Gonzales	44	43	51	16	2
Sturgess	42	41	37	3	4

	E.	EP.	TP.	G.	Sets.
Gonzales	89	67	154	26	3
Sturgess	87	40	129	17	0

Umpire—Harcourt Wood. Time of match—1:38.

MRS. DUPONT VS. MISS BROUGH

FIRST SET

Point Score

	Point Score — Pts.	G.
Mrs. duPont	0 5 2 4 0 4 1 5 1 2—24	4
Miss Brough	4 3 4 1 4 0 4 3 4 4—31	6

Stroke Analysis

	N.	O.	PL.	SA.	DF.
Mrs. duPont	5	14	2	2	3
Miss Brough	5	15	8	1	0

SECOND SET

Point Score

	Point Score — Pts.	G.
Mrs. duPont	0 4 2 5 2 4 1 4 7 4—33	6
Miss Brough	4 0 4 3 4 1 4 2 5 0—27	4

Stroke Analysis

	N.	O.	PL.	SA.	DF.
Mrs. duPont	7	11	11	1	0
Miss Brough	8	11	8	1	2

THIRD SET

Point Score

	Point Score — Pts.	G.
Mrs. duPont	2 4 4 5 3 4 2 11 1 4 2 3 3 4 1 4 0 4 3 4 1 4 3 4 0 4 4 4—94	15
Miss Brough	4 0 6 3 5 2 4 9 4 0 4 3 5 0 4 1 4 2 5 2 4 1 5 1 4 2 2 2—88	13

Stroke Analysis

	N.	O.	PL.	SA.	DF.
Mrs. duPont	29	26	40	2	1
Miss Brough	26	24	27	5	2

RECAPITULATION

	N.	O.	PL.	SA.	DF.
Mrs. duPont	41	51	53	5	4
Miss Brough	39	50	43	7	4

	E.	EP.	TP.	G.	Sets.
Mrs. duPont	96	58	151	25	2
Miss Brough	93	50	146	23	1

Umpire—Louis Shaw. Time of match—2:52.

Breaks Through Once

Three times Sturgess lost his service in the opening set while breaking through Gonzales' once. The seventh game proved the sterling worth of the American's backhand as he broke through for the third time, and pulled out the eighth from 0—40 for the set.

The second set saw Gonzales still the master and making the fewer errors, although his service was still not functioning at its best. The poise and headiness of the youngster were shown as he broke through for the second time in the ninth game with the aid of a half-volley lob followed by a winning lob volley, and finally a a beautifully turned drop shot that Sturgess saluted.

With the third set Gonzales began to explode service aces in his best fashion, and it was not entirely because of the poor light. It was well that he did, for Sturgess now began to play better and better. Gonzales went to 3—1 and 30—0 and his opponent drew even at 4-all. From then on it was a bitter fight and after Gonzales had passed up two match points in the twelfth game he was fighting to stay even.

Twice he had narrow escapes and, with Sturgess playing so brilliantly and holding his service so easily, it seemed that the match might well go to a fourth set on the morrow. Then the referee appeared upon the court and Gonzales, realizing that the play might possibly take an altogether different turn if there was a postponement, immediately took his cue and lifted his game to win in a sensational finish.

Three Service Breaks

Miss Brough and Mrs. duPont, partners in winning innumerable doubles championships at home and abroad, were so evenly matched all the way that there was little to choose between them. There was just one break in service in each of the three sets. Neither played at her best, although both rose to brilliant heights at the net, particularly in their smashing, and the inability to return service resulted in a steady succession of errors.

Mrs. duPont worked into her best form after the first interruption by rain. Her footwork was faster and her clever volleying ability was asserted as she won the second set. In the final set Miss Brough was three times within a point of 5-3 but failed to get it. She stood at match point in the twelfth game but Mrs. duPont came through with some of her most dazzling volleys to save the day.

Thereafter Miss Brough was the one in trouble. She saved herself several times but finally she failed in her volleying, was broken through in the twenty-seventh game, and Mrs. duPont scored on three fine volleys in the twenty-eighth.

When the match finally came to an end, amid a great wave of cheering, Mr. duPont, who had watched the match from the stands directly behind the court without so much as changing expression, was overwhelmed by friends who rushed to congratulate him upon his wife's victory. Mrs. duPont had finally achieved her ambition after standing among the three or four best players of the country since 1941.

Victor Seixas of Philadelphia, one of the leading younger players of the country, received the award of the William Johnston Trophy in a brief ceremony in the stadium. The trophy, given on the basis of sportsmanship as well as excellence of play for the season, was presented by Julian S. Myrick after introductory remarks by Harold Lebair.

Members of the Australian Davis Cup team were honored by the West Side Tennis Club. President Renville McMann presented to Captain Adrian Quist three watches and a camera as tokens of the general esteem for the Australians' sportsmanship and expressed the hope the men from Down Under would be back here in 1949.

September 20, 1948

Gonzales Downs Schroeder, Retains U. S. Singles Title; Mrs. du Pont Victor

CHAMPION RALLIES TO SCORE IN 5 SETS

Gonzales Drops Record First Tilt, 18-16, Second at 6-2, Then Rises to Triumph

MISS HART BOWS, 6-4, 6-1

Florida Girl Beaten in Final by Mrs. du Pont — Hall Wins Veteran Title 6th Time

By ALLISON DANZIG

Richard (Pancho) Gonzales' reign as national amateur tennis champion was extended for a second year yesterday and no holder of the crown has shown more perseverance in enduring and surmounting the barbs of adversity than did the 21-year-old six-footer from Los Angeles to defeat Frederick R. (Ted) Schroeder of La Crescenta, Calif., in the Forest Hills stadium yesterday.

Beaten in a record-breaking 34-game opening set—the longest ever played in a championship final—after five times requiring only a point to win it, and outplayed by a wide margin in the second as the inevitable reaction brought on the blight of apathy, Gonzales took the gallery of 13,000 and his tiring older opponent by storm as he came back to win at 16—18, 2—6, 6—1, 6—2, 6—4.

The women's title also was carried off for the second successive year by Mrs. William du Pont, the former Margaret Osborne, of Wilmington, Del., in a one-sided final that contrasted with last year's epochal marathon. She defeated Miss Doris Hart of Jacksonville, Fla., 6—4, 6—1.

Scores in Straight Sets

The veterans' championship was won for the sixth successive year by J. Gilbert Hall of New York. In the concluding round on the grandstand court he won from Wilmer Allison of Austin, Tex., former men's national titleholder, 6—3, 6—2, and maintained his record of never losing a set in all the years he has held the crown.

The mixed doubles tournament will be brought to a conclusion today. The final will be held at 1 P. M. between Miss Louise Brough and Eric Sturgess of South Africa and Mrs. du Pont and William Talbert. Darkness set in at the end of the semi-finals making it impossible to continue play.

Gonzales, the victim of repeated setbacks during the year both at home and abroad, showed his characteristic genius for bringing his game to its peak in the big match

ON THE STADIUM COURT AND STARS WHO DEFENDED TITLES

Pancho Gonzales, background, returning a shot to Ted Schroeder in the final at West Side Tennis Club

Gonzales holding the trophy after he defeated Schroeder

Mrs. William du Pont with prize
The New York Times (by George Alexanderson)

that counts. He did that in the Davis Cup challenge round and he did it again in the championship.

One can hardly give the champion too much praise for his moral fiber. Almost invariably the loser of an opening set of anything like the length of yesterday's, which broke the 16—14 record set by John Doeg and Frank Shields in the 1930 final, loses heart as well and never is able to overcome the discouragement of the setback. So it seemed would be the case yesterday, as Gonzales slumped badly in the second set and appeared to be resigned to his fate.

Hits 17 Service Aces

For an hour and thirteen minutes through that thirty-four-game opener the champion had fought his rival in a tremendous duel of service and volley. Seventeen times he had scored on unquestionable service aces, which must have set a record for one set, and he had matched Schroeder in winning one love game after another.

So devastating was Gonzales' service that never until the twenty-fifth game was Schroeder able to get to "deuce" against it. The only other time he got that far was the thirty-first game until the lone break of the set was effected in the thirty-third.

In the thirtieth game came the most painful experience of all for the champion. Schroeder was behind at 0—40 as the champion threw two perfect lobs over his head, and the big crowd was ready to let loose with a thundering roar. Instead it cheered the Wimbledon titleholder for the great fight he made to pull out of that seemingly hopeless situation, twice as Gonzales' backhand failed on the return of service, as it did so often in the match, and the third time with one of Schroeder's overhead smashes.

Gonzales refused to become discouraged after missing that golden opportunity and won his next service. Then came the bitter blow. Behind at 0—40 in the thirty-third game, he emulated his rival in pulling up to deuce, to the thunderous applause of the crowd, and after Schroeder had gained advantage point on a net-cord shot, one of several by which he benefited, the champion brought the house down again with a searing service ace.

Loses Close Decision

Then came a particularly bitter pill for the titleholder. In the next rally, an exciting exchange of lightning strokes, he executed one of his adroit drop volleys. The side linesman cried "out" and immediately an outburst of protests came from the stands.

Gonzales cried out too, then immediately accepted the decision with the fine sportsmanship Schroeder was to exhibit on the final point of the match and which both men shared throughout. In the next rally, the last of the set, the champion slipped as he made his volley and a gasp went up from the crowd as the ball fell into the net.

It seemed that the fates were against Gonzales. All the luck in the match had been with Schroeder, though it had not amounted to much, and that fact and the memory of the great opportunity he had missed at 40—0 were enough to have broken the spirit of most players after making so great a fight for seventy-three minutes—as long as many entire matches last.

To all appearances Gonzales was a beaten champion as the second set ended. But with the start of the third the big fellow lost no time in reassuring his admirers that he was in the fight again for all he was worth. It was the Gonzales of the first set with whom Schroeder had to reckon now, with his mighty service going full blast, his footwork speeded up and his volley doing deadly execution.

Four games in a row went to Gonzales without deuce being called once. Rifled service aces and blazing passing shots and volleys were speeding from his racquet in a barrage of winning shots that had his rival helpless.

The ten-minute rest period did not serve to restore the vigor of Schroeder's game. He was offering more resistance, but his play lacked the vitality of his rival's. He could not return service nor was he attacking at the net as often or making the dazzling volleys for which he is feared.

With the final set, Schroeder dug in and made so strong a fight that the crowd was kept on tenterhooks almost to the very end. This was the famous fifth set, and no one had beaten him down the wire in four long matches at Wimbledon or in two in the championship against Frank Sedgman and Talbert.

Schroeder saved the first game from 0—30 and then had the crowd holding its breath as he got to 30—0 against Gonzales' service in the fourth. This was his chance, and, as it proved, his last one. His backhand failed him in trying to pass on an easy volley, and he never threatened to break through again. Nevertheless, he held his own service to 4-all even though Gonzales was both serving and returning service the better of the two.

As the play went on, the crowd could sense Schroeder's weakening in the opportunities he wasted with errors unworthy of him when he is fresh. Gonzales was missing chances, too, but not because of fatigue so much as from the nervous tension as he sighted victory.

Then came the break that decided the match. Against a clearly tiring Schroeder, Gonzales went on the attack. The return of service which had been so recalcitrant for most of the match now was functioning beautifully, to keep the ball at Schroeder's feet to extract the error or elicit a half-volley that enabled the champion to take the net position away from his opponent.

Every point in this final game brought cheers or groans, so worked up was the crowd. When Gonzales double-faulted to make the score 15—all, his first in three sets, they groaned. When he fell behind, 30—40, as he reached high up and hit a ball that was going out, they groaned again in extreme anguish.

A sigh of relief went through the crowd as the score reached deuce on Schroeder's backhand drive beyond the line. Then came a smash from Gonzales' racquet that set the crowd wild with delight. Now came the final rally and Schroeder whipped a forehand down the line past Gonzales at the net. A gasp went up and then the place turned into bedlam as the linesman signaled it was out.

Schroeder, stunned by the call, cried out, and there were outcries from the stand. But the Wimbledon champion accepted the decision which meant failure to his great fight. Breaking into a grin, he pretended he was going to throw his racquet at the official and then ran forward to offer his congratulations to the happy Gonzales as the crowd cheered.

In the mixed doubles semi-finals, Miss Brough and Sturgess defeated Miss Gertrude Moran and Gonzales, 6—8, 6—3, 15—13, and Mrs. du Pont and Talbert won from Mrs. Patricia Todd and Jaroslav Drobny, 6—0, 6—2.

September 6, 1949

Details of the Matches

GONZALES VS. SCHROEDER

FIRST SET

POINT SCORE

		G.	Pts.
Gonzales	4 1 4 3 4 1 4 1 4 1 4 0 4 0 4		
	0 4 2 4 4 4 1 4 2 5 4 4 2 4 5 5 0 4 4	16	101
Schroeder	0 4 2 5 1 4 1 4 0 4 2 4 0 4 2		
	4 2 4 2 6 2 4 0 4 3 6 0 4 0 7 3 4 6 6	18	104

STROKE ANALYSIS

	N.	O.	P.	SA.	DF.
Gonzales	38	31	38	17	3
Schroeder	24	21	27	5	1

SECOND SET

POINT SCORE

		G.	Pts.
Gonzales	5 0 2 0 3 1 4 2	2	17
Schroeder	3 4 4 4 5 4 0 4	6	28

STROKE ANALYSIS

	N.	O.	P.	SA.	DF.
Gonzales	10	7	5	4	1
Schroeder	6	1	10	0	1

THIRD SET

POINT SCORE

		G.	Pts.
Gonzales	4 4 4 4 2 4 4	6	26
Schroeder	2 2 2 1 4 1 2	1	14

STROKE ANALYSIS

	N.	O.	P.	SA.	DF.
Gonzales	5	5	11	5	0
Schroeder	2	7	4	0	1

FOURTH SET

POINT SCORE

		G.	Pts.
Gonzales	4 4 1 4 2 4 4 6	6	29
Schroeder	2 1 4 2 4 0 2 4	2	19

STROKE ANALYSIS

	N.	O.	P.	SA.	DF.
Gonzales	5	7	8	0	0
Schroeder	10	10	5	2	1

FIFTH SET

POINT SCORE

		G.	Pts.
Gonzales	3 4 1 4 2 4 2 4 4 5	6	33
Schroeder	5 1 4 2 4 0 4 1 2 3	4	26

STROKE ANALYSIS

	N.	O.	P.	SA.	DF.
Gonzales	7	9	7	1	1
Schroeder	13	10	8	1	2

RECAPITULATION

	N.	O.	P.	SA.	DF.
Gonzales	65	59	69	27	5
Schroeder	55	49	54	8	6

	E.	EP.	TP.	G.	Sets
Gonzales	129	96	206	36	3
Schroeder	110	62	191	31	2

Umpires—Harold Le Bair. Net umpire—Louis Shaw. Linesmen—Frank Guernsey, Harold Ammerman, Ovin Spellman, Donald Dickson, Harold (Bud) Young, Frank Tybeski, Fred Krais, Herbert Lewis, John Stahl, Harold Young. Time of match—2:25.

MRS. DUPONT VS. MISS HART

FIRST SET

POINT SCORE

		G.	Pts.
Mrs. du Pont	4 1 5 4 5 1 5 5 4 4	6	38
Miss Hart	6 4 3 1 3 4 7 3 1 2	4	34

STROKE ANALYSIS

	N.	O.	P.	SA.	DF.
Mrs. du Pont	6	14	12	2	2
Miss Hart	12	18	12	0	0

SECOND SET

POINT SCORE

		G.	Pts.
Mrs. du Pont	4 4 4 5 1 5 4	6	27
Miss Hart	2 0 0 3 4 3 2	1	14

STROKE ANALYSIS

	N.	O.	P.	SA.	DF.
Mrs. du Pont	4	6	9	0	0
Miss Hart	7	11	4	0	0

RECAPITULATION

	N.	O.	P.	SA.	DF.
Mrs. du Pont	10	20	21	2	2
Miss Hart	19	29	16	0	0

	E.	EP.	TP.	G.	Sets
Mrs. du Pont	32	23	64	12	2
Miss Hart	48	16	48	5	0

Umpire—W. Harcourt Woods. Net umpire—Arthur Knight. Linesman—Chas. Villanueva, Mrs. J. Mann, Mrs. E. Lake, Mrs. Peter Reutz, Sam Keats, Frank Hammond, Miss Gerry Mallory, T. G. Campbell, Thos. Rudolph and Mrs. Edna Ammerman. Time of match—42 minutes.

GONZALES ACCEPTS PRO TENNIS OFFER

To Open Tour Against Kramer Here Oct. 25—1-Year Pact Guarantees $60,000

Richard (Pancho) Gonzales, 21-year-old national singles champion from Los Angeles, yesterday joined the professional tennis ranks. The Californian signed a one-year contract to tour as a pro under the direction of Bobby Riggs.

Formal announcement of the signing of Gonzales to a contract was made yesterday by Riggs, making his first venture in the role of promoter, at a press conference at the 21 Club. Pancho will be opposed by Jack Kramer, former national titleholder, on the tour, slated to begin at Madison Square Garden Tuesday night, Oct. 25.

Declaring that he was "glad to turn pro," Gonzales has been guaranteed $60,000, with the privilege of 30 per cent of the net gate for the engagements with Kramer. They are expected to play between 90 and 100 matches in every major city in the country.

Gonzales flew in from California yesterday to sign the contract with Riggs. Riggs, who said he would concentrate on the promotion end of the tour, may take part in the doubles play. Riggs is also a former national champion.

Riggs said that Richard (Pancho) Segura of Ecuador also would make the tour. Segura turned professional with Kramer two years ago. Riggs also said that a fifth outstanding player had been invited to join the troupe. While the identity of that player was not disclosed, it was believed in tennis circles that it might be Frank Parker of Los Angeles.

The youngest tennis champion to turn pro, Gonzales said: "I'm glad to turn pro because I need the money and I have a family to support. I'm getting a good deal. Bobby has been very fair to me, and I expect this to be a very exciting tour. I'd like very much to take Jack Kramer's pro title away from him next season."

"I don't have to tell you that tennis is my business," Riggs declared. "I have a lot of faith in the sport and that's why I'm putting my money and my time in it.

"I went out and got Pancho here to play Kramer because I know that's the match the people want to see. They must know that a match between Gonzales and Kramer is the match of a decade," Riggs added.

September 21, 1949

TILDEN SELECTED GREATEST NETMAN

Kramer Is Second, Budge Third in Poll but Big Bill Has His Own List of Stars

HOLLYWOOD, Calif., Feb. 3 (AP) —William T. Tilden II—Big Bill, the ultra-sophisticate of the world's tennis courts—was genuinely gratified that he had been named the greatest tennis player of the past 50 years.

He showed his delight in undisguised manner, hardly in keeping with some of the disdainful characteristics of the great Tilden of the golden Twenties. He meant it when he said, "I am truly grateful for this honor."

But at the same time Tilden didn't hesitate to take issue with some of the findings of the 391 participants in the Associated Press poll which voted him this signal distinction by overwhelming ballot.

His criticism was not with the choice of Tilden as the greatest. He offered no protestations over this decision. It was with the runner-up candidates' ratings that he differed—not directly, mind you, but in tabbing the other greatest of the past five decades, Tilden listed many who didn't make the first five.

Didn't Know Runners-up

In fairness to Tilden, it must be noted that at the time of this interview he was not aware of the personnel of the also-ran division. But anyone knowing Tilden would appreciate that these were his convictions, and a conviction with the old master was always something that man, beast or the august officials of the United States Lawn Tennis Association could never, never budge.

Tilden got 310 votes out of the 391. Rated far back, in order, were Jack Kramer, Don Budge, Mrs. Helen Wills Moody Roark and Suzanne Lenglen.

Tilden's nominees—behind Tilden—included Frenchmen Henri Cochet and Rene Lacoste, Little Bill Johnston, Budge, Fred Perry—he mentioned Francis T. Hunter and Vinnie Richards—and Ellsworth Vines. He flatly refused to pick one over the other; all, he said, were so tightly grouped, separation was impossible.

Older Stars First

The older stars came first. Then —whether by afterthought or intention, who can say?—came Kramer. Bobby Riggs, and then unstinted but delayed praise for Ted Schroeder, Pancho Gonzales and others of the more modern era.

The great women players? He gave them in rapid one-two-three order—Lenglen, Alice Marble and Helen Wills Roark. Fourth, down a marked step, came Helen Hull Jacobs. After that the drop was much greater.

Tilden has been having grave personal problems, but he presented no picture of concern as he sat and talked in his small but gaily decorated little apartment in Hollywood.

Following is the result of the Associated Press poll:

Players	Votes
1—Bill Tilden	310
2—Jack Kramer	32
3—Donald Budge	31
4—Helen Wills Moody Roark	12
5—Suzanne Lenglen	2

One vote each: Little Bill Johnston, Fred Perry, Ellsworth Vines and Mrs. Molla Bjurstedt Mallory.

February 4, 1950

Title Tennis Admits First Negro, a Girl

Miss Althea Gibson, New York Negro girl, was accepted yesterday for the United States tennis championships and will be the first of her race to compete in the national grass court competition.

The tournament acceptance committee of the United States Lawn Tennis Association announced Miss Gibson as one of fifty-two women who will begin play at the West Side Tennis Club, Forest Hills, on Monday.

Lawrence A. Baker, president of the U. S. L. T. A., said Miss Gibson "was accepted on her ability."

Miss Gibson, 22, a Florida A. and M. student, was runner-up to Miss Nancy Chaffee, Ventura, Calif., in the national indoor play this year. She won the Eastern indoor title and competed in both the national clay court and Eastern grass court tournaments.

August 22, 1950

LOUISE BROUGH BEATS MRS. DU PONT IN WIMBLEDON FINAL

GAINS NET SWEEP

Singles, Doubles, Mixed Doubles Won by Miss Brough in England

By The Associated Press.

WIMBLEDON, July 8—Miss Louise Brough, the blonde from Beverly Hills, Calif., scored a tennis grand slam today when she retained two of her All-England titles and shared another before an admiring throng of 20,000 on Wimbledon's ancient center court.

Miss Brough began her all-conquering afternoon by defeating Mrs. Margaret Osborne du Pont of Wilmington, Del., in an all-American women's singles final, 6—1, 3—6, 6—1. She had beaten her Delaware rival in the final a year ago, too.

After a two and one-half hour break during which the Australian veterans John Bromwich and Adrian Quist took the men's doubles, she joined forces with Mrs. du Pont to win the women's doubles. They downed Miss Doris Hart of Jacksonville, Fla., and Miss Shirley Fry of Akron, Ohio in another all-United States match, 6—4, 5—7,

6—1.

Then, following a thirty-minute rest, Miss Brough and Eric Sturgess of South Africa defeated Mrs. Pat Todd of La Jolla, Calif., and Geoff Brown of Australia, 11—9, 1—6, 6—4 in the mixed doubles.

The Californian thus equaled her 1948 sweep.

Singles Finalist 4 Times

Louise virtually has owned Wimbledon since the war. She's gone to the finals in singles four years out of five and won the last three. With Mrs. du Pont she's captured the doubles four times out of five. With Tom Brown, then Jack Bromwich and now with Sturgess, she's shared the mixed doubles crown the same number of times.

In the other title decided today Bromwich and Quist defeated fellow Australians Brown and Billy Sidwell, 7-5, 3-6, 6-3, 3-6, 6-2.

Budge Patty of Los Angeles tucked away the men's singles title yesterday with a decisive victory over Frank Sedgman of Australia.

This gave the Americans three and a half out of a possible five titles, about par for the post-war course at Wimbledon.

Miss Brough's victory over Mrs. du Pont was unexpected only in so far as it was one-sided. When the two women met a year ago Miss Brough came out on top, 10—8, 1—6, 10—8.

Today she was vastly superior. She had things all her own way in the first set which she won in 15 minutes. The second set started off like a carbon copy of the first, only that Mrs. du Pont won the first five games. Miss Brough obviously was coasting in anticipation of a long afternoon of tennis. She fought back briefly to put the score at 3—5, then bowed without a struggle at 3—6.

Service in High Gear

Miss Brough returned to form the moment the third set opened. Her service was in high gear, her drop shots fell just where she wanted them and her passing shots left Mrs. duPont helpless. She raced through the first three games, lost the fourth after it had gone to deuce eight times, and then finished her business at 6—1.

Despite the apparent ease with which it was won, her singles victory obviously had tired Miss Brough.

Mrs. duPont carried her much of the way in the doubles match as she lost her service four times.

What really saved the champions in doubles was the poor form of Miss Hart. She lost her service four times and her drives from the baseline, usually point-makers for the Florida girl, rarely stayed in the court.

It turned into a private battle between Mrs. duPont and Miss Fry, and although the Akron girl played well and brilliantly at times she was not quite a match for the veteran.

Two service breaks against Miss Hart gave the winners the first

set. Miss Fry and Miss Hart cashed in on Miss Brough's errors to win the second, but Miss Hart lost her service again in the second game of the final set and when Miss Fry lost hers for the first time in the match in the fourth game, it was all over but the shouting.

The mixed doubles, which didn't start until after 7 P. M. local time, brought some of the best tennis of the day.

The first set lasted 20 games as it seesawed back and forth on fine serving, excellent net play and point-making passes down the sidelines before Sturgess and Miss Brough finally pulled it out, 11—9.

It looked as if Miss Brough and Sturgess were through when they dropped six out of the seven games in the second set. But they jumped to the front early in the final set only to find it all square at 4—4 when Miss Brough dropped her service.

With Sturgess holding the advantage on Brown's service in the vital ninth game, Brown missed with his first serve and his second appeared to graze the net as it came across. Sturgess returned it mildly and Mrs. Todd, making no effort to play the ball, batted it into the net.

The referee called it a played point and gave the game to Sturgess and Miss Brough. Mrs. Todd angrily tossed her racket into the air but the damage was done. Sturgess held his service and the match was over.

July 9, 1950

CHAPTER 2

THE AUSTRALIANS: UP FROM DOWN UNDER

Rod Laver is the only man to have won two
"grand slams." His repertoire included every shot.
He had speed and power—and grace, as this
1962 photo demonstrates.

AUSTRALIA CLINCHES DAVIS CUP, BEATING U. S. IN DOUBLES;

TRIUMPH IN 5 SETS

Bromwich-Sedgman Top Schroeder-Mulloy at Forest Hills Net

AUSSIES' SCORE NOW 3-0

Davis Cup Victory Over U. S. Is First Since 1939—Final Singles Matches Today

By ALLISON DANZIG

Four years of American tennis supremacy as the champion Davis Cup nation ended in the Forest Hills Stadium yesterday and Australia became the holder of the trophy for the first time since 1939.

John Bromwich, member of that winning team from Down Under of eleven years ago, and 22-year-old Frank Sedgman sealed the verdict as they defeated Ted Schroeder of La Crescenta, Calif., and Gardnar Mulloy of Coral Gables, Fla., 4—6, 6—4, 6—2, 4—6, 6—4.

With the victories of Sedgman and Kenneth McGregor over Tom

The Americans, Ted Schroeder (left) and Gardnar Mulloy, and the Australians, John Bromwich and Frank Sedgman (right), before yesterday's match.

Brown Jr. of San Francisco and Schroeder, respectively. in Friday's two opening singles, both gained in the minimum of three sets, Australia had the necessary three points to clinch matters in the Golden Jubilee challenge round.

It marked the first time since 1935 that an American team had been put to rout in the first two days of play. and the prospect is that the United States will have to develop new blood if it is to win back the cup.

The Australians, with their exceptionally talented group of extremely youthful players, are going to be difficult to defeat for some years, defending on their home turf and at a time of the year when American's thoughts are of Christmas turkey, rather than on tennis.

An Historic Occasion

The end of America's reign was a rather historic occasion, comparable to that day in 1927, when the Four Musketeers of France, finally toppled Big Bill Tilden and William Johnston, who had kept this country at the top for seven years.

Like the French, the small group of Australians in the gallery of 10.000 were carried away with joy, and Americans, who had cheered on the defenders so exuberantly in their unexpectedly prolonged but losing fight, were cast down.

No one, however, begrudged the Australians their victory, in preparation for which they had taken bad lickings year after year, as had the Four Musketeers, and which they had accepted with such good sportsmanship. It was agreed that it was a good thing for tennis that the cup should not remain too long in any one nation.

So there was nothing insincere about the congratulations that Capt. Alrick H. Man and the referee, Dr. S. Ellsworth Davenport, extended to Capt. Harry Hopman on the court and which other American officials offered to Sir Norman Brookes, president of the Australian Lawn Tennis Associatio.

Two concluding singles matches remain to be played to bring the 1950 challenge round to a close and

The Australian team in the foreground with Sedgman (left) chopping the ball across net to Mulloy (right, far court) in the first set.
The New York Times (by Edward Hausner)

Maureen "Little Mo" Connolly (near court) won three consecutive U.S. titles (1951-53) and a grand slam in 1953. Her opponent in this 1953 match is Althea Gibson, who won the U.S. and British championships in 1957 and 1958. She was the first black woman to achieve major tennis status.

they will be staged today even though nothing is any longer at stake. In the first, at 2 o'clock, Sedgman, champion of his country, will face Schroeder.

In the finale McGregor, the remarkably gifted youngster of 21 who projected himself to the fore as a potential world champion with his superlative performance against Schroeder, will meet Brown. This last match should be of particular interest, and if Brown can find his true form, now that the pressure is off in his first challenge round series, it will be well worth seeing.

The victory of Bromwich and Sedgman yesterday was clearly won on merit. They were the superior team, more proficient in their collective play and armed with the better weapons for the doubles game.

Schroeder and Mulloy did more than was expected of them in carrying the match to five sets. They made a stirring fight to the end in the effort to defer the decision in the series to the final day, but it was beyond their capacity against so smooth-working a combination that presented an almost impenetrable defense, that could maneuver for the opening so inexorably and take advantage of it with such conclusiveness.

The Australians won in the final analysis because they had command of the net for the most part. Schroeder and Mulloy did not assert themselves enough in seeking the volleying position. Their formation in receiving service, with both men back, was not in conformity with the tradition of winning doubles.

Against an opponent so clever in keeping the ball at the opponents' feet as Bromwich, it was imperative for the Americans to get in close to intercept the veteran's "dink" shot, and too often they were trapped, with the result that they erred or set up the winning "down" shot for the Australians.

A Sterling Performance

But Bromwich did not play the major role in the defeat of the defending team. Sedgman was the outstanding man on the court for the last four sets. Erratic in the first, in which his faulty volleying was responsible in good part for his side's failure to win the set after it had broken through service twice for a 3-0 lead, the youthful Australian champion gave a sterling performance thereafter, especially at the net.

The stroke analysis shows that Sedgman made 41 errors in the match and 37 earned points. In the last four sets his totals were 30 errors and 31 earned points, a remarkable performance.

So deadly was he at the net that he became almost terrorizing with his volley and smash, and he was strong, too, with his return of service. Bromwich made the fewest errors and the fewest earned points. He set up numerous winning shots for his partner and, except in the fourth set, when he was shaking his head dolefully over his persistent volley errors, he was close to his best form.

On the American side Mulloy was the more effective of the two, even though he made the more errors. The Florida veteran had only one less earned point than Sedgman and he played extremely brilliant doubles at times, stand-

ing off the oponents in exciting volleying passages and working up winning shots in beautiful fashion.

Schroeder erred grievously at times and after the first set he was unable to get the right length with the lob, which the Americans used so advantageously to gain command in the opening set after falling behind at 0—3. In the final set, when he and Mulloy were fighting for their lives after getting into the hole early, his errors cost them chances to break through Bromwich in the sixth and through Sedgman in the eighth.

Some Murderous Volleys

It was not for lack of effort that Schroeder failed. He fought in his characteristic fashion and there were occasions when his volleying was absolutely murderous. But the 29-year-old Californian is not quite the player of former years.

He hasn't the same control of the ball. His return of service, so low and wrathful heretofore, was permitting the Australians to score winners forthwith, and he did not have the wonderful reaction at the net that made him one of the most effective volleyers in the world.

The Americans found the Australians a little too quick for them in the volleying duels. Sedgman, particularly, laid about him like a demon in these passages, and Bromwich, too, was quick on the trigger though not so decisive as his partner.

Following the doubles match, commemorative ceremonies in observance of the Golden Jubilee of the Davis Cup were held. Walter Merrill Hall, chairman of the Davis Cup Committee, made an introductory talk and then Lawrence A. Baker, president of the United States Lawn Tennis Association, presented the medallions awarded to players who have represented the United States in the cup matches and also to team captains and Davis Cup chairmen. Sir Norman Brookes also spoke.

Among those present to receive the medallions were Holcombe Ward, only living member of the first United States team of 1900; William J. Clothier, Beals C. Wright, Richard Norris Williams 2d, Watson Washburn, Samuel Hardy, Vincent Richards, Francis T. Hunter, Wilmer Allison, Arnold Jones, Frank Shields, Sidney Wood and Clifford Sutter.

Also, Donald Budge, Robert Riggs, John Kramer, Mulloy, Schroeder, William Talbert, Donald McNeill and Brown. Also captains Walter D. Pate and Alrick Man, chairmen Julian S. Myrick, Jones W. Mersereau, Lt. Col. James H. Bishop and Walter Merrill Hall. Dwight F. Davis Jr., son of the donor of the cup, also received a medallion.

A mixed doubles exhibition concluded the day's program. Miss Beverly Baker and Jaroslav Drobny defeated Miss Nancy Chaffee and Talbert, 6—4, 6—8, 6—4.

The point score and stroke analysis of the cup match follow:

FIRST SET
POINT SCORE

				G.	Pts.
Australia	4 4 5 1 1 3 2 4 0 2—4				26
United States	1 1 3 4 4 5 4 0 4—6				30

STROKE ANALYSIS

	N.	O.	P.	S.A.	D.F.
Bromwich	3	1	1	0	0
Sedgman	3	8	6	0	0
Schroeder	3	3	5	1	0
Mulloy	3	8	5	4	2

SECOND SET
POINT SCORE

Australia	7 4 3 4 1 4 2 4 0 4—6	33
United States	5 2 5 0 4 0 4 0 4 0—4	24

STROKE ANALYSIS

	N.	O.	P.	S.A.	D.F.
Bromwich	6	2	4	0	0
Sedgman	2	6	6	0	0
Schroeder	4	4	4	1	0
Mulloy	8	7	3	0	0

THIRD SET
POINT SCORE

Australia	1 4 1 6 4 4 4 4—6	28
United States	4 2 4 4 2 2 1 2—2	21

STROKE ANALYSIS

	N.	O.	P.	S.A.	D.F.
Bromwich	5	2	3	0	0
Sedgman	2	2	10	0	0
Schroeder	2	5	3	1	0
Mulloy	6	2	5	1	0

FOURTH SET
POINT SCORE

Australia	2 4 2 4 6 4 2 4 3—4	34
United States	4 1 4 1 8 1 4 2 5—6	35

STROKE ANALYSIS

	N.	O.	P.	S.A.	D.F.
Bromwich	8	2	6	0	0
Sedgman	4	6	10	0	0
Schroeder	3	5	4	1	0
Mulloy	7	1	9	1	2

FIFTH SET
POINT SCORE

Australia	2 4 4 4 2 4 2 6 0 4—6	32
United States	4 0 2 0 4 2 4 4 4 0—4	24

STROKE ANALYSIS

	N.	O.	P.	S.A.	D.F.
Bromwich	4	1	5	0	0
Sedgman	5	3	5	0	0
Schroeder	7	6	2	1	0
Mulloy	8	1	8	0	0

RECAPITULATION

	N.	O.	P.	S.A.	D.F.
Bromwich	26	8	19	0	0
Sedgman	16	25	37	0	0
Schroeder	19	23	18	5	0
Mulloy	32	19	30	6	4

	E.	E.P.	T.P.	G.	Sets
Australia	75	56	153	26	3
United States	97	59	134	22	2

United States started service.
Umpire—Winslow Blanchard. Net umpire—Donald Dickson. Foot fault judge—Irving Wright. Linesmen—Frank Tabeski, Herbert Lewis, Orrin Spellman, Bud Young, Richard Moore, C. Zarilla, Olin Parks, John Fowler, Clark Peck, Louis Shaw. Time of match—2 hours

August 27, 1950

Staid Wimbledon Warns Women To Exhibit Tennis, Not Charms

LONDON, June 22 (AP)—Staid old Wimbledon's tennis officials drew the line today—"no Bikini bathing dresses"—on their famed courts. "We don't like this business of running the thing into a dress show," fumed Wing Commander Sir Louis Greig, chairman of Wimbledon's All-England Tennis Club.

Women players at Wimbledon's championships, which will start next Monday, are getting discreet motherly advice about how far they can go to get freedom of movement with peekaboo shorts and brief sun top dresses without exhibiting too many of their physical charms.

Gussie Moran in the costume she wore at Wimbledon in 1950.
Associated Press

But a British tennis writer who said the advice was aimed at American girls alone was incorrect, said Sir Louis. Two or three British girls and a couple of fashion designers who are promoting brief costumes are the main targets.

The girls have been trying to outdo each other ever since Gertrude Moran of Santa Monica, Calif., startled Wimbledon by wearing panties with a lace fringe. Gussie's costumes, designed by Teddy Tinling of England, gained world-wide publicity for the Californian.

"There's a growing tendency among young and little-known players of trying to get publicity with their costumes," said Sir Louis.

"The American girls are great tennis players and they come to play tennis, not show off."

But Mrs. D. C. Shepperd-Baron, tactful "mother" of the British Wightman Cup team which she chaperons and captains, has been asked to talk with all the girls.

"We want to tell them not to spend a lot of money on some designer's ideas which might make a bad impression on the British public," said Sir Louis.

Lieut. Col. Duncan Macaulay, secretary of the All-England Club, confirmed there was no specific rule governing what the girls may wear, except that "it must be white."

June 23, 1951

Miss Connolly Turns Back Miss Fry in Final of National Tennis Tournament

16-YEAR-OLD STAR WINS BY 6-3, 1-6, 6-4

Miss Connolly, Youngest U. S. Champion, Tires Out Rival With Powerful Tennis

---

LOSER'S STRATEGY FAILS

Miss Fry Shuns Net for Play on Baseline—Australians Honor Arthur MacArthur

By ALLISON DANZIG

A sixteen-year-old California girl sits on the tennis throne, the youngest within memory to win the championship of the United States, at least since May Sutton was crowned in 1904.

Inevitably, Helen Wills Moody comes to mind with the elevation of Miss Maureen Connolly. The Berkeley belle of another generation was two months short of her eighteenth birthday when she won the title for the first time with her dreadnaught drives in 1923.

The golden-haired junior miss from San Diego will be seventeen the seventeenth of this month. No player since Mrs. Moody has hit a ball of such velocity from both sides as Miss Connolly did yesterday at Forest Hills in defeating Miss Shirley Fry of Akron, Ohio, 6—3, 1—6, 6—4 in the final round of the championship.

Only 2,500 Watch Final

No more than 2,500 people were in the stadium of the West Side Tennis Club to witness the elevation of a player who, if she can develop a strong service, may take her place on a pedestal with Mrs. Moody, seven times the winner of the championship. It was a slim gathering, compared to the galleries of 15,000 and 12,000 of the two previous days, and those who stayed away missed one of the tensest and most wearing fights of the entire tournament.

The final was so nerve-wracking in the concluding stages, with the outcome hanging in the balance to the last stroke, that Miss Eleanor Tennant, Miss Connolly's coach, was near collapse at the end. She had to be administered to in a box in the marquee as her pretty little protégée let out a scream of joy and ran forward to greet her beaten opponent.

Miss Fry, winner of the French championship, and the national and British doubles titles with Miss Doris Hart, was a wonderfully game antagonist who deserved a better fate for the adamant resistance she offered to the jolting drives that had exacted forthright

Maureen Connolly, the victor, making a return to Shirley Fry on the stadium court

The New York Times

capitulation from Miss Connolly's every other opponent in the tournament. Not even Miss Hart, champion of Wimbledon, had been able to wrest a set from the businesslike, remarkably poised youngster in the semi-finals, though she led at 4—0 in the first.

This was strictly a battle of attrition fought out almost entirely from long range. The pattern of the play was pretty much the same in game after game, rally after rally. Both girls might as well have left the volley at home, so little did it figure in the outcome.

Miss Connolly did not voluntarily seek the net until the last game of the second set and it was not until the sixth game of the final set that Miss Fry did so. Not a single passing shot was made until the very last game.

Miss Fry on Defensive

Perhaps had Miss Fry sought the net more often it might have been a different story, for she showed how good a volleyer she can be in the closing stages. But she was committed to a plan of battle that was predicated on defense rather than attack. She had seen Miss Hart's volleying ventures come to grief in the face of the lightning drives that streaked past her after gaining the 4-0 advantage, and the Ohio girl was resolved to fight it out on different lines.

It was a defense in depth that Miss Fry relied upon. Throughout the first set she made her stand well behind her baseline. There she took Miss Connolly's bombarding full-length drives at the top of the rise, after the full force of the blow had been spent in part.

With a tenacity that never wavered and a quickness around the court that permitted few balls to escape her racquet, Miss Fry kept sending her opponent's lethal drives back. Her backhand bore the brunt of the defense, for it was to the backhand that both players were directing their shots.

As strong as was her resistance, Miss Fry in the opening set could not quite contain the barrage that was beating down in the vicinity of her baseline and making the chalk fly. But she made Miss Connolly pay dearly for almost every point she got in the expenditure of energy in long rallies.

Miss Fry led at 2—1 in the set on a break through service in the third game, but then her backhand had to yield to the constant hammering, and she lost the next four games and eventually the set. Miss Connolly did not find the net but once in the first four games and only three times in the set, despite the riskiness of her length and low trajectory, but she knocked many balls out of court in trying to

break down her rival's resistance, and she also double-faulted three times.

When Miss Fry lost her service to start the second set it seemed that her tactics were a mistake and that she would be wise to bring the volley into play, as dangerous as it was to go forward against such length. Up to this time, she not only had not gone in but she also had hardly used a change of length.

Then came a turn in the play and Miss Fry's methods began to pay dividends, such big dividends as to throw fear into the gallery, which patently was devoted to the cause of her 16-year-old opponent though it was almost won over by the pluckiness of the Ohio girl.

Miss Connolly began to tire from the effort called for in sustaining her offensive barrage. She began to lose in length until Miss Fry was able to play inside of the baseline, and then Miss Connolly's control broke badly, on both the backhand and also the forehand, which was figuring more in the play now.

Miss Fry proceeded to take six games in a row, the last three of them going to deuce. Double faults contributed to Miss Connolly's loss of two of the six, but it was the Californian's fatigue that had brought about the turn in the tide.

Miss Fry was so steady, kept the ball so deep with her backhand and powerful forehand, and made her rival run so much that Miss Connolly broke under the strain. She became so discouraged, in fact, in trying to outhit Miss Fry that it was the champion who resorted to changes of length and the drop shot, which she did in the fifth game.

When Miss Connolly lost that game after leading at 40—15 it was evident that the match was to go to a third set. The second set ended with Miss Connolly seeking the net for the first time and bringing off a smash in the final game, only to lose it as she missed a volley.

Winner Makes 30 Errors

The stroke analysis shows how the situation had changed. Miss Fry netted the ball only three times in the second set and made only eleven errors to Miss Connolly's thirty. The Californian scored seven placements to one for her rival, as she did in the opener, but her mistakes were beating her now.

The third set was an even fight every inch of the way in long, exhausting rallies. Miss Connolly broke through in the opening game and led at 40—15 in the second, only to yield it. From there on, service held until the final game in a fight that had the gallery on edge.

Both players in this set showed more variety in the way of changes of length, and the drop shot and lob were brought into play, as also were the volley and overhead. Miss Fry scored on her first volley of the match in the long sixth game.

Miss Connolly missed the chance

to break through in that game but she passed up a bigger opportunity in the eighth, in which she led at 40—15 and then failed on four successive shots. It was almost too much for Miss Tennant. But, the little Californian eased the tension by taking the ninth quickly, with Miss Fry definitely showing her weariness, and then came the end.

Trailing at 15—40 as Miss Fry scored on a smash and the first winning passing shot of the day, Miss Connolly set the gallery wild as she won with an overhead, a drop shot and a magnificent backhand down the line that stopped the weary Miss Fry in her tracks. Two outs by Miss Fry followed, and it was all over.

The closeness of the match is evidenced by the fact that both players won thirteen games and there was a difference of only three points in their point totals.

The Point Scores

FIRST SET

Point Score		G. Pts.
Miss Connolly	4 4 2 4 6 4 5 1	4—6 34
Miss Fry	0 6 4 1 4 2 3 4	1—3 25

Stroke Analysis

	N.	O.	P.	SA.	DF.
Miss Connolly	3	18	1	0	3
Miss Fry	10	16	1	0	1

SECOND SET

Point Score		G. Pts.
Miss Connolly	4 0 2 1 3 3	5—1 18
Miss Fry	2 4 4 4 5 5	7—6 31

Stroke Analysis

	N.	O.	P.	SA.	DF.
Miss Connolly	13	15	7	0	2
Miss Fry	3	7	1	0	1

THIRD SET

Point Score		G. Pts.
Miss Connolly	2 6 4 1 4 4 4 4	7—6 39
Miss Fry	4 4 0 4 2 6 1 5	1 5—4 32

Stroke Analysis

	N.	O.	P.	SA.	DF.
Miss Connolly	13	13	13	1	0
Miss Fry	16	19	6	0	0

RECAPITULATION

	N.	O.	P.	SA.	DF.
Miss Connolly	29	46	21	1	5
Miss Fry	19	44	8	0	2

	E.	EP.	TP.	G.	Sets.
Miss Connolly	80	28	91	13	2
Miss Fry	63	8	88	13	1

Umpire—Herbert Lewis. Time of match—1:18.

In a doubles exhibition that followed, William Talbert and Hamilton Richardson of the newly named United States Davis Cup team defeated Kenneth McGregor and Don Candy of Australia, 11—9, 6—4.

In a brief ceremony, Esca Stephens, manager of the Australian group of players, presented a racquet on their behalf to Arthur MacArthur, son of General of the Army Douglas MacArthur, the man whom Australians revere for his leadership in saving their country from invasion.

It was announced by Ralph Gatcomb, president of the West Side Tennis Club, that the receipts from the seventieth national championships were approximately $113,000, second only to the 1946 gross. The profits ran roughly to $50,000.

September 6, 1951

Youngest Net Champion Was May Sutton, in 1904

Miss Maureen Connolly is not the youngest women's United States tennis champion after all.

The 16-year-old San Diego, Calif., girl was believed to be the youngest champion when she defeated Miss Shirley Fry of Akron, Ohio, in the final Tuesday.

But research by the United States Lawn Tennis Association revealed that May Suton won the title in 1904 at the age of 16 years 9 months, The United Press reported yesterday. Miss Connolly was 16 years 11 months.

September 8, 1951

Sedgman Wins Wimbledon Title as Miss Connolly and Miss Brough Gain Final

AUSTRALIAN STAR SETS BACK DROBNY

Sedgman Captures All-England Tennis Laurels, Winning by 4-6, 6-2, 6-3, 6-2

By ALLISON DANZIG
Special to THE NEW YORK TIMES.

WIMBLEDON, England, July 4—Frank Sedgman won the All-England lawn tennis championship today, the first Australian to do so since 1933, and Maureen Connolly and Louise Brough will meet in an All-California women's final tomorrow.

The 24-year-old Sedgman, holder of the American title, lost the opening set to Jaroslav Drobny of Egypt and then went on to victory, reversing the result of their meeting in the final of the French championship.

The quality of the tennis was not particularly good and Drobny, discouraged by a gusty wind that made it risky to use his drop shot and lob, chief instruments of his victory at Paris, slumped badly in the middle of the third set and was helpless against the scintillating volley attack of the Australian. The score was 4—6, 6—2, 6—3, 6—2.

Sedgman succeeds Richard Savitt of Orange, N. J., who was ousted in the quarter-finals by Mervyn Rose of Australia. Jack Crawford was the last previous player from Down Under to win here.

Displays Hitting Power

Miss Connolly, 17-year-old American champion from San Diego, gave a most convincing demonstration of her hitting power and volleyed with real skill to gain the women's final after an alarming start.

Trailing by 1—4 against Shirley Fry of Akron, Ohio, who gave her so punishing a three-set contest in the Forest Hills final last year, the little blonde Californian swept through her opponent's defenses in seven successive games and won by 6—4, 6—3.

In arriving at the final of her first Wimbledon championship, Miss Connolly has duplicated the success of Helen Wills, who got to the title round here in 1924, a year after she won the American crown at the age of 17. Should she win tomorrow, she will have surpassed the achievement of her famous predecessor, who was beaten in the final, and will have duplicated the feat of May Sutton of California, who triumphed in the United States championship in 1904 at the age of 16 and won at Wimbledon the following year.

A Difficult Task

It is a difficult task that awaits Miss Connolly tomorrow in her meeting with Miss Brough, who won by 6—3, 3—6, 6—1 over Mrs. Patricia Todd of LaJolla, Calif., victor over the defending champion, Doris Hart. Miss Brough has carried off the championship at Wimbledon three successive times and the doubles on four occasions with Mrs. Margaret Osborne du Pont. Also, she defeated Miss Connolly in May in the Southern California championship at Los Angeles. With her experience, her power at the net and a variety of shots, she is a formidable antagonist when she plays up to her full capacity.

Nevertheless, Miss Connolly's severity of stroke off both forehand and backhand, her ability at the net and her speed of foot are assets that should challenge Miss

Frank Sedgman of Australia holding the trophy aloft after his tennis victory over Jaroslav Drobny at Wimbledon yesterday.

Brough's very best. Also, for a 17-year-old she has rare poise and coolness and she is a fighter who reacts admirably to adversity. In three different matches here she has demonstrated these qualities when things were going badly against her.

Big Crowd Looks On

Wimbledon's center court was filled to its capacity of 17,000 for the men's final and for Miss Connolly's match with Miss Fry, while 10,000 more saw Miss Brough become rampant in the third set and overwhelm Mrs. Todd with her attack on court No. 1.

Semi-finals of the doubles also were held. Sedgman and Kenneth McGregor of Australia defeated Drobny and Budge Patty of Los Angeles, 6—3, 6—4, 7—9, 6—4, failing by a stroke to end matters in the third set. Victor Seixas of Philadelphia and Eric Sturgess of South Africa stopped Australia's sensational pair of 17-year-olds, Lewis Hoad and Kenneth Rosewall, 6—4, 8—6, 7—5.

The final of the women's doubles, like the singles, will be an all-American affair. Miss Hart and Miss Fry, defending champions, defeated Susan Partridge and Mrs. Jean Quertier Rinkel of England, 7—5, 6—3, and Miss Brough and

Miss Connolly overcame Mrs. Todd and Mrs. Thelma Long of Australia in an exceptionally good match, 5—7, 6—1, 6—4.

The weather took a marked change after the extreme heat of the past week. The temperature dropped more than 20 degrees and the skies were overcast and there was a chill in the wind that came up.

The wind boded no good for Drobny, with his delicately shaved strokes, and particularly with his lobs and drop shots, which stopped Sedgman on the wet, hard surface in Paris. Repeatedly the self-exiled Czech showed his discouragement over his inability to gauge the gusts as the ball went astray and he used his drop shot very little, though this may have been in part because Sedgman was so quick in getting to it on the dry turf.

Sedgman did not play well in the first set except at the net. His ground strokes were erring constantly and his strategy in attacking Drobny's supposedly weak backhand did not pay dividends after the first few games. His service, too, was not functioning at its best. In the ninth game, Drobny put three returns of service at Sedgman's feet and his errors on the volley and half-volley enabled the French champion to effect the lone break.

In the second set, the Australian went on the attack in earnest, and Drobny was put on the defensive and kept there. Sedgman was going in on both his service, which was now sharper, and his return of service, and his passing shots discouraged his opponent from coming in. Drobny was clearly outplayed, with his backhand highly vulnerable.

The third set found both men playing rather badly and the first four games went against the server. Drobny's ripostes and drives down the line from backhand were forcing Sedgman into backhand volley errors.

To 3—all there was nothing to choose between them and then Drobny weakened and it was entirely Sedgman's match. The play turned into a stampede with the Australian winning seven games in a row. A point from 0—5, Drobny rallied to win two games with his passing shots and volleys before yielding.

Winner Is Elated

Sedgman, seeded first here three times in a row, finally achieved the last of the big turf court titles to elude him. He threw his racquet joyfully to the side of the court and went forward to greet his beaten foe, who never has won one of the major grass court championships. The Duchess of Kent came down from the royal box to greet the players and present the cup to Sedgman.

Miss Connolly started so raggedly against Miss Fry that it seemed she would be beaten in no time at all. She hit four balls into the net to lose the opening game at love and dropped her service on four more errors. She won the third game and then lost the next two quickly on her mistakes.

Miss Fry was keeping the ball deep and had no need to go to the net, so quickly was her opponent giving her the points on errors. Suddenly, it became a contest for a few minutes and then the match turned into a procession again, this time for Miss Connolly. The American champion found her control in the sixth game and from then on she was so accurate with her powerful drives, so quick in retrieving drop shots and so decisive at the net that Miss Fry was helpless to hold her off.

With hardly an inexcusable mistake, Miss Connolly took five games in succession as Miss Fry's control failed badly under pressure.

Miss Connolly continued to win almost as she pleased until she led at 2—0 and 40—0 in the second set. Here Miss Fry rallied and salvaged the third game and broke through at love in the sixth for 3—all.

It looked as if Miss Connolly might find herself in difficulties again but the little Californian attacked with so much speed, used the drop shot so well and volleyed and smashed overhead so decisively that Miss Fry had to yield the next three games and the match.

July 5, 1952

MISS CONNOLLY WIMBLEDON VICTOR

BEATS MISS BROUGH

Miss Connolly Takes the Wimbledon Tennis Final, 7-5, 6-3

FORCED TO RALLY TWICE

At 17 She Becomes Youngest U. S. Victor Since 1905— Sedgman's Teams Win

By ALLISON DANZIG
Special to THE NEW YORK TIMES.

WIMBLEDON, England, July 5

Hail to a new Queen of Wimbledon, the youngest American to be crowned All-England champion since May Sutton won in 1905.

On the famed center court, where Helen Wills scored eight triumphs, 17-year-old Maureen Connolly of San Diego, Calif., today won the prize of all lawn tennis prizes and did it on her first quest for the title. Not even the peerless Helen did that, her bid ending in defeat in the final of 1924, the year after she had won the first of her seven American championships at the age of 17.

With 17,000 persons filling the center court to the last bit of standing room on this warm day of brilliant sunshine, the blonde little champion of the United States overcame the dangerous challenge of Louise Brough of Beverly Hills, Calif., in a punishing first set of superlative tennis, then won more comfortably in the second. The score was 7—5, 6—3.

Miss Brough, champion of Wimbledon in 1948-49-50, played as fine a quality of tennis in the opening set as has come from her racquet in years. When her varied and powerful attack went for thought after she had broken through for a 5-4 lead, victory was beyond her ebbing strength against the quick, bustling youngster, who hammered away relentlessly with her jolting forehand and backhand, never lost her poise and concentration in any circumstance and was tireless in going up for drop shots and scurrying back for lobs.

Associated Press Radiophoto

Maureen Connolly receiving the championship trophy from the Duchess of Kent after she defeated Louise Brough at Wimbledon yesterday.

Tosses Perfect Lobs

Miss Brough led at 2—0 in the second set, lost a long third game and could do no more except for a final despairing stand. Miss Connolly pounded her out of the back-court, whipped magnificent backhand passing shots and tossed perfect lobs beyond reach of her racquet and went to 5—2.

In the next game, the petite San Diego dynamo they call "Little Mo" led by 40—0, match point. When the tall, blonde Miss Brough, a big favorite with Wimbledon galleries, pulled out the game with her volleys, escaping disaster thrice by a stroke, the fans cheered her delightedly. In the ninth game she needed only a point to break through and she was playing more and more like the Louise Brough of the first set, attacking incessantly.

But Miss Connolly, sensing the danger of the situation if she should lose her service, set herself for the kill and stopped the threat on her fifth match point.

It was a joyously excited youngster who ran to the net to greet her opponent and doubles partner as Miss Brough, going forward to the last, knocked the ball into the net on her approach shot. There were tears of happiness in her eyes as the Duchess of Kent left the royal box to come on the court to present the championship gilt plate to Miss Connolly and congratulate both players on a match of stirring excitement.

Her Royal Highness then departed from the enclosure and left the new queen of Wimbledon to hold court while a score of cameramen swarmed feverishly around her. There wasn't a question in the mind of any one present that the little 17-year-old girl was a queen of the courts every inch, worthy to wear the double crown of Wimbledon and Forest Hills and a vibrant personality who has invested women's tennis with more interest than it has attracted in years.

Miss Connolly cannot yet be said to be invincible. She does not yet command complete control of her wonderfully sound and fluent ground strokes. Her service and overhead are a bit shaky and, as much progress as she has made since last year with her net attack, the powerful passing shots of Miss Brough exposed a lack of strength on her volley that Miss Connolly will have to repair through hours of work on the practice court.

But recognizing these shortcomings, the San Diego youngster is still so good a tennis player and has so extraordinary a match temperament that none of her rivals can hope to beat her with anything less than an exceptional performance. No woman player since Helen Wills Roark has had such weight of stroke from both forehand and backhand as Miss Connolly. Few have matched her in quickness and celerity around the court and none within memory has excelled her in fortitude of spirit. She is so dead game, so unflinching in adversity and so clearheaded and poised when the going is rugged and discouraging, that one is almost tempted to predict it will be a rare occasion when she is beaten in championship play.

The confidence she gained from rising to the challenge of one trying test after another and winning at Wimbledon, where nervousness has afflicted more experienced players on the center court, in her first appearance here should make her all the more formidable an opponent henceforth.

Australia Takes Honors

This 17-year-old girl won over Wimbledon in spite of unfortunate publicity of which she was an innocent victim early in the tournament, and she came through to the championship where our ranking players in the men's tournament failed.

Honors in both men's singles and doubles went to Australia. Frank Sedgman, who defeated Jaroslav Drobny in the singles final, and Kenneth McGregor retained the

doubles title. defeating Victor Seixas of Philadelphia and Eric Sturgess of South Africa, 6—3, 7—5, 6—4.

Doris Hart of Coral Gables, Fla., who yielded her singles crown when she lost to Mrs. Patricia Todd of La Jolla, Calif., and Shirley Fry of Akron, Ohio, won the women's doubles for the second year in succession. They overcame Miss Connolly and Miss Brough, 8—6, 6—3.

The opening set of the women's singles was perhaps the finest of the tournament. Miss Brough, whose three-year reign as Wimbledon champion ended last year when she had an arm ailment, was at the peak of her game, with every stroke so obedient to her dictates that she seldom gave away anything.

Strong and deep off the ground and mixing her attack skilfully with changes of length and pace, she kept Miss Connolly under a pressure that never relaxed. Her service was much the stronger, though later it was to weaken and cost her rather dearly on double faults, and she hit with such power on her passing shots that Miss Connolly could not control her volleys.

Every game and almost every point was a fight. Miss Brough broke through in the fifth game with her passing shots. Then Miss Connolly, staying back, showed the beauty of her own passing shots and lobs to go ahead, 4—3. Miss Brough again gained the upper hand and broke through for a 5-4 lead. She was extracting errors with drop shots and attacking Miss Connolly's backhand successfully.

The tenth was the crucial game

of the set and probably of the match. Miss Brough needed only to hold service to take the set and a terrific fight developed. Deuce was called repeatedly and three times Miss Brough was two points away from winning the set. Then Miss Connolly whipped through a terrific backhand passing shot and a strong cross-court forehand, each in answer to a volley, and took the game for 5—5.

Misses Her Chance

Miss Brough had missed her chance and Miss Connolly took the next two games for the set.

In the second set Miss Brough started strong for a 2-0 lead and yielded the third only after a wearing fight. The fourth game marked the beginning of the end for her. She double-faulted twice, the second time on a footfault. The penalty seemed to unnerve her and she was tiring. Her errors mounted on her forehand as Miss Connolly hammered away and she began to chop and seek the net at every chance.

She could not stay in the backcourt and her volleying ventures were stopped dead by her opponent's passing shots.

Miss Connolly went to 5—2 and 40—0. Then Miss Brough made her game rally and saved four match points before the little Californian brought play to a close.

On television after the match ended, Miss Connolly said "This is the happiest day of my life."

A delegation of American officials was in the gallery. Among them were Russell Kingman of Orange, N. J., president of the United States Lawn Tennis Association; James Dickey of Orange, vice president of the Eastern

association; Perry Jones of Los Angeles, secretary of the Southern California association, and Frederick Small of New York, member of the championship committee of the West Side Tennis Club.

Kingman made known that a number of ranking Americans who planned to play in a German tournament were instructed to withdraw. He reported that unusual financial inducements were offered to them and both the German and International Lawn Tennis Federations were opposed to the arrangements.

Miss Connolly said she would compete in Dublin and then go home to play the circuit.

WIMBLEDON, England, July 5 (UP)—Frank Sedgman and Doris Hart won the mixed doubles final today over Mrs. Thelma Long of Australia and Enrique Morea of Argentina, 4—6, 6—3, 6—4. Morea and Mrs. Long earlier beat Kenneth McGregor and Louise Brough in the semi-finals, 6—3, 7—5.

All-England Champions

The champions crowned in the tournament follow:

Men's singles—Frank Sedgman, Australia.

Women's singles—Maureen Connolly, San Diego, Calif.

*Men's doubles — Sedgman and Ken McGregor, Australia.

*Women's doubles—Doris Hart, Coral Gables, Fla., and Shirley Fry, Akron, Ohio.

*Mixed doubles — Sedgman and Miss Hart.

*Retained title.

July 6, 1952

Sedgman and Miss Connolly Retain National Tennis Singles Championships

DEFENDERS SCORE IN STRAIGHT SETS

By ALLISON DANZIG

Frank Sedgman of Australia and Maureen Connolly of San Diego, Calif., remain enthroned for a second year as the national tennis champions of the United States.

In one of the most crushing victories scored in the final round of the championship, Sedgman defeated 38-year-old Gardnar Mulloy of Miami, Fla., 6—1, 6—2, 6—3, in forty-seven minutes yesterday as 13,000 looked on in the Forest Hills Stadium of the West Side Tennis Club.

Among those present were Gov. Thomas E. Dewey and his son, seated in a box in the marquee.

Mulloy, the oldest player to reach the final of the tournament since William Larned won his sev-

enth title in 1911, could offer little resistance after his exhausting matches in the semi-finals and quarter-finals and got exactly the same number of games as the 24-year-old Sedgman allowed Victor Seixas a year ago.

Probably never before has any player won two successive championship finals by such overwhelming margins. Nor is it recalled that anyone ever went through a tournament with the loss of so few games as did the blond, quick-footed Australian, who yielded only forty in winning twenty-one successive sets in seven matches.

Only two other players from overseas have won the United States championship two years running. René Lacoste of France did it in 1926 and 1927, and Fred Perry of England in 1933 and 1934, as well as in 1936.

Forest Hills-Wimbledon Rulers

Miss Connolly, who had rather a close call in her semi-final match Saturday with Shirley Fry, won with less difficulty yesterday from Doris Hart of Coral Gables, Fla., 6—3, 7—5. Like Sedgman,

the blonde little Californian, the second youngest player at 16 to win the women's title in her first triumph a year ago, retained her crown after having scored her first triumph at Wimbledon last July.

There Miss Connolly succeeded Miss Hart, who had the unhappy experience yesterday of finishing as runner-up for the fourth time in the national championship, while Sedgman succeeded Richard Savitt as all-England titleholder. Very few players have won both the British and American women's titles the same year.

Russell B. Kingman, president of the United States Lawn Tennis Association, presented the cups to the winners of the singles. The mixed doubles champions remain to be decided. It was not possible to bring the tournament to a conclusion yesterday.

The final will be played today at 2:30 between Miss Hart and Sedgman and the winner of the unfinished semi-final between Miss Connolly and Mervyn Rose of Australia and Mrs. Thelma Long and Lewis Hoad of Australia. Holders of tenth-day ticket stubs will be

admitted free, and for others the admission charge will be $1.50.

The final of the men's singles was not much of a show for the big crowd that turned out in the unusually cool weather, and Mulloy, speaking over the public address system after it was over, expressed his regret that he had not made more of a contest of it. His apology was accepted with good humor by the crowd, which understood that he had been unable physically to play up to his full capacity after his ordeals of the two previous days.

Even had Mulloy been in full vigor he hardly could have hoped to defeat so young, fast and accomplished an opponent as Sedgman, with his speed around the court, his unerring anticipation and his great talent in taking the ball on the volley from any depth, angle and level below or above the net.

World No. 1 Amateur

The graceful Australian, who moves about and strokes the ball with less effort than any other player within memory—not even excepting Henri Cochet of France

—has established himself beyond any question as the world's foremost amateur. The ease with which he dispatched his Davis Cup team-mate, Mervyn Rose, after Rose had overcome Savitt's most desperate efforts with a lightning-swift southpaw service and stabbing volleys, should have convinced even the most skeptical.

Mulloy never was able to offer any kind of a challenge in the first two sets, although he won his service at love in the sixth game of the opener and brought roars from the crowd after falling behind at 4—0 in the second. He won the fifth game with two fine volleys and in the seventh his play sparkled for the first time as he passed, smashed and served in a manner to keep Sedgman running and on the defensive.

Other than that, Mulloy was slow on his feet, lethargic in his hitting and could not get any life into his service or his ground strokes. His passing shots failed badly and Sedgman worked his will at the net, to which he advanced with impunity.

In the third set the gallery was stirred to enthusiastic applause as Mulloy threw off his years and fatigue and attacked with a brilliance that even Sedgman could not resist at times. The American's passing shots, particularly from the backhand, stopped the Australian repeatedly. His forehand was pummeling the ball for winners and his service was much stronger.

Sedgman Thwarts Rally

Breaking through service in the second game amid cheers, Mulloy won the third quickly, with Sedgman falling to the ground in going after the ball. Mulloy carried his lead to 3—2, with the Australian unable to return service, and hope was born that Mulloy might make a match of it. But Sedgman stopped his opponent after Mulloy had come within a point of 4—2, with two passing shots, and won four successive games, three of them going to deuce, to end the match.

Miss Connolly's greater strength of ground strokes and her speed of foot won her the victory over Miss Hart. It was a closely fought match, in which neither player came up to her best, but once the champion had taken the lead by breaking through in the fifth game, she always held the upper hand.

Miss Hart drove with good length and at times outhit Miss Connolly, but she could not do that more than occasionally against an opponent with such powerful, fluent drives on both sides. Perhaps Miss Hart would have fared better had she used the tactics employed by Miss Fry and softened her strokes to slow down the pace.

Miss Connolly won four games in a row in the first set to lead at 5—2, faltered and lost her service in the eighth as she double-faulted twice and then broke through from 0—30 for the set with a lob and a backhand passing shot.

The champion set sail in earnest in the second set and won the first three games with the loss of only two points. It seemed that Miss Hart was helpless against her rival's hammering blows and was resigned to defeat.

Miss Hart Pulls Up

But the Florida girl had not given up by any means. She won the fourth game at love on the strength of her service and the sixth, as Miss Connolly erred badly and then, trailing at 2—5, she had the gallery cheering as she pulled up to 5—all. The champion could get only three points in three games, with her control failing grievously, and it seemed that the play might well go to a third set.

But Miss Connolly recovered and summarily put a halt to Miss Hart's rally by sweeping through the next two games with a succession of unreachable drives. Miss Hart made the mistake of keeping the ball on the backhand and the champion hit no less than five winners from that side in the two games, two of them passing shots. The match ended as Miss Connolly's backhand drive hit in the far corner, a hair short of going out.

It was announced that the estimated attendance for the championships was 63,400.

THE SUMMARIES

WOMEN'S SINGLES
Final Round—Maureen Connolly defeated Doris Hart, 6-3, 7-5.
MEN'S SINGLES
Final Round—Frank Sedgman defeated Gardnar Mulloy, 6-1, 6-2, 6-3.
MIXED DOUBLES
Quarter-Final Round—Miss Connolly and Mervyn Rose defeated Anita Kanter and Ken Rosewall, 6-1, 3-6, 7-5; Shirley Fry and William Talbert defeated Mrs. Nellie Adamson and Phillppe Washer, 5-7, 6-2, 6-1. Semi-Final Round—Miss Hart and Sedgman defeated Miss Fry and Talbert, 6-2, 13-11; Miss Connolly and Rose won the first set, 5-4, while Mrs. Thelma Long and Lewis Hoad won the second set, 6-2, with the third at 10-all when play was called because of darkness (to be played off today at 2 P. M.).

September 8, 1952

Tennis Point Scores

MEN'S FINAL

FIRST SET
Point Score

										G. Pts.
Sedgman	4	4	4	4	4	0	4—6			24
Mulloy	0	2	0	1	2	4	2—1			11

Stroke Analysis

	N.	O.	P.	SA.	DF.
Sedgman	0	7	5	3	1
Mulloy	9	7	3	0	0

SECOND SET
Point Score

										G. Pts.
Sedgman	4	4	4	4	0	4	1—6			25
Mulloy	0	2	0	2	4	2	2—2			14

Stroke Analysis

	N.	O.	P.	SA.	DF.
Sedgman	2	4	7	3	0
Mulloy	7	8	8	0	0

THIRD SET
Point Score

										G. Pts.
Sedgman	4	4	1	4	6	6	4	5—6		35
Mulloy	1	6	4	1	4	4	1	3—3		28

Stroke Analysis

	N.	O.	P.	SA.	DF.
Sedgman	6	5	13	2	2
Mulloy	10	10	15	0	0

RECAPITULATION

	N.	O.	P.	SA.	DF.
Sedgman	8	16	25	8	3
Mulloy	26	25	26	0	0

	E.	EP.	TP.	G.	Sets.
Sedgman	27	33	84	18	3
Mulloy	51	26	53	6	0

Umpire—Harold A. Lebair, New York—Time of match—0:47.

WOMEN'S FINAL

FIRST SET
Point Score

										G. Pts.
Miss Connolly	1	4	3	4	4	4	1—6			29
Miss Hart	4	1	5	1	2	2	4—3			21

Stroke Analysis

	N.	O.	P.	SA.	DF.
Miss Connolly	3	8	10	0	3
Miss Hart	7	11	8	2	1

SECOND SET
Point Score

										G. Pts.
Miss Connolly	4	4	0	4	1	4	1	2	4—7	32
Miss Hart	1	1	4	2	4	1	4	4	0—5	26

Stroke Analysis

	N.	O.	P.	SA.	DF.
Miss Connolly	6	13	16	1	0
Miss Hart	6	9	3	2	0

RECAPITULATION

	N.	O.	P.	SA.	DF.
Miss Connolly	9	23	26	1	3
Miss Hart	13	20	8	4	1

	E.	EP.	TP.	G.	Sets.
Miss Connolly	35	27	61	13	2
Miss Hart	34	12	47	5	0

Umpires—Herbert G. Lewis, White Plains. Time of match—0:42.

Maureen Connolly Wins, 6-3, 6-2, From Miss Sampson in Australia

U. S. Champion Beats Team-Mate for Title in Singles—Rosewall Sets Back Rose for the Men's Crown by 6-0, 6-3, 6-4

MELBOURNE, Australia, Saturday, Jan. 17 (AP)—Maureen Connolly of San Diego, Calif., added the Australian women's singles championship today to her United States and Wimbledon titles by beating her team-mate, Julie Sampson of San Marino, Calif., 6—3, 6—2, in the all-American final of the Aussie national tennis tournament.

After Miss Connolly's victory, 18-year-old Ken Rosewall, who had eliminated Vic Seixas of Philadelphia, in the semi-final, won the men's singles championship by beating his countryman, Mervyn Rose, 6—0, 6—3, 6—4.

Maureen, at 18, is the youngest ever to win the title. She is the fourth American to do so.

"Little Mo" took only 35 minutes to triumph. She amazed the crowd of 5,000 with the depth of her accurate drives and passing shots.

The victor lapsed just once. In the sixth game of the second set Julie forced errors from her to take the champion's service for the only time during the match.

Rosewall, like Miss Connolly in the women's division, became the youngest ever to win the Australian men's title.

He dazzled the left-handed Rose with uncanny accuracy, giving the first-seeded Australian the most humiliating drubbing of his major tennis career.

MELBOURNE, Jan. 16 (AP)—The 18-year-old Australian wonder boys of big tennis—Ken Rosewall and Lewis Hoad—today became the youngest Australians ever to take the national doubles title.

They defeated countrymen Mervyn Rose and Don Candy, 9—11, 6—4, 10—8, 6—4, at the Kooyong courts.

The doubles triumph followed a victory earlier in the day of American girls, Maureen Connolly and Julie Sampson, in the women's doubles. They took the title by defeating Mary Hawton and Beryl Penrose of Australia, 6—4, 6—2.

The American girls will be opponents in the final of the mixed doubles. Miss Sampson and Rex Hartwig of Australia reached the mixed final yesterday. Ham Richardson of Baton Rouge, La., and Miss Connolly beat Clive Wilderspin and June Ryan, 3—6, 6—2, 6—3, and followed that by defeating Don Tregowning and Pam Southcombe, 6—0, 6—4, in the semi-finals.

The victory for Rosewall and Hoad gives them a chance of playing doubles for Australia in Davis Cup challenge matches at the end of this year.

January 17, 1953

Rosewall and Miss Connolly Gain Singles Crowns in Paris Tennis

By The United Press.

PARIS, May 30—Ken Rosewall, the 18-year-old Australian champion, upset Vic Seixas of Philadelphia today to win the men's singles title in the French international tennis championships as Maureen Connolly of San Diego, Calif., won the women's crown.

The youngest player ever to win the championship, Rosewall downed the United States No. 2 player, 6—4, 6—4, 6—2, while Miss Connolly defeated the defending champion, Doris Hart of Coral Gables, Fla., 6—2, 6—4.

It marked only the second time in twenty years that an Australian had won the men's singles title, Jack Crawford having taken it last in 1933. Miss Connolly, 18, became the first woman of her age ever to win all four world major women's singles titles—the United States, Wimbledon and Australian, in addition to the French.

Rosewall's triumph was his third over Seixas in as many matches. The blond Australian had defeated the Philadelphian in the semi-finals of the Australian championships in January and in the fourth round of the United States championships at Forest Hills, N. Y., last September.

Rosewall left the 10,000 fans crowding the concrete stands of Roland Garros Stadium gasping with admiration with his faultless tennis. The young Australian's mastery in all phases of the game disheartened Seixas as Rosewall beat him repeatedly with perfectly placed shots.

Rosewall, committing only twenty-six errors against thirty-nine for Seixas, required only one hour 35 minutes to defeat his favored opponent. He broke through Seixas' service in the second game of the first set and built up a 3-0 lead, making only two errors in the 15 points. Holding his own service with the help of three aces, Rosewall won the first set in sixteen minutes.

He broke Seixas' service twice in the second set to lead, 4—0, but then Seixas improved his game, held his own service and broke Rosewall's to make it 4—2. He held his own service again to come within a game of the Australian, but then Rosewall merely held his own services to win the second set in 33 minutes.

Rosewall's uncanny precision began to fail him in the third set and Seixas, playing more confidently, moved into a 3-0 lead. He then broke Rosewall's service again and made it 5—0 when he held his own service, thanks to three Rosewall errors. After losing the next game, Seixas ran out the set after losing one set-point to a brilliant cross-court volley by the Australian.

Following the ten-minute interval, Rosewall began strongly by holding his own serve, breaking Seixas' and then holding his own again for a 3-0 edge. He won his own service at love to make it 4—0 and then broke Seixas' service again to make it 5—0. Seixas then held his serve and broke Rosewall's to make it 5—2. On Seixas' serve, Rosewall took a 30-0 lead but Seixas drew level at 30—30, and moved to advantage point when Rosewall missed an easy half-volley. Seixas lost the next point by mishitting a volley and Rosewall won the next two points and the match, ending it with a deep backhand volley in the left-hand corner of the court.

Near-Perfect Tennis

Miss Connolly, too, played near-perfect tennis to dethrone Miss Hart, who had won the title in 1950 and again in 1952. Little Mo's stylish ground shots, sweeping the court from right to left, pinned her opponent to the base line, thus preventing the defending champion from playing her usually sharp volleying game.

Making a minimum of errors, Miss Connolly was clearing the net by only a few inches with her sizzling cross-court shots in the first set, in which she stormed to a 5-0 lead. Miss Hart opened with a double fault and didn't have a chance until she finally broke through Miss Connolly's service and then held her own to trail, 5—2. Then Little Mo won her service at love to run out the set.

Miss Hart improved in the second set with each player holding service until the score reached 2—2. Then Miss Hart held her service to lead 3—2. Each held service until 4—4, when Miss Connolly came back from 15—40 to win the game after a long backcourt exchange. Leading by 5—4, she served to a 30-0 lead, but Miss Hart drew level at 30—30 with well-placed forehands. Miss Connolly had match-point when Miss Hart netted a forehand and then won on the next set when Miss Hart again netted a forehand drive.

The defeated singles finalists, Miss Hart and Seixas, reached the mixed doubles final by beating Julia Sampson of San Marino, Calif., and Rosewall, 4—6, 6—3, 6—2. They will meet Miss Connolly and Mervyn Rose of Australia tomorrow. Little Mo and Rose defeated Shirley Fry of Akron, Ohio, and Enrique Morea of Argentina, 6—4, 6—8, 6—4 in the other semifinal.

May 31, 1953

Seixas Defeats Nielsen in Straight Sets for Wimbledon Tennis Championship

U. S. STAR CONTROLS MATCH FROM START

Seixas Easily Beats Nielsen 9-7, 6-3, 6-4, to Gain His First Major Net Title

By FRED TUPPER
Special to THE NEW YORK TIMES.

WIMBLEDON, England, July 3 —Playing some of the finest tennis of his long international career, Victor Seixas of the United States trounced Kurt Nielsen of Denmark in straight sets today to win the coveted All-England championship before a capacity crowd that sat under cold, gunmetal skies.

Seixas triumphed by 9—7, 6—3, 6—4 to give America its sixth Wimbledon crown in the eight post-war years. It was his first major championship and he won it strictly on merit. His was the harder half of the draw. He defeated Phillipe Washer, the Belgian, and George Worthington, the New Zealander, in straight sets and then had to come from behind in two tremendous five-set struggles to defeat Lewis Hoad and Mervyn Rose of Australia.

Moreover, Seixas was the fittest man in the field. These championships last for a full, grueling fortnight and most of the big names broke down completely under the stress and strain.

That was how Nielsen reached the final. Unseeded, he caught a tired Gardnar Mulloy with a pulled muscle, an overtrained Ken Rosewall with stomach trouble and then defeated a Jaroslav Drobny so patched together with tape that he had to have a pain-killing injection before going on court.

Nielsen at His Peak

Seixas, seeded No. 2, was favored today but the great Dane with the great serve had killed off the giants with ease and obviously had reached his peak.

Vic was in control right from the start. He won the toss and his service with it, broke through a hesitant Nielsen at love and then took his service again for a 3-0 lead. His whipped forehand across court was pulling the Dane far out of position and his volleying, as always, was crisp and decisive.

They held service to 4-2 and then Kurt varied his attack. Not trusting his ground strokes, he chopped short to the forecourt and as Seixas continued to force the net, threw him back with some beautifully timed lobs. Two of them dusted the lines in the seventh game for the break.

Takes Serves Easily

On they went, Seixas winning his serves easily, the Dane always fighting to hold his. In the finest exchange of the match, Vic dug out a volley from his shoetops in the sixteenth game, a double fault put him to advantage and that lovely, spinning forehand diagonally across court meant the first set.

Seixas was all over his man now and Nielsen cracked under such pressure. Twice he double-faulted in the fourth game and Vic was through again to lead, 3-1.

It was simply a question of holding service and the Seixas formula never varied. If his first serve failed, he hit the second with a violent spin to the Dane's backhand and then rushed the net. Kurt rarely got by, his lobs were shorter now and the Seixas volley still rang clearly off the corners. It was Seixas at 6—3.

With his strokes failing critically, Nielsen's serve started to crumple. Game after game he double-faulted and then pulled himself out of difficulty with an ace. He lost the third game in the third set that way on another double and again Seixas was at 3—1. His fine service held right through for the match.

Duchess Presents Bowl

"I have never seen him play so well," said the 22-year-old Nielsen after the match. "I tightened up. It was like wearing a mental corset."

The Duchess of Kent presented the huge silver bowl to Seixas on midcourt after the match.

"I may or may not defend it," said Seixas. "I would like to play in the Davis Cup against Australia this year but it is time I joined my father's plumbing business." Vic is a month short of 30 and has played tennis since his fifth birthday.

The defending champions in the women's doubles, Shirley Fry and Doris Hart, routed Jean Rinkel-Quertier and Helen Fletcher of Great Britain, 6—0, 6—0, in twenty-five minutes. In the lower half, Maureen Connolly and Julia Sampson, the other American seeded team, won from Ann Shilcock and Angela Mortimer of Great Britain, 6—2, 6—3. The winners will meet in the final tomorrow.

Miss Hart will have a busy day. She plays Miss Connolly in the singles final and will also pair with Seixas in the mixed doubles on the strength of their 6-3, 7-5 victory over Miss Sampson and Hoad today. The opposition will be Enrique Morea of Argentina, who was in this final last year, and Miss Fry. They defeated Worthington and Pat Ward of England, 6—2, 6—2.

July 4, 1953

Ken Rosewall stopped Lew Hoad from completing a 1956 grand slam when he beat him in the finals at Forest Hills. Fourteen years later, in 1970, Rosewall, who had long since turned pro, took advantage of open tennis to win a second U.S. crown.

MISS CONNOLLY KEEPS TENNIS TITLE

4 OF 5 FINALS TO U.S.

Maureen Connolly Beats Miss Hart in Thrilling Wimbledon Match

By FRED TUPPER
Special to The New York Times.

WIMBLEDON, England, July 4 —In what assuredly must rank as one of the great matches in the history of women's tennis, Maureen Connolly of San Diego, Calif., needed all her bludgeoning ground strokes and bulldog determination today to defeat Doris Hart of Miami at the very top of her game, 8—6, 7—5, for the huge silver loving cup emblematic of the All-England singles championship.

"Little Mo" was defending her crown and in between she had garnered the American, Australian and French titles, but she has never ground out a victory against so stubborn an opponent as she faced for seventy minutes in this ivied crater today.

Gone were the timidity and looseness that had characterized Miss Hart's play in continental tourneys earlier this year. This was an old campaigner reaching into her memory book for all the shots that had made her a champion in her own right of every country in which she had ever competed. Here were the fluent forehand mixed with the hard slice, the beautifully timed lob with the deceptive drop shot. They were all on display in this brilliant final and yet, as the points and games rolled by, it was apparent that they were just not enough.

For Maureen has more pace and length off the ground — perhaps more than any other woman ever— and she is faster afoot. This year she has added an overhead and ironed out the wrinkles in her service and net play. More than all these, she has concentration in the clutch. In the final analysis, it was her sheer tenacity that brought her home.

A Variety of Strokes

In the first few exchanges the crowd could sense the drama ahead. Tired of the inevitable net storming that has become almost a disease in male competition, the spectators could watch the full use of the court as Maureen hammered her strokes for the sidelines and Doris played hers long and short in an effort to break her opponent's rhythm.

Little Mo opened service and held it perfectly to 4—3. Finally, in a long game, she blasted a cross-court forehand out of reach for the break. Then she became human just long enough to double-fault twice and Doris was back to 5—4.

In the fourteenth game, a Connolly drop shot left Doris standing, a passing backhand ripped down the line and another cross-court forehand gave Miss Connolly game and set after trailing 40—0.

Miss Hart was through service in the first game of the second set but Maureen came right back and added another on Doris' service to lead at 3—1. Two delightful punch volleys evened it again and on they went to 4—0. Doris made a last effort in the ninth game six times the score was deuced and twice she had the advantage. On the last attempt, she made the big gamble, hitting all out with a flat forehand down the side. It hit the top of the net and caromed back.

That was the breaking point. Maureen held her service to 6—5 and then took Doris' delivery at love. An ovation from 15,000 throats echoed through the arena for more than four minutes. It was superb tennis.

Helping the United States contingent capture four of the five all-England titles, Miss Hart paired with Shirley Fry to get quick revenge in the women's doubles final. In taking their third consecutive championship here, they shut out Miss Connolly and her California partner, Julia Sampson, 6—0, 6—0, in a match that lasted barely 25 minutes. Miss Sampson was strangely nervous and Little Mo had spent all her concentration in the singles. The Hart-Fry team waltzed through the entire draw with the loss of only four games.

The 18-year-old Australians, Ken Rosewall and Lew Hoad, finally came of age at Wimbledon with a 6—4, 7—5, 4—6, 7—5 victory over their compatriots, Mervyn Rose and Rex Hartwig to give them three-fourths of the grand slam in tennis. They have already won the Australian and French titles and are entered in the American doubles at Longwood.

Play of Fine Order

Yet for too long today they were uncertain in the crises. Four times in the first set they missed sitters when leading 5-4 on Hoad's service. Again at the same score in the second, on Rosewall's, they fumbled about and lost.

In the third, still again, they were even at 4—all when a tremendous Hoad passing shot that rifled down the alley put them at 0—40 on Rose's service but they managed to drop that and Rosewall's delivery at love for the set. Eventually they made it uncertainly in the fourth.

Save for these moments of anguish, the youngsters' play was of fine order and it was Rosewall's sharp, low-angled return of service that finally proved the tiny margin of difference.

Miss Hart and Victor Seixas paired in the mixed doubles against Miss Fry and Enrique Morea of Argentina. What started out as a carefree exchange that could have been played any Sabbath morning on any vicarage lawn developed into a rousing battle. Miss Hart and Seixas led at 5—4 with Vic serving and strangely lost the game. Twenty minutes later they took the first set at 9—7 and broke Shirley twice in the second to win 7—5.

It was also the third in a row for Miss Hart in the mixed doubles

The Duchess of Kent, a faithful follower of tennis here for the past fortnight, presented the awards.

July 5, 1953

The Little Girl With the Big Racquet

Seeking her third successive Forest Hills crown, Maureen Connolly is a teen-age tennis queen who has long since 'come of age.'

By ALLISON DANZIG

MAUREEN CONNOLLY, at 18 the top woman tennis player in the world and the only one in history who has held all four of the world's major crowns—American, British, Australian and French—at one and the same time (in fact, at any time), is going after her third successive national championship this week at Forest Hills. If she makes it, she will have equaled the feat of the illustrious Don Budge in scoring a grand slam of the four big titles all in the same year.

Yet—take it from the lady champ herself—tennis is still a man's game, and there is no queen of the courts as yet discovered who has defeated a prominent player of the opposite sex, in an exhibition or practice match, without benefiting from unusual gallantry on the man's part.

"An average male tournament player could beat the top woman, 6—0, 6—0," the blond, blue-eyed little girl from San Diego, who pummels a ball harder than any woman since Helen Wills, said the other day. "He would simply annihilate her. I know. I was annihilated myself yesterday by a pro no one has ever heard of."

Bracketing Budge and Maureen is a natural. Both are Californians. Both are full of bounce, personality and good sportsmanship and have made countless friends for themselves and for their country. Both also play a big game that flattens the opposition and starts a stampede toward the box office. But bracket them in a tournament, with Maureen on one side of the net and Don on the other, and it would be murder in the nth degree.

"Men hit so much harder and run so much faster than women," Maureen says, "that we don't have a ghost of a chance against them. It's not only a matter of power and speed. They have variations of spin and tactics and they are so much stronger at the net. They can pass us every time we try to volley, while we can't do much about it when they follow their service in. Even when they stay back it doesn't make much difference. The pro I played yesterday hardly volleyed once and still he killed me. I won only two games."

WOMEN'S tennis today, Maureen thinks, is faster than it was a generation ago, but the margin between the sexes is just as great as it was when Bill Tilden persuaded Suzanne Lenglen, then world's champion, to play him in a set in the early Nineteen Twenties and defeated her, 6—0.

"Women have more freedom of movement today," she points out, "with their abbreviated skirts and shorts. They run faster, too, because they're not thinking about being sedate on the court. They train more to become good athletes, running sprints and skipping rope. More women now go to the net and they have more confidence when they volley and smash. The racquets now are strung more tightly, and that makes for faster hitting."

So far as the average is concerned, Maureen believes that there are more good women players today, but she doubts that any of them is better at the net than Alice Marble was or more formidable from the baseline than Helen Wills; nor does she believe that any has had to overcome stronger rivals in winning the championship than did those two.

"Helen Wills was my model in building my game," she says. "I tried to develop a baseline game like hers. I played against her once, in mixed doubles, and it was an experience I will never forget. She always knew where the ball was coming and she was always there ready to meet it."

Like Helen Wills, Miss Connolly practices against men because there are so few players of her sex who can give her a match and extend her sufficiently for her to profit from the workout. Not since Miss Wills was in her prime has any woman played with such force as the little girl from San Diego. Possibly Helen may have hit harder from the forehand, with her greater weight behind the racquet, but from the backhand Maureen, with her perfect timing, fluency, balance and confidence, has developed the most overpowering stroke of its kind the game has known.

Again like Miss Wills, Miss Connolly wins largely from the back of the court. She does not need to go to the net often when she can hit winners from the baseline. Miss Wills had no affinity for the volley. She could hold her ground up forward and, with her height and reach, it was not easy to pass her or to lob successfully against her, but she was happier in the back court. Her footwork was not too good and that was another reason why she preferred to remain at the baseline.

Maureen, much faster afoot and quicker in her reaction, has no inhibitions about attacking up forward, but it is only since she won her first na-

Maureen Connolly—"She pummels a ball harder than any woman since Helen Wills."

tional title that she has worked to any great degree on her net attack. Eleanor (Teach) Tennant, who was her coach, wisely had her develop her ground strokes before she let her do much volleying.

Maureen gives Harry Hopman much of the credit for the improvement in her game this year. "Mr. Hopman helped me with my game when I was in Australia, and he worked with me in Europe. I have a lot more confidence in my volley and overhead now and I feel my service is better. It still needs improving, though. My swing is wrong. It's too jerky. I am trying to correct it and swing like a man."

HOPMAN, the astute and successful captain of the Australian Davis Cup team, also persuaded Maureen to run and skip rope to improve her physical condition. Of training in general, the women's tennis champion says:

"Tennis can be a grind and there is always the danger of going stale if you think about it too much. You can get embittered if you train too hard and have nothing else on your mind. You have to be able to relax between matches and between tournaments. There are also certain sacrifices you have to make. You have to go to bed early and be careful about what you eat—cut down on pastries, but have plenty of sugar and steak. And you have to avoid dancing too much and going to the movies too often, and swimming is out completely."

These sentiments come from the heart since Miss Connolly loves a good

time as much as any teen-age girl and tries to have as much fun as any player of the top flight. Her hobbies are dancing and music of any and every kind. She likes to eat hamburgers and drink cokes, go to baseball games and parties. On the court she is all business and has no thoughts for anything but beating her opponent into submission as quickly as she can. But once she is finished, she becomes a different person, a bubbling 18-year-old full of gaiety and friendliness for everyone.

SOME in recent months have accused Maureen of letting success go to her head and of developing an exaggerated sense of her importance. They find fault with her because she doesn't play in every tournament to which she is invited. Possibly some of the top-ranking players have made a habit of competing abroad too much and not supporting the tournaments at home enough, but they can hardly be blamed if they find it more exciting to travel and see the world, particularly when they are in their teens.

No player can compete week after week for months without feeling the strain and grind. All of them have to take time off now and then for relaxation. From all one observer has seen of Miss Connolly, he finds nothing on which to fault her. She is just as friendly and unaffected as she was when she came East seeking her first big victory.

August 23, 1953

Trabert Takes U. S. Tennis Title By Crushing Seixas in Big Upset

Ex-Sailor Victor, 6-3, 6-2, 6-3 —Miss Connolly Wins and Completes Grand Slam

By ALLISON DANZIG

An ex-sailor, less than three months out of the Navy, won the amateur tennis championship of the United States yesterday in as stunning a final-round reversal as Forest Hills has seen in many years.

With an onslaught of the leveling fire power of 16-inch rifles, Tony Trabert of Cincinnati silenced the guns of the favored champion of Wimbledon, Victor Seixas of Philadelphia, and in exactly one hour won the match, to the acclaim of 12,000 in the stadium of the West Side Tennis Club. The score was 6—3, 6—2, 6—3.

Preceding the triumph of the 23-year-old six-footer, one of the few to go through a championship without losing a set, Maureen Connelly of San Diego, Calif., carried off the women's crown for the third successive year.

In so doing she completed the first grand slam of the world's four major national tournaments scored by a woman. She, too, went through the ten days of play without yielding a set.

Miss Connolly previously had won the Wimbledon, Australian and French grass-court titles.

The little, blonde Californian, who will shortly attain the age of 19, repeated her victory of last year's final over Doris Hart of Coral Gables, Fla., whom she also defeated in a magnificent final at Wimbledon in July.

In forty-three minutes Miss Connolly, with her devastating speed and length off the ground and showing vast improvement since last year, took the match, 6—2, 6—4.

Miss Hart, a finalist five times and a strong hitter in her own right, resorted to every device, including changes of spin, length and pace, in an effort to slow down her opponent. But Miss Connolly went implacably on to victory in one of her finest performances. She was irresistible except for a momentary wavering when she stood within a stroke of ending matters at 6—2 in the final set and yielded two more games to Miss Hart.

In the final event of the seventy-second annual tournament, Miss Hart paired with Seixas to win the mixed doubles title. They defeated Julia Sampson of San Marino, Calif., and Rex Hartwig of Australia, 6—2, 4—6, 6—4. It was the third time in a row that Miss Hart shared in the crown, which she carried off with Frank Sedgman of Australia in 1951 and 1952.

The victory of Trabert over Seixas, the player with whom he is expected to shoulder the burden of America's challenge for the Davis Cup at Melbourne, Australia, in December, was achieved with the finest tennis to come from his racquet this observer has seen.

Food for Thought

It was disturbing enough for Australia that its two 18-year-old aces, Kenneth Rosewall and Lewis Hoad, failed to win a set in the semi-finals. The performance of Trabert in crushing the Wimbledon champion by almost as decisive a margin as did Sedgman in the 1951 final should be of even more concern Down Under.

On the best day Rosewall and Hoad ever had they could hardly have stood their ground against the all-court attack Trabert turned loose against Seixas.

Two years ago the rugged ex-sailor, who has the proportions of a football player, carried Sedgman to five sets in the championship. In 1952 he laid aside his racquets to serve in the Navy and was out of major competition except for the French championship while his aircraft carrier was in the Mediterranean Sea.

Since leaving the service in June, Trabert has been laboring hours daily in practice and physical conditioning work to bring his game back to where it was in 1951 and to get his weight down and regain his speed of foot.

At the Merion Cricket Club he met Seixas in the final and was crushed after a promising start. He won the Baltimore tournament, lost to Rosewall at South Orange and then met Seixas again at Newport.

The Philadelphian, with his speed and agility and his faultless volleying, won the first two sets, 7—5, 6—0, and then injured his knee early in the third set and lost the match. Trabert got little credit for the victory, under the circumstances.

Yesterday he went on the court again against Seixas. This time the Wimbledon champion was thoroughly fit, with his knee completely healed, and primed with the confidence gained from his earlier victories over Hoad, Kurt Nielsen of Denmark and William Talbert of New York.

Seixas was favored in the final in spite of the excellence of Trabert's tennis against Rosewall. How was any one to suspect that Trabert would show the most punishing and solid ground strokes on display at Forest Hills in recent years or that they would wreak such havoc against an opponent who had made a shambles of the highly respected back court game of Talbert?

The explanation of the massacre that was perpetrated in the last two sets yesterday came down to the fact that Trabert on this day suddenly caught fire as he never had before and attained the mastery toward which he has strived over the years. On this day he measured up to a Donald Budge, a Jack Kramer in the fearful toll taken by his forehand and backhand, particularly the latter.

It is premature to rank him with those two former champions, but if he can sustain the form he showed against Seixas, the time may well come when Trabert will receive that recognition. At any rate, Australia has much to worry about as it prepares for the defense of the Davis Cup.

In his powerful serving and deadly play in the forecourt and in his speed in bringing off one amazing recovery after another for spectacular winners, Trabert was a foe for the best to reckon with. But his ground strokes were what broke Seixas' resistance and turned the match into something of a rout in the second set. The Wimbledon champion was harried at every turn, driven to the far corners and tied in knots as he tried to get his racquet on the ball at the net.

The New York Times

TO THE VICTOR: Maureen Connolly, center, who defeated Doris Hart, left, for the women's national singles tennis title yesterday, receives trophy from Mrs. Hazel Hotchkiss Wightman.

Tactics Fail to Work

In the final analysis, it was Trabert's top-spin backhand that made the match a nightmare for Seixas. The Philadelphian had beaten Hoad by putting his twist service high on the backhand preparatory to rushing in for the finishing volley. Such tactics also had worked successfully against other opponents. They did not succeed against Trabert.

In his overspin backhand Trabert had the antidote, and his return of service from the left side, falling low below the level of the tape and usually wide of Seixas' racquet, wrecked the loser's net attack.

In game after game Seixas came rushing in, only to find himself passed or unable to take the ball at his feet with a regularity that finally left him at his wits' end, discouraged and baffled, though he kept going forward to the last.

The Wimbledon champion had little alternative. From the back of the court, with his looping forehand and undercut backhand, he was not sufficiently equipped to stand up to the long, heavy strokes that stemmed from Trabert's racquet. He had to get in.

The inadequacy of his ground strokes was revealed in his inability to return Trabert's powerful service, which was usually directed to the backhand, or to make the passing shot on the run from the forehand as the Cincinnatian angled his following volley across the court. Trabert was using the tactics that his rival had employed so successfully against others.

The play turned into a rout for Seixas beginning with the fourth game of the second set, just before the players donned spikes, with a light rain falling.

In the opening set it had been an even fight until Seixas missed his chance to break through in the 18-point fifth game. Then he lost his service in the seventh as Trabert's returns forced him into volley errors. That was the margin of the difference between them in the set.

Up to this time there had been no inkling of the beating in store for Seixas. Indeed, few of his backers had lost faith in his capacity to win. When he took the opening game of the second set at love and won the third on the strength of his service, he seemed to be strongly in the running.

Then the storm broke and the spectators forgot about the sprinkle of rain as they looked on spellbound at the whirlwind that engulfed the clean-cut and wonderfully conditioned 30-year-old as Trabert swept through seven games in a row.

Trabert's service, with its length and varying speed and spin, extracted errors or scored outright in the fourth game. In the fifth his return of service had Seixas reeling and diving for the ball, to set up scorching passing shots and volleys. His service won at love in the sixth and Seixas had got just 2 points in the last three games.

Seixas Fights Hard

Then came a magnificently fought seventh game, with Seixas battling might and main and scoring thrice at the net and yielding finally as Trabert scored six outright winners, four with his ground strokes. When Seixas lost the

---

The Point Scores

MEN'S SINGLES FINAL

FIRST SET
Point Score

										G.Pts.
Trabert	4	0	4	1	10	4	4	2	4—6—33
Seixas	0	4	2	4	8	2	2	4	0—3—26

Stroke Analysis

	N.	O.	P.	SA.	DF.
Trabert	7	9	12	0	1
Seixas	9	13	9	0	0

SECOND SET
Point Score

										G.Pts.
Trabert	0	4	3	4	4	4	7	5—6—31
Seixas	4	1	5	1	1	0	5	3—2—20

Stroke Analysis

	N.	O.	P.	SA.	DF.
Trabert	7	6	17	2	0
Seixas	7	5	7	0	0

THIRD SET
Point Score

										G.Pts.
Trabert	4	5	0	4	4	1	4	5	4—6—31
Seixas	0	3	4	1	6	4	0	3	1—3—22

Stroke Analysis

	N.	O.	P.	SA.	DF.
Trabert	6	10	14	0	0
Seixas	10	7	6	0	0

RECAPITULATION

	N.	O.	P.	SA.	DF.
Trabert	20	25	43	2	1
Seixas	26	24	22	0	0

	E.	EP.	TP.	G.	Sets
Trabert	46	45	95	18	3
Seixas	50	22	68	8	0

Umpire—Winslow Blanchard. Time of match
—1:00.

WOMEN'S SINGLES FINAL

FIRST SET
Point Score

										G.Pts.
Miss Connolly	2	4	5	4	5	4	1	6—6—31
Miss Hart	4	1	3	2	3	1	4	4—2—22

Stroke Analysis

	N.	O.	P.	SA.	DF.
Miss Connolly	8	13	11	2	0
Miss Hart	12	6	6	0	0

SECOND SET
Point Score

										G.Pts.
Miss Connolly	4	3	4	4	4	5	3	4—6—38
Miss Hart	1	5	6	0	1	2	3	5	0—4—28

Stroke Analysis

	N.	O.	P.	SA.	DF.
Miss Connolly	8	12	14	3	1
Miss Hart	13	8	7	0	1

RECAPITULATION

	N.	O.	P.	SA.	DF.
Miss Connolly	11	25	25	4	1
Miss Hart	25	11	13	0	1

	E.	EP.	TP.	G.	Sets
Miss Connolly	37	29	69	12	2
Miss Hart	40	13	50	6	0

Umpire—Herbert J. Lewis. Time—43 minutes.

---

eighth game also, after leading by 40—0, it was seen to be all over.

Trabert continued his string of games to seven by breaking through at love in the first of the final set, making a sensational recovery of a cross-court volley, and taking the second game with a volley and two beautiful backhand drives. Seixas had a brief reprieve as his service picked up to win a love game in the third. Then he pulled out the fifth after being down 0—40.

When the Philadelphian broke through service for the first time in the match to draw even at 3-all, a spark of hope was revived. But Trabert came back like a tiger. The Cincinnati youth broke through in the seventh at love with another of his amazing recoveries and two passing shots down the line, won the eighth with two overhand smashes and then hit two hammering forehand returns of service that Seixas could not volley and finished matters with a tremendous backhand passing shot down the line.

With a cry of joy, Trabert tossed his racquet into the air and then, after shaking hands with his opponent, turned and blew a kiss to his fiancee, Shauna Wood of Salt Lake City, Utah, who was seated in the marquee. Miss Wood, whom Trabert will marry in January, was called on the court to receive the winner's prize from Col. James H. Bishop, president of the United States Lawn Tennis Association.

September 8, 1953

U.S.L.T.A. TO MAKE CHANGES IN CODE

The controversial rule that prohibits an amateur tennis player from working for a sporting goods firm will be tossed out when the United States Lawn Tennis Association holds its annual meeting here next Saturday. The Associated Press learned yesterday.

Thus, from now on, the United States will be able to compete on even terms with the rest of the world. This will be one of the most radical rule changes in the history of the U. S. L. T. A., which has been under fire for many years for its sacrosanct attitude toward amateurism.

The entire amateur code of the organization will be eliminated and in its place the rules of the International Lawn Tennis Federation will be substituted. The I. L. T. F. permits amateurs to work for sporting goods companies. Until now the United States was the only country which prohibited its players from holding these jobs.

Question Arose Last Year

This question came up at last year's meeting, but instead of immediate action, the problem was turned over to a committee for study.

An official of the U. S. L. T. A. said there was a resolution was drawn up specifying that a player who had reached the age of 21 and had been working for a sporting goods outfit two years, would be eligible.

But when the presidents of the fifteen sectional organizations of the U. S. L. T. A. met in secret session Sept. 2, they decided to eliminate the two-year employment stipulation.

"At first," the U. S. L. T. A. official said, "there was a feeling that if a player worked for a sporting goods company for two years, he would be serious in the work and not be merely a front man. Then, it was decided that if the two-year stipulation were kept in effect, it would deprive many of the tournaments of young players."

Strangely, the sporting goods companies were all for the two-year rule.

Col. Jim Bishop of Culver, Ind., president of the U. S. L. T. A.—who is slated to be elected for another term—was non-committal, but in a letter to delegates said:

"The will of the sectional associations is the rule of the national association."

Jim Moffet of San Francisco,

---

second vice-president of the national organization and representative of the Pacific section, was credited with pushing the rule through. It finally passed the regional group by a 14-1 vote.

Moffet, along with First Vice-President Renville McMann of Forest Hills, who has been running the national championships for some years, long have been regarded as two far-thinking members of the organization. It's fairly certain that the former had the solid backing of McMann.

The effects of the new rule could be far-reaching—enough to win back the Davis Cup from Australia in the near future. Until now, there was no incentive for a youngster to take tennis seriously. He had to have some sort of an independent income since he was permitted only expenses and a living allowance in tournaments. If he was knocked out in an early round, he received nothing.

Now, if he is working for a sporting goods company he will be able to concentrate on his game and also know where his next meal is coming from.

"I really don't look at the proposed change with winning the Davis Cup back in mind," said Alrick Man, chairman of the Davis Cup Selection Committee. "That's important, of course, but it's something that should have been done long ago by the U. S. L. T. A. If the rule is changed I'll be happy. The older members of the organization kept it in, but it is inevitable that it will have to be changed. The sooner the better.

Aussie Version of 'Amateur'

The change will not make the term "amateur" as loose as the Australian interpretation. Down Under, they take the kids out of school and if they are promising —as was the case of Lewis Hoad and Ken Rosewall who won the Davis Cup this year—they are assigned to tennis full-time.

Before they turned professional last year, Frank Sedgman and Ken McGregor, the Aussies' three-time cup winners, were employed by sporting goods firms.

The amateur rules will be liberalized right down the line. Now a boy will be permitted to teach tennis if he is acting as a counselor at a summer camp and a teacher will be permitted to coach a school or college tennis team and still remain an amateur if he is a regular member of the faculty.

If they did either in the past, they were declared professionals.

Otherwise the meeting will be routine. Along with Bishop, the entire slate of officers is scheduled to be re-elected. They include McCann, Moffet, Percy Rogers of Exeter, N. H., secretary, and Dr. S. Ellsworth Davenport Jr., treasurer.

The tentative rankings will be approved. They list Tony Trabert No. 1, and down the line, in order, Vic Seixas, Art Larsen, Gardnar Mulloy, Straight Clark, Hamilton Richardson, Bernard Bartzen, Tom Brown, Noel Brown and Grant Golden.

Maureen Connolly, of course, has no rival for the top ranking in the women's division.

January 10, 1954

Drobny Tops Rosewall in 4 Sets to Gain Wimbledon Title in 11th Attempt

SOUTHPAW, 32, CAPS QUEST OF 16 YEARS

Drobny Captures Wimbledon Singles, Beating Rosewall by 13-11, 4-6, 6-2, 9-7

By FRED TUPPER
Special to The New York Times.

WIMBLEDON, England, July 2 — Jaroslav Drobny of Egypt defeated Ken Rosewall of Australia, 13—11, 4—6, 6—2, 9—7, today for the men's singles title in the all-England lawn tennis championships. And the thunderous applause that rang down the crowded center court at Wimbledon must have echoed wherever tennis is played.

For "Old Drob" had finally made it. He had been eleven times trying, first in 1938 as a 16-year-old ball boy from Prague. He had reached the semi-finals six times, the finals thrice, and at long last his dream had come true.

King Gustav of Sweden, Princess Margaret of Britain and the Duchess of Kent saw him achieve his goal.

"I was holding thumbs for you all the way," said the Duchess as she presented the huge silver loving cup to the left-handed Drobny. "The finest tennis I've ever seen," she added.

The finalists went on the court in the early afternoon. Drobny, 33 next month, faced Rosewall, 19—the aging tactician with the all-court game against the subtle, young genius with the delicate lob and the best backhand in tennis.

Drobny Loses Two Games

Two rapier backhands knifed down the line meant the service break and a 2-0 lead for Rosewall as Drobny started shakily. But, cross-courting brilliantly off his own backhand, he was quickly even and then had four games running as Ken seemed tense and stiff under increasing pressure. Drobny was 5 to 4, with his own big serve to hold for the set.

But Rosewall came alive, as he was to do all afternoon in the crises. A gorgeous forehand passing shot down the line meant the game.

Drobny broke through again at 7—6; again Rosewall smashed him back, always forcing him on the backhand. Ken suddenly had a set point at 11—10, but Drobny just saved with a lunging smash return that clicked off the baseline.

Drobny was staying in the backcourt now, chopping deeply to either side, but concentrating chiefly on Ken's backhand in de-

fiance of its reputation. His own strokes grew sharper and two forehands down the ribbon gave him the break and then the set at 13—11.

Pattern Becomes Clearer

They were 4—3 in the second when Drobny lost his concentration briefly. A missed volley off his shoestrings and a flubbed drop shot had him in trouble. Then Ken whipped a flashing backhand across court to lead at 5—3. The pattern was becoming clearer.

It is axiomatic in big-time tennis that a server should follow his delivery to the net. But Rosewall's service has not the power of Drobny's and Ken went up only on service return.

Twice Drobny saved, once with an incredible return of a Rosewall smash, but the Australian made sure of his net volley and the set.

With the tide running against him, Drob abruptly shifted his whole game. He had been staying in backcourt; now he followed up his return of service.

Ken tried to pass him, but Jaroslav cut off his volleys dead to the corners. Then Rosewall pushed

up a series of lobs but Drobny was simply lethal overhead. Quickly, the former Czech had the third set at 6—2.

This was beautiful tennis as each contrived for the narrow opening, the single shot that would pull the other off balance for the thrust and kill.

Scores With Forehand

They were 3-all in the fourth set when a pair of searing forehands into the corner gave Drob the advantage. Three times he had it before Ken stumbled and his volley just drifted beyond the baseline.

At last Drobny was at 5—4 with his service, just where he wanted to be. There was hardly a sound in the huge crater as he toed the line.

He was 15—love. Then, as they had been all this long fortnight, the gods were with Rosewall. A backhand nipped the cord and popped in. Another backhand straight down the line and an overhead smash on the gallop broke Drobny's service. It was 5—5.

So near had Drobny come. He hadn't failed under the tremen-

dous tension; he had been outgunned by a man who dared to fire all when he had to.

Still scrambling desperately, Drobny had an advantage in the fifteenth game, one more chance to break through. They traded drives and Drob hammered at the top of the net. The ball stuck there for a tantalizing split-second, then dropped over. Luck had evened up. Again he was ahead, again he had service to come.

Rosewall seemed exhausted now —a limp, little figure bent almost double over the baseline as he waited for service. Once more Drobny was 15—love. Then Rosewall fired a backhand down the side and produced a roaring forehand across court, falling as he swung, to leave Drobny bewildered at the net.

Another point and it was 15—40. Drobny seemed about to fail again. Then it was level and a service ace that popped off the wood made it match point. Drobny smashed to the backhand. Ken netted.

For fully five minutes the 15,-000 spectators cheered and waved. Some of them had queued all night to root for their favorite. Tickets sold as high as $30 apiece.

[A ticket speculator tried to sell Drobny a seat when the athlete showed up for the match, The United Press reported. "Sorry, I shall have to stand during the match," Drobny said.]

After the match, Drobny said, with a smile, "That's it—and that's all. From here in it will be fun."

Misses Hart-Fry Win

The two best doubles teams in women's tennis will meet in the final tomorrow.

In today's semi-finals, Doris Hart of Coral Gables, Fla., and Shirley Fry of Akron, Ohio, defeated Angela Mortimer and Ann Shilcock of Great Britain, 6—2, 6—1, and Louise Brough of Beverly Hills, Calif., and Mrs. Margaret Osborne du Pont of Wilmington, Del., won from Kay Hubbell of Boston and Mrs. Heather Brewer of Bermuda, 6—1, 6—1.

Miss Hart and Miss Fry have won at Wimbledon three times running; Miss Brough and Mrs. du Pont have scored four times previously.

In some spirited mixed doubles, Mrs. du Pont and Rosewall won from Maureen Connolly of San Diego, Calif., and Lew Hoad of Australia, 6—8, 6—4, 6—4. They will meet the defenders, Miss Hart and Vic Seixas of Philadelphia, who had easier passage through Judy Burke and Mark Otway of New Zealand, 6—4, 6—1.

The women's singles final also will be played tomorrow. Miss Connolly, seeking her third title in a row here, will meet Miss Brough.

Associated Press Radiophotos
Drobny moves in for a shot in his match against Rosewall

July 3, 1954

MISS CONNOLLY TENNIS VICTOR

NO. 3 FOR MAUREEN

Miss Connolly Is Victor Over Miss Brough at Wimbledon, 6-2, 7-5

By FRED TUPPER

Special to The New York Times

WIMBLEDON, England, July 3 – Let it be placed on the record that Maureen Connolly of San Diego, Calif., won her third Wimbledon singles title today. In a swirling wind that raised eddies on the famous center court she defeated Louise Brough of Beverly Hills, Calif., 6—2, 7—5, and the manner in which she did it put her closer to her rightful niche among the tennis immortals.

Little Mo took the first set just as she had been expected to do, purposefully and ruthlessly, in 18 minutes. There was scarcely a chink in her armor.

She was firing her ground strokes for the corners, and as Louise raced from side to side retrieving, she would increase the pace and put the ball firmly away.

When the mood seized her, she would vary the tempo, and time and again, after a long base-line rally, out would come the most delicate of drop shots to spin just over the net and fade away.

All this was in the best Connolly tradition. Another chapter in the saga of invincibility that has carried her to triumph in every major tournament in which she has appeared the world over for the past three years.

But today she was meeting another champion in her own right, winner of Wimbledon three times herself in 1948, '49, '50 and now on the comeback trail after being sidelined with a "tennis elbow."

There is only one way left to play Miss Connolly. There is no use in slugging it out with her outright; it is foolhardy to force the net against the lightning of her passing shots. And so Louise attacked her down the middle.

Diet of Slow Chops

She fed her a diet of slow chops, high and deep, just inside the baseline. Maureen would take the cut-off with her drive, but Louise would slice it back interminably.

As Louise persisted, Maureen became impatient. Her fine edge was gone now and, disconcerted, she was having trouble with her service. Monotonously Louise kept pushing away, occasionally switching to her drive on the

Associated Press Radiophoto

REPEAT PERFORMANCE: Maureen Connolly of San Diego, Calif., reaching to make a backhand return during her match against Louise Brough in women's singles title final at Wimbledon. Miss Connolly defeated Miss Brough, 6—2, 7—5, and won the championship for the third straight year.

forehand, but always keeping the ball deep in play.

The points started to come now, and then the games. She was 5—2 and the packed stadium, prepared by the press for a slaughter, was clapping Miss Brough's every winner.

Then came the deluge. Clenching her fists and muttering her own private words of encouragement, Maureen started to hit out. She produced the big shot on nearly every shot, the scorching backhand across court and the flat forehand down the line. Louise was back to the treadmill again, scampering all over the court in an increasingly hopeless attempt to retrieve.

Maureen was dead on target, each shot a bullseye. Against such cannonading, all resistance collapsed. Little Mo took five games running for the match.

"I thought I was a goner in the second set," she said later, after accepting the loving cup from the Duchess of Kent. "But I did what I knew I must. I aimed for the winner and it came off. Lucky for me."

Louise had a different version. "I made the biggest mistake ever. I worked too hard to break Maureen's service when I had her down, 5—2. It took that little bit out of me that I needed to hold my own," she said.

But Louise got some revenge. She and Mrs. Margaret Osborne du Pont, her lifelong friend, out-lasted the defending champions, Shirley Fry of Akron, Ohio, and Doris Hart of Coral Gables, Fla., in a fantastic comeback, 4—6,

9—7, 6—3, in the women's doubles final.

The Brough-du Pont team led, 4 to 1, in the first set before Doris and Shirley turned to the lob. Under their skillful touch, it proved the best offensive weapon of all. Smashes, volleys and ground strokes they blocked, angling high floaters unerringly to deep court until they produced a rash of errors.

Five games consecutively they had for the first set and were out front at 5—3 in the second with two match points. They lost the first on a sliced volley down the center, dropped the second as Doris hit out.

It was superlative doubles now as the former champions hung on, then broke Miss Hart's service. Four set points for Louise and Mrs. du Pont and then they won it at 9—7.

The sun broke out briefly and the stands packed as they went to 3-all in the third. Shirley was broken on serve, and Mrs. du Pont led, 4—3, with seven advantages before she pulled out the eighth game as Shirley hammered an overhead just beyond the chalk. And that meant the match. Triumphantly, Mrs. du Pont fired a smash through the middle to end it.

Miss Brough and Mrs. du Pont had their fifth Wimbledon crown. They won it first in 1946, again in 1948, 1949 and 1950.

Hartwig-Rose Score

Ever since 1949 the men's doubles event has been considered an Australian preserve. And it was today. Between bouts of showers, Rex Hartwig and Mervyn Rose defeated Vic Seixas of Philadelphia and Tony Trabert of Cincinnati, 6—4, 6—4, 3—6, 6—4, to add this title to the American and Australian ones they already hold.

In the final analysis it was return of service that decided it. Hartwig hits flatly down the middle on both forehand and backhand. Rose produces the intricate, skimming, soft shot and the angled slice close to net.

Between them they had Seixas badly off balance on his serve. Four times in all, they broke it and, in such power tennis, it meant the first two sets and a 5-3 lead in the fourth.

The Americans, in a last burst, broke through Rose then as Seixas scored three times on passing shots. With Trabert serving at 4—5, Mervyn hit a forehand deep that caught the edge of the alley line. It was match point and he buried an overhead into the backcourt to clinch it.

As shadows darkened the area, Seixas and Miss Hart gave America her third victory at Wimbledon this year by defeating Ken Rosewall of Australia and Mrs. du Pont in the mixed doubles.

They had to come from behind to do it. At 5—4 and set point in the first, Doris netted and later lost her service, but they stormed back to win, 5—7, 6—4, 6—3. They had defended the crown and for Doris it was the fourth straight in the mixed doubles.

July 4, 1954

U. S. Recaptures Davis Cup In Seixas-Trabert Triumph

Vic Seixas

The New York Times

Tony Trabert

Associated Press

By The Associated Press.

SYDNEY, Australia, Tuesday, Dec. 28—After four years of bitter frustration, the United States won back the Davis Cup today. Half a world from home, Tony Trabert and Vic Seixas defeated Australia's Lew Hoad and Ken Rosewall, 6—2, 4—6, 6—2, 10—8, in the doubles match to decide the challenge round.

The victory gave the Yanks an insurmountable 3-0 lead in the best-of-five event. Tomorrow's final two singles matches are mere formalities.

Thus the ancient trophy, the coveted symbol of world amateur tennis supremacy, will journey back to the United States after nestling here since 1950. That was the year the Frank Sedgman-Ken McGregor team began to cut a swath through the tennis world.

Seixas and Trabert were virtual giants of the court the past two days. They completely dwarfed the efforts of Hoad and Rosewall, the same two youngsters who licked them by a 3-2 margin last year.

A throng of 25,578—taking up every seat in White City Stadium—watched the match. The fans let loose a great cheer for Seixas and Trabert when the final point was safely put away. The two Americans and their captain, Billy Talbert, were almost beside themselves with happiness as they went off the court.

After the opening two singles victories yesterday there was hardly anyone in all Australia, with the possible exception of Captain Harry Hopman, who thought the home-grown lads had a chance. Trabert and Seixas constitute the most fearsome doubles combination in the world and they lived up to expectations.

So confident were Seixas and Trabert that they only occasionally reverted to their patented criss-cross strategy that won them the doubles last year. In it, the man at the net, on signal, may cross the court for a volley.

This, properly executed, is confusing to the enemy and the Americans showed little of it during practice sessions. As things turned out, they didn't need it. A few times, just to keep the Aussies in a state of bewilderment, they used it. But in the main, they stuck to standard power tennis.

The result was foreshadowed after the first set when Hoad and Rosewall failed to take advantage of two openings. For one thing, Trabert's service was not quite up to par. His delivery had been a source of worry to Talbert for some weeks, but the rest of his "big" game carried him just as it did today.

If there was any turning point in the match it probably came in the third game of the first set. The Aussies had a chance then to break Trabert. They were at advantage, but let the chance slip away.

Winners Break Through

From there on, Seixas and Trabert just sailed right along until they broke through Hoad in the sixth game. Both Lew and Ken were playing erratically, and even at this early stage their only hope was to settle down. They never did.

The Americans won that set in fast order by breaking through Rosewall in the eighth game.

Hoad and Rosewall took the second set. For a short while the home folks thought the young stars might come out of it. But, at that, their winning set was close and they managed to break through only once—on Trabert's delivery in the sixth game. That was the only time in the match they smashed the Americans' service.

That made it a brand new match going into the third set. The crowd refused to give up its hopes that Hoad and Rosewall would rally.

In the third set, however, the Aussies did nothing more than go through the motions. Trabert won his opening delivery after two deuces and then the match went according to service until the sixth game.

At that point, the set still was technically tied, but Seixas and Trabert broke through Rosewall and then Vic held his own service to make it 5—2. The Yanks then broke through on Hoad in the eighth game.

Seixas, the American champion, was by far the steadiest player on the court. He and Trabert were so superior in this set that they were not charged with a single netted return. The Aussies sent fourteen shots into the barrier.

There was only one service break in the final set and that was in the eighteenth game when the match was decided. Trabert smashed a fine passing shot down the sideline to clinch the set and match.

Until that final point, the Aussies looked their best. They fought for every point and brought the crowd to its feet for the first time since the second set when they fought off three match points in the tenth game.

Rosewall was serving and he made a fine showing coming from 0—40. By this time the crowd—sensing just a bare chance for their favorites—cheered every point.

Aussies Miss Chance

At that, the Aussies had a good opportunity to break Trabert in the thirteenth game. They went to two game points before Tony pulled it out.

So now Seixas, the Philadelphia star whose one remaining ambition after more than a decade of tennis campaigning, was to play on a winning Davis Cup team, can sit back and rest. He'll probably get tomorrow off and Hamilton Richardson, the national intercollegiate champion from Tulane, will take his place against Hoad. Trabert probably will play his scheduled match against Rosewall.

It might have been prophetic that the United States should win back the cup after the Aussies held it four years. When Hopman's players took the cup Down Under in 1950, they broke a four-year monopoly by the United States.

The 1938 and 1939 challenge rounds—the last two before the war—were divided by the Aussies and Yanks. In 1937, the Americans defeated Great Britain. The last time the United States failed to qualify for the challenge round was in 1936.

Seixas and Trabert won the first set 6—2, although Tony was not serving up his old cannonball delivery. In fact, in the third game, the Aussies had two chances to break him. They were at advantage once, but missed the opportunity.

The Americans broke through in the sixth game and that was

Associated Press Wirephotos via Radio from Australia

Tony Trabert makes backhand return during match with Lewis Hoad. Trabert scored 4-set victory over Australian.

all they needed. It was on Hoad's delivery and the blond youngster could score only one point.

The Americans seemed more confident than the Aussies, although Trabert was making more than his usual number of errors in the early games. Tony and his partner only occasionally reverted to the scissors and criss-cross strategy that won the doubles for them last year. In this, the net-man on signal may criss-cross for a volley.

Once the Americans broke through in the sixth game, the Aussies could do nothing and Seixas and Trabert broke through Rosewall, who was the steadier of the Australians, in the eighth game.

Hoad and Rosewall won the second set, 6—4. Seixas and Hoad each won service and it was 1-all when the Aussies got back in business by breaking through Trabert in the third game. Rosewall held his own delivery and the Aussies went ahead, 3-1.

Aussie's Game Picks Up

Hoad's game seemed to pick up in this set and he appeared determined to make a fight of it.

Seixas closed the gap to 3—2 when he held his own delivery on a deuced game, but Hoad came back again and held his service. Trabert held his own and Rosewall made it 5—3 by winning a love game.

Seixas served the ninth game and he, too, had a love game until he netted a return. But that was the only point the Aussies got as the Americans again cut the score to 5—4. But Hoad again held in the tenth game to run it out, although the Americans fought off one set point.

The Americans also won the third set, 6—2. The set started as though the Aussie youngsters were going to fight it right down to the barrier, but in the end they were discouraged.

The Seixas-Trabert duo won the first game on Tony's service, but it went to deuce five times. Then the games followed service until the Americans came back from 0—30 to break Rosewall in the sixth game for a 4-2 lead.

This also broke the Aussies spirit and they meekly lost the next two games. The Americans ran out the set by breaking through Hoad in the eighth game.

The Americans won the final set, 10—8. The young Aussies put up a good fight and Rosewall won two of his last three services. But in the eighteenth game Trabert and Seixas broke through.

In the tenth game Rosewall came from 0—40 to win and the Americans had two match points. The Aussies had a chance to break Trabert in the thirteenth game when they went to two game points, but Tony pulled it out.

The eighteenth game was the only break in the set.

December 28, 1954

CINCINNATI STAR WINS, 6-3, 7-5, 6-1

Displaying Power, Trabert Halts Nielsen of Denmark —Miss Hard Pair Bows

By FRED TUPPER
Special to The New York Times

WIMBLEDON, England, July 1—Tony Trabert is the Wimbledon tennis champion. In a crushing display of power worthy of the best players of bygone eras, the American routed Kurt Nielsen of Denmark, 6—3, 7—5, 6—1, in the men's singles final of the all-England championships today.

It was Tony's thirteenth victory in his last fourteen tournaments. And it was the seventh triumph for the United States in the ten post-war championships here.

Not since Don Budge swept through in 1938 had any man so dominated Wimbledon. The Cincinnati siege gun with the wide grin and crew cut played twenty-one events of singles during the fortnight and he won them all.

Even big Jack Kramer, considered the finest of the recent champions, dropped a set in taking the title in 1947.

"I've been dreaming of winning this one since I was in knee pants," said Trabert. "And I've been working on it for the past five years."

An overflow crowd of 18,000, including Princess Margaret, jammed every inch of this historic oval for the final. A thousand persons had queued all night.

Dane Is Unseeded

Trabert was top-seeded and the favorite; the 24-year-old Dane, unseeded, was here because of his brilliant victory over Australia's Ken Rosewall in the semi-finals.

Trabert has the all-court game without a sign of a weakness. Nielsen has the big serve, the sharp volley and a suspected weakness on his ground strokes, particularly the forehand.

Kurt won the toss and the first game on service. Tony took his own and then went to work. A ripping backhand down the line, a passing shot, a double fault and then another backhand with a full swing and he was through to 3—1.

The pattern was already clear. Trabert was spinning his service to the Dane's forehand, pulling him out of court with the kick, and darting in to volleying position. Almost automatically he was slapping the return away.

The Dane's first serve is fast, but Tony was getting a good piece of the ball. He had two game points for another breakthrough at 4—2 but an ace pulled Kurt out of the hole.

It was 5—3 now, Kurt serving, and five times Tony had set point. Five times Kurt saved it, once magnificently with a backhand cross-court volley on the dead run. Tony finally tossed up a rolling lob that hit just inside the chalk and bounced away. It was his set, 6—3.

Strokes Become Sharper

It now was 2—2 in the second set. Nielsen was much more accurate on return of service. His strokes were sharper and he was no longer blocking the ball but hitting for that thin bit of space open on either side as Tony charged the net.

Suddenly Kurt had game point, then another and finally slapped a cross-court volley off the damp grass to lead, 3—2. He held his service for 4—2 with an ace and the gallery, inevitably rooting for the underdog, was swaying with excitement.

Up to this point, Trabert had controlled his power. Now he opened up a notch. He had service for 4—3 and then he swung out with two full backhands, one across the court and the other savagely down the line. Kurt missed an overhead from mid-court and then, after a long exchange, Tony floated another spinning lob over his head for the break. It was 4-all, then 5—4 as Trabert hit his hardest serve of the day.

Quickly it was set point, but Kurt hammered an overhead down the ribbon and outgunned Tony from center with two perfectly punched volleys. The stay of execution was temporary.

Succeeds on First Chance

Again Trabert had service easily and was at love-40 on two backhand passes and a swinging volley that nicked the line. He had three chances. He made it on the first, taking Kurt's service on the rise and backhanding it into the corner for set No. 2 by 7—5.

With his cramped forehand, Kurt couldn't break Tony's spinning deliveries and he was having increased trouble holding his own.

Utterly confident now, Tony was putting full weight into his volleys but still using his three-quarter serve. When Kurt did manage to get to the net, the American forced him back with a series of lobs, all delicate and all, almost monotonously, to the backhand corner.

With the score 1-all in the third set, Tony served and took the next game. Then the Dane double faulted and that game was gone. Tony won again for 4—1 and it was Kurt's serve. Another double fault and Nielsen's spirit and control were gone, too. Tony slashed a backhand down the tapes to break service.

Three serves, three dumped volleys and, finally, another lob that dropped tantalizingly into the corner slot. Trabert: 6—1.

The match was over. Tony flung his racquet across court and bowed to the royal box.

The Duchess of Kent went to the court to award the large silver loving cup emblematic of the highest honor in amateur tennis.

For three years, Trabert has been considered the world's best. Today he proved it.

Starved for any victory here for a generation, the British clapped and cheered their two women's doubles teams into the final.

Pat Ward and Shirley Bloomer defeated Mrs. Beverly Baker Fleitz of Long Beach, Calif., and Darlene Hard of Montebello, Calif., 6—3, 9—7, while Angela Mortimer and Ann Shilcock overpowered Mrs. Jennifer Hoad and Fay Muller of Australia, 6—2, 6—1. It will be the first all-British final in twenty-six years.

Vic Seixas of Philadelphia and Doris Hart of Coral Gables, Fla., twice holders of the mixed doubles title, won from the two Hoads, Lew and Jennifer, 6—3, 9—7. They will meet Enrique Morea of Argentina and Louise Brough of Beverly Hills, Calif., in tomorrow's final. Morea and Miss Brough rallied to defeat Neale Fraser and Beryl Penrose of Australia, 7—9, 6—4, 6—4.

July 2, 1955

LOUISE BROUGH TAKES FINAL

MRS. FLEITZ BOWS

Miss Brough Captures Wimbledon Title by 7-5, 8-6 Score

By FRED TUPPER

Special to The New York Times

WIMBLEDON, England, July 2—Louise Brough entered the hall of Wimbledon fame today. She drew on every shot in her memory book and improvised a few more on the spur of the moment to defeat Mrs. Beverly Baker Fleitz of Long Beach, Calif., 7—5, 8—6, for the all-England women's tennis championship.

The 31-year-old Beverly Hills (Calif.) player won at Wimbledon three times running, 1948-50. Her fourth victory, a desperate struggle, placed her on a pedestal near Suzanne Lenglen and Mrs. Helen Wills Moody Roark. These two alone have won the title more often. Mlle. Lenglen won six times and Mrs. Roark eight times.

And with the triumph of Vic Seixas and Doris Hart in the mixed doubles on top of Tony Trabert's singles title victory yesterday, the United States took three of the five championships in the tournament. Australians won the men's doubles, British the women's.

20,000 Fans Thrilled

This singles match will live long in Wimbledon tradition. It rang on a high note from the first serve and enthralled a crowd of nearly 20,000.

Mrs. Fleitz was the favorite. She had smothered Doris Hart in straight sets to reach the final and she had beaten Louise four times in a row around the world. She was rested and confident, faster afoot and infinitely better on ground strokes.

Louise played her the only way. She sliced one shot, drove another, always trying to break the lovely rhythm of Mrs. Fleitz' two-handed game. She lobbed and she drop-shotted. She even went to the net, but that proved damaging. Mrs. Fleitz passed her with consummate ease.

Quickly in stride, Louise broke service and held hers. She was 3—1 when Mrs. Fleitz double faulted twice and Louise dumped a teaser just over the barrier.

Slugger Finds Range

Then the little slugger found the range. She barreled the ball down one side, put away the return on the other. Her shots were faster and deeper and all at once she led, 4—3, and again at 5—4 when Miss Brough unaccountably hit a short volley far over the baseline.

Louise took measures. She won her serve immaculately and then pulled the drop shot out of her repertoire. Mrs. Fleitz simply cannot handle the short ball and

Broughie, biding her time, kept rallying from deep court and suddenly pushed in a couple of floaters for outright winners. She had broken service at love.

In a tremendous rally Mrs. Fleitz fell down and then, unsettled, banged the next shot into net. Louise had the set.

In the ascendancy now, Louise mixed every wile and stratagem she has picked up in the fifteen years since she was the American junior champion.

A crisis came in the sixth game, Miss Brough serving. Five times Mrs. Fleitz had advantage, eight times in all the game went to deuce and finally Louise ripped a beautifully sliced backhand down the tape to lead 4—2.

Mrs. Fleitz merely hit the ball harder. No woman could stand against her pace now. She won ten points in a row on a brilliant barrage that left Louise shaking her head, helplessly, as the shots thundered by. The audience roared as Mrs. Fleitz reached 5—4.

Louise took her serve, broke her rival's and then the 25-year-old mother fired four rockets down the lines and it was 6—6 and anybody to win.

Louise was clearly tired now. She was resting between points and having difficulty throwing the ball into the air for service. Miss Brough finally struggled up to advantage on Mrs. Fleitz' service. Then came the shot of the match.

A Fleitz drive down the left-hand side was weakly returned and Mrs. Fleitz hammered it down the other. Across court raced Louise. She lunged desperately and pulled off a gorgeous stop volley that just trickled over the net. It was, as

she said later, a "determined bit of stretching."

That shot did it. It was Louise to serve and 7—6. She was 40—15, faltered long enough to double fault and then leaped in the air as Mrs. Fleitz weakly netted.

"I couldn't have gone on any longer," said Louise later. "The heart was there but the legs were gone."

The Duchess of Kent went to the court to present the large silver plate. "Wonderful tennis," she said. "Finest I have seen in years."

Seixas, of Philadelphia, and Miss Hart, of Coral Gables, Fla., won their third straight mixed doubles title in a spirited match with Miss Brough and the gigantic Enrique Morea of Argentina, 8—6, 2—6, 6—3. It was five in a row for Doris in this event. Eclipsed all week in the singles and women's doubles, she broke up the rallies with her superb overhead play.

Lew Hoad and Rex Hartwig of Australia, supposedly the combination that Capt. Harry Hopman has set for the Davis Cup doubles competition, defeated their team-mates, Ken Rosewall and Neale Fraser, 7—5, 6—4, 6—3. They broke Rosewall's service in each set and never lost theirs.

The women's doubles crown returned to Britain for the first time since 1939, as Angela Mortimer and Anne Shilcock defeated Pat Ward and Shirley Bloomer, also of Britain, 7—5, 6—1.

In all, more than 285,000 people jammed the Wimbledon oval during the fortnight to establish an attendance record. An orange sun hung high in a blue sky today and the weather was fine the whole way.

July 3, 1955

AUSTRALIA TAKES DOUBLES TO CLINCH DAVIS CUP, 3-0

TEST GOES 5 SETS

Hoad and Hartwig Beat Trabert and Seixas in 2½-Hour Match

By ALLISON DANZIG

Only eight months after it lost the Davis Cup to the United States at Sydney, Australia regained the world team tennis championship yesterday at Forest Hills.

In a truly great doubles match of two and a half hours, Lewis Hoad and Rex Hartwig defeated Tony Trabert and Victor Seixas for the clinching victory before 12,000 fans. The score was 12—14, 6—4, 6—3, 3—6, 7—5.

With the 2 points scored in the singles on Friday by Hoad and Kenneth Rosewall, Australia had the necessary 3 to give it possession of the cup. Thus it

had emulated the success of the American team in 1954 in gaining the decision by the end of the second day of play.

The final two singles will be played today. Of course, they can have no bearing on the disposition of the cup, which will travel back across the far reaches of the Pacific again.

In the first match, at 2 o'clock, Hoad is scheduled to play Seixas. Then Hamilton Richardson will go on against Rosewall in the closing contest. Captain William Talbert named Richardson to re-

place Trabert.

The first set yesterday was the longest in doubles played in a cup challenge round since William Tilden and R. Norris Williams 2d defeated James O. Anderson and John B. Hawkes of Australia in 1923 in an opening set that went to 17—15.

Three Times at Set Point

Three times Hoad and Hartwig, champions of Wimbledon, stood within a stroke of winning the set. They had their first chance in the twentieth game

GOING AFTER A HIGH ONE: Tony Trabert of the U. S. team leaves his feet in attempt to return a shot during doubles match with Australia's Rex Hartwig, left background, and Lewis Hoad. Victor Seixas is at the lower right.

Associated Press

and two more in the twenty-second.

That they rallied, after missing these opportunities, to go on to victory, was a testimonial to their spirit. Most often the team that loses so prolonged an opening set becomes discouraged and yields forthwith.

Too much credit can not be given the young players from Down Under for their tenacity. At the same time, Trabert and the 32-year-old Seixas showed a fortitude of their own in the great fight they made when they seemed to be clearly on the defensive at the intermission.

So close and exciting was the battle, which had the crowd roaring throughout the five sets, that the outcome was never evident until the last stroke. Indeed, a few minutes before the end, it seemed that victory was at hand for the defending team.

To 5-all the teams fought without a breakthrough in service in this final set, just as they had fought to 12-all without a break in the long opener. Then, in the eleventh game, the Stadium was boiling with excitement.

Break Through Seixas

Three times Trabert and Seixas stood within a stroke of breaking through Hoad. That practically meant they had three match points, from the way service had been standing up. But Hoad's volcanic service and

the deadliness of the two young Australians at the net saved the day and killed the United States last chance.

Leading by 6—5, the Aussies broke through Seixas in the next game. Hoad whipped a backhand return of service at Seixas' feet and Hartwig scored with a backhand volley.

The next instant the two partners were throwing their arms around each other in joy and Umpire Herbert Lewis was announcing Australia as the winner of the Davis Cup.

This was the first time that Australia had won the challenge round doubles in three years. Last year Trabert and Seixas defeated Hoad and Rosewall. In 1953 they had beaten Hoad and Hartwig.

That was the first time Hoad and Hartwig had joined forces. They were hastily paired as a scratch combination against the wishes of Capt. Harry Hopman.

Yesterday Hoad and Hartwig were a far more effective team. Certainly Hartwig was a far better player. Indeed, the wiry 26-year-old Australian was the outstanding man on the court. It was to him in the main that the credit was due for the victory.

Hoad, who rose to such scintillating heights in defeating Trabert in the singles Friday, after Rosewall had beaten Seixas, was not nearly as consistent as his partner. His service was tremendous and he was great with the volley and the smash, but off the ground he was not nearly so effective.

Hoad's return of service, chief-

ly from the backhand, was glaringly off until the last stages. Had his return of service not been so at fault, Australia might have won the opening set.

Hartwig was strong in every department. His return of service stood out all the more by comparison with Hoad's. Hoad seemed to be thrown off by the system of signals that the Americans used.

The man at the net signaled to the server whether or not he would cross over to protect against the cross-court return of service. Trabert often would fake crossing over. It may have been that this motion bothered Hoad.

Seixas gave a splendid account of himself until he began to tire a bit. He was in trouble more often than Trabert on his service, but he was so sterling a fighter and Trabert was so good in poaching that they were able to pull out of the hole most of the time.

The opening set was won on just one break through service, through Hartwig in the next to last game. There was just one break in the second set, also, through Seixas in the final game.

In the third set Trabert was broken through in the sixth game. Then, to the amazement and delight of the gallery, Hoad was broken through in the ninth after he had led at 40—0, with Seixas magnificent on the return.

To break Hoad's service under any circumstances is an achievement. To rally from 0—40 against it is almost incredible, particularly in doubles.

But hardly had the crowd quieted down from its uproarious demonstration when the Americans were in trouble

again. Seixas lost his service in the eighth game as Hoad and Hartwig did some mad volleying behind the return of service. Hartwig then served out the set in invincible style.

So the Australians, who were thought to be doomed to defeat at the end of the 57-minute opening set, left the Stadium arena with a lead of 2 sets to 1. At that time they were the decided favorites to win the match. So strong were they in service and at the net that the crowd was prepared to see them finish the match in the fourth set.

Seixas in Trouble

The Australians had their opportunity. They led at 30—0 on Seixas' service in the third game, but both failed with their return of service and Seixas pulled out of the hole. Then the Americans broke through Hoad in the next game.

Trabert rose to superb heights in this game. He brought off a two-handed push volley, in self defense, that sent the ball off at a tangent into the unprotected alley as the Australians stared unbelieving and the crowd gasped.

A smash by Trabert and his cross court volley contributed 2 more points. Trabert's return of service was dumped into the net by Hoad for the final point. That was the set, as it turned out, for the Australians missed an opportunity to get even when they led at 30—0 again on Seixas' service in the eighth game and lost it.

The fans cheered as the United States took the set to square the match. There was still hope, and strong hope, that the fate of the cup might be deferred until Sunday in the final singles matches.

This final set was a tense, gripping battle every minute, with the crowd hanging on every stroke. The suspense mounted every time the pitcher, meaning the server, got behind the batter, meaning the striker or receiver.

Hartwig was behind at 0—30 in the first game. Trabert was 30—40 on his serve in the second game and was carried to deuce in the sixth. Then service was devastating to 5-all, and then followed the tremendously stirring eleventh game.

Three times, as related, Trabert and Seixas stood within a stroke of breaking through Hoad after leading at 30—0. But Hoad's cannonball service and the brilliance of both Australians at the net pulled them out of the fearful situation.

It was a keen disappointment to the crowd when the game was lost by the Americans. Then followed the final blow.

Seixas, serving, netted two volleys. Hoad knocked Vic's service back for a winner from the backhand that had failed so often. Hartwig's backhand volley brought the match to an end.

Hoad Loses Racquet

Two developments in the opening set remain to be commented on. In the fifteenth game Hoad hit a volley down the center of the court for a winner,

Tennis Joins Parade of Synthetics

but his racquet flew from his hand into the opponents' court.

At first it was ruled that the ball was dead before Hoad's racquet crossed the net. Seixas and Captain Talbert protested and the referee, Dr. S. Ellsworth Davenport Jr., ruled that the ball was still in play as the racquet crossed the net. So the Australians lost the point, but they went on to win the game.

In the twenty-fifth game, in which Hartwig was broken through, the final point was won by the United States as Hartwig put his volley into the net in answer to the return of service.

Hoad claimed that the service had been a let and both he and Seixas, who was of the same opinion, made no move to change courts. But the net umpire, Hollis Dann, ruled that the serve had not ticked the net, and so the point stood.

That was the only time in the match that Hartwig lost his service. It was the first time in twenty-seven service games against Japan, Italy and the United States that he had lost his service.

The blond, wiry Hartwig, the runner-up for the United States title last year, was judged to be too erratic for singles in spite of his great brilliance. But in doubles yesterday he was the most dependable man on the court and added greatly to his stature as an international player.

The stroke analysis shows that Trabert had the best average, with 44 earned points against forty-six errors. That is a rather remarkable percentage of winning shots. Hartwig scored 49 times and made sixty errors. Hoad had exactly the same number of earned points and seventy-one errors.

In an exhibition match, Richardson and Gilbert Shea, the other two members of the United States team, took on Neale Fraser and Ashley Cooper of Australia. The Americans won the first set, 6—4, and lost the second, 17—15.

But Experts Say It's Too Early to Judge Ball by Its Cover

By MICHAEL STRAUSS

Tennis balls, like suits and shirts and hose, have joined the synthetic parade. The newest ball has nylon and dacron in its cover and its manufacturers claim it is the best ever.

The new ball is a far cry from the type used by Dr. James Dwight and Richard D. Sears, who are to American tennis what Lewis and Clark are to American history. Dwight and Sears were among the first tennis trail blazers in this country some eighty years ago. In those days almost anything that bounced was used.

Today, manufacturers are offering a ball that is as new as the supersonic plane. It's a move toward producing a ball that will give longer and more uniform wear. Manufacturers say the ball is easier to control. So far, there have been neither squawks nor praise. The idea is that new.

When he was asked about the ball at Forest Hills last week, Bill Talbert, the non-playing captain of the United States Davis Cup team, said:

Ball May Be Faster

"Some of our players believe the new ball plays a bit faster. But it's still too early to tell. It has to be used some more."

Jack Kramer, the former amateur champion who is now a professional, said just about the same thing:

"I believe the new ball plays lighter at the start. But after you have hit about ten or twelve points worth, it "heavies up" just right. I think we'll have to wait awhile before being definite about it."

The rule book has a long list of stipulations for a tennis ball. Before leaving the factory the ball is put to an exhaustive test. Room temperatures, atmospheric pressure and even the corrosive qualities of the metal used in the test, are considered. After the ball passes the preliminaries it is dropped from a height of 100 inches to a concrete base to prove its bouncing qualities.

When the ball is finally put into the can for packing it is grade "A." An "A-minus" rating relegates a ball to the discard. The ball has to be "more than two-and-a-half inches and less than two-and-five-eighths inches in diameter." It has to be "more than two ounces and less than two-and-one-sixteenth ounces in weight." Brother!

In 1875 a tennis ball was large, rubbery and uncovered. Children of that era used the same ball to play street games. Early courts were not rectangular as they are today. They had that hour glass figure so popular with the women of the time —narrow at the net and wide at the baselines.

From the simple rubber ball, tennis pioneers moved to one with feathers on it. Even an India-rubber ball was tried before something resembling the present-day ball was adopted for the national championships in 1887.

Uniformity became essential. The importance of uniformity became highlighted when international play was begun between this country and England. One year, the American-type ball was described by an English writer as being "small, light and soft enough to be almost squashy."

The truth of the matter was that Malcolm Whitman, an American star at the turn of the century, had developed a service that was then known as the "reverse twist." His service sliced the ball so as to make it become a bit egg-shaped in flight.

Today more than 515,094 dozen tennis balls are sold every year in the United States. There are two types, one made for lawn tennis and one for harder surfaces. The hard-surface playing balls are made with fuzzier covers, which last longer.

The ordinary tennis player generally uses a ball until it falls apart. In championship play, new balls are put into play often, as agreed upon by tournament officials or team captains.

In the recent Davis Cup matches at Forest Hills new balls were tossed to the players every seven games.

September 8, 1955

The Point Scores

FIRST SET

Point Score

											G. Pts.
Australia	6	1	4	0	4	2	4	3	6	2	4	1
	4	1	5	0	4	0	4	3	4	4	1	2	1—12 74
United States	4	4	1	4	1	4	2	5	4	4	0	4
	1	4	3	4	0	4	2	3	1	6	1	4	4—14 80

Stroke Analysis

	N.	C.	P.	SA.	DF.
Hoad	18	6	14	2	0
Hartwig	14	12	12	0	0
Trabert	9	11	17	2	1
Seixas	14	11	10	1	0

SECOND SET

Point Score

										G. Pts.
Australia	4	1	4	3	4	4	4	0	4	4—6 32
United States	0	4	1	5	2	6	1	4	2	2—4 27

Stroke Analysis

	N.	O.	P.	SA.	DF.
Hoad	5	5	8	3	0
Hartwig	4	7	7	0	0
Trabert	4	2	4	0	0
Seixas	3	5	2	0	0

THIRD SET

Point Score

										G. Pts.
Australia	4	0	4	2	4	4	6	1	4—6 35
United States	3	4	2	4	1	2	8	2	1—3 36

Stroke Analysis

	N.	O.	P.	SA.	DF.
Hoad	11	3	9	0	0
Hartwig	2	3	8	0	1
Trabert	1	5	6	0	1
Seixas	5	7	0	1	0

August 28, 1955

Trabert Defeats Rosewall and Doris Hart Also Captures U. S. Tennis Final

OHIO ACE REGAINS CROWN IN 3 SETS

Trabert Wins, 9-7, 6-3, 6-3 —Miss Hart Victor Over Patricia Ward, 6-4, 6-2

By ALLISON DANZIG

Tony Trabert regained the national championship yesterday and completed the finest record in amateur tennis since Donald Budge's grand slam of 1938 in the world's major tournaments.

Following Saturday's 6-4, 6-2, 6-1 victory over Lewis Hoad in the semi-finals, the 25-year-old Trabert defeated Kenneth Rosewall, 9—7, 6—3, 6—3, in the final round before 9,000 in the Forest Hills Stadium of the West Side Tennis Club.

Thus, without yielding a set to them, the big fellow from Cincinnati disposed of the two 20-year-old Australians who had regained the Davis Cup from the United States in a 5-0 sweep.

It was Trabert's second United States championship. His first was gained in 1953.

Earlier in the day Doris Hart of Coral Gables, Fla., retained the women's title with a 6-4, 6-2 victory over Patricia Ward of England.

All Straight-Set Victories

Trabert went through the entire tournament without the loss of a set. Rosewall, the champion of his country, was the only player to get more than four games from him in any one set.

Trabert won the Wimbledon championship, also without yielding a set. The French crown fell to him, too, together with our national indoor and clay court titles and numerous other prizes.

Lacking only the Australian crown among the world's four major championships, Trabert probably has a better claim to world pre-eminence than any other amateur, though Davis Cup success carries great prestige. In his position, he would be a big attraction for professional tennis. Jack Kramer, the promoter, is ready to sign him to a fat contract, if he says the word.

"I think now is the time for Tony to start on a professional career if he intends to do so," said Kramer yesterday. "It would be risky for him to put it off. He can net $50,000 clear for himself in his first year."

Kramer doesn't know what Trabert will do. The champion is entering upon a business career following the Pacific Southwest championships at Los Angeles. He will be manager of the Los Angeles office of the Security Banknote Company, of which William Talbert, Davis Cup captain, is vice president.

Issue Before Trabert

Talbert has been trying to persuade Trabert that he will be better off and happier sticking to his job and playing amateur tennis than he will be in making a big haul for a year or two as a professional and giving a good part of it to Uncle Sam in taxes.

That is the question that Trabert is weighing. And whether he will be available for the United States Davis Cup team in 1956 is in the balance.

Trabert's clear-cut victories over Rosewall and Hoad brighten the United States' hopes of regaining the cup if he elects to remain an amateur.

Neither of the Australians was as keen or had as great an incentive in the championship as in the cup matches. Nevertheless, the improvement in Trabert's play was immensely heartening to American tennis officials. He was better prepared to show at his best than he had been in the challenge round following a four-week lay-off.

Neither Trabert nor Rosewall came up to his form of the semi-finals, and the match did not quite measure up to expectations. The condition of the court, badly scarred and barren of grass in spots, was not conducive to the best grade of tennis. Nor was the cloudy, threatening weather, which kept many at home at their television sets.

Control Shaky at Times

Rosewall, possibly a bit more at a disadvantage than Trabert on the patchy turf because of his greater dependence upon his ground strokes, was shaky in his control at times. But he never gave up the fight. Unlike Hoad, who lost interest in his semi-final in the second set, the little Australian champion gave his best to the final point, though he seemed discouraged early in the final set.

In each of the three sets, Trabert was out in front and Rosewall rallied, only to falter each time against the American's stiffening opposition.

The New York Times (by Carl T. Gossett Jr.)

Pat Ward leaps off ground to drive home overhand smash to score on Doris Hart.

It appeared that Trabert was going to win almost as quickly as against Hoad when he broke service twice for a 4-1 lead in the opening set. Then Rosewall found his control with his lightning forehand and unsurpassed backhand, and Trabert broke badly in his volleying.

When Rosewall drew even at 5-all, breaking through in the sixth and tenth games on Trabert's errors at the net, there was concern for the Ohio star's prospects. It was believed that if he lost the set after dissipating his commanding lead, there would be no stopping Rosewall.

Trabert's service kept him in the running to 7-all and then Rosewall, who won four of his games in the set at love, weakened in his serving in the fifteenth game. He double-faulted, faltered in control, and Trabert sent a scorching crosscourt forehand past him for the deciding break.

Once he had pulled out the set, Trabert was never headed. He went ahead again at 4-1 in the second set and once more in the third. His powerful serving, the depth and speed of his volley and his strong return of service kept him on top.

Rosewall's ground strokes, blazing sharp and bringing gasps from the gallery in the first set, failed to stand up under the constant pressure on the patchy turf. He made considerably more errors than is his wont, both from the back of the court and at the net.

In the second set Rosewall, at 1—4, broke Trabert at love, won the seventh game and had 40—15 in the eighth. There Trabert braced and his cannonball service, a clear drop shot made on the dead run, and a resounding overhead smash scored for him as he took the next eight points. The champion was too powerful, too alert and too good a shotmaker to be resisted.

When Trabert won the first three games of the third set, two of them at love, Rosewall seemed resigned to defeat. His superb backhand was failing him badly and he could not resist Trabert's volley, smash or his return of service. In every quarter Rosewall was being outplayed, and no one could have blamed him much if he had lost heart and submitted.

But, unlike some of his teammates, the little Australian fought to the bitter end. He broke service in the seventh with his lobs as Trabert's volley slumped again. And the gallery, though favoring Trabert, cheered Rosewall for his courage. But in the next game Rosewall's volley failed him three times, and Trabert sent a short crosscourt forehand past him at the net to break through at Love.

Trabert's powerful service, which scored ten aces in the match to Rosewall's one, brought the play to an end in the ninth. Soon Col. James H. Bishop of Culver, Ind., president of the United States Lawn Tennis Association, was presenting the the cup to the new champion.

Miss Hart's victory over Miss Ward in the women's final was gained after a faltering start. For a time it even seemed that Miss Ward might become the first English player to win the crown since Betty Nuthall triumphed in 1930.

Driving beautifully and deep from her underhit backhand and mixing her attack, Miss Ward won the first three games with the loss of only 4 points. She was outhitting the champion and she showed much the better control.

Then Miss Hart began to work into her best form and won the next two games, pulling out the fifth from 0—30. The use of the drop shot helped to stem the tide. Then the Florida girl failed with her volleys and lost her service, to make the score 4—2 against her. And she was down 0—40 in the seventh.

The gallery hardly knew what to expect. But Miss Hart thenceforth had command of her game and of the match. She took four games in a row, pulling out the seventh and forcing her opponent on the run with her changing length in the long rallies.

In the second set Miss Ward took the first game and then was on the defensive against Miss Hart's strong attack and service. She did not get another game until Miss Hart was at 5—1 and 40—15. She saved 2 match points and then Miss Hart ended matters in the eighth.

Miss Hart and Victor Seixas won the mixed doubles championship for the third successive year. In the final they defeated Shirley Fry and Gardnar Mulloy, 7—5, 5—7, 6—2. They had won the mixed doubles title at Wimbledon, also for the third year in a row.

Tennis Point Scores

MEN'S FINAL

FIRST SET

Point Score

		Pts.	G.
Trabert—	0 4 4 4 4 2 0 4 0 3 2 4 0 4 5 4—44		9
Rosewall—	4 2 2 1 2 4 4 1 4 5 4 1 4 1 3 2—44		7

Stroke Analysis

	N.	O.	P.	SA.	D.F.
Trabert	15	14	12	7	2
Rosewall	12	11	13	1	2

SECOND SET

Point Score

		Pts.	G.
Trabert	4 4 3 4 6 0 2 5 4—32		6
Rosewall	1 2 5 1 4 4 4 3 0—24		3

Stroke Analysis

	N.	O.	P.	SA.	D.F.
Trabert	3	11	11	2	0
Rosewall	13	6	10	0	0

THIRD SET

Point Score

		Pts.	G.
Trabert	4 4 4 5 5 3 1 4 4—34		6
Rosewall	0 2 0 7 3 5 4 0 2—23		3

Stroke Analysis

	N.	O.	P.	SA.	D.F.
Trabert	10	4	11	1	0
Rosewall	12	10	9	0	0

RECAPITULATION

	N.	O.	P.	SA.	D.F.
Trabert	28	29	34	10	2
Rosewall	37	27	31	1	2

	E.	E.P.	T.P.	G.	Sets.
Trabert	59	44	110	21	3
Rosewall	66	32	91	13	0

WOMEN'S FINAL

FIRST SET

Point Score

		Pts.	G.
Miss Hart	1 1 2 4 5 2 6 5 5 4—35		6
Miss Ward	4 4 4 1 3 4 4 3 3 1—31		4

Stroke Analysis

	N.	O.	P.	SA.	D.F.
Miss Hart	7	16	12	1	0
Miss Ward	5	17	8	0	0

SECOND SET

Point Score

		Pts.	G.
Miss Hart	4 4 4 4 4 3 5—32		6
Miss Ward	6 0 1 1 2 1 5 3—19		2

Stroke Analysis

	N.	O.	P.	SA.	D.F.
Miss Hart	4	7	13	0	0
Miss Ward	9	10	8	0	0

RECAPITULATION

	N.	O.	P.	SA.	D.F.
Miss Hart	11	23	25	1	0
Miss Ward	14	27	16	0	0

	E.	E.P.	T.P.	G.	Sets.
Miss Hart	34	26	67	12	2
Miss Ward	41	16	50	6	0

Tony Trabert stretches to return a low ball to Kenneth Rosewall in the first set of their match in final at the West Side Tennis Club stadium.

Hoad Downs Rosewall in Wimbledon Final

LEW GAINS CROWN BY 6-2, 4-6, 7-5, 6-4

Hoad Halts Rosewall to Win Third Major Title of Year —Brough-Fry Duo Bows

By FRED TUPPER
Special to The New York Times.

WIMBLEDON, England, July 6—Lew Hoad advanced a step closer to tennis immortality today. As the crowd in the jammed stadium whistled in amazement he cut loose with a five-game burst of flawless hitting in the fourth set to defeat Ken Rosewall, 6—2, 4—6, 7—5, 6—4, for the men's singles title in the All-England lawn tennis championships.

It was a triumph of power over touch and it meant a third major crown on the world circuit so far this year for the 21-year-old Australian. Earlier Hoad won the Australian and French championships. He needs the American crown to reach the top pedestal of tennis. Only one man, Don Budge of the United States in 1938, has achieved a grand slam.

"Now you've done it," said the Duchess of Kent as she arrived from the royal box to present the huge silver challenge trophy. "And it's high time."

Hoad competed here for the first time at the age of 17.

In an upset Louise Brough of Beverly Hills, Calif., and Shirley Fry of St. Petersburg, Fla., were beaten by Althea Gibson of New York and Angela Buxton of Britain, 7—5, 6—4, in the semi-finals of the women's doubles. The victors next will meet Fay Muller and Daphne Seeney of Australia, who dethroned the Wimbledon titleholders, Angela Mortimer and Ann Shilcock of Britain, 6—4, 6—2.

Larsen Pair Beaten

Hoad and Rosewall went on the court later to win from Bob Howe of Australia and Art Larsen of San Leondro, Calif., 4—6, 6—2, 7—5, 6—3, in a men's doubles semi-final. They will face Nick Pietrangeli and Orlando Sirola of Italy for the crown tomorrow.

For the first time in years the United States is sure of only one title, the mixed doubles. Vic Seixas of Philadelphia and Miss Fry defeated Darlene Hard of Montebello, Calif., and Howe, 6—3, 7—5, and Gardnar Mulloy of Denver and Miss Gibson won from Trevor Fancutt of South Africa and Miss Seeney, 6—4, 6—4, in the semi-finals.

The stocky Hoad is a man of moods. When Lew is on his big

Associated Press Radiophoto
AUSTRALIAN WINS AT WIMBLEDON: Lew Hoad receiving yesterday from Duchess of Kent tennis trophy he won in men's title play. He defeated a countryman, Ken Rosewall.

game nobody in amateur tennis can stand against him.

At 2-all in the first set he struck his first streak. With three running forehands that shot into the corners he was through Rosewall for the first service break.

He held his own service and then broke through his fellow Australian again with a fantastic half-volley off a Rosewall smash and a forehand down the line. Serving well, he wrapped up the set.

Rosewall had yet to make his bid. He was slowly solving the secret of Hoad's service, a blur at times on the lightning-fast grass of the center court, and in the fourth game he hit two forehands on the rise that rocketed into the corners.

Crowd Cheers Shot

The exchanges were furious now and in one long rally Ken ran off the court, just got his racquet on the ball and whipped it across to the far court as the crowd rose to its feet cheering. He riveted another forehand into the identical spot and the game was his. He led, 3—1.

Both were at the peak of their games now. Rosewall had the range of his ground strokes and Hoad, trying to break through the only way he knew how, went to the net on Rosewall's second serve in hope of controlling the volley.

Time and again Rosewall would push up lobs that fell inside the baseline or whip the ball through the tiny gaps at the net. Yet Hoad hung on.

Service seemed meaningless. They broke each other four times in row and Ken finally took the set at 6—4.

At 1-all in third, Rosewall double-faulted. Each point was so precious that every mistake was damaging. He made another, slipping on the grass while returning a volley. Hoad broke through his rival for a 3-1 lead. Yet minutes later, Rosewall somehow got the game back.

Stretching, Ken dumped a stop-volley over the net and then pulled out his fine forehand across court. On they went to 5-all. Again Ken fell, this time on a volley. Again he double-faulted. Hoad smashed down the line for the game and held his service at love for the set, 7—5.

With his back to the wall Rosewall made a final bid. A backhand volley into the open court broke Hoad's service in the second game. A backhand down the line followed by a stop-volley meant the fourth game. There he was at 4—1 in the fourth, still in the fight and a final set almost inevitable.

Gambles for Corners

Then Hoad made his run. Three aces and it was 4—2. A drop-volley deftly sprinkled between two forehands and it was 4—3. Every shot clicked as he gambled for the corners.

He held service and Rosewall was helpless under the cannonading. Ken was forced into error after error. Two backhand volleys dropped sadly into the bottom of the net, two more were

lofted over the back line. Hoad led, 5-4, and served beautifully to take the match.

Lew smiled now and waved his racquet at his wife, who was in the stands. From the royal box came nods of recognition from Princess Margaret, Sir Anthony Eden, the Prime Minister of Britain, and Robert Gordon Menzies, Australia's Prime Minister.

The defeat of America's top women's doubles team was a surprise. With other partners Miss Brough and Miss Fry had controlled every big title the world over for years. Together they were regarded as invincible.

But Miss Gibson was having a day of days. Her fine service was booming into the corners and her overhead was infallible. With Miss Buxton setting up the plays for her, Althea dominated the court.

The scratch pair of Larsen and Howe frightened Rosewall and Hoad, the 1953 champions, into producing their best under pressure.

At 1 set-all, Larsen and Howe led, 5-to-2, in third and lost five games running; at 3-1 in the fourth, they dropped five more in row. Australia was having its day.

Tomorrow Miss Fry will meet Miss Buxton, the first Briton to reach the women's singles final in seventeen years.

July 7, 1956

Rosewall Defeats Hoad, Miss Fry Beats Miss Gibson for U.S. Tennis Titles

MEN'S LOSER FAILS IN QUEST OF SLAM

Hoad Bows to Rosewall, 4-6, 6-2, 6-3, 6-3 — Miss Fry Triumphs by 6-3, 6-4

By ALLISON DANZIG

Lewis Hoad's quest for the first grand slam in tennis since Don Budge's history-making success of 1938 fell short yesterday in the final of our Diamond Jubilee national championships.

Kenneth Rosewall, the little master of the racquet who is Hoad's Davis Cup team-mate and doubles partner, administered the jolting checkmate to the rugged, blond youth who holds the championships of Wimbledon, France and his own Australia.

With a gallery of 12,000 looking on in the Forest Hills stadium and marveling at the breath-taking, rapid-fire brilliance of the world's two ranking amateurs, the 21-year-old Rosewall defeated Hoad, 4—6, 6—2, 6—3, 6—3.

It was the first championship final between foreign players since 1933, and that year, too, another Australian, Jack Crawford, was thwarted in his bid for a grand slam by Fred Perry of Great Britain.

Shirley Fry of St. Petersburg, Fla., was crowned as the new women's champion. In a rather one-sided final she defeated Althea Gibson of New York, 6—3, 6—4.

Presentation by Dewey

Former Governor Thomas E. Dewey presented the Diamond Jubilee championship cup to Rosewall, the winner of our crown for the first time and the runner-up to Hoad in the Australian and British championships. Dewey hailed Rosewall as one of the greatest players he or anyone else ever had seen.

If there were any doubts about the little Australian measuring up to the caliber of a truly great player they were dispelled by his play in the championship. His performance in breaking down the powerful attack and then the will to win of the favored Hoad was even more convincing, considering the conditions, than his wizardry in his unforgettable quarter-final round match against Richard Savitt.

Against the powerful, rangy Savitt, Rosewall's ground strokes were the chief instruments of victory in a crescendo of lethal driving exchanges seldom equaled on the Forest Hills turf.

Yesterday's match between possibly the two most accomplished 21-year-old finalists in the tournament's history was a madcap, lightning-fast duel. The shots were taken out of the air with rapidity and radiance despite a strong wind that played tricks with the ball.

The breakneck pace of the rallies, the exploits of both men in scrambling over the turf to bring off electrifying winners, their almost unbelievable control when off balance and the repetition with which they made the chalk fly on the lines with their lobs, made for the most entertaining kind of tennis.

In time the gallery was so surfeited with brilliance that the extraordinary shot became commonplace, particularly by Rosewall.

Pace Wilts Hoad

The strain of the killing pace began to tell on Hoad, and when Rosewall got to his service in the second set and began to take the net away from him. Hoad's fortunes began to dwindle.

The blond Australian became shaky overhead and then his volleying went off, particularly on the backhand. It was fancied that his tremendous service and his powerful volley would be too much for his little opponent, but neither was up to its best standard, or at least it was made to seem so by the superlative quality of Rosewall's return of service and passing shots.

Rosewall's backhand has been rated the best in amateur tennis. It was terrorizing yesterday, so much so that Hoad's backhand, which had shown so much improvement this year, broke down.

It was not Rosewall's backhand alone but the accumulative pressure of his whole game that started Hoad on the road to defeat. The little fellow was a whirling streak on the court, on the ball like a hawk with unerring instinct and lightning reflex action, his racquet flashing in perfect timing from the back of the court and in the furious give-and-take at the net.

How Rosewall managed to maintain such accuracy in the strong wind was a wonder to the thousands in the stands, and in time it was too much for Hoad and gave him a sense of his impending doom. He got off to a good start in the third set, leading at 2—0, but then Rosewall was on him with a fury that broke down his game.

Success After 16 Years

In the women's match Miss Fry was finally rewarded with success after competing for the title sixteen years, just as was Doris Hart two years ago. After winning the championship a second time in 1955, Miss Hart turned professional, as did Tony Trabert, the men's champion. Miss Fry also won the Wimbledon crown this season and stands as the world's leading woman amateur player.

Miss Gibson, the first Negro player to reach the final of the championship, had lost to Miss Fry at Wimbledon and also in our clay court championship but was confident that she could reverse the outcome this time. Unfortunately for her, she was unable to produce her best form more than momentarily, and her lack of control under the pressure of Miss Fry's forcing strokes hastened her defeat.

Miss Fry's volleying skill contributed to her success in the first set. In the second she stayed back almost entirely and her deep, accurate ground strokes broke up her opponent's net attack. Miss Gibson showed how strong she could be with the volley at the beginning of the second set, but then she faltered both in her volleying and overhead, and her service did not come up to expectations either.

In the final of the mixed doubles Mrs. Margaret du Pont of Wilmington, Del., and Rosewall defeated Darlene Hard of Montebello, Calif., and Hoad, 9—7, 6—1.

Ceremonies commemorating the Diamond Jubilee anniversary of the United States Lawn Tennis Association were carried out on the stadium turf. Jean Borotra of France, Ted Avory and William Mellor of England and Clifford Sproule of Australia were introduced by Renville H. McMann, the president of the U. S. L. T. A. Each delivered a short speech and presented gifts to the U. S. L. T. A. and its president.

Borotra paired with Watson Washburn of New York in an exhibition against R. Norris Williams of Philadelphia and Vincent Richards of New York. Former champions served on the lines, with Budge in the umpire's chair and William J. Clothier, the national champion half a century ago, as the net umpire. Borotra and Washburn won, 6—2.

September 10, 1956

Tennis Point Scores

MEN'S FINAL

FIRST SET
Point Score

										G.Pts.
Rosewall	5	6	2	1	4	4	9	0	4	0—4—36
Hoad	3	8	4	4	2	2	11	0	4	4—6—42

Stroke Analysis

	N.	O.	P.	SA.	DF.
Rosewall	16	9	9	0	0
Hoad	12	14	16	1	0

SECOND SET
Point Score

								G.Pts.
Rosewall	5	4	5	3	5	4	4	7—6—37
Hoad	3	6	3	5	3	2	1	5—2—28

Stroke Analysis

	N.	O.	P.	SA.	DF.
Rosewall	8	11	15	0	1
Hoad	11	11	8	0	0

THIRD SET
Point Score

								G.Pts.
Rosewall	2	2	4	9	6	4	1	4	5—6—37
Hoad	4	4	0	7	4	2	4	0	3—3—28

Stroke Analysis

	N.	O.	P.	SA.	DF.
Rosewall	9	8	8	2	1
Hoad	10	17	10	0	0

FOURTH SET
Point Score

								G.Pts.
Rosewall	1	4	4	4	3	4	4	4—6—32
Hoad	4	0	6	1	5	2	2	0	2—3—22

Stroke Analysis

	N.	O.	P.	SA.	DF.
Rosewall	5	7	14	1	0
Hoad	11	6	8	2	0

RECAPITULATION

	N.	O.	P.	SA.	DF.
Rosewall	38	35	46	3	2
Hoad	44	48	42	3	0

	E.	EP.	TP.	G.	Sets.
Rosewall	75	49	141	22	3
Hoad	92	45	120	14	1

Umpire—Herbert Lewis. Time of match—1:45.

WOMEN'S FINAL

FIRST SET
Point Score

									G.Pts.
Miss Fry	4	4	4	4	5	4	2	1	4—6—32
Miss Gibson	1	2	1	2	7	1	4	4	1—3—23

Stroke Analysis

	N.	O.	P.	SA.	DF
Miss Fry	6	9	55	0	0
Miss Gibson	16	10	5	2	1

SECOND SET
Point Score

									G.Pts.
Miss Fry	3	4	4	1	4	4	4	3	4—6—35
Miss Gibson	5	2	6	1	4	1	2	2	5	1—4—29

Stroke Analysis

	N.	O.	P.	SA.	DF.
Miss Fry	7	11	12	0	0
Miss Gibson	13	9	11	0	1

RECAPITULATION

	N.	O.	P.	SA.	DF.
Miss Fry	13	20	17	0	1
Miss Gibson	29	19	16	2	2

	E.	EP.	TP.	G.	Sets.
Miss Fry	34	17	67	12	2
Miss Gibson	50	18	52	7	0

Umpire—Winslow Blanchard. Time of match—54 minutes.

Davis Cup Play Is Organized on Challenge Basis

Only Four Countries Have Taken Bowl Put Up in 1900

By ALLISON DANZIG
Special to The New York Times.

ADELAIDE, Australia, Dec. 21—Next to the Olympic Games, Davis Cup tennis matches are the most international of all sports competitions.

The tennis event started as a dual match between the United States and England in 1900, when Dwight F. Davis of St. Louis, a Harvard student, offered the trophy for competition. The cup now is played for annually by countries of every continent. As many as thirty-three nations have challenged for it in a single year.

Only four nations have won

the cup, a massive silver bowl with tray and a huge base on which are inscribed the names of its winners. The United States, Great Britain and Australia were the only winners up to 1927. They are the three grass-court playing nations.

In 1927 France's four musketeers of the court—René Lacoste, Henri Cochet, Jean Borotra and Jacques Brugnon—ended the sway of the United States on the Germantown Cricket Club courts.

Seven-Year Reign Ended

That was one of the great moments in French sports history. The celebrated Tilden and Johnston, the Big and Little Bills who had kept America supreme for seven years, were toppled. Those seven years set a record for consecutive cup victories.

In 1928 France staged the challenge round on composition courts. That was the first time it was ever played on any surface other than grass. The regulations specify that the matches may be played only on turf or on a natural or artificial fine gritty surface.

The challenge round is the climactic match of play for the cup. It brings together the nation that holds the cup and the team that survives months of qualifying play. The cup-holding nation takes part only in this one match. Its opponent may have faced as many as half a dozen other nations or more to earn the right to play in the challenge round.

The qualifying matches are held in zones. There are European, American and Eastern zones. Most of the nations compete in the European zone. This year there were sixteen in the European, five in the American and three in the Eastern.

The winners of the three zones meet in interzone matches. Italy, the winner in Europe, and the United States, the winner in America, met in the first interzone final in late September at Forest Hills. The United States was the winner by four matches to one.

Then the United States and India, the winner in the Eastern zone, met in the second interzone final in Perth, Australia, on the Indian Ocean. Again the United States won by a score of four matches to one. It thereby qualified to face Australia in the challenge round Dec. 26 to 28.

Match Lasts Three Days

A cup match between nations is known as a tie. It lasts for three days and consists of four singles and a doubles contest. Teams of not more than four players are nominated by each nation ten days in advance of a tie.

The day before play begins each captain names two men to play the singles and a draw is made. The names are put into the cup and drawn out blind to determine the pairings. On the third day the players switch opponents. The doubles match is played the second day. The doubles players may be the same as in singles or a different pair.

The team winning three of five matches advances to the next round of competition and the defeated opponent is eliminated.

The participating nations file their entries each year with the country holding the cup. That country has the responsibility of setting up the organization for conducting play. It holds the draw after the closing of entries, and the nations are drawn in the three zones. They may enter in any zone they choose.

The cup holder delegates authority to other nations to conduct play in foreign zones. The United States was in charge of play in the American zone. England usually conducts the matches in the European zone.

When Australia holds the cup, the challenge round is held in December during its summer season. When the United States, Great Britain or France holds it, the challenge round is staged at the height of their seasons, in late August in the United States.

The American season reaches its climax in the national championships at Forest Hills in early September.

Our team assembled on the West Coast in late October after defeating Italy in the interzone match at Forest Hills the previous month. It arrived in Australia the first week of November and played in several big tournaments preparatory to flying 2,500 miles across Australia to Perth to play India. It returned east to Adelaide for eight days of preparations preliminary to meeting Australia in the challenge round.

State Tournaments Held

The Australian team meanwhile had been competing in big state tournaments comparable to our Eastern grass court events. Its players arrived here at the same time as ours for intensive practice to prepare them for the defense of the cup.

Such is the interest in tennis in this country that every one of the nearly 18,000 seats in the stadium here has been sold out for more than two months. The best seats cost approximately $6

each, and the two teams will share in approximately $125,000 profit from the matches. The money goes into the exchequers of national tennis associations for the development of the game.

December 22, 1956

Australia Keeps Davis Cup as Seixas and Giammalva of U.S. Bow in Doubles

HOAD, ROSEWALL WIN IN FOUR SETS

Australian Tennis Duo Gains 1-6, 6-1, 7-5, 6-4 Victory Over American Pair

ADELAIDE, Australia, Thursday, Dec. 27 (P)—Kenneth Rosewall and Lewis Hoad, staggered and bewildered at the start, came back to win the Davis Cup for Australia today with a 1—6, 6—1, 7—5, 6—4 victory over Victor Seixas and Sam Giammalva, the United States' doubles team.

Not even the most optimistic American had dared to expect so close a match. Time and again, Seixas, the 33-year-old Philadelphian, who was playing tournament tennis when his opponents were still in knee pants, and Giammalva, a 21-year-old University of Texas student from Houston, appeared ready to spring the upset of the decade.

They didn't quite have enough steam to carry them through. But they worried Rosewall and Hoad—rated the best doubles combination in the world—right to the end. What they did with Rosewall's service in the first two sets amazed the capacity crowd of 18,000 at War Memorial Drive Stadium.

Rosewall dropped two of his first three services. No one could remember such a thing happening before.

The Aussies now lead the series, 3—0, so tomorrow's final two singles matches will be nothing more than exhibitions.

Seixas is down to play Hoad and Herbert Flam is scheduled to go against Rosewall, but with the competition decided, both captains, Billy Talbert of the United States and Harry Hopman of Australia, could alter their line-ups.

Flam was beaten by Hoad yesterday in the opening singles match, 6—2, 6—3, 6—3. Seixas lost to Rosewall in the second match, 6—1, 6—4, 4—6, 6—1.

Second Straight Conquest

Australia's victory was its second straight in the challenge round. The United States won it in 1954, breaking a four-year Australian stranglehold, but Hopman's lads went to Forest Hills last year and brought it back.

Giammalva played splendidly in his first appearance in the Davis Cup. The Americans won the first set on a combination of Sam's booming drives and Seixas' uncanny placements.

Seixas won the first game on his service at love and that set the tenor of the entire set. The American team broke Rosewall in the fourth game and smashed through Hoad in the sixth.

The second set started as though the biggest tennis upset of the year were in the making. Here was a patchwork American team—one that hadn't been decided upon until a couple of hours before the start of the match—running the greatest doubles team in the world all over the court. Giammalva had been selected as Seixas' partner in preference to the more experienced Flam.

Seixas and Giammalva blasted through Rosewall's service in the first game of the second set

and the crowd began to grow uneasy.

But the upset was not to be. The tide changed right there. The Aussies won the second game, breaking Giammalva, and then raced through the next five games in short order.

Trouble With Service

Giammalva, an excitable youngster, was having trouble with his first service and committed numerous foot faults. At one point Talbert went to the court and tried to get a better look at what was troubling Giammalva. Apparently his left foot was too close to the line.

Giammalva kept up a steady stream of chatter to the experienced Seixas and remonstrated with himself on almost every point, to the enjoyment of the crowd.

The third set, too, presented doubts until the Aussies broke through in the eleventh game. Until that point, the Yanks had been playing them on even terms. Seixas and Giammalva went ahead, 3—1, by breaking in the fourth game.

They couldn't keep the advantage, though, and the Aussies came back in the fifth game. That's how it went until they broke in the eleventh.

The final set went to 4-all, and the Americans by this time had changed their strategy. Giammalva, instead of blasting away, was trying merely to get his first service in. He was successful in that he didn't lose a point in two games.

But Seixas, who had been all over the court, dropped his service twice and that was the break the Aussies needed. Seixas didn't get his delivery in quite as fast as in the first three sets and had a double fault called on him.

December 27, 1956

Anyone for Tennis? Yes, Gonzales

From boy wonder of the courts to king, Pancho has found it fun all the way.

By ALLISON DANZIG

THE world champion in sport, so the book says, reaches the top only after years of striving to improve himself through sacrifice and abnegation. To remain there entails a continuation of the hard work and the abjuring of the things of the flesh.

Not so with Richard (Pancho) Gonzales

The supreme ruler of the tennis courts came up the easy way in an almost unbelievably sudden ascension. And staying on top has meant no more for him than doing what comes naturally. It has been fun all the way, and no sacrifice at all. That's his story, and what this handsome, 6-foot three-inch athlete from Los Angeles tells you, in his positive, uninhibited way, you believe.

Twenty-nine years old this month, Pancho Gonzales is sitting on top of the world, with money in the bank, a pretty, tiny wife, Henrietta, who bubbles with fun (except when anyone calls her Richard "Pancho"), three healthy sons, and no one on the immediate horizon to challenge his suzerainty of the courts. He expects to receive around $60,000 from promoter Jack Kramer when the American phase of his tour with Kenneth Rosewall of Australia—which began in Melbourne last January—ends May 27 in California. And he could add another $25,000 during the year from tournaments in this country and abroad, although he may have contract trouble with Kramer if his demand for a greater share of the take than the 25 per cent he has been getting is not granted.

"THE only worry I have," says Gonzales, "is the income tax." Possibly the fact that Uncle Sam will take so large a percentage of anything additional he makes in 1957 may help to explain his decision not to go on a South American tour with the Kramer ensemble in June. He says the reason is that he wants to rest and be with his family.

On the subject of what being the world's top player has meant in the way of hard work and denying himself the pleasures of life, Pancho says:

"I never felt I had to sacrifice or work, because I enjoy tennis so much. To me this is fun—as a professional the same as it was when I was an amateur. The hardest part of it is when you lay off and have to work to

---

ALLISON DANZIG of The Times sports staff was reporting the world of tennis before Mr. Gonzales was born. He is the author of several books on tennis and a history of football.

keep in condition. While on tour I don't regard it as work. I can't go to the movies or watch television as often as I would like because of the eye strain. There are eight hours during the day when you have nothing to do, lying around for the match in the evening. It can get boring. But once I'm on the court I'm doing the thing I want to do, and I am very happy with my life."

IT may have been fun for Gonzales as an amateur, but until he got to the top he had lean pickings and very little change in his pocket to satisfy his big appetite. In 1947, his first year on the Eastern grass court "circuit," the leggy, swarthy kid from the Coast was grubbing it in a small, isolated rooming house, some miles away from the club where he was competing in the national doubles championship matches. When a tennis reporter asked him to dinner, the home-cooked meal was a royal treat. And his host's children took a greater liking to him than they have to almost any other tennis player.

It was only a year later that Gonzales won the championship of the United States at Forest Hills. He had had no professional coaching—in fact, he was entirely self-taught. It was not only his second season of play on grass courts but his second in men's competition on any surface, incredible as it seems. In all the history of tennis no one has even approached this amazingly quick rise to the pinnacle. William Tilden, recognized generally as the greatest player of all time, had slaved for years on the practice court and in tournaments before he won the national championship for the first time at the age of 27.

PANCHO began to play in boys' tournaments in 1942 at the age of 14, two years after his mother had given him a 50-cent racquet for Christmas (he had quickly come to the decision that tennis, rather than baseball, was his game because of its speed). In 1943 he was ranked as the No. 1 boy in Southern California.

Then his tournament career came to an abrupt halt.

He was disqualified for not going to school ("I was playing hooky," he admits with a grin). Not until 1947, after a hitch in the Navy, did he play against ranking players. He won the Southern California championship in May of that year to gain the first ranking ever accorded him—No. 17 nationally. Sixteen months later, in September, 1948, he won the national crown at Forest Hills as an outsider who was seeded last.

ONCE he became national champion, Gonzales' fortunes began to improve. He was a drawing card with his "big" game, his speed and grace of movement, superb physique and swarthy handsomeness. He no longer had to room out in the sticks. He ate regularly and to his fill.

But he wasn't getting rich, as tennis champions are commonly supposed to. He won the championship again in 1949, played on the Davis Cup team, helping the United States retain the trophy, and then in October, 1949, began his professional career, going on tour with Kramer.

"As an amateur," says Gonzales, "I saved enough from the expense money I received to be able to practice and play occasionally in the off season." You can't hold a steady job and hope to be a top amateur player. You have to keep in competition most of the year to keep your game up with the others' and maintain the physical condition tennis requires. I just managed to get by when I was out of competition, but I had to scrape. When I got married, I really had to pinch pennies. Lucky that Henrietta is so small and doesn't eat much."

Now, as a professional, Pancho lives it up the year round with no financial worries. He travels in style, with his brother Ralph at the wheel, in one of his hot-rod cars that he loves to tinker with—a Ford with a 350-horsepower Cadillac engine. A drag racing enthusiast who has driven 114.8 miles per hour (his service, recorded electronically, travels 112.88 miles per hour), Pancho is taking no chances while in the prime of his tennis career and earning power. He will have no part of road racing but drives only in carefully supervised tests on airstrips.

Comparing professional and amateur tennis, Gonzales says that there is a certain amount of strain to playing now that was missing when he was competing just for the fun.

"There is more involved now," he explains. "As an amateur you don't work at it as a business, but purely for the enjoyment. As a pro, every time I lose or come close to losing it is a strain. It takes away from your livelihood. You never let up on your opponent. Every victory helps to ensure your ending up on top in the tour and staying in the big money the next year. Also, the amateur plays under ideal conditions and in the daytime. The pro plays mostly at night, indoors. He jumps from town to town.

"But, in one respect, there is more strain in amateur tennis. When you play on the Davis Cup team, the pressure is greater than I have known as a pro. You are representing your country and you can't let your team down. Also, you are younger and not as able to overcome the nervousness.

"The top amateur meets a lot of rich people and gets invitations to their homes. But if he isn't careful all the partying can hurt his training. The pro doesn't find himself in the limelight as much. The only thing comparable in professional tennis is when you play in Australia, where they go mad about any kind of tennis.

"The competition is tougher in pro

tennis. It stands to reason that it should be. You are playing against the best men in the world."

ASKED to compare his game now with what it was when he was amateur champion and to rate himself with the other professionals, Pancho does so with his characteristic realism. He has no false modesty. He believes he is the world's best player and says so. He said so publicly a short while ago when he announced that he was dissatisfied with his contract and threatened to break with Kramer.

"I'm the best player in the world," he declared. "I am in a position to call the shots."

At the same time, Gonzales readily admits to weaknesses in his game, says that his forehand and backhand are not so good as were Kramer's and Donald Budge's ground strokes, and agrees that he would not be on top were it not for his service and quickness of movement and the advantage these give him on indoor courts.

"I AM more consistent now than I was before I turned pro," he says. "As an amateur I was good one day and bad the next. Now I keep my game on a high level fairly regularly, though I have my losses. My service has always been strong. It came to me naturally and has been my biggest asset. My service is no better now than it was in my amateur days, but I volley and hit my ground strokes better. My return of service has always been the weak part of my game. I have a tendency to step backward instead of forward.

"I think I am entitled to the top position in pro tennis and that my record against Tony Trabert and Ken Rosewall and against other players in tournaments proves it. [Pancho defeated Trabert, 74 matches to 27, on tour last season and has won forty of his first sixty matches with Rosewall on their current tour.] It is my service and the fact that the matches are played mostly indoors that give me my advantage. My serve is strongest indoors and I have the reach for the net attack which is so important in the indoor game.

"My toughest opponents have been Frank Sedgman and Kramer. Sedgman is capable of lifting his game to great heights. Kramer was too good for me when I first turned professional [he defeated Gonzales, 96 matches to 27,

in their 1949-50 tour], but I think that my game has improved since then. Segura is a tough little opponent, too."

Francisco (Pancho) Segura, a little South American from Guayaquil, Ecuador, who has the best two-handed forehand the game probably has known, won the Australian professional championship recently. He rates Gonzales the world's No. 1 player, but only because of his service.

Little Pancho goes so far as to declare that big Pancho would not be an outstanding player were it not for his serve. He says that on any surface Rosewall is a better player than Gonzales, except in the service department. "Rosewall," says Segura, "is sounder off the ground. He returns service

more consistently and his passing shots are better. Gonzales has more great shots but he is not as reliable. He uses a little too much wrist. He flicks the ball and has no long follow-through."

But no one, Segura concedes, is more consistent than Gonzales in getting his first service into play. When he does, he adds, "You can't attack him. You can't make him work indoors. Outdoors, you can return his service with more length and make him work more to win the points.

"Pancho is a natural athlete. If he worked more on his strokes and trained more, he could be even tougher than he is. He misses a lot of returns of service and he could improve his lobbing and passing shots."

As Segura points out, Gonzales does not work or train as seriously as do others. On tour, Rosewall is in bed half an hour after his match. Pancho will go out for a steak, and it may be

2 or 3 in the morning before he is in bed. "Pancho is a very individual person," says Segura. "He likes to be alone and doesn't pal around much. But he's a good guy."

Gonzales admits to taking training less seriously than Rosewall. "That little guy is in bed at 11," he objects. "His determination and incentive keep you on your toes to beat him."

Big Pancho likes to stay up late and to sleep late. He likes to bowl and play snooker, to go hunting in the mountains. On Sundays when he is at home in Los Angeles, he and Henrietta spend the entire day at the drag races. "Tennis has been good to me," he says. "You wonder why some players get so much and others who work so hard get so little."

Gonzales is one of the few top professionals who have declared themselves ready to take part in an open

tournament should one be held. He thinks that an open championship would give a tremendous boost to tennis, just as it has to golf, awakening wider interest in the game and helping to build up the standard of play.

"I would like to be a part of an open tournament," says Pancho, "and would help even though it would hurt me financially. It would hurt me, the top

amateur who turns professional and the promoter who books our tour But the top pros should play even if they take a loss."

GONZALES finds the standard of amateur play in the United States very poor and sees no chance of Australia's losing the Davis Cup this year. He considers Ashley Cooper, the new Australian champion, probably the best amateur in the world.

"We keep using the older players," he objects. "We don't give the younger players enough of a chance. Sam Giammalva was given a chance last year and made the best showing in

Australia. We should work with the kids coming up and see that they get in shape. Those who show the desire and work hard should be sent to Wimbledon and put on the Davis Cup team."

It can be pointed out that the state of American amateur tennis is not quite so bad as it seems, considering the many losses of top players to the professional ranks. It can be pointed out further that had not a certain Pancho Gonzales turned pro after licking the Australians in 1949, the United States probably would still have the Davis Cup.

"You got a point," Pancho admits with a grin.

May 19, 1957

MISS GIBSON WIMBLEDON VICTOR

MISS HARD ROUTED

Althea Gibson Becomes First Negro to Take Wimbledon Tennis

By FRED TUPPER
Special to The New York Times.

WIMBLEDON, England, July —Althea Gibson fulfilled her destiny at Wimbledon today and became the first member of her race to rule the world of tennis. Reaching a high note at the start, the New York Negro routed Darlene Hard, the Montebello (Calif.) waitress, 6—3, 6—2, for the all-England crown.

Later Miss Gibson paired with Miss Hard to swamp Mary Hawton and Thelma Long of Australia, 6—2, 6—1, in the doubles for her second championship.

But the match of the day and the sensation of the year saw Gardnar Mulloy gain the honor of being the oldest man in Wimbledon history to win a title. The 42-year-old Denver executive teamed with 33-year-old Budge Patty, the Californian who lives in Paris, to upset the top-seeded Neale Fraser and Lew Hoad, 8—10, 6—4, 6—4, 6—4, and break an Australian domination in the men's doubles that went back seven years.

The shirt-sleeved crowd jammed in this ivy-covered inferno hailed Mulloy with a roaring ovation that must have echoed wherever he has played. The applause was deafening as Queen Elizabeth went down on the court to present a silver trophy to the American.

With the pressure off Miss Hard played magnificently with Mervyn Rose to win from Miss Gibson and Fraser, 6—4, 7—5, in the mixed doubles.

U. S. Takes Three Titles

In all, the United States took three titles and divided another of the five contested here. It was the best American showing since 1953. Australia's Hoad won the singles yesterday.

The ladies took the stage amid a sea of waving programs as the temperature touched 96 in the shade. Miss Gibson was in rare form. She had beaten Darlene three times running in the past year and was off in high. Her big service was kicking to Miss Hard's backhand with such speed that Darlene could only lob it back.

Behind her serves and her severe ground shots, Althea moved tigerishly to the net to cut away her volleys. Quickly she had four games running against one of the finest net players in the game. Darlene, white-faced in the heat, kept shaking her head at her failure to find an offensive shot. The set was gone in 25 minutes at 6—3.

Althea was unhurried. Her control was good and she calmly passed Miss Hard every time she tried to storm up to the barrier. The game grew faster as Miss Gibson's service jumped so alarmingly off the fast grass that Darlene nodded miserably as her errors mounted. It was all over in 50 minutes.

Queen Presents Trophy

"At last! At last!" Althea said, grinning widely as the Queen congratulated her and presented the trophy. Althea flies home with her prize Monday evening.

It was Mulloy who was the master strategist in the staggering American victory over Fraser and Hoad. The artful ancient abandoned all pretext of playing the smash-grab Australian game. Cunningly he pitched the ball just over the net, mixing soft floaters with angled chop shots and invariably he was the man who put the ball away at the end of every exchange.

The games went with service in that long first set, but while the Australians were winning theirs easily, the Americans were struggling to hold service. Mulloy saved a set point at 5—4 as he and Patty tangled racquets, but Budge was finally broken at love as he popped three volleys into the net.

Then Mulloy took command. He hit four shots, all of them outright winners, to break Fraser in the first game of the second set. And then he had the crowd in stitches as he chased a Hoad overhead right into the stands and moved a spectator over so he could sit down.

Returning on court, he won the point for the break-through in the first game of the third set. The Americans took both sets at 6—4 as Patty backed Mulloy with his delicate volleying.

Hoad was making errors now, unable to dispatch the tantalizing soft stuff around his ankles. The Americans broke through him again to lead at 4—3 in the fourth. A Patty ace saved the next game and then Mulloy majestically served his game out at love for the match.

Tenth Wimbledon Event

This was Gardnar's tenth appearance at Wimbledon. Patty has played here since the war. He won the singles in 1950. The delighted audience gave a concerted cheer, something reserved for old friends, at the Americans' victory.

After watching Mulloy's performance. Miss Gibson must have regretted discarding him as a partner. Together they reached the final last year in the mixed doubles. Obviously tired after her ordeals in the steaming crater. Miss Gibson was broken four times on service in the mixed doubles as Miss Hard suddenly found her touch overhead. Ecstatically, Darlene bounced about the court and fired Rose to such perfection that they were off court in under an hour.

Miss Gibson and Miss Hard had only to go to the net to command the play against Mrs. Hawton and Mrs. Long.

And to round out a fine American day, the junior champion, Mimi Arnold of Redwood City, Calif., avenged her defeat at the hands of Rosa Reyes of Mexico in the ladies' event by winning, 8—6, 6—2, for the Wimbledon girl's crown.

July 7, 1957

Anderson and Miss Gibson Capture National Tennis Titles at Forest Hills

COOPER IS BEATEN FOR MEN'S CROWN

Bows to Anderson, 10-8, 7-5, 6-4—Miss Gibson Defeats Louise Brough, 6-3, 6-2

By ALLISON DANZIG

A lean, swift-moving athlete, striking rapier thrusts with his racquet, yesterday became the first unseeded player within memory to win the national lawn tennis championship.

That was one of two counts on which history was made before 11,000 in the Forest Hills Stadium as unheralded Malcolm Anderson, from a cattle station in far off Queensland, dispatched top-seeded Ashley Cooper in the second successive all-Australian final. The scores were 10-8, 7-5, 6-4.

Althea Gibson wrote the second red-letter entry for the archives. The first Negro player to win the crown of tennis crowns at Wimbledon, in July, and the first to represent the United States in the Wightman Cup matches, in August, she became the first also to carry off our national women's grass court title.

The girl who was playing paddle tennis on the streets of Harlem some fifteen years ago found herself, at the age of 30, at the pinnacle of tennisdom as she completed a year of almost uninterrupted conquest with a 6-3, 6-2 victory over Louise Brough.

Seven-Year Quest

It was against the same Louise Brough that Miss Gibson played the match that brought her into national prominence in 1950, when she came within inches of defeating the then Wimbledon champion. Althea had made history on that occasion, too, as the first player of her race to compete in the national championship.

The Vice President of the United States, Richard M. Nixon, introduced by President Renville H. McMann of the United States Lawn Tennis Association, presented the championship trophy, filled with white gladioli and red roses, to Miss Gibson. He made the presentations also to Anderson and to the runner-up in each event.

Miss Gibson, responding to the Vice President's congratulations, bespoke her gratefulness to every one in the stands and to all in tennis for the opportunity to play at Forest Hills. She offered thanks to God for her ability. She ended with an expression of hope that she might be able to wear her crown with dignity and humility.

Her remarks were followed by the longest demonstration of hand-clapping heard in the stadium in years.

Miss Gibson won the championship without the loss of a set. The most games any opponent was able to win from her in a set was four. Karol Fageros gave her her stoutest opposition in the opening round in a match that ended at 6—4, 6—4.

A Surprise Package

Sentimentally, the final day of the seventy-seventh annual tournament belonged to Miss Gibson. But no one fortunate

117

enough to be in the stadium will soon forget the transcendent performance given by Anderson, a thin, dark-haired youth of 22 who was scarcely mentioned among the possible winners when the championships began.

Anderson's performance ranks with the finest displays of offensive tennis of recent years. His speed of stroke and foot, the inevitability of his volley, his hair-trigger reaction and facileness on the half-volley, the rapidity of his service and passing shots and the adroitness of his return of service, compelling Cooper to volley up, all bore the stamp of a master of the racquet.

It was offensive tennis all the way, sustained without a let-up. The margin of safety on most shots was almost nil. The most difficult shots were taken in stride with the acme of timing, going in or swiftly moving to the side.

Cooper, playing at his best, or the best he could under the strain of defending against so lethal and unrelenting an onslaught, shook his head over and over or stared at his opponent, unable to comprehend prodigies he was performing. Could this be, he seemed to be asking himself, the Anderson whom he had beaten in five of six previous meetings?

It was not the same Anderson, for those six meetings had been in Australia. The Anderson Cooper was facing now had "arrived" only in the past month.

Road to the Peak

Laid low by nervous exhaustion at home in February, stricken by heat prostration and also a broken toe at Wimbledon, and underweight and lacking in confidence in successive defeats in his early weeks in this country since then, Anderson did not find himself until he arrived at Newport. There he defeated Hamilton Richardson, our ranking player, breaking his serve at the start with four blistering returns of service that Richardson could scarcely touch.

Winning the Newport tournament gave Anderson the confidence he had been lacking. He came to Forest Hills primed for execution, and the fact that he was left out of the seeding of eight players, headed by Cooper, made him all the keener for victory.

Richard Savitt, who had beaten him at Orange and was thought to be our strongest hope, was crushed by Anderson, 6—4, 6—3, 6—1. That was a real shock, even though Savitt was ailing with a virus cold.

Next Anderson faced Luis Ayala, the fiery little Chilean who had beaten Richardson at Wimbledon and had come so close to defeating Savitt at Rye. The Australian youth knocked Ayala's searing service back so fast and whipped passing shots by him so regularly that Luis hardly knew what had hit him in a 6-1, 6-3, 6-1 rout.

Sven Davidson, the big, strong Swedish champion, holder of the French title and a winner from Victor Seixas at Wimbledon, was next in line. There were many who thought Davidson

the most dangerous man in the field. They were almost right.

Davidson led Anderson by two sets to one before the latter won the match, one of the most magnificently fought of the tournament.

And then yesterday it was Cooper, rated at the age of 20 potentially the top amateur of the world. Victory in the final would establish Ashley definitely as the world's best, as holder of the American and Australian crowns and runner-up to Lewis Hoad at Wimbledon.

But it was Malcolm's match from the second game. He let loose with a blaze of savage hitting, projecting three whistling service aces. Then he shook Cooper's confidence with a half-volley, a backhand passing shot and a perfect lob to break service.

Cooper knew from this moment how accomplished and skilled a foe he had. There

never was a moment when he was able to forget it.

Anderson wavered for one of the few times in the match in the eighth game when he double-faulted and failed three times with the volley. After that he hardly gave Cooper anything he did not earn, and only Ashley's strong service enabled him to prolong the match to the length he did.

Women Tense, Cautious

The women's final was on the disappointing side in the quality of the tennis. Miss Brough, a former American and British champion, could not find her control. Miss Gibson, too, was erratic in the opening set. Both double-faulted, perhaps disturbed by numerous foot faults, and both erred off the ground and overhead.

They seemed tense and played cautiously. Both were tentative in their hitting. Miss Gibson let a lead of 30-0 escape her as she

double-faulted twice in the second game. She led at 40-15 in the third and lost this game also. But after trailing at 2-3, Althea began to work into her stride and won the next four games.

In the second set Miss Gibson showed the tennis of which she is capable and her opponent, nervous and losing in confidence, continued to miss, particularly from her forehand. Miss Brough hit out boldly in the first game, to score twice on passing shots and break service. But her errors cost her the second game and from then on her hopes sank. The end came after she had saved two match points in the final game.

Miss Gibson shared in another title. In the final of the mixed doubles she and Kurt Nielsen of Denmark defeated Darlene Hard of Montebello, Calif., and Robert Howe of Australia, 6-3, 9-7.

September 9, 1957

BRITISH TAKE TENNIS TROPHY

MISS GIBSON BOWS

Miss Truman Defeats U. S. Ace as British Win Wightman Cup

By FRED TUPPER

Special to The New York Times.

WIMBLEDON, England, June 14—It had to happen, sooner or later. After a twenty-eight-year famine, Britain won the Wightman Cup tennis honors today, 4 to 3, before a wildly excited crowd that watched the matches on the historic No. 1 court at Wimbledon.

It had to happen, perhaps. But the way it happened was hardly credible to followers of world tennis form.

The amazing 17-year-old Christine Truman came from behind to trounce Althea Gibson, the Wimbledon and American champion, 2—6, 6—3, 6—4, after the team score had been tied at 2—all. Then Ann Haydon, a 19-year-old left-hander who had reached three world table-tennis finals, outlasted little Mimi Arnold of Redwood City, Calif., 6—3, 5—7, 6—3, to clinch the cup.

Earlier, Mrs. Dorothy Head Knode of Forest Hills, Queens, America's No. 2 player here, had beaten Shirley Bloomer, England's No. 1, 6—4, 6—2. Later, when the cup winner had been decided and the pressure was off, Miss Gibson

paired with Janet Hopps of Seattle, Wash., to defeat Ann Shilcock and Pat Ward, 6—4, 3—6, 6—3.

String of 21 Victories Ends

It was the first British victory in the competition since 1930. America had won twenty-one times running, mostly by lopsided scores. The matches were not played during World War II.

The Duchess of Kent went onto the court to present the trophy to the British captain, Mrs. Mary Halford, as the applause rolled down into this ivied amphitheatre.

"Too much Christine," said the American captain, Mrs. Margaret Osborne du Pont, after the matches. "That's the one we expected to win," she added, alluding to Miss Truman's victory over Miss Gibson.

It was Christine who made the difference. The six-foot schoolgirl was the architect of three of the four British triumphs, beating Mrs. Knode in singles and pairing with Miss Bloomer to win from Mrs. Knode and Miami's glamour girl, Karol Fageros, in doubles yesterday.

U. S. Victory Hopes Rise

Those victories were possible, even expected. But it was incomprehensible that she should have a chance against Miss Gibson, conceded to be the world's best. They had met three times before; Althea had won all three—at Beckenham, Kent; in the Wimbledon semifinals last year and in the

Wightman Cup matches at Sewickley, Pa., in 1957.

Christine won the first two games today and then the New Yorker, right on top of her big game, rolled off six in a row for the first set with such consummate ease that the match and cup seemed assured for the United States.

But much had changed in Miss Truman's game over the winter. The blazing forehand, on which she made her reputation, is still there—and steadier. Her sliced backhand is almost impregnable and she has added pace to her service and speed to her all-court game through daily bouts of weight-lifting and sprints. In the second set, she was ready.

She won three games she might well have lost, pasted forehand drives firmly down the line to break Miss Gibson for 5—1, dropped two games because of uncertainty and then exploded forehand drives all over the court to take the set. The crowd by now was almost hysterical. A horde of school children, here to cheer their idol, was squealing and tossing straw hats in the air, and the umpire had to call for order.

Miss Truman was as stoical as ever, attending strictly to the business of opening a hole down the lines for her forehand and chopping her reliable backhand dead to Althea's feet as she pounded up to the barrier. She broke Miss Gibson to lead 3-2 as Althea double-faulted, then foot-faulted.

Miss Arnold Shows Courage

Christine lost the next game and broke through again at 5—4 with two forehands riveted into the corners. A smash gave her two chances for the match; she double-faulted on the first and then hammered a smash cross court that Althea volleyed weakly off her shoe tops into the alley. There was pandemonium in the stands.

It all depended, then, on the Haydon-Arnold match. Ann is a left-hander who chops off both wings and covers the net like an angry octopus. Little

Mimi, trying to emulate her mother's feat (Mrs. Ethel Arnold defeated Kay Stammers in three sets iin the 1935 Wightman Cup match) has little equipment, but a big heart.

This was a ding-dong baseline struggle for nearly two hours, ending only when Miss Haydon charged up the net to cut off the volleys. At 3-all in the last set she abandoned the long rallies at baseline, most of which she had been losing, and ventured forward for all or nothing. So quick are her reflexes that she always had the winner in the clutch, taking three games in a row for the clincher.

Mrs. Knode, beaten twice yesterday, had her armory intact this afternoon. Against Miss Truman she had opened the hole for her cross-court forehand, but never had the weight of stroke to put it away.

She played Miss Bloomer the same way, pulling the British ace far out of court with angled backhand shots and then whipping her forehand away into the grass for winners. After taking the first set, she trailed at 1—2 in the second before running off five consecutive games for the match.

Miss Hopps, a last-minute addition to the United States team, was the big difference in the doubles. Pig-tail flying, she crossed court continually to intercept service returns and held her own delivery all the way as she and Miss Gibson scored a three-set victory over the Misses Shilcock and Ward.

Miss Truman had a word to say in the dressing room after the matches. "I thought I'd do better than when I was last here," she said. When last here she won just two games from Miss Gibson.

June 15, 1958

RULE, BRITANNIA! British team members who won the Wightman Cup tournament at Wimbledon, England. Seated, from left, are Ann Haydon and Shirley Bloomer. Standing are Mrs. Mary Halford, non-playing captain; Christine Truman, Ann Shilcock, Pat Ward.

The Times, London

Cooper Subdues Fraser in 4-Set Struggle to Take Wimbledon Tennis Title

RALLY BY AUSSIE STOPS COMPATRIOT

3-6, 6-3, 6-4, 13-11 Victory Gained by Cooper—Althea Gibson Duos in 2 Finals

By FRED TUPPER
Special to The New York Times.

WIMBLEDON, England, July 4—Ashley Cooper is the new champion at Wimbledon.

The burly, brooding Australian traveled half way around the world for a 3-6, 6-3, 6-4, 13-11 victory today over Neale Fraser, who lives a stone's throw from him across the Yarra River in Melbourne. Princess Margaret and a center-court crowd cheered happily in shirt sleeves and summer frocks.

It was the third successive Australian victory in these All-England lawn tennis championships. And it was the eighth time running that Cooper had beaten Fraser in tourneys over the globe.

This was the one that mattered. The 21-year-old Aussie had been close before. He reached the final here a year ago and was slaughtered by Lew Hoad the day before Hoad turned professional. He made the American final at Forest Hills, Queens, and was trounced by a team-mate, Mal Anderson.

Congratulated by Duchess

Earlier this year he took the Australian title and tonight he had the cup that is emblematic of the world championship.

"I won't talk about turning professional and I will play for Australia in the Davis Cup challenge round," he said after he had been congratulated by the Duchess of Kent on the center court.

Cooper will pair with Fraser against Sven Davidson and Ulf Schmidt of Sweden in the doubles final tomorrow.

America's Althea Gibson is in three finals here, just as she was a year ago. The defending champion goes on the center court tomorrow against Britain's forgotten girl, the unseeded Angela Mortimer, for the women's crown.

She and the 18-year-old Brazilian, Maria Bueno, will meet Mrs. Margaret Osborne duPont of Wilmington, Del., and Margaret Varner of El Paso, Tex., in the women's doubles final. Then she will join the great Dane, Kurt Nielsen, against Bob Howe and Lorraine Coghlan of Australia in the mixed doubles.

Grounded in Fundamentals

Cooper is a schoolmaster's son and he has grounded himself perfectly in the tennis fundamentals. In this rock-'n'-sock era you must have the big serve, the decisive volley, the overhead smash. And it's helpful too—if not absolutely necessary—to own a sound forehand and backhand drive. Cooper has them all and they stood him in good stead today.

For a time Ashley was uncertain. The 24-year-old Fraser is a faster starter and is faster around court. Leading, 2—1, in the first set, he smiled gratefully as Cooper outthought himself and presented a sitter right back for Fraser to smash. He accepted a double-fault and took the service break on a Cooper volley just over the far tapes. That was enough in a service struggle like this. Fraser held his own for the set.

But the pattern was clear even at this early stage. The left-handed Fraser's serve is the better of the two and his volleying is acrobatic and accurate. But he has a weakness on the backhand, and Cooper exploited it from the start.

Every serve, every volley and most of his ground shots were directed against Neale's vulnerable right side. The tactics paid off. In the eighth game of the second set, Cooper thrust three ripping backhands through that right-side hole and forced him so hard with a fourth that volleyed out, and Cooper won the next game for the set.

Break in Seventh Game

On they went. Cooper still applying relentless, remorseless pressure. He got the break he wanted in the seventh game of the third set. Fraser double-faulted, grimaced as a backhand shot roared by him and then dumped a blooping volley into the bottom of the net.

Neale made a last stab in the fourth set. Leading, 2—1. he hit all out with his suspect backhand. Three passing shots and he was at 40—0. Cooper saved twice and then cut off a stop-volley that hung above the barrier and just dropped over.

Fraser had a single set point when the games were 10-all and was promptly aced.

Suddenly the roof fell in. A gorgeous running backhand off-balance from far out of court put Cooper in front and then the breaks came. He had the next point on a netcord, a third on another and then buried a smash into the far corner.

With his own service to come, it seemed all over. Cooper raced to 40—0, but was passed by Fraser and then came a twinge of center-court nerves. He double-faulted, then sprayed an overhead against the stands. It was deuce now. Then he won it.

"I played those two awful shots from memory," he said later, "and what a memory!"

MacKay and Rose Bow

Cooper and Fraser, the top seeds, won from the scratch pair of big Barry MacKay of Dayton. Ohio, and Mervyn Rose of Australia, 3—6, 8—6, 7—5. 7—5. MacKay had dominated the first set with his servicing and Rose was slapping the set-ups with élan.

Then Mervyn's serve went to pieces. He was broken twice in the second set, again in the last game of the third and in the fourth.

Earlier, the Swedish Davis Cup pair of Sven Davidson and Ulf Schmidt had squeaked by the laughing Italians, Nicky Pietrangeli and Orlando Sirola. 8—6. 3—6. 6—3. 7—5, despite a last-ditch stand by Nicky. Trailing, 4—5, in the fourth set, he hit three outright winners on Davidson's service to tie it, then lost his own serve. Schmidt fired his thunderbolts for the match.

Miss Gibson and Senhorita Bueno reached the women's final on sheer power, defeating the Australians, Mrs. Mary Hawton and Mrs. Thelma Long. 6—3. 6—2. The New Yorker also advanced to the mixed doubles final today.

Mrs. duPont and Miss Varner upset the fourth-seeded Mexicans, Yolanda Ramirez and Rosa Reyes, 6—2, 6—3, as Mrs. duPont gave an exhibition in the angled chop and running lob to the astonished throng. Mrs. duPont has taken the Wimbledon doubles title five times and the American doubles thirteen. She and Miss Varner were unseeded here.

July 5, 1958

Cooper and Althea Gibson Win National Tennis Titles

By ALLISON DANZIG

Ashley Cooper and Althea Gibson rule the world of tennis. The supremacy of the 22-year-old youth from Australia and the young woman from Harlem was established beyond question yesterday as each added the American title to the British singles titles they won last July.

Cooper made a stirring recovery from a seemingly crippling injury late in his final-round match with Malcolm Anderson at Forest Hills.

To the consternation of the 11,000 in the stadium, the 22-year-old Australian had fallen to the ground clutching his right ankle in the fifth set of the two-hour contest.

Squirming with pain, Cooper managed to rise. He took a few hops and fell to the ground again. Apparently it was the finish for the game champion of Wimbledon and Australia, who had escaped defeat in the fourth set and again in the fifth. Now, though he was leading at 6—5, the loss of the match and the championship by default seemed inevitable.

He Stages a Comeback

But after being administered to, Cooper resumed the battle. No more than five minutes later, he walked off the court a 6—2, 3—6, 4—6, 10—8, 8—6 winner over Anderson, his Davis Cup teammate and the defender in this tournament.

Cooper's dramatic victory over the favored Anderson followed Althea Gibson's successful defense of her crown in the women's final.

With her uncanny exploitation of the lob, Miss Gibson overcame Darlene Hard, an unseeded player from Montebello, Calif., 3—6, 6—1, 6—2. The 31-year-old champion stood as the first woman player to win at both Wimbledon and Forest Hills in successive years since Maureen Connolly of San Diego, Calif., did so in 1952 and 1953.

Secretary of State John Foster Dulles presented the trophies to Miss Gibson and Cooper and congratulated them on their victories.

Will Not Defend Title

In responding to Mr. Dulles, Miss Gibson, who in 1951 became the first Negro player ever to compete in the championship, announced that she would not defend her title in 1959.

She is retiring from the courts for a year to devote herself to her singing career and the promotion of her forthcoming book on her rise from the slums of Harlem to the pinnacle of tennis and world fame.

The black-haired Cooper, a perfect physical specimen with an intensity of purpose that could not be shaken by any amount of discouragement, had looked to be beaten long before his mishap.

He had averted disaster with the score 40—0 against him on his service at 7—all in the fourth set. In the fifth set Anderson, leading at 5—4 after breaking through at love in the fifth game, prepared to unleash his whiplash service for what was accepted as inevitably the final game of this tremendous match.

Then came four thrilling backhand returns of service by Cooper, all knocked back at the feet of Anderson to break his service at love.

The shots drew storms of applause. It was one of the most stunning feats under maximum pressure that the championship has known. Anderson's virtuosity with the racquet had approached genius from the time he took command late in the second set, but this was a shock from which he never recovered.

Then followed the most dramatic happening of the day, after Cooper, buoyed by his almost miraculous reprieve, had won the eleventh game also, to go ahead at 6—5.

In the twelfth game with Anderson leading, 30-15, the defender hit a cross-court forehand drive. Cooper rushed across the baseline to retrieve the shot and managed to get it back.

As Anderson volleyed the ball for a winner into a defenseless court, Cooper fell to the ground. He was holding his right ankle and appeared to be in great pain. Then he managed to rise, only to drop again.

The umpire, J. Clarence Davies Jr., and linesmen rushed to his aid. After a few minutes, Cooper was assisted to his feet and limped to the umpire's stand.

It appeared out of the question for him to continue play and the sympathetic gallery resigned itself to his wonderful come back ending with a default.

But after Cooper's shoe had been removed and he had been administered to, he got to his feet once more and took a few steps gingerly. To the amazement of the crowd, he picked up his racquet and walked back on the court, ready to resume the match. There was a prolonged burst of applause.

With the resumption of play, four or five minutes after Cooper's mishap, Anderson served and Cooper knocked the ball out. It was Anderson's game, making the score 6-all.

But within five minutes, Cooper had won the match he had appeared to be on the verge of losing three times.

Whether it was Cooper's superior play or Anderson's slump that was accountable is food for speculation. Certainly Cooper played extremely well, amazingly well, considering how crippled he had appeared only a few minutes before the end. Anderson hardly could have been prepared for his opponent's mobility and brilliance of execution.

Cooper at Match Point

Cooper won the eleventh game on service with a volley and overhead smash, and Anderson's two errors. By now Anderson knew it was no cripple he had to reckon with. But aroused as he was, and fight as he did to save a match he had come so close to winning, it was not his destiny to win. He met his fate in the next game.

Anderson won the first point of this final game as Cooper hit a backhand out of court. Then Ashley's return of service, so true for the first set and most of the second, got in its deadly work.

Anderson erred in taking the return of service, to make the score 15-all. He then put a backhand volley out of court and it was 15-30.

Now came a magnificent backhand return of service. The ball plummeted at Anderson's feet and he was a half-step too far forward to deal with it. His backhand half-volley found the net and it was 15-40, match point.

Anderson served. Cooper's return of service was a beauty. It set up the championship shot. Anderson returned it with a defensive volley and Cooper pounced on it to volley it for a winner and the match.

Few players have received a greater hand in the stadium in recent years than Cooper got for his salvaging of this match against an opponent who had beaten him in three successive sets in the Newport final a few weeks ago and at Forest Hills last year.

The defeat was the cruelest of disappointments for Anderson, as bitter a pill as this quiet, mannerly youngster with the flaming strokes and the touch of an artist has had to take in his career.

Miss Gibson, too, gained her victory after taking a f... that caused some concern. In the prolonged second game of the final set against the blonde, bouncing Miss Hard, the champion fell in rushing across court for the ball.

She was wringing her right hand as she got to her feet and it was feared that she had suffered a sprain. She walked to the umpire's chair and there was a brief pause as she wiped her hand.

Miss Gibson then took her place again on the court, to the applause of the gallery. Al-

The New York Times (by Allyn Baum)

HE GOT UP TO WIN: Ashley Cooper is offered aid by Malcolm Anderson, his opponent, and an official after injuring ankle in U. S. tennis championships at Forest Hills.

though she said after the end of play that she had sprained two fingers, she proceeded to take immediate command of a match in which she had been desperately pressed.

In the very first rally following the resumption, she threw up the fourth of her amazingly accurate lobs in this game. Miss Hard, rushing back to retrieve the ball at the baseline and then coming forward again, put a backhand volley into the net. Tired from her exertion in pursuit of the parabolas, she failed on another backhand volley in answer to the return of service, and lost her service.

That was the turning point in the set. Miss Gibson had lost her service in the first game, proceded to pull out the third game from 15—40 as the weakening Miss Hard lost her control, and then the champion broke service again in the fourth.

In this fourth game Miss Hard double-faulted and then Miss Gibson tossed up two more of those deadly lobs. Both fell squarely on the baseline and the sturdy Californian was done for.

Discouraged, though never quitting on the fight, she could win only one more game, the sixth. A lob helped Miss Gibson win the fifth and also the seventh.

Weary, Miss Hard double-faulted to start the final game. Then she failed on three volleys, once after being driven back by a lob, and her splendid challenge to the champion had come to naught.

Until Miss Gibson brought the lob into play, it had appeared that Miss Hard, who won the national doubles championship two weeks ago in her first tournament of the season, had at least an even chance of victory. The Californian's speed around the court, her volleying skill, particularly from the backhand, and her straight backhand return of service had won the opening set for her.

Miss Gibson in this set was making unworthy errors and was unable to return service from the backhand. Miss Hard was making double faults, but her first service was so deep, so well paced, that the champion could not deal with it. Miss Gibson served well herself and her volleying was decisive, but her ground strokes were losing the match.

It was in the second set that Miss Gibson began to resort to the lob. It brought results, though nothing like the sensational success of the third set. In the third game Miss Hard went to 40—0 on three fine volleys and then lost it. Miss Gibson played her best tennis of the match to this point, and two lobs enabled her to reach deuce.

Breaking through at 8—6, she won the fourth at love on Miss Hard's errors. Then Miss Hard went to 40-0 again in the fifth game, making a sensational recovery of a lob, and lost it on her volley errors. It was Miss Gibson's return of service that was provoking the errors now.

When the Californian lost the sixth game also, after leading at 30—0, it was seen that a third set was inevitable. She volleyed well in the seventh game, but her double fault ended the game after she had been trapped by a lob.

The champion was a much improved player in this set, refusing to make errors when the big points were at stake. Her volleying was sharp and decisive and her return of service was more effective as Miss Hard's delivery weakened.

September 8, 1958

U.S. Regains Davis Cup as Olmedo Beats Cooper of Australia at Brisbane

Alex Olmedo Halts Ashley Cooper for Deciding Point

By The Associated Press.

BRISBANE, Australia, Wednesday, Dec. 31—The United States won back the Davis Cup from Australia today.

In the biggest upset in the history of the competition, Alex Olmedo, a nerveless young Peruvian, won the deciding singles match from Ashley Cooper. The scores were 6—3, 4—6, 6—4, 8—6.

Olmedo's triumph gave a 3-1 lead to the United States in the three-out-of-five-match series for the cup, the symbol of world amateur tennis supremacy. It made the subsequent singles match between Barry MacKay of Dayton, Ohio, and Mal Anderson a mere formality.

It was young Olmedo, the 22-year-old National Collegiate champion from Southern California, who sparked the American team to its victory. First he defeated Mal Anderson on Monday. Then he teamed with Ham Richardson yesterday to win the doubles from Anderson and Neale Fraser.

Today he was the complete master of Cooper, generally acclaimed as the finest amateur player in the world. But for the last three days, the greatest amateur player in the world was Olmedo, who almost didn't make the American team.

Last summer there was doubt whether he should be chosen, because he was not a United States national. However, he had resided in the United States for five years and that made him eligible for the team. Until he joined the squad captained by Perry Jones, he never had seen a Davis Cup match.

As a result of his efforts, the Davis Cup is returning to the United States for the first time in four years. This was the fifteenth straight challenge round between the United States and Australia. Australia has won eight of those and the United States seven.

It was almost incomprehensible to the throng of 18,500 packed in the Milton Tennis Stadium that Olmedo was the complete master of Cooper.

It was Cooper who had a bad case of nerves, double-faulting at numerous critical spots. It was Cooper who permitted himself to be fooled. And it was Cooper who got rattled when the chips were down.

The lad from Peru kept pressing. In the first three games of the first set, Cooper won only 4 points while Olmedo was holding his own service twice and breaking the Aussie once.

Cooper is a notoriously slow starter and the crowd confidently waited for him to settle down.

He did break through Olmedo in the fifth game of the first set with several booming drives.

Aussie's Spirit Broken

Back roared Olmedo to shatter Cooper at love. That apparently broke the Aussie's spirit for the set and quite possibly the match.

Cooper was nervous, but he certainly was not one to give up. He fought right down to the final point. After trailing at 4—3 in the final set and being down 0—40 in the eighth game, he broke Olmedo after going to deuce four times.

Olmedo made the key break in the thirteenth game of the final set, when he gave Cooper only 2 points . By that time Cooper was a bundle of nerves and didn't get a single first service into play.

Cooper was at his best in the second set. He seemed to regain some of his lost confidence and moved to the net quickly behind his service.

He broke Olmedo for the first time in the match in the eighth game to go ahead, 5—3, and then ran out the set on service.

Yet even in that set a mere inch kept Olmedo from breaking through Cooper and perhaps sweeping through in straight sets.

Olmedo was ahead, 4—3, 40—30, and shot a return of Cooper's service deep in the back court. Ashley couldn't get to it, but it hit the ground just about an inch outside the chalk.

Olmedo came right back and broke Cooper in the ninth game of the second set, but permitted Ashley to break him again in the tenth for the set.

That was as far as Cooper progressed, though. The rest of the match was strictly Olmedo's. He whipped to a 3-0 lead in the third set and by that time it was just a question of how far Cooper could run it out.

It was a hot, sunny day with the temperature hovering around the 100-degree mark. But it wasn't as humid as the first two days of the series for world tennis supremacy.

Cooper seemed somewhat nervous and didn't have his usual poise at the start. Olmedo took full advantage of the big Aussie's lapses and quickly ran up a 5-2 lead, breaking Cooper's service once.

Cooper Goes Ahead

Cooper held his service in the eighth game, but Olmedo ran out the first set in the ninth game, although it went to deuce and Cooper had advantage once.

Olmedo, confident, was serving with greater power than in the first two days of the challenge round. He was on the offensive and had Cooper befuddled on several shots.

Olmedo held his own service for a 1-0 lead at the start of the second set, giving up 2 points.

Then Cooper served a love game, smashing three aces and it was 1—1.

Cooper took the lead in the third game of the second set, holding service. Now he seemed to be steadying down. His first service was good and he moved in on the net with confidence.

Olmedo then held his own delivery, although he fell reaching for one shot by Cooper, and it was 2-all.

Cooper went in front, 3—2, holding service with another love game. Back came Olmedo

on his service for 3—3.

Cooper was behind in the second game, 15—40, but rallied and won his service to go ahead, 4—3. With the score 30—40, Olmedo returned the ball over the baseline by about one inch. That was all that prevented him from breaking through Cooper.

Cooper broke through Olmedo for the first tiem in the match in the eighth game. He went ahead, 5—3, when Alex sent the final ponit into the net.

But the young Peruvian broke through Cooper's service in the next game. With the pressure on him, Cooper double-faulted. That made it 5—4 for Cooper.

Then Olmedo lost his service after trailing at 0—30, and Cooper took the second set, 6—4. Olmedo missed a volley at set point.

Olmedo broke Cooper in the first game of the third set. The Australian ace double-faulted on two of his points, hitting

three balls into the net and one over the baseline. That made it four service breaks in a row as the pair began applying pressure in the home stretch.

Olmedo went ahead 2—0, holding his own service.

Olmedo broke Cooper again in the third game and went ahead, 3—0.

Cooper again was getting

nervous. He was down, 0—30, then double-faulted and enabled Olmedo to get to game point.

Olmedo, apparently sensing victory, whipped into a 4-0 lead, holding service. He had a clean ace on a second service, following a fault—which is unusual.

Cooper barely held his service in the fifth game, ralling from a 30—40 deficit.

Then Olmedo made it 5—1 by winning a love game.

Cooper held service and it was 5—2, in Olmedo's favor.

Cooper then broke through Olmedo after the game went to deuce three times and cut the

deficit to 3—5.

Cooper held his own service and Olmedo led, 5—4.

Then Olmedo held and won the third set, 6—4.

Olmedo Gains 2-0 Lead

Olmedo broke Cooper's service in the first game of the fourth set, then held his own to run his margin to 2—0. Cooper won the third game and it was 2—1.

Then he broke Olmedo's service and it was 2—2. He held and Olmedo held for 3—3.

Olmedo broke through again for 4—3, only to have Cooper break right back after trailing 0—40. It was 4-4 in games.

Then Cooper held to make it 5—4, but Alex made it 5—5. Cooper led at 6—5 with a love game. Olmedo held and it was 6—all. Olmedo then broke through service again on a cross-shot for 7—6, then held his own service for the match and cup.

December 31, 1958

Olmedo Beats Laver in Straight Sets and Takes Wimbledon Championship

PERUVIAN PUZZLES AUSSIE WITH LOB

All-England Tennis Laurels Go to America as Olmedo Scores at 6-4, 6-3, 6-4

By FRED TUPPER
Special to The New York Times.

WIMBLEDON, England, July 8 Alex (The Chief) Olmedo has won Wimbledon. The top-seeded Peruvian from Los Angeles enchanted a center-court crowd of 15,000, including Princess Margaret, with miracles of his own making in defeating unseeded Rod Laver of Australia today, 6—4, 6—3, 6—4.

His straight-set triumph was the climax of an amazing year for the 23-year-old University of Southern California senior. It established him as the best amateur tennis player in the world today.

Almost single-handedly, Olmedo brought the Davis Cup back to America from Australia last winter and later took the Australian and United States indoor titles.

Today he brought back the all-England lawn tennis championship, last won for America by freckle-faced Tony Trabert in 1955.

Olmedo Resorts to Lob

There's an extra dimension to Olmedo's game. He has the weapons essential for the modern game: the big serve, volley and glorious freedom of swing

on his ground strokes. But there's more. Today he confounded the red-headed Australian by deliberately using the lob to attack.

With his mind invariably on the move ahead, Alex shifted the

Brazil's Maria Bueno won Wimbledon three times and took four U.S. titles.

From her astonishing first round upset of Margaret Court at Wimbledon in 1962, to her many triumphs at that stadium and at Forest Hills, to her fight for more money for women's tennis, Billy Jean King has been the spark in the female side of the sport for over fifteen years.

20-year-old redhead around the court like a chess piece. He was feinting for the coups to come.

Olmedo started fast against the left-handed Australian. He broke service in the first game, just as he had done against Ramanathan Krishnan, Luis Ayala and Roy Emerson in the earlier rounds.

Olmedo was tuned up and Laver was not. The Australian has had a gruelling fortnight. It took him nearly four hours to subdue Barry MacKay of Dayton, Ohio, in a furious five-setter Wednesday and he has been further involved with doubles and mixed doubles. Laver was slow afoot and he was nervous.

Rout Appears in Making

Quickly, the Peruvian was 5—1, outpacing Laver on his ground shots and forcing him to err off the volley. There was a stunned silence in the packed stadium. It appeared to be a rout.

Then the redhead switched his various services. He served flat on the left side down the middle and he swung it to the right side, always to the Olmedo backhand. He came alive with his heavily spun ground shots. Soon Laver was back in the match at 4—5. The Peruvian was unruffled. He held service for the set.

The battle was now joined in earnest. Rod was a step quicker getting up to the net and he led at 3—2 in the second set. It was the trap Olmedo had baited. He saved his service game and then came the lobs, high to the baseline and short to the sidelines. Backward pedaled Laver. Here came the drop shots, pulling the redhead in. Laver lunged up and netted. Olmedo had broken through at love.

It was deft, thinking tennis and it paid dividends. Off balance, Laver was confused and he was caught. Four games went to Olmedo in a row and the second set at 6—3 as he lobbed Laver off a volley with fingertip control.

Two Match Points Saved

Games went with service as Olmedo took a 5-4 lead in the third set. The panther had his man and it was time for the kill. He moved far inside the baseline to take service. A backhand passed Laver cleanly. A double fault gave Alex his second point. A flat forehand that hugged the sideline gave him match point.

Desperately, Laver saved with a volley. A backhand pass and a second match point for Olmedo. Laver saved it with a smash. Alex slashed another backhand into open court. A third match point. It came off. Laver, stumbling, volleyed into the net.

The Duchess of Kent went on the court to award Olmedo with the challenge cup presented by the late King George V as the applause rang down from the terraces.

"I won't tell you my strategy," said Olmedo to the press. "It's a professional secret."

It was there for all to see.

July 4, 1959

MARIA BUENO TENNIS VICTOR

MISS HARD LOSES

Bows to Maria Bueno, 6-4, 6-3, in Final of Wimbledon Tennis

By FRED TUPPER
Special to The New York Times

WIMBLEDON, England, July 4—Gay, graceful Maria Esther Bueno of Brazil is the new queen at Wimbledon. The 19-year-old senhorita from Sao Paulo today realized all her enormous potential and defeated Darlene Hard of Montebello, Calif., 6—4, 6—3, on the center court oven. This snapped a string of American triumphs that dated back to 1938.

For Maria, the talent has been there a long time; the will to win grew this fortnight. Her fluent and almost flawless performance in 85 degree temperatures this afternoon was the second major triumph for South Americans in two days. Alex Olmedo of Peru, representing the United States, won the men's singles yesterday.

America salvaged half of the All-England lawn tennis titles. Miss Hard paired with Jeanne Arth of St. Paul to win the women's doubles from Britain's Christine Truman and Mrs. Beverly Baker Fleitz of Long Beach, Calif., in a scorching slugfest, 2—6, 6—2, 6—3, and then joined Rod Laver of Australia to take the mixed doubles from Neale Fraser of Australia and Senhorita Bueno, 6—4, 6—3.

Laver in Three Finals

The red-headed Laver, a tremendously popular figure here, had figured in three finals. Unseeded, he was beaten by Olmedo and, despite a last ditch stand, he and Bob Mark were edged by their team-mates from Down Under, Fraser and Roy Emerson, 8—6, 6—3, 14—16, 9—7, in a three-hour duel of service.

In a major surprise, Tomas Lejus, a Russian still two months short of his seventeenth birthday, defeated Ronald Barnes of Brazil, 6—2, 6—4, to win the Wimbledon Junior championship on his first trip to England.

Senhorita Bueno was born across the street from a tennis club and had a tiny racquet in her hands at the age of 6. She burst like a comet into the big time a year ago and the wonder was simply when she would win her first crown. She took the Italian title then, but a combination of temperament and a strained shoulder cut her down for the rest of the season. Her game is modeled on a man's. There are both the kicking and swinging serves, impeccable ground strokes and cat-like coverage of court. She has everything except restraint and that she had against Miss Hard today.

Darlene broke through service to win the first game, lost her own on two glorious passing shots that roared by her and then utterly failed to handle Maria's blazing service. She was cleanly aced by the Brazilian three times and barely got her racquet on a dozen more serves.

The break that mattered occured in the long tenth game. So uncertain was Darlene of her own service that she failed to follow it to net and a double fault gave Maria her first set point. Miss Hard saved it, but on the second she outrageously blooped a volley way behind the baseline.

At a game apiece in the second set, Darlene apparently pulled the same leg muscle that gave her trouble against Ann Haydon. She said later that it affected her game, but she was treated by a masseur before her doubles match.

Miss Hard Slows Down

Miss Hard was notoriously slower around the court and the senhorita, slashing her volleys away beautifully behind service, ran to 4—1. Darlene must dominate the net to win, but she was unable to force the pace against a girl who hits with more length and authority than any player since Maureen Connolly.

Senhorita Bueno had her own service to win and, as Darlene again volleyed long on match point, the Brazilian threw her racquet high on court and burst into tears.

"I have never played better," she said in five languages to the journalists who clustered about her. "I am going back to Brazil and I am coming to Forest Hills."

"That service", said Miss Hard ruefully. "It's as good as Louise Brough's or Althea Gibson's."

Darlene was the mainspring in her doubles triumph with Miss Arth. Two years ago she paired with Miss Gibson to win this title and last year she and Miss Arth took the nationals at Longwood.

The American string in the ladies singles here goes back to the days of Helen Wills Moody. She won the title in 1938 for the last time. Helen Jacobs took it the next year and there have been thirteen consecutive American victories in the postwar period.
July 5, 1959

Forest Hills Invites Bunche Application; Head of Club Quits

The governors of the West Side Tennis Club announced yesterday that they had accepted the resignation of the club's president and would give "courteous and prompt attention" to a membership bid in behalf of Dr. Ralph J. Bunche or his son.

The governors' statement also said that "it is the policy of the club to consider and accept members without regard to race, creed or color."

Dr. Bunche, a Negro, said on July 8 that the club's president, Wilfred Burglund, had made it clear to him that neither Negroes nor Jews would be accepted for membership.

Statement Welcomed

Last night, Dr. Bunche, United Nations Under Secretary for Special Political Affairs, who won the Nobel Peace Prize in 1950, welcomed the club's statement as "a very full, very clear one." However, he said there seemed no immediate likelihood that he or his son, Ralph Jr., would apply for membership.

The club statement noted that it "presently has members of Oriental and other ancestry and there is representation of the Jewish faith among the membership," but "to the best of our knowledge, no Negro has ever applied for membership."

It called Mr. Burglund's remarks to Dr. Bunche "personal opinions of one individual to another," and said that "some of these reported opinions are contrary to opinions and beliefs of the board of governors and other club members."

The report of Dr. Bunche's conversation with Mr. Burglund touched off a storm and scores of public figures and organizations denounced the club. Most of them demanded that the Davis Cup matches be switched from the Forest Hills, Queens, club to another site.

The governors' statement said that while the club was a private membership corporation receiving no outside subsidies of any kind, "it has achieved and holds a status of public importance throughout the sports world, and feels a deep obligation in this respect."

"Recent questions concerning possible racial bars to membership in the club are a matter of deep regret and embarrassment to the board of governors," the statement said. "They have come about as the result of misunderstanding."

"In order that there will be no remaining vestige of misunderstanding, and in order to avoid further embarrassment to the United States Lawn Tennis Association and to the club, Mr. Wilfred Burglund has asked the board to accept his resignation as president."

No successor to Mr. Burglund has been named.

Earlier yesterday, before the club's statement, Victor Denny, president of the United States Lawn Tennis Association, said the matches would be held at the club because "no other suitable facility is available."

Last week, Acting Mayor Abe Stark ordered the Department of Licenses to investigate the club, and yesterday License Commissioner Bernard J. O'Connell said no license was required to put on sporting events at the club.

Mr. O'Connell said that the West Side Tennis Club's stadium, where Althea Gibson, the Negro tennis star, won her national women's championship,

was a "sports arena" like Yankee Stadium. No license is required for the Yankees to play at the stadium, he said.

In another aspect of the case, the city's Commission on Intergroup Relations will meet today with private and civic organizations to discuss ways of eliminating "discriminatory action" as such places as the tennis club.

Dr. Bunche, in commenting on the tennis club's statement, said that he had never had any interest in membership for himself, and that the idea that his son might join had come from George Agutter, the club professional who had given young Ralph tennis lessons.

He explained that his son

was now at the Choate School in Wallingford, Conn., and that that removed the question of the boy's membership for the time being.

Dr. Bunche said that if Mr. Burglund had taken the stand that the club governors had taken "there would not have been any West Side Club story."

"The whole episode from the standpoint of notoriety affecting my family was highly distasteful," he said, "but I did feel that a club such as this, heavily tinged with the public interest, was not entitled to immunity from public opinion about its policies."

July 15, 1959

Laver Beats Fraser for Australian Tennis Title in 3-Hour 15-Minute Match

LOSER COLLAPSES IN DRESSING ROOM

Fraser Beaten After Taking First 2 Sets From Laver— Margaret Smith Wins

Camera Press-Pix
WINS TENNIS TITLE: Rod Laver, who upset Neale Fraser in five sets to capture the Australian national tennis title yesterday.

BRISBANE, Australia, Feb. 1 (UPI)—Rod Laver, rallying in a match that had both men on the brink of exhaustion, won the Australian national tennis title today by upsetting Neale Fraser, 5—7, 3—6, 6—3, 8—6, 8—6.

Fraser, who holds the United States crown and led Australia's 1959 Davis Cup triumph over the United States, sank to the

grass as Laver tossed up his racquet to celebrate his first national title. The match lasted 3 hours 15 minutes.

Fraser later collapsed in the dressing room and was unable to move about for nearly an hour because of cramps and fatigue. Laver, who won the United States junior title in 1956, ruined Fraser's hopes of sweeping the Australian, French, Wimbledon and United States crowns this year.

Girl, 17, Is Champion

Before the Laver-Fraser match, Margaret Smith, 17, became the youngest player ever to win the national women's title. She defeated 18-year-old Jan Lehane, 7—5, 6—2.

Laver lost to Alex Olmedo in

straight sets in the 1959 Wimbledon final. He appeared in for another disappointment when Fraser won the first two sets today.

Then Laver began his rally. He took the third set after cracking Fraser's serve in the eighth game. Fraser got to match point in the tenth game of the fourth set but Laver won the game when a lob by Fraser was long by inches. Laver evened the match by winning the fourteenth game with three aces.

Fraser slumped to his knees in the seventh game of the final set. He appeared pale when he walked to the umpire's stand for a drink. He held service in the ninth game after seven deuces had been called and Laver got to match point five

times.

Laver broke through in the thirteenth game for a 7-6 lead and took a 40-0 lead on his own service in the fourteenth before Fraser began a final, futile rally. Fraser fought off six match points. On the seventh match point, he finally won when Fraser dunked a backhand return into the net.

Miss Smith's triumph over Miss Lehane capped a title drive in which she upset Maria Bueno, the Wimbledon and United States champion from Brazil, and Mary Reitano, the 1959 Australian champion.

Miss Lehane and Trevor Fancutt of South Africa won the mixed doubles title by defeating Miss Reitano and Bob Mark, 6—2, 7—5.

February 2, 1960

Grass Courts Being Weeded Out

Trend in Tennis Is Toward Clay and Hard Surfaces

By CHARLES FRIEDMAN

When three United States Davis Cup players failed to show up for the Eastern grass court championships at South Orange, N. J., the tournament chairman naturally was miffed.

But there was an explanation. The three—Barry MacKay, Earl Buchholz and Chuck McKinley —had been playing on clay courts for weeks in preparation for the conquests of Canada and Mexico. They didn't think it would be "smart" to switch to grass competition.

This points up an old argument. Some fans and officials have been saying it may be time to take the "lawn" out of tennis. By this, they mean that major

events, including all Davis Cup matches, should be staged on more universal surfaces, such as clay, hard-top or cement.

Only four cup countries play on grass courts when they are hosts—the United States, Britain, Canada and Australia. This year, for some reason, Canada chose to meet the United States on clay. The Europeans would be particularly pleased to by-pass grass.

Defender Gets Choice

In a significant move, the international committee recently agreed on a United States proposal to permit the country defending the cup to play the challenge round on cement if it wished.

True, tennis was born on grass. But where are the grass tournaments? The few that remain are concentrated in the East. Players who enter them must adapt themselves to that strange surface after spending

all their time on the other, more common types.

Then, too, for the legions of non-tournament players grass courts are so rarely available as to be considered oddities. A reason is the expense of construction and maintenance.

Of the familiar surfaces, hard-top may consist of macadam or asphalt mix, specially treated to provide resiliency. Brick composition courts are finding favor. Har-Tru is increasingly in demand. This is pulverized, natural green rock, chemically treated.

What are the differences to the player? A grass court is easy on the feet and eyes and, in the opinion of many, furnishes an almost perfect medium for spin and bounce. On clay the bounce is slower, affording more time for retrieving. Both surfaces call for a distinctive sort of footing; one must learn how to stop short and prevent sliding after a run.

125

Cement and asphalt, in the "all-weather" family, are the fastest courts. They require no upkeep except for painting lines once or twice a year. Hard-top is considered slightly slower than cement, while brick composition, also known by its French origin as En Tous Cas, gives a slow, medium bounce. Footing in all these is no problem.

The excessive speed of the California game is attributed to the hard courts used almost exclusively there. But such surfaces have disadvantages. They are tiring on the feet and, unless given a dark tinge to reduce the sun's glare, a strain on the eyes. Also, the tennis balls wear out more quickly and become discolored.

Since matches are sometimes won and lost on bad bounces, the maintenance of courts is important. In Queens there is a man on the sidelines who winces whenever he sees a ball bounce erratically. His eyes rivet on the point of contact on the court and he mutters: "Unforgivable! It should never happen."

This is the sort of perfectionism that has earned a reputation for Joe Molfetto, a builder and operator of courts for thirty years. Millionaires, schools and clubs all know his handiwork. He runs the public Sterling Tennis Club, where fifteen clay courts get a steady pounding seven days a week and stay beautifully manicured.

Molfetto, whose two sons work with him, says Long Island clay is "best for tennis." It is dug out of banks, pits and underground veins and screened to eliminate silt and sand. Molfetto's first step in building a court is grading the land with a bulldozer. Then he does fine-grading by hand. Now he is ready to pitch the ground, mainly so that water will run off easily.

As a base he lays a bed of stone and cinders to a minimum depth of four inches. Then he applies two to four inches of clay. This is topped by green or red surface clay, the color being important to reduce glare. The final phase is squaring off the court area and painting lines. The cost ranges from $2,000 to $4,000.

Rain Problem Licked

Molfetto is such a craftsman that he has mostly neutralized his greatest enemy, rain. Even after the heaviest downpour, he says, he can whip all the courts into shape in about an hour and forty-five minutes. For this, he lines up an impressive array of equipment, including a 1,200-pound power roller and eight-foot brushes. By contrast, most Park Department courts are forced to shut down for twenty-four hours after a rain.

"As far as maintenance goes," Molfetto says, "the big difference between clay and grass courts is that clay can take constant use for hours and hours, while grass wears out, needs lots of water and rest to allow it to grow. You also must remember that grass, when it is moist or uneven, won't give you that true bounce."

August 21, 1960

MISS HARD TENNIS VICTOR

Miss Hard Halts Maria Bueno—Fraser Beats Laver for Title

By MICHAEL STRAUSS

Maria Esther Bueno, considered the queen of them all in women's tennis for these past two years, ran into an unexpected uprising in the national tennis championship final at Forest Hills yesterday.

The Brazilian senhorita, defending her crown, was beaten by Darlene Hard, America's No. 2 player, from Montebello, Calif., 6—3, 10—12, 6—4. As a result, the title won by Althea Gibson in 1957 and 1958, was returned to the United States.

In the men's final, Neale Fraser, the sharpshooting stylist from Australia, conquered Rod Laver, his red-headed countryman, in a duel of southpaws, 6—4, 6—4, 10—8. Service breaks in the last game of each set enabled Fraser to win the championship for the second straight time.

Fraser's Service at Peak

Fraser has a service that he can make "kick" in either direction. It is his most feared weapon. Yesterday his tricky delivery was at its best. Laver was only able to pierce it once—in the third game of the second set.

The contest was a rubber-match. Laver beat his Davis Cup team-mate for the Australian crown early this year. In June, however, Fraser bounced back to conquer the red-headed bomber in four sets at Wimbledon. Yesterday Fraser was, by far, the more consistent performer.

There is little doubt that the developments in the women's encounter took the gallery of 7,000 by surprise. Senhorita Bueno has been winning the important matches with a sparkling well-rounded repertoire of strokes. She was the big pre-match favorite.

But Miss Hard was unimpressed. She sailed into the South American senhorita at the start with a confidence that gave her the role of aggressor. Her service was superb and her overhead deadly. After ten minutes, she boasted a 3-love lead in games.

Senhorita Bueno, famed for her poise, power and poker-face, never seemed able to gain full control of her game there-after. She displayed moments of brilliance and long sieges of obstinacy. But after 1 hour and 45 minutes of play, she succumbed.

A Dream Come True

For the American, the victory represented a dream come true. Five times before, she had failed in her quest of the national title. In 1958, she was beaten by Miss Gibson in the final. In 1959, she bowed to Senhorita Bueno in the semi-final, 6—2, 6—4.

"I never thought I'd do it," the Californian said after the match. "That girl never gives up. She hits winners when least expected. It's been a long time coming. It's great."

The gallery also thought it was "great." It rose and gave the American girl, a 24-year-old junior on leave of absence from Pomona (Calif.) College, an ovation. The American had helped provide one of the most gripping women's matches seen in the big cement saucer in years.

Suspenseful moments were liberally sprinkled throughout the contest. The second set, by itself, had more thrills than often seen in a whole day's programe on the field courts. The set was filled with drawn-out games.

The ninth game, for example, was settled after twenty-four points. It was an old fashioned neck-twister. With Miss Bueno on the service line and trailing, 3—5, Miss Hard tried to end it then and there. The best she could do, however, was to gain one match point.

Senhorita Bueno finally broke Miss Hard in the twenty-second game after gaining a triple set point. The Californian held off the threat temporarily by acing her rival on the fourth point and volleying her out of position on the fifth. But, Miss Hard then erred on a shot from the base line.

The situation appeared far from right for Miss Hard. She had missed numerous opportunities and seemed unable to provide the important shots when most needed. Miss Bueno, who had been having trouble with her short ground strokes, seemed to have finally found the touch.

But, when the girls returned for play, the Californian demonstrated that she was not ready to concede anything. She broke her opponent's service in the first game and took her own. Then the players exchanged breaks in the seventh and eighth games.

It seemed that Miss Hard's task might be made easier late in the ninth game when Senhorita Bueno went sprawling on the heavy turf after trying to return a drop shot. When the South American girl arose, she

TRIUMPHANT: Darlene Hard holds trophy awarded her after she won the women's national singles crown at Forest Hills.

wa shaking her right hand.

Nevertheless, she was able to withstand her foe's charges during the game, which was the match's big breath-catcher. The South American took it on her service on the twenty-fourth point, a cross-court volley and a near-service ace settling the issue.

Miss Bueno's Reign Ended

The long ninth game was a violation of the law of averages. Although it was teeming with sparkling shots by both players, Miss Hard gained only one match point in the seventh. After that, the advantage points all went to the South American. But having weathered the one threat, the Brazilian couldn't survive the second. In the nept game, Miss Hard rushed into a 40-15 lead. Then she ended matters with a short forehand shot that caught her rival out of position.

For the 21-year-old Miss Bueno, the Wimbledon champion, the defeat marked the end of a reign that had made her the toast of courts around the world. In her younger days, Miss Hard beat her frequently. Lately, however, the job had become difficult.

In their get-together yesterday, Miss Bueno seemed to adopt the strategy of watchful waiting. She was careful with her strokes at the start, always waiting for her opponent to make errors. Instead, the South American got into difficulties as Miss Hard clicked repeatedly, particularly with decisive cross-court volleys.

In the wake of Miss Hard's triumph, the developments in the men's engagement were only anti-climactic. Indeed, the match, pairing foreign players in a final for the fourth time in five years, seemed to be watched by the railbirds with only passing interest.

Fraser Makes Move

Fraser made his big move late in the first set. From 4—all, he moved to a 2-love lead in the second set. Laver retaliated with a service break in the third game, but he could not keep pace with his countryman. Neale broke him again in the tenth game to take the set.

Throughout the match, Laver's volley, his most potent weapon, missed connections repeatedly. Fraser, on the other

126

hand, made fine use of his opportunities at the net and kept pecking away at his rival until able to get in his pay-off shots.

A big factor, too, was Neale's lobs. His lofting thrusts were flawless. But, it was the service that made the big difference. Fraser works on the delivery line like a spitball pitcher in baseball. He masks his offerings. As a result, Laver never was sure what to expect.

Because of conflicting reports circulating for the past week concerning a robbery of last week-end's tournament receipts, West Side Tennis Club officials saw fit to clear the picture yesterday. They said the intruders had forced their way into a safe in the club's basement and had made off with $40,000. The loss is partly covered by insurance.

In the concluding match for 1960, Margaret Osborne du Pont, Wilmington, Del., and Fraser defeated Miss Bueno and Antonio Palafox, Mexico, in the mixed doubles final, 6—3, 6—2. The victory marked the ninth time Miss du Pont had been a party to such a victory since 1943.

September 18, 1960

The New York Times (by Allyn Baum)

Laver gets shot past fallen Fraser. Fraser captured U. S. championship by 6-4, 6-4, 10-8.

Laver Trounces McKinley in Straight Sets to Gain Wimbledon Tennis Title

AUSSIE CAPTURES 55-MINUTE FINAL

Laver Turns Back McKinley by 6-3, 6-1, 6-4—Fraser Team Takes Semi-Final

By FRED TUPPER

Special to The New York Times.

WIMBLEDON, England, July 7—Rod (The Rocket) Laver of Australia is the new champion at Wimbledon. And high time. The lithe, 22-year-old redhead, the runner-up the past two years, demolished Chuck McKinley of St. Louis, 6—3, 6—1, 6—4, on the center court in fifty-five minutes today.

It was the quickest men's tennis final here since Jack Kramer won from Tom Brown in forty-five minutes back in 1947.

And it confirmed what everybody from connoisseur to bookmaker knew: Laver is the best amateur in the world.

The Australian left-hander has been knocking at the door for some time. He was a finalist with Alex Olmedo here in 1959 and he lost to Neale Fraser of Australia in 1960. Over the past year, Laver has been the runner-up in the American, Australian and Italian championships.

Suspension Lifted May 1

Laver was tough and tournament-tested. McKinley was under suspension until May 1 for throwing a racquet in Perth during the Davis Cup interzone final against Italy in Australia last winter. The stocky 20-year-old American has been studying at Trinity University in Texas. He played in his first tourney this year in Oklahoma late in May.

Since arriving in England, he won at Bristol, lost in the final of the London grass championship and then acrobatically wove through the field into the Wimbledon final.

Laver was seeded second here, McKinley eighth.

For a few minutes it was a fine match. McKinley started confidently, ripping his bullet service into the corners and sprinting up court behind it to volley. In the sixth game he had his one and only chance to break through.

Chuck was ahead 3-2 and 0-40 on Laver's service. Two flat passing shots and a wide Laver volley got McKinley to deuce and a cross-court volley to advantage. Sadly, he popped the service return low into the net.

7 Games in Row to Laver

Then Laver was away on a brilliant seven-game winning streak, continually forcing McKinley into errors. Chuck volleyed wide over the baseline, double-faulted on a netcord, volleyed into the net and stared at a running Laver forehand that streaked by him.

Laver was serving continually to McKinley's backhand, alternately using his reverse-twist jumper or cutting the ball low to the right side. The Rocket took the eighth game at love and he had the next one and the first set on a backhand pass riveted to the sideline.

Nothing went right for McKinley. The little breaks never came. He couldn't handle Laver's service cleanly and he had no better luck with his own. The second set was soon gone. McKinley had won only 10 points in thirteen minutes.

Chuck thumped his racket on the burned grass and dug in. He was roaring around the court, chasing the redhead's looped ground strokes and the spinning lobs that arched over his head and disappeared.

Bravely McKinley held service to 4-all in the final set. Then came the holocaust. Laver braced himself for the breakthrough. He slapped a backhand down one line, banked a forehand down the other and then hammered a backhand squarely into the corner—three outright winners. McKinley hadn't touched one.

It was love-forty now. McKinley hurtled forward behind his service. Laver threaded his looped forehand through the hole for 5—4.

Princess Lauds Victor

Quickly the redhead was at 40—15 and match point. Only then was there a flicker of nerves. He blooped a volley out and watched a flat backhand sail by him. He had match point again and bashed the ball in off the wood. That did it. Laver had won the all-England championship and Princess Marina, the Duchess of Kent, went to the court to praise him.

"I aimed every point for a winner," said the Australian. "Chuck was hanging around the edges and playing well."

"If I played well," said McKinley, "The Rocket played awful well."

The defending men's doubles champions, Fraser and Roy Emerson, won from their Australian team-mates, John Newcombe and Ken Fletcher, 10—8, 11—9, 6—1. They face another pair from Down Under, Fred Stolle and Bob Hewitt, in the final tomorrow.

Two Americans reached the finals in the junior events. Kathy Chabot of San Diego, Calif., has won all her matches without dropping a game. Clark Graebner of Lakewood, Ohio, defeated Claude de Groncel of Belgium, 6—3, 6—2, today.

July 8, 1961

Laver Downs Emerson

SOUTHPAW WINS ON PASSING SHOTS

Laver Gains 8-6, 0-6, 6-4, 6-4 Victory as Emerson's Net Game Fails in Third Set

SYDNEY, Australia, Jan. 15 (AP)—Rod Laver of Australia clinched the world amateur tennis laurels today by defeating a countryman, Roy Emerson, in a four-set final of the Australian national championships.

The 23-year old left-hander required 105 minutes in sweltering heat to subdue Emerson, 8—6, 0—6, 6—4, 6—4. A crowd of 3,000 watched the match at White City Stadium.

In beating the 25-year-old Emerson, Laver added the Australian crown to his Wimbledon title and spectacular successes against the Italians in the Davis Cup challenge round last month. Emerson holds the United State championship, which he won at Forest Hills, Queens, last September.

The poised, precision-hitting redhead now has beaten Emerson four straight times in major tournaments in Australia. Laver won the state titles in New South Wales, Victoria and Queensland. Emerson won the South Australian and West Au-

Associated Press

WINS IN AUSTRALIA: Rod Laver, who beat Roy Emerson for tennis title.

stralian championships, but did not meet Laver in those tournaments.

Emerson jumped to a 3—0 lead in each of the first two sets. Laver fought back to capture the first set after fighting off several set points, but couldn't hold off his rival in the second. Emerson couldn't do anything wrong and Laver couldn't do anything right in that second set.

The tide turned in the third set, however. Laver held his

serves easily in the last two sets and broke through Emerson's delivery when he felt the time was ripe. He wound up each break-through by deftly passing the net-storming Emerson with deadly volleys.

January 16, 1962

Laver Turns Back Emerson in 5 Sets

By United Press International.

PARIS, June 2—Rod Laver of Australia gained his second championship en route to tennis' Big Four today when he rallied from a two-set deficit to beat a countryman, Roy Emerson, 3—6, 2—6, 6—3, 9—7, 6—2, in the French championships.

Margaret Smith, one of the world's top-ranked players at 19 years of age, lost her first set of the tournament to Lesley Turner, but rallied to win the women's title, 6—3, 3—6, 7—5.

Earlier this year, the red-haired Laver had taken the Australian championship. He now needs victories at Wimbledon and Forest Hills to become the first player since

Don Budge in 1938 to win all four major titles in the same year.

The last three sets were excellently played, and the fourth and fifth brought the 3,500 fans in Roland Garros Stadium to their feet cheering on a number of occasions.

Laver got off badly when he had trouble volleying. His only good shot in the first two sets was an excellent lob on the base line. He finally got rolling in the third set, winning it with a smashing forehand cross that Emerson netted.

Rod took the fourth easily the best set of the match after trailing 3—0. He went to his big game and finally tied it at 3—3. With each player winning his service, it went to 7—6 in Emerson's favor. Once again, however, Laver bounced back, taking advantage of a break in Emerson's next service to make it 8—7.

The last game then went to 40—love with three match points before Laver took it with a wonderful cross-volley.

In the last set, Emerson led at 1—0 and 2—1 but fell behind when Laver, with excellent passing shots, lobs and volleys, forged in front, 4—2. Laver broke Emerson's service to make it 5—2, and finished it with a sharp back hand that Emerson put out of bounds.

In the mixed doubles semifinal today, Fred Stolle of Australia and Miss Turner beat Ned Neeley of Atlanta and Judy Tegart of Australia, 6—3, 3—6, 6—4.

June 3, 1962

Billie Jean Moffitt of U.S. Beats Top-Seeded Margaret Smith at Wimbledon

18-YEAR-OLD GIRL WINS, 1-6, 6-3, 7-5

Miss Moffitt's Opening-Card Upset Is Earliest Ever of Its Kind at Wimbledon

By FRED TUPPER
Special to The New York Times.

WIMBLEDON, England, June 26—Billie Jean Moffitt made tennis history at Wimbledon today. The 18-year-old Californian rallied from the brink of defeat with an extraordinary display of grit and nerve and beat top-seeded Margaret Smith of Australia, 1—6, 6—3, 7—5. A

stunned center-court crowd of 18,000 watched the match.

Never before had a top-seeded woman been beaten on the first day of singles competition in that division.

Miss Smith was a prohibitive favorite to win this world championship—and with good reason. So far this year she had won the Australian, French and Italian titles and appeared on her way to the "grand slam" of tennis.

She had trounced both Maria Bueno and Darlene Hard, the only girls given a chance against her here. For nine consecutive months she had gone without defeat before reaching England. Margaret is a big girl with a big game. She is a devastating hitter off the ground, her service is the fastest in tennis and her overhead and volley are considered superb.

Miss Smith Starts Well

And yet she was beaten by

little Miss Moffitt, beaten by raw courage on this raw, blustery afternoon.

It was all so innocuous to begin with. Miss Smith ripped off the first set with the loss of only one game. Billie Jean, who is from Long Beach, won her service at the start of the second set. Then she hit three magnificent shots. Two backhands flashed down the line and a forehand hit the chalk. Billie Jean had broken Margaret's service for the first time. She was on her way.

Miss Moffitt soon was at 5—0 and set point. She was at 5—1 and set point. She was at 5—3 and set point. The waiting seemed interminable. Finally Miss Smith banged one into the net.

A good effort by the American, but hardly decisive. Miss Smith applied the pressure. She gained leads of 3—0, 4—1 and 5—2. Then Billie Jean went to work. She won her own service and

then she hit a tremendous running backhand.

Forehand Shots Have Zip

"It was the crucial point of the match," she said later.

The backhand enabled her to break through to 4—5. Then she won her service at love. Nothing seemed beyond her talents now. She was ripping her forehand shots across court to Miss Smith's forehand deliberately, probing for the errors. And they came.

It was 6—5, Billie Jean to serve, and suddenly 40—love as the capacity crowd hushed. A forehand went out. Then a double-fault. One more chance for Miss Moffitt. She slashed a backhand volley into the corner for the match, hurled her racquet skyward and then jumped into the net.

June 27, 1962

TO THE VICTOR: Queen Elizabeth II awards the trophy to Rod Laver of Australia on his victory in the men's singles championship at Wimbledon. Laver defeated Martin Mulligan, another Australian, in straight sets in final.

United Press International Radiophoto

Laver Crushes Mulligan, 6-2, 6-2, 6-1, to Win Singles Title at Wimbledon

ONE-SIDED MATCH LASTS 53 MINUTES

Laver Wins With Brilliant Tennis

By FRED TUPPER
Special to The New York Times.

WIMBLEDON, England, July 6—Rod Laver has won at Wimbledon again. The red-haired Rocket demolished unseeded Martin Mulligan of Australia, 6—2, 6—2, 6—1, in fifty-three minutes of flawless tennis today before the Queen and a jam-packed Center Court to take the all-England lawn tennis championship.

A year ago Laver had allowed Chuck McKinley of the United States seven games in a fifty-five minute final.

Laver's one-sided triumph today confirmed what everybody has known all along: that the 23-year-old Australian is the best player in amateur tennis today and one of the great ones of our time.

With the Australian and French titles already his, Laver is gunning for the American championship at Forest Hills to complete the Grand Slam won only by Donald Budge in 1938.

Today, Laver was in a militant mood all the way. There was no hesitation here, no temporizing. That whole lovely range of strokes was on show from the start. The redhead had three games running before Mulligan did what he had to do, hammer it hard for the tiny holes.

Three Glorious Backhands

Three glorious backhands and a loose volley by Laver gave Mulligan a game at 1—3. Then he salvaged another at 2—5 on an off-balance overhead smash. Yet the set was gone in seventeen minutes.

So incredible was Laver's speed afoot and so diabolically did he mask his shots that there was no recourse for a player of Mulligan's talents. He was outhit, out-thought and outrun.

Laver toyed with Mulligan's service, either riveting his backhand down the line or caressing the ball on his racquet long enough to stroke it toward the spot that Mulligan had just left. Rod won the second set in seventeen minutes also.

There were two wonderful games in the third set. Martin was behind, 3—0, in games when, for the first time in the match, he had Laver at full stretch. It was tennis like this that gave Mulligan the Australian junior championship a few years back and brought him to match point against Laver in the 1962 French championships.

Martin won one of those games as the crowd roared him on and he should have won the other. It vanished, however, as Laver short-volleyed and smashed him.

The Coup de Grace

Then Mulligan was serving for the match: Four backhands, one after the other, exploded into the corners. Mulligan bowed his head in respect.

"I thought I played very well," said Laver.

July 7, 1962

129

Laver Defeats Emerson to Win U.S. Title and Complete Tennis Grand Slam

AUSSIE'S SWEEP FIRST SINCE 1938

Laver Wins, 6-2, 5-7, 6-4 in Tennis Final— Margaret Smith Beats Miss Hard

By ALLISON DANZIG

Rodney Laver of Australia achieved the first grand slam in men's tennis since 1938 when he won the national championship yesterday. For the first time, the women's title also went to an Australian player.

The holder of the Wimbledon, Australian and French championships, the red-haired, left-handed Laver completed his sweep of the world's four major titles by defeating his Davis Cup team-mate, Roy Emerson, in the final round. The scores were 6—2, 6—4, 5—7, 6—4.

A year ago, Emerson had beaten Laver in the final here in three sets.

The gallery of 9,000 in the Forest Hills stadium of the West Side Tennis Club acclaimed the 24-year-old champion with a standing ovation as he walked off the court.

Waiting to congratulate him as he reached the marquee was Donald Budge, also a redhead, and the only other player to achieve the grand slam.

Laver was born the same year that Budge won four titles.

"I feel so happy, I don't know what to say," said Laver after the championship cup had been presented to him by James B. Dickey, the first vice president of the United States Lawn Tennis Association. "I only wish I may be able to come back next year and defend this cup."

The Tongue in Check

Emerson, whom Laver had also defeated in the Australian French and Italian championship finals, said: "I would like to congratulate Rod for his fantastic record in matching Don Budge in winning the four major championships."

"He has beaten some great players in the finals," he added, as the crowd roared in appreciation.

Budge, called to the microphone, said, "If any one ever deserved winning the grand slam, Rod Laver certainly deserved to win it. I was lucky in not having to compete against such a player as Rod, and Roy's sportsmanship has been impeccable. A lot of our boys and players from other countries could learn something from them."

Margaret Smith is the Australian girl who made history in carrying off the women's crown. Like Laver, she too is red-haired.

The tall, 20-year-old Miss Smith ended the two-year reign of Darlene Hard of Long Beach, Calif., defeating her, 9-7, 6-4, in the final after saving set point in the fourteenth game.

Only once before had an Australian reached the women's final. Nancy Wynne of Australia was the runner-up to Alice Marble in 1938.

Miss Hard, who practically ruined her chances of winning with sixteen double-faults, was so emotionally distraught that she gave way to tears after losing the sixth game of the second set.

Calls Go Against Miss Hard

Miss Hard had been aggravated by close calls on the lines against her, as well as by her lost opportunity in the first set and her five double-faults in the third game of the second set. She found it too much when another call went against her in the sixth game.

Fighting to break service and get back on even terms in the set, she had volleyed the ball deep at advantage point for Miss Smith in the game. Miss Hard was going back to receive service, thinking she had won the point, when the official on the base line belatedly called the ball out.

Miss Hard stopped in her tracks as if stunned by the call, which gave the game to Miss Smith. She put her hand to her eyes and wept. Then she walked to the rear of the court and stood with her face to the canvas backstop, continuing to weep.

It was a trying ordeal for Miss Smith, and it became more difficult for her when the gallery roared its encouragement to Miss Hard as the American got back into the fight and won the seventh game with her skillfully turned volleys.

In the next game, the Australian girl broke badly. After Miss Hard had scored with a return of service, Miss Smith double-faulted and missed twice on her fine backhand, which had been so steadfast and had scored so often for her. She lost her service at love.

Miss Smith Fights Back

It seemed that the defending champion was strongly back in the running. Miss Smith, however, regaining her composure and, returning service beautifully from both sides, broke through easily in the ninth game as the California double-faulted.

Miss Smith then ran out the last game at love with her powerful service, which had been so big a factor in her victory along with her strong backhand volley. Miss Hard appeared to slam her last two returns of service carelessly out of court and into the net, as if in a hurry to have the match over with.

Laver, for the first two sets of the men's final, was almost as irresistible as he had been in overwhelming Rafael Osuna of Mexico in the semi-finals.

Emerson is one of the world's toughest competitors. He had led Laver, two sets to none, in the French final, and two sets to one in the Italian. He was not serving at his best, however, and he could not cope with Laver's rifle-fire return of service, failing on his lift volleys.

Laver, even though he was not getting his scorching first service in play as often as usual, was completely in command in the first two sets. He was both chipping and stroking his backhand return and hitting his forehand with topspin. At the net, he was ruthless with his volley and overhead.

Laver Breaks Though

In the very first game, Rocket Rod hit four of his fearful backhand returns of service and broke through. He broke service again in the eighth as Emerson double-faulted three times, and his emphatic volleys ended the set in the tenth.

Emerson's service improved in the second set and he showed what a masterly volleyer he is. He won his games decisively, but he had one letdown and yielded the long seventh game to Laver's cracking backhand returns of service.

Emerson had not once reached 40 on Laver's service, and it appeared he would never do so. Then Rod began to weaken in his serving and return of service. The gallery cheered Emerson on as he broke through for the first time in the eighth game of the third set. Two lucky net-cord shots helped.

Roy's two double-faults in the ninth enabled Laver to retaliate, and the latter saved three set points to even the score at 5—all. Then in the twelfth game, Emerson returned service from the backhand in the fashion of Laver, both chipping and stroking for winners, and he won the set. It was only the second set Laver had yielded in the entire tournament.

The crowd applauded Emerson enthusiastically as he left for the rest period, and it continued to cheer him as he broke Laver's service in the fourth game of the fourth set to get back on even terms after losing the first game.

The Big Break

Then came the break that sent Laver on his way to victory. Emerson faltered in his volleying, missing twice on high backhands as Laver tossed up lobs, and yielded the fifth game.

Emerson had one chance to save himself. He got to 40—30 in the last game, scoring with a marvelous cross-court forehand passing shot. Then Laver ran the next three points and it was over. He had his grand slam.

The mixed-doubles championship also went to Australia. In the final, Miss Smith and Fred Stolle defeated Lesley Turner of Australia and Frank Froehling 3d of Coral Gables, Fla., 7—5, 6—2.

Froehling and Miss Turner had defeated Ron Holmberg, of West Point, N. Y., and Jan Lehane of Australia, 6—4, 6—2, in a semi-final match. Stolle and Miss Smith had defeated James McManus of Berkeley, Calif., and Miss Hard in the other semi-final, 6—3, 6—4.

So ended the most exciting and most international championships held in recent years. Thanks to Col. Edward P. F. Eagan's People-to-People Sports Committee, which airlifted some seventy players from Europe in a chartered plane, thirty-five nations were represented in the tournament. The Soviet Union sent players here for the first time.

The attendance far exceeded last year's Colonel Eagan presented a citation to Mrs. Gladys Heldman, the editor and publisher of World Tennis, who represented his committee in marshaling the players, raising the funds for their transportation and housing and dining them for two weeks.

September 11, 1962

U.S. BREAKS AUSTRALIA'S 4-YEAR HOLD ON DAVIS CUP

M'KINLEY IS HERO

Beats Newcombe in Finale for a 3-2 Victory by U.S.

By The Associated Press

ADELAIDE, Australia, Sunday, Dec. 29—The Davis Cup, symbol of world tennis supremacy, is heading back to the United States. And the two young men chiefly responsible for it—Chuck McKinley and Dennis Ralston — look good enough to keep it there for the next several years.

These two college boys combined to break Australia's four-year domination in the 52d challenge round that ended yesterday on a note of high excitement.

It remained for McKinley, the 22-year-old senior from Trinity University of San Antonio, Tex., to strike the clinching blow. As for Ralston, a University of Southern California student from Bakersfield, Calif., he contributed one singles victory and joined McKinley in winning the doubles point.

McKinley Victory Decides

In a match charged with tension, McKinley broke a 2-2 deadlock by blunting the cannon-like power of 19-year-old John Newcombe and winning, 10—12, 6—2, 9—7, 6—2.

Australia's reliable national champion, Roy Emerson, who had never lost a Davis Cup singles match, played some of the finest tennis of his career in crushing Ralston, 6—2, 6—3, 3—6, 6—2, in yesterday's first match.

The Americans had taken a 2-1 lead when Ralston and McKinley beat Emerson and 31-year-old Neale Fraser in the doubles on Friday.

In the opening singles last Thursday, Ralston defeated Newcombe in five hard-fought sets and Emerson whipped McKinley in four.

After scoring their Davis Cup triumph, McKinley and Ralston said that they were not immediately interested in a pro career.

Aussie Players in Revolt

McKinley, who recently rejected a $60,000 offer to become a pro, said he expected no new bid. He plans to finish his college course next spring and defend his title at Wimbledon.

Meanwhile, a dark cloud fell over the tennis picture in Australia, which has been dominant in the sport since World War II.

Leading players, headed by Emerson, have been feuding with the national association over restrictions on foreign play and expense allowances and have threatened either to move to Britain or turn professional.

The latest development came shortly after the final of the Davis Cup matches. Frank Sedgman, the president of the Professional Players Association, said he had made a bid to dissatisfied players offering them a spot on a professional tour.

Besides Emerson, the group includes Fred Stolle, Bob Hewitt, Ken Fletcher and Martin Mulligan, all ranking players.

If all or part of them go through with their threat the strength would be drained from Australia's Davis Cup team and it would not be a serious threat for years.

The United States now has won the Davis Cup 19 times, but trails Australia in their series, 13—12. Since 1950, the Aussies had captured the cup 11 times, losing to the United States in major upsets in 1954 and 1956. Over all, Australia has been Davis Cup champion 18 times.

With Bob Kelleher, the tall, soft-spoken Los Angeles attorney serving as captain, the American team won in the American Zone competition, then proceeded to beat Britain's European champions and India's Far East champions en route to the challenge round in Australia.

Kelleher obtained the services of Pancho Gonzalez, the former professional tennis champion who worked with the squad two weeks before he left for home just before Christmas.

The full load of winning the cup was placed on McKinley when Ralston lost to Emerson in the opening match of the final day's play.

Emerson, the 27 - year - old Queenslander who hit his peak form just in time for the cup series, played too well for Ralston. The American was well below the form he had shown earlier when he won two Australian state tournaments and finished as the runner-up in a third.

The McKinley - Newcombe match was called one of the classics of Davis Cup competition, dating back to 1900.

Newcombe, a big strong boy with a service like a rocket and powerful ground strokes, finally won the marathon opening set after McKinley had fought off 4 set points.

McKinley won the first four games of the second set with a loss of only 2 points. He won chiefly on his excellent service returns and the type of court-covering acrobatics for which he is famous. But the key play came in the third set.

McKinley was trailing, 2—4, but got a 40-30 lead on Newcombe's service and a chance to rebreak. Newcombe unleashed a blazing cannonball second service that at first was assumed good since there was no call from the lineman.

But the lineman later indicated that he hadn't seen the ball, so the umpire ruled it out. It was a double fault and a break for McKinley, who went on to win the long set when Newcombe, showing strain, double-faulted at game point in the 15th game.

The fourth set was easy for McKinley as he played with confidence and speed.

December 29, 1963

Women's International Tennis Is Set

WIMBLEDON GETS TEAM COMPETITION

Women's Tennis, Patterned After Davis Cup, Will Be Staged in U.S. in 1964

By ALLISON DANZIG
Special to The New York Times.
NEW YORK.

An international team competition for women, comparable to the Davis Cup matches for men, will be started in tennis this summer.

The United States and Britain meet annually for the Wightman Cup, playing alternately here and in England. This fixture, in which five matches in singles and two in doubles are contested, will continue to be held.

The new international competition will be open to the teams of other countries, as well as Britain and the United States. The play will be confined to one week and to one club and will not involve the month of competition and travel and expense associated with the Davis Cup which has its American, European and Eastern zones of qualifying matches.

Competition Set for June

The first competition is scheduled at Wimbledon, England, in June. It will begin two weeks before Wimbledon's famed championship tournament.

The United States will stage the matches in 1964 and Australia will act as host in 1965. Mrs. Nell Hopman, wife of Harry Hopman, captain of the Australian Davis Cup team, hopes that a plane can be chartered to take players to the matches Down Under, as was done to take some 80 players from Europe to the United States championships at Forest Hills last August.

For some years there had been talk of broadening the Wightman Cup competition and opening it

131

to other nations, particularly Australia. Efforts in this direction failed for the reason that the plan was to pattern the competition after the Davis Cup and it would have been too costly and entailed more travelling than was thought advisable.

William Kellogg of La Jolla, Calif., will have charge of making the arrangements for the American team that will take part in the opening matches and will head the selection committee. he is a representative of the United States Lawn Tennis Association

of the committee of management of the International Lawn Tennis Association.

Australia, with the world's top-ranking player. Margaret Smith, and other strong representatives in Jan Lehane and Leslie Turner, is expected to prove a formidable rival for the United States, which has won the overwhelming majority of Wightman Cup matches. Miss Smith is the champion of Australia, the United States and France.

February 6, 1963

Associated Press Wirephoto

Chuck McKinley in action against Fred Stolle at Wimbledon

McKinley Defeats Stolle in Three Sets to Capture Wimbledon Tennis Title

Men's Tennis Crown Is First Such for U.S. Since 1955

By FRED TUPPER
Special to The New York Times

LONDON, July 6—Chuck McKinley has won the Wimbledon title, the highest honor in tennis.

Hitting hard and flat from the start, the 22-year-old American scored a 9-7, 6-1, 6-4 triumph over Fred Stolle of Australia in 100 minutes today.

Princess Margaret and the Duchess of Kent were among the 17,000 spectators at the famed center court.

McKinley is the first American-born player to take the men's title since Tony Trabert in 1955. Mrs. Karen Hantze Susman, a Californian, won the women's championship last year.

A Peruvian, Alex Olmedo, captured the title in 1959. At the time he was attending the University of Southern California and said he had won "for Peru and the United States."

McKinley's triumph was one of technique over textbook, of intelligence over indecision and it was achieved with as fine a court-covering exhibition as Wimbledon has seen.

"I had planned to break down

his forehand but he knocked it down my throat," said Stolle later. "In the end I didn't know where to serve or what he was going to do."

Neither did the crowd. McKinley bounced from one crisis to another. He scrambled, he slid and he got his racquet on everything. He tumbled and he dived headlong and he came up with blood on his knees and elbows. But he kept running and running.

For a long time in that tense first set there was no quarter and no sign of a service break. The 24-year-old bank clerk from Sydney had reached this stage on merit with his fine, fast serving and impeccable stroking.

Stolle looks fragile but he moves well. His brilliant performances as a doubles player result from a sound overhead and firm volley.

Australian Confident

The Australian was fit and ready and confident. Just three weeks ago, he had trounced McKinley in the final at Bristol and he was playing better in these championships than he had been then.

McKinley had ideas of his own —to mix up his flat service with his kicking service, to vary his shots and his pace and to run and then run faster for every ball in sight.

Stolle served first and he served hard and deep.

McKinley was serving first to the forehand with his flat

one, then to the backhand with his kicker. He was up at the net fast, but his reach is short and he was straining to put away the passing shots.

At 3—4, the American was in trouble. He double-faulted and he pitched a volley in the alley. Stolle rapped one through the middle. McKinley dived at it, hit the ball on the half-volley and got it over the net. He saved that game.

The tempo was increasing. Stolle had the range now and was hitting the lines, or just missing them, from deep court. McKinley was running through his repertoire, trying for the big stroke through the middle, or chipping the ball short to the sides.

Stolle's Service Fails

It was 7—7 when the break came. Stolle had lunged for a high volley and knocked it off balance into the net. Then he double-faulted trying to put speed on his second service. Chuck aimed for the corner with a spinning forehand and hit it. Straining now, Stolle double-faulted. McKinley held his own service at love for the first set.

Rampant now, Chuck let loose a barrage. Everything came off. He lured Stolle to the

net with his drop shots and then lobbed him.

The Australian seemed a step slower and his plan of attack had disintegrated. In a brilliant burst, McKinley had the second set at 6—1.

Not once in this period had Stolle been at game point on Chuck's service. Then McKinley, for once, was careless. He pushed an easy volley into the net at one-all in the third game but held it. Two backhands had Stolle at game point in the fifth and he lost it.

The Final Point

At 5—4 McKinley did it. He lashed a backhand inside, crosscourted off a volley and it was match point. Chuck played it perfectly. He chipped the return back, then lobbed Stolle. He hit a forehand to the sideline that forced Stolle to the baseline. The return collapsed in the net.

McKinley jumped up and down. Then he leaped over the net, emitting a war whoop.

The Duchess of Kent came down from the royal box to the court to give him the huge silver cup.

Later, he said he had received a $50,000 offer from Tony Trabert, who was at the match, to turn professional. "I

Associated Press Radiophoto

A study in perpetual motion
(McKinley after triumph at Wimbledon)

PARTICIPANT: Chuck McKinley clears net after victory

Margaret Smith Beats Miss Moffitt in Wimbledon Final

AUSTRALIAN GIRL WINS BY 6-3, 6-4

Breaks Through Service in Last Set to Halt Late Surge of U.S. Star

By FRED TUPPER
Special to The New York Times

LONDON, July 8—Margaret Smith has won Wimbledon. The 20-year-old Australian triumphed over nerves and a last ditch surge by Billie Jean Moffitt of Long Beach, Calif., and took the one crown that had eluded her. The scores were 6—3, 6—4.

She confirmed what everyone had known all along—that she's the best woman tennis player in the world.

Later on, Miss Smith paired with Ken Fletcher of Australia and won the mixed doubles from Darlene Hard of Los Angeles and Bob Hewitt, 11—9, 6—4.

The finish of the women's doubles had a center court crowd of 17,000 squirming in its seats. Miss Hard and Maria Bueno of Brazil led 5—2 and 40—0 in the second set. They then dropped 5 match points before they downed Miss Smith and Robyn Ebbern of Australia, 8—6, 9—7.

In the men's doubles, Rafael Osuna and Antonio Palafox, the Davis Cup combination from Mexico, defeated Pierre Darmon and Jean Claude Barclay of France, 4—6, 6—2, 6—2, 6—2.

Miss Smith was top-seeded at Wimbledon in 1961 but lost to Christine Truman. She was top-seeded again in 1962 only to be rudely dispatched by Miss Moffitt after she led in the third set by 5—2.

Miss Smith Stands Firm

Under enormous pressure today Big Margaret, as Miss Smith is called, stood firm in the clutch and became the first Australian to win the All-England women's championship. Bruising the ball with the speed of her ground strokes, she broke through the 19-year-old Billie Jean at love to lead 3—2 in the first set and then hit two devastating forehands to reach deuce at 5—3.

Miss Moffitt swung a first service wide that creased the line as Miss Smith hit it into the net. It was called out. The umpire reversed the call. Margaret slashed a forehand across court, then banged a backhand down the line. She had the set at 6—3.

The Australian was keyed for the kill and her service bit into the corners. She roared up to the net to punch away the volleys and she ate up Miss Moffitt's weak second serve.

Suddenly Miss Smith was at 4-0, and it seemed over. In a final desperate stand, Miss Moffitt shook off the malaise that had hobbled her serve and had taken the sting from her volley.

The American had been in serious straits before in this tournament and had survived. She had rallied to beat Lea Pericoli of Italy in three sets, and had upset Lesley Turner of Australia in three more.

There still was time. Billie Jean banged a backhand through the hole. Miss Smith foot-faulted and then double-faulted. Miss Moffitt tossed up a lob and cut off the volley. She rapped another drive and broke through at love.

Billy Jean Rallies

Serving, she dumped a half-volley off her shoetops across court, hit a volley away and then caught Margaret off-balance. Seven points in a row and it was 2-4 Miss Smith held her service and slashed a forehand across court for match point.

Billie Jean smashed it. She volleyed into one corner and then the other. It was 3-5, Miss Smith to serve. Miss Moffitt was hitting the ball with all she had. She had broken through to 4-5, with her own serve due.

This was the test for the Australian. She had cracked before in the crises because of nerves. She had temporized when she should have hit out. Now she went for the big shot. A forehand ripped down the line, another forehand hit the tape and a third disappeared out of reach into the far corner. Two more match points to come. Billie saved the first and then volleyed across court.

Margaret moved in on the dead run and lashed the ball to the line. She had won.

July 9, 1963

---

made him a firm offer" said Trabert.

McKinley said he would continue his studies at Trinity University in San Antonio, where he will be graduated in January.

"The offer will be open then," said Trabert.

McKinley is the first man in the 77-year history of these all-England lawn tennis championships to win without meeting a seeded player.

He became the third man to win without losing a set during the tournament. Don Budge of the United States did it in 1938 and Trabert in 1955.

The San Antonio player avenged four defeats by Stolle in six previous meetings. He also atoned for his straight-set loss here to Rod Laver of Australia in the 1961 final.

Rafael Osuna and Antonio Palafox of Mexico reached the final of the men's doubles by beating the South African pair, Gordon Forbes and Abe Segal, 6—3, 5—7, 6—4, 6—4.

Osuna set up the openings and Palafox put the ball away.

Darlene Hard and Maria Bueno won from Anna Dmitrieva of the Soviet Union and Judy Tegart of Australia, 6—4, 9—7. Then Margaret Smith and Robyn Ebbern of Australia defeated Renee Schuurman of South Africa and Ann Jones of Britain, 7—5, 3—6, 6—3, to enter the women's doubles. But first Miss Smith has a date with Billie Jean Moffitt for the singles championship.

July 6, 1963

TENNIS ALTERS CODE ON EXPENSE MONEY

PARIS, July 10 (AP) — The International Lawn Tennis Federation today revised its rules on amateurs to make the regulations more realistic.

J. Eaton Griffith of Britain, newly elected president of the federation said, "National associations have found it difficult to enforce the rules. We hope that the new rules will be easier to apply."

The regulation limiting a player to 210 days of expense money during a year was dropped.

The basic $14-a-day expense limit was retained, with the provision that nations can apply to the international federation for approval to exceed this allowance if the cost of living justifies it.

The value of prizes given in tournaments was increased from $56 to $140. A new rule was adopted forbidding a player to enter two tournaments being played at the same time and then taking his pick at the last minute —usually on the basis of the highest offer.

The international federation management committee will draw up each year a list of about 50 men and 25 women considered the best in the world. These will not be considered as ratings, but the hope is that more attention will be paid to controlling the expenses of the top players. Almost all the abuses are in this category.

Edward A. Turville, president of the U.S.L.T.A., said: "I think we've got a set of rules now that can be enforced. I think it will do a lot of good."

The Federation Cup, an international team event for women started this year, and won by the United States, will be played in America in 1964 and in Australia in 1965.

July 11, 1963

U. S. Captures Wightman Cup for Third Time in Row

MISS HARD GAINS DECIDING TRIUMPH

Beats Miss Truman, 6-3, 6-0, for 4th Victory After Miss Richey Downs Miss Catt

By ALLISON DANZIG
Special to The New York Times

CLEVELAND, Aug. 11—One of the great matches in United States women's tennis was played on the hard clay courts of the Skating Club today as the United States Wightman Cup team defeated Britain for the third successive time.

The parties to the match were only the third-string players. They are also two of the tiniest girls in competition. Their names are Nancy Richey of Dallas and Deidre Catt of Britain, and they put on a slugfest of savage, unbelievably accurate hitting from the back of the court worthy of a Helen Wills and a Maureen Connolly.

Miss Richey won, 14—12, 6—3. She saved six set points in the 80-minute opening set, the second longest in Wightman Cup competition. Following her victory, which opened the final program, Darlene Hard of Los Angeles defeated Christine Truman, 6—3, 6—0, and the United States had the necessary four matches for a decision in the international team match.

With the issue resolved, Billie Jean Moffitt of Long Beach, Calif., Wimbledon finalist, overcame Mrs. Ann Haydon Jones, 6—4, 4—6, 6—3, and in the concluding doubles Miss Richey and Mrs. Donna Floyd Fales of New York, defeated Miss Catt and Elizabeth Starkie, 6—4, 6—8, 6—2. The final score was 6 to 1.

On Saturday the defending

team had won two of the first three matches in the series. To begin with Miss Hard, the United States' ranking and most experienced player, suffered a stunning defeat against Mrs. Jones, 6—1, 0—6, 8—6 after she had won nine successive games and led at 3—0 and 40—0 in the final set.

Then Miss Moffitt beat Miss Truman, 6—4, 19—17. The 100-minute second set of 36 games set a cup record. In doubles, Miss Hard and Miss Moffitt won from Miss Truman and Mrs. Jones, 4—6, 7—5, 6—2.

A Match to Remember

Long after the winner of the cup has been forgotten, the gallery of 1,800 here will remember the thrilling exposition of classic ground strokes put on by Miss Richey and Miss Catt. From forehand and backhand they hammered the ball with a length, velocity and control nothing short of astonishing in rally after rally and game after game.

The volley was virtually excluded from this onslaught of murderous drives. The reason was apparent enough in the deadly accuracy of the passing shots from the backhand on the few occasions either ventured to the net.

It was from the backhand that both excelled in style and rapacity of angle as well as speed. But with both the forehand was a bludgeon of overpowering weight.

At the beginning, Miss Richey's forehand was overhitting under the provocation of Miss Catt's depth of stroke. The British girl, hardly missing except on the return of service, won the first three games and then led at 4-1.

Now the little Texan, inscrutable under her eyeshade, began to let up a bit on her forehand. Her whole game became more secure. She was dead game in pursuit. So was Miss Catt. They went at it hammer and sledge hammer, and bit by bit Miss Richey pulled up.

Miss Catt missed one chance after another and not because of any weakening. Miss Richey was running down everything and replying with winners when she had to have the point. The British girl was within a stroke of 5-1, of 5-2 and of 5-3. She lost all of them, and the score was 4-all.

Then came Miss Catt's big chance, at 5-4 and 40-0, after her opponent had double-faulted twice in the 10th game. She had triple set point, she missed them all. Then she lost her service in the 17th game, broke back, lost it again in the 19th and broke back again. The fight and stamina of the two girls under punishment was beyond belief.

At last came the big break. Miss Catt's superb backhand failed her and she lost her service in the 25th game. The set went to Miss Richey in the long 26th after the British girl had saved herself twice by a stroke.

It is most often the case that the outcome of so long a set decides the eventual winner of the match, and so it was today. Miss Catt lost her service in the third game of the second set, after she had led, 40—0, to Miss Richey's five scorching returns of service and passing shots.

Then the Texas girl slumped and lost her service on her errors in the sixth and it seemed she might be tired. But immediately she renewed her bombardment with pitiless accuracy, and Miss Catt was helpless to resist. The British girl got only four points in the final three games. She double-faulted twice in the last game.

August 12, 1963

A TENNIS REVOLT BREWS AT MIAMI

University's Star Resents Addition of Girl to Team

MIAMI, March 7 (AP)—All because of a girl, Rodney Mandelstam, the University of Miami's No. 1 tennis player, says he, and maybe the rest of the squad, will refuse to play intercollegiate tennis.

The girl is 20-year-old Fern Lee (Peachy) Kellmeyer, who has been named the No. 7 player on the squad by Coach Dale Lewis. Mandelstam, for one, doesn't like it.

"For years tennis has been striving to overcome the notion it's a sissy game," Mandelstam said. "This will set it all the way back. I would rather lose than win with a girl."

Mandelstam, from Johannesburg, South Africa, also says he "did not come 10,000 miles to play on a team with a girl."

"It makes a mockery of the team," he asserted. "For instance, we play Army this season. What if some West Pointer came down here and got beat by Peachy? Can you imagine the reaction when he returned and confessed he'd been beaten by a girl?"

Coach Lewis shrugs off Mandelstam's comments as "strictly one boy's opinion," and said he had no intention of removing Peachy from the squad. Miami has won 126 straight dual meets.

There are generally six players on a team. A dual meet consists of six singles matches and three doubles matches. Lewis said he would use Miss Kellmeyer only if one of the six regulars was injured.

Mandelstam said, "I know the feelings of the fellows on the team. I spoke to each one and all felt insulted."

Mandelstam said his feelings were not "derogatory to Peachy . . . she would be an asset to any woman's team. It's the principle of the thing."

Miss Kellmeyer is ranked 15th nationally among women players.

March 8, 1964

Soviet Tennis Star Withdraws Rather Than Play South African

WIMBLEDON, England, June 25 (UPI)—The Soviet Union provoked the first political controversy in the 78-year history of the Wimbledon tennis championships today by ordering Aleksandr Metreveli to withdraw from the tournament rather than play against a South African, Abe Segal.

Hungary followed suit by ordering Istvan Gulyas to dissolve his doubles partnership with Segal. Gulyas, in withdrawing, said he was acting on instructions from the Ministry of Sport in Budapest.

Soviet officials hedged on whether they would resort to the same measures in the Olympic Games at Tokyo.

Metreveli, the 19-year-old second-ranked Soviet player, insisted it was "a personal decision" that he hoped would register as "a moral protest against the apartheid policy of the South African government."

However, Soviet officials had announced prior to the start of the tournament that they would not compete against a South African.

The Soviet move, coming only five years after it had entered international tennis competition, caused immediate repercussions that may severely limit the Soviets' campaign to become a leading tennis power.

One Wimbledon official said, "They've only been in top-line tennis for five years now—and already they have introduced the only major political hassle in the history of the tournament."

An official of the British Lawn Tennis Association said it was possible tournament managers might refuse Soviet entries hereafter if South Africa also is entered.

Segal said the loss of his singles opponent, Metreveli, and his doubles partner, Gulyas, as "regrettable and childish."

June 26, 1964

Emerson Wins Wimbledon Title by Beating Stolle, 6-4, 12-10, 4-6, 6-3

AUSSIE ACES DUEL FOR OVER 2 HOURS

Emerson's Speed Decisive— Miss Moffitt, Mrs. Susman of U.S. Gain in Doubles

By FRED TUPPER
Special to The New York Times

WIMBLEDON, England, July 3—Roy Emerson won the Wimbledon lawn tennis championship today after nine years of trying. In an all-Australian final, the dark, superbly conditioned 27-year-old whipped Fred Stolle, 6—4, 12—10, 4—6, 6—3, in 2 hours 10 minutes of slambang serve and volley.

Roy threw his racquet high, jumped the net and hugged Stolle as applause thundered down and Princess Marina came on court to present him with the prize he wanted most, the highest accolade in tennis.

"I've won the one I've never won," said Emerson. Now he has won, at one time or another, all the titles that matter: of England, Australia, France and the United States. He has proved beyond doubt that he is the best amateur in the game today.

Through the luck of the draw, the sixth-seeded Stolle was the only seeded player Emerson met here. He paraded through the early rounds with ease, losing only one set—to Nicola Pilic of Yugoslavia—on his way to the final.

Great player though he is, Stolle seems doomed to the role of an also-ran. He lost the Wimbledon final to Chuck McKinley of the United States a year ago, dropped the Australian title final to Emerson at Brisbane early this year and was beaten by Jan Erik Lundquist of Sweden in the Italian championships.

A Match of Power

This had to be a match of big serve and volley. The Australians don't play it any other way. In the first set, before their ground strokes, five games were served at love and there were four rallies.

Emerson, faster afoot, got the break in the ninth game and he earned it. He swung a forehand into the corner, slapped a volley through a hole and reached advantage with a high backhand that pinned the line. In a furious exchange at the net, he slipped a volley across court to gain a 5-4 lead. Then he held service for the set.

They were at it hammer and tongs now and the return of service was stronger. In the seventh game of the second set, Roy caught Stolle wrong-footed on a lob that was smashed out.

Emerson rifled the next return down the middle. Stolle half-volleyed it off his shoe tops and it sailed out.

Emerson led, 4—3, on his service, and he had yet to lose it. Then the 25-year-old Stolle made four points running, breaking through on a change-of-pace as he steered a forehand shot across court to win the game at love.

Rain Halts Play

Intermittent rain broke up the long set three times and at 10—10 Stolle came out of the dressing room to serve again. He was cold and had no pace on his second delivery. Emerson hit two enormous forehands for the breakthrough and served out for the set.

The pattern became clearer in the third set. When it came to a rally, Emerson had the better of the exchanges. His anticipation was quicker and he was faster to the ball. He bungled a chance at 0—40 in the first game, however, and he was fallible again at 4—5 as Stolle pounded the lines to take the set game at love.

Gradually Stolle's control of service disintegrated. He double-faulted in the first game of the fourth set, hit a half-volley out and then dropped his racquet and clapped in admiration when Emerson hit the shot of the day — an angled backhand that slid obliquely across court. Stolle double-faulted again and that game was gone.

With victory looming, Emerson served like a giant, rattling his thunderbolts downcourt as Stolle swung futilely.

Fred had fought his fight, but Roy was untouchable. He lost just four points on the serve in that last set and broke through with a glorious forehand down the middle for the

July 4, 1964

135

Roy Emerson, twice a winner at Wimbledon and Forest Hills, was always somewhat overshadowed in the 1960's by Rod Laver, a fellow Australian.

BRAZILIAN UPSETS MARGARET SMITH

Frustrates Australian's Bid for Tennis Grand Slam by Taking Final in 3 Sets

By FRED TUPPER
Special to The New York Times

WIMBLEDON, England, July 4—Maria Bueno rules again at Wimbledon. The graceful Brazilian upset Margaret Smith of Australia, the defending champion, in a match that was sheer tennis delight. The scores were 6—4, 7—9, 6—3.

Miss Bueno's last shot was a half-volley that blooped over the net and dropped dead on the turf. It marked the fourth straight game she had taken in a magnificent burst of hitting.

To achieve victory Miss Bueno reached into her memory book to play the kind of tennis that brought her the title here in 1959 and 1960. She proved beyond doubt that she had recovered from the ill health that wrecked her game for most of three years.

As a crowd of 17,000 at the center court roared with applause, Miss Bueno threw away her racquet and jumped with joy.

"It was the finest win of my career," the 24-year-old champion said. "People said it would be too hard to come back, but I made it. I was determined to make it."

In so doing she ended one of the great winning streaks in tennis. Miss Smith, 21, had won the championship of Australia, Italy and France, beating Miss Bueno in a three-set final for the French crown at Roland Garros stadium. She had seemed on her way toward achieving the grand slam in tennis, which includes the British championship at Wimbledon and the United States crown at Forest Hills.

The Australians clamped a stranglehold on the tournament. They took four titles — men's singles and doubles, women's doubles and mixed doubles. But they lost the one they had been surest of, the women's singles.

Fred Stolle avenged his loss to Roy Emerson in the men's final by pairing with Bob Hewitt to defeat Emerson and Ken Fletcher in the all-Australian men's doubles. Fletcher dropped his service each time for the crucial break. The scores were 7—5, 11—9, 6—4.

Billie Jean Moffitt of Long Beach, Calif., and Mrs. Karen Hantze Susman of San Antonio, Tex., doubles champions here in 1961 and 1962, did not make it this time.

They played well, but not at the same time, and were beaten by Miss Smith and Lesley Turner of Australia, 7—5, 6—2.

At 5-all in the first set, the Americans each flubbed smashes, while Miss Smith hit a couple in. That was the break that mattered. Miss Smith was devastating in the second set.

Service Balky

Miss Bueno goes as her service goes, and for a long time today it did not obey her. She took the first game on a flicked cross-court forehand, a lunging return from far off the sideline and a double-fault by Miss Smith.

But she lost the second at love as Miss Smith hammered her heavy ground shots for winners.

The Brazilian, lifting her game, was taking the ball on the rise and making powerful returns down the sidelines. She was passing Miss Smith before the Australian could get up to the volleying position.

In the ninth game Miss Bueno suddenly broke through with three drives into the corners. Miss Smith, under pressure, double-faulted. First set to Miss Bueno.

The defending champion seemed nervous. Her serve failed her when she needed it, and she was pushing her ground strokes mechanically, rather than taking a full cut at the ball.

She survived a dreadful first game in the second set, then ran up a 4-0 lead with the crushing power of her service and with deep volleys.

Miss Bueno had reverted to playing hot and cold. Now she caught fire. Her drives ripped into the corners and her delicate volleying touch returned. Incredibly she was at 4-all and five times was a point away from a break-through.

Fans in a Turmoil

The stands were in a turmoil, continually breaking into applause during Miss Bueno's rally.

Miss Smith was shaking and seemed to be set up for the knockout. But Miss Bueno could not put over the finisher.

The Australian braced and fenced her off. She won two service games at love, and finally took the set, 9—7, on a lob that Miss Bueno knocked out of the court.

The third set was an epic. The girls were serving with venom, acing each other until they reached 3-all.

Miss Bueno scored on a beautiful forehand, then flicked a cross-court volley through a hole. She was charging to the net to attack.

Miss Smith hit one return wide, the next floated just over the line. That gave Miss Bueno

United Press International Radiophoto

A JUMP FOR JOY: Maria Bueno of Brazil leaps into the air after beating Margaret Smith of Australia to win the women's singles championship at Wimbledon, 6-4, 7-9, 6-3.

the lead at 4—3, with her service coming up. She held it.

The stands were hushed. Could Miss Smith be beaten after all?

The Brazilian slashed a forehand down the line for the first point. Miss Smith double-faulted, then volleyed into the net.

With two match points in her favor, Miss Bueno reached down to her ankles to hit a half-volley off the edge of the racquet. It popped over the net and died. The crown was hers.

"I felt the pressure," Miss Smith said later. "I clamped up. I guess I beat myself again, but Maria played so well."

Peaches Bartkowicz, the 15-year-old player from Hamtramck, Mich., who has never been beaten by a girl her age,

moved into higher tennis society today. She won the Wimbledon juniors for girls 18 and under by vanquishing Elena Subirate of Mexico, 6—3, 6—1.

In the early evening a mixed doubles streak was snapped. A year ago Fletcher and Miss Smith made the grand slam across the world. The record book showed they had never lost a match.

But this evening they were beaten by Stolle and Miss Turner, 6—4, 6—4. It was Miss Turner who won the critical points.

The attendance for the two-week tournament totaled 286,000 the second largest in history.

July 5, 1964

Best and 'Best-Paid' Amateur

By HARRY GORDON

MELBOURNE.

IN Brussels for the space of just one day, during the first trip overseas he had ever made, Roy Emerson enjoyed a reputation as a large-scale tipper. For a tennis player, his handouts were surprisingly generous; for an Australian tennis player—a notoriously careful breed, this—they were massive. As a result, the staff at his hotel lavished special care upon him; headwaiters bowed deeply, bellhops fawned and the man who looked after room service arrived breathlessly, within seconds, every time he was summoned.

Roy Emerson was 17 at the time, and until that journey had spent the bulk of his life on a farm in the Queensland outback, milking 160 cows every morning. Because he could hit a tennis ball hard and accurately, he had been yanked from the bosom of his family and exposed suddenly to the wonders of the international circuit. Emerson was traveling as a member of an earnest young team, under the management of Harry Hopman, and Hopman, who believed in asking his youngsters to shoulder some small responsibilities, had asked him to handle the petty cash for several of the team who were flying from Paris to Brussels ahead of the main party.

In France that summer, 11 years ago, an Australian pound was worth about 1,000 francs; in Belgium it brought a little over 100 francs. Mervyn Rose, the oldest member of that Hopman team, recalls today, "To Emmo then a franc was a franc was a franc. That was all there was to it. He had noted that the usual tip in France was 100 francs, or a tenth of an Australian pound, and he just kept on tipping 100 francs when we arrived in Brussels. That meant he was giving away a pound every time a waiter approached him, and that was often; this at a time when 20 pounds a week was an excellent wage in Australia.

"We were having a lot of food in our room, and those waiters loved Emmo. They wouldn't leave him alone. Sure . . . the rest of us knew he was paying out 10 times too much, but we figured it was Australian Lawn Tennis Association money anyway. Hopman arrived next day and he looked as if he was going to explode when he saw what had happened. From then until the tour ended, he didn't let Emerson handle another penny."

HARRY GORDON is a Melbourne newspaperman who often covers international tennis events. His book, "Below the Surface" — about Dawn Fraser, the Australian Olympic swimmer — will be published here next week.

WINNING FORM—Roy Emerson hits hard and, by common consent, covers the court more efficiently than anyone else now in the game. His serve is only B-plus and he is not a great tactician, but teammates say he is the fastest man they have ever seen on a tennis court.

ROY EMERSON has come a long way since that first trip in 1954—as a tennis player (he is a prime choice to win the men's singles in the French matches starting tomorrow), a sophisticate and a handler of finance. A regular visitor to such places as the Caribbean, Panama, Naples, Rome, Barcelona, Paris, Berlin, Deauville, London, Istanbul, Athens, Beirut, New York and Los Angeles, he can nowadays convert pesetas to dollars and marks to drachmas almost without a blink. He mixes easily with movie stars, wears the finest clothes, drinks the best wines, stays at the plushest hotels. He is the best amateur tennis player in the world, and it follows, in the phony, twilight zone of amateurism which belongs exclusively to lawn tennis, that he is the "highest paid."

Emerson, who is a very honest young man, has often observed that "there is no ..... thing as amateur tennis." This isn't a very profound remark, really. What it means is that, at the international level of tennis, amateurs are not amateurs in the accepted, dictionary sense. They earn money out of tennis, just as emphatically as the professionals do.

The big difference is simply the method of payment. Whereas the professionals earn their money openly, and sign receipts for it, the amateurs have to resort to various subterfuges. They get their money from "expenses," which are not expenses so much as appearance fees, and from retainers paid by manufacturers who want to cash in on their reputations. Sometimes patriotic individuals pay them large lump sums so they can afford to reject professional offers and stay "amateur" and available for Davis Cup matches.

If the set-up smacks of hypocrisy and deceit, it is not the amateurs-who-really-aren't who should be blamed; it is the administrators who condone the massive masquerade. There are, of course, rules which limit expense payments, and one of the bizarre niceties of the game is the fact that promoters and clubs are often willing to go to extraordinary lengths to pretend to observe them. Understandably, most players are not willing to talk about these methods until they have either turned professional or retired — and Emerson is no exception.

But Australian professionals joke openly about the manner in which they used to earn their extra "expenses." Sometimes they would perform some simple feat like jumping over a suitcase on a "bet"; sometimes they would be asked to play poker, knowing that their hand was loaded with aces; sometimes they might just find an envelope, packed with bills, wedged inside one of their shoes in the locker room.

None of this is very new. A well-known story of the tennis circuits concerns the way Continental officials used to bet Suzanne Lenglen's father £1,000 (sterling) that she wouldn't arrive for a certain tournament. She would turn up and he would pocket the £1,000.

So lively is the bidding in expense payments that one corner of the Wimbledon grandstand, where organizers meet each year to haggle over terms with players, is called "the cattle market." Here officials from the Caribbean circuit try to outbid the men from Lebanon and the Mediterranean tourist resorts. They aren't offering their own money, of course; invariably, the clubs making the offers are subsidized by groups who profit from the tourist trade.

IT would be wrong to infer from all this that players like Emerson are guilty of any misbehavior. They simply conform to the accepted pattern. It is a fair bet that every top amateur player since the last war has been, by the strict Olympic standards of Mr. Avery Brundage (in charge of the Games since 1952), a professional. And it is significant that in the face of constant, often quite blatant evidence of payments, no lawn tennis association makes any move to have any of its players declared professionals.

The players, most of whom point out that they didn't invent the system, are usually realists; they regard themselves as performers whose incomes are determined by simple box-office economics— the bigger the reputation, the bigger the fee. A player like Emerson, who has the largest reputation in the business— and therefore the largest income — looks upon amateur tennis as an industry which allows him to move around the world in reasonable luxury, sometimes accompanied by his family, and so far he has refused to swap it, even for an offer of $85,000, for the life of a professional.

EMERSON is in the top income bracket of amateurism for one reason: he is remarkably good at winning. He has won virtually every title of any significance, singles and doubles, in the world. This year it is generally conceded that he has an excellent chance of winning the quartet of major singles championships which constitutes the "grand slam"—the Australian, French, Wimbledon and American titles. Only two players in history, Donald Budge and Rodney Laver, have won the four in any one year.

Even more imposing, though, than his string of tournament wins is Emerson's record in Davis Cup play. He is unbeaten in Cup singles, and is undoubtedly the reason why Australia holds the Cup today. He has been a member of the Australian Davis Cup squad since he was 17 and has played in six challenge rounds. Only one Australian, the late Sir Norman Brookes, ever played in more, and Emerson seems certain to top his record of eight if he remains an amateur.

Several times before Emerson has been tagged as a likely winner of the "grand slam." In 1963, after Laver turned professional and left the amateur field comparatively clear, the slim and lanky (6 feet, 165 pounds) Queenslander got half-way there by winning the Australian and French singles titles. Then he went down in a quarter-final at Wimbledon, and was bundled out of the American championship by the unseeded Frank Froehling. After that defeat Emerson announced, "I reckon I'm ready for the pasture"—but he was back, the following year and won three of the four big ones.

He took the Wimbledon title (his ninth try), but missed out in the French championship. This past January, after he won the first of the 1965 major titles—the Australian— he was asked how he ranked his "grand slam" chances. "Well," replied Emerson, who has a quiet, dry humor, "I reckon I've got a better chance than anyone else this year."

Emerson's biggest asset as a tennis player is his superb physical fitness. He was a schoolboy track and field champion. At 14 he covered 100 yards in 10.6 seconds and, as a 16-year-old student at Brisbane Grammar School he established broad jump and hurdling records in competition against the rest of Queensland's top private schools.

Harry Hopman, who is something of a fanatic on the subject of conditioning, says that he has never handled a fitter, more athletic player than Emerson.

Mervyn Rose remembers, more earthily, "Harry Hopman used to take us for early-morning runs around Hyde Park in London and the Bois de Boulogne in Paris, and most of us weren't crazy to put too much effort into them. Emmo had a beautiful loping stride, and he loved to run. So we'd get him to hare out in front. Harry, who was very jealous of his own fitness, used to go really hard to catch Emerson, and leave the rest of us alone.

"We'd fall behind in the mist and wait until the pair of them caught us next time around. In the Bois we found that there was plenty of small change lying about on the riding tracks where we used to run. Apparently it used to get jolted out of pockets when people were galloping on horseback. We used to spend a lot of time picking up money, while Emerson and Hopman were going hell for leather round the Bois."

THE Emerson game is neither colorful nor dramatic, and it is doubtful whether he would ever be a great drawing card as a professional. He hits the ball very hard, and spreads himself around the court more efficiently than any other man in the game. He is not a great tactician; he moves more by instinct than by generalship, and the weakest single factor of his game is his service—which probably rates a B-plus in top professional and amateur company. He wins matches mainly by just hitting the ball back and wearing his opponents down.

His fitness and his great courage make him very hard to beat in a long match. He demonstrated his fighting qualities in this year's Australian singles final, when he came back to win after losing the first two sets and trailing 1-3 in the third against his Davis Cup partner Fred Stolle. "No," said a dejected Stolle afterward, "I was never confident that I had the match won. How can you think that way against a bloke like Emmo?"

Neale Fraser, who was Emerson's Davis Cup buddy in three winning doubles matches, is frank in his assessment of Emerson's ability.

"Roy is the fastest man I've ever seen around a tennis court, amateur or pro," he says. "You can never be sure of winning a point against him until the ball is out of play.

JUMP FOR JOY—Emerson defeats Chuck McKinley of the U. S. (right) in 1964 and regains the Davis Cup for Australia.

His forehand is not as strong as his backhand, which can be a matchwinner. I've often been amazed at the way he punches back his return of service, and some of his interceptions at the net are unbelievable. One big fault is his inability to alter his game when things are going against him. He's very stereotyped, and has trouble changing a losing game into a winning one."

Alf Chave, a veteran Queensland official who has known Emerson since he was a boy and has managed him on several overseas trips, claims that his one real failing is his lack of variety. "On grass courts, his speed gives him the ability to win any tournament," says Chave. "But there's a sameness about his stroke-making that makes him vulnerable when anything goes wrong. His shots come off the court at the expected height and pace. There just isn't much element of surprise in his equipment."

Rod Laver, who was unbeaten in six singles and two doubles during Davis Cup challenge rounds, claims that the only possible way to beat Emerson is to hustle him. "You've got to keep the pressure up from the first ball, and just not relax concentration," he says. "The German, Wilhelm Bungert, who isn't a great player, proved at Wimbledon a couple of years ago that Emerson can falter under pressure."

HOPMAN believes that the toughest of the three major titles which now stand between Emerson and the "grand slam" is the French. "The ball comes off the clay surface at the Roland Garros Stadium in Paris comparatively slowly," he says, "and it's obvious that the faster grass surface at Wimbledon and Forest Hills suits his style a lot more."

Hopman claims that Emerson has improved his forehand and his service greatly in the last 18 months, and that he has finally achieved excellent ball control. "He used to hit that forehand far too flatly, but he's worked on it desperately hard in the last year or so. I'd say that the only aspect of his play that bears improvement now is his second service. When he gets the big one in, it's a beauty. But the second ball is too flat. It lacks spin and just isn't penetrating."

Emerson's service, to which he has devoted large amounts of practice time during the last few months, is a weird thing to behold. He is the only player in the world who winds up three times, in the manner of a baseball pitcher, before he belts down on the ball. His corkscrew action

WINNER—Australian Roy Emerson won three of the four big titles of tennis last year (above, at Wimbledon). This year he could make it four; he has won the Australian and goes after the French tomorrow.

has earned him the nickname "Old Crankshaft."

Emerson explains that the elaborate wind-up is aimed at giving him a smooth rhythm rather than extra power. But the action is anything but smooth; he hesitates twice as he whirls the racket about—and, in fact, starts the serve proper halfway through the windup. So far, despite all his work, the result is still less than perfect.

"I used to be able to attack on my second service," says Rose, who played the professional circuit for a couple of seasons before settling down as a coach. "Emmo could never do that. His second one is just plain crook. But on his day, when he's getting the first ball in, nobody could beat him."

EMERSON admits that he doesn't bother a great deal about strategy. "If I know an opponent has a weak point, I attack it," he says. "That's elementary. But I don't think you need to keep changing your game. All you can do is play your bloody best. You either have the ability to win or you don't. That's all there is to it." This attitude is characteristic of Emerson's whole approach to the game.

Even as a very young teen-ager, Roy Emerson never wanted to be anything other than an international tennis player. Born in the peanut-growing township of Kingaroy, he grew up on his father's 800-acre dairy farm near Blackbutt, about 100 miles from Brisbane, with his

parents, two older sisters (Daphne and Hazel), 160 cows and a tennis court for company. (The tennis court was not a remarkable feature for an Australian farm. The sport is not limited to any income group Down Under, and many homes - both in the country and in suburban areas—are equipped with either lawn, entout-cas or asphalt courts.) Emerson claims quite seriously that the steady milking helped his tennis by making his wrists grow big and strong.

In 1951, his father sold half his share in the farm and moved to Brisbane. Mr. Emerson admits today that the major motive for the move was to promote the tennis ambitions of young Roy. By the time he was 17, and a member of the Australian Davis Cup squad, the lad had won every junior Queensland title from under-11 up.

When he took his first overseas tour, in 1954, it was generally expected that he would soon develop into one of the world's top singles players. This conviction was reinforced during the trip when he beat Lew Hoad in a tournament at at Newport, R. I.

During the next few years, though, Emerson seemed unable to fulfill his early high promise. He found himself low man among a batch of remarkably gifted Australian youngsters which included Hoad, Ken Rosewall, Ashley Cooper, Neale Fraser and Mal Anderson. Anderson, a close friend whose lithe, clean-cut, toothy good looks bore an astonishing resemblance to

Emerson's own, began to overshadow him. The pair became known as Queensland's tennis twins, and the fact that they could double for each other caused much confusion among referees and fans.

Several times, outside the locker room after a match that Anderson had won, Emerson would find himself being congratulated; in such cases his own straight-faced brand of humor would take over and he would mutter, "Thanks . . . I was seeing 'em pretty well today." Anderson, who later married Emerson's sister Daphne, went on to play in two challenge rounds before he turned professional in 1959.

AT 21, Emerson, disappointed by his own lack of improvement but still nagged by his tennis ambitions, made a difficult decision. He withdrew from the official 1958 Australian touring team and spent the winter at home, brushing up his forehand and his service under the guidance of Frank Sedgman.

The sacrifice of the trip paid dividends the following year: after taking his bride, Joy, on a honeymoon tour around the world circuits, he joined the Australian Davis Cup team for the challenge round in America. He shone first as a Cup doubles player, with Neale Fraser; later, after Fraser was forced out of the game by a knee injury and Rod Laver decided to join the Jack Kramer troupe, he inherited the world singles championship.

Although most of his early rivals turned pro with Kramer, it would be wrong to assume that Emerson earned his place in amateur tennis simply by default. At Wimbledon last year, and in the last couple of challenge rounds, the quality of his tennis was generally rated superior to that of many recent amateur "greats."

Emerson is a devoted family man. He lives across the street from his parents in a fashionable suburb of Brisbane with his wife and two very young children. Last year he took his wife and son, Anthony, around the world with him; this year he is traveling alone, having delayed his departure until after the birth of his daughter, Heidi, at the end of March. When he rejected the offer of $85,000 to turn professional last November, he explained, "It would mean spending too much time away from my family . . . a lot more than I do now."

He is a gracious young man who does not conform to the old Australian tradition of dumb tennis players. Bob Mitchell, a Melbourne businessman who acted as Emerson's patron in the late nineteen fifties, is emphatic that he is the most intelligent Australian player since the war. "He has gained something from every trip overseas," he says. "He doesn't hang around with tennis people when he's away from the courts. He's an excellent conversationalist, interested in everything that's happening. He's a music lover, a student of Spanish dancing, and he has a very discriminating palate for wine. He's a real cosmopolitan." On the less cosmopolitan side, Emerson plays a reasonable game of golf.

STRANGELY, in view of his urbanity, Emerson is something of a rebel. He has skirmished often with the Establishment of Australian tennis, mainly on the subject of expense payments, and has at times refused point-blank to play in championships rather than accept expenses which he considered inadequate.

He founded the Australian Tennis Players' Association, which is a kind of militant trade union in white shorts, and last year he led a mutiny against the L.T.A.A. With five other players, he refused to accept an order to play in Australian bush towns rather than visit the Caribbean, where the pickings are excellent.

They were all suspended, and thus banned from last year's challenge round in Cleveland, Ohio. But after some vigorous off-stage maneuvering by Harry Hopman and a face-saving demand by officials for an apology, the L.T.A.A. climbed down and allowed Emerson and Fred Stolle to play. This surrender undoubtedly won back the Cup for Australia, but it also cost the L.T.A.A. much respect.

For three years now, Emerson has been employed as a public relations officer for the Philip Morris cigarette company. At home he does office work and travels for the company, but mostly the job consists of looking good on the tennis court and carrying packs of cigarettes around (even though he's not an enthusiastic smoker). Before that he was on Bob Mitchell's payroll and from 1954 until 1958 he worked for a firm which manufactures tennis equipment.

The fact that he hasn't worked for a sports firm in more than 10 years has undoubtedly allowed him to show more independence than most Australian players. These firms, which used to employ all the amateur talent, are an important part of the structure of Australian tennis. They work closely with administrators and would certainly never

tolerate their employes to buck the system.

ABOUT his future, Emerson is noncommittal. Early this year he said that his two big ambitions were to win the "grand slam" and help Australia keep the Davis Cup. At 28 he figures that he has a couple of good tennis years left in him. He is very serious about his work with Philip Morris, whose president, Joseph Cullman 3d, has been generous with him. He receives a retainer of around $8,000 a year, and close friends like Mitchell say that he is keen to remain with the company—possibly in the United States or Latin America—after he retires from tennis.

But it is possible that he will receive another big offer to turn professional this year. Despite his unwillingness to leave his family for long periods, he has let it be known that he is "always willing to listen." Even when he turned down the $85,000 last year, he mentioned that he might have been swayed had the figure been $100,000.

"Take the pro money while you can," Mervyn Rose advised Emerson before he left on this trip. "Nobody looks after you when you're all washed up. Neale Fraser and John Bromwich stayed amateur, and look what happened to them." Fraser is working, at a comparatively modest salary, for a sporting goods firm, and Bromwich, a prewar Australian idol, works long, hard hours at the job of selling newspapers.

As he makes his 10th journey round the world and contemplates the future, Emerson will undoubtedly remember Rose's warning, but it is unlikely that he will take it too seriously. He has complete confidence in his own ability to do well, inside or outside tennis. If he does finally join the professionals, it will almost certainly be because he wants to measure himself against the best men in the business — not because he's scared.

May 16, 1965

MISS SMITH IS VICTOR
Miss Bueno Bows, 6-4, 7-5, In Wimbledon Tennis Final

By FRED TUPPER
Special to The New York Times

WIMBLEDON, England, July 3 — Margaret Smith has her Wimbledon title back.

With a four-game burst down the stretch, the 22-year-old Australian defeated her arch-rival, Maria Bueno of Brazil, 6-4, 7-5 today in a match that had sustained spells of magnificence.

It was revenge indeed. Just a year ago the fiery Brazilian won her third Wimbledon tennis title with a four-game streak to knock Miss Smith off her throne.

For the first time, Australia has taken both all-England singles titles at Wimbledon. Yesterday the defending champion, Roy Emerson, thrashed Fred Stolle in straight sets.

It was not a patch on this 55-minute final, an almost inevitable meeting between the best women in tennis.

Miss Bueno was the top-seeded, Miss Smith No. 2 and the betting favorite. Margaret had a 13-to-4 lead in their matches around the world and had won the Australian championship when Miss Bueno collapsed with bursitis and cramp.

Before a center-court crowd of 16,000, some of whom had queued all night, the Australian stormed to a 5-2 lead in the first set on sheer weight of serve and stroke. She had a set point then as Maria double-faulted. It was the spur that fired Miss Bueno to battle.

Maria is a law unto herself and she can hit shots out of the realm of mortal ken. They rolled off her racquet now. A sweeping backhand down the line saved that game. A darting volley off Miss Smith's shoelaces and a backhand that ripped across court like a shaft of light had her suddenly at 4-5 on her own service.

A windblown lob bounced off the baseline and Miss Bueno hit an astonishing over-the-shoulder, back-to-court, not-looking shot that hung on the top of the net and fell back. She was in trouble again, with a second set point against her. Another lob floated over her head and she watched motionless in despair as it dropped just inside the chalk. First set to Miss Smith.

Margaret had played beautifully up to now. Not a mistake had she made overhead, and her speed around court was amazing. Yet Miss Bueno was still forcing the pace.

Uncoiling like a snake about to strike, she hit deeper and flatter with her services. The volleys wre skipping into the corners and the game came running. A backhand through the hole and she was at 4-2 in the second set and on the dead-run she slapped a volley home to lead at 5-3.

Two points she had then on Margaret's service and two more she needed for the set. Miss Smith's speed saved her. A foot faster to the ball than any other woman in tennis, she hurtled across court and with her long reach struck an off-balance volley for a winner. A great forehand and she was at 4-5.

Miss Bueno reached 30-all in the tenth game, still two points away for the set she had to have. She never got them. Margaret cross-courted a forehand for advantage. And again in the crisis Maria double-faulted.

With victory in sight, the Australian had the next game too, on the luckiest of netcords —Miss Bueno to serve.

A backhand fled by her and then she was foot-faulted for a double-fault as a sigh echoed around court. Her next volley was long and then Miss Smith scraped a tiny lob. With the whole court open, Maria pushed it into the net.

The stadium exploded with applause as Princess Marina went on court to present Miss Smith with the silver challenge trophy.

Miss Bueno paired with Billie Jean Moffitt of Long Beach, Calif., to defeat Françoise Durr and Janine Lieffrig, 6-2, 7-5, in a rousing doubles final. The French duo had recorded the surprise of the year by upsetting the defending champions, Miss Smith and Lesley Turner, in the third round.

Completely unorthodox, they used topspin lobs to attack and came from behind to tie it at 5-5 in the second set before Miss Durr hit a smash awry off the wood and served out to lose the match.

It was Miss Bueno's fourth doubles title at Wimbledon, Miss Moffitt's third.

Australia is having its best year ever on the tournament circuit. All five titles in the French championships went Down Under, four more were won at Wimbledon over this fortnight.

The brilliant young combination of Tony Roche and John Newcombe, seeded second, won from two peripatetic Australians. Bob Hewitt and Ken Fletcher. 7-5, 6-3, 6-4.

Miss Smith took her second prize as she paired with Fletcher to defeat Roche and Judy Tegart of Australia in a fascinating mixed-doubles final, 12-10, 6-3, getting the service break as Miss Tegart was foot-faulted to groans on game point.

Fletcher and Miss Smith have lost only one mixed match in their lives, to Stolle and Miss Turner in last year's final.

It may be a sign of the times that the Americans took the veterans' doubles as Gardnar Mulloy and Bill Talbert beat George MacCall and Al Martini of Los Angeles, 6-3, 6-1, and the Russian won both the junior events.

Vladimir Korotkov took the boys' singles from Georges Goven of France, 6-2, 3-6, 6-3, and Olga Morozova won the girls final from Rachael Giscafre of Argentina, 6-3, 6-3.

July 4, 1965

1965 Wimbledon Champions

Men's singles—Roy Emerson, Australia.
Women's singles — Margaret Smith, Australia.
Men's doubles — John Newcombe-Tony Roche, Australia.
Women's doubles — Billie Jean Moffitt. Long Beach, Calif.; Maria Bueno, Brazil.
Mixed doubles — Ken Fletcher and Margaret Smith, Australia.
Veterans' doubles — Gardnar Mulloy. Miami-Bill Talbert, New York.
Boys' Singles—Vladimir Korotkov, Soviet Union.
Girls' Singles—Olga Morozova, Soviet Union.

Santana Beats Ralston and Becomes First Spaniard to Win Wimbledon Title

By FRED TUPPER
Special to The New York Times

WIMBLEDON, England, July 1 — Manuel Santana defeated Dennis Ralston of the United States, 6-4, 11-9, 6-4, today in a fiesta of glorious tennis and became the first Spaniard to win the Wimbledon championship.

As Manolo's last stop-volley died on the scarred turf, a vast cheer erupted that must have echoed wherever the game is played. For the popular Santana is a legend around the circuit and he has added the most important title of all to those he had won in Paris and at Forest Hills.

Universally recognized as the world's best on clay courts, the 28-year-old former ballboy from Madrid has established his claim on grass where America and Australia have reigned supreme over the last 20 years.

Seeded only fourth when these championships began, Santana survived two classic five-set struggles with Ken Fletcher and Owen Davidson of Australia along the way to become the first European to win here since Jaroslav Drobny defeated Ken Rosewall in 1954.

An Artistic Game

Beautifully as the Spaniard played — and there was hardly an error in his artistic game those 110 minutes on center court—the result of this match hinged on the double-fault, an affliction that dogged Ralston all through his march to the final at Wimbledon.

It was a double-fault in the ninth game that helped give Santana the break that meant the first set. And it was two double-faults after a questionable call on a smash in the 19th game that broke up the long second set just when it appeared that the American was getting on top.

Through the match Ralston served magnificently to score five games at love with an occasional ace on his second delivery, but his nine double-faults invariably in the crises were too much to give away to a man of Santana's class.

Until the end today there was hope for Ralston. At 17 he was the best young player to come out of California for a generation and he teamed with Rafael Osuna then to take the doubles at Wimbledon.

In the years since he has twice achieved America's top ranking, and in 1963 he was on the American team that took the Davis Cup away from Australia at Adelaide. At 23, he was trying for his first major title.

Dennis held service to 4-3 in the first set. He was getting his high hard one in most of the time and hitting his second serve so flat that he had Santana continually off balance.

Suddenly Ralston had a chance for the service break he needed in that eighth game. A forehand pass, a forehand drive across court and an attacking l b that brushed the chalk put him at 15-40 with two chances to reach 5-3. A Ralston net and an ace bailed Santana out of trouble.

Magic Wand Is Waved

Then the Madrid magician reached into his bag of tricks. A backhand pass hit directly across court, that important Ralston double-fault and a forehand down the line put him at advantage.

Ralston pushed a volley short into midcourt, and Santana hurtled forward and hit it with the best running forehand since Fred Perry. The ball glanced off the net cord into paydirt. Santana had the set in 24 minutes.

Ralston tried harder. He was mixing up lob and chop now in an effort to break the Spaniard's rhythm, and in the fourth game of the second set he hit a ball from the baseline that tottered on the net top and fell over. With the court wide open Manolo angled it on the wrong side of the net.

A backhand across court gave Dennis the break to 3-1, but Santana got it back on a running lob to 4-3. At 6-5 Ralston had his chance. In a furious game that saw the score deuce four times, Dennis finally had a set point. He chopped it weakly off his backhand into the net.

At 9-all, Ralston hit a smash that appeared well inside the line. It was called out. Frustrated and disconcerted, he served one double-fault then another. The game and then the second set were gone.

Ralston survived two more double-faults to take the first game of the third set and then made his desperation bid. A backhand down the line, a forehand that jumped through a hole and another forehand nailed to the chalk gave him an advantage point in the very next game.

Santana was equal to the emergency. Down came an ace that Ralston waved at futilely. He never threatened again.

Santana ran it out at 6—4 with a stop-volley and turned on the familiar toothy grin as he faced his wife in the stands. As the crowd roared its appreciation, Princess Marina walked out to the court to present the silver loving cup to him. A courtier, he bent to kiss her hand.

"I worried a little when I twisted my back early, but it didn't hurt long," said the Spaniard. "I think perhaps grass is now for Santana."

Tomorrow Mrs. Billie Jean King of the United States will meet Maria Bueno of Brazil, three-time champion here, for the women's crown.

Although the Australians are out of the singles finals for the first time in 11 years, they have the finalists in the men's doubles. Bill Bowrey and Davidson, who beat Mark Cox and Alan Mills of Britain, 6—2, 6—4, 9—7, will meet Fletcher and John Newcombe, who had an easy victory over two Americans, Clark Graebner and Marty Riessen, 6—3, 7—5, 6—1.

Nancy Richey of the United States pairs with Miss Bueno against Margaret Smith and Judy Tegart of Australia in the women's doubles final.

July 2, 1966

MRS. KING RETURNS WIMBLEDON TENNIS TITLE TO U. S.

MISS BUENO BOWS

Loses by 6-3, 3-6, 6-1

By FRED TUPPER

Special to The New York Times

WIMBLEDON, England, July 2 — Mrs. Billie Jean King has won Wimbledon after six years of trying. The bespectacled 22-year-old from Long Beach, Calif., whipped her arch-rival, Maria Bueno, 6-3, 3-6, 6-1, with absolute mastery of lob and volley today before Princess Marina, the dowager duchess of Kent, and a crowd of 15,000—some of whom had queued all night — in this most exciting Wimbledon in years.

Mrs. King's decisive triumph over the three-time champion from Brazil brought this title back to the United States for the first time since 1962. It brought the bustling little Californian to the top in tennis—a feat that, somehow seemed inevitable after she had upset Margaret Smith in a first-round stunner here four years ago.

Billie Jean walloped Miss Smith in the semi-finals this year, 6-3, 6-3, with a six-game burst in the second set. She attributes her victory streak in this tournament to a change in attitude.

"I've stopped chattering. I've started concentrating," she said.

Manuel Santana had won the men's singles yesterday when he beat Dennis Ralston of the United States, 6-4, 11-9, 6-4. The Spaniard was seeded fourth here as was Mrs. King.

Although Australia was shut out of the men's singles final for the first time since 1956, she retained the men's doubles as Ken Fletcher and John Newcombe won from their countrymen, Owen Davidson and Bill Bowrey, 6-3, 6-4, 3-6, 6-3.

In a fantastic finish that had the center court in an uproar, Miss Bueno paired with Nancy Richey of Texas to win the women's doubles, 6-3, 4-6, 6-4, from Judy Tegart and Miss Smith.

Trailing by 15-4 at 5-4, Miss Richey hit an incredible half-volley off a smash by Miss Smith and brought off an outright winner. Then Miss Bueno drove a smash down the middle and won the match with an ace. It was her fifth doubles title here.

Miss Smith had her revenge later. She paired with Fletcher to take the mixed-doubles for the third time as they defeated Ralston and Mrs. King, 4-6, 6-3, 6-3, with a four-game burst at the end.

Bill Talbert and Gardnar Mulloy of the United States kept their veterans doubles title by defeating two fellow Americans, Bob Sherman and Bob Freedman, 6-8, 6-2, 6-3.

It may be a sign of the times that a Russian won the junior title for the second year. Vladimir Korotkov defeated Brian Fairlie of New Zealand in the final, 6-3, 11-9. Christina Lindstrom of Finland won the girls junior title from Judy Congdon of Britain, 7-5, 6-3.

To the purists, the King-Bueno match was not a classic Wimbledon final. There is no more gifted hitter in tennis than Miss Bueno. She can either soar to the sublime or make the heinous mistake.

There were moments today when her shots traveled like shafts of light, there were too many when she erred on the easy ball. Yet for perhaps the first time in all her wonderful years of play, the Brazilian did not dictate the pace of the match.

A Workable Plant

Mrs. King had a plan, and she stuck to it. She served wide to the Brazilian's forehand and she chopped her returns to Miss Bueno's shoetops. After she had diced Miss Bueno into the net, she tossed up a barrage of high lobs that rained softly and persistently on the baseline. And, in between, she proved again that she is the best volleyer in women's tennis.

Mrs. King played an impeccable first set. The crowd was clapping in delight at some of those scintillating exchanges early on when Miss Bueno was taking the ball on the rise and hammering it for the lines, and Mrs. King was lunging in to make the interceptions and stabbing the volleys away.

Mrs. King had the service break that mattered in the fourth game on a backhand pass and a tiny backhand chop that fled away to the sideline. And she had the set at 6-3 behind such punishing serving that only 6 points were lost on it, half of them by double-faults.

Mrs. King had the advantage point, too, in the first game of the second set on one of those lovely lobs that nicked the baseline chalk. Then Miss Bueno attacked in earnest.

She salvaged that game on a pair of deep smashes from midcourt and a half-volley on the run into open space. The Brazilian had the next game on a backhand pass, a double-fault and a forehand hit so hard that Mrs. King volleyed it into the alley.

The Brazilian was at 3-1 now, still trying to fend off the American. Three times Mrs. King had a chance to break her, but her shots were skimming the line or hitting the top of the net. At 2-5 she was at 15-10 and couldn't make it.

Discouraged, Mrs. King played one wretched game. Three times she double-faulted at game point, yet still won it. But Bueno then held service for the second set, 6-3.

The hangover was still with Mrs. King at the start of the third set. She stared at a rippling pass, double-faulted sadly and was at 30-40 as a forehand sped by her. She got that game, however, dropped the next and then was off on a streak of such masterly tennis that Miss Bueno could only shrug her shoulders in dismay.

Mrs. King had the service break to 3-1 at love as her backhand found the holes. She was exerting such pressure now that the Brazilian was missing even the easy shot. Quickly the Californian was at 5-1 with the stadium hushed for the kill.

A smash, a great volley off balance, another volley off the net cord and she was at match point. A backhand volley creased the line as Mrs. King rushed up to the net for the handshake. She hurled her racquet high and backward as the hand clapping swelled. She had won Wimbledon.

Princess Marina walked down on court to make the presentation. A spontaneous shout went up from the standees, who have followed Mrs. King for years. She held up the big silver tray and pushed it toward them.

July 3, 1966

Stolle Beats Newcombe in 4 Sets for U.S. Tennis Title; Miss Bueno Victor

12,500 FANS SEE ALL-AUSSIE FINAL

Stolle Controls Serve-Volley Battle—Brazilian Downs Miss Richey, 6-3, 6-1

By ALLISON DANZIG

Fred Stolle of Australia won the grass-court tennis championship of the United States yesterday, the first unseeded player to do so since 1957, and Maria Bueno of Brazil carried off the women's title for the fourth time.

The runner-up for the title to Roy Emerson in 1964 and also at Wimbledon in 1964 and 1965, the blond, 6-foot 3-inch Stolle gained the biggest individual triumph of his career in defeating his teammate, John Newcombe, before 12,500 in the Forest Hills Stadium in Queens. The scores were 4-6, 12-10, 6-3, 6-4.

Newcombe also was unseeded in the draw, and for the first time the final was played with all of the players in the favored list out of the tournament. They were, in order of their rating: Manuel Santana of Spain, the defending champion; Emerson, a former titleholder; Dennis Ralston, first in the United States ranking; Tony Roche of Australia, the French and Italian champion; Arthur Ashe, second in the American ranking; Cliff Drysdale of South Africa, the runner-up last year; Clark Graebner and Cliff Richey, third in the United States ranking.

Miss Richey Starts Fast

Miss Bueno, the winner at Forest Hills in 1959, 1963 and 1964 and also at Wimbledon in 1959, 1960 and 1964, defeated Nancy Richey of San Angelo, Tex., in the women's final, 6-3, 6-1. She won 10 of the last 11 games of the match after Miss Richey had started promisingly by breaking service for a 3-2 lead. The Texas girl, who shares the No. 1 ranking with Mrs. Billie Jean King (who was eliminated in an early round), was also the runner-up for the French title.

The only honors to accrue to a player of the United States came in the mixed doubles final in which Mrs. Donna Floyd Fales of New York and Owen Davidson of Australia defeated Mrs. Carol Aucamp of St. Louis and Edward Rubinoff of Miami, 6-1, 6-3. Mrs. Fales stands as the only American to share in one of the three championships since Darlene Hard retained the

women's singles title in 1961.

The set that the 27-year-old Stolle lost to Newcombe was the first he had dropped in the tournament, in which he had defeated Emerson, Ralston and Graebner, among others. The 22-year-old Newcombe, who was seeking his first major national championship, put out Santana, Ashe, Wilhelm Bungert of Germany and Mark Cox of Britain, the victor over Roche.

Following the excitement of Saturday's semi-finals, in which Stolle annihilated Emerson and Newcombe beat Santana in a block-busting double reversal, the men's final yesterday was rather tame entertainment for much of the 2 hours 15 minutes of play.

Service Is Predominant

Service was so predominant a factor that neither man could get the ball in play more than occasionally to generate a rally. Over and over both rushed for the net behind powerful serves for the finishing volley or smash, and in game after game there was the monotony of the same pattern.

Stolle, who had put on one of the finest displays ever seen at Forest Hills in winning 14 of 15 successive games from Emerson with his unbelievably accurate returns of service and lobs, could not get his ground strokes functioning in anything like the same fashion until late in the second set. His service, so potent, too, against Emerson, failed him at the start yesterday, and when he lost the opening game on two double-faults and Newcombe's two winning returns of service, he said good-by to the set.

Newcombe, serving magnificently and returning service a little more often than his opponent, showed not the slightest weakening in the 55-minute set until, in the 10th game, Stolle reached set point as he hit a straight backhand return of service and a forehand passing shot. Newcombe's service and volley extricated him and in his five service games he was so tough that he gave up only one point.

Stolle Breaks Through

It was not encouraging for Stolle, but finally came the turning point. In the 22d game, he got his touch on his ground strokes, and his returns of service enabled him to break through at love for the set as he scored on a final short backhand across court, so typical of him against Emerson.

A big cheer went up for Stolle as he evened the match, and his whole game picked up as he won the opening game of the third set at love and went to 30-0 in the second, making 14 successive points he had won. Newcombe, a dead-game fighter, pulled out of the hole from 15-40, but he was having more and more difficulty and Stolle, getting to his service,

broke through in the eighth, throwing up a final lob.

At the start of the fourth set, Stolle broke through again, despite two service aces by Newcombe, and then Newcombe set the gallery to cheering as he broke back with his dazzling return of service and a passing shot.

That was Newcombe's last big effort. Thereafter he was straining to hold off an opponent who was getting stronger and stronger in his serving and return of service and who was infallible overhead, as he was throughout the match. Escaping disaster in the fifth game, Newcombe yielded to Stolle's stunning ground strokes in the ninth, double-faulting on the final point, and Stolle then served out the match with a love game.

Miss Bueno, whose career has been interrupted twice by hepatitis and knee operations, was a happy champion at the end of her match with Miss Richey. At the outset, her prospects did not seem too good. She was not serving well and Miss Richey's jolting returns from the forehand, as well as her lobs, were beating her or forcing her into errors.

Winner Double Faults

When she double-faulted twice in the fifth game and lost her service at love, it looked serious for Miss Bueno. But in the sixth game she came back strong to retaliate and in the seventh she hit four stunning winners — a passing shot, a smash, a volley and a final great return of a lob, hitting the ball over her shoulder with her back to the net. From then on she was in command.

Miss Richey lost in confidence and aggressiveness and her control failed her, particularly on her fine forehand. She won the first game of the second set and that was her last, though she led, 40-15, in the second and third and had chances to win the sixth also.

Sargent Shriver, director of the Office of Economic Opportunity, and Martin Tressel of Pittsburgh, president of the United States Lawn Tennis Association, presented the cups.

Ernest Oberlaender, chairman of the championships committee of the U.S.L.T.A., announced record figures of more than 85,000 in attendance and in excess of $200,000 in gate receipts for the 11-day championships.

September 12, 1966

Indoor Tennis Is Booming as Winter Nears

Park Players Press for 'Bubbles' but Cost Is Factor

By CHARLES FRIEDMAN

Whether it's played in a nylon "bubble" that looks like a bloated sausage, a converted television studio, an old chemical warehouse, a gloomy armory, a crowded school gymnasium or a "house" built specifically for its purposes, indoor tennis is entering the second year of an eye-opening comeback in many parts of the country.

More players are participating and more investors are extending funds, although in tennis, unlike other businesses, potential profit may not always be the deciding factor.

Around here, for instance, the builder of indoor courts could himself be an avid player like Joe Struhl. He determined to put up courts because he couldn't reserve them elsewhere at the time he preferred.

Thus the boom is self-de-

veloping. Of course there's always the hazard that it may outpace itself. Right now there are some 30 indoor centers in the metropolitan area.

Escape From Boredom

Actually tennis players don't ask much—just an escape from a peculiar melancholia triggered by the oncoming of winter, when outdoor courts close, and the opportunity to get into a few tournaments rather than read about those going on in warmer climes.

Some swingers with polar bear instincts hold out until the first snowfall before reluctantly retreating indoors. At places like the Town Club, though, they pitch in, brush off the snow and keep playing to the accompaniment of chattering teeth.

The 500 or so public park courts here stay open until the end of November. It's a long season, starting in April, for the permit-holders, but some are now petitioning Commissioner Tom Hoving to install bubbles for indoor play when it rains or gets cold. The bubbles could cost $15,000 apiece.

"The Commissioner is throwing money around for a lot of park projects, but there's nothing in it for the 25,000 people who buy tennis permits at $7.50 every year," says a Central Park buff. "He promised to put in lighting for night tennis, but didn't do it. We are getting a little mad at him."

Top Players Compete

A major factor that heightens indoor-tennis interest is tournament activity, and some owners have been obliging in that respect.

Last year saw a burst of tournaments at Geza Gazdag's Vanderbilt Club, Luke Sapan's Midtown Club, Nick's Indoor Courts, Struhl's and Chick Soloway's Tennis Indoors of New York, Freddie Botur's Park Avenue Tennis and Joe Martucci's Bergen Tennis Center in Waldwick, N. J.

By far the best was the international event at the Vanderbilt, which brought together Manuel Santana of Spain, Rafael Osuna of Mexico, Arthur Ashe, Gene Scott, Frank Froehling, Chuck McKinley and Charlie Pasarell. It ran for four days in a crazy

quilt place that used to be a television studio, and proved a big hit with the public.

Expense Is a Factor

Gazdag, who opened the Vanderbilt last year, plans to put on that tournament again, as well as the Eastern women's indoor championship.

"There was no profit, but it was good for tennis and the club," he says.

The Midtown will again sponsor the Eastern junior indoor clay championship. Sapan, a Long Island University basketball star in the Clair Bee era, has been partial to making his courts available to youngsters.

While most operators say they are satisfied with the public's response to indoor tennis, a bugaboo remains: It's expensive to play.

Membership fees generally range up to $500 for an hour a week in a 30-week season. The fee can be split among four persons who wish to play doubles. But for singles it's steep. Nonmembers pay $8 to $10 or more an hour, when a court is available.

"We haven't been able to attract the public park element," says one operator.

Charlie Masterson, a high-ranking Eastern senior player, serves in match at Tennis Indoors of New York, Woodside, Queens. There are some 30 indoor tennis centers here.

"They can't get used to the idea of paying more than $7.50 for the season."

"Our best customers? Doctors and stockbrokers, who else?"

October 30, 1966

Pro Tennis Obtains Five-Year Contract for Tournaments at Garden

FIRST OF SERIES WILL OPEN JUNE 7

Laver, Ralston in Field for $25,000 Event—Garden to Help Develop Tour

By THOMAS ROGERS

The establishment of an annual professional tennis tournament at Madison Square Garden and plans for pro tournaments "in other major arenas of the United States, Canada and Mexico" were announced yesterday.

These were the major items in a five-year agreement between the Garden and the International Professional Tennis Association.

Irving Mitchell Felt, chairman of the Garden Corporation, and the association's five-man executive committee made the announcement at a news conference at Toots Shor's restaurant on West 52d Street.

Under the agreement, the first tournament at the Garden will be held June 7 to 10. The event, for $25,000 in prize money, will present a field of 12 or 14.

The New York Times

ANNOUNCE TENNIS TOURNEY: Irving Mitchell Felt, right, the chairman of the Madison Square Garden Corporation, with Rod Laver, professional tennis star, at Toots Shor's restaurant yesterday. Laver will play in new tennis tournament scheduled at the Garden June 7 to 10.

Prize Money to Grow

Rod Laver, Ken Rosewall, Mal Anderson, Dennis Ralston, Fred Stolle, Earl Buchholz and Mike Davies have agreed to participate. The rest of the field, the draw and the breakdown of prize money will be announced later.

In following years, the prize money will be increased. Next year, for instance, when the tournament will be in the new Garden atop Pennsylvania Sta-

tion, the purse will be $35,000; in 1969, $45,000, and for the last two years of the agreement, $50,000.

Under the contract, Madison Square Garden Attractions, Inc., in conjunction with the executive committee of the I.P.T.A., will coordinate the scheduling of all North American events and television programing.

At present there are no plans for televising next month's tournament.

Television in Prospect

In the future, according to Fred J. Podesta, the president of Garden Attractions, Inc., "we will coordinate an international schedule with a sound television series."

"The program will substantially contribute to the growth of pro tennis by drawing larger audiences to the arenas and creating new fans for the sport through the medium of television," he declared.

The members of the pro association's executive committee are Wally Dill, who has been serving as association director; Buchholz, Davies and two businessmen, Joseph F. Cullman 3d, board chairman of Philip Morris, Inc., and Edward Hickey, vice president of the New England Merchants National Bank.

Dill, who took over the association in January, 1966, was enthusiastic about the agreement.

"The Garden has displayed far-sighted optimism on the future of tennis as a spectator sport," he said. "Our relationship is a natural one that will prove of the greatest value to tennis."

Last month the Garden entered a similar agreement with the United States Lawn Tennis Association, the governing body for amateur competition.

Under it, an international amateur tournament will be presented annually at the new Garden. The first is scheduled next March. 25.

May 9, 1967

Newcombe Captures Wimbledon Crown by Trouncing Bungert, 6-3, 6-1, 6-1

ONE-SIDED FINAL TAKES 70 MINUTES

German Unable to Handle Aussie's Powerful Game After Brief Early Lead

By FRED TUPPER
Special to The New York Times

WIMBLEDON, England, July 7—John Newcombe has won Wimbledon. The 23-year-old Australian demolished Wilhelm Bungert of West Germany, 6-3, 6-1, 6-1, over 70 minutes today in an anticlimax to this wonderful fortnight where reputations were shattered, upsets were routine and a new tennis generation made its breakthrough.

There have been other disappointing finals since the war. Jack Kramer allowed Tom Brown six games in 1947 in just 42 minutes, the fastest final ever; Lew Hoad lost five to Ashley Cooper in 1957, and Rod Laver five to Martin Mulligan in 1962.

Newcombe's shattering victory was the eighth for an Australian in the last 11 years, and the big, burly man from Sydney, seeded third, was one of only two seeded players to reach the quarter-finals.

"I've wanted to win Wimbledon since I was 10," said Newcombe. "I thought I could win it when I got the service break I lost back in the first set."

Career Started at 6

Newcombe had a relative picnic all the way through: He dropped two sets in all, one to Stan Smith, the American No. 11, and the other to Nikki Pilic of Yugoslavia, the only player to extend him.

The Australian has learned his trade well. He started playing tennis at 6, was coached weekends until he was 10, played his first Wimbledon at 17 and at 19 was the youngest Australian ever to play in a Davis Cup challenge round, with the United States the opponent.

Newcombe's shots are out of the textbook, hit with tremendous power. He is a net rusher and crowds it, probably too closely, but he is fit and fast enough to retreat for the smash or lob. His most effective weapon is that huge service, which he banged in game after game with brutal consistency this afternoon. It was like a hammerlock on Bungert. He broke it in the third game but never after that.

Bungert is one of the last true amateurs, a shy, humorous man who enjoys his tennis and plays about six weeks a year mostly for the fun of it. Yet the rigid stance, the jerky movement, the stoical mien all portray the Prussian image. He hit some ground shots standing at attention.

Wilhelm had a miraculous Wimbledon until this afternoon. The 28-year-old Dusseldorf sports dealer is a touch player and somehow always found it in the crisis. He takes the ball quickly on the rise, hits it suddenly at awkward angles for winners and is an effective volleyer. He played four five-set matches, dropped nine sets on his way to the final and, he said later, "packed my bags four times during the fortnight."

In the early minutes the German looked dangerous. At a game-all, he struck like lightning. A forced error, a forehand rifled across court, a backhand down the line and another forced error gave him the game at love. He led, 2-1, with his service to come and promptly made a botch of it. Three times he double-faulted in that long game, missed an easy smash and flubbed two volleys. Newcombe smiled with relief when he won it.

They were at 3-4 on service, Bungert leading, 40-15, when the vital break came. Wilhelm just missed with a couple of volleys, and at ad-out, Newcombe crashed a forehand across court into the clear to lead, 5-3. He had the set in 25 minutes.

From there on it was just a formality. Newcombe hurtled his service thunderbolts, Bungert became impatient and hurried his shots. Big John won his last service at love, and beamed as Princess Marina came on the court and handed over the silver cup. "Champagne tonight," he said.

July 8, 1967

MRS. KING SWEEPS 3 TENNIS TITLES AT WIMBLEDON

MRS. JONES LOSES

Billie Jean Scores, 6-3, 6-4, in Singles—First Sweep Since 1951

By FRED TUPPER
Special to The New York Times

WIMBLEDON, England, July 8—Mrs. Billie Jean King has done it again. The bouncing, bespectacled 23-year-old from Long Beach, Calif., defeated an old rival, Mrs. Ann Jones of Britain, in precisely one hour today to take the coveted Wimbledon tennis crown for the second year in a row.

Before an enormous center court crowd—some of whom had queued all night—the top-seeded Mrs. King won, 6-3, 6-4, in a fascinating, fluctuating battle of styles amid gusts of wind that whipped the canopies over the Royal Box, kicked up puffs of dust on this sacred patch of turfdom and made playing conditions far from easy.

Today was Billie Jean's finest four hours. She came off court shortly after 7 P.M. wearily grinning in delight with all three women's titles—singles, doubles and mixed doubles—for the first triple sweep since Doris Hart pulled it off in 1951.

Yesterday, John Newcombe of Australia beat Wilhelm Bungert to take the men's singles.

Tournament of Upsets

In this topsy-turvy Wimbledon, where six of the eight male seeded players were gone by quarter-final time and the reigning champion, Manuel Santana, was upset by Charles Pasarell of the United States on opening day, Billie Jean was the only player in the field to justify her singles seeding.

The emergence of Roger Taylor of Britain into the semi-finals and of third-seeded Mrs. Jones into the finals, after six years reaching the semi-finals, brought vast crowds through the gates. The final attendance figures of more than 300,000 were the largest in the 81-year history of the All-England lawn tennis championships.

By her singles victory this afternoon Billie Jean became the first woman to win the title twice since Maria Bueno of Brazil did it in 1959 and 1960.

Mrs. King was the favorite because over the years, around the world, she had won 10 of her 13 matches against Mrs. Jones on the big occasions. Billie Jean was favored, too, because this was where she first made her reputation at the age of 18 by knocking out the great Australian, Margaret Smith, and where she blasted Miss Bueno to reach her first final at 19.

The Californian's big serve and volley game thrives on the fast grass of center court, and she was off to a splendid start. She held her first service, with three advantage points against her, but then she dived pell-mell into the attack.

Mrs. Jones Storms Net

Mrs. Jones had a plan today. She had survived an early onslaught by Rosemary Casals in the semi-finals by discarding her stonewall base-court game and taking command of the net. So on her opening service Ann bustled netward and Billie Jean fired her rockets.

A backhand ripped down the line, another shot across court, a lob pulled Mrs. Jones back so that Billie Jean could volley a winner, and then another backhand streaked down the tape for the breakthrough.

Billie Jean just held her service to 3-love and suddenly was at 4-1 with a point for another break. It was beginning to look like a rout. The partisan crowd clapped perfunctorily as Mrs. King had the first set at 6-3.

Billie Jean quickly broke service again with two breathtaking ground shots through the holes. So there she was at 2-1 in the second set, riding high, with her booming service to come.

But Ann is not that easy to beat. Patiently she was slowing down Billie Jean, giving her a mixture of spin chops and lobs. Six times in that vital fourth game, the Briton had points to win it.

As the wind swirled around the court, Mrs. King began to miss the low volley. "I can't do it," she cried in distraction, but she held service to 3-1.

Mrs. King lost her next service, though, as Mrs. Jones increased the pressure, slapping a backhand shot down the line as the stadium exploded. They were at 3-all now, with Mrs. Jones toeing the service line.

Backhand Is Superb

With a magnificent volley, Billie Jean was at deuce and had the game as she wrong-footed the Briton with a background down the line. It was more than the crowd could bear.

Billie Jean was serving for the match and, in a dying surge, Mrs. Jones was at advantage. Four times this afternoon she had been poised for a break-through. Once she had made it.

With the scent of victory near, the American fired her cannonballs into the corners. A last looping Jones drive slipped over the baseline, and Mrs. King again had her Wimbledon.

"It was my service that did it," she said. "And I wanted to win this one for my coach." Her coach, Frank Brennan of Upper Saddle River, N.J., suffered a heart attack here yesterday and was said to be rest-ing comfortably in a hospital.

In one of the best doubles finals seen here in years, Billie Jean took her second title. Serving four love games in the last two sets, Mrs. King and tiny Rosemary Casals of San Francisco dethroned Maria Bueno and Nancy Richey, the 1966 winners, 9-11, 6-4, 6-2.

The doubles crown was the fourth here for Billie Jean. She won it in 1961 with Karen Hantze, again in 1962 with Mrs. Karen Hantze Susman and in 1965 with Miss Bueno.

And then, in early evening, Owen Davidson of Australia hit a shot off the wood that touched the baseline on match point to give him and Mrs. King the mixed doubles title, 7-5, 6-2, over Ken Fletcher of Australia and Miss Bueno. For Billie Jean, it was a day to remember.

Hewitt Triumphs Again

Bob Hewitt, long considered one of the world's great doubles players, paired with Frew McMillan, a South African who plays double-handed, to defeat Roy Emerson and Fletcher of Australia with surprising ease, 6-2, 6-3, 6-4.

Hewitt, an Australian who now represents South Africa, had won the title in 1962 and 1964 with Fred Stolle, now a professional.

The Americans won both singles in the Plate, confined to players who had been defeated in either the first or second rounds. Eighteen-year-old, freckled-face Patti Hogen of La Jolla, Calif., defeated Gail Sheriff of Australia, 6-2, 9-7, and Jim McManus of Berkeley, Calif., won from Gene Scott of St. James, L. I., 6-3, 6-2.

In the junior event, Mike Estep of Dallas took only two games from the new Spanish prodigy, Manuel Orantes.

July 9, 1967

Plays Tennis Like a Man, Speaks Out Like — Billie Jean King

WHEN she first started playing in tennis tournaments, little Billie Jean Moffitt found her aggressive net-rushing style ineffectual against the "backcourters" — "the kids that are very steady, and play from the back court, and hit lobs all day" waiting for the opponent to make the first mistake. "They used to say, 'Ha, ha, all we need to do is get two or three back on you and you'll miss the fourth shot.' And I said, 'We'll see who's winning when we're 16.'"

It didn't take that long. When she was 15 she won her first big tournament with her own hard-hitting style, and since then she hasn't slackened a bit: she still plays a man's game, darting toward the net and glowering over it like an angry bear, covering the court as a fly covers a sugar bowl, slamming serves and mixing ground shots the way Juan Marichal mixes pitches. Her hard, grueling game has led her to the top of women's amateur tennis, and following this summer's capture of the "Triple Crown" at Wimbledon—her second consecutive women's singles title, her fourth women's doubles championship and the mixed doubles title—Mrs. Billie Jean Moffitt King is now comfortably lodged as the world's No. 1 women's tennis player.

One of the few honors still to elude the dynamic Mrs. King is, oddly enough, the championship of her own country. But she will have a chance to remedy that this week when she goes into the United States Lawn Tennis Association tournament at Forest Hills beginning Friday. The odds are strong in her favor.

THE world's top-ranked women's player is 23 years old, stands 5 feet 6 inches tall and weighs 140 pounds

("That is, when things are going right—I love to eat"). Unlike most men tennis players, who wear a sweat band around one wrist, Billie Jean—as if to emphasize her femininity—wears a gold bracelet which a friend gave her several years ago and which she hasn't taken off since. With short wavy brown hair, blue harlequin glasses, 5 million freckles and a Doris Day face, King seems an ordinary attractive young lady.

But she is probably amateur tennis's most colorful and controversial player today. "I have a tendency to say things that should be off the record," she admits. "I don't know if our men really want to be the best in the world," she once told a reporter asking about American tennis players. "There's no glory in this country!" And when a Chicago newspaperman recently approached Billie Jean with a request to interview her for a feature on the women's page, she blurted angrily: "That's the trouble with this sport. We've got to get it off the society page and onto the sports pages!"

Recently, in the clubhouse of the élite Town Club in the Milwaukee suburb of Fox Point, where she was playing in the National Clay Courts Championships, Billie Jean held forth in her usual outspoken way on one of her favorite subjects: what's wrong with American tennis. "Tennis is a very good sport," she began, "but you've got to get it away from the club atmosphere and into the public places, the parks, arenas like Madison Square Garden. You've got to get tennis into places where everyone feels welcome. I don't think the average person feels welcome in a

HAL HIGDON, a freelance writer, is the author of "Heroes of the Olympics."

147

club atmosphere like this unless he's a member"—and she looked pointedly around her at the ornately fashioned bar and the ornately fashioned men and women sitting around it. "If you're a member, it's great! You get to meet all the players. You can see all your buddies. And after the match you can wander into the bar and drink.

"You look at Sports Illustrated when it has a tennis article in it. Too clubby. Much too clubby. Drawings of Forest Hills. Well, let's get away from all that. Tennis takes stamina, so much stamina, but you never think of it as a sport. You picture people sipping mint juleps under an umbrella, and it's not that way. People think of tennis as a sissy sport and this is what we have to get away from." She talk such as this, of course, that causes many members of the staid and usually stuffy tennis world—especially those in the dominant United States Lawn Tennis Association—to shudder.

MRS. KING is as outspoken and controversial on the court as off. "Billie Jean's a ham," says her husband Larry. "She likes to play before fans. And she lets them know when she's angry." If the call of an official displeases her, she does not hesitate to raise her voice to tell him. After one close line call in Fox Point, she snapped at the line judge: "How can you see from that position?" The line judge lifted his nose as if to indicate that he had been judging for 30 years and would do as he damn pleased, but following game point, when he thought no one was looking, he shifted his chair so he could see straight down the line.

In addition to haranguing officials, Billie Jean maintains a constant conversation with herself, particularly after a bad shot and always in a voice clearly audible in the grandstand. "Oh, Billie, think!" she'll shout, or "Boy, I'm telling you!" or "You've got the touch of an ox!" or her favorite expression: "Nuts!" She also has been known to mutter a few other less homey expressions under her breath, and in fact several years ago the U.S.L.T.A. apparently considered censuring her for her language on court. Billie Jean grumbles: "In basketball or football the players are cussing out there like troopers. But if you're a tennis player you've got to be jolly nice all the time." She admits, however, that lately her language has changed like her tennis game, to become less flamboyant and more mechanical. Billie Jean also dislikes the sepulchral atmosphere at most tennis tournaments and would like to see the fans shout and cheer and even boo for a change. The conservatives within tennis — that is, practically everybody — raise their eyebrows at this suggestion, too.

Controversy seems to snap around Billie Jean's heels. After the 1965 season, during which she reached the finals at Forest Hills (losing to Australia's Margaret Smith) and won for the third time the women's doubles crown at Wimbledon (with Brazil's Maria Bueno as partner), Billie

Probably the amateur ranks' most colorful, controversial player, a 23-year-old Californian (seen here at the recent Wightman Cup matches) has slammed and agonized her way to the top of women's tennis.

Jean seemed assured of being ranked No. 1 in America. The U.S.L.T.A.'s national ranking committee did list her in that position, an action approved by its executive committee. But Al Buman, president of the Texas Lawn Tennis Association, wanted the top ranking for Nancy Richey of Dallas, who had won the National Clay Courts Championships, a tournament Billie Jean had skipped. Buman's proposal that Billie Jean be dumped to No. 2 lost before the executive committee and again the following day before the U.S.L.T.A. membership. Finally Buman suggested that Billie Jean and Nancy be allowed to share the No. 1 ranking. This compromise proposal passed, partly because Buman had the votes of the clay-courters, angry because Billie Jean usually bypassed their national championships. The result of the vote did less to discredit Billie Jean than to discredit the U.S.L.T.A.

Billie Jean won Wimbledon the following season, but when she appeared at Forest Hills for a second-round match with Australia's Kerry Melville, she found Texas official Buman sitting in the raised umpire's chair. She promptly kicked up a

storm and asked that another umpire be substituted, but the officials denied her request and Buman himself declined to move. Billie Jean proceeded to blow higher than a lob to the baseline, losing her match in straight sets even though she had beaten Kerry Melville just two weeks before, 6-1, 6-2.

Billie Jean today prefers to forget all that. "I feel a lot of the trouble was my own fault," she admits. "I shouldn't have come unglued at the seams." Yet she dislikes Forest Hills as a tournament: "It's run more for the officials than for the players." And she still harbors a grudge against the U.S.L.T.A., although she prefers to discuss it off the record. "Don't get me wrong," she insists. "I have a lot of friends in the organization—but let's say we've had our differences."

Billie Jean King has risen to the top of women's tennis by following a daily training regimen that would impress even Jim Ryun. When not traveling the tournament circuit, the Kings live in a one-bedroom apartment in Berkeley, Calif., where Larry attends the University of California. They selected their apart-

ment because of the view across the street, which happens to be of the Berkeley Tennis Club.

BILLIE JEAN rises between 8 and 8:30 and by 10 she is on the court for two hours of drills aimed at perfecting her shots and improving her conditioning. She also may mix in some exercises or run short sprints preferring speed work to long-distance running. She practices at Berkeley seven days a week unless Rosemary Casals — who herself reached the semifinals at Wimbledon this year—is in town and then the two girls will split their practice time between Berkeley and Golden Gate Park near Rosie's home.

Following lunch Billie Jean will play a match with one of the men players ("because men are tougher") and three or four sets of doubles with Rosie. Although Larry, a handsome blond law student, lettered on his high school tennis team and does some coaching during the summer to help the family treasury, he rarely plays tennis with his wife, figuring she can benefit more by playing different players. He is a shrewd analyst of tennis style, but prefers to leave the actual coaching of his wife to Frank Brennan, who runs a tennis clinic in Upper Saddle River, N. J., and with whom the Kings stay between summer tournaments. At Wimbledon this year Larry talked a play-by-play account of Billie Jean's matches into a tape recorder, but admits he did it not for analysis but to keep himself from being nervous. "The previous year I ate bonbons," he says.

Billie Jean finishes practice around 6 or 7 and then cooks dinner, usually steak. She likes to read, particularly books on psychology, and eventually hopes to complete her college degree in that subject. Partly to aid her concentration, Larry taught his wife to play bridge and in her first duplicate bridge tournament they finished fourth. She thus owns one-third of a Master Point.

"Billie Jean also likes to dance," says her father, Bill Moffitt, "although she probably won't admit it." Moffitt, a fireman in Long Beach, Calif., likes to tell the story of the high school teacher who once told Billie Jean that, though a good tennis player, she could never master anything as complex as modern dance. Billie Jean accepted the challenge, joined the dance class and became so proficient that the teacher later urged her to concentrate on dancing instead of tennis.

BILLIE JEAN seems to have been endowed with a certain athletic talent at birth on Nov. 22, 1943. Her father played basketball, baseball and ran track; her mother is an excellent swimmer. This summer Randy Moffitt, her 18-year-old brother, pitched three no-hitters and one one-hitter in four games in the local Connie Mack baseball tournament. "Whenever the Fire Department had a picnic," says her father, "the men would always want Billie Jean to play shortstop or third base. She had natural ability in hitting the ball and fielding and throwing."

When Billie Jean was 10 she

played shortstop with a group of girls mostly 14 and 15 years old. Her team won the Long Beach softball championship, but Billie Jean realized her potential in that sport was limited: "I told my mother, 'You know I love softball, but · d still like to be in a sport where you could be considered a lady.' My parents, especially Dad, suggested I play tennis, and I said, 'What's tennis?'"

When she learned tennis. was a game in which you could both run and hit a ball, Billie Jean decided to try it, but her parents, aware of the changeableness of children, made her pay for that first racquet out of her earnings from odd jobs. Billie Jean placed a glass jar in the cupboard and when it finally contained $8, she became a tennis player.

Tennis professional Clyde Walker gave free lessons once a week at each of five public parks in Long Beach, and Billie Jean soon would trail him from park to park. She played few games those first years, spending most of her time standing with a bucket of balls hitting them one at a time over the net. For a while she walked three-and-a-half miles to school each day to strengthen her legs. When she started entering tournaments, she invariably would lose in the first round to the backcourters, who would play steadily while Billie Jean charged all over the court. "I've always played a net game," she says. "It's part of my personality. It's *me*! One day Clyde asked me; 'What are you doing at the net?' I said, 'I don't know. This is fun, whatever I'm doing.' He said, 'You get back in the backcourt and learn those groundstrokes first!'"

Billie Jean's groundstrokes, relatively speaking, remain the weak point of her game, but she feels that she now profits from the flexibility she learned at that early age. "I was very erratic when I started playing tournaments," she says. "But I learned an all-round game, and it paid off, even though I suffered. Now a lot of children don't realize this, or they realize it but can't stand to lose. I couldn't stand to lose. It used to just *kill* me! But I felt in the long run if I really wanted to achieve my goals I would have to lose."

I N 1958 Billie Jean won the Southern California championship in her age group, so a number of tennis fans from Long Beach raised money to send her and her mother (as chaperon) to the National Girl's 15 and Under Championships in Middletown, Ohio. Billie Jean lost in the quarter-finals, then watched sorrowfully as most of the other girls continued east to play in the 18-and-under tournament: "I nearly died, but we couldn't afford to go any further. When we arrived home in Long Beach my mother had only a few dollars in her purse."

The following year Billie Jean played in the Eastern Grass Court Championships against 1959 Wimbledon champion Maria Bueno. She lost, but her showing impressed tennis coach Frank Brennan. "You're going to be good some day," he said, "but how come you use a nylon racket?" Billie Jean admitted she couldn't afford gut, so he sent her some and has continued as her coach and adviser to this day.

In 1960 Billie Jean reached the finals of the National Girl's 18 and Under Championships, losing to Karen Hantze. The following year she traveled to Wimbledon, where she and Karen won the women's doubles title. Billie Jean was 17 and Karen 18, the youngest pair to achieve such a victory.

Billie Jean returned to Wimbledon in 1962 and startled the tennis world by defeating top-seeded Margaret Smith in the opening round, the first time a first-ranked player had lost that early. She made the quarterfinals and with Karen repeated her doubles victory. In 1963, though college now left her little time for practice, she went to Wimbledon and, still unseeded, upset three seeded players—Maria Bueno, Ann Jones and Leslie Turner—to make the finals, where she lost to Margaret Smith. Margaret told her: "You know, Billie Jean, you've got all the shots, but I always wear you out. I know you don't practice. You just don't play enough. I know you could win Wimbledon. Why don't you give it a·go?"

But Billie Jean wasn't yet ready to give it a go. "I was in love," she says of 1964. "I was in another world." She had met Larry King one night in the library and soon they began to talk of marriage. Nevertheless, she made the semi-finals at Wimbledon that year on what amounted to a week's practice, then decided she either had to take tennis seriously or give it up. Billie Jean and Larry became engaged that fall and two weeks later she left for Australia to train three months under Mervyn Rose.

"T HE first three or four weeks I thought I was going to die," she remembers. "Every day I could hardly drag myself out of bed, and I was just learning what tennis was all about." The Australians had her running, doing exercises and participating in two-on-one drills where two players guard one side of the net with the single purpose of returning all shots to the remotest possible corners of the court. When she first began two-on-one drills she found herself unable to last more than five minutes; after three months she could retrieve shots for an entire hour.

Learning a whole new game did not come easy for Billie Jean. In an attempt to improve her consistency, Rose shortened all her strokes, which immediately affected her timing. For instance, when she tossed the ball up for a serve it would be in the wrong place when her racket came around. "In one match I had 35 double faults," she remembers. "Merv said, 'Don't get discouraged if it takes three months, or even a year. I promise you that in six months you're going to notice the difference.' And September, 1965, is when I played Margaret Smith and realized that the work I had done had made all the difference in the world."

Billie Jean lost in the finals at Forest Hills to Margaret, but said: "I realized I could beat her and that I could beat anyone in the world." The following spring she did beat Margaret in the South African championships, then won the singles title at Wimbledon in 1966 and again this year. Even the U.S.L.T.A. has had to

acknowledge her as the best woman tennis player in the world.

I T is Billie Jean's early-developed ability to play an all-round game that has brought her to this peak, plus the sheer speed of a well-tuned body. "She's a hell of an athlete," says Arthur Ashe, the top-ranked American amateur. "That's the most important thing for a woman. Forget the strokes—if you can move on your feet, you can win." And her husband Larry adds, "She can run down balls that other girls won't even try for."

Billie Jean originally used a "Continental" grip which permitted her to hit both forehand and backhand shots without shifting her hand on the racket, but now she has modified this so it is closer to the more standard "Eastern" grip. Within the last month she also has changed rackets. She now uses a new steel-frame racket which she claims is faster and whippier than the old wooden ones.

Her strongest shot is her volley at the net. Her backhand (which she can hit with topspin, underspin or even sidespin) is stronger than her forehand. Her main serve is the standard slicer, although occasionally she will change pace by offering a flat serve, harder for the server to control. For the second serve she can utilize either the spin or the American twist, the latter a serve most other girls can't master because of the strain imposed on back and stomach muscles. It is in areas such as this that Billie Jean's abilities as an "athlete" give her the edge over the backcourters who merely know how to hit the ball back.

Yet echoes of her erratic past occasionally return to haunt her. In the National Clay Court Championships in Milwaukee Billie Jean lost in straight sets in the semi-finals to Rosemary Casals, seemingly unable to control either her serves or returns. The suggestion that she might be unable to play well on clay continues to irk her. "Look at the record," she snaps, then ticks off on her well-manicured fingers the high-ranked opponents she has defeated on clay. "Sure I lose on clay, but I also lose on grass, too!"

The difference between tennis played on clay and on grass courts is subtle but simple: the ball bounces higher and slower on clay than on grass. Thus, the tennis player has more time to reach balls hit away from him and aces come less frequently. A strong first serve is less important, and the effectiveness of the volley from the net is somewhat muted. "You have to put three balls away to win a point on clay compared to one on grass," says Larry King.

Larry insists that his wife's speed still gives her the edge on clay as well as on grass, but a backcourter able to return balls and wait for a Billie Jean error will at least look better against her on clay—and sometimes may upset her. Significantly, however, three of the four tournaments Billie Jean will need to win to achieve the grand slam (Australia, Wimbledon and Forest Hills) are played on grass, and the fourth (France) is played on a bouncier clay surface that she likes better than the clay in America.

D OES Billie Jean King deserve to be ranked with the great women tennis players of the past? Perry T. Jones, president of the Southern California Tennis Association, says: "Mrs. King so far is the best of her day. That is, 1967. But if she should continue to have losses as she did in Milwaukee she'll have to go down. Now she can lose occasionally, but the great players didn't lose occasionally. So I can't put Mrs. King in the same class with somebody like Suzanne Lenglen, or Helen Wills Moody, who won Wimbledon eight times. She's going to have to stand the test of time before she can be ranked as one of the all-time greats. But if she continues to dominate women's tennis for the next three or four years, she will go down as one of the greats." Perry Jones suspects that Billie Jean might have beaten Doris Hart but at present may rank a shade behind Maureen Connolly, who won Wimbledon three times and achieved the grand slam in 1953.

According to Jack Kramer: "I don't think she's reached the caliber of the real best of the Americans I've seen —such as Helen Wills Moody, or Alice Marble, or Maureen Connolly, or Pauline Betz — and I think that Margaret Smith and Maria Bueno at their top would have an edge. But I think she's about ready to jump into that group."

Meanwhile, Billie Jean figures that she has another two or three years of highly competitive tennis before time comes to settle down and raise a family. At the present she has focused her eyes on one goal: winning the grand slam. But that will have to wait at least until next year, since she did not play the Australian championships this year, being laid up with stomach trouble, and she lost the French championships.

Seated in the clubhouse of the Town Club, she speculated on her future: "It's really hard to commit yourself to win the grand slam. I may never win it. Roy Emerson tried for 13 years and never won it. But as long as you try your hardest, that's all you can do. I think it's good to set goals even if you never achieve them. At least try. I think a lot more people should do it, a lot more often in every field. Not just sports, school. It's no disgrace losing as long as you try, and give it all you have at the moment. Sometimes your spirit is good but the flesh refuses, because I've had days when I'm trying like crazy and I can't find the court. You've got days like this, in business or anything. But you always bounce back and you always keep going.

"You know, one tennis match to me is almost like life. There are so many ups and downs. You can be down to where you think there's no way possible you can win a match. You just keep trying step by step and finally you win. The next time you're in a position when you're ahead and you lose. It's just like life. Life's like that." ∎

Steel Racquet Kicking Up a Storm

By CHARLES FRIEDMAN

"It's faster, whippier."

"It takes a lot of adjusting."

"My serve is 30 per cent more effective."

"I wouldn't trust it; too dangerous to control."

Fans at Forest Hills are excited about the controversial steel tennis racquet being used in the national championships for the first time. In fact, the round-headed racquet, developed by René Lacoste, the old-time French Musketeer, is almost as popular a topic of conversation as who will win what has become, through casualties, a wide-open tournament.

Borotra Flails Away

On opening day, Jean Borotra, the 70-year-old Bounding Basque, another of the unforgettable Musketeers, walked onto the court and unveiled the racquet. It had already been used in United States tournaments, but never at Forest Hills.

The old warrior flailed away with it and gallantly went down to defeat in the senior division. He missed a lot of shots, but never, as many players do, did he look at the racquet as if to say, "You're to blame, you rat, not me."

And, at the end, he lovingly tucked it under his arm, convinced that it was not his comrade, Lacoste, who had let him down, but plain old hardening of the arteries.

The racquet is made of chrome-plated tubing and stainless wire, a frame supposedly more durable and resilient than wood, much like the steel-shafted golf clubs, which first gave Lacoste the idea. It takes conventional nylon or gut stringing, but with a special technique. A major innovation is the open throat, which reduces wind resistance in the act of stroking. The theory is that this results in a faster, more powerful shot.

While many top players have besieged the Wilson Sporting Goods Company, which manufactures it, for information about the racquet, only nine have made the switch from wood for the nationals. They are Mrs. Billie Jean King, Rosemary Casals, Kathy Harter, Chuck McKinley, Clark Graebner and his wife, Carole; Stephanie DeFina, Gene Scott and Joaquin Loyo-Mayo of Mexico.

Others are eager to try it, including Charlie Pasarell, but they are committed to the wooden racquets put out by rival manufacturers, which they get free, or are unwilling to change at this point of the season. Of course, they could buy the steel racquet, but they'd better not get caught playing with it, or the free service ends. Also, they would have to spend $40 to $52 for it, the current retail price. That

Steel racquet with insert showing stringing method.

is about $10 to $22 more than what a first-class wooden racquet costs.

Praised by Champion

For players who don't get racquets free, the difference in price apparently is not a great obstacle to sales of the Wilson T2000, as the "steelie" is labeled. It has hit the market hard in recent weeks through a combination of published advertising and comments by those using it.

For instance, when Mrs. King and Miss Casals showed up with it at the Eastern grass tournaments, they told everyone they were getting better results. Mrs. King, the Wimbledon champion and the top favorite in the nationals, said it gave her a faster, whippier stroke.

Immediately a host of players began looking for Joe Boggia, Wilson's liaison man, who travels the tournament circuit.

McKinley, the former Davis Cup hero and now a part-time player, surprisingly began showing the form of his glory years, earning the respect he used to command.

"I'm a little guy, which puts me at a disadvantage in serving," he said. "But the racquet, I found, has put more power into my serve and I'm getting the ball in more often."

Scott said the only complaint he had was that the racquet was so easy to maneuver that sometimes "I don't feel I'm part of the game." He conceded that it took time to adjust to it, "just as when the steel shaft was introduced in golf."

Mrs. Graebner, who has come back strongly after a year's retirement, during which she had a baby, wanted to play with the racquet at Wimbledon, but Boggia couldn't get her more than two. Her husband confiscated one and she didn't want to be left with just the other for the big tournament.

"I did pretty well with the wooden one at Wimbledon, so I'm continuing to use it for the rest of the season," said the attractive star. "But I'm going to switch to steel next year.

"That racquet does all the work. The ball comes off so fast that your opponent finds it hard to tell where it's going. It gives you more touch and you can make more flick shots."

Her husband chimed in: "I like the feel of the ball on the strings. For me, it's easier to serve and volley."

For the average swinger, however, a few doubts persist, mainly on the matter of control.

"It seems that you just tip the ball and it goes over the baseline," said one. "I've found it good for certain shots and not so good for others. And I'm not sure whether to have it strung loosely or tightly, or with nylon or gut."

Another had this to say:

"It's strictly a fad thing. Let's face it. It's the player wielding the racquet who tells the ball what to do, not the racquet."

A woman club player said she was through with the racquet after having given it a week's trial.

"See this," she said, pointing to a blood-scabbed shin. "That damn steel hurts like hell." Unfortunately she had a serving flaw.

September 3, 1967

Newcombe and Mrs. King Capture National Tennis Crowns at Forest Hills

GRAEBNER BOWS BY 6-4, 6-4, 8-6

Aussie Is Sharp While Foe's Serve Fails—Mrs. Jones Hurt in 11-9, 6-4 Loss

By ALLISON DANZIG

John Newcombe of Australia and Mrs. Billie Jean King of Berkeley, Calif., added the United States championship to their Wimbledon titles yesterday and stand indisputably as the monarchs of amateur tennis the world over.

The 23-year-old Mrs. King became the first player of this country since 1961 to win the women's title when she repeated her victory in the Wimbledon final over Mrs. Ann Haydon Jones of Britain, 11-9, 6-4, as 10,000 looked on in the stadium of the West Side Tennis Club at Forest Hills, Queens.

Mrs. King stands also as the first woman player to win the triple crown of singles, doubles and mixed doubles in both the British and American championships since Alice Marble garnered them in 1939. Rosemary Casals of San Francisco and Owen Davidson of Australia were her doubles partners.

Newcombe, also 23, who was runner-up a year ago to Fred Stolle of Australia, ended the striking progress of Clark Graebner of Beachwood, Ohio, through the tournament by winning the final, 6-4, 6-4, 8-6. They had met also at Wimbledon, where Newcombe was the winner, 17-15, 6-3, 6-4.

So the title went to a player other than a representative of the United States for the 12th successive time since 1955, when Tony Trabert was the winner.

Harold Brown, the Secretary of the Air Force, presented the trophies to the champions and runners-up. He was assisted by Robert J. Kelleher, the president of the United States Lawn Tennis Association, and Henry Benisch, the president of the West Side Club.

10,000 in Stadium

The presence of a home player in the final of the men's

championship for the first time since 1963 probably accounted for the crowd of 10,000 that turned out despite threatening weather following a morning rain.

Graebner's unexpected success in having defeated Roy Emerson in a match lasting almost three hours and his sensational comeback victory over Jan Leschly of Denmark, after he had lost the first two sets, in another marathon of 2 hours 37 minutes had nurtured hopes that at long last a player of this country would win the championship.

These hopes were dispelled before the match was 10 minutes under way Newcombe had not been playing too impressively in the tournament, but now he demonstrated imediately that he was razor sharp and in the mood for swift execution.

Fast on on his feet, merciless in fighting with all his fury for every point and'intimidating with his service and backhand return of service, he got on top at once. After Graebner had won the opening game on service, the big Australian took the next five games, and the glum gallery had a sense of Graebner's impending doom.

Graebner's service was not functioning. He was double-faulting and failing to get the first ball in lay, and Newcombe was knocking back the second serve for winners or to provoke the volleying error to set up the winning shot for him.

When Newcombe broke service at love to start the second set as Graebner double-faulted on the final point, the futility of the Americans' cause was apparent. Graebner made a brave fight in the long second game, only to be thwarted by two successive aces, and Newcombe won his next three service games at love.

Serves Ace After Ace

Then came a turn, and hopes began to revive. Newcombe lost some of his fire in the third set and Graebner's service began to hit for aces, while his backhand was suddenly performing like his opponent's. He was passing Newcombe and forcing him into repeated volleying errors.

Could Graebner be on the way to repeating his rally against Leschly? It seemed he could as he went ahead at 5-2, breaking service with four beautiful backhand returns and serving aces galore in game after game to the cheers of the gallery.

But Newcombe, regaining his control, came back on the attack with power and accuracy and a deadliness at the net that put him again in command. He ran through three games with the loss of only 3 points.

Graebner caused a final stir as he hit three successive aces to win the 11th game, but after that he could win only 3 more points.

Mrs. Jones gave Mrs. King

Mrs. Jones Displays Courage in Defeat

The New York Times (by Don Charles)

Mrs. Ann Haydon Jones, foreground, and Mrs. Billie Jean King during their final-round match at Forest Hills yesterday. Mrs. King was extended to 20 games in the first set.

United Press International

In the fourth game of the second set Mrs. Jones, who had pulled a muscle, collapsed. When she failed to rise, Mrs. King ran to her aid. Mrs. Jones, however, continued play.

her stiffest fight of the tournament, in which the champion, did not back down. The performance of the left-handed British player was all the more commendable because she was handicapped by the recurrence of a pulled hamstring muscle that had her hobbling at times in the first set and caused her to fall in pain in the fourth game of the second set.

Mrs. King ran to her opponent's assistance, as did the referee, Dan Johnson, and linesmen. Mrs. Jones resumed play shortly to a burst of applause.

Mrs. King won largely on her speed and volleying ability. But she was challenged severely throughout. The games were unusually prolonged and the two sets required an hour 37 minutes.

Brian Tobin of Australia won the championship for men 35 years and over. He defeated Jack Darrah of San Mateo, Calif., 6-3, 6-3.

September 11, 1967

CHAPTER 3

OPEN TENNIS

Chris Evert was the darling of the Forest Hills
crowd when as the latest teenage wonder, she
first made her mark in 1971.

British Vote Open Tennis, Admitting Pros to Wimbledon

WORLD OFFICIALS DEFIED BY ACTION

Plan Accepted by Margin of 295 Votes to 5—Aussies Will Contest Move

By ANTHONY LEWIS
Special to The New York Times

LONDON, Dec. 14—The tennis barons of Britain agreed today to abolish the ancient line between amateurs and professionals and throw Wimbledon open to all.

The action, taken at the annual meeting of the Lawn Tennis Association, is the most serious challenge yet to the many countries that have long resisted open tennis. It could lead to a major struggle between different national tennis groups.

The International Lawn Tennis Federation, which has repeatedly rejected open tennis proposals, has threatened massive retaliation against the British move. It would boycott tournaments here and suspend any players who participated.

Today's meeting approved by an overwhelming margin a tentative decision for open tournaments, made by the British association's council on Oct. 5. There were only five no votes in a meeting of 300.

Deadline is Put Back

As a final gesture to permit international agreement, the association put off the effective date of its new rules for four months. Instead of Jan. 1, they will operate from April 22.

The delay makes no practical difference here, since the regular series of spring tournaments leading to Wimbledon begins after April 22. The new rules will be used first at the Bournemouth meeting, starting April 24.

But the delay will give the I.L.T.F. another chance to consider the problem. It has a meeting scheduled for April 19 and 20.

A further strong stand by the I.L.T.A. against open tournaments could, in theory, lead to a last-minute backdown by the British authorities. But most of the tennis world believes the decision now is final.

The idea of open tournaments is to end what authorities all over the world have complained about for years — the shamateurism that plagues high-class tennis.

Amateurs in name are known to bargain for extravagant expenses. Many play virtually full-time and live in considerable luxury without any visible source of income.

"We feel we can no longer endure the present situation," Derek Penman of the British association said in seconding the motion for a change in the rules today. "We must take action on our own account to make the game honest.

"For too long now we have been governed by a set of amateur rules that are quite unenforceable.

"We know that so-called amateur players bargain for payments grossly in excess of what they are entitled to but without which they cannot live.

"We know that tournament committees connive at this, else there would be no players at their tournaments."

An Australian representative of the I. L. T. F. at today's meeting made clear that the fight against open tennis was likely to go on. Ben Barnett said:

"If this decision is passed, Australia will not let its players compete in Britain, and any who did so would be suspended. The international federation's committee of management fervently hope you will not break away from the federation."

But the world's leading pro's would now be able to play at Wimbledon and about a dozen more leading amateurs who are expected to sign professional contracts in the next two months would presumably join them.

December 15, 1967

U.S.L.T.A. VOTES FOR OPEN TENNIS

Threatens to Leave World Federation Over Issue

By ALLISON DANZIG
Special to The New York Times

CORONADO, Calif., Feb. 3—The United States Lawn Tennis Association took its strongest position in favor of open tennis today, but voted unanimously to maintain the distinction between amateur and professional and preserve its schedule of tournaments.

At the 87th annual session, the delegates posted the threat of resigning from the International Lawn Tennis Federation if it did not sanction open competition between amateurs and professionals.

At the same time they demanded self-determination in setting up realistic amateur rules, and expressed their resolve to enforce the rules and end the "shamateurism" of excessive expense payments.

The U.S.L.T.A. did not go all the way in giving the British Lawn Tennis Association the backing it had asked in its rebellion against the federation. Britain is scheduled to be suspended from the federation April 22 if it goes through with its plan to conduct Bournemouth as an open championship on that date, and Wimbledon in June.

The delegates took a stronger supporting position than did the Lawn Tennis Association of Australia, which voted Jan. 30

for open tournaments and ending the amateur-pro distinction, but only within the framework of the federation.

They were to have voted on a proposal to allow our amateurs to play in an open Wimbledon. However, a substitute proposal was offered by the New England Association, in which self-determination on open tournaments was requested. Thus the federation was presented with the prospect of the United States withdrawing from membership if it did not grant sanction at its forthcoming special meeting.

The special meeting has been tentatively scheduled for Paris March 30 in the hope that the crisis precipitated by Britain's threatened suspension may be resolved.

Next Saturday or Sunday representatives of tennis's Big Four—the United States, Britain, Australia and France—will meet in Paris to set up the date and agenda.

Robert J. Kelleher of Beverly Hills, re-elected today as president of the U.S.L.T.A., likely will be the United States representative at Paris. He will be accompanied by Alastair B. Martin of Katonah, N. Y., also re-elected first vice president.

Dissent by Sorlien

The New England resolution, seconded by Henry Benisch of the Eastern Association, was adopted with one dissenting vote, by the Middle States Association. The vote was cast by Richard Sorlien of Philadelphia, who pleaded for a new effort to obtain open tournaments within the framework of the federation.

In settling on the language of the resolution, there was considerable debate as to whether it should read the U.S.L.T.A. "may tender" or "will tender" its resignation from the federation.

How far Kelleher would be permitted to go in pressing the federation for sanction of open tournaments was also strongly debated.

Melvin Bergman of Toledo and Martin Tressel of Pittsburgh, a former president, warned against going to the special meeting "with a shotgun" and on the possible risk of disqualification from the Davis Cup matches.

John Sisson of San Marino felt that Kelleher should be given the strongest possible hand, as did Martin and Edward Turville of St. Petersburg, a former U.S.L.T.A. president.

John Newcombe's concentration, evident in this 1975 photo, helped him to win three Wimbledon titles. The most exciting came in 1971 after a great battle with Stan Smith.

Sees Strong Federation

Martin said the resolution would make for a "strong federation, legalized open tennis and the withering of sham amateurism."

Turville argued that Kelleher "will make the federation realize we are serious and will no longer countenance what has been going on, and that he is not going over there on a mission of folly."

Lawerence A. Baker of New York, counsel for the association and a former president, was asked his interpretation of Kelleher's mandate at the federation meeting. He said he considered it restrictive and, should the meeting fail to sanction open tournaments, Kelleher would refer back to the U.S.L.T.A. on the possibility of taking it out of the federation.

Kelleher said:

"We do not want to defy the federation, as Britain has done, or to be thrown out. We believe in rules and going to the federation to do legally what we think they should do. We want the rules to be changed so they can be honestly administered."

Later, at a news conference, he said he was satisfied with the action taken and felt he could present the strongest case for a change at the federation session.

On amateurism, he said the resolution was significant in that "the U.S.L.T.A., as a matter of policy, has declared itself in favor of honest rules honestly enforced, and is determined to see that they are enforced."

The delegates agreed to reconvene "by April 20 or 20 days after the I.L.T.F. special meeting to consider the report and act on the recommendations of our delegate and at that time to take such action as may be desirable."

William J. Clothier 2d of Philadelphia received the Samuel Hardy Award from the National Tennis Educational Foundation for outstanding service over a quarter of a century.

Bill Lufler, head professional at the West Side Tennis Club in Forest Hills, Queens, and Perry T. Jones, president of the Southern California Association, also received awards.

Re-elected with Kelleher and Martin were Robert S. Piatt of Louisville, secretary and J. Clarence Davies Jr. of New York, treasurer. Robert B. Colwell of Seattle was elected second vice president.

Davies, in the treasurer's report, said the association had a profit of $14,115 in 1967 and a balance of $149,861.

W. Harcourt Woods of Short Hills, N. J., the chairman of the Davis Cup committee, said the United States could look forward to playing four of its five possible cup matches at home this year.

February 4, 1968

Open Tennis Is Approved by World Federation

NO DISSENT HEARD

Kelleher of U.S. Says 'Incredible Result' Gained in Paris

By FRED TUPPER
Special to The New York Times

PARIS, March 30—In a historic decision, the International Lawn Tennis Federation voted unanimously today for open tennis. That means that professionals will be allowed to compete against amateurs in a limited number of tournaments.

Not one dissenting voice was heard as the entire agenda was approved with resounding applause at this extraordinary general meeting, fittingly enough held in the Place de la Concorde.

"It was an incredible result achieved here," said Bob Kelleher, president of the United States Lawn Tennis Association, "in a spirit of highest co-operation and friendliness."

Victory for British

Until today, the federation had adamantly voted down over the years all attempts to introduce open tennis. In 1967 at Luxembourg, the open proposal was defeated, 139 votes to 83.

The British had made approval possible. In an unparalleled decision, they announced last October they would make the 1968 Wimbledon tournament an open. They said that in the future all players in Britain would be simply "players," not amateurs or professionals. And the British said they were ready to risk expulsion from the federation to make open tennis possible.

Country after country fell into line, and today the world agreed.

Amateurism Not Dead

Specifically, the federation approved these things:

¶"Retention of the notion of amateurism in the rules of the I.L.T.F., as its removal would indisputably weaken the ideals which the I.L.T.F. has the duty to protect and develop." Creation of officially recognized amateur championships; for example, championships of Europe, etc.

¶Right of national associations to self-determination regarding the status of their players, except where relations with professionals are concerned. On this point, in view of international implications, a common international policy must be established by the federation. Professionals may play against other players only in events organized by a national association or an affiliated body if that event has been declared open to all by the federation.

¶Creation of a strictly limited number of open tournaments under the authority of the federation, each one sanctioned by the federation.

The words need translation. What the federation is prepared to recognize is the following categories of tennis players: the "amateur," who is not paid; the "registered" player, who can profit from the game while not making tennis his profession, and the "professional," who makes his money from teaching or playing in events not organized by the national association.

Everybody seemed happy.

"It's a wonderful thing," said 70-year-old Jean Borotra, who had won Wimbledon as long ago as 1924. "Amateurism is preserved. I've been repaid for the six months it took out of my life to make this possible."

The British were pleased. They continue their own interpretation of "players," as just that, neither amateurs nor pros, but they recognize the rights of other nations to call them what they want.

The United States voted for open tennis at Coronado, Calif., in February and had worked here solidly behind the scenes all week for its success. Kelleher now will reconvene the adjourned Coronado meeting next Saturday at Dallas to decide where and if the U.S.L.T.A. will stage an open tournament this year.

Under the new conditions, the open tourney would logically be held in Forest Hills, Queens, the site of the national amateur championships, in early September.

"I don't know whether Forest Hills wants an open," said Kelleher. "We'll know at Dallas."

Another site, he intimated, might be Cleveland, where

Davis Cup and Wightman Cup matches have been successfully held.

There is bound to be bickering in a Committee of Managements meeting tomorrow, when it must be agreed how many open tournaments will be apportioned to each country this year. The British, for example, have asked for nine. That number will undoubtedly be reduced under protest.

The Australians are reported to want opens for their various states, possibly as many as six. The French will probably have one to replace their national championships at Roland Garros Stadium in Paris in May.

Further difficulties are foreseen in the administration of when and where some categories of players can play others. But in the flush of victory today, these matters seem irrelevant.

"You have to creep before you can crawl," Kelleher said, "and the evolutionary process will take time."

The federation has 65 member nations. The meeting was attended by 66 representatives from 47 nations.

March 31, 1968

Laver Trounces Roche and Is First Since 1936 to Win 3d Wimbledon Title

THREE-SET FINAL TAKES ONE HOUR

Laver Is First Since Perry to Win 3 Times—Some Fans in Line All Night

By FRED TUPPER
Special to The New York Times

WIMBLEDON, England, July 5—Rod Laver has taken the first open Wimbledon tennis championship. The 29-year-old Australian redhead dazzled Tony Roche of Australia with his wristy volleys and topspin backhands to win by 6-3, 6-4, 6-2 in exactly an hour before Princess Marina and a sun-spattered, sellout center-court crowd, some of whom had queued for 24 hours.

A mild little man with the look of a drowsy cockatoo off court, Laver is a terror on it. He has been the scourge of tennis for nearly 10 years, and his shattering victory this afternoon ranks on a par with his under-an-hour destructions of Chuck McKinley and Marty Mulligan in 1961 and 1962. He

is the first man since Fred Perry (1934-35-36) to take the most coveted award of the game three times. A check for $4,800 goes with it this time.

Tomorrow Mrs. Billie Jean King of Berkeley, Calif., tries for her third singles title in a row against Judy Tegart of Australia.

In his last year as an amateur in 1962 Laver won everything in sight—the grand slam of Wimbledon, Forest Hills, France and Australia and the Italian and German titles as well. In the hazy world of professionalism, where newspaper scores pop up in tiny type and records are hard to trace, Laver has been supreme.

The bookmakers had quoted him "evens" against one of the finest tennis fields of all time.

Laver One Step Ahead

Laver was a step faster and a thought ahead of the 23-year-old Roche. It took him time to solve the spinning southpaw serve and the record shows that he was able to get only 4 points in as many service games from Roche at the start.

Typical of Laver, the 4 points were enough. They gave him the service break he needed in the eighth game of the first set. A backhand chip to the sideline caught Roche floundering, a backhand heavy with topspin jumped clear and a

forehand drive streaked down the line to put Laver at advantage.

Then Tony sadly double-faulted for the only time in the match to trail at 3-5. Then Roche tried to zero in. Three times in the next game he had a point for the break, battering the ball to force Rod into error. Not good enough. First set to Laver, 6-3.

The talents that took the redhead to the top are unique. In his private world of slice and spin, loops and twists, live inspiration and imagination. And there were shots off his racquet that must be etched in memory.

Roche hit the shot of the day midway through that second set, a running, offbalance forehand from far out of court that rocketed diagonally past the redhead. Laver swung his racquet out, inches off the burned turf, and scooped the ball over as the cheers rang down. Seconds later, in case anybody had missed it, he did it again.

Redhead Runs Wild

In a brilliant streak now, Laver ran wild. Backhands and forehands sped by the lunging Roche, and a last whipped forehand across court forced Tony into error. The redhead was at 4-3 on the break and he had the second set in 20 min-

utes on a love game as Roche sprayed that flat first service high into the screen.

There was little that Roche could do. Primarily a clay-court player (French and Italian champion in 1966), he has been the top money-winner in the "handsome eight" pro group, and by defeating Ken Rosewall here earlier he had proved his aptitude on grass.

The shots were there, but today the flare was missing and Laver ran out five consecutive games to lead, 4-0, in the third set. Game, set and match soon came at 6-2 as the crowd rose, applauding.

For Laver, it was "my greatest thrill ever." En route, he had eradicated four of America's first 10 and its former No. 1, Dennis Ralston.

"Perhaps that was my toughest match," said Laver of the engagement with Ralston.

It is pointless to explain that if this Wimbledon had not been open, the United States was a sure shot for the title, as one amateur, Arthur Ashe, lost to Laver in one semi-final, and another amateur, Clark Graebner, lost to Roche in the other.

July 6, 1968

MRS. KING TAKES THIRD WIMBLEDON CROWN IN ROW

VICTOR BY 9-7, 7-5

Miss Tegart Is Beaten in Final—Newcombe, Roche Win Doubles

By FRED TUPPER
Special to The New York Times

WIMBLEDON, England, July 6—Mrs. Billie Jean Moffitt King is still queen of Wimbledon.

The bespectacled Californian, wan and listless most of the way, won her third title in a row on raw courage and some knifing volleys in beating seventh-seeded Judy Tegart of Australia, 9-7, 7-5, over 70

minutes on the center court today.

Mrs. King seemed a pale carbon of the exuberant extrovert who set tennis aflame here a few years back. Wide of grin and brash of manner, she made history in 1962 by bouncing out the favorite, Margaret Smith (now Mrs. Court) in the first round. The public loved it. The "Moffitt Mob" would hem in the sidecourts to hear as much as watch her.

"Throw in your nickles and dimes," she would say. "This is the worst show on earth."

A Subdued Champion

It was far from that today, but it was not vintage King. She was subdued. She moved slowly around the court, and it was not until early in the second set that a flicker of a

smile glinted across her face.

On the other side was Miss Tegart, a big broth of a girl who, at 30, had blossomed late. She had been trying for seven years and the pieces suddenly had fallen into place.

She had beaten second-seeded Mrs. Court over three sets and demolished third-seeded Nancy Richey of the United States, 6-3, 6-1, with the finest tennis of this tournament. A laugh on her lips, ponytail askew, she had overnight become the darling of Wimbledon.

Luck Also Helps

Mrs. King was lucky to be on the court at all. In the semi-final, Mrs. Ann Jones of Britain had led her by a set and 5-4 with her service to come. She had Mrs. King on the hook and

couldn't reel her in. Great match player that she is, Mrs. King had the resolution and somehow found the shots to win.

Today Miss Tegart was uncertain. Her devil-may-care attitude vanished, carried away by center-court jitters.

The American had the first service game and the service break, too, in a long, vital game. She was at advantage point four times as Miss Tegart volleyed into the net, missed a forehand down the middle, foot-faulted and then stared at a cross-court forehand that fled by her. In an exchange around the net, Mrs. King whipped a topspin forehand short to the sideline to lead, 2-0, and then 4-1.

But there was trouble ahead. Mrs. King was not getting her

157

first service in, and her second was short without much pace.

Miss Tegart began to bang the ball. In the seventh game she slashed a backhand pass down the line, hit a forehand that Mrs. King muffed and then pasted another backhand to the line for the break to 3-4.

The American was shaking her head. She seemed unable to move. Bravely she held her service, because she could still get up to the net in time to scythe away those lovely backhand volleys.

Miss Tegart was scampering around the court, but doublefaults were haunting her, and she blew the 16th game with her sixth double-fault and three flubbed volleys as the crowd groaned with her.

With that hurdle cleared, Mrs. King was happier. A wild yell at an error was a familiar sign. She served her first ace in the third game, hammered a couple more in the fifth and smiled at her parents in the players' stand.

Determined to Fight

Miss Tegart was determined to make a fight. She had length and spin on her service and was booming up for the volley. With the crowd's cheers to nourish her, she hit three splendid shots, one after the other, in the ninth game with the score at 4-all.

In some frantic infighting at the barrier, the Australian slapped a volley through a hole, scored with a forehand on the run and then slammed a backhand to Mrs. King's shoelaces for vantage point.

This was the test. Mrs. King met it with courage, volleying away the dangers to hold service.

Five-6 now, the Australian serving. Shrewdly Mrs. King changed tactics. She dinked a return just over the net, placed a forehand to the wide side and chipped another return short as Miss Tegart underhit. Love-40, three match points to come.

A delicate lob drifting on the breeze left Miss Tegart wrong-footed. She blooped it out. Mrs. King threw her racket aloft and hurtled up to the handshake. The wide grin was back. She had become the first woman to win here three times since Maureen Connolly swept the titles in 1952-53-54.

"There was nothing wrong with me," Mrs. King said later. "Judy goes fast, and I went slow. I've had to learn to go slow to concentrate."

She thought about it, then said: "I guess I won this Wimbledon on sheer fight. I wasn't prepared either mentally or physically. But I'll be back one more time."

For her victory in this first Wimbledon open, Mrs. King earned $1,800, but she said it would go toward her $40,000-a-year guarantee as a pro.

In the almost inevitable five-set

United Press International

WIMBLEDON WINNER: Mrs. Billie Jean Moffitt King of the United States as she defeated Judy Tegart of Australia in 70 minutes yesterday and became the first to capture women's singles for three years in a row since Maureen Connolly won in 1952-53-54.

match that is played when Australians meet in the doubles final, John Newcombe and Tony Roche defeated Ken Rosewall and Fred Stolle, 6-3, 6-8, 5-7, 14-12, 6-3, in an all-pro slugfest that ebbed and flowed nearly three hours.

The break that meant the match was a deep smash from the baseline by Rosewall that Roche, by reflex, volleyed squarely into Stolle's stomach. Roche picked up just over $4,000 for the victory and as the losing finalist to Rod Laver in the singles yesterday.

Mrs. King did it again later. She paired with Rosie Casals to win from Francoise Durr and Mrs. Jones in thrill-stabbed doubles final, 3-6, 6-4, 7-5. It was agony for the crowd that was trying to root Mrs. Jones to her first Wimbledon triumph since she began playing here in the mid-nineteen-fifties.

Once on a seeming bad call against Mrs. Jones, yells of protest echoed around the court, and both Miss Durr and Mrs. King decided

to sit it out until the noise had subsided.

The Americans were a long time in winning. They had four advantage points in the ninth game of the third set, and lost them, and five more in the 11th game before Mrs. King buried a smash in deep court to take it.

Miss Casals, the "Mighty Mouse," made it home at last with a flat backhand down the alley.

Mrs. King won the doubles with Miss Casals last year, with Maria Bueno in 1965 and with Mrs. Karen Hantze Susman in 1962 and 1961.

Ken Fletcher of Hong Kong and Mrs. Court of Australia beat the Russians, Alex Metreveli and Olga Morozova, for their fourth mixed-doubles crown since 1963. The victors, both amateurs, were playing for prize money and shared $1,080.

John Alexander of Australia took the junior title by beating Jan Thamin of France, 6-1, 6-2. Kristy Pigeon, 17, of San Francisco, who

trades stock shares, paints landscapes and strings rackets in her odd moments off the court, won from the talented Leslie Hunt of Australia in the girls final, 6-4, 6-3.

Herb FitzGibbon and Kathy Harter, American finalists in the singles plate event, were beaten by Gerald Battrick and Virginia Wade of Britain for the mixed-doubles plate.

Gar Mulloy and Sam Match lost to the defenders, Jaroslav Drobny of Britain and Al Martini of Los Angeles, in the veterans' doubles final 6-2, 7-5.

Rain and a rail slowdown militated against what had been expected to be a Wimbledon attendance record. About 277,000 fans paid over the 12 days. The record is last year's 301,111.

July 7, 1968

Capital Club Bars Integrated Tennis

By NAN ROBERTSON
Special to The New York Times

WASHINGTON, Aug. 24—An exclusive Washington country club whose members include some of the nation's most famous names has refused to play tennis with teams that have Negro members.

The focus of the controversy is the Chevy Chase Club in suburban Maryland. Among its members are Secretary of Defense Clark M. Clifford, Mrs. Hugh D. Auchincloss, the mother of Mrs. John F. Kennedy, and David K. E. Bruce, the American Ambassador to Britain since 1961.

There was no indication that these members were aware of the situation.

The central figure involved is Mrs. Carl T. Rowan, a Negro. Her husband, also a Negro, is a syndicated columnist who was a high State Department official, the American Ambassador to Finland in 1963 and 1964 and former head of the United States information Agency.

Six years ago, Mr. Rowan, then Deputy Assistant Secretary of State for Public Affairs, was refused membership in the Cosmos Club here, one of Washington's oldest and most distinguished social and intellectual organizations.

The disclosure of his rejection in 1962 precipitated an upheaval within that club. Admission rules were changed and important members resigned. The controversy also led to the withdrawal of a membership application submitted in behalf of President Kennedy.

The present dispute also involves the Columbia Country Club in Chevy Chase, the Washington Golf and Country Club in nearby Arlington, Va., and the Kenwood Golf and Country Club in Bethesda, Md. But the issue of discrimination is not nearly as clear-cut at these clubs.

Last spring, the Rowans were among several Negro couples to be accepted by the Indian Spring Country Club in Glenmont, Md. Mrs. Rowan, a good tennis player, was invited to play on the women's second-ranked or "B" tennis team. This team plays in a league that has included 10 Washington area country clubs. She has been the only Negro to participate.

The news touched off a flurry of telephone calls, letters and secret meetings in the women's league, marked by dissension and acrimony.

Shortly thereafter, the Chevy Chase Club, the Columbia Country Club and the Wash-

ington Golf and Country Club dropped out of the women's "B" league, giving various reasons. The most prevalent was that the clubs could not find enough players to field a team in the league.

It appears likely at this time that the Kenwood Club will drop out of the same circuit next spring, when a new round of inter-club matches will be scheduled, rather than be host on its courts to a team that includes a Negro.

Mrs. Helen Yanowitz, captain of the Indian Spring "B" team and 1968 tournament chairman, said that the league's executive committee offered her three choices at one closed meeting:

"One. I could make up a team excluding Vivien Rowan; two, we could drop out of the league; three, we could be host to those clubs which would not permit Negroes on their own courts."

Mrs. Yanowitz reacted sharply against the first two suggestions and decided for the time being to choose the last course of action. Chevy Chase, Columbia and Washington Golf withdrew from the league.

There appears to be no conflict with six other clubs in the league. The Kenwood Club is still playing in "B" team games

with Indian Spring at the host this year.

Next year it is Kenwood's turn to be host. Almost everyone interviewed expected trouble by spring. At least a half-dozen women involved in meetings and calls agreed that race was the primary issue in the dispute, particularly the Chevy Chase Club.

Mr. Rowan's reaction to the undercover debate combined amusement and bitterness.

"When we first heard the rumors we just laughed," he said. "We found it morbidly funny that at the time this nation was deeply involved in a great struggle in Southeast Asia, when the great cities were facing chaos and decay, when the dollar was in great trouble, that the supposedly elite people of this country could be running around holding secret meetings to figure out how to keep one Negro woman off a tennis court."

His wife described the "whole business" as "so childish I have not attempted to check the truthfulness of the rumors."

The 10-woman team is due to play on home ground against Kenwood early in October.

Mr. Rowan commented that "the crux of the matter is that at some of these clubs, the members don't have a single reason on earth for feeling proud of themselves except for

the so-called racial exclusivity of their country club."

"They're afraid," he said, that somebody is going to take away from them the last reason for them to feel important. They are struggling to keep the last preserve of white supremacy."

The president of the Chevy Chase Club, Harrison Brand 3d, disclaimed knowledge of any dispute. When Mrs. Rowan was mentioned, he replied: "Who's she?"

Mr. Brand said that enough players could not be found to field a "B" team this year and that "we are cutting back participation in inter-club matters in all sports" because of overcrowded facilities.

He added that he had received complaints from members that other clubs participating in matches at Chevy Chase were forcing them off the courts on weekends.

However, the Chevy Chase Club fielded a strong "A" or first-rank women's tennis team this year in a league that included no Negroes. This team won the league championship in 1967.

Mrs. Robert Hanson, captain of Columbia's "B" women's team, said that it had been such a strain to find players that last year "we defaulted 50 per cent of our games."

The club's nationally prominent members include Barry Goldwater, the Republican candidate for President in 1964, and Mr. Clifford.

Of Mrs. Rowan, she said: "I didn't even know she was playing" in the league. Mrs. Hanson said Columbia's decision to withdraw had been made last fall.

However, members of clubs other than Indian Spring said they had been invited to play women's matches informally at Columbia.

Mrs. Vida Geiger, captain of the Kenwood team and president of the Women's Inter-Club Tennis League, said there was "no reason to talk about" the dispute at this time. "Each club has a right to do what it wants to do," she said.

The Washington Golf and Country Club, whose members include Justice Byron R. White of the Supreme Court, informed the league one week after a spring meeting involving Mrs. Rowan that it was "impossible" to field a team for lack of players.

The Chevy Chase Club has also been the target of complaints from Jewish members of other country clubs, including predominantly Jewish Indian Spring.

They said that although Chevy Chase in recent years had allowed Jews to play on its tennis courts, it had been made clear to them that they were not welcome to use its bathrooms and locker facilities. They had to change in their cars, they said.

August 25, 1968

Miss Wade Upsets Mrs. King, 6-4, 6-2, and Wins U.S. Open Tennis Title

OKKER AND ASHE ADVANCE TO FINAL

Dutch Star Earns $14,000 by Defeating Rosewall— Graebner Eliminated

By NEIL AMDUR

The first United States Open tennis championships took another unpredictable turn yesterday when two nonprofessionals playing for prize money hit the jackpot.

Tom Okker, a 24-year-old acrobatic Dutchman, won the $14,000 men's singles prize by defeating Ken Rosewall, the 33-year-old Australian pro, 8-6, 6-4, 6-8, 6-1, in a semi-final round match on the Forest Hills Stadium court.

Before the excited West Side Tennis Club crowd of 14,088 had quieted down from this upset, Virginia Wade of Britain beat top-seeded Mrs. Billie Jean King for the women's singles title and the $6,000 prize. Playing the best 42 minutes of tennis of her career, the 23-year-old Miss Wade overwhelmed the world's top professional, 6-4, 6-2.

Both Okker and Miss Wade are classified as nonprofessionals under new international rules, which allow amateurs to register for prize money, rather than expenses, in open tournaments.

Okker's Earnings Near $20,000

Today, Okker will try to write his name officially into the record books when he plays Lieut. Arthur Ashe of Richmond for the singles crown. Ashe defeated Clark Graebner, his Davis Cup teammate, 4-6, 8-6, 7-5, 6-2, in yesterday's first semi-final.

Since Ashe is an amateur, and thus eligible only for $15 a day expenses, the outcome of the men's final will have no effect on Okker's earnings, which now total almost $20,000 since his tennis federation in the Netherlands informed the world that he was playing for prize money.

Okker won more in men's doubles yesterday—$1,149.22—than he did as a losing quarter-finalist to Ashe at the first Wimbledon Open this year. His Wimbledon singles earnings were $1,100. Okker has beaten Ashe only once in five matches.

Yesterday's lightning turn of events was another advertisement to the hectic tone of this

$100,000 event, which has brought professionals and amateur players together for the first time with dynamic results. Seventeen pros beaten by amateurs in singles: 13 in the men's division, four in the women's.

Okker Too Quick and Strong

Okker, who was the world's first "registered player," also must be most improved. He was too quick and strong for the venerable Rosewall, who had never lost to an amateur and who had replaced Richard (Pancho) Gonzalez as a reigning pro champion. Ironically, Okker's looping forehand placements and speed afoot were too much for Gonzalez, who was a four-set loser in the quarter-finals, the second of the pros ousted by Okker.

"I was probably soft on my volleys and serves," the dejected Rosewall said afterward. "I was trying to make Tom work as hard as he could. But everytime I gave him a good shot, he came back with one better."

Okker scored his big service break in the 10th game of the second set when Rosewall, leading, 40-15, lost control of his service. After five deuce points, Okker won the set with a backhand passing shot down

the line and a backhand return of service down the middle that hung on Rosewall's racquet as he futilely tried to hit a half-volley.

"I think it's the best I've ever played," said Okker, who broke Rosewall in the fourth game of the fourth set when the Aussie double-faulted on game point. "My return of serves and passing shots were sound and I was moving well."

Until Ashe broke Graebner's stinging, flat serve with a cross-court backhand passing shot in the 14th game of the second set, the Army lieutenant's personal singles victory streak seemed in jeopardy.

Then Ashe hit two lobs and another backhand cross-court to win the 12th game of the third set. When he broke Graebner's serve in the fourth game of the fourth set with a sliced backhand return-of-service placement down the line, his string—now at 25 singles matches since the national clay-court championships—was assured. So was his claim to the No. 1 spot in American amateur tennis.

Miss Wade, who is classified simply as a "player" under Britain's rules, has always been a player of promise. Yesterday, however, as one close friend said, "she tamed a wild game"

with the right mental attitude and excellent strokes.

A marvelous forehand lob broke Mrs. King for the first time in the seventh game of the opening set after the bespectacled Californian volleyed away a 15-40 lead on Miss Wade's serve a game earlier.

With her first serve keeping Mrs. King on the defensive and with a growing sense of confidence, Miss Wade broke service in the opening game of the second set. When Billie Jean went ahead, 0-30, on Miss Wade's serve in the fourth game, the pretty Britisher boldly hit two overheads and a backhand volley and held service, then broke Mrs. King at love three games later.

"I don't think I ever expected to win this event," the surprised Miss Wade said, clutching a victory bouquet of red roses. The sixth-seeded player in the draw, Miss Wade survived an opening three-set match with Stephanie DeFina, beat Rosemary Casals, a professional; third-seeded Judy Tegart and second-seeded Mrs. Ann Haydon Jones, another pro, en route to the final.

September 9, 1968

Ashe Beats Okker for 2-Hour-40-Minute Match U.S. Open Tennis Title in

Ashe Beats Okker to Win Tennis Open

By DAVE ANDERSON

Lieut. Arthur Ashe won the men's singles title yesterday at Forest Hills Stadium in the first United States open tennis championships. The triumph was the most notable achievement made in the sport by a Negro male athlete.

Serving a total of 26 aces, the slender Army officer defeated Tom Okker of the Netherlands, 14-12, 5-7, 6-3, 3-6, 6-3, but he was ineligible to receive the $14,000 top prize in the $100,000 event, the richest tournament in tennis history.

As an American amateur, Ashe collected a total of $280 in expenses, at $20 per diem for 14 days, including two days of practice. As a Davis cup player, he had his room at the Hotel Roosevelt paid for by the United States Lawn Tennis Association.

The 25-year-old Ashe, who grew up in a middle-class Negro neighborhood in Richmond, also won the United States amateur singles championship Aug. 25 in Longwood, Mass.

Four touring Australian pro-

fessionals — Rod Laver, Tony Roche, Ken Rosewall and John Newcombe—were seeded ahead of Ashe, in that order, but the expected dominance of the pros never materialized. Seventeen pros were defeated by amateurs in singles: 13 in the men's division, 4 in the women's.

Unfortunately, the drama of Ashe's glory was diminished somewhat by the size of the crowd. An estimated turnout of 7,100 was scattered throughout the 13,500-seat stadium for the final, postponed a day be-

Arthur Ashe, like Althea Gibson, has been a pioneer among black tennis players. *The Times* called his victory in the 1968 U.S. Open "the most notable achievement made in the sport by a Negro male athlete."

cause of the rain that wiped out last Friday's program.

The introduction of open tennis in this country produced an 11-day attendance of 97,000, according to the daily totals issued by the tournament officials. The box-office receipts were expected to approach $400,000. Additional income was realized from television, concessions and parking.

And for the first time since 1955, when Tony Trabert won the national amateur title in the West Side Tennis Club stadium, an American has conquered the men's field in this country's most distinguished tennis tournament.

Okker, as a "registered" player eligible to compete for prize money as a nonprofessional under new international rules, earned the $14,000 men's prize Sunday with a four-set victory over Rosewall, the only professional to reach the semi-finals.

In the women's division, another nonprofessional, 23-year-old Virginia Wade, of England, received $6,000 for winning the women's singles title on Sunday.

In yesterday's women's doubles final, Mrs. Margaret Smith Court of Australia and Maria Bueno of Brazil, a pair of non-professionals competing for prize money, defeated two American pros, Mrs. Billie Jean King and Rosemary Casals, 4-6, 9-7, 8-6.

In the men's doubles, an all-United States Davis Cup final is possible today.

Clark Graebner and Charles Pasarell were leading Ashe and Andres Gimeno, a Spanish professional, 4-6, 6-3, 6-4, 12-12, when their semi-final match was halted by darkness. They will resume this morning at 10:30, with free admission to the stadium.

Gestures of Triumph

Awaiting the winning team were two other Davis Cup members, Robert Lutz and Stan Smith.

Ashe returned to the center court for his doubles match, which resumed with the start of the fourth set, nearly an hour after drilling a forehand volley past the nimble Okker on his first match point to end the 2-hour-40-minute final.

As the curly-haired Dutchman waved helplessly at the grass-stained ball, Ashe spun, stood at a crouched attention and aimed his racquet handle at the tarpaulin-covered stadium wall. Then he turned and shook hands with Okker at the net.

Although the bespectacled bachelor later said that he "wasn't particularly excited about winning," his gestures in that moment of triumph betrayed his emotional involvement.

Striding slowly behind the umpire's chair, Ashe clasped his hands and held them high, in the traditional gesture of a

CAUGHT off guard by return of Lieut. Arthur Ashe, Tom Okker sprawls on court as he tries to reach for the ball.

victorious boxer. Moments later, he cupped his hands behind his head and walked around, staring down at the turf.

Introduced as "General Ashe" by Robert J. Kelleher, president of the U.S.L.T.A., at the presentation ceremonies, Ashe laughed and hugged his father, a guard in the Recreation Department in Richmond.

During his poised acceptance speech, Ashe mentioned that he was "grateful that he was able" to win.

Ashe Lobs Cleverly

Ironically, had the United States Davis Cup team been eliminated in the world-wide competition, Ashe would have been ordered to return to duty as a computer-programming instructor at the United States Military Academy at West Point, N. Y.

But with the United States awaiting its interzone series with either West Germany, India or Japan in November, Ashe's participation in the open championships was considered to be Davis Cup preparation, thus permitting a furlough.

Ashe's triumph over Okker

was his 25th consecutive singles victory. He hasn't lost since a surprise defeat in mid-July by little-known Patricio Cornejo of Chile in the third round of the national clay-court championships at Milwaukee.

Upon entering the fifth set yesterday, Ashe and Okker had battled for more than two hours to a standstill. Ashe had depended on clever lobs, a rare stroke for him, as well as his scorching serve while Okker performed tenaciously.

Okker is a small, slight 24-year-old athlete with remarkable speed, both afoot and with his racquet. He had conquered the experience of the old pro, Richard (Pancho) Gonzalez, and the cunning of Rosewall in attaining the title round.

In the second game of the decisive set, Okker's serve faltered and Ashe, sleek and smooth and crouching to remind himself to bend his knees, floated a lob beyond Okker but inside the chalk-dusted baseline to produce a 30-40 situation.

Moments later, Ashe angled a forehand that Okker was unable to retrieve near the west sideline.

Ashe had the service break and all he required to win was to hold his serve four consecutive times. He coasted to a 4-2 lead, but suddenly in the seventh game, he lost the flowing form that often had reduced Okker to helplessness.

On his second serve at 30-all, Ashe spun the ball to Okker's backhand, but the Dutchman ran around and swatted a forehand passing shot. Should his rival attain the next point, Ashe would have lost his serve.

Instead, on his second serve again, Ashe maneuvered Okker into swatting a backhand return wide. Deuce.

On his next serve, also a second ball, Ashe earned the advantage when Okker swooped a backhand return long. On the next serve, again on the second ball, Okker chipped a backhand return into the net. Ashe had held for 5-2.

In the ninth game, serving for the match, Ashe powered an ace on the second point in producing a love game as the spectors stood and applauded.

Gesture of Surrender

Ashe served 15 aces during the 64-minute first set. After two consecutive aces thundered by him in the 11th game, the Dutchman positioned himself for the next serve, then turned his back on Ashe, as if to signify his surrender.

Actually, it would be more than two hours before Okker would surrender. In winning the tournament, Ashe also defeated his Davis Cup teammate, Graebner, in the semi-finals, and two pros, Cliff Drysdale of South Africa and Roy Emerson of Australia.

Ashe had been expected to oppose Rod Laver, the top-seeded Wimbledon open champion, in the quarter-finals, but Drysdale had eliminated Laver in an upset.

Asked later how he rated himself with Laver, who is considered the ruler of the touring profesionals, Ashe replied that "Laver has won 20 big ones, I've only won two big ones," meaning the national amateur and the national open.

Ashe, however, is the only male amateur to have won any of the six national open events throughout the world.

Laver won Wimbledon, Rosewall the French open, Newcombe the German open, Drysdale the Swiss open and Okker, the "registered" player who is something of an amateur with an asterisk, won the Irish open, with its first-place prize money.

Ashe is the only tennis player to have won an open at $20 per diem and with a free hotel room.

Non-Open Tennis Events to Offer Prize Money

By NEIL AMDUR

Tennis tournaments in the United States, other than the five sanctioned opens, will be allowed to offer prize money to nonprofessionals, the United States Lawn Tennis Association said yesterday.

The announcement by Alastair B. Martin, the new president, was the association's second major policy revision in four days. Last Saturday, at the annual meeting in Belleair, Fla., delegates approved a "player" category that will permit American nonprofessionals 19 years and older to register for prize money in open events.

Yesterday's move further defined the categories of "player" and "amateur." It also gave tournament directors the opportunity of soliciting corporate and individual sponsorship similar to the successful professional golf program.

Hopefully, the rule in principle will eliminate the under-the-table hypocrisy or "shamateurism" that led countries to join in a revision of the international conditions governing players.

The new rule also will apply to foreigners who declare for prize money and play in American tournaments.

"We intend to work as fast as possible to incorporate the mechanics of the new rule into our program," Martin said through Bob Malaga, U.S.L.T.A. executive secretary. "This should further the expanding and professionalizing concepts of the association."

As applicable to tournaments other than opens, the rule reads as follows:

"The U.S.L.T.A. will require all applications for sanctions in events of which prize money will be offered to set forth expressly the amount or amounts of prize money offered in each event. No prize money will be permitted except as expressly permitted by U.S.L.T.A. sanctions."

"The rule sounds good," said Don Hobart, chairman of the Eastern grass-court championships at South Orange, N.J. "I hope it will eliminate the expense problems. I've been doing it for so long I don't know who's the better bargainer, me or the players."

Stan Smith, the third-ranking amateur and recent winner of the national Johnston Sportsmanship award, agreed and said he would register for prize money as a "player."

"My idea is to get money above the board," Smith, 22, said from Salisbury, Md., where he is competing in the national indoor championships. "Make a tournament competitive instead of a guarantee. I think most of the players in this country agree with this idea and approve of the new categories."

Hobert said his tournament, the first grass-court event of the summer, would consider approaching sponsors and offering prize money.

"I'm sure other grass-court tournaments also will review their contracts, since it's bound to give us a more attractive schedule," he said.

Several companies active in tennis promotion also praised the move.

"This is the type of thing I'd be looking for in making a pitch to our company," said Roy Fishman, director of publicity and educational services for Standard Brands, Inc. "Certainly it's the biggest step tennis has taken in trying to attract company interest in the sport."

February 13, 1969

Mrs. Jones Wins Wimbledon Title, Ending Mrs. King's Bid for 4th in a Row

BRITISH TRIUMPH FIRST IN 8 YEARS

First Also for Mrs. Jones, a 3-6, 6-3, 6-2 Winner— Fans Taunt Mrs. King

By FRED TUPPER
Special to The New York Times

WIMBLEDON, England, July 4—Mrs. Ann Jones ended today the three-year reign of Mrs. Billie Jean King as Wimbledon women's tennis champion. The 30-year-old British left-hander, a dogged competitor, won by 3-6, 6-3, 6-2 in 70 minutes before 15,000 excited fans jammed around center court.

Some of the fans had yelled "Out! Out! at close line calls and at one point the yelling prompted Mrs. King to curtsy to the crowd.

"The crowd was making the calls before the balls hit," Mrs. King said after the match. "The curtsy was a nice way of saying be quiet."

An official request for quiet came from the umpire, Laurie McCallum.

"I wanted to win fair and square," Mrs. Jones said. "I

Mrs. Ann Jones of England in action on Wimbledon court yesterday as she defeated Mrs. Billie Jean King of the United States to win the women's singles title. Mrs. Jones is the first left-hander ever to win the women's title as well as first British victor since 1961.

did not want the crowd to put Billie Jean off. I felt slightly embarrassed about being in England. I wanted to win, but I wanted to win fair and square."

First Briton Since 1961

Mrs. Jones was the better player and she became the first British woman to win since Angela Mortimer defeated Christine Truman in 1961. Mrs. Jones had been in the semi-finals eight times in the last 11 years and lost to Mrs. King in the final two years.

Her inspiration came from her tremendous victory over the world's No. 1, Mrs. Margaret Court of Australia, in the Wednesday semi-finals. Given little chance then, she blew an early lead and lost the first set, but stuck to her guns and triumphed on persistence.

Early in the match, Mrs. King dominated the court, serving well, volleying beautifully and finding wide openings for her backhand. At a game apiece, she was dead on target. She slapped a backhand down the tape, a backhand into the clear across court and another backhand through a hole for a service break.

Soon she was at 5-3, with Ann serving. That backhand thumped into the corner to put her at set point and in some infighting around the net, Mrs.

King volleyed into open space for 6-3.

Mrs. Jones in Trouble

Mrs. Jones had been having trouble reaching the low bouncers and was not swinging true on the shot. Mrs. King had the first game of the second set at love and was at game point on Ann's serve with a lob to the base line and a wristy shot that slid over the net and dropped dead. But that game eluded her.

Three times she hoisted windblown lobs to deep court as Ann smashed back, curving one to the corner for deuce and starting a blazing run that gave her game after game. Mrs. Jones was transformed now, coming in on everything and jerking Mrs. King around court with low spinning volleys.

Billie Jean was at 2-1 with three points for the break and missed them all. She was down 1-4, and then pulled herself together. Sharp volleys and a forehand into the corner brought her to 2-4, deep serving to 3-4.

She was love-30, Ann serving, with 10 points in a row. It looked like a new game. But Ann rushed to advantage and a swinging southpaw serve pulled Mrs. King far out of court and into error.

A forehand from the baseline was so accurate that Billie Jean

could get only the wood on it as it thundered by. Set to Mrs. Jones at 6-3.

Mrs. King was at 15 - 40, Ann's service, in the first game of the decider on a backhand across court that nicked the line. The crowd didn't like it. A group in the open stand behind Mrs. King shouted "Out! Out!" The umpire called for silence.

Needling Takes Effect

Billie Jean lost that game, then won the next, but she was demoralized. She couldn't get her first service in. She lost her touch on the volley. Those spinners were fluttering around her shoetops as she became enmeshed in a defensive web. She tried to blast her way out, but Mrs. Jones was in control, with cheers driving her on. At 1-4, Mrs. King flubbed some volleys and double-faulted on game point.

The match was there for the taking and so were the butterflies for Ann.

"I kept thinking of Nancy Richey," she said, alluding to the quarter-final match in which she had led, 5-1, and was pulled back to 5-all.

Ann served a wild game and lost it. She was soon at 15-40 with two match points. Mrs King saved them both with volleys and wristed a dropshot

over for ad-in. The postponement was futile. At the third match point she double-faulted again. There was bedlam.

Princess Anne came on court to present the huge silver platter. Mrs. Jones takes $3,600 for winning (Mrs. King won $1,800). She receives honors as a Member of the British Empire next Tuesday. Her cup is full after 13 years of trying.

The Australians, John Newcombe and Tony Roche, retained their doubles title by defeating Tom Okker of the Netherlands and Marty Riessen of Evanston, Ill., 7-5, 11-9, 6-3. Marty was the culprit. He lost his serve for the second set and Roche banged the ball off his chest for the service break that meant the match.

Rod Laver, winner in 1968, meets Newcombe, winner in 1967, for the men's singles crown tomorrow. It will be the first time since Henri Cochet faced Jean Borotra in 1929 that two former champions have met in the final.

July 5, 1969

LAVER TAKES WIMBLEDON TENNIS TITLE FOURTH TIME

Laver Triumphs in 4 Sets Over Newcombe in Final

By FRED TUPPER
Special to The New York Times

WIMBLEDON, England, July 5—Rod Laver has won the Wimbledon championship for the fourth time.

The Australian carrot-top fought back with an irresistible seven-game surge today to defeat John Newcombe, 6-4, 5-7, 6-4, 6-4, in one of the best finals in Wimbledon history.

And so the wiry left-hander enters the halls of tennis immortals. He is the first man to take the title four times since the challenge round was abolished in 1922 and the first man to take it four times in as many attempts. He won it in 1961 and 1962 as an amateur, turned professional in 1963 and then won the first open last year.

Laver has also taken the Australian and French crowns this year and needs the United States title at Forest Hills next

month for the grand slam. The last man to do it was Laver in 1962, and then the pros were not competing. The only other man to do it was Don Budge in 1938.

Laver was top-seeded and a 5-to-4 betting favorite when this wonderful Wimbledon began. But he never had a tougher match over his years here than against Newcombe this afternoon.

Big John burst into the limelight this spring. He won the Italian and British hard-court titles and made a mockery of his sixth-seeded position here by demolishing the second favorite, Tony Roche.

This final was supposed to be a contrast in styles, the blazing ground strokes and imaginative improvisations of the 30-year-old redhead against the big

serving and inflexible tactics of the 25-year-old Newcombe.

It didn't work out that way. Rod served beautifully and Newcombe dinked and lobbed and hit soft shots with such consummate cunning that at one stage it seemed probable that he would win.

It was a slugfest at the start, tennis as good as you could see with the ball moving as fast as the eye could follow. In a marvelous point, with the players scrambling all over the court, Laver shot out of nowhere to slash a volley down the line and then break Newcombe's service for 2-1.

The redhead went to 4—3 and was serving when John tried another ploy. He teased Laver with a running lob, hoisted another high and deep that was smashed out and then dropped a dink over the net that pulled Laver up, whereupon John pitched a topsin lob over his head for the breakback. He was in the set at 4-all.

For a moment there Laver had looked mortal. Not so.

Taking dead aim he whipped a backhand across court and fired another one down the tape for the next game and took the set with an ace.

Newcombe persevered. In the eighth game of the second set he floated a chip to the sideline, threaded a backhand through a needle and then chipped to Laver's feet to lead, 5-3. But the big Australian double-faulted to start the next game and double-faulted to end it.

Twice he had broken Laver, Twice he had been broken back immediately. Then he made it. He hammered a forehand down the middle and Laver was long on the return. He stretched him with a cross-court backhand, which Laver netted. Second set to Newcombe as the crowd roared approval.

Seems to Lose His Touch

Laver was losing his touch. At 1-2 in the third set he messed up a low volley, sprayed a shot too far, hit a half-volley over the line and double-faulted.

Newcombe held his serve to 4-1 and there were mutterings in the stands. He seemed clearly on top. Was the unthinkable to

RETAINS TITLE: Rod Laver in action against fellow Australian, John Newcombe, at Wimbledon yesterday. Laver kept Wimbledon crown, defeating Newcombe in four sets.

Associated Press

happen? The great Margaret Smith Court was a certainty to win the women's title and she had fallen. And a crisis was staring Laver in the face.

He hit a couple of lobs to take the first point in the seventh game and then he struck a wonder shot. With a snap of his wrist he hit a backhand spinner at such an inconceivable angle that it cleared the net by inch fractions. Then he backhanded a shot through the middle and was at 3-4.

It was savage, searing stuff and turned the whole match in a twinkling. The winners streamed off Laver's racket, hit to impossible places.

In the seven-game streak he had the third set and was 2-love in the fourth. Then it was a question of holding service. As he toed the line at 5-3, one match point escaped, but he buried a high lob diagonally across court for the set and match.

Serves 10 Aces

Along the route he had 10 aces, 12 winning smashes and six winning lobs.

"You've got to believe you can beat anybody in the place," he had said earlier. "You give your best performances when you're charged up for the big ones."

It was Laver at his best. The Duke of Kent came down from the royal box, walked through

an aisle of ballboys and handed the silver cup to Rod as the crowd clapped for minutes.

"It was my toughest match here ever," Laver said. The victory was worth $7,200 of the $80,000 purse in the open tournament. Laver goes to Boston

next week for a tournament, then will rest in California before Forest Hills.

The Americans did not win a major title as Mrs. Billie Jean King was dethroned in the singles and she and Rosemary Casals lost their doubles crown.

Patti Hogan, 19, and Peggy Michel, 20, a pair of upcoming Californians, reached the doubles final by upsetting third-seeded Mrs. Ann Jones and Francoise Durr along the way. Playing for the title, they led Mrs. Court and Judy Tegart on service throughout the first set, but the top-seeded Australians broke through to win, 9-7, 6-2.

Fourth-seeded Fred Stolle and Mrs. Jones took the mixed doubles crown from third-seeded Roche and Miss Tegart, 6-2, 6-3.

The beauteous Betty Ann Grubb of Santa Monica, Calif., won the plate for the first-round losers by defeating Laura Rosscuw of South Africa, 6-3, 4-6, 6-4. And in the cool of the evening two former Wimbledon singles champions, Vic Seixas (1953) and Jaroslav Drobny (1954) paired to defeat Ellis Slack and Dick Sorlien of the United States, 9-7, 8-6, in the senior doubles final.

After a rainy first day, perfect weather helped bring the total attendance to 300,000. This Wimbledon was to be remembered for Pancho Gonzales's record 5-hour-12-minute, 112-game victory over Charles Pasarell, the fantastic first-set performance of Arthur Ashe against Laver and the victories of Mrs. Jones over Mrs. Court and then Mrs. King.

July 6, 1969

Rumania Advances To Challenge Round

By The Associated Press

WIMBLEDON, England, Aug. 16—Ilie Nastase, a 23-year-old former shepherd boy, defeated Mark Cox of Britain, 3-6, 6-1, 6-4, 6-4, today and sent Rumania's tennis team into the challenge round for the Davis Cup for the first time.

The Rumanians won, 3-2. They led, 2-1, at the start of the final day but Graham Stilwell kept Britain's hopes alive by downing Ion Tiriac, 6-3, 6-2, 6-4.

The Rumanians next will meet the United States for the trophy at Cleveland, Sept. 19 to 21.

They are the first team from a Communist country to reach the challenge round.

A crowd of 7,000 surrounded Wimbledon's No. 1 court and was kept on edge as Britain's hopes rose and then faded.

Nastase, after losing the first set of the deciding singles, raised his game while Cox became flustered and faltered badly, especially with his backhand.

Wildly excited Rumanians danced and shouted as Nastase hit the last few winning points.

It took Cox only 17 minutes to win the first set, and it looked as if Britain was heading for the challenge round for the first time since 1937.

But then the English left-hander lost control of his backhand. Nastase won four games in a row at the start of the second set and his confidence went sky high.

The agile Rumanian sped around the court, hitting spectacular retrieving shots and volleying faultlessly.

Stilwell Crowd's Hero

Earlier in the afternoon Stilwell was the crowd's hero.

As in the previous round against Brazil, he pulled Britain back from the abyss.

Tiriac had dominated the first two days, both in singles and doubles. But Stilwell threw himself into the attack and broke Tiriac's service at the first attempt in all three sets.

Tiriac, 30, was under pressure from the start. By the end of the second set he appeared tired.

The Rumanians did not break his opponent until the third set. But Stilwell moved ahead again at 4-3, lobbing cleverly and then following up with a smash, when Tiriac retrieved desperately from the baseline.

In previous rounds the Rumanians defeated the United Arab Republic, Israel, Spain, the Soviet Union and India. Until this encounter on Wimbledon grass, they had played all their games on clay courts.

August 17, 1969

Laver Beats Roche in U.S. Open Final and Gains His 2d Tennis Grand Slam

RECORD ACHIEVED IN 4-SET TRIUMPH

Favorite Takes $16,000 Top Prize and 4th Major Title by 7-9, 6-1, 6-2, 6-2

By NEIL AMDUR

Rod Laver achieved the second grand slam of his tennis career yesterday.

With all the competitive trademarks of the true champion, the 31-year-old king of the court overcame Tony Roche, his 24-year-old Australian countryman, 7-9, 6-1, 6-2, 6-2, in the final of the United States Open championship at the West Side Tennis Club in Forest Hills, Queens.

With the $16,000 first prize, the richest singles payoff in the sport, Laver lifted his professional earnings this year to a record $106,000. He also entered the record books as the only player to have achieved two sweeps of the Australian, French, British and American championships, the international events that make up the grand slam.

Budge Did It First

Don Budge registered the first slam in 1938. Laver completed his initial sweep in 1962, but as an amateur and with such established pros as Richard (Pancho) Gonzales, Ken Rosewall, Lew Hoad and Tony Trabert ineligible for the competition. That situation has been changed with the approval of open tournaments.

"Tenniswise, winning this slam was a lot tougher because of all the good players," the modest, freckle-faced redhead said.

"Pressurewise, I don't think it was any tougher. There's always pressure when you're playing for something over nine months."

Laver and Roche had to wait 1 hour 35 minutes until a rented helicopter could dry the center court, which had been dampened by the morning rain.

"The playing conditions made it very difficult," Laver said. "The ground was very soft, the speeds of the bounce made it tough to return and you were sliding all over."

Switches to Spikes

Before the 10th game of the first set, after having lost his serve at 5-4 on Roche's backhand passing shot down the middle and three errors off his

first volley, Laver made a strategic switch from sneakers to spiked shoes.

"The spikes helped me considerably," he said. "I lost the first set using them, but I felt good and I was able to move better." Roche wore sneakers throughout.

The fine line that separates Laver from Roche, Arthur Ashe, Roy Emerson and others is his ability to concentrate on the big serve or decisive volley at 15-30 or 30-40.

Laver trailed, 30-40, in the opening game of the second set. A service break at this point could have carried Roche to a two-set lead. But three strong first serves saved the game. Laver won the last three service games of the set at love.

The crucial moment in the match, when it seemed to turn dramatically, came in the second game of the third set, after play had been suspended by rain.

Roche had won his serve at love for a 1-0 lead. When the players returned 30 minutes later, the pressure was on Laver. On Sunday he saw the result of the strain of serving first following a delay. At 12-12 in the third set of his match with Ashe, Arthur had to serve the first game. Laver broke him immediately and won the match in the next game.

Roche pushed Laver to deuce twice in that second game. But two more big serves, hopping deep to Roche's backhand, gave Laver the impetus to hold service and then break Roche in the next game, in which he was helped by Tony's netted forehand approach volley and long overhead at deuce.

Runner-Up Gets $8,000

"Tony didn't seem to be digging in as much," Laver said of the player who had beaten him in five of their seven previous meetings. "I felt his concentration was off."

Roche, who collected $8,000 as runner-up, could have felt the physical strain of his three-hour, five-set semifinal with John Newcombe on Sunday, particularly after the 30-minute cooling-off period in the third set (he never got beyond 30 on Laver's last six serves).

But when the big money goes on the line, the winning strokes are Laver's. Except for last year's first Open here, when he lost to Cliff Drysdale in the quarter finals, Laver has won every major tennis money event in the world.

Alastair B. Martin, president of the United States Lawn Tennis Association, called Laver "the greatest player ever," and the 5-foot-9-inch, 155-pounder said "that makes me feel humble and proud and grateful."

Comparing Laver with the stars of other eras—Gonzales, Jack Kramer, Budge and Tilden—might be treasonous in tennis's sacrosanct society, but the Rocket has met every challenge with the discipline and dedication worthy of a place in the hall of heroes.

"Red showed this year that he's still the best," said Roche, who is considered Laver's successor. "He's won so much money this year that maybe the money might slow him down."

Laver has three years to go on a five-year, $450,000 contract with the National Tennis League. He keeps whatever amount he makes in prize

money above his guarantee.

The pressure began for him last January after he had beaten Emerson, Fred Stolle, Roche and Andres Gimeno en route to the Australian title. In the French and Wimbledon championships, he trailed, two sets to love, twice in the early rounds, but salvaged each match and went on to the crowns despite persistent pains in his left elbow.

In winning here at Forest Hills, the richest tournament in the world with its $137,000 purse, Laver overcame psychological hazards as well as such quality pros as Dennis Ralston, Emerson, Ashe and Roche, his chief tormentor this year. Rain had washed out two complete sessions and delayed the final one day. His tense semifinal match with Ashe had been halted by darkness in the third set and finished the following day.

Meanwhile, in Newport Beach, Calif., Laver's wife, Mary, had also been experiencing delays. The couple's first child was three days' overdue and Laver had been calling every morning to make sure everything was all right.

Mrs. Laver reported yesterday by phone before her husband walked onto the stadium court for the final. "I've been telling him everything's fine and to concentrate on his tennis," she said.

If there was a touch of nostalgia to this tournament, it came in the women's doubles final yesterday, in which Francoise Durr and 33-year-old Darlene Hard upset the top-seeded team of Mrs. Margaret Court and Virginia Wade, 0-6, 6-4, 6-4.

The crowd of 3,708 (6,200 tickets had actually been sold) cheered lustily, particularly for Miss Hard, a former national champion who had replaced Miss Durr's regular partner, Mrs. Ann Haydon Jones.

"I guess Frankie (Miss Durr's nickname) cried when she saw my name on the doubles list," said Miss Hard, who is a teaching pro in Los Angeles and lost to Miss Durr in the second round of singles. "But everything worked out great, and a win like this convinces me I should get back to full-time tennis."

One day remains in the tournament to complete the men's doubles. Naturally Laver is still playing for the $3,000 top doubles prize, even though his mind is elsewhere.

"I want to get home as soon as possible," he said, flashing a familiar half-smile. "If you had a baby on the way, wouldn't you?"

September 9, 1969

Laver hefts U.S. Lawn Tennis Association's Open trophy

Independent Net Pros Form New Unit

By EUGENE L. SCOTT
Special to The New York Times

HAMPTON, Va., March 7— Thirty-two international tennis stars announced the formation of a new players association today at the United States Lawn Tennis Association's indoor championships.

The organization, to be known as the Association of Independent Tennis Professionals, will establish a player force to counteract the bargaining strength of the contract professionals.

Independent pros are players who maintain allegiance to their national tennis associations and their eligibility for Davis Cup competition. Contract professionals sign agreements with one of two promoters—George MacCall of Los Angeles and Lamar Hunt of Texas—to play for a fixed minimum salary.

The contract pros cannot play in the Davis Cup because they have abandoned their national associations.

Problems have arisen because the promoter's prime source of revenue is a management fee extracted from individual tournaments in addition to the prize money, which goes to the contract professional directly.

Independent professionals have insisted they were entitled to the equivalent of a management fee. Better yet, they requested that no appearance fees be paid at all—just prize money.

The International Tennis Players Association, made up of athletes from both groups, was formed last June to obtain equal treatment for all competitors, but its futility became evident quickly.

Its president, the former Wimbledon and United States champion, John Newcombe, could not bring about reforms concerning guarantees because those reforms conflicted with the aims of his boss, Lamar Hunt. The group, recognizing this conflict, began to disband and only a skeleton organization remains.

The new association includes among its purposes the creation of a "unified and independent voice when dealing with contract professionals, agents, and international tennis bodies to secure equal treatment for its members." The group will also assist its players with all phases of financial management.

The association, whose members include Arthur Ashe, Stan Smith, Clark Graebner and Cliff Richey, all members of the United States Davis Cup team, elected a player advisory committee from four parts of the world.

Jim McManus, ranked 10th in the United States, was chosen as North America's representative; a British Davis Cup player, Peter Curtis, was selected to represent Europe; the Brazilian star, Tom Koch, represents South America and Dick Crealy, a high-ranking Australian, is Australia's representative.

A president, who will be granted broad powers, was not elected. But it is certain he will not be a player.

The players intend to stick to what they do best, playing tennis, and leave the leadership to a strong professional administrator.

The man certain to be chosen is Bill Riordan of Salisbury, Md., who has many duties with the U.S.L.T.A., including those of player coordinator, chairman of the indoor circuit, and sectional delegate. The players insist their leader should have no formal connection with the U.S.L.T.A., though a cordial relationship between the two is expected.

Riordan will, no doubt, confer with the U.S.L.T.A. president, Alastair B. Martin, this week to request release from association duties. Martin sent his official blessing to the new group by telegram and said he was looking forward to "a working relationship with its leaders" and hoped to meet them shortly to discuss "common aims for the progress of lawn tennis throughout the world."

The writer of this article is a former United States Davis Cup player.

March 8, 1970

Mrs. Court Sets Back Mrs. King, 14-12, 11-9, in 2½-Hour Final at Wimbledon

AUSTRALIAN WINS TITLE FOR 3D TIME

Leg Injuries Beset Rivals in Long Struggle—Roche and Newcombe Take Doubles

By FRED TUPPER
Special to The New York Times

WIMBLEDON, England, July 3—Mrs. Margaret Court won her third All-England tennis title at Wimbledon today. The great Australian defeated Mrs. Billie Jean King, 14-12, 11-9, in a battle that raged 2½ hours and left the windblown crowd on center court drained on emotion.

It was the longest women's final in 21 years, since Louise Brough beat Mrs. Margaret Osborn du Pont, 10-8, 1-6, 10-8, and it ended with a crescendo of drama as Billie Jean, hobbled by leg cramps and unable to go to net, hit five shots of outrageous imagination to save as many match points before the last ball dribbled weakly into the net.

Mrs. Court, too, had her physical troubles. Before she went on court, she took pain-killing injections for the torn ankle ligaments sustained in a Monday match with Helga Neissen.

"Whether I would have lasted three sets, I don't know. When I came off court in the end, I had a cramp in the ankle quite badly," she said.

More Surgery Looms

Billie Jean's cramps set in midway through the second set.

"It's my bad right knee; I keep getting leg cramps," she said. "I may need another operation, but I don't know if I want to go through the mental anguish. I may not play at Forest Hills. I'm not sure I have any further plans."

Billie Jean injured both knees in an automobile accident in 1963 and later had surgery on the left knee.

So now the grand slam lies temptingly ahead for Mrs. Court, with the Australian, French and Wimbledon titles already won and the fourth looming at Forest Hills. No one has achieved the grand slam since the late Maureen Connolly did it in 1953.

For the fourth time and for the third year in a row, the men's doubles title went to the Australians, John Newcombe and Tony Roche, who defeated their countrymen, Ken Rosewall and Fred Stolle, 10-8, 6-3, 6-1. Earlier, Rosewall and Stolle had taken the deciding set in play held over from yesterday in defeating the Rumanian combination of Ion Tiriac and Ilie Nastase, 6-4, 3-6, 10-8, 0-6, 6-3.

Tomorrow, Newcombe plays Rosewall for the singles championship.

On the Razor's Edge

Break points became a numbers game for Mrs. Court and Mrs. King, so many time did the girls live on the knife edge. Billie Jean, in the first set, was through to 5-4 with love-40 and five breakpoints and was two points away from the set before Mrs. Court evened it with a lob that bounced off the chalk.

Four times in that marathon first set Billie Jean broke service. It should have been good enough. Service dominates even the women's game and the Californian is a server of repute and the best volleyer in tennis. Invariably, Mrs. Court shook her off.

There was sort of a jangled pattern most of the afternoon. Up to the net would hurtle Billie Jean, inevitably hungry for the volley. Mrs. Court would tease her back with lobs and as she became more and more accurate, fastened her shots on the lines. The whole court was there for both of them to be explored and exploited.

A set point loomed for Margaret in the 24th game. Billie Jean slapped a volley away, was at 12-13 and love-40 and grimacing in pain as a high backhand slice floated by her into the corner for the set.

Imagination Saves Day

With her strength ebbing, Mrs. King no longer followed her first serve to net. For a while imagination saved the day, as she aimed her lobs and dropshots for the angles.

Mrs. Court reached her first

Margaret Court faced Billy Jean King in many crucial games throughout her career. In this 1970 photo, she moves to return the ball to Billy Jean in the finals at Wimbledon. Court won this time.

United Press International

Mrs. King strains to return the ball during losing effort

NEWCOMBE BEATS ROSEWALL IN WIMBLEDON FINAL

A 5-SET STRUGGLE

Newcombe's Service, Volley Prevail After Foe Fights Back

By FRED TUPPER
Special to The New York Times

WIMBLEDON, England, July 4—John Newcombe has won his second Wimbledon singles title in four years.

The big, well-built Australian slammed the door shut on Ken Rosewall in the closing stages after little Ken, with all but hope gone, had set the center court on fire with a five-game burst for the fourth set.

Newcombe won, 5-7, 6-3, 6-2, 3-6, 6-1, in the first five-set final since Ted Schroeder defeated Jaroslav Drobny in 1949, and to his credit he hauled his wandering concentration together after the victory that had seemed certain began to fade in the gloom and drizzle.

Mrs. Billie Jean King, beaten in that 46-game classic by Mrs. Margaret Court for the women's crown yesterday, teamed with Rosie Casals to defeat Virginia Wade of Britain and Francoise Durr of France, 6-2, 6-3, and take their third doubles title here in the last four years.

Notable Age Gaps

It was heart-rending for Rosewall. The 35-year-old Australian was having what might be his last fling for the only major title that had escaped him. This was the third time he had reached the final, the first 16 years ago against Drobny and the second 14 years ago again Lew Hoad.

Those are prodigious age gaps in tennis, a game that makes such demands on speed, reflexes and stamina.

Rosewall reached the heights at a precocious 18 to take the Australian and French titles,

and the sands of time seemed to have run out for him when Wimbledon became an open as he lost to Tony Roche two years ago and Bob Lutz last year early in the championships.

Besides the handicap of age, Rosewall was no physical match for the 6-foot, 26-year-old Newcombe. A little man at 5-7½ and 150 pounds, Ken must rely on the weapons that are peculiarly his—a backhand that flashes like lightning, a feathery touch on the lob and the intelligence and imagination to crease openings.

But Newcombe has mastered his trade. His bulldozing service is the most penetrating in tennis, his ground strokes are strong and he covers court like an octopus, arms flailing about for remarkable gets.

A searing backhand gave him a chance for the service break in the second game and Rosewall was love-40 on a running forehand at 4-all.

Watches a Point Drop

At 5-4 John spun a forehand through the middle that Ken surprisingly let go, and it dived inside the baseline to give him set point. A backhand volley off his shoe tops saved Rosewall, and a backhand put him at set point seconds later. He won it as Newcombe volleyed into the alley under pressure.

All the nostalgia for Ken broke out in prolonged applause that once was Drobny's when the self-exiled Czechoslovak beat him in 1954.

That devastating backhand gave the little man a break point again as the second set started, but scrambling up to net he put a volley out.

Now he was in trouble. Again he awtched a returnable forehand drop into the court, then he bungled a volley, stared at another forehand that whipped by him and double faulted to trail, 2-4.

Three break points Ken had in the next game, once hoisting a wavering lob that plopped just behind the line as John wiped his forehead in relief.

Then the set was Newcombe's as he galloped up to punch a volley into the clear.

Again Rosewall had 3 points

Mrs. Court during 2½-hour match, longest Wimbledon women's final since 1949. She beat Mrs. King, 14-12, 11-9.

Associated Press

match point at 7-6. As the umpire called for quiet, Billie Jean hammered the volley across court and made her final bid. At 7-all she reached advantage point, but Margaret stormed up to put the volley away. A forehand had Billie Jean at ad point again, but sadly she plumped the ball low into the net.

Mrs. Court fell, her ankle began to ache, but the pain seemed to give her purpose. Suddenly she was at 10-9 and

15-40, victory a stroke away.

Billie Jean hit a deep smash to save a second match point and blasted an ace to save the third. Ad Margaret again. A King backhand drew chalk as it nailed the line. Another ad Margaret. Billie Jean hit a running forehand deep across court to save. A sixth match point to Margaret. There were no more miracles. Mrs. King pushed it into the net.

July 4, 1970

United Press International

LOVE THAT TROPHY: John Newcombe of Australia with his prize after he defeated Ken Rosewall at Wimbledon.

for the break in the second game of the third set, but Newcombe fobbed him off. So near so often was Rosewall. He seemed discouraged, trudging around the baseline with head down and shoulders sagging.

A Miserable Game

Then Ken served a miserable game. He his his seventh double-fault and pushed successive volleys into the net to lose the game at love and trail, 1-2. The next service was lost, too, as Newcombe came roaring up for the kill, and so was the third set.

All the fire had gone from Rosewall's game and when he double-faulted twice again to drop his service at the start of the fourth set, the match seemed over. Newcombe was completely in command, dominating the net and drilling his first serve in consistently.

It was almost embarrassing, so the crowd clapped for Rosewall spontaneously when he changed courts, trying to inject some strength and purpose into the bedraggled figure now bent into a crouch with weariness and disappointment.

12 Points in a Row

Behind by 1-3 and love-30, Rosewall suddenly took heart. He had 4 points running to keep his service, then ran amok. A backhand forced Newk into an error, a forehand put him back on his heels and then a backhand streaked away and Ken was at love-40. He slapped his thigh and dug in. Then John double-faulted. Twelve points in succession for Rosewall as he got his second wind.

At 3-4 Ken had a break point In this exuberant mood he decided to go for it, whipping a backhand acutely through a hole. He served out masterfully to take the fourth set. Five games in a streak, match all even.

Newcombe Bears Down

Then Newcombe proved his mettle. A tough, brutal competitor, he bore down. He made returns that seemed impossible, his service thundered down on the shrinking Rosewall.

Game after game came running and on his second match point he cranked up a forehand and fired it cross-court as the applause came down.

Victory meant a check for $7,200 of the $100,000 purse, and Princess Margaret came on the court to bestow the silver platter, emblematic of the most prized title in tennis.

"I felt sorry for Ken, but not too sorry," said Newcombe. "I wanted to win the darned thing myself."

"Had I played just a fraction better—a few passing shots, a few volleys, a few points here and there," said Rosewall, who won $3,600. "But John is a good, hard-working match player, and he played enough good shots."

Sharon Walsh, the 18-year-old Californian who had played so beautifully to upset Patti Hogan, Helen Gourlay and even lead Miss Durr, 5-4 and 40-love in women's play, took the junior title by beating M. Kroshina of the Soviet Union, 8-6, 6-4.

Bobby Riggs, the champion here way back in 1939, teamed with Drobny to defeat Pancho Segura and George MacCall, the former United States Davis Cup captain, 6-2, 6-2, in the veterans' doubles final.

Mrs. Court earned $3,600 for the women's single crown and Mrs. King $1,800 as runner-up.

Miss Casals won her second title of the day when she and Rumania's Ilie Nastase won the mixed doubles, 6-3, 4-6, 9-7, from the Russian pair of Alex Metreveli and Olga Morozova.

July 5, 1970

U.S. Open Adopts Sudden-Death Set

By NEIL AMDUR

In the most revolutionary step in tournament tennis scoring since "love" became synonymous with losers, a sudden-death scoring system will be instituted for all matches in the $160,000 United States Open championships, Sept. 2 through 13, at the West Side Tennis Club in Forest Hills, Queens.

A 9-point tiebreaker, recently approved for experimental use by the International Lawn Tennis Federation, will decide all sets reaching 6-6. The player who wins 5 of the 9 points in the playoff wins the set or match. Conceivably, as much as $20,000, the top prize in men's singles at Forest Hills, could ride on one serve or shot, if the score reached 6-all in games in the fifth set and 4-all in the tiebreaker.

"We consider this to be a major step forward for the game of tennis," said William F. Talbert, the former national doubles champion and the tournament director of the third Open.

"It provides tennis with a finish line, such as we have in racing, basketball, football and other major sports. No longer will a tennis match drag on for hours. It will be played within a sensible, predictable amount of time, enabling spectators to estimate the length of a match and make their plans accordingly."

How Tiebreaker Works

Talbert explained the 9-point tiebreaker as follows:

When a set reaches 6-all, Player A serves 2 points and then Player B serves 2 points, after which the players change ends. Player A then serves 2 points, if necessary, and Player B serves the final 3 points, if necessary. The player who serves last then serves first in the following set to equalize service in the event of another deuced set. The set is scored, 7-6. After the fourth set, in the event sudden-death has been used twice or four times in the match, a racquet is tossed and the winner chooses either to serve or receive.

Talbert said the tiebreaker should have tremendous impact, artistically and psychologically. It also should improve the sport's chances of gaining national television exposure, which, undoubtedly, have been hindered by the unpredictability and length of many matches.

As a further means of streamlining the competition,

Talbert said the customary rest period, after the third set in men's matches and after the second set in women's play, would be eliminated.

"Sudden-death retains the element of stamina in lengthy matches," he said. "But it will force players to improve one of the most ignored aspects of the game, the return of serve. Now the guy with the big serve will also have to learn how to hit the serve back."

Tiebreakers have been utilized for many years, in various forms, from the Van Alen Simplified Scoring System (VASSS), which is similar to table-tennis scoring, to seven, eight, nine and 12 point tiebreakers.

¶Laver, who achieved his second Grand Slam by winning the men's title last year, played 25 sets of singles, six of which went to 6-all. He won five of the deuce sets.

¶Of the 20 men's singles finals played at Forest Hills since 1950, 10 of the 72 sets have reached 6-all.

¶Eight of the 10 longest men's singles matches on record have been played on grass courts.

Conventional scoring in tennis is based on 4 points to a game (15, 30, 40, game) and six games to a set. "Love" is zero. In matches involving players who are evenly matched, games and sets can run to "deuce." In this case, a player must win either two consecutive points or games.

The problem of deciding "deuce" games and sets is compounded on faster surfaces such as grass, cement or wood, because the ball moves faster, points are played out more quickly and the server has the advantage of making the first offensive stroke.

Disputes May Develop

Since one player could serve five times in the 9-point tiebreaker, controversy may surround its introduction at Forest Hills. Several top players, including Rod Laver, the world champion, already have called the 9-point system "unfair."

A statistical look at last year's Open, however, reveals the significance and excitement that the tiebreaker might generate at this year's tournament:

¶In men's singles, 68 sets, or about 15 per cent of the total number of sets played, reached 6-all, including 13 matches that were decided by deuce sets. In women's singles, 13 of the 134 sets played were deuce sets.

July 26, 1970

Women Tennis Stars Threaten Boycott Over Unequal Purses

Some of the world's leading women tennis players threatened yesterday to boycott future tournaments because men get more prize money.

"It's discrimination," Rosemary Casals said at the West Side Tennis Club, in Forest Hills, Queens, where the United States Open is being played. She is seeded second in the championships.

"We expend the same amount of energy," she said. "We practice as much, we play just as hard. We contribute our share to the success of the tournament."

Mrs. Margaret Court of Australia, the world's leading woman player, said the women's prize money should be "at least half and possibly three-fourths that of the men."

Addressing a meeting of the Lawn Tennis Writers Association, the women players indicated that they might refuse to compete in a major tournament starting Sept. 21 in Los Angeles.

This tournament, the Pacific Southwest, offers a first prize of $12,500 for men and $1,500 for women. The women players, insisting that their demands have nothing to do with the women's liberation movement, want a purse at least one-third as large as the men's.

In the Los Angeles tournaments, a woman must reach the quarter-finals to get any money at all. Men losers customarily get first-round money. A man who loses in the first round at Forest Hills collects $300. A woman gets $150.

Other women players at the meeting were Mrs. Gail Chanfreau of France, the former Gail Sherriff of Australia; Mrs. Mary Ann Curtis of St. Louis; Francoise Durr of France; Kerry Harris of Australia; Mrs. Ingrid Bentzer of Sweden; Kathy Harter of Seal Beach, Calif., and Esme Emanuel, a South African now living in San Francisco.

They laid down a three-point program for future tournaments:

1, Prize money commensurate with that of the men; 2, equal exposure in center-court matches; 3, better treatment by the news media, which subordinates women's to men's tennis.

They said another meeting tonight would decide whether most of the top players would compete at Los Angeles, a tournament run by Perry Jones, or play in a proposed women's tournament at Houston with a $5,000 first prize.

Jack Kramer, Pacific Southwest director in place of the ailing Jones, said, "We will have a women's tournament regardless. We have 57 entries from our area alone. We can't change the prize money now. It is already fixed."

Miss Emanuel said she and Ceci Martinez of San Francisco polled spectators at the Open on Sunday, getting 2 per cent of the 13,000 turnout.

"Eighty-two per cent said they preferred both women and men playing rather than just the men," she said. "But 5 per cent said women shouldn't be playing tennis at all."

Miss Durr said she believed that women with their ballerina skirts added sex appeal to a tournament.

The women were asked if they believed the tours could be separated permanently for men and women.

"No," said Miss Durr. "How would we play mixed doubles?"

John Newcombe of Australia, who headed the now defunct International Tennis Players Association, thinks women players have little cause for argument in regard to their demands for more prize money.

Arthur Ashe was even more adamant on the subject.

"Without a doubt," he said, "women's play will disappear soon from men's tournaments except for the large ones like the United States Open."

He added, "Men are doing this for a living now. They have families, and they don't want to give up money just for girls to play. Only three or four women draw fans to a tourney, anyhow, so why do we have to split our money with them?"

September 8, 1970

Mrs. Court Completes Grand Slam at Forest Hills; Rosewall Wins in 4 Sets

ROCHE IS BEATEN IN U.S. OPEN FINAL

Mrs. Court Gains Her 4th Major Title of Year by Defeating Miss Casals

By NEIL AMDUR

Mrs. Margaret Court swept everything, including her grand slam in singles, and little Ken Rosewall collected his biggest payday as a professional on the final day of the $160,000 United States Open tennis championships yesterday.

The 35-year-old Rosewall, who received a gold ball and a handshake for winning the National Amateur event 14 years ago, drove out of the West Side Tennis Club in Forest Hills, Queens, with a new Ford Pinto and a check for $20,000 after his 2-6, 6-4, 7-6, 6-3 victory over Tony Roche. It was the biggest payoff for a tournament since the Open era began in tennis three years ago.

Roche, the Australian left-hander beaten by Rosewall in the semifinals at Wimbledon and seeded fourth here, received $10,000 as the runner-up for a second straight year.

"I felt the pressure quite a bit at times," Mrs. Court said after her final. "I played very tentative, but I sort of made myself concentrate. I'm tired. I guess I haven't realized that it's all over."

Victor in Mixed Doubles

Mrs. Court, who at 5 feet 9 inches is two inches taller than Rosewall, overshadowed the women's field. She achieved the last leg of her singles grand slam with a 6-2, 2-6, 6-1 triumph over Rosemary Casals, a victory worth $7,500; teamed with Marty Riessen for the mixed doubles crown, 6-4, 6-4, over Mrs. Judy Dalton and Frew McMillan, worth $1,000, and received $1,000 more from Saturday's women's doubles championship.

In a move that may help to make her the first woman athlete to earn $100,000 in a single year, Mrs. Court received another 500 shares of stock from her racquet manufacturer, the Chemold Corporation of Jamaica, Queens. In addition to the victory, coupled with her titles in the Australian, French and Wimbledon championships, Mrs. Court has at least 2,000 shares of stock, currently valued at about $1.50 a share, a new contract for 1971 and countless opportunities for commercial endorsements.

The only other woman player to win the grand slam was the late Maureen Connolly as an amateur in 1953. Mrs. Court had won three of the four amateur events three times in the past. Two men, Rod Laver and Don Budge, have successfully completed the men's grand slam, Budge in 1938, Laver in 1962 and last year.

Rosewall's comeback delighted the record crowd of 14,502, the second sellout in two days. Not since Bill Tilden, at the age of 36, beat Francis T. Hunter in the 1929 amateur final here, has a player so late in his career successfully withstood the physical and mental pressures of potential five-set matches on grass courts over 12 long days.

Added Pressures on Rosewall

The pressure on Rosewall was compounded by the record prize money, the institution of the sudden-death nine-point tiebreaker and the depth of the professional talent in the 108-player field.

Yesterday, the dark-haired Australian survived the loss of the first set, three break points at 5-6 in the third set, a tense sudden-death playoff and a cracked frame in his favorite wooden racquet, which he continued to use because of its marvelous touch.

"It's my biggest win," said the modest soft-spoken Australian, who reached the semifinals here at the age of 18 in 1953 and ended Lew Hoad's bid for a grand slam in the 1956 final. "I'm very touched. It's such a long time between wins."

For the 25-year-old Roche, who grew up watching Rosewall play Davis Cup matches, defeat brought intense disappointment. Though he is considered one of the world's top five singles players, the blocky left-hander has yet to win a major grass-court championship.

"This is getting to be a bad habit for me," he said. "I thought I was going along well there, but Kenny hit some great shots."

As so often happened during the tournament, the momentum seemed to sway during the tie-breaker for the third set, after Rosewall held service for 6-all with a running forehand placement down the line and Roche's forehand error at deuce.

Roche had won all four of

his previous tiebreaker sets during the tournament, including one in a straight-set victory over Cliff Richey in the semifinals. But the third-seeded Rosewall employed his strongest weapons, ground strokes and the return of serve, to push his rival out of position and take an early 2-0 lead in the playoff, with Roche serving the first 2 points.

The shot that brought the tense crowd to its feet was a forehand cross-court placement at 3-1, a ground stroke that Rosewall executed time after

Road to the Slam

AUSTRALIAN OPEN
Defeated Evonne Goolagong, 6-3, 6-1; Karen Krantzcke, 6-1, 6-3, and Kerry Melville, 6-3, 6-1.

FRENCH OPEN
Defeated Marijke Schaar-Jansen, 6-1, 6-1; Olga Morozova 3-6, 8-6, 6-1; Lesley Hunt, 6-2, 6-1; Rosemary Casals, 7-5, 6-2; Julie Heldman, 6-0, 6-2, and Helga Niessen, 6-2, 6-4.

WIMBLEDON OPEN
Defeated Sue Alexander, 6-0, 6-1, Maria Guzman, 6-0, 6-1; Vlasta Vopicova, 6-3, 6-3; Helga Niessen 6-8, 6-0, 6-0; Rosemary Casals, 6-4, 6-1 and Mrs. Billie Jean King, 14-12, 11-9.

UNITED STATES OPEN
Defeated Pam Austin, 6-1, 6-0; Patti Hogan, 6-1, 6-1; Patricia Faulkner, 6-10, 6-2; Helen Gourlay, 6-2, 6-2, Nancy Richey, 6-1, 6-3, and Rosemary Casals, 6-2, 2-6, 6-1.

time in knocking down Charles Pasarell, Nikki Pilic, Stan Smith and John Newcombe, the Wimbledon champion, en route to the final.

With Roche attacking, Rosewall dug the ball out of the browned turf, refused to jerk the motion or top it, but fluently lifted it into an open spot, as if he were reproducing it from an instructional guide. The tie-breaker ended, 5-2, with Roche driving a backhand return of serve wide.

"That's what happens when you do 'Muscles' a favor," Roche said afterward of his Australian countryman. "I did his laundry for him yesterday and look what he does to me."

In winning the second set, the 21-year-old Miss Casals became the first player in two years here to take a set against Mrs. Court.

Both women appeared nervous and admitted afterward that the play had been "tentative and spotty" because of the stakes.

"I had a lot of trouble with my serve," said Miss Casals, a Californian who won $3,750 as the runner-up. "And Margaret has such long arms that they seemed to go all around the court."

Mrs. Court broke Miss Casals inthe second and sixth games of the third set, concentrating her attack on her rival's backhand volley and driving deeply off the ground.

"There was a lot of tension," she said. "I was praying on that last serve that Rosie hit into the net."

Mrs. Court's husband, Barry, was one of the first to congratulate her after the match.

"What was the first thing she said to you afterward?" a friend asked Barry.

"She said she couldn't believe it," he answered.

September 14, 1970

WOMEN NET REBELS PLANNING OWN TOUR

HOUSTON, Sept. 24 (UPI)—The women tennis stars who bolted the United States Lawn Tennis Association to play in this week's Virginia Slims invitation tournament plan to make their break with the U.S.L.T.A. permanent and form their own tennis tour, Mrs. Billie Jean King said today. She said they hoped to start the tour with a series of tournaments on the West Coast, Texas, Boston and in Florida next January and February.

Eight women revolted yesterday because the U.S.L.T.A. would not sanction the Virginia Slims tournament if it paid the $5,000 prize money it was offering. The sponsors offered to pay the money as expenses, but the women said they did not want the money under the table and decided to become contract pros.

They signed for $1 each with Gladys Heldman, editor and publisher of World Tennis Magazine. Her daughter, Julie, ranked second in the nation and fifth in the world, signed today to bring the total to nine.

The original eight and their world rankings are Mrs. King (2), Nancy Richey (4), Rosemary Casals (6), Kerry Melville (7), Mrs. Judy Tegart Dalton (3), Peaches Bartkowicz (10), Krisy Pigeon and Valerie Ziegenfuss.

In first-round play of the Virginia Slims tourney, Mrs. King, playing for the first time since knee surgery in July, lost, 6-3, 6-3, today to Mrs. Dalton of Australia at the Houston Racquet Club.

September 25, 1970

N.C.A.A. NET TITLE GOES TO CONNORS

U.C.L.A. Freshman Defeats Tanner in Four Sets

SOUTH BEND, Ind., June 19 (AP)—Jimmy Connors, a freshman at the University of California, Los Angeles, used a tremendous serve and consistent placements to capture the National Collegiate tennis championship today by defeating Roscoe Tanner of Stanford in the final, 6-3, 4-6, 6-4, 6-4.

The Bruin star, the No. 1 junior in the nation and 14th in the men's ranking, became the first freshman ever to win the singles title. Tanner lost in the final for the second straight year. Both are left-handers.

Connors dropped his service only once in 19 games while winning his eighth match of the week-long event. He defeated his teammate, Haroon Rahim, in yesterday's semifinals while Tanner beat Jeff Borowiak of U.C.L.A., the defending champion.

Tanner, a member of the Junior Davis Cup team, lost his service three times. He had seven double-faults to only four for Connors.

Connors will play in the Wimbledon tournament in England beginning Monday.

The Uclan duo of Borowiak and Rahim captured the doubles title with a 7-6, 7-6 victory over Bob McKinley and Dick Stockton of Trinity of Texas.

June 20, 1971

Miss Goolagong Wins at Wimbledon

By FRED TUPPER
Special to The New York Times

WIMBLEDON, England, July 2—Evonne Goolagong won at Wimbledon today. The 19-year-old daughter of an Australian aboriginal sheep-shearer won the All-England women's tennis championship on the storied center court by defeating the great Mrs. Margaret Court. The margin by which she destroyed her 28-year-old Australian opponent defies belief.

With a four-game burst at the start and a streak of six games in a row to end it, the amazing youngster won by 6-4, 6-1 from the three-time Wimbledon champion who has taken more major titles than any other woman.

Of all the reputations that have been shattered here over the past fortnight, this was the most formidable. Rod Laver, Ken Rosewall and Mrs. Billie Jean King have been beaten on occasion, but Mrs. Court, the 1970 grand slam winner (the Australian, French, Wimbledon and American titles) was a 2-1 favorite to win today.

This year she had lost only to Miss Goolagong in the Tasmanian tournament and to Mrs.

Associated Press

Evonne Goolagong in action against Mrs. Margaret Court

Gail Chanfreau in the French championships, when she was suffering with the flu.

Miss Goolagong was discovered at the age of 9 by Vic Edwards, British-born head of the largest coaching school in Australia.

He adopted her at the age of 14 and brought her to Europe a year ago. She was put out in the second round here by Peaches Bartkowicz, 6-4, 6-0. "Wimbledon champion by 1974," was the Edwards target. The rest is now history.

Shades of Maria Bueno

Evonne is the first girl in her teens to win Wimbledon since Karen Hantze did it at the age of 19 in 1962, and her spontaneous shotmaking and her grace around court are reminiscent of Maria Bueno, who was 19 when she won in 1959. Maureen Connolly of California was 17 when she won in 1952.

Evonne said she had received a good luck cable before today's match from her parents in the room in the tiny Australian town of Barellan, 365 miles southwest of Sydney. The parents and six of their children watched the match on television.

Her father, Ken Goolagong, was quoted in dispatches as saying that when Evonne won, "the kids ran all around the room shouting and leaping." But he said that Evonne, the third eldest child, "will be treated just like all the others when she comes home."

American fans, however, will not see her perform before she does go home. Her schedule does not embrace the United States Open at Forest Hills, Queens, because Edwards, her coach, said he decided "it would be too much for her to go on to the United States this time."

"She'll be there next year," he said.

Regal Surroundings

Among the 15,000 Wimbledon fans who saw her today were Prime Minister Edward Heath and former Prime Minister Harold Macmillan, who joined Princess Margaret in the royal box. Princess Alexandra, president of the All-England Club, came down on court and awarded Miss Goolagong the silver platter. Her victory was worth $4,300.

Her plan for tonight was typical of a teen-ager who takes the pressures of championship tennis in stride.

"Guess a group of us will go to a 'disco' tonight to celebrate," she said. "Come to think of it, I was going to celebrate anyway."

Alf Chave, an Australian newsman who has been staying with Edwards and his wife, said Evonne "hasn't got a nerve in her body. She showed me her gown for Saturday's Wimbledon ball last night and then I knew it was curtains for Margaret."

Evonne has lived with Edwards and his wife while on the tennis circuit since she was 14. Edwards had persuaded Evonne's parents to allow him and his wife to adopt her and she moved with them as a member of the family.

This year, she brought her foster family a major honor when she won the French championship. At Wimbledon, she was seeded third on the strength of her French title, and she dropped just one set all the way, to Lesley Hunt of Australia in the fourth round. She beat Mrs. Nancy Gunter easily and upset the second-seeded Mrs. King on Wednesday.

Off to Fast Start

Evonne was off the mark today like a sprinter. A cross-court forehand angled shot beat Margaret completely for the service break at the start. A buzz of expectancy ran through the stands. Evonne was enjoying herself.

She cut off a backhand volley to take the second game and bounced happily around the court to beat Margaret repeatedly to the decisive volley. Quickly she was at 4-love and 15-40 on Margaret's service, still cool and confident.

For a time the errors crept in. Evonne's backhand is feared, her forehand is not, and the mistakes were being made off her stronger side. Her lead drifted away. She was 4-3 and 15-40 on service and Mrs. Court seemed ready to charge.

Miss Goolagong was magnificent in the crisis. She rapped a volley across court, pulled up Margaret with a drop shot and then lobbed to the baseline. Two more volleys took her to 5-3 and she had the

first set at 6-4.

In the second set, Margaret's strokes shortened and her volley became tentative. Invariably in the deuce games, Evonne was winning the big point, the mark of a champion. She soon was at 5-love and love-40, three match points. Margaret bravely saved them all. Match point again and Mrs. Court double-faulted and lost to Evonne for the second time in eight matches.

AS A WINNER: Miss Goolagong with trophy after she defeated Mrs. Court for women's singles championship.

Those older Australians, Roy Emerson and Rod Laver, came from behind to win the doubles title from Arthur Ashe and Dennis Ralston, 4-6, 9-7, 6-8, 6-4, 6-4. Tomorrow, John Newcombe, winner as an amateur in 1967 and as a contract pro last year, faces fourth-seeded Stan Smith of Pasadena, Calif., for the men's title.

July 3, 1971

NEWCOMBE TENNIS VICTOR

AUSSIE WINS TITLE

Fights Back to Topple Smith Over 5 Sets in Wimbledon Final

By FRED TUPPER
Special to The New York Times

WIMBLEDON, England, July 3—At the stroke of 5 today John Newcombe slashed a low volley into the clear to end one of the great finals in Wimbledon history.

The Australian beat Stan Smith of the United States in a dour, uncompromising battle of battering serves and fierce volleys with the result in dispute right down to the wire.

The scores were 6-3, 5-7, 2-6, 6-4, 6-4.

As that volley fled away, wave after wave of applause rolled down. Newcombe, over 170 palpitating minutes, took his second All-England final in a row and third in five years.

The victory confirmed the 27-year-old Australian's status as the world's No. 1, but in Smith's golden moments halfway through, it seemed that America would have its first champion here since little Chuck McKinley took this coveted crown in 1963.

Avenge Their Defeats

The United States salvaged one title as Mrs. Billie Jean King and Rosie Casals avenged their singles defeats by beating Mrs. Margaret Court and Evonne Goolagong of Australia, 6-3, 6-2, for their fourth doubles championship in five years.

Bob Kriess, 18, a sophomore at the University of California, Los Angeles, won the junior title by defeating Stephen Warboys of Britain, 2-6, 6-4, 6-3.

No quarter was given or asked in the wildly fluctuating men's final, and only one lapse by Smith under tremendous pressure in the fifth set settled this issue of resolution and character.

Newcombe had been second-seeded and the favorite. He had raced through six rounds with the loss of only one set and he had granted the great Ken Rosewall a meager five games in reaching the final.

There was no way to fault Newcombe's play at the start. He was crashing his first serve into the corners, volleying like a madman and covering so much court that the giant Smith seemed leaden in comparison.

In the sixth game John was at 15-40 on a backhand that streaked cross court, and though Stan saved then, he later reached for a ball that appeared to be going out and volleyed over the line to give the Australian the break at 4-2.

In this mood John had the set and was 4-all and 15-40 in the next set with another backhand pasted against the line.

It was now or never for the American army private. Smith had come far over the last couple of years and a fortnight ago had beaten Newcombe in straight sets for the London grass title. A smash from deep court, a blazing serve and a volley put him at 5-4, and when Newcombe double-faulted to 30-40 in the next game, there was Stan surprisingly at set point.

It hardly seemed possible. Until then he had never had a break point on Newcombe's service or had even reached deuce. John dug himself out of that morass, but the whole complexion of the match was to change in a twinkling. The 24-year-old Smith had found inspiration and was ready to roll.

Unleashes His Weapons

All his glorious weapons came immediately to hand. A flat forehand to an empty spot, a Newcombe double-fault and a backhand that found the net put the American again at set point in the 12th game. Then Smith hit a backhand through the middle that was volleyed out by Newcombe, and Stan had the set at 7-5 for one apiece.

Trailing at 0-2 in the third, Smith went berserk. That huge first serve was caroming off the grass and his ground strokes were finding the corners. Under this nonstop assault, Newcombe lost his concentration.

"I know about center court," he had said before the match. "You can go into coma out there."

Suddenly Stan was invincible. In that streak he had six games running and the third set at 6-2. What price the fourth-seeded Smith now?

Newcombe shook off the malaise. He jumped up and down on the service line and snapped back to attention. It's on the record now that he played to perfection.

In the finest sustained serving streak since Bob Falkenburg won here in 1948, he had four service games at love and was 5-4 and 40-love.

Not a single point had Smith won against service all the way through the set. Desperately he fought off three set points to get to deuce. At advantage John aced him for 6-4 and two sets each.

It was a question now of toughness of fiber and high resolve. At 2-all, the man from Pasadena served a dreadful game. A forehand passed him, he double-faulted twice and pushed a volley low into the net to lose at love.

AWKWARD MOMENT: John Newcombe in match against Stan Smith. Ball boy is at front.
Associated Press

Could Smith break back? A forehand winner off the tape, a backhand off John's shoetops and a volley through the middle put him at break point in the next game. Newcombe, off balance, smashed deep and, on the run, Smith got his racquet on the ball. With the court wide open, his lob drifted inches over the baseline.

Newcombe's 12th ace took him to 4-2 and when that low volley scooted across court like a rabbit he had wonderfully won.

"I kept telling myself out there that 'fortune favors the brave,'" he said. His reward was a cup presented by the Duke of Kent and $9,000.

"I'll be back," said Smith, who received $5,400.

In the all-American senior final the evergreen Gardnar Mulloy, now 57 years old, and Tony Vincent beat Vic Seixas, the 1953 Wimbledon men's champion, and Straight Clark, 6-2, 6-4, as Gar served out the match at love.

With the great names disappearing — Rod Laver, Rosewall, Mrs. King and Mrs. Court were all crushed in straight sets —the crowds came running to this $120,000 85th tournament. Attendance reached 299,000 over the fortnight, 2,000 short of the record set in 1967, the last year before Wimbledon became an open.

July 4, 1971

Smith Beats Kodes for U.S. Open Title

4-Set Triumph-Mrs. King Wins by 6-4, 7-6

By NEIL AMDUR

Stan Smith, a rejected ballboy, won the United States Open tennis championship yesterday.

The second-seeded Californian, currently serving a two-year tour of duty in the Army, put down the grass-court heroics of Jan Kodes, the unseeded, 25-year-old Czech, 3-6, 6-3, 6-2, 7-6, before a crowd of 12,879 at the West Side Tennis Club in Forest Hills, Queens.

The women's singles final, also delayed three days by rain, went to top-seeded Mrs. Billie Jean King, who beat second-seeded Rosemary Casals, her keenest rival on the tour, 6-4, 7-6, for the ninth time in 10 meetings this year.

It was the first time in 16 years that Americans had swept the singles titles.

Smith's victory was the finest achievement in a career that has brought continued artistic improvement. With this title and as runner-up to John Newcombe at Wimbledon earlier the angular, 6-foot-4-inch blond must be considered among the top three or four players in the world, perhaps behind Newcombe, Rod Laver and Ken Rosewall.

Graceful Performer

Such status is a far cry from that gloomy day a decade ago when Smith, an ambitious junior, offered his services as a ballboy for a Davis Cup match, but was turned down because officials thought he was too clumsy to run across the court and pick up balls.

Yesterday he moved on the lawn in the stadium with the controlled grace of an athlete who had spent long, perhaps frustrating hours jumping rope and exercising to improve his balance, coordination and timing.

He leaned into returns of serves with adroit skill, was impeccable on the difficult half-volley and managed 68 per cent of his first serves (66 of 97), with enough diversity to thwart his rival's potent passing game.

"I changed strategy after the first set," the mustachioed victor said, sipping champagne sent by his racquet manufacturer. "I was serving hard in the first set, and I was hitting everything back. So I slowed it down and tried to hop the ball on the grass."

Contrast Stands Out

The contrast of Smith's range and power with Kodes's tenacious talents off the ground made for an exciting, well-played match despite four service breaks in the fourth set.

Early in the second set, the players hit five successive winners on returns of serves, volleys, and shots from difficult angles. Smith broke Kodes for 2-1 in the third set off a short second serve, which he ran around to take on his forehand and hammer cross-court for a winner.

"I was feeling very tired," said Kodes, who needed five sets to beat Ashe in the semi-finals on Tuesday and perhaps felt the effects of a hot, mid-afternoon sun. "My serve was very weak."

Kodes converted 62 per cent of his first serves. But Smith demonstrated in the 12th game of the fourth set, and again in the tiebreaker for the match, that his serve had precision and power.

Serving at 5-6 in a tense stadium, Smith carried the game at love without hitting a volley. The last 3 points were an unreturnable flat serve deep to Kodes's forehand and two aces, the second of which took a bad bounce, bolstering the Czech's contention that grass courts might not be the joke he thought they were, but that "grass is grass, you know."

Smith and Kodes had won four tiebreaker sets apiece during the tournament.

"The tiebreaker really demands a different technique," said Smith, whose concentration on the court is another outstanding trademark. "You have to change your thinking."

Kodes won the first 2 points of the tiebreaker on serve. Smith put in a spin-serve ace for 1-2, but the trim, inspired Czech slapped a fore-hand cross-court winner.

Leading by 3-1 and with an opportunity to win the 5-of-9 point playoff and the set on service, Kodes lost the next 2 points. More specifically, Smith won them.

The Californian again ran around his backhand on Kodes's second serve and slapped a forehand winner cross-court. Then he answered the Czech's best flat first serve with another cross-court return for a winner, this time off the backhand.

Spectator Last Year

Mrs. King had not won a tournament in the metropolitan area since 1967. The only match she had lost to Miss Casals this year was in an indoor tournament here.

Billie Jean had said she was eager for this year's Open after having watched last year's as a spectator, the result of knee surgery.

Miss Casals carried her bespectacled doubles partner to a tiebreaker in the second set, the only time in the tournament that Mrs. King had seemed in jeopardy of losing a set. Billie Jean won the tiebreaker, 5-2, and the match.

She earned $5,000 in prize money, $2,500 in travel allowance and a new car. She needs less than $20,000 to become the first woman athlete to top $100,000 in a year.

The 24-year-old Smith said that his $15,000 winner's check would be deposited with the Davis Cup fund. He also got $5,000 for expenses.

Since his parents in Pasadena, Calif., recently sold his old Mustang, Smith said he hoped to keep his new cham-

Mrs. Billie Jean King returning shot to Rosemary Casals, whom she defeated for title

pionship car. a Ford Torino.

Smith and Erik Van Dillen, who may play the doubles in the Davis Cup challenge round against Rumania next month in Charlotte, N. C., lost a close battle in the doubles final to Newcombe and Roger Taylor of Britain.

Playing into darkness, the teams split four sets, then agreed to settle the match and $2,000 first prize with a tie-breaker game. The scores were 6-7, 6-3, 7-6, 4-6, 5 points to 3.

September 16, 1971

Center Court Cinderella

Cinderella came to Forest Hills last week, and there was no doubt that she was the belle of the center court ball. Christine Evert, a 16-year-old high school beauty from Fort Lauderdale, Fla., arrived for the United States Open tennis championships unheralded and unseeded. But as she defeated one, then two, then three, then four older and more experienced opponents—often coming from behind—to reach the women's semi-finals, Chrissie became the darling of the crowds. She was such a hit that the tournament's promoters, who otherwise had a rather lackluster show, moved her matches to the prestigious center court. TV cameras focused on Chrissie's matches, and her postmatch interviews produced standing-room crowds. The girl's hypnotic grip on the galleries, according to one tennis writer, "arose from a combination of her youth, poise under pressure, her status as an amateur against the established professionals, her impeccable court conduct, her tactical baseline game and the natural sports instinct that follows an underdog." But as with Cinderella, midnight eventually came. On Friday, Chrissie was defeated by Mrs. Billie Jean King, the veteran top-seeded player, in straight sets. Miss Evert, who is the daughter of a professional tennis teacher, said quietly, "Billie Jean is just too tough." Her mother added, "I'm glad we can go back to reality."

September 12, 1971

MRS. KING POSTS EARNINGS RECORD

Tennis Star First Woman to Exceed $100,000 in Year

PHOENIX, Ariz., Oct. 3 (AP) —Mrs. Billie Jean King of Long Beach, Calif., won the Virginia Slims-Thunderbird tennis tournament today and became the first woman athlete in history to earn $100,000 in a single year.

Mrs. King defeated Rosemary Casals of San Francisco, in the final match, 7-5, 6-1.

"I'm thrilled," Mrs. King told an overflow crowd at Phoenix Tennis Center. "I think I played the best game I've ever played today and I feel very lucky because my husband and my parents were here to share this with me."

Mrs. King and Miss Casals doused each other with champagne after the match.

With the victory, Mrs. King's official earnings reached $102,-600. First place in the tournament was worth $4,000.

Mrs. King and Miss Casals won the doubles by defeating Francoise Durr of France and Mrs. Judy Dalton of Australia, 6-3, 6-2.

The tournament completed this year's Virginia Slims circuit.

October 4, 1971

175

Mrs. King Wins, 6-3, 6-3, for 4th Wimbledon Title

Miss Goolagong Falls Victim to Backhand Play

By FRED TUPPER

Special to The New York Times

WIMBLEDON, England, July 7—Mrs. Billie Jean King has won her fourth Wimbledon title. In 50 nerve-racked minutes on the center court, the bustling 28-year-old from Long Beach, Calif., won from Evonne Goolagong of Australia, 6-3, 6-3, and avenged her semifinal loss here a year ago to the 20-year-old daughter of an aboriginal sheep-shearer.

And so Billie Jean enters the Wimbledon "Hall of Fame" with the half-dozen others who have won this tennis title as many times over the years, including Suzanne Lenglen and Mrs. Helen Wills Moody after World War I and Louise Brough after World War II.

This was not a vintage affair for the classicist. Strangely for her, Billie Jean was a bundle of nerves at first and carefree Evonne, the slowest of starters, didn't find her lovely range of shots until the first set had escaped her.

In those early minutes Little Bo Peep seemed to have lost her way.

Mrs. King gave her every opportunity. She was serving badly, sprinkling her first two service games with four double-faults, and there was Evonne waving futilely with a racquet that was more like a crook.

A Sign of Revival

There was a sign of revival then. Through most of her last three matches here happy-go-lucky Evonne had been behind. She was down 4-5 and receiving in the third set to Olga Morozova of the Soviet Union; behind by 5-6 in the first set and 2-5 in the second against Françoise Durr of France, and down a set and 3-love in that scintillating battle of styles with 17-year-old Chris Evert.

In those crises the Australian came alive, finding inspiration under pressure, responding to the challenge, moving with the grace of a superb athlete to hit winners and make a farce of the odds. Now the Australian won her service game at love with a volley like a dagger thrust into the far corner. It was a beginning.

Mrs. King shook off her vapors and began to go forward, volleying as only she can. She was leading by 4-2 now, at 40-30 and served what seemed to be an ace into the backhand corner. To the call of out, Billie Jean came forward, started to protest and retreated.

She lost that game and the crowd, overwhelmingly for the Australian, loosed a huge cheer. At game point down in the next the American forced a stream of errors for the break and served out the set at love to 6-3.

Half an hour had gone then and it was a new ball game. These are the best female players in tennis and here was the proof. Four first serves creased the corners and Miss Goolagong had the first game at love, floating up to the net to bury the volley.

And here was Billie Jean to counter, her nerves on tight rein, mentally disciplined and finding the range on her ground shots. She scurried behind the baseline and a long, low backhand streaked into the corner and there they were at 3-all.

In the end, the match was decided in the furious seventh game. When Evonne could get the first serve in, there was no reply. But her second is often short and slow, and Mrs. King moved in to attack it, commanding the net behind her return.

Back in 1962, as young Miss Moffitt, she hit a backhand that destroyed the then Margaret Smith (now Mrs. Court) and won from the top-seeded player in the first round. Today she did it again, rolling the backhand into the far corner for the breakthrough to 4-3. With the crowd in silence, she had had four games in a row with a last blinding backhand for the match, 6-3, 6-3.

Silver Symbol of Success

Mrs. King threw her racquet high, shook her fist in delight and was presented with the silver plate by the Duke of Kent.

"There is nothing more really for me to accomplish now, but I love my tennis and will go on playing." she said.

What Billie Jean has done is to become the first woman in tennis to win more than $100,000 a year. This year, for the first time, she won the French championship, beating Evonne in the final. And then today she took her fourth Wimbledon crown after a lapse of three years. She won in 1966, 1967 and 1968.

Her smile as wide as ever, Evonne was gracious in defeat. "I went on my usual 'walkabout,'" she said. "I'm quite satisfied with the way I'm going. My coach, Vic Edwards, told everyone he did not expect me to win Wimbledon until I was about 24."

Miss Goolagong had a word to say about the crowd, with its massively one-sided sympathy for her and against Mrs. King. "When she hits a bit short or hits out and everybody claps, it upsets me. I just don't think it's fair."

Bob Hewitt and Frew McMillan of South Africa won the men's doubles from Stan Smith and Erik Van Dillen of the United States, 6-2, 6-2, 9-7, in a repeat of their triumph in 1967, the last year before the pros came to Wimbledon.

Smith has a date in the final with Ilie Nastase tomorrow.

July 8, 1972

Smith Wins Wimbledon Crown, Defeating Nastase in Five Sets

Missed Smash by Rumanian Ends Match

By FRED TUPPER

Special to The New York Times

WIMBLEDON, England, July 9—In one of the great finals in Wimbledon history, Stan Smith won today from Ilie Nastase, 4-6, 6-3, 6-3, 4-6, 7-5, and what it came down to in the end were all the words that mean courage.

This marvelous match throbbed and pulsated for 160 minutes on center court and in the dying moments the Rumanian saved three match points and then muffed the simplest shot of all—a straightforward smash when he was standing at net—because every nerve in his body had been tuned to handling a difficult one.

And if there was a precedent, go back 18 years to another classic final when Jar Drobny at match point deliberately served an easy ball to the best backhand in tennis and won from Ken Rosewall.

Only this time it wasn't deliberate.

And so the big fellow from Sea Pines, S. C., has done what for so long didn't seem possible.

Only a fortnight ago he lost to little-known John Paish of Britain at Queen's Club and round by round here he stuttered uneasily through matches against opponents way below his class.

At 25, look at Smith's record. He has won Forest Hills, the Grand Prix and all those Davis Cup matches, and with this tremendous triumph today, he becomes the first American since Chuck McKinley in 1963 to win Wimbledon and with Mrs. Billie Jean King, victor over Evonne Goolagong Friday, the first Americans to share the coveted double since freckled-faced Tony Trabert and Louise Brough took the titles in 1955.

And Smith said it himself: "80 per cent guts and a little luck."

Nastase was all that he had been thought to be. This is no longer the deadpan comic with the throwaway shot nor the bad-tempered showoff. The Rumanian muttered a bit, mostly in Italian, and queried a decision or two, but when it mattered most in those final sets, he played the kind of tennis to dream about.

Unexpected Shot When Needed

What an artist this man is. No shot is impossible for him to fashion. His speed around court is phenomenal. His antici-

pation and quick reflexes turn a gone ball into the outright winner. And to Smith's eternal credit, he never panicked and the only gesture he made on court was to leap over the net at the end.

The American's game, by contrast, seems limited to the huge serve, the onrushing volley and baseline ground shots, but on those crucial points with the match in the balance, out would come a delicate drop shot or the concealed stop volley.

The test of his talents and courage came as early as the fifth game of the first set. He was serving at 40-15, double-faulted then and Nastase's running save with the ball seemingly put away made it deuce. Then Natase had three advantage points before Smith rescued himself.

In the sixth game, Stan was unlucky. At game point, Smith's backhand down the line rattled the net cord. The Rumanian ticked the ball off the wood of his racquet for a winner. It could have been Smith 4-2 and serving. Instead there he was

at 3-all, then 4-all and in trouble.

Nastase was dipping his returns off the American's shoelaces and Smith could only volley defensively. Five times Stan staved off game points. Nastase finally broke him, took the set at 6-4 and broke him again for 1-0 in the second set.

With the match drifting away, Smith began his charge. The shots that he had just missed were now falling sweetly. "I feel confident," he had said all through this Wimbledon, "I'll get better."

Indeed he did. Three games running and then he had the second set, 6-3. Smith trailed, 0-2, in the third set and then won another brilliant patch of three games in a row, taking the set at 6-3.

Battle of Wills in 5th Set

They were at four-all in the fourth when Nastase struck again. This time with a running forehand pass that left Stan staring. That game was gone and so was the fourth set to Nastase at 6.4.

All square now, and then the battle of wills in that nail-biting fifth game. Smith led, 40-0, and the Rumanian exploded. All afternoon he had penetrated Stan's defense with a whipped topspin lob off the backhand—the most difficult of shots—and now he did it again. Deuce, then add in.

Five times Smith was at game point and Nastase reached for the stars. One break point, another and another he had, and Smith saved them all. A diving stop volley, a forehand into the corner and then the big serve. And finally that little drop shot that drifted over to put the big fellow ahead at 3-2.

"That game was crucial," said Smith later. "I slowed myself down and took a couple of deep breaths."

Now there was Smith at 5-4 and Nastase serving at 15-40. Two match points. A forehand was saved by Ilie's volley and a backhand fell over the line. Smith at 6-5 and down 40-0. The points came in a bunch and then the third match point. A forehand and Nastase bashed it away. Now the fourth match point. Up floated that easy return and Nastase netted.

The Duke of Kent came down on center court and presented Stan with a golden trophy. A check for $13,000 came with it. Then Smith came into the interview room drenched in perspiration and champagne.

He grinned crookedly at the newsmen. "It was never in doubt."

In all, the United States gained the two singles and shared in two doubles as Mrs. King and Betty Stove of the Netherlands defeated Judy Dalton of Australia and Francoise Durr of France, 6-2, 4-6, 6-3. And then Rosie Casals paired with Nastase to win from Kim Warwick and Miss Goolagong, 6-4, 6-4.

And in the veterans doubles, the 1953 Wimbledon champion Vic Seixas, and Straight Clark of the United States won from Gar Mulloy and Tony Vincent of the United States, 6-3, 9-8.

July 10, 1972

Nastase Turns Back Ashe in U.S. Open Final

Rumanian Scores in Five Sets Despite Temperamental Show

By PARTON KEESE

Ilie Nastase of Rumania won the United States Open tennis championship yesterday at Forest Hills, a top prize of $25,000 and the right to be called the world's best player on grass.

Nastase, by defeating Arthur Ashe of Miami, 3-6, 6-3, 6-7, 6-4, 6-3, before a record crowd of 14,696 and coming out on top in a tournament that included the world's best contract and independent professionals and amateurs, earned those honors at the age of 26.

So, for the second year in a row a soldier has taken the Open crown, though admittedly neither Stan Smith, who won the championship last year as a Specialist 4, nor Nastase, a lieutenant in the Rumanian army, has done much soldiering other than carry a racquet in a militant manner.

Although the Nastase-Ashe match showed how close are the two men in skills, the result tended to prove this: When he wants to be, and puts his mind entirely to the task, Nastase has no peer on grass.

On the other hand, when Ashe is serving at his best (which he was not yesterday) and returning serves with his scintillating backhand and rapier forehand (which he was for the most part against Ilie)), he could be the winner.

Ashe started with a bang, getting his big first serve in and volleying consistently, while Nastase seemed to be concentrating more on establishing relations with the linesmen.

Once, Nastase, acting shocked over a call by Jack Stahr, the service linesman, threw a towel and bounced a ball lightly in Stahr's direction. The crowd immediately got on Nastase. Earlier, Nastase took exception over a foot-fault call by Titus Sparrow, a black linesman, and dropped his racquet in disbelief, one of many times he dropped his racquet in exasperation, tiredness or just for fun.

Ashe had a few words to say about Nastase's behavior. At the presentation of the prizes—Ashe picked up $12,000—Arthur said of Ilie: "When Nastase brushes up on his manners, he'll be an even better player. Maybe I ought to do the same thing."

Afterward, Ashe refused to elaborate on the remarks other than to say: "Ilie and I are good friends off the court, although I must say his table manners are just like his court manners."

Those antics out of the way —at the expense of losing the first set Natase started making untouchable returns and volleys, sweeping the next three games on the way to an easy second set victory at 6-3.

Nevertheless, if the match did not appear lackluster at this point, it was mostly because of its significance as a championship contest. And a tiebreaker in the third set, which brought out four of Ashe's most terrific shots, helped break the monotony of short rallies and forced errors, and gave Ashe the lead.

Behind, two sets to one, Nastase had a roused-up Ashe to contend with, and when Arthur broke his service in the third game of the fourth set, it looked as if Ashe would return to the pinnacle he reached in 1968 when he won the Open.

This is where Nastase's superb ability, when confronted with disaster, took over. He outdueled Ashe at the net, broke even on the passing shots and served far better, especially on his first serve. This might have been the key in the late going: Ashe could not put in that first hard one enough times.

By winning, Nastase fulfilled a potential his rivals knew was **late in arriving. He had developed his electric strokes on the slow clay courts of his native Bucharest, and it may have been this background that delayed his development on grass, the surface on which major tourneys of the world, except the Franch open, are played.**

His erratic behavior, however,

may have been—and may still be—his major bugaboo toward staying on top. His flashy, temperamental spirit, though, is definitely a crowd-pleaser, and mischief under the severest kind of pressure is always to be admired, though not necessarily practiced.

Although he wouldn't admit the victory had made this his happiest day, Nastase said he hoped it was. "I won the tournament, didn't I?" It probably was his most important triumph, though one never knows, talking with Ilie. He also won a car, and announced that since he had won another car recently and owned several already, he might "open a garage in Rumania."

This year Nastase advanced to the final at Wimbledon before losing in five sets to Smith. In 1967 Nastase took over from Ion Tiriac his country's championship and a ranking of No. 1. Together with the tall, glowering Tiriac, they made Rumania a key force in the Davis Cup, gaining the final round in 1969 and 1971, but losing both times to the United States in this country.

Significantly, they are again in the final of the Davis Cup competition, again with the United States as defender. So when the site was announced for here, Nastase and Tiriac objected strenuously enough to have it changed to Bucharest, where the surface is clay, the linesmen Rumanians and the crowds wildly partisan.

Nastase also increased his lead in Gran Prix points (he won the Masters playoff last year in Paris), and he was awarded $1,250 for an early round match with Roger Taylor that a panel voted the most memorable in the tournament. Nastase won in five sets, with a tiebreaker at the end.

The women's doubles title was taken by Francoise Durr of France and Betty Stove of the Netherlands, who beat Mrs Margaret Court of Australia and Virginia Wade of Britain, 6-3, 1-6, 6-3, while the mixed doubles was won by Mrs. Court and Marty Riessen of Evanston, Ill., 6-3, 7-5, from Nastase and Rosemary Casals of San Francisco.

In an innovation for the Open, the third and fourth places in singles were decided by playing one set. Cliff Richey of Sarasota, Fla., took third and an extra $1,000 by defeating Tom Gorman of Seattle, 6-4.

It was the best Open yet in terms of attendance, with a total of 130,010 on hand for the 12 days.

September 11, 1972

This pose is not untypical for Ilie Nastase. ''Nasty'', as he is sometimes called, is here registering a mild disagreement with a linesman's call. It is sometimes almost overlooked that, his manners not withstanding, Nastase is a fine tennis player.

Often brash and arrogant like his good friend Ilie Nastase, Jimmy Connors dominated men's tennis for much of the 1970's.

Bjorn Borg swept Wimbledon from 1976-78, challenging Jimmy Connors for number one ranking in men's tennis.

Riggs Defeats Mrs. Court, 6-2, 6-1

By NEIL AMDUR
Special to The New York Times

RAMONA, Calif., May 13—Bobby Riggs let his tennis racquet do the talking today.

After having softened up Mrs. Margaret Court with a Mothers Day bouquet of roses, the ebullient 55-year-old former national champion routed the current queen of the women's professional tour, 6-2, 6-1, in their $10,000 winner-take-all challenge match.

The victory was the latest and perhaps the most amazing chapter in the colorful career of one of the game's most underrated players and one of sport's most successful hustlers.

It was Riggs who had issued the initial challenge to Mrs. Court and who had heightened the interest for this unusual happening with his continuous putdown of women's tennis ("it stinks").

Today, Riggs gave a 57-minute demonstration of why tennis, at any level, remains a game of mind over muscle. No sooner had the match finished before he was preparing yet another page for his hustler's handbook—a winner-take-all match against Mrs. Billie Jean King, hopefully for mid-July.

"I want her, she's the Women's Libber leader," Riggs, the Muhammad Ali of tennis, said of Mrs. King, who had turned down his first challenge before Mrs. Court stepped in. "She can name the place, the court and the time, just as long as the price is right."

Riggs, who labeled today's victory "the greatest hustle of all time," had put up $5,000 as an invitation for Mrs. Court. His total take from the nationally televised match amounted to $12,500, excluding the private wagering that has always characterized his matches ("that's for me and the I.R.S. to find out," he quipped.)

Mrs. Court's Mothers Day began on an ominous note when her 14-month-old son, Danny, threw her only pair of tennis sneakers into the toilet of their hotel room at the San Vicente Country Club, site of the match, 38 miles northeast of San Diego.

No Resemblance

The sneakers dried in time for Mrs. Court to wear them, along with a new lime and gold dress specially designed for the match. But from the first game, which Riggs carried at 15, the 30-year-old Mrs. Court looked little like the dominant force she has been in winning 89 of the last 92 singles matches on the women's tour.

To neutralize Mrs. Court's powerful stroke and 5-foot-10-inch reach, Riggs wisely softballed her on everything from dink serves to sliced groundstrokes. Sometimes, the pace on Riggs's strokes was slower than you might expect in a weekend country club match, but it achieved the objective of breaking Mrs. Court's rhythm and concentration.

When Mrs. Court netted her first overhead attempt in the second game to fall behind, love-30, her nerves, always a problem for her in championship matches, increased, and her confidence wilted. Meanwhile, Riggs calmly played each point with almost effortless expertise.

"I didn't hit out enough," Mrs. Court said, depressed over her showing but willing to play a rematch. "I didn't expect him to mix it up so much at the start."

Credits Soft Touch

"It went exactly as I thought," said Riggs, who rarely needed to resort to gamesmanship as a tactic. "I thought if I could get her out of her rhythm and change her concentration that I'd have it, and that soft stuff did the trick."

Riggs, the Wimbledon champion four years before Mrs. Court was born, had termed this meeting "the greatest mystery match of all time." It must have been that to many in the capacity crowd of 3,500; a poll of newsmen taken before the match favored Mrs. Court, 18-6.

"The whole thing was pressure," Riggs said, and no one was more responsible for creating such tension. As late as two hours before the match, after he had swallowed what he said was his 207th vitamin pill of the day, Riggs was still trying to hustle Mrs. Court's husband, Barry, on the potential money value of a rematch.

It also was Riggs who demanded coaches at court side, Davis Cup-style, even though he unquestionably knew more about tactics and strategy than the two teaching pros who chatted with him during the crossovers.

Mrs. Court had looked crisp and confident in workouts here. But in retrospect, her preparation was poor. Instead of practicing against players who could have drilled her on off-speed serves and ground strokes to adjust her rhythm and timing, she chose all-out hits with Tony Trabert and Vickie Berner.

Riggs faulted only seven of 41 first serves and hammered successive aces at 30-all for a decisive 4-1 lead in the second set. By contrast, Mrs. Court faulted 19 of 37 first serves and had so little rhythm that she committed 10 return errors on serves having less pace than she would see in most women's matches.

The most ironic note to the bizarre tone of the match, however, was that Riggs won by playing the backcourt game more synonymous with women's tennis than the serve-and-volley tactics associated with the men.

"That's the trouble with the women's game," said Riggs, tugging at his sun visor. "Those women think they're men, and they go off hitting all over the place. They'd be better off if they'd played like women."

May 14, 1973

MRS. KING ACCEPTS NEW GROUP'S PACT

Newcombe Is Also Signed With World Team Tennis

By NEIL AMDUR

Lured by the chance to make more money for less work, Mrs. Billie Jean King and John Newcombe have signed long-term contracts with World Team Tennis.

The newly organized 16-team league, which hopes to begin a 44-match schedule in May, 1974, with men and women players, announced the two signings before its first player draft yesterday.

Mrs. King, currently the top-ranking women's player, was signed to a five-year contract by the Philadelphia franchise, which outbid four other cities, including New York, for the bespectacled Wimbledon champion. The terms of Mrs. King's contract were not disclosed, but it is believed she will be guaranteed in excess of $100,000 a year.

Newcombe, the mustachioed Australian, was signed by Houston at terms estimated at $75,000 a year. A desire to cut down tournament travel and remain closer to his family and business interests in Texas were regarded as major factors in Newcombe's decision.

10 Players Signed

Mrs. King and Newcombe were among a group of 10 players who signed contracts with the league and then allowed individual cities to bid for their services. League officials declined to identify the other players under contract, but Linda Tuero, Clark Graebner and Jimmy Connors reportedly have agreed to play next year.

Miami won the special league drawing for the No. 1 choice and predictably selected Chris Evert, the teen-ager from nearby Fort Lauderdale. One men's and one women's singles match, plus some form of doubles, will constitute the team concept.

Six women were drafted in the first round and 15 in the first 32 players chosen. But the most conspicuous note was the failure of any city to select the world's top two men players, Stan Smith and Ilie Nastase, in the opening two rounds.

The ommissions were the most significant indication from the various club owners that they were content to settle or players they felt would participate in the league, regardless of ranking.

No Sanction Received

The league has not received sanctioning from the International Lawn Tennis Federation, the sport's governing body. And it has not won any endorsement from the Association of Tennis Professionls, which speaks for most of the world's top male players.

As a result, any player who joins the league next spring risks being banned from I. L. T. F.-sanctioned tournaments, which, of course, include Wimbledon and the United States

Smith, the game's biggest money-winner at the moment, was selected by Minnesota on the third round ("with honor and a little luck," a team official said). He was the 43d player chosen, behind Alex (Sandy) Mayer, the New Jersey collegian, who was drafted by the New York entry, nicknamed the Sets.

New York's No. 1 choice was Roy Emerson, the 37-year-old Australian, who also may be eager to cut down tournament commitments. Pam Teeguarden, the ninth-ranking American woman, was selected by the Sets in the second round.

The club also gambled that it may be able to convince Arthur Ashe to join. Ashe was New York's fifth-round choice. The Sets also drafted Manuel Santana of Spain and Haroon Rahim, the colorful Pakistani professional.

Nastase, the tempestuous Rumanian, was the 62d player chosen. He joined two other East European players, Alex Metreveli of the Soviet Union and Jan Kodes of Czechoslovakia, plus Rod Laver and two great names from the past, Mrs. Karen Susman and Maria Bueno, on a strange San Diego roster.

August 4, 1973

Mrs. King Defeats Riggs, 6-4, 6-3, 6-3, Amid a Circus Atmosphere

By NEIL AMDUR
Special to The New York Times

HOUSTON, Sept. 20—Mrs. Billie Jean King struck a proud blow for herself and women around the world with a crushing 6-4, 6-3, 6-3 rout of Bobby Riggs tonight in their $100,000 winner-take-all tennis match at the Astrodome.

In an atmosphere more suited for a circus than a sports event, the 29-year-old Mrs. King ended the bizarre saga of the 55-year-old hustler, who had bolted to national prominence with his blunt putdowns of women's tennis and the role of today's female.

Mrs. King, a five-time Wimbledon champion and the most familiar face in the women's athletic movement, needed only 2 hours 4 minutes to reaffirm her status as one of the gifted and tenacious competitors in sport, female or male.

A crowd of 30,492, some paying as much as $100 a seat, watched the best-three-of-five set struggle, the largest single attendance ever for a tennis match. Millions more viewed the event on national television. The match also was seen in 36 foreign countries via satellite.

Mrs. King squashed Riggs with tools synonymous with men's tennis, the serve and volley. She beat Bobby to the ball, dominated the net and ran him around the baseline to the point of near exhaustion in the third set, when he suffered hand cramps and trailed, 2-4.

Most important, perhaps for women everywhere, she convinced skeptics that a female athlete can survive pressure-filled situations and that men are as susceptible to nerves as women.

It was Riggs, for example, who only yesterday had claimed "I have no nerves," who double-faulted at 4-5, 30-40 to decide the first set.

And it was another Riggs double-fault, at deuce in the ninth game of the final set, that gave Mrs. King her third match point. An uproar of cheers followed when Riggs drove a high backhand volley into the net.

Later, away from the tumult and the shouting, Mrs. King admitted that she, too, had suffered cramps in her leg in the sixth game of the final set.

"It was a combination of nerves and just all that running," she said. "When I felt the first twinge, I said, 'Oh God, not now—not this close.' I was really worried."

Riggs did not leave the match empty-handed. Like Mrs. King, he was guaranteed a minimum of $75,000 for ancillary rights to the promotion. His other endorsements and contracts should swell his take to over $300,000.

Mrs. King, the biggest money-winner in the history of women's athletics and the foremost spokesman for equality in sport, is certain to reap even greater financial returns from tonight's victory. But as she said yesterday, "pride matters a lot more than money."

Riggs, who had hoped to use another triumph as a springboard to greater riches, praised Mrs. King.

"She was too good," said the 1939 Wimbledon singles champion. "She played too well. She was playing well within herself, and I couldn't get the most out of my game. It was over too quickly."

In the first set alone, in what represented an incredible testimony to her quality of play, Mrs. King won 26 of her 34 points with outright winners, balls which Riggs never touched with his racquet.

After having lost her serve to open the second set, she immediately broke back at 30 with the shot she relishes, the running backhand crosscourt.

As he pressed to put more pace on his serve and first volley, Riggs's game gradually deteriorated. He found himself being passed on return of serve, chasing lobs that HE was supposed to be stroking, and stretching in vain for Billie Jean's assortment of passing shots and deadly volleys.

At the finish, Mrs. King's statistics spoke for themselves: 70 of the 109 points she won, or over 64 per cent, were outright winners. Such perfection might compare favorably with a quarterback who completes 20 of 24 passes for six touchdowns.

Even before the first ball was struck, it became even more evident that this was to be no ordinary tennis event.

Instead of the traditional walk onto to the court, the players entered the stadium with the flourish of something out of a Cecil B. DeMille movie.

Mrs. King came first on a Cleopatra-style gold litter that was held aloft by four muscular track-and-field athletes from nearby Rice University and an Astrodome employe. One of the toga-clad carriers was Dave Roberts, one of the world's finest pole vaulters.

Riggs was transported into the stadium in a gold-wheeled rickshaw pulled by six professional models in tight red and gold outfits who had been dubbed "Bobby's Bosom Buddies" during his stay here. It was apparent why.

A band, seated behind what would have been home plate for baseball, blared brassy march music while brightly colored costumed characters from Astroworld frolicked for the large crowd.

Large banners, seldom displayed at staid country clubs where tennis languished as a sport for the classes for much of this century, were sprinkled throughout the stadium.

The circus atmosphere contrasted sharply not only with conventional tennis events but with the challenge match between Riggs and Mrs. Margaret Court last Mother's Day.

That match, which Riggs won in a 6-2, 6-1 rout, was held at a wilderness site in Ramona, Calif., before 3,000 fans sitting in make-shift seats.

Tonight's courtside crowd sat in $100 seats sipping champagne from several improvised bars. Some spectators arrived in suits or evening dresses.

Mrs. King even went one-up on Riggs at the courtside introductions. After Bobby had presented Billie Jean with a large candy sucker (he had given Mrs. Court a bouquet of roses before their match), Mrs. King gave her gift—a brown baby pig.

September 21, 1973

Kodes Captures Wimbledon Crown

By FRED TUPPER
Special to The New York Times

WIMBLEDON, England, July 7—The Wimbledon tennis title went to a Soviet-bloc nation for the first time today as Jan Kodes of Czechoslovakia won from Alex Metreveli of the Soviet Union, 6-1, 9-8, 6-3, over 107 minutes.

And if this Eastern European men's final was a pedestrian affair, earlier on Mrs. Billie Jean King treated the sunlit center court to a tennis masterpiece as she defeated 18-year-old Chris Evert, 6-0, 7-5, to take her second straight crown and her fifth in the eight finals she had played here.

"It's the Old Lady's house," Rosie Casals, her doubles partner, has said of Mrs. King on the center court.

There was no way that the game could have been played better than in the flawless exhibition that Mrs. King put on in the 17-minute first set. Some of her shots were breath-taking, and all the more so because her intelligence demanded that against the sharp-shooting of young Chris, she must abandon her normal serve-and-volley tactics and play chiefly from the baseline.

Quick and Assured

With her little gray cells ticking over, Billie Jean came netward only when her forcing ground shots had tipped Miss Evert off balance. And when she did hurtle up there, her quickness on the volley and assurance on the slam made winners certain.

"Billie Jean would have made anybody look like a beginner," said Miss Evert later. "She played great. She hardly made an error."

"It's the best set I've ever played," said Mrs. King, and in 13 years of having watched her at Wimbledon the press box veterans agreed.

In the match, held over because of rain yesterday, Mrs. King won eight games before Chris made a move. Then the Floridian used a weapon she has mastered. A perfect lob, a King mistake and then a drop off a drop shot put her to 1-2. Then a forehand volley, recently

Chris Evert in action against Mrs. Billie Jean King, who defeated the 18-year-old player

Associated Press

acquired, put her at 2-3 in the second set.

With 10 points in a row, Chris was very much back in the match. She broke Mrs. King at love with a drop shot off the net cord, and she held her service to love at 4-3. The crowd came to life and was roaring in delight. The fight was on.

An Incredible Volley

Billie Jean reached for her all with an incredible volley from midcourt off her shoetops, but Chris was at 5-4, her confidence back and hitting those double-handers into the far corners.

They were at 15-all in the next game, when Billie Jean swung two serves to the outside to make it 40-15, and then hit a lovely low volley — her trademark — for 5-all.

Chris had two points for 6-5, but Mrs. King broke her with a volley across court and an Evert over-the-line lob. She then held service for the match.

"I wanted to keep her guessing," Mrs. King said. "I was changing the rhythm, mixing up the slice and topspin. I felt I had to get into the lead right off to win. Then she played better. I was losing length and getting a little tired in the wind."

She laughed, and said: "Now I'm ready to play Bobby Riggs. I've challenged him."

It took Kodes only a minute longer than Mrs. King to win his final. Hunched in the shoulders, shaking himself to get a good grip on the racquet

and then beating Metreveli to the punch with the sheer velocity of his shots, the Czechoslovak had the first set at 6-1.

Over the years they have played interminably and the results have been close. Now Metreveli broke to 2-love in the second set with a backhand riveted to the line, and was broken back. Again Alex took Jan's service and was at 4-2, and again the Czechoslovak came back to 4-4.

At 4-5 the Soviet star from Georgia had a set point with a crosscourt forehand blazed into the clear. Inexplicably he hit a simple second serve off the forehand into the net. That did it. With his nerves jumping, he was bouncing the ball as many as seven times before serving, and was looking vainly on high for help.

In the tiebreaker Alex made another error on a simple short forehand volley. That set was gone too at 9-8, and Kodes ran out the match at 6-3.

He jumped the net, smiling for the first time, and held up the huge golden cup for all to see. Jaroslav Drobny, a Czechoslovak then living in exile in Egypt, won here in 1954.

Kodes received $12,500 for his victory, Mrs. King $7,500.

The Old Lady, nearly exhausted by her efforts, took her fifth doubles title here with Miss Casals. They were trailing Evonne Goolagong and Janet Young of Australia, 2-5 and love-40, in the first set of the semifinal before winning, 7-5, 7-5. And they were behind against Francoise Durr of France and Betty Stove of the Netherlands, 4-5 and 15-30, in the third set of the final before pulling it out on the third match point, 6-1, 4-6, 7-5.

Mrs. King's fifth victory in the singles meant that only Helen Wills, with eight titles,

and Suzanne Lenglen, with six, had won here more times, and her doubles titles now total eight—the five with Rosie, two with Mrs. Karen Hantze Susman and last year with Miss Stove.

She Also Wins Double

She did the sweep, which in-

cludes the mixed doubles, in 1967 and will be trying for that again tomorrow.

"And I'll be back next year," she said.

Ilie Nastase and Jimmy Connors won the men's doubles title from Neale Fraser and John Cooper of Australia, 3-6, 6-3, 6-4, 8-9, 6-1. Fraser won the singles here in 1960, and was the best man on the court today.

Billy Martin, America's fast-rising 16-year-old from Palos Verdes, Calif., defeated Colin Dowdeswell of Rhodesia, 6-2, 6-4, to win the junior crown.

Despite the boycott by the Association of Tennis Professionals, the attendance reached 299,718, the second highest since the tournament began in 1877. It was surpassed only by 2,000 in 1967, the year before Wimbledon was opened to the pros.

There were rumors of peace between the warring factions, with the differences reportedly narrowing. The International Lawn Tennis Federation wants to create a new seven-man board, with four of its members and three from the A.T.P. The A.T.P. wants three each, with four additional men who run the four major world tournaments, or the presidents of the tennis associations in those four countries.

July 8, 1973

Associated Press

Mrs. Billie Jean King in action against Chris Evert

Mrs. Court Takes Open Title; Smith Upset, Newcombe Wins

By PARTON KEESE

The largest crowd in the history of Forest Hills tennis —15,137—was treated yesterday to a full gamut of thrills in the United States Open championships.

It began with Mrs. Margaret Court of Australia winning her fifth United States title as she beat Evonne Goolagong, 7-6, 5-7, 6-2, and ended in the moonlight with Jan Kodes of Czechoslovakia defeating top-seeded Stan Smith in a fantastic men's semifinal, 7-5, 6-7, 1-6, 6-1, 7-5.

In between, another pair of Australians battled for a berth in the final, with John Newcombe routing Ken Rosewall, 6-4, 7-6, 6-3.

From noon until 7:30 P.M. the two best of 64 women players and the four best of 128 men battled on the center court. It was like a Mets' double-header in which they clinched the division title in the first game, then played 18 innings to qualify for the World Series.

The 31-year-old Mrs. Court now has won 24 major world titles in her career. She received the top prize of $25,-000, a new automobile, a silver trophy, a wristwatch and a kiss from her husband, Barry.

The acrobatic Kodes, 27, and the ramrod-straight Smith, 26, played the top match of the tournament. There was hardly a point that wasn't earned, and the pair traded scintillating returns of bullet serves, followed by volleying duels that had the crowd in a frenzy.

The match had the added significance of pitting Kodes, the Wimbledon champion, against Smith, last year's Wimbledon champion, who did not defend that title this year. What's more, in gaining the final Kodes will play another "undefeated" Wimbledon champion in Newcombe, who won in 1971 but did not play there the next two years.

When Kodes lost the final point of the second-set tiebreaker on what looked like a bad call by the service linesman, he patted the linesman on the head in muted anger, then kicked a hole in a chair.

He lost the third set, 6-1, and it looked as if the fight had left him. But like a tiger, Kodes came tearing back to win the fourth, 6-1, and then he saved one match point in the thrilling fifth set, which he won in near-darkness.

Though five inches taller than her opponent, Mrs. Court gave up 9 years in age and speed to the bouncy Miss Goolagong. No matter that their styles differ—Margaret is a harder server and rangier at the net; Evonne has quicker reflexes and faster legs —their weaknesses and strengths added up to an even match.

However, as even as they were on paper, Miss Goolagong raced to a 4-1 lead in the first set. Her first serve, fast and deep, was working and gave Mrs. Court few chances to rush the net.

Margaret, who admits she plays better when behind "because it makes me concentrate more," found herself just in time—behind by 15-40 on her serve — and pulled out the game.

Just as suddenly, Evonne could not get her first serve in the court, and her puffy, arching second serve was pounced on repeatedly.

So the pattern was set early on: When Evonne put her first service in, she attacked the net, usually successfully. When she had to resort to a second serve, Margaret returned a spinning shot into a corner, rushed to the net and volleyed home a winner.

Each broke the other's service to make it 6-6 and bring on the 5-of-9-point, sudden-death tiebreaker. Miss Goolagong picked this crucial time to make her first of only two double-faults, hit an easy overhead wide and made two more errors, while picking up only 2 points for herself, and dropped the set, 7-6.

Now it was Margaret's turn to garner an early lead, breaking through in the sixth game for 4-2. When Evonne sent three backhand volleys astray in that game, Margaret seemed to have the money in the bank and could foresee a victory that would put her second only to Mrs. Helen Wills Roark, who won seven times at Forest Hills.

But Miss Goolagong had played Mrs. Court before, beating her for the Wimbledon championship in 1971, and she began playing carefully, one point at a time.

"I really enjoy playing Margaret, she's such a fine player," said the gracious Evonne later, "She brings me up to a higher level."

As is her wont, Miss Goolagong reached that higher level, taking five of the last six games to even the match at a set apiece. But it was nervous tennis at this point, as each competitor knew she had to go to the net to win, but, probably in fear, hesitated to do so.

Fearful or not, Margaret jumped on every opportunity in the final set to go in, and it paid off, as Evonne tried in vain to pass htre. Also, Miss Goolagong's first serve was missing, and one could almost hear the crowd saying, "Oh, oh," when it missed, knowing full well what Margaret would do with the simple No. 2 ball.

Evonne had an alternative, which she attempted only rarely: lobbing over Margaret's head. The day before Chris Evert had employed the lob against Margaret, and it seemed as effective as any other stroke in forcing Mrs. Court to fall back.

Taking the sharpest returns that Evonne continued to send directly at her, Margaret cake-walked through the games she served, losing only 4 points the set.

Though nearly everybody in the capacity crowd was aware that Miss Goolagong could catch fire at any moment and win every game, it didn't happen.

"I'm exhausted," said Margaret at the trophy presentation. "I won't be able to walk tomorrow."

"You won't have to," said an official of the Virginia Slims circuit. "Here are the keys to a 1973 Mustang."

Newcombe, nine years Rosewall's junior at 29, had too much power and accuracy for his compatriot, even though he had not played many tournaments this year.

"We had a couple of close games at the start, but when I got my first service in, I was happy," said John. "You can't beat Kenny with the first service only. You've got to earn the point." Newcombe won here in 1967, the year before the first Open.

Rosewall hit few of his great backhands, and age and his lack of a big service finally went against him, and he was denied a chance to take a third title to go with those he won in 1956 and 1970. The men's first prize is also $25,000 from the purse of $227,000.

In the Pepsi Cola junior international final, Billy Martin of Palos Verdes, Calif., fought back to defeat Colin Dowdeswell of Rhodesia, 4-6, 6-4, 6-3.

September 9, 1973

Chris Evert Captures The Wimbledon Title

By FRED TUPPER
Special to The New York Times

WIMBLEDON, England, July 5—This is the year of Chris Evert. In just an hour today she defeated Olga Morozova of the Soviet Union, 6-0, 6-4, and added the Wimbledon tennis title to the Italian and French titles that she won a few weeks ago. She was the runner-up a year ago in all three of these tournaments.

At the age of 19, Miss Evert of Fort Lauderdale, Fla., became the youngest winner of the women's singles here since Maureen Connolly took the title in 1952 at 17.

Miss Evert, who was beaten in two sets by Mrs. Billie Jean King in the 1973 championship round, said she was surprised at winning this year. "I know I'll be playing at Wimbledon for years to come. But I was thinking a few years ahead when Billie Jean and Margaret [Court] might retire. I never expected to win Wimbledon this year."

To her baseline accomplishments she put on parade today a volley and overhead game. That was the deciding factor in those last minutes down the stretch, when the Russian had pulled up from 2-4 to 4-all in the second set just as she had rallied yesterday in upsetting Virginia Wade.

In the men's singles final tomorrow, Jimmy Connors of Belleville, Ill., will play Ken Rosewall, who left center court in a state of shock when he came out of the abyss to win a match that had seemed irretrievably lost. Here was little Ken, semi-retired and approaching 40, two sets and match point down to Stan Smith, the 1972 champion, from Sea Pines, S.C. The script looks incredible, but it's now on the record, a tale of tennis to be told in years to come as the Australian triumphed, 6-8, 4-6, 9-8, 6-1, 6-3.

Henri Cochet came from two sets and 1-5 down to beat Bill Tilden here in 1927, but not from match point.

Connors reached the final by stopping young Dick Stockton of Dallas, 4-6, 6-2, 6-3, 6-4.

A sentimental journey with his family had seemed the reason for Rosewall's presence. He was seeded ninth on his reputation, not on his recent record. He had quit the World Championship Tennis circuit this year, played one tournament back in March and came back in May to be a manager-player of Pittsburgh in World Team Tennis.

He knocked out John Newcombe, the top-seeded player and three-time champion to gain the semifinal round here. Today he was 6-8, 4-6, and 4-5 down with big Stan serving for the match. Ken had played well earlier with a point to break to 5-3 in the first set.

But then it had been all Smith. The American served harder, volleyed better and was invincible overhead. Even the vast crowd, Rosewall lovers since he first enchanted this stadium at 17, was beginning to drift away.

So 6-fot-4-inch Smith toed the line and served, and Ken changed his tactics. Instead of trying to pass on the flanks, he dinked a return to the feet as Stan charged in for the volley. Twice Smith fluffed the short ball and the third caromed off his shoe-tops and Rosewall reached 15-40. Stan half-volleyed the next return and Rosewall backhanded the ball to the far corner and tied the game at 5-all.

It didn't seem that important then and in the tiebreak that followed at 8-8, Smith reached match point at 6-5 and backhanded into the net. Then that Rosewall backhand streaked across court and he had that set 9-8. He broke in the first game, again in the third and once more in the seventh and had the fourth

set at 6-1 with the stadium a well of sound.

Stan was shaken, his confidence fading. At 1-2 serving in the fifth set he missed a simple smash at the net and netted again as another backhand flew by him. Ken now was serving for the match at 5-3 and 40-0. Almost by script a backhand return like a shaft of lightning seared the chalk. The last shot had gone from the Australians' sling, the giant had been slain.

Rosewall is in a Wimbledon final for the fourth time over 20 years, winning in five sets in 3 hours 8 minutes. Now he has another chance for the one big title that has always escaped him. There was a standing, cheering ovation as he and Smith trudged off court.

Connors proved the better man on the big occasion. Stockton, who had upset Ilie Nastase and Alex Metreveli, a 1973 Wimbledon finalist, **started the stronger. A couple of volley errors, a lob that spun over his head and a lob that he hit out cost Jimmy a break in the third game and then the first set at 6-4.**

They exchanged service breaks. Another timely lob, as Connors charged in, put Stockton at 2-1. But suddenly his game disintegrated. Jimmy had slowed the pace a bit and seemed to be more flexible on the volley. The games

came running. He had eight in a row now and the match comfortably by taking the next three sets.

Asked about Rosewall, who played before he was born, Connors said: "How do you play a legend?"

Connors got no help from Newcombe and Tony Roche, the Australian doubles team, which lost the first two sets and won in five from Nastase and Connors in the semifinals. They were hitting most of the balls to Jimmy.

Connors and Miss Evert are engaged to be married. The wedding is scheduled for November. A tradition of Wimbledon is the ball that follows completion of play at which the men's singles champion and the women's champion dance the first dance. Chris is hoping that the first dance tomorrow night will be with Jimmy.

Miss Evert has beaten Miss Morozova repeatedly, in a semifinal at Rome, in the final at Paris and over three tough sets on grass in a tune-up at Eastbourne, which seemed the key to today's play.

The Russian has a game of serve and volley built for a fast surface such as Wimbledon's, and she came to center court tired but confident after dethroning Mrs. King and eliminating Miss Wade.

In a long first game that

lasted 13 minutes with Olga three times at advantage, Chris won and raced to 6-0 in 14 more minutes. On clay she lobs continually, today she was hitting her ground strokes deep and making occasional sorties to the net. Her overhead was sharp and her volley deadly placed in the direction Olga was not going. Quickly she reached 4-2 in the second set, breaking service at love.

Miss Morozova was still in the hunt. She hit a blazing forehand passing shot and a forehand volley to break to 4-3 and held her own service with a drop shot and a deep smash for 4-all.

At 30-all in-the ninth game, a vital stage, Miss Evers hit a forehand cross-court shot for an outright winner. That did it. The Russian volleyed over the line and then double-faulted on match point, 6-0, 6-4.

"To beat her you have to win all the points," said Olga later. "There is no other way."

Miss Evert missed out on a chance to share another title. Paired with Miss Morozova, she was beaten in doubles by Evonne Goolagong of Australia and Margaret Michel of Pacific Palisades, Calif., in the semifinals, 7-5, 6-2.

July 6, 1974

Connors Crushes Rosewall, 6-1, 6-1, 6-4; U.S. Sweeps Wimbledon Singles Crowns

By FRED TUPPER
Special to The New York Times

WIMBLEDON, England July 6—With the world waiting in the wings, Jimmy Connors beat Ken Rosewall for the Wimbledon men's tennis title today. Rosewall, the sentimental favorite, had staged one of the great turnarounds by coming from two sets and match point down against Stan Smith to reach his fourth final here over 20 years. But today he was given no chance, demolished by weight of stroke and serve as Connors won, 6-1, 6-1, 6-4, over 93 minutes.

The victory gave the United States a sweep of the singles titles, with Chris Evert, Connors's fiancée, having beaten Olga Morozova in the women's final yesterday.

Despite everybody's willing him on, Rosewall never got in the match. He was outrun and outhit, a weary 39-year-old man who had left his game in the dressing room. It was the most one-sided final since John Newcombe granted Wilhelm Bungert of West Germany a meager five games in 1967.

Connors was superb. He has never played better and said so. The 21-year-old left-hander, joint No. 1 in the States with Smith, had a plan of attack and kept to it. He stayed in the backcourt at first, hitting hard and deep to get the feel, taking the ball on the rise and swinging it from side to side. Rosewall could do little about it. He was beaten to the punch, battered by those two-fisted

backhands, which knocked him off balance.

The little Australian won the first game and then the avalanche hit him. Connors held service and went to work on Ken's service. A forehand pass, a smash on a short lob, a two-hander into the corner and then the break to 2-1 as Rosewall backhanded over the line.

Quickly Connors was at set point, slipping a backhand through the hole for 6-1. Only 21minutes had passed and the crowd was mute in sympathy.

Rosewall kept waiting for a lift, some inspiration of thought or stroke. In the opening game of the second set, he unsheathed what is recognized as the best backhand in tennis.

Connors Overcomes Rosewall, Mrs. King Victor in U.S. Finals

Jimmy was brimming with confidence. First off the chair between changes, he would beat his thigh and then berate the ball. His percentage of good shots was incredible as the two-fisters brought up the chalk from the lines and the overheads jumped off the grass. The second set was on the board at 6-1, then Jimmy had the break at 1-0. Was Rosewall ever going to move?

Leading by 2-1, Ken made his bid. He was at 30-40 on a backhand rifled to Connors's feet, then was brought back to deuce. He was at ad-out on a backhand pass. Deuce again. One more advantage on a backhand volley. Could he get the break that might mean the set? Connors squashed his hopes, smashing for that game, breaking service for another, reaching 5-4 and serving for the match.

But Smith had been in that position against Rosewall yesterday and had lost the edge and the match in five sets. So had Connors been earlier on in the sprinkle against Phil Dent and lost the edge, then had been 2 points from defeat at 5-6, love-30, and had to go five sets to win.

Jimmy made no mistake now. "Boom! Boom! Boom! I got to 40-love," he said. In a last gasp Rosewall made two marvelous returns, then he pushed a backhand low into the net for the match.

The Duke of Kent came down onto the center court to award a gold cup to young Jimmy. There was also a check for $24,000 of the $234,000 purse.

The crowd rose to clap for Rosewall. He had been there so often before—in the final against Jaroslav Drobny in 1954, against Lew Hoad in 1956 and John Newcombe in 1970.

Newcombe paired with Tony Roche to beat Smith and Bob Lutz, 8-6, 6-4, 6-4, for their fifth doubles title. But there were other American successes.

Miss Evert took the women's championship yesterday. Peggy Michel of Pacific Palisades, Calif., and Evonne Goolagong of Australia won the women's doubles from Karen Krantzcke and Helen Gourlay of Australia, 2-6, 6-4, 6-3. Mrs. Billie Jean King and Owen Davidson captured the mixed doubles for the fourth time by beating Mark Farrell and Lesley Charles of Britain 6-3, 9-7.

Billy Martin, 18, of Palos Verdes, Calif., won the junior singles, 6-2, 6-1, from Ashook Amritraj of India, and that fountain of eternal youth, Gardnar Mulloy, paired with Ronald Dunas to take the veterans' doubles, 6-3, 6-2.

July 7, 1974

...my Connors after winning U.S. Open title.

Connors, Mrs. King Win Singles Crowns In U.S. Open Tennis

By PARTON KEESE

Jimmy Connors, overwhelmingly, and Billie Jean King, excruciatingly, became the United States Open tennis champions yesterday. The title was the first for Connors and the fourth for Mrs. King at Forest Hills. Each won $22,500, an automobile and other prizes.

Age withered before the onslaught of youth as the 22-year-old Connors, from Belleville, Ill., crushed Australia's Ken Rosewall, 6-1, 6-0, 6-1. It was the worst defeat suffered by a men's finalist in the national tournament.

Rosewall, who will be 40 in November, played his first match in the Forest Hills stadium before Connors was born and had won the tournament twice, in 1956 and 1970.

The victory by Mrs. King, who had previously won in 1967, 1971 and 1972, was almost painstaking in comparison to Connors'. She triumphed over Evonne Goolagong of Australia, 3-6, 6-3, 7-5.

"Whoever calls her 'the Old Lady of Tennis' has never played her on the court," said Miss Goolagong. At 30, Mrs. King is 7 years older than Miss Goolagong. Later, Billie Jean teamed with Rosemary Casals to win the women's doubles crown.

The result of the men's final duplicated that at Wimbledon in July, when Connors gained the British crown by routing Rosewall, 6-1, 6-1, 6-4. But yesterday he was even more devastating.

A crowd of 15,303, which helped set a total attendance mark of 153,287 for the 12-day event, sat hushed in awe as the left-handed Connors made the sad-faced Rosewall look like a refugee from a 35-years-and-over tournament.

The first set lasted 19 minutes, the second 20 and the whole match just 1 hour 18 minutes, with a lot of time used up by Rosewall's looking at his opponent as if he were a wizard.

Jimmy came out swinging. As he said later: "I woke up this morning feeling just the way I did at Wimbledon. From the moment I took the court and hit the first ball, I felt I was gliding. I was on a cloud. It was a terrific feeling."

Attacking Rosewall's serve from the start with his two-handed backhand, he made the ball land on the line or inches from it. With his forehand, he passed Rosewall at will or lobbed a winner over his head. His volley had no answers. Rosewall was mes-merized.

Dejected, a beaten and tragic figure, the Australian picked up only 12 points in the first set and 12 in the second. As the score mounted, it became embarrassing, especially for those familiar with the legend that Rosewall had established.

Showing little respect for an elder, Connors was subjected to some heckling.

"You're a bum, Connors!" someone shouted.

"I agree," he answered, and completed the romp without emotion.

"In the back of my mind," he said, "I held the thought that if I let down, Rosewall

"From the moment I took the court and hit the first ball, I felt I was gliding."
—*Jimmy Connors*

Billie Jean King exulting after her victory.

could win it. My heart was going boom-boom against my shirt. I was afraid I'd come down. I had to keep the pressure on."

The crowd was ready for the King-Goolagong battle long before the women were. After the mismatch, it wanted something tight, surprising, fluctuating. And it was rewarded with a splendid contest.

Miss Goolagong, a fast starter normally, reached her heights sooner than Mrs. King, and lashed her marvelous backhand past her opponent time and time again. It gained her the first set.

But the Australian is known for her letdowns, and with Mrs. King growing more consistent, Evonne appeared to become tentative which is not her best style. Second set to the onrushing Billie Jean.

Both are known for their play under pressure, and the third set was filled with it. The spectators became more excited and began "calling" balls hit close to the lines and whistling at the lineswomen. Most of the fans seemed to favor Miss Goolagong.

As she had done the day before in ending Chris Evert's 56-game victory skein, Evonne ran off a 3-0 lead in the deciding set. She was at the top of her gracefully powerful game, and the crowd waxed ecstatic as it rooted the underdog on.

On one crucial point, Evonne sent a passing shot whizzing down the line, but Billie Jean leaped and intercepted it. Evonne sent a backhand across court, and Billie Jean leaped to her left and somehow got it back. Evonne then rammed another potential winner down the line, and this time Billie Jean blasted it back for a winner.

The crowd stood and gave both a tremendous ovation in appreciation of the most extraordinary kind of tennis. But that point also indicated the resurrection of the determined Mrs. King, who went on to tie the set at 3-3.

Then it was 5-5, and the verdict seemed to rest on whether Evonne could put in her first serve with sting. However, in the last two games, Billie Jean allowed her only 1 point as she proved the stronger-willed.

"It's the best I've seen Evonne ever play," said Mrs. King, who put this victory at the top of a list almost overburdened with sensational triumphs. "I was in a daze at the end. I said if she can keep it up, she's the better player. I don't even remember what I did. How did I win? I don't have a clue."

September 10, 1974

South Africa Given Cup; No Penalty Against India

ROME, Nov. 7 (AP)—South Africa was awarded the 1974 Davis Cup today, but no disciplinary action was taken by the International Lawn Tennis Federation against India, which refused to play South Africa in the final.

South Africa also was named as the eighth member of the I.L.T.F. Davis Cup committee, which handed down the decisions after an eight-hour session.

"The cup was awarded to South Africa by India's re-fusal to play because of its opponent's apartheid policy," said W. Harcourt Woods of the United States, chairman of the Davis Cup committee.

Woods also said the format of the Davis Cup would almost certainly be changed.

It was the first time the cup final would not be played. South Africa was also the first country except the United States, Australia, Britain and France to win the competition.

Woods denied reports that each country had asked the committee to expel the other from the Davis Cup.

"South Africa proposed to expel India, but the matter was withdrawn after the official documents were produced," Woods said. "There has been no such proposal from India."

Woods said that South Africa had been included in the North American Davis Cup Zone for 1975 and "no objection from any country" had been made against the South Africans' participation in the event.

November 8, 1974

Connors Beats Laver, 6–4, 6–2, 3–6, 7–5

Late Comeback by Aussie Is Thwarted

By LEONARD KOPPETT
Special to The New York Times

LAS VEGAS, Nev., Feb. 2—Both the caliber of tennis and the intensity of competition proved worthy of the circumstances today as Jimmy Connors defeated Rod Laver, 6-4, 6-2, 3-6, 7-5 for a $100,000 prize.

The 22-year-old Connors, who has powerful ground strokes and a reputation for disruptive behavior in the usually genteel atmosphere of the tennis world, displayed the strokes but no histrionics while he dominated the first two sets.

Then the 36-year-old Laver, an Australian transplanted to California after reigning unchallenged as the world's best player through most of the nineteen-sixties, seemed to find his stride and brought the challenge to the younger man. With striking improvement in his serve and aggressiveness, Laver won the third set decisively and started the fourth by breaking Connors's service.

But Connors responded in turn and the rest of the fourth set was spectacularly even through 5-5. Connors had squared it at 1-1 by breaking Laver, and both held after that until Laver was serving and trailing at 4-5. At that stage, Laver held off match point five times before finally winning the 22-point game.

No Pressure at First

Connors, however, started the next game with an ace, won his service with the loss of only one point, and broke through at love in the final game.

"That's the toughest match I've ever played," declared Connors afterward. "And if Rod is willing, I'd like to arrange to play him again soon."

Laver, calm and contained as ever, said he'd think about it, and ascribed his defeat to taking "too long to get into the groove."

"I wasn't able to put pressure on him at first," said Laver. "Later I served better, and that helped my confidence. I got more depth on my ground shots, and that gave him different problems.

"But he played great tennis today, and he has the power and talent to be a championship player — he's proved that by winning them — and he plays aggressively, which is what today's game is all about.

"And I enjoyed the challenge of playing him enormously. It got me properly back in the game, and I'm glad about that because I don't want to just fade out."

The age factor did not seem to matter in physical conditioning. Actually, Connors eventually left the building with cramps in his legs, while Laver walked off easily, saying he could have played seven sets if necessary. But age makes a difference in other ways, pointed out Pancho Gonzales.

said Gonzales. "The surface is fast, and that means reflexes; and indoors, sharp

vision is important and Jimmy has exceptional vision. Laver did years ago, too, but it's not quite as sharp when you get older.

"Whatever the explanations, the battle followed a distinct pattern. In the first two sets, Connors kept Laver on the defensive — and on several occasions when Laver maneuvered Connors out of position, Laver missed the openings.

The key games in those two sets came early. Connors broke through in a deuce game for a 2-1 lead, and then held his service in the next game through 22 points (deuce tight times). That made it 3-1 and he ran out the set. In the third game of the second set, he broke Laver again, with passing shots, and won the fifth game, too, off Laver's service.

But in the third set, Laver suddenly found the ball going where he wanted it to, and in the five games he served he lost only 3 points. Connors lost his serve in the sixth game on three straight errors after leading, 30-15, giving Laver a 4-2 lead.

And the third game of the final set was a spectacular one, also. Connors lost his service in the first game, exciting the pro-Laver crowd, but broke through in return at 30-30 when Laver missed two shots. Now Connors succeeded in holding service through a four-deuce game, and the see-saw began through mounting tension.

February 3, 1975

French Title to Miss Evert

By FRED TUPPER
Special to The New York Times

PARIS, June 14—It took all her vaunted composure under pressure for Chris Evert to come back from a first-set hammering and retain her French tennis title with a 2-6, 6-2, 6-1 victory today over Martina Navratilova, the 18-year-old wonder from Czechoslovakia.

Bjorn Borg gained the men's final and will defend his title tomorrow against Guillermo Vilas of Argentina. The 19-year-old Swede won from Adriano Panatta of Italy, 6-4, 1-6, 7-5, 6-4, and Vilas beat Eddie Dibbs, the 11th-ranking American who had upset Raul Ramirez, 6-1, 6-4, 1-6, 6-1.

In the steaming caldron at Roland Garros Stadium, Miss Evert won the first game and then was overwhelmed by fiery smashes and cutoff volleys that blazed by her. Forever charging the net, Miss Navratilova in one inspired streak took 14 points and shortly was at 5-1.

There seemed little that Miss Evert could do. Her touch was off and she was not taking the ball on the rise. Straining, she staved off three set points in the seventh game, but a forehand gave Martina the set.

The stadium was bulging with more than 12,500 people pressed around the center court, entranced by the Czechoslovak's daring.

"I did not think anyone could serve or volley that well on clay," Miss Evert said later. "Martina had never taken a set from me on clay before. I thought I could get the second set and then have a chance, but if she kept on playing like she did at the start, then she would be the champion."

Miss Evert, admittedly tight at first, sent her returns short and was punished for it. But then she got length and accuracy. She had the first game of the second set and the second game was crucial.

Six advantage points she had and two against her. The one that mattered most came with Martina serving at ad-

in. Chris rifled the ball across court, but the Czechoslovak was stranded, thinking her serve had been out. After a dispute, deuce was called, but Miss Navratilova was never quite as good again.

Three games were gone now and she saved the fourth with a lunging volley when the ball seemed by her. Now the American was merciless, her shots on target. She went to 5-2 on her trademark drop shot and had the second set as her tiring opponent double-faulted.

The third set was a formality. Wearing the canary dress in which she won a year ago, the 20-year-old from Fort Lauderdale, Fla., had it in 19 minutes, granting a measly 10 points.

June 15, 1975

Mrs. King Wins Her Sixth Wimbledon Singles Title, 6-0, 6-1

Mrs. Cawley Is Trounced in 39 Minutes

By FRED TUPPER
Special to The New York Times

WIMBLEDON, England, July 4 — Billie Jean King trounced Evonne Goolagong Cawley, 6-0, 6-1, in just 39 minutes today to win what she says will be her last major singles tennis title and to leave Wimbledon in a blaze of glory.

"What a way to end my career," she said happily. "It's as close as I've ever come to a perfect match."

By ending her career, she means she will no longer play in major singles competition. "That's it," she said. "I will not play singles at Forest Hills. When I say I'm quitting, I mean it.

"I may come back here for doubles. And I'll go on playing in World Team Tennis."

Mrs. King won the first game at love today with a backhand volley to the corner, and she ended the match, racquet thrown on high, with a clean forehand volley into a corner. In between, she so completely dominated the court that Mrs. Cawley, the champion here in 1971, could garner only 24 points, one of them on Mrs. King's lone double-fault.

The scores of 6-0, 6-1 equaled the modern record for one-sidedness set by Doris Hart over Shirley Fry in 1951. And the title here was Mrs. King's sixth in singles and 19th over all, tying the long-time record held by Elizabeth Ryan, a Californian whose successes were solely in doubles play.

The women's prize money amounts to $15,400 at the current pound rate, but Mrs. King said she didn't know the figure after all the hub-

bub about creating equal prize money for women here, as in the case of Forest Hills.

"I've dreamed of winning Wimbledon ever since I was a little girl," she said. Playing here for the first time in 1961, at the age of 17, she won the doubles title with Karen Hantze. Her first singles title came in 1966 when she defeated Maria Bueno. This was her ninth final, which tied a mark set by Helen Wills Moody.

Now, at 31, she has no further tennis worlds to conquer, and she has gone out with a devastating triumph. The great volleyer never volleyed better than today. Her ground strokes were riveted on target, and there were fewer than a half-dozen errors from her racquet in those fleeting minutes she was on public view.

Mrs. Cawley, by contrast, won the service toss and double-faulted to 15. The game was gone at love. The Australian is a slow starter, and in the semifinals she had lost her first service game in each set against Margaret Court, whom she beat, 6-4, 6-4.

Mrs. King romped to 40-love in the second game, volleying beautifully, and then double-faulted, was past on a net cord and pushed a forehand volley into the net. There were three deuces then, and on one of the few decent rallies in the match, Billie Jean slapped a forehand volley down the line for 2-love.

The games came running. Mrs. Cawley, a gifted athlete and the best mover in women's tennis, seemed mired in midcourt, mesmerized by the accuracy of the shots that breezed past her. Mrs. King served out for the first set at 6-love, and it was hard to find an unforced error. Mrs. Cawley had won 10 points.

"If I got ahead, I was not going to let her up," said Mrs. King. "I was going to watch the ball, play the ball and not think about whom I was playing."

Starting the second set, Mrs. King played a superb game, employing a backhand to the line, a backhand pass, a backhand across court and, almost inevitably, another backhand that beat the Australian coming in. They changed courts and the crowd, muted for so long, let out a cheer for Mrs. Cawley, trying to give her encouragement.

There were brief signs of revival then. But they petered out under Mrs. King's charges to net. Four-love now and Mrs. Cawley serving. A forehand volley, a smash and a drop volley gave her a game. That was all. Mrs. King had three match points, finally planting that volley into the corner for her sixth championship. None had been easier. No other one, she said, had she wanted so much.

"I wanted to go out on a high. It's time for the youngsters to take over."

"Anybody who plays like that" said the beaten Australian, "there's nothing I can do."

With the men's final between Jimmy Connors and Arthur Ashe tomorrow, the United States is assured to three titles. America won a second today when Sandy Mayer of Wayne, N.J., and Vitas Gerulaitis of Howard Beach, Queens, beat Colin Dowdeswell of Rhodesia and Allan Stone of Australia, 7-5, 8-6, 6-4, in the doubles final.

Mayer and Gerulaitis are respectively ranked 17 and 21 at home, but their victory in the final was not surprising in light of upsets that had come earlier. None of the eight seeded teams even reached the semifinals, and only one reached the quarter-finals.

It was the first American doubles victory since 1957, when Gardnor Mulloy, then 43, paired with Budge Patty to defeat Neale Fraser and Lew Hoad.

And the passing of the years has not dimmed historic figures. Mulloy, old Rip Van Wimbledon himself, pairs with Don Budge, the grand slam winner in 1938, to face Patty and Lennart Bergelin in the veterans' final tomorrow.

July 5, 1975

Ashe Topples Connors for Crown at Wimbledon

'Junk' and Solid Serving Produce 4-Set Victory

By FRED TUPPER
Special to The New York Times

WIMBLEDON, England, July 5—Jimmy Connors, the man everybody thought unbeatable, was thrashed by Arthur Ashe in the Wimbledon men's final today.

Before a stunned center-court crowd, Ashe won, 6-1 6-1, 5-7, 6-4, over 125 minutes and became the first black man to take the highest honor in tennis. Althea Gibson, a black, won the women's title in 1957 and 1958.

For many years Ashe had waited in the wings, his best efforts here having been a losing semi-finalist in 1968 and 1969. He will be 32 next week, and had set two objectives for this year—to win the World Championship Tennis and Wimbledon crowns. Amazingly, he has achieved both.

Connors was a 3-to-2 favorite to win the title for the second straight time. Three times he had beaten Ashe, never having lost to him. Jimmy had waded through the draw without dropping a set, and his massacre of Roscoe Tanner, the huge server in the semifinals, was thought to have contained the hardest hitting ever seen at this historic shrine.

Ashe confounded him. He threw "junk" at Jimmy, he chipped and dinked, mostly to the backhand. He tossed up lobs. He served solidly all the way through, and his forehand volley, admittedly his weakness, was a tower of strength at the infighting around the net.

"I played well, I was confident," he said.

Arthur had found his game plan by watching the Connors-Raul Ramirez match on tape, not the Tanner match. "It may have looked suicidal," he said of his tactics, but the result was there for all to see.

He took the pace off the ball and gave the slugger little to bang at, and he served wide to the backhand to pull Connors off balance.

For a time it seemed unreal. Cocky and cool, Connors won the first game and then was swamped. After 20 minutes Ashe had the set at 6-1, without a break point against him.

This match brought alive what had been a dull Wimbledon. On the changeovers

Ashe playing against Connors on the Center Court

Ashe sat still, eyes closed, meditating, relaxing for the task ahead. He had nine games in a row now, leading by 3-love in the second set.

Was this the great Connors, winner of everything in sight, champion here and at Forest Hills, conqueror of Rod Laver and John Newcombe in challenge matches? "Come on, Connors!" a voice yelled in the distance. "I'm trying, for crissake!" replied, Jimmy, tearing around the court, mop of hair flying.

Then he won a game, a single flare in the gloom.

Outwardly unemotional, Ashe pressed on with the plan. He had the second set in 25 minutes, getting it on his fourth set point, the crowd exploding in applause.

A backhand volley took ~~him~~ to break point and a backhand into Jimmy's body brought Arthur to 3-2 in the third set. It seemed like a mirage, the fans could hardly believe what they were seeing.

Finally Connors found the reins. A two-handed pass, a backhand dumped at Ashe's feet as he came in and a teasing lob that Ashe smashed out brought Jimmy back to 3-all.

With two ads against him, the 22-year-old bravely held service for 4-3, staved off two more break points and took the set at 7-5 with a blistering forehand across court as he threw a fist high in defiance.

Connors had climbed out of the coffin, but could he stay alive? Suddenly he was at 3-love in the fourth set, the two-fisters streaming down the lines. Ashe cut him off. In the fifth game he slid a little chip to the side for deuce, smashed an overhead deep for ad out and,

sprinting across court, lashed a forehand down the line for the break back to 3-2.

Deliberate and careful, Ashe stuck to the battle plan. A backhand wafted high to the corner was good as Connors let it drop, thinking it out. A backhand pass slid down the sideline. Now came a gossamer touch on the chip, putting Ashe at 15-40. Jimmy backhanded a volley wide and there was Ashe serving for the match, the center court enthralled.

A serve for 15, a desperate dash by Connors for a rocket, down the side, and finally a big, jumping serve

that Jimmy could push up only feebly near the net. Arthur smashed it away. At last he had won his Wimbledon title.

The winner received $23,000 and the loser $13,800.

"I just didn't have it today," said a crestfallen Connors, but the bravado was still there. He had played a wonderful Wimbledon.

"I came here with my head high and I'll walk out that way, and I'll be back with my head even higher," he added.

July 6, 1975

Miss Evert Takes Open Crown; Connors, Orantes Reach Final

By PARTON KEESE

Chris Evert won her first United States Open singles championship on her fifth attempt yesterday, defeating Evonne Goolagong of Australia, 5-7, 6-4, 6-2.

Before her victory, worth $25,000, Jimmy Connors beat Bjorn Borg to gain the men's final. And then, in a 3-hour-44-minute match under the lights in the Forest Hills stadium, Manuel Orantes outlasted Guillermo Vilas in the second semifinal to earn the right to meet Connors.

A crowd of 15,720 braved a threat of rain to see Miss Evert and Connors move one victory away from duplicating their "lovebird" Wimbledon triumphs in singles last year. The three matches yesterday lasted more than nine hours, however, forcing many persons to leave early and tournament officials to postpone the men's doubles final until this afternoon.

Connors defeated his Swedish rival 7-5, 7-5, 7-5. The sets not only were identical in the number of games, but also in the manner that Connors succeeded. In each instance, the top-seeded American broke Borg's service in the 12th game to take an otherwise even set.

Orantes, a Spaniard, made an amazing comeback against the second-seeded Vilas of Argentina. Trailing by two sets to one and down 0-5, in the fourth set, Orantes saved 5 match points before winning, 4-6, 1-6, 6-2, 7-5, 6-4, in the longest match of the tournament.

Cheered on by his followers, Orantes simply lasted longer than his exhausted

The New York Times/Robert Walker

Chris Evert during her final match in the U.S. Open at Forest Hills against Evonne Goolagong

foe. Seeded third, he continued his jinx over Vilas with his fourth victory in four meetings this year.

Today's final program will start at 11:30 A.M. with the Hall of Fame doubles, followed by the women's doubles and the men's singles, the men's doubles, in which Connors will also play, and the mixed doubles.

Miss Evert's victory stretched her winning streak on clay to 84 matches and increased her year's earnings to $280,027. In her keen

rivalry with Miss Goolagong over the last three years, she has won 12 of 21 matches.

Both were battling for a title they had never won, but had come close to winning. Chris had reached the semifinals four times before this year, her furthest advance, while Evonne had played in the final without success in 1974 and 1973.

Though she outdueled Miss Consistency from the baseline to take the opening set and barely lost the second on the only service break,

Miss Goolagong faded badly in the third set, winning a total of only 3 points in the last three games.

"I felt sort of tennised out," she said afterward. "She was getting too much back, and I'm not patient enough to play that type of game and keep going."

Capturing the last five games with little resistance, Miss Evert raced on to a triumph she termed "more satisfying than Wimbledon."

Not that she wasn't worried and even "quite down on myself" when Miss Goolagong looked as if she would win in straight sets.

"I had two thoughts when things were really tight," Miss Evert said. "The first one was how Evonne always seemed to win our close matches. The second one was on how hard I'd worked to come this far and lose."

There was little to choose between Connors, 22, and the 19-year-old Borg except in the final game of each set. The defending champion hit the ball consistently harder and flatter than his rival, but Borg's tremendously accurate topspin returns and placements matched everything Connors could hurl at him.

Credit Connors with figuring out what to do.

"Every time Bjorn passed me in the beginning," he said, "it was on a helluva shot. Then, after 30 of these shots it began to dawn on me. They were all hit down the line. When I realized this, I was there when it counted

and cut them off."

Jimmy started in his normally cocky way, joking with the crowd, which seemed to favor Borg. When a baby cried loudly in the stands. Connors shouted, "I hope it isn't mine!"

In the second set he showed some anger. He had hit two straight shots into the net, and on the second asked to see the ball. Feeling it, he contended it was too soft and tossed it to Frank Hammond, the umpire, to confirm this and perhaps replay the point.

Hammond agreed on a new ball but not the point, letting it stand, and the crowd began getting on Connors, who shouted at one heckler, "Shut up!" Then, when he took the court again, he held up his little finger derisively as the stands hooted. But that was the end of the show.

September 7, 1975

The New York Times

Jimmy Connors slamming ball back to Bjorn Borg during semifinals at the U.S. Open

Orantes Takes U.S. Open Title, Beating Connors by 6-4, 6-3, 6-3

By NEIL AMDUR

Like a matador taunting a bull, Manuel Orantes destroyed Jimmy Connors, 6-4, 6-3, 6-3, yesterday for the men's singles title in the United States Open tennis championships.

Less than 18 hours after he had survived five match points in an exhausting five-set struggle with second-seeded Guillermo Vilas, the 26-year-old Spanish left-hander brought the top-seeded Connors to his knees before a stunned crowd of 15,669 at the West Side Tennis Club in Forest Hills, Queens.

Off-speed ground strokes and passing shots from both sides were two of the tactics that blunted the bullish tactics of the defending champion. But Orantes's most devastating weapon was the forehand topspin lob, a shot that typified the tone of a tournament that had switched from grass to the clay-like Har-Tru surface.

Time and again, with time to spare on a slower playing surface, Orantes looped the deceiving lobs over his net rushing rival for outright winners, while cheers and chants of "Viva Orantes" emanated from a small, but vocal rooting section high above Portal 9.

"If he wins, do you think they'll give him one of Jimmy's ears?" a spectator in a courtside box joked after Orantes broke Connors in the opening game of the third set with two winning lobs.

The third-seeded Orantes collected $25,000 and a Pinto

The New York Times

Orantes exulting after the final point at Forest Hills

automobile for his biggest tournament achievement. More important, the gracious self-effacing Spaniard finally may have achieved the respect and recognition due him after being almost totally ignored and shunted to obscure field courts in the early rounds of the 12-day event.

How Orantes managed to control the tempo against Connors after his 3-hour-44 minute match with Vilas and a sleepless night at his midtown hotel was a tribute to the Spaniard's competitive instinct and clay-court artistry.

The Vilas struggle did not end until 10:28 P.M. Saturday and only after Orantes had rallied from two sets to one down and 0-5 in the fourth set.

He ate no dinner after the match, did not reach the Roosevelt Hotel until 2 A.M. yesterday and could not get to sleep until 3 A.M. because of running water in the bathroom that forced him to summon a plumber.

"It was a very hard night," he said.

Connors, seeking to become the first two-time singles winner since Neale Fraser 15 years ago, had outslugged Bjorn Borg of Sweden in a straight-set Saturday afternoon semifinal. But just as Arthur Ashe had changed speeds and kept Connors from finding a hitting groove in the Wimbledon final on grass, Orantes left him uncomfortable in pursuit of a pattern.

"I tried to give him soft balls," said the soft-spoken Spaniard who joined his countryman, Manuel Santana, as a champion here. "Let him do everything. I know he is not as consistent that way, and I am lucky he miss so many shots."

Connors had said after his first match that "everyone's a challenger on clay." Subconsciously, however, he may have wondered how Orantes could recover from the Vilas encounter.

"He played unbelievably," Jimmy told the stadium gathering, after receiving his runner-up check for $12,00. "I didn't think it would be possible for him to play the way he did and hit the kind of passing shots he did. Unfortunately for me, he did."

Starts With Flourish

Connors started with a flourish by breaking his rival at love and holding at 15 for 2-0. But Orantes turned matador, his drop-shots and slicing backhands teasing Connors with the same effect as a red cape.

Jimmy netted a routine forehand approach that brought Orantes to 2-all. He stroked a forehand volley past the baseline at 30-40 that moved Orantes ahead, 4-2.

A forehand passing shot down the line gave the Spaniard the first set after Connors tried to attack on a weak approach shot.

Orantes appeared ready for the kill at 3-1, 40-love

Connors-Evert Win Doubles

By FRED TUPPER
Special to The New York Times

in the second set only to have Connors charge back to 3-all. But the earlier matches against such clay-court proponents as François Jauffert, Ilie Nastase and Vilas had toughened Orantes, and he broke for 5-3 by blocking a serve with a forehand that bounced on the baseline.

Connors strung together 13 straight points in the third set to reach 3-all and continued to banter with the crowd, responding to pleas of "C'mon Jimmy," with "I'm comin' baby!"

Orantes was too deliberate, conserving energy and patience just as Chris Evert, another clay-court specialist, had done in beating Evonne Goolagong for the women's singles crown.

"I had a point for 4-2 and blew it," Connors noted, referring to a netted forehand service return that got Orantes to deuce from 30-40.

Orantes delivered the final blows with successive service breaks in the seventh and ninth games, each time with forehand passing shots down the line.

Connors was boring in on the second match point when Orantes took the big backswing for the clincher, a shot that might not have been possible with a skidding ball on a faster surface such as grass.

As the ball landed for the final winner, Orantes dropped to his knees, smiled in relief and turned immediately toward his wife, who was seated at courtside.

Lament by Connors

"Another day, another final, another loss," Connors lamented, of his defeats in the Australian, Wimbledon and United States Open finals.

Asked about the tirelessly effective play of his rival, Connors said, "A lot of times it happens that way. The guy is still playing from the night before. You forget to sleep, you forget to eat. I don't think he had time to get tired."

Connors returned and teamed with Nastase for a 6-4, 7-6 victory over Tom Okker and Marty Riessen in the men's doubles final. Afterward, he said that Orantes had become the top opponent for next February's $250,000 challenge match in Las Vegas.

Connors did not appear pleased with the partisan Orantes crowd, although underdogs generally draw considerable support from West Side galleries, even against Americans.

"The American public is spoiled with its tennis players," America's top-ranking player said. "There are too many good tennis players now."

The women's doubles title was won by Margaret Court and Virginia Wade over Rosemary Casals and Billie Jean King, 7-5, 2-6, 7-6. In mixed doubles, Miss Casals and Dick Stockton beat Mrs. King and Fred Stolle, 6-3, 6-7, 6-3.

September 8, 1975

LAS VEGAS, Nev., Dec. 6 —Jimmy Connors and Chris Evert, ranked the best players in the world separately, paired as underdogs and defeated Marty Riessen and Billie Jean King, 4-6, 6-3, 6-4, 7-5, in a $150,000 mixed doubles match today. The contest at the Caesars Palace indoor pavilion lasted nearly 2½ hours and was nationally televised.

Riessen, 34 years old, and Mrs. King, 32 were 7-5 favorites, but were giving away 22 years and had been out of competition for three months. Spectacular at the start, with Billie Jean slashing away the volleys, they were worn down by the slugging of Connors and unexpectedly solid net game of Miss Evert, who held the combination together in the crisis. The winners received $100,000 and the losers $50,000.

"I never hit the ball that hard before at a lady," said Connors, 23. "It takes a lot of guts to stand up to two men pounding the ball."

Miss Evert, two weeks short of her 21st birthday, was shaking at the thought.

"I couldn't sleep," she said.

"I had only four hours. I've never been so nerves, not even before Wimbledon."

In the end, though, she threated a two-handed backhand through a narrow opening to reach match point, then served wide and deep to force Billie Jean to sky out.

"Four points cost us the match," lamented Riessen. Perhaps the two that mattered most came in the fourth game of the second set. At game point Mrs. King smashed wide and at advantage out she smashed wide again to put Connors-Evert at 3-1, from where they went on to take the second set.

Riessen, introduced accurately as the world's best mixed-doubles player, was responsible for the 2 other points. He and his partner were leading, 2-1 and 30-40 in the third set on Miss Evert's service. A huge hole opened down the alley, but Riessen drifted his backhand just over the line. Later, he had a miserable serving game, losing his delivery for the first time with a weak push shot that Connors crashed through the middle for 5-4, after which Jimmy held his service for the set.

The favorites never threatened again. Brilliant as Billie Jean had been at the start, she tired toward the end. Serving at 5-all in the fourth set, the best volleyer of her time lost her touch on the low volley. Three times she pushed the ball into the net. Then, at 15-40, Miss Evert rocketed a forehand across court for the breakthrough. Chris held service for the victory.

The match had its magic moments, most of them fashioned by the genius of Connors, to spark the 3,300 fans into prolonged applause.

Mixed doubles is new to most crowds and Mrs. King believes it has a future. "There are 35 million people playing tennis, and most of them are couples playing mixed," she said.

Connors and Miss Evert now will be challenged by John Newcombe and Margaret Court, who holds every major mixed-doubles title.

As the crowd drifted away to the gaming tables, Connors was asked, "What will you do with your prize money?"

"Put it on red," he replied.

December 7, 1975

Sweden Victor In Davis Cup

STOCKHOLM, Dec. 21 (AP) —Bjorn Borg scored one of his greatest victories today in leading Sweden to a 3-2 triumph over Czechoslovakia in the 1975 Davis Cup final series and to its first victory in the world's most prestigious team tennis competition.

The 19-year-old Borg cut down Jan Kodes, a former Wimbledon champion in straight sets, 6-4, 6-2, 6-2, on a fast indoor court. It was Borg's 19th straight Davis Cup singles victory, giving Sweden an unbeatable 3-1 lead in the three of-five match series.

"This was my finest victory ever, I've always dreamt of winning the Davis Cup since I played my first match in the tournament three years ago," said Borg after being tossed in the air by his teammates.

After Borg's performance, watched by a sellout crowd of 4,500 fans in the Royal Tennis Hall, Jiri Hrebec of Czechoslovakia defeated Ove Bengtson, 1-6, 6-3, 6-1, 6-4, in the closing match, which was virtually meaningless.

Associated Press
Bjorn Borg being carried by enthusiastic supporters after defeating Jan Kodes in the Davis Cup final at Stockholm yesterday as Sweden won first Davis Cup.

The Swedish team's triumph was the finest sports achievement for this country since Ingemar Johansson won the world heavyweight boxing crown in 1959 by knocking out Floyd Patterson.

It was sweet revenge for Borg, who previously had failed to win a major tournament in his home town. He repeatedly flopped in the Stockholm open—the world's biggest indoor event—and only three weeks ago lost the final of the Masters tournament to Ilie Nastase of Rumania.

"I'm very happy. I finally made it in a tournament like this, which I think surpasses everything else in world tennis," said Borg who now lives in Monte Carlo.

"I've never been so nervous before a big match. I could only sleep four or five hours in the night, but after the first game felt very relaxed."

The young Swede, with his whipping forehand working to near perfection, was in the lead throughout the 1-hour-55-minute match. He got off to an explosive start, breaking Kodes's serve at once.

In the opening set, Kodes bounced back briefly to score his only break of the match in the eighth game, leveling to 4-4 after a superb forehand cross.

But Borg stayed cool and broke back immediately to lead 5-4 after saving one break point for Kodes with a forehand deep into the corner. He then held his serve easily to win the set in 45 minutes.

After breaking Kodes's serve again in the first game, Borg raced to a 4-1 lead in the second set with another break in the fifth game in which he won four straight points.

Kodes fought back and had two chances at 15-40 in the eighth game to go to 3-5 with service in the next. But Borg saved both, one with a lucky net cord. Then he banged in two booming serves for the set.

The third set was just a formality for the long-haired Swede, although he had some troubles in the last two games, missing four match points before clinching victory.

He broke to love twice in the first and fifth games and led 4-1.

In the seventh game, Kodes survived one match point at 30-40 with a forehand volley into the corner and then fired two good serves to trail, 2-5.

Serving for the match, Borg aced his way into a 40-15 lead. He missed the first match point, hitting out an easy smash and then Kodes passed him with a backhand.

The Czech got two break chances, but Borg came back each time with forehand winners. Kodes then saved another match point — his fourth in the match—before finally netting a backhand on the fifth after Borg had forced the Czech backward with some sizzling forehands.

December 22, 1975

Chris Evert Takes 2d Wimbledon Title

By FRED TUPPER
Special to The New York Times

WIMBLEDON, England, July 2—Chris Evert has won the All-England tennis title for the second time. In a nail-biting final that raged over 2 hours on center court, the 20-year-old No. 1 seeded player rallied to take three games running and the match from archrival Evonne Goolagong, 6-3, 4-6, 8-6, for the first American title at this sunniest of Wimbledons.

"It was a battle of the minds, a question of who was going to hang in longest and who was going to rise to the occasion," said Miss Evert, who was beating the Australian for the first time on grass. "I never gave up. I just tried to stay in there—to guts it out."

It was also the first three-setter since 1969, and may well determine who is to be the world No. 1 for 1976. In their perennial rivalry, Miss Evert has won 17 of 27 in her career, 4-2 so far this year, but was beaten in another three-setter at the Virginia Slims final a few months ago.

The victory brings her $17,700 at current British exchange rates. "I don't really care how much winning Wimbledon is worth to me. I'm absolutely determined not to defend my title next year unless the women get equal parity."

For a clay-court specialist, the Floridian has done well here. Semifinalist to Miss Goolagong in 1972 at 17, finalist to Billie Jean King in 1973, winner in 1974, semifinalist to Mrs. King last year when she led, 3-0 and 15-40, in the third set, she started fast and she finished strong. If there were lapses here and there, for a long time she was put under intense pressure by a woman who had won 26 consecutive matches on all surfaces until she bowed this afternoon. And this victory runs the Chris Evert streak to 17, dating from that Virginia Slims loss in Los Angeles.

On the eleventh day of bright sun and cloudless sky at this 90th Wimbledon, the smart opinion was that Miss Goolagong would win. She had been in four Wimbledon finals, taking the 1971 title at a precocious 19, and her flowing strokes and superb volleying invariably favor her on grass.

Her marriage to Roger Cawley of Britain a year ago has given her confidence, and she is a much better player now than at any time since she came out of the sheep country, around her Barellan, Australia, birthplace.

They were off and running at 2:02, both scared stiff of each other and jockeying for position, Miss Evert taking the first game by ramming a forehand down the counter, and the second at love by driving the Australian back and using the corners.

"I was tentative," said Miss Goolagong later, "I was not getting my ground stroke deep enough."

Miss Evert was quickly at 4-2, finding room for a forehand across court, and forcing a backhand error on a forehand down the line. Serving at 5-3, she hit a great pass to reach 30-15 and had the set in 28 minutes on a backhand that kicked up the chalk.

The rallies were longer now, as they fenced for position, Miss Goolagong wanting to come up for the volley, Miss Evert often racing in on the short ball. The American had a point for the first game, and a point again in the third.

Miss Goolagong fought her off and aced her for 3-2, and had the break to 4-2 as a return died on a bald spot, a forehand shot into the clear. Bravely, Miss Evert broke back with two stunning backhand volleys, and soon they were locked at 4-all.

At 4-5, with the crowd cheering her on, the Australian attacked. A smash to deep court and a forehand volley had her poised at set point, and she won it on her second try in the longest rally of the match. The tide was changing.

Miss Goolagong was hitting deeper and then sliding in a backhand slice to force her opponent off balance. She held her serve, broke to 2-0, and had three more break points for 3-1. Miss Evert saved them all, charging up for a forehand volley, at net again for a low volley into the corner, and then hammering a forehand down the line.

It wasn't good enough. At 3-all, she dropped service on a tactical mistake. A short lob loomed up and she backed away, preferring to hit it on the bounce. And so into the net it went.

The line calls had been provoking whistles from the stands, and at 4-all an Evert shot soared out, there was no call and the rally continued—then the umpire took charge.

"One moment," he said sternly, "the ball was out."

The rest were in, and now the American No. 1 was serving for the match. She lost it at love, head bowed a little as the Australian dispatched a backhand volley for 5-all, and held her serve to 6-5 as a loose forehand wandered over the line.

Miss Evert has a curious way of jumping to a stop, feet together and surveying the scene, something like Jack Nicklaus before a putt. Now she gallivanted into action. A backhand rabbited into a hole, a forehand volley raised white dust, and then a drop volley sat down on the scarred turf. She was 6-all and 7-6, with match point looming.

Miss Goolagong tore into the net for a short forehand and braked to a stop. Too late—an Evert backhand lob jumped over her head and plopped a foot inside the back line.

The cheers rang out and the racquet was thrown high. The Duchess of Kent came on court to present a silver platter to Miss Evert, and to enormous applause Miss Goolagong came on for a medal and handshake.

One of the great Wimbledon finals? Perhaps not, but it was vastly exciting, and a match to remember.

Brian Gottfried of Fort Lauderdale, Fla., and Raul Ramirez of Mexico justified their top seeding by going the full route before beating Geoff Masters and Ross Case of Australia, 3-6, 6-3, 8-6, 2-6, 7-5, and taking the men's doubles title.

It ended on a sad note as little Case double-faulted on match point.

In semifinal mixed-doubles

Chris Evert

competition, Dick Stockton and Rosie Casals of the United States defeated Bob Hewitt and Greer Stevens of South Africa, 6-3, 9-8, and Tony Roche of Australia and Francoise Durr of France eliminated Frew McMillan of South Africa and Betty Stove of the Netherlands, 6-3, 6-3.

Tomorrow the 20-year-old wonder boy, Bjorn Borg, has a date with the tempestuous Rumanian, Ilie Nastase, in the first European final since Fred Perry of Britain faced Baron Gottfried Von Cramm of Germany 40 years ago.

Over the years since 1972, Nastase has won seven times, Borg three, and the last one was in Hawaii in the Avis Challenge Cup semifinal with Nastase coming from 2-4 down to win the fifth set at 6-4. They have never played each other on grass.

Partly retired Billie Jean King will play a doubles final tomorrow with Miss Stove against Miss Evert and Martina Navratilova. Mrs. King is tied for career Wimbledon titles at 19 with Elizabeth Ryan.

July 3, 1976

Borg Beats Nastase in 3 Sets for Wimbledon Title

By FRED TUPPER

Special to The New York Times

WIMBLEDON, England, July 3—Bjorn Borg won the men's Wimbledon title today and became the youngest champion in 45 years.

For 107 minutes, the bearded Swede—just 20 years and 27 days old—belted the cover off the ball with such nonstop aggression that even a last-stand rally by the favored Ilie Nastase of Rumania was fruitless in the 6-4, 6-2, 9-7 victory.

A year ago, Arthur Ashe achieved his ambition of winning both the World Championship Tennis circuit final and the Wimbledon title in the same year. Now Borg has done that, too. He also has held the titles of France and Italy, the United States professional title and last year took Sweden to its first victory in the Davis Cup final.

For his triumph today, Borg won $22,250 and he did it without losing a set, a feat unparalleled since Chuck McKinley did it in 1963.

Tender though his age may be — Sidney Wood took the Wimbledon title by default from the late Frank Shields in 1931 at 19 years 7 months —the Swede has been beating everybody for years, defeating Onny Perun of New Zealand in a Davis Cup match at 15.

The margin of his victory over Nastase today almost defies belief. In 10 previous meetings, the Rumanian had won seven matches, granting Borg only five games in winning the Grand Prix Masters last December and beating him again in Hawaii over five sets. Everybody was beginning to think this would be Nastase's year to win the All-England tournament.

Like Borg, he had plowed through the opposition without losing a set and seemed to have regained the touch that had brought him the Italian title twice as well as the French, Forest Hills and four Grand Masters titles. He was runner-up here before, in 1972, when he lost a five-setter to Stan Smith that is still talked about with reverence.

The serving today was tremendous. Borg, who seemed to grow an inch or two in stature on court, hit 71 first serves in 111 attempts and Nastase had 69 of 107. Borg returned much the better, his aim being to hit every ball as hard as he could with a semi-Western forehand that imparts a heavy topspin.

They went on court in stifling heat without a bit of a breeze before a royal box containing the King and Queen of Greece, the Queen Mother of Denmark, the Duke and Duchess of Kent, the Rumanian and Swedish Ambassadors, the Lord Mayor of London, assorted generals and admirals. More than 14,-000 fans, some of whom had lined up for 50 hours and others of whom had paid $180 for a pair of tickets, also were on hand.

On a backhand struck by Nastase like a lightning bolt, Borg was at 30-40 break point and hit a forehand down the line. He did it again in the next game, watched his volley go out and saw Nastase stroke a delicate backhand just inside the far corner that gave the Rumanian a 2-0 lead.

Nastase fired an ace and, serving beautifully, reached game point again on a forehand pass. He got it by burying a forehand in the corner for a 3-0 edge.

Then came the game that might have decided the match, a furious head to head clash in which Nastase had three break points and muffed the simplest of volleys astride the net, which would have brought him to 4-0.

The Rumanian was like a robot, wound up tight and ready to explode. No matter how deftly he would slide the ball into little pockets across the court, up would charge Borg and spin it away for winners, holding the ball on the racquet until Nastase committed himself.

"I had those points for 4-0 and I wish I knew what happened," said Nastase later. "I never knew him to serve so well."

A double-fault and a forehand that blazed by him cost Nastase his service and the Swede held his to 3-all. Still, Nastase stuck to it. He hit four first serves, deep and fast, in the next game and won it at love.

But Borg was devastating. He held service easily, then attacked. A backhand volley seared a line then he lunged and stabbed a forehand volley clear. He reached 40-15 on a forehand that spun across court and took a 5-4 lead as Nastase's forehand volley soared over the line.

Nastase had little answer; he was being forced back, with the heavier ball winning the day. Borg captured the first set at 6-4 as his crashing serves won the final points outright.

The Rumanian fretted. A camera clicked and he glared. A ball boy gave him an extra ball and he hit it contemptuously back. Psychological warfare was in order. He held his hand on a stomach muscle, presumably to annoy Borg, who applies freezing spray there during changeovers and had three cortisone injections early this morning.

The phlegmatic Swede paid no attention. Down by love-1 and 15-40 in the second set, Borg struck two aces, reached advantage playing cat and mouse at the net and whipped a forehand free for a 1-1 tie.

He broke Nastase as he went up by 2-1, held his service and eventually had the second set at 6-2, taking the last service game at love. The stands were thunder-struck at the destruction going on below, with Borg having won 12 of the last 15 games.

It was 4-2 for Borg in the third set before the crowd started yelling for Nastase to fight back. The Rumanian stirred. He held service and he was at 30-40 in the next game when Borg backhanded the ball into the net. A marvelous forehand jumped into a corner and Nastase had another chance. Borg rifled another serve and suddenly it was 5-4 with Borg serving for the match.

Two break points for Nastase and a roar went up. A drop shot and Nastase raced in too late. A forehand volley and the Swede was at match point, the crater stilled. Nastase banged a shot at the body, Borg halfvolleyed it high. It was hammered away and Nastase quickly broke to 5-5, a final gasp. In the 15th game, Borg slugged a backhand into one corner, another across court for the break point and went up by 8-7 as a forehand streaked in. That virtually did it.

Borg Wraps It Up

Borg served out at love and made the other statistics meaningless. He had five aces and two double-faults, Nastase had four and three.

"Are you disappointed?" somebody said.

"No, I am very happy," said Nastase. "Next stupid question."

"This was probably my last chance," Nastase added, underlining the fact that he turns 30 this month. "It will be very hard for me to concentrate for another year."

There was another disappointment. A year ago, Billie Jean King won the Wimbledon final for the sixth time and said she would come back only "for a hit and a giggle." What she wanted was a 20th title to go with her nine doubles and four mixed doubles victories here.

Mrs. King and Sandy Mayer were put out early in the mixed doubles and today in the women's doubles final she and Betty Stove led by 3-0 in the final set but were beaten by Chris Evert and Martina Navratilova, 6-1, 3-6, 7-5.

Among the older men, the stylish Budge Patty, 53, paired with Lennart Bergelin, Borg's captain and coach, and won the veteran doubles for the second year, from Homer Richards and Dick Sorlien, 6-4, 4-6, 6-1.

And in the mixed doubles, Tony Roche and Françoise Durr won from Dick Stockton and Rosie Casals, 6-3, 2-6, 7-5.

The crowds totaled more than 313,000 for the fortnight, second highest in the tourney's history.

July 4, 1976

Connors Defeats Borg for Open Crown

Tiebreaker in 3d Set Is High Point

The New York Times/Don Hogan Charles
Jimmy Connors with victor's cup and $30,000 check at Forest Hills yesterday

By NEIL AMDUR

It was everything anyone could have asked for. And more. Courage and greatness flowed across the stadium of the West Side Tennis Club yesterday on the men's final of the United States open championship. A little blood trickled, too.

And when it was over, when the crowd of 16,253 had given the last of what seemed like one continuous standing ovation, it was hard to tell whether top-seeded Jimmy Connors or second-seeded Bjorn Borg had taken the 130,000 first prize.

Connors won 6-4, 3-6, 7-6, 6-4, in a 2 hour-10-minute struggle that rivaled the most satisfying moments in the 24-year-old American's brilliant career.

"We killed each other out there," Connors said, so emotional that it took him almost five seconds to realize that the match was over after Borg's final backhand had landed limply at the net.

The match began under sunny, late afternoon skies and finished under lights. and as the crowd left the concrete horseshoe in Forest Hills Queens, for the last time in the 12-day tournament, many were using superlatives to describe their sentiments.

The national television audience that watched might have felt that way too. No recent Open men's final contained the countless highs and lows in which the two players, like courageous prize fighters, refused to be counted out.

'He Hit Everything on Lines'

"Since Forest Hills changed to clay and I'm not supposed to be a clay-court player, it was very satisfying," Said Connors, who won here on grass in 1974 but lost last year's final to Manuci Orantes, a straight-set embarrassment that gnawed at his pride.

"It was a very good match." the 20-year-old Borg said. "It was the best Jimmy has ever played against me. He hit everything on the lines, everything in the corners. I couldn't do anything. Usually, you play like that for one and a half sets and start missing. But he was very consistent"

The third set alone took 1 hour 10 minutes almost as long as their straight-set semifinal victories, and embodied the spirit of this classic. It began with Connors losing his serve at love and ended with Jimmy saving 4 set points and winning the longest tiebreaker he had every played—20 points.

Borg also showed the depth of his game and character Down a break point in the second game, Connors drove a backhand deep into the corner that sent Borg diving and rolling on the ground in futile pursuit. As he got up, the back of his shirt was conered with the green clay and a thin stream of blood trickled from a scrape the size of a quarter on his right knee.

Although he insisted later "it was nothing." Borg received treatment and assistance on the court changeover and acknowledged that the knee "felt strange." He suddenly fell behind, with Connors serving at 4-2, 40-0, before fighting back to 6-all.

on Borg and the Swede's backhand went wide.

"The tiebreaker was very important for me," Borg said. "When I lose the tiebreaker, I was disappointed."

Temptation Becomes Costly

Connors had started the match strongly, ramming 14 winners to only three for the Swede in the first set. But the temptation of trying for the good shot too soon, particularly off the forehand, became costly for Jimmy in the second set.

By the fourth set he was on his fourth game plan. "I just wanted to get to the net and say, 'Pass me,' " he said later.

Borg, ever the opportunist, did. With Connors serving at match point—5-4, 40-30—the imperturbable Swede looped a topspin forehand cross-court with such pace and angle that Connors, at the net, could not reach it.

Borg netted a backhand, giving Connors a second match point. Perhaps overanxious, Jimmy drove a forehand wide.

Attacking again. Connors got the advantage a third time when Borg lobbed too deeply.

It was the sixth victory for Connors in their seven matches, including the last six in a row. But with both young, eager and fit, these street fights are just beginning.

Marty Riessen and Tom Okker, a familiar international team and fourth-seeded here, took the men's doubles title and $10,000 with a 6-4, 6-4 victory over the surprising unseeded duo of Paul Kronk and Cliff Letcher.

The women's doubles crown went to the fifth-seeded team of Linky Boshoff and Ilana Kloss over third-seeded Virginia Wade and Olga Morozova, 6-1, 6-4.

An interesting mixed-doubles final paired Betty Stove and Frew McMillan aganst Billie Jean King and Phil Dent, both leftovers from World Team Tennis summers.

"We entered as a joke because we had played together on the Sets," Mrs. King said. It was no joke, however, when the pair recovered from 2 match points at 4-5, 15-40 in the final set and won 3-6, 6-2, 7-5. The winning team split $6,500.

In other final-day developments, the U.S. Open tournament committee fined Ilie Nastase $11,000 for five offenses during his early-round match against Hans-Jurgen Pohmann. The money will be deducted from Nastase's $7,500 as a losing semifinalist.

Nastase will appeal the fine, his agent, Mitch Oprea, said yesterday. If the fine is upheld, Nastase faces an automatic 21-day suspension because he already had accumulated $2,700 worth of fines earlier this year. A $3,000 total in any single year is grounds for suspension under rules of the International Professional Council.

September 13, 1976

A Memorable Sequence

The tiebreaker was one that fans might store in their memories, with Arthur Ashe's victory at the first Open in 1968, the Grand Slam finishes of Rod Laver and Margaret Court, and Ilie Nastase's five-set comeback victory against Ashe in the final of the 1972 Open.

"You have to be very, very lucky to win tiebreakers," said Borg, who had won the Wimbledon, United States Pro and World Championship Tennis titles

this year. "He made some unbelievable points then."

Each time Borg reached set point, Connors went all out with shots that had weekend hackers shaking their heads in disbelief. A backhand volley winner at 4-6, a slashing forehand down the line at 5-6, an overhead at 7-8, another overhead at 8-9.

Borg was just as cool when Jimbo held 2 set points. But at 9-all, Connors nearly blasted the fuzz off the ball with a backhand cross-court winner.

Serving at 10-9, Jimmy put pressure

Issue and Debate

Are Tennis Rules Strong Enough To Stop Misconduct on Court?

By ROBIN HERMAN

Ilie Nastase is losing a tennis match to Roscoe Tanner. Annoyed at the turn of events and at an official's call against him, Nastase turns his back on the tournament referee, calls him an obscene name, walks off the court and sits in the stands, his feet on the railing, refusing to continue to play. The crowd becomes restless. "Play tennis!" someone yells.

Virginia Wade loses a point. In a fit of rage she screeches, then slams a ball into the fence, just missing a linesman. She shrugs apologetically, but the official remains visibly intimidated for the rest of the match.

Is this tennis? The rules of the game say it is not, yet misbehavior by players of "the gentlemanly sport" seems to be on the rise. Saturation coverage by television networks begging for "colorful" personalities and the advent of World Team Tennis, with its encouragement of showmanship and clowning, have made questionable behavior part of the sport. The war of nerves between players and officials is taken for granted.

Rules governing the behavior of tennis players and fines and punishments for violations are in the books

of all major international and national tennis bodies. Should these sanctions be escalated to bring the game under stricter control?

The Background

"Mercurial" is the kindest of the many words used to describe Nastase, the gifted Rumanian whose oncourt antics have overshadowed his athletic talent. Nastase is the focus of most arguments over the control of tennis behavior because he is the most frequent and flagrant violator of the rules.

Tennis has always had its troublemakers, but television has brought worldwide notoriety to Nastase. Television has also helped to inflate the dollar value of tournaments and has lured sponsors into huge investments. But stalling tactics and defaults, once merely disappointments to the crowds at matches, now mean a prohibitive cost to commercial sponsors and disappointments as well to hundreds of thousands of home viewers.

Fines, disqualifications and suspensions have been the main weapons of behavioral control wielded by those sanctioning the tournaments. Provoked into action largely by Nastase's misbehaviors, the International Professional Tennis Council last December issued a "code of conduct" with fines for violators as high as $10,000.

Violations under the code include physically or verbally abusing umpires, linesmen, opponents or spectators; defaulting or withdrawing from a match without medical authority after a tournament has started; throwing or kicking a racquet or hitting or kicking a ball out of the court in anger, and the use of obscene language.

In the 1975 season alone Nastase lost three matches through disqualification. The Men's Professional Tennis Council fined him $6,000 last September for "conduct detrimental to the game"; in the final of the Canadian open, he had made obscene gestures and comments to the crowd during an indifferent performance.

When Nastase did not pay the fine, the council suspended him from tournaments. One day after the suspension had gone into effect, Nastase begrudgingly paid the fine, saying: "I pay and I can play."

But just 10 days later Nastase was at it again, this time in the $200,000 American Airlines Tennis Games in Palm Springs, Calif. Charles Hare, the referee, defaulted him out of the tournament.

Nastase has not been the only violator of behavioral rules. Harold Solomon questioned a line call and walked out of a semifinal with Adriano Panatta in the 1976 Italian open.

The usually cool Arthur Ashe quit in a rage over Nastase's stalling tactics in the first round of the 1975 Grand Prix Masters last November. Both players were disqualified, but Ashe was later reinstated.
ous."

Misbehavior becomes a problem in the sport, Ashe said, "because tennis has no time limits." Then he stressed: "You can't have anyone at his whim interrupting the rhythm of the game. Play must be continuous."

Are the rules governing behavior strong enough to keep play continuous or are modifications needed?

Proponents

Jack Stahr, coordinator of the United States Tennis Association's new Umpires Council, said:

"Most of the players subject to such fines are so rich it makes no difference to them."

Existing rules for fines and sanctions just don't work, at least not in Nastase's case. After Nastase had learned of his suspension following the Canadian open incident he said:

"How nice. How nice to tell me that. No problem. They cannot suspend me. The world is free. I have to eat. I make my living playing

tennis. If they don't let me play, I play somewhere else."

If a top player is suspended by a national or international organization, he would find it hard to draw an income. The tours operate under sanctions from the governing bodies. He could make money from televised challenge matches and exhibition appearances.

Although codes of behavior and punishments for violations have been outlined in detail by the U.S.T.A. and other organizations, many tennis officials are voluntary workers who, charged with upholding the rules, often lack the experience or fortitude to hold their ground against an enraged world-class player.

"For a long time no referee would stand up to Nastase," said Hare, who will be the referee at the United States Open at Forest Hills next month. "They've been afraid, saying the crowd had to be considered. But what about the other guy in the match?" Before Nastase was disqualified in the match with Tanner, he had beaten Dick Stockton to reach the quarterfinals.

"It's hard to play when a guy is doing the things Nastase does on the court," said Stockton. "He did everything to win the match in an unfair way. He stalled around. He called the umpire and referee every name in the book. He called me names. There's no excuse for it. They let him get away with it."

August 3, 1976

Issue and Debate

Women's Demands for Equality in Money Are Threatening $11 Million Tennis Tour

By NEIL AMDUR

Jimmy Connors collected $30,000 for beating Bjorn Borg in a 3-hour-10-minute men's singles final at the United States Open tennis championships on Sunday.

The preceding day Chris Evert received $30,000 for defeating Evonne Goolagong, 6-3, 6-0, in 52 minutes for the women's title.

Equal pay for equal play has become only one of the issues that threaten to disrupt the $11 million professional tennis tour.

Members of the Women's Tennis Association have voted to boycott next year's Wimbledon championships and hold their own $300,000 tournament in the United States unless they receive parity with the men. The present Wimbledon prize-money ratio favors the men by 80-20.

But the Association of Tennis Professionals, with 203 male players from 40 countries, says future United States Open money breakdowns should reflect where the action is, and the action, it insists, is clearly with the men.

The battle lines are defined, but the question remains: Should women players receive the same prize money as men at major international tournaments?

The Background

Unlike most professional sports, in which separate tours remain in effect for men and women throughout a competitive year, the top men and women tennis players assemble for such world championships as Forest Hills, Wimbledon and the French and Italian opens.

The early years of open tennis provided no equality for women. At the first United States Open in 1968, for example, the men's first prize was $14,000, with $6,000 going to the women's winner.

In 1970, with little hope for improvement of the women's share, two players, Ceci Martinez and Esme Emanuel, surveyed several hundred Open fans on whether spectators would pay to see women play. The favorable results of the survey and the financial support of a company, Philip Morris, whose board chairman, Joseph F. Cullman 3d, was a tennis fan and player, produced the first all-women pro tournaments that year.

The women's push for equality gained its strongest momentum in 1971 with the emergence of 16-year-old Chris Evert at the Open. The following summer the long-awaited first meeting between Miss Evert and Evonne Goolagong in the semifinals at Wimbledon upstaged the men's draw

A men's boycott of Wimbledon in 1973 allowed Mrs. Billie Jean King and Miss Evert to bask in the final-round spotlight. With the financial backing of Ban, a deodorant manufacturer, the women received parity with the men for the first time at the 1973 United States Open.

Few international tournaments, however, offer equal prize money. At Wimbledon this summer Miss Evert received $20,000, compared with $25,000 for Borg, the men's champion. The difference between the men's and women's first prize at the Italian open was $15,000.

The Proponents

"If you look at drawing power, which is what you're considering as a promoter, the women are as big as the men," says Jerry Diamond, executive director of the W.T.A.

Says Mrs. King: "Walking down the street, if you ask Joe Six Pack, he doesn't know any more than the top tour players—men or women."

The W.T.A. also stresses that women's pro tennis has opened the doors to a new group of sports fans—women —who might not otherwise attend matches.

Mrs. King, Miss Evert and other women pros agree that the men may have more depth in a comparison of each tour's top 64 players. "But they've also

had more opportunities," says Mrs. King. "You're not going to see the kind of depth among the women for another five to 10 years. We haven't had the same kind of opportunities or programs."

Says Diamond: "You're not going to make women stars until you treat them as stars." He calls European promoters the worst offenders in short-changing the women.

The W.T.A. cites the record attendance on the Virginia Slims circuit last year and higher national television ratings than comparable men's events as examples of the women's drawing power. It also contends that the fragmentation of the $8 million men's circuit and the inability of the men's council to control its players and promoters, make the men's circuit less attractive than the unified women's.

Mrs. King and others maintain that the equal pay-equal work principle "is bad logic" and should have no bearing on prize money, since promoters have never requested the women to play longer matches. At a recent W.T.A. meeting, the players voted to play three-of-five-set matches, "just like the men," if that policy would equalize the prize money at Wimbledon.

"We're not fighting for more money," said Betty Stove of the Netherlands, the newly elected W.T.A. president. "All we want is equality."

Connors Tops Nastase In 4 Sets for $250,000

The Opponents

"Equality?" said Jimmy Connors at the United States Open. "They ought to play the women's final on opening day. Everybody knows who's going to be in it."

Bob Briner, executive director of the A.T.P., believes that "when the two groups play together, the men bring so much more to a tournament."

"It's a question of market value," says Arthur Ashe, a top-ranking player for the last 10 years. According to him, the market value of the women, beyond Misses Evert and Goolagong, is not as great as the men's.

Although he won the Open mixed doubles title with Mrs. King at Forest Hills, Phil Dent, an Australian, does not believe in equality.

"We spread tournaments all over the country every week and they all draw crowds," he says. "The women only have one tournament a week."

Dent argues that the men's matches at Forest Hills "were the mainstay of the tournament," a statement that drew a concurring nod from Mrs. King during their news conference after the mixed doubles final. Mrs. King, however, blamed the slow playing surface for the lack of excitement in women's matches.

"The equal money does disturb a few of the guys," Dent says. "I'm a man. I'd like to see a more proportionate amount go to the men. We deserve it."

The Outlook

In the aftermath of the Open, the United States Tennis Association will review the equal prize-money situation, Stanley Malless, the president, said yesterday.

"It seems there are only two girls that are outstanding," he said by phone from Indianapolis in what could represent a shift in association policy for future Opens. "It doesn't make much of a show."

Briner believes the market place should decide. "The best way to do that is separate men's and women's events at Wimbledon and Forest Hills," he says. "Let the women play at a separate time from the men, maybe a week later. If the women empiracally produce equal dollars, they deserve it."

Briner and Diamond agree that the men's and women's associations should confer more than they do. "There's a wide area of commonality of interest," Briner says, citing mixed doubles events and consistent administrative and player policies as potential areas of agreement.

Diamond hopes that the women can reach an accommodation with Wimbledon and convince other promoters to upgrade their share of prize money.

"The trouble with the women," says Colin Dibley, an Australian player, "is that their bargaining power decreases every time Evert and Goolagong play in another final."

September 14, 1976

By STEVE CADY
Special to The New York Times

DORADO BEACH, P.R., March 5—For a player whose nickname is Nasty, it was a sweetheart of a battle plan: Let Jimmy Connors destroy himself. Hit him lobs, chops, spins, whatever he's apt to whack into the net or out of bounds with his overstated attack.

For more than two hours today, the plan worked well for Ilie Nastase as he challenged the defender in what CBS Sports and Bill Riordan, the outspoken promoter, called the "heavyweight championship" of tennis. While 2,400 spectators at the Cerromar Beach Hotel and millions of television viewers watched, the tempestuous 30-year-old Rumanian stunned his 24-year-old rival in the first set and looked like a possible winner.

But eventually, the slugger started tagging the boxer. Though it took more time than the allotted three hours of television, Connors retained his title, 4-6, 6-3, 7-5, 6-3. If it had been a prize fight instead of a television-created tennis spectacular, the fans would have been satisfied. The hour-long first set, in which Nastase forced Connors into repeated errors, provided enough suspense to make the three-of-five-set match exciting.

Even before the end of the first set, Connors was grunting like a man trying to carry a piano up a flight of stairs. He was still grunting at the finish. But by then, the piano was at the top of the stairs. The slugger was in complete control. Connors, making the third defense of the title he won in 1975 by beating Rod Laver, had the winner-take-all purse of $250,000 safely stowed away.

His First Match Since Injury

Afterward, his nose and face burned by the sun, he explained how he had been able to beat a player who had defeated him regularly in the past, including four of five times last year.

"Maybe I just waited for this one," said Connors. Then, in a modest appraisal, he said: "I started the day and ended the day the way I wanted to: the best."

This was his first match since he injured his left knee last month in Toronto. There was no evidence of an ailment today. Said Nastase: "We both ran a lot, but maybe I did more running. I was tired by the end of the second set."

Riordan called it a $900,000 package, with television putting up $400,000. Some of that, though, was regained by the commercials, each of which ran 90 seconds instead of the usual 60. Despite suggestions by skeptics that the two friends might have agreed beforehand to split the purse, Nastase insisted the battle was "for real." He called it a "million-dollar title" if he could win it.

Nasty failed, but he had the crowd on his side as he found himself in the good-guy role. Connors, whose previous defenses had been against John Newcombe and Manuel Orantes, found Nastase a "worthy opponent," as the announcer put it. And Riordan and CBS did their best to sustain the "title fight" motif. Nasty even had a fighter's robe with "Nasty, the Greatest" inscribed on it, though he didn't wear it going on the court.

There was also a tale of the tape, similar to prize-fight statistics, but the tropical setting destroyed the image. There was no smoke-filled arena for those two high-living gladiators. A few hundred yards from the court, avalanches of dazzling white surf slid down off green waves that thudded toward the beach at this se-

cluded resort 21 miles west of San Juan.

For sights like that, plus palm trees and tropical flowers and ocean breezes and plenty of service, guests at the Cerromar Beach Motel pay $104 a day, single or double occupancy, and that doesn't include meals.

The tennis match was played on a cement-base court covered by a rubberized surface. Tickets cost $20 to $80.

As far as Riordan was concerned, the match should have been covered by The Wall Street Journal. Past and future business deals were involved, with some pending lawsuits.

"This is just a front for the real money," Riordan said. "The real money is in the litigation."

Riordan, who discovered Connors but eventually split with him, is suing him for a "considerable amount" in a case involving an alleged breach of endorsement contract. And Riordan is being sued by Barry Frank, vice president of CBS Sports, because the promoter allegedly had promised him a piece of the action in the "title fight" series. Riordan has more matches planned.

March 6, 1977

The New York Times/Barton Silverman

Ilie Nastase walking with his wife, Dominique, after losing to Jimmy Connors yesterday at Dorado Beach, Puerto Rico.

195

Ban Is Voted In Davis Cup Withdrawal

LONDON, June 29 (UPI)—The Davis Cup tennis nations voted today to impose automatic one-year suspensions on countries that refused to play matches on political grounds. The proposal was carried by 40 votes to 12.

The new regulation reads, "If, after the draw has been made, any nation withdraws from the competition, that nation shall not be eligible to take part in the competition the following year. In the case of a natural disaster, the committee of management may resolve by a two-thirds majority that no penalty be imposed.

The previous regulations had laid down a maximum fine of $850 for offenders and it was up to the management committee to vote additional penalties, such as the one-year ban on the Soviet Union for withdrawing from last year's match against Chile.

Earlier today, at the annual general meeting, the Davis Cup nations voted against barring South Africa from entering the 1978 competition. The proposal failed to gain the necessary 80 percent majority, 29 nations voting against South Africa's entry and 25 in favor.

Mexico had previously refused to meet South Africa and India had also withdrawn from a match, saying that its leading player was injured. The Soviet Union, Hungary, Rumania and Czechoslovakia have also withdrawn from sporting competitions in which South Africa has taken part.

In other action, the annual meeting:
¶Rejected a proposal by Hungary, India and the Soviet Union that called for the reinstatement of the Russians, who had been suspended from the 1977 competition after failing to play Chile.

¶Decided against bringing back the Challenge round system, which was dropped in 1970-71. Under the old format, the champion nation was exempt from the qualifying rounds.

¶Deferred a decision on a proposal to change the format for the final stages of the competition. Brazil proposed that the final matches be played during a 12-day period in one country among the defending champion, zone winners and the host nation.

David Gray, secretary of the Davis Cup Nations, said the committee was looking for a sponsor for such a 12-day final series, which he believed would attract lucrative television coverage and provide financial benefit for all Davis Cup nations.

June 30, 1977

Virginia Wade Beats Betty Stove in Wimbledon Final, 4-6, 6-3, 6-1

Briton Wins Her First Singles Title in 16 Attempts to Delight of Crowd

By NEIL AMDUR
Special to The New York Times

WIMBLEDON, England, July 1—They waved the Union Jack, cheered wildly and sang "For She's a Jolly Good Fellow." The Duchess of Kent held her arms high in the royal box. And in the middle of the madness, Queen Elizabeth II praised Virginia Wade for winning Wimbledon today and said, "It must be hard work."

It was. Miss Wade had kept her eager subjects waiting and nervous. She lost the first set of the women's singles final to Betty Stove of the Netherlands and lingered close to the brink at 3-all in the second before winning nine of the next 10 games and the match, 4-6, 6-3, 6-1, for her first Wimbledon singles crown.

Could it have gone any other way in a summer when the Silver Jubilee and a tennis centennial have sprung excitement and hope throughout the land? Yet even cynics who have sat through Wimbledon finals for 50 years were unprepared for the unrestrained center-court joy and emotion that followed the victory by the 31-year-old Miss Wade, Britain's tennis heroine for the last decade.

Like a Fairy Tale

"The whole thing was like a fairy-tale situation," Miss Wade said afterward, visibly elated to have erased her self-view as "the best player who had never won Wimbledon," after 15 unsuccessful attempts.

"It was a young-people's affair," Roy McKelvie, a longtime lord of the press box, observed, referring to the spontaneous post-match celebration. "They had something to celebrate and they did it, Wimbledon or no Wimbledon."

If a new era has dawned at the All-England Lawn Tennis Club, and the large crowds of the fortnight would seem to indicate such a trend, Miss Wade's title and the first appearance of the Queen at Wimbledon since 1962 will be remembered long after the tennis world has forgotten the details of the 1-hour-37-minute match.

Nine Double-Faults

The quality of play was patchy on both sides. The 32-year-old Miss Stove, the first Dutch player to reach a Wimbledon final, served nine double-faults and struggled through a break point at 5-4 and 30-40 before winning the first set.

United Press International
Virginia Wade holds aloft women's singles trophy she won at Wimbledon

Miss Wade, seeded third in the 96-player women's singles draw, could hardly have been expected to reach the heights of her semifinal-round upset of Chris Evert, the top-seeded defending champion. The daughter of a former Archdeacon of Durban also was clearly carrying the dreams of British citizens, many of whom had crowned her even before today's match was played.

"Ginny Tonic," read one front-page headline in a Fleet Street tabloid after her victory over Miss Evert. "It's Wade to Win—Stove is Not in Her Class," another headline proclaimed today.

A less-confident player might have caved in under such anticipation. But there is a new Virginia Wade these days, from her stylish, fluffy Vidal Sassoon hairdo, minus pins and ribbons, to a positive mental approach. Once nervous and uncertain, Miss Wade felt that she was the "strongest person in the dressing room" for this Wimbledon fortnight. She dreamed of playing before the Queen, of holding up the gold victory plate and of opening the 1978 tournament on the center court as defending singles champion.

Avoid Hearing the Phone

Years ago, if curious photographers had showed up at her flat at 9 A.M. on the day of a big match, she might have sent them packing. She was shocked to see them today at such an early hour, she said, but let them get on with their business anyway, although she turned up the volume of the Rachmaninoff records on the stereo to avoid hearing the ring of the telephone.

Miss Wade also went to an empty center court hours before the match, to picture herself playing there, a mental tactic she might have ignored in the years when beautiful tennis took priority over what she now describes as the "intellectual experience."

Miss Wade had beaten the seventh-seeded Miss Stove in 17 of their 19 previous meetings. But Miss Stove had eliminated second-seeded Martina Navratilova and fourth-seeded Sue Barker in successive matches and remains a difficult opponent for most players.

Can Be a Great Threat

When she is serving crisply and volleying with authority and finesse, Miss

Stove, at 6 feet 1 inch and 160 pounds, can be very, very good. But when she inexplicably overstrokes volleys and ground strokes, hits routine service returns standing straight up or nervously manages only 52 percent of her first serves, as she did today, she nullifies the physical skills and technical potential that could carry her to loftier heights.

The problem, of course, is that no one knows when or how Miss Stove suddenly will string it together. She wears a rubber pad on her right knee as a precaution against tendonitis, but insists there is nothing wrong with the knee.

Yet at 3-4 and 15-all in the second set, she double-faulted and then lost her service when Miss Wade, by now settled into stride after some sluggish early moments, knocked off consecutive forehand winners on short balls that sat high in the forecourt.

The match drifted out of Miss Stove's reach at 0-2 in the last set. She saved a break point and got the advantage to 1-2. But she lost advantage and the game on a careless volley, Miss Wade's sliced backhand service return winner and a game-ending double-fault.

"I thought Virginia played very well, particularly in the middle of the second set," said Miss Stove, a bright, thoughtful, popular pro, who is president of the Women's Tennis Association. "Virginia had a lot of pressure on her. I thought she handled it well."

Miss Stove collected about $12,000 as the runner-up. Miss Wade, the first British champion since Ann Jones in 1969, earned almost $23,000.

The center-court meeting between the champion and the queen was a memorable moment. They chatted for several minutes, although the cheers of the capacity crowd of 14,000 made it difficult for Miss Wade to hear much of Her Majesty's thoughts other than, "well-played and the tribute to her determination."

"I think she must have loved the atmosphere," said Miss Wade, who will return to World Team Tennis with the New York Apples next week. "Even if our match wasn't like Borg and Gerulaitis. [one of yesterday's men's semifinals], which would have turned anyone on to tennis, I think she must have loved it."

The crowd did. Some paid as much as $75 for an $8.60 center-court seat; others had camped out for days outside the club just for standing room.

"The atmosphere was so wonderful," Miss Wade said, now assured of a permanent spot in the hearts of British fans, regardless of her future. "I'd never seen it before," neither had anyone else.

July 2, 1977

Borg Defeats Connors for Wimbledon Title

By NEIL AMDUR
Special to The New York Times

WIMBLEDON, England, July 2— Wimbledon's first 100 years wound up in a blaze of glory today as Bjorn Borg outlasted Jimmy Connors in five sets for his second consecutive men's singles tennis title.

In what he described as "for sure the happiest win of my career," the normally stolid 21-year-old Borg crowned himself No. 1 "for the moment" on the men's professional tennis tour with an exhausting 3-6, 6-2, 6-1, 5-7, 6-4 victory that took 3 hours 14 minutes under a warm midafternoon sun.

The 10th meeting of the sport's two biggest men stars was a heavyweight title match that went the distance, with both coming off the floor when it seemed they were about to be counted out.

The heavy-hitting Connors, top-seeded in the 128-player draw, had a set and four break points for a 2-1 lead against an admittedly tired opponent, who had whipped Ilie Nastase and Vitas Gerulaitis in strenuous matches en route to the final. Then the second-seeded Borg slowed the pace and counterpunched his way to a 4-0 lead in the fifth set with two break points for 5-0, only to see the 24-year-old Connors amazingly punch back to 4-all.

Cynics will suggest that Borg's triumph was inevitable. In the year of Queen Elizabeth's Silver Jubilee and Wimbledon's centennial celebration, which saw Virginia Wade of Britain win the women's title and produced record crowds and such exciting new faces as Tracy Austin and John McEnroe. Didn't Connors snub the All-England Club's opening-day parade of champions, while Borg paid his dues? Borg won the decision in the last round, not so much because he was stronger physically at the finish, but because of his mental endurance. He played it cool, jabbing for points instead of flailing. The victory was worth $25,500.

When Connors broke the bearded Swede for 4-all in the fifth set with a reflex volley, he was shaking his fists, slapping his sides, exhorting himself to go, go, go. But Connors did not have the benefit of a one-minute court changeover to assess where he was, where he had come from and what he now needed to do, with victory within sight.

"I thought the match might slip away then," Borg said in a rare admission for someone whose inner thoughts often are buried.

United Press International

Bjorn Borg kissing his trophy after beating Connors for Wimbledon title

Connors said: "Maybe I got a little excited and rushed into things instead of being calm and collected."

Connors won the first point of the ninth game with a high backhand volley placement. But just when it seemed that the momentum was with him, he served a double-fault.

"It came out of nowhere," Connors said. No, it came out of being too fired up. So did an instinctively obscene gesture with his finger as some of the center-court crowd applauded the double fault. It was hardly the time for an expression of individuality at the expense of concentration. Connors lost the next 3 points and the game, missing first serves on each point and overhitting two backhands by several feet at 15-30 and 15-40.

"It seems as if when I was down, I played my best tennis," he said.

He had come out swinging, with the same aggressive ground strokes and bullish tactics that had produced a four-set victory over Borg in last year's final at Forest Hills and seven triumphs in their nine previous matches.

"If Connors had kept going on, playing more net, I think he had to win," said Lennart Bergelin, Borg's Swedish coach. "When he stayed on the baseline, to play Borg that way, it was a mistake."

Connors and Borg have different personalities—Jimmy is aggressive, brazen, brash; Bjorn is quiet, sensitive, stoical—but they share an indomitable will.

Borg double-faulted on game point and dropped service at love at 3-4 in the opening set. He was reeling at 1-1, 15-40 in the second, still seemingly stiff and uncomfortable from the tough five-set semifinal against Gerulaitis on Thursday. But he saved one break point by forcing Connors to chase a low forehand passing shot, which he netted, then firing an ace for deuce.

The game went to deuce four more times, with Connors twice more primed for the break ("If he broke my serve then, I think I would have lost the second set." Borg acknowledged.) But Connors stroked a backhand volley long, and Borg held serve with another ace.

Borg has been exceedingly popular here since first captivating the teen-age set by reaching the quarter finals in 1973 as a 17-year-old too young to shave. He still does not shave for Wimbledon, but the motives now are different; he won last year with a beard and had a three-week mustache and beard this time, saying, "This is lucky," as he playfully stroked his chin during the news conference.

The difference between Borg and Connors also involves maturity.

In their previous matches, Connors had seemed to intimidate Borg with his power and presence. But as Borg improved his serve and dissected the Connors left-handed style, he closed the gap and has now won their last two matches.

"Before it was mentally tough to play against Jimmy," Bjorn said. "Always he hits the ball hard, with such depth. Now I know I can come back, I have the confidence I can win."

That confidence was reflected when Borg began his slowdown in the middle of the second set. Instead of driving every ball with the same pace, he looped two-handed backhands higher and shorter and teased Connors with forehand cross-court shots that landed around the service line.

Connors thrives on pace, which he showed by winning here in 1974 and by blitzing Stan Smith in the fifth set of their match earlier in the tournament. If he is at all vulnerable, it shows in the form of impatience on the short ball, a blind spot that Arthur Ashe first exploited successfully in their 1975 Wimbledon final.

But few players can match Connors for fight. Nowhere was this relentless spirit more evident than when he held serve from 0-4, 30-40 in the fifth set, driving to the net and whacking winners with an intensity that belied the state of the match. He broke Borg in consecutive service games to reach 4-all, opening each game with running forehand passing shots down the line that seemed to demoralize the Swede.

"Are you disappointed?" he was asked. "I'm pretty satisfied with my career after five years," he replied.

Borg has earned a special spot, the first player to have won singles titles in successive years at Paris and Wimbledon since World War II.

"I'm a little happier this year," he said, when asked to compare today's triumph with his straight-set victory over Ilie Nastase in last year's final. "I play Jimmy in the final, and I want to beat him badly."

Borg has been pictured as icy and unemotional. But on the final point, he unwrapped his feelings, throwing his head back in relieved exasperation. He looked toward his fiancee, Mariana Simionescu, dropped his racquet, looked again, then smiled and put his hand on his head. It was over, indeed.

Lea Antonoplis of Glendora, Calif., beat Maureen Louis of San Francisco, 7-5, 6-1, to capture the junior girls' title. Van Winitsky of North Miami Beach downed Eliot Teltscher of Palos Verdes Calif., 6-1, 1-6, 8-6 for the boys' title.

The senior doubles crown went to Glen Davidson and Torben Ulrich, who defeated Rex Hartwig and Vic Seixas, 8-6, 6-4.

July 3, 1977

Golden King of the Courts

Bjorn Borg

By NEIL AMDUR
Special to The New York Times

WIMBLEDON, England, July 3 — There was no way Bjorn Borg could win Wimbledon this year, the insiders said. He was too involved with team tennis, his fiancée and his countless commercial endorsements to get match-tough on grass courts in time. The centennial Wimbledon fortnight ended yesterday at the All England Lawn Tennis Club. When the Duke of Kent presented the gold trophy to the men's singles champion, the recipient for the second consecutive year was not Jimmy Connors, Ilie Nastase or any of the so-called big guns on grass, but Bjorn Borg.

Man in the News

Borg won it the hard way, rallying from two sets down and 4-all in the third against Mark Edmondson of Australia in a difficult second-round match. Then he beat three formidable opponents in succession for the title —Nastase, Vitas Gerulaitis and the top-seeded Connors, acknowledging after the 3-hour, five-set final with Connors, "I have never been so tired on the tennis court before."

Few players could have handled the physical and mental strain of such a draw. But then the 5-foot-10-inch, 150-pound Borg has been a source of amazement to the tennis world ever since he arrived from Sweden with his long, angelic blond hair, soft blue eyes and seemingly detached demeanor and fluttered the hearts of British schoolgirls as a 17-year-old quarterfinalist in the 1973 Wimbledon.

Sweden's Favorite Son

At a time when most tennis players are trying to determine if they have the will power and talent to succeed as professionals, the 21-year-old Borg has won twice at Wimbledon, twice in the French open (1974 and 1975), the Italian (1974), three United States Pro titles (1974-75-76) and the World Championship of Tennis (1976). He helped lead Sweden, a country with only modest tennis success in the past, to its first Davis Cup crown in 1975, an achievement that catapulted Borg past Ingemar Johansson, the heavyweight boxer, as Sweden's favorite son.

Borg's tour earnings in 1976 totaled $424,420. He probably doubled that in commercial endorsements ranging from racquets and clothes to headbands and shoes.

Borg was born on a Swedish national holiday, June 6, 1956. His parents, Rune and Margaretha Borg, operated a small food store in the town of Sodertlage, near Stockholm. Until the age of 8, Bjorn's early sporting interest was hockey, the national sport. Then, his father brought home a tennis racquet one day as a first prize from a table tennis tournament.

During the next few years, Borg created his own Sweden vs. United States Davis Cup matches, hitting ball against the garage door, hour after hour, until his mother would beg him to stop.

"If I hit the ball five times against the door, I got the point," he once recalled. "If less than five, the United States got the point."

Borg settled on tennis over hockey at 13. At 14, he swept Sweden's junior titles. At 15, he made his debut for Sweden against New Zealand in the Davis Cup and then took the Swedish men's championship.

Part of Borg's strength is his natural athletic ability. He is more athlete than classical tennis player, and his two-handed backhand and topspin forehand are unorthodox strokes seldom taught in traditional tennis lessons.

Borg's movements on the court, particularly his rocking gait, have been emulated by hundreds of young players. His short, quick steps often give the impression that he is a squirrel racing to a hideout to store nuts for the winter. The geometry of his strokes is amazing, particularly his flicking, reflex returns on shots that few other players have the quickness and instinct to reach.

Borg seldom beats himself in a match, but he is sensitive to those who suggest that his behavior is mechanical.

And anyone who sat at center court for the Wimbledon final or watched on television could sense the emotional satisfaction in Borg after the final point of the match against Connors. In a moment of jubilation, Borg's arms were outstretched, his head looking upward.

Until he met Mariana Simionescu, an attractive Rumanian tennis player, Borg had few outside interests other than music and comic books. They became engaged on Nov. 4, 1976, and their desire to be together as much as possible was the reason why they signed with the Cleveland Nets of World Team Tennis.

Borg has had to change his residence and lifestyle because of his popularity and financial status. He now lives in Monte Carlo, where his parents operate a tennis boutique, and where the tax bite is considerably less than in Sweden.

With his victory over Connors, Borg considers himself "No. 1 for the moment." Their diverse personalities and interesting rivalry have heightened spectator interest in tennis, although Borg insists, "I don't think Jimmy and I can dominate the game.

"The competition is so hot, and there are many good players about. I think we are, just at the moment, more consistent than the other players."

July 4, 1977

Renee Richards Ruled Eligible for U.S. Open

By NEIL AMDUR

Dr. Renee Richards has won the right to qualify for the United States Open tennis championships without passing a sex chromosome test.

State Supreme Court Justice Alfred M. Ascione issued a preliminary injunction yesterday barring the United States Tennis Association, the United States Open Tennis Championship Committee and the Women's Tennis Association from excluding the 42-year-old transsexual from the world's richest tournament because of her inability to pass the Barr body test.

In a 13-page decision that could become a landmark, Ascione said the requirement that Dr. Richards pass the test in order to become eligible for the United States Open was "grossly unfair, discriminatory and inequitable, and violative of her rights under the Human Rights Law of this state."

Ascione also criticized the defendants for adopting the sex test for women players last year after Dr. Richards had filed an entry for the United States Open.

"It seems clear that defendants knowingly instituted this test for the sole purpose of preventing plaintiff from participating in the tournament," he wrote. "The only justification for using a sex-determination test in athletic competition is to prevent fraud, i.e., men masquerading as women competing against women."

Lawyers for the U.S.T.A. and the W.T.A. said they would review the decision before deciding whether to file an appeal. The women's qualifying event for the United States Open will begin Aug. 25.

Sources close to the U.S.T.A. believe the association may not contest Dr. Richards's right to play this year and then appeal yesterday's court decision at a later date. The U.S.T.A. concern, according to sources, is more over the long-range implications of transsexuals in women's tennis than the threat of a player who is probably past her prime as a professional.

The ruling capped a year-long struggle for acceptance by Dr. Richards, a New York ophthalmologist who, as Richard Raskind, underwent a sex-change operation in 1975. Ascione made reference to this in a section of his decision, which was unusually long for a preliminary injunction.

"When an individual such as plaintiff, a successful physician, a husband and father, finds it necessary for his own mental sanity to undergo a sex reassignment," Ascione wrote, "the unfounded fears and misconceptions of defendants must give way to the overwhelming medical evidence that this person is now female."

"I feel ecstatic, I can't believe it," Dr. Richards said when informed of the ruling. "It's really a vindication of everything I've tried to prove in the last year. Whether I win the tournament doesn't mean anything in the long run."

W.T.T. Lawyers Interested

Dr. Richards said she was prepared to play in the qualifying next week, although she felt her record in nine tournaments over the last year was good enough to gain direct admittance to the 96-player championship draw. The United States Open, with $462,000 in prize money, begins on Aug. 31 at the West Side Tennis Club in Forest Hills, Queens.

"I had faith in our cause, faith in Renee and, most of all, faith in our system of justice," said Michael Rosen, the attorney for Dr. Richards.

Rosen said he was prepared for an appeal.

"If they want to be archaic and litigate it further, they can," he added. "They acted as true professionals throughout. They were decent and honorable. But somebody's got to win and somebody's got to lose, just like on a tennis court."

The effect of Ascione's ruling may be felt before the United States Open. Lawyers for World Team Tennis ordered copies of the decision to determine if Dr. Richards would be eligible to play for the Cleveland Nets tomorrow night in a playoff match against the Boston Lobsters.

Joe Zingale, owner of the Nets, said Dr. Richards had signed a contract with Cleveland on June 2d and the contract had been approved by Butch Buchholz, the W.T.T. commissioner.

"Now that Renee is eligible, we want her to play," Zingale said, realizing that a match between Dr. Richards and Martina Navratilova, Boston's top women's player, would be a box-office attraction.

Dr. Richards, however, was uncertain over whether she would accept the team tennis assignment on such short notice, saying, "all my training has been geared toward Forest Hills."

Lawyers involved with international sports also began studying the decision for its potential impact on the 1980 Winter Olympics, which will be held at Lake Placid, N.Y. The Barr body test has been a medical requirement for all female olympic athletes since the 1968 Games.

Barr Test Not Voided

"This court is not striking down the Barr body test, as it appears to be a recognized and acceptable tool for determining sex," Ascione wrote, referring to the test that Dr. Richards failed on two occasions earlier this year in an attempt to play in the Italian and French championships. "However, it is not and should not be the sole criterion where, as here, the circumstances warrant consideration of other factors."

Ascione's ruling nullified the contention of the tennis establishment that Dr. Richards, as a former male, enjoyed an unfair physical advantage over other women players.

"Most of the medical testimony indicates she is a woman, not in the sense that she gives birth, but socially and physically," Ascione said. "She can't test out as a woman in all aspects, but she is a woman."

Later, during an interview, Ascione conceded that there were "a lot of ramifications" to the decision, particularly in areas of criminal law and the long-range question of whether younger males might undergo operations to become eligible for women's professional sports.

"This was no open-and-shut case," the judge said. "The transsexuals are going to lose, I guess. According to the psychiatrists, they want to be recognized. This is another step that recognizes them."

Ascione said he had confined the decision to "Dr. Richards today. Tomorrow, somebody else, and the decision may be entirely different."

"I don't see a sudden rash of transsexuals applying for Wimbledon, Forest Hills or college baseball teams," said Dr. Richards, who won two of the nine tournaments she entered but had not faced any of the big names on the women's tours. "It does have major significance in pointing out that persons oppressed, regardless of where they come from, have recourse in the law and in the courts."

August 17, 1977

Tracy Austin Triumphs
Special to The New York Times

PHILADELPHIA, Aug. 16 — Tracy Austin of Rolling Hills, Calif.,defeated Kathy Jordan, King of Prussia, Pa., 6-2, 6-2, today and won the United States Tennis Association girls' 18-and-under national championship on the grass courts of the Philadelphia Cricket Club.

Miss Austin, the third-seeded player here who had been beaten in the third round at Wimbledon by Chris Evert, equaled the 1957 feat of another Californian, Karen Hantze, by winning the title at age 14. Miss Hantze also was victorious in 1959 and 1960.

Miss Austin is eligible to play in this event for four more years. No one, including such stars as Helen Wills Moody, Helen Jacobs, Sarah Palfrey, Maureen Connolly and Chris Evert, has ever won the girls'-18 title four times.

A near-capacity crowd saw Miss Austin end the 38-minute final with a cross-court forehand return of service that passed Miss Jordan, the 14th-seeded player, as she charged the net.After having established a 3-2 lead in the first set, Miss Austin allowed her opponent, a strong volleyer, only 11 points, seven of them during the second set.

Miss Austin's sharp, short stroke resulted in only 13 errors in the match, as she netted the ball only four times, hit it out of the court seven times and served two double-faults.

Her returns of service from her forehand and two-handed backhand were very effective as they either produced outright winners or forced Miss Jordan to reply ineffectively with shots to Miss Austin's feet as she attacked the net. Nothing seemed to elude Miss Austin's racquet as she ran up 24 placements with passing shots, drives across the court or sharply-angled volleys.

Miss Jordan, the 17-year-old Middle States girls' grass-court champion who will attend Stanford University in the fall, made 14 placements and 32 errors.

Miss Jordan and Lea Antonoplis, the Wimbledon junior champion from Glendora, Calif., won the doubles title by 6-0, 6-1 over Trey Lewis of San Pedro, Calif., and Ann Henrickson of Mahtomedi, Minn. Mareen Louie of San Francisco defeated Miss Lewis, 7-5, 6-3, in the third-place singles consolation.

August 17, 1977

Has TV Killed the Goose That Laid the Golden Tennis Ball?

By LEONARD PROBST

Starting at noon today, CBS television will carry seven straight hours of the tennis finals from the U.S. Open at Forest Hills, thereby topping the "unprecedented" six-and-a-half-hour NBC broadcast last July 2 when covering the finals at Wimbledon. That appears to be the networks' counter to falling ratings for televised tennis: stretching out the coverage of major matches. But the question arises: Has television killed the goose that laid the optic-yellow ball?

There is disagreement on the subject, but in a series of interviews with television sports vice presidents, producers, programmers and program analysts, as well as with players and organizers of the sport, one thing comes through: The love affair between tennis and television has peaked, and it happened sooner than expected.

At times it seemed as though the networks had rounded up the top six players, flown them to a camera-infested island, taped their playing for a week and then doled out the same endless series of sets weekend after weekend. Carl Lindemann, vice president of NBC Sports from 1964 to 1977 and now consultant to the New York Olympics Committee, says, "Tennis died on television. It was not clear which tournaments were important. You would see the same half-dozen players live and on tape. It was apparent two years ago tennis was overexposed."

Billie Jean King, who understands the game as a fierce competitor as well as a business woman, claims she saw the decline of the game on television coming years ago. "I knew tennis was not going to make it on TV," she recently said. "That's because everybody was greedy. We had canned tennis, which meant you were watching a six-month-old match. Next year very little tennis is going to be on TV and rightly so. We deserve it, because we didn't do it properly."

The confusing canned tennis Miss King referred to usually turned up on Sunday afternoons. For instance, home viewers on Sunday, May 16, 1976, could have seen Bjorn Borg hitting his topspin forehand in mixed doubles with Virginia Wade against Rod Laver and Evonne

Leonard Probst, NBC News drama critic for the past 15 years and author of "Off Camera," is a veteran observer of tennis court theatrics.

Goolagong on ABC's "World Invitational Tennis Classic" from 2:30 to 4 P.M., as well as in a singles match against Guillermo Vilas, from 1:30 to 4:10 P.M. on NBC. NBC's coverage was live from Hawaii; ABC's had been taped months earlier at Hilton Head, S.C., and was one of 11 Sunday matches to come out of that taping session.

And earlier, on Sunday, May 4, 1975, viewers might have thought they were suffering from double vision when watching Billie Jean King, live on CBS, playing against Margaret Court in Scottsdale, Ariz., while she was simultaneously appearing in a doubles match taped by ABC earlier at Hilton Head.

On six Sundays in 1975 alone, NBC was carrying live tennis from cities in Europe and the United States while the other networks were telecasting taped matches—often with the same players.

•

Switching networks and finding tennis on all of them, but not knowing which is live and which is on tape, as well as not knowing whether any or all of the matches are important or where the players really are, and then not being able to find press accounts the following day of what was seen on television, has left many viewers highly confused.

The confusion takes many forms. For instance, on Saturday, July 3, 1975, NBC showed Chris Evert defeating Evonne Goolagong in a Wimbledon match taped earlier that week; the following day ABC showed these same two players in a match taped several months earlier at Hilton Head.

Evonne Goolagong was playing graceful, rhythmic tennis last May 1 against England's Sue Barker and again on May 24 in mixed doubles, both times on ABC taped matches. Actually, she was otherwise engaged, giving birth to a daughter, Kelly Inalla Cawley, in Beaufort, S.C., May 12, 1977.

•

Nielsen ratings for network tennis in 1976 averaged 4.4, a drop from an even 5 the previous year. Each rating point represents 700,000 homes. In 1976, tennis accounted for 10 percent of network sports shows, a drop from 13 percent the previous year.

The answer to that, says Lindemann, is clear: "The numbers, the ratings, weren't there except for the major tournaments. When you've got important events like the Rose Bowl or the Kentucky Derby, you seemingly can't get too much of it, but there are limits."

On television, "big events" cost big money to cover. By scheduling more hours of the same event, the networks stand a chance of recouping their costs, which, for example, in the case of the U.S. Open has gone up sevenfold. Last year, CBS paid $300,000 for the television rights to the U.S. Open. This year, the head of the United States Tennis Association, W.E. "Slew" Hester, says his organization is receiving "in excess of $2 million." CBS executives confirm that figure.

NBC Sports producer Richard Auerbach believes that the future of tennis on television lies in spectaculars. He says, "Last year we carried a dozen tennis tournaments. This year we plan to carry only two: Wimbledon and one other." Auerbach produced the Wimbledon coverage, which this year hit a record audience high, 6.1 on a Saturday with an estimated 4,340,000 homes tuned in.

Why is NBC cutting back on tennis? Auerbach replies, "We stuck with it for six years and poured everything in it we could, and the ratings have been steadily declining. Tennis is no longer believable on TV."

"We definitely are going to be more selective as to the amount of tennis we carry in the future," says George Page, WNET's director of program development and programming. "There have been times when we have run tennis and gotten BMS—basic minimum ratings, so low the audience could not be measured." What happened to the tennis boom? "We all just rushed in with so much coverage that it is a case of overkill."

•

Only at CBS will there be more hours of tennis, principally the result of that network's doubling its coverage of the U.S. Open. Last year, CBS devoted 14 hours to the tournament; this year 29.

Barry Frank, CBS vice president for sports, recently admitted that he did cut back on a couple of tennis telecasts scheduled for earlier this year. He added, however, that "there will be more tennis on CBS than there has been in the last couple of years, but not more than when we had the CBS Tennis Classic." He says the network dropped taped tennis shows such as the "Classic," which had a four-year run ending in 1975, because "they don't work out so well—they get no press, promotion or publicity, while a tournament like the

U.S. Open has on-going publicity."

Has scandal affected audience ratings? No one knows for sure. As to the recent embarrassment surrounding the CBS "Winner-Take-All" matches, for which the network later admitted the loser had been paid substantial sums of money, Mr. Frank said that was "sloppiness" which would not happen again.

He added, facetiously, "We are going to come to the time when there are going to be more disclaimers [on the broadcasts] than competition."

By using the language of boxing and by treating tennis as though it were a contest between opponents in the ring, CBS sought to increase the TV audience with the "Winner-Take-All" illusion in its "Heavyweight Championship of Tennis" title matches. There have been four, each won by Jimmy Connors. None was of any significance in the official standings of the players involved; they were events produced solely for television.

'At times it seemed as though the networks had rounded up the top six players, flown them to a camera-infested island, taped their playing for a week and then doled out the same sets weekend after weekend.'

At ABC, tennis has been regarded "as a sport of the élite," according to James Spence, vice president in charge of sports program planning. "We did not think the tennis boom on television was as big as NBC and CBS did." He said ABC would maintain about the same 24 hours of tennis broadcasts this year as last and would continue its taped series. Asked if taped tennis was "dishonest" to the viewer, he replied, "A taped show is what it is, and we say it was pre-recorded. It is not dishonest—though it can be confusing."

Three years ago on these pages I wrote about television's infatuation with tennis. At the time, it was a love match —with the rules of the game being altered to make it more colorful on color TV. The optic-yellow ball was introduced, as were optic-blue court surfaces, and fines were beginning to be levied against players who failed to wear contrasting colored shirts. Now, as one student of the game who has closely watched television's effect on tennis puts it, "A game I love has been corrupted. The players have advertisements every place but the soles of their feet. It has become a business, a relentless business."

The football Joe Namath is tossing, the basketball Walt Frazer is dribbling and Bobby Orr's hockey stick are not the

stuff of commercials. But in tennis, the products advertised tend to be the balls, racquets and shoes the players can be seen with in play.

The future? John Newcombe, the Australian ace player, an NBC sports commentator and the president of the Association of Tennis Professionals, says, "I don't believe that tennis on television has peaked. Television jumped on the bandwagon and did a good butcher job by putting on too many taped shows, which only confused the public. I don't think the sport has been overexposed; it has been exposed in the wrong way. It is a

case of too much going on in too many events."

Newcombe strongly believes it is up to tennis to get its house in order. "Next year," he says, "the whole circuit is being organized so that tennis will come up with something the public can identify and comprehend. If tennis can show it is forming itself better and the top players are playing together in tournaments and the whole sport is better organized, the networks will start coming back."

We shall see.

September 11, 1977

Tracy Austin, a competitor in this year's U.S. Open.

Vilas Captures Open Title
From Connors, 2-6, 6-3, 7-6, 6-0

by NEIL AMDUR

It was a farewell to remember at Forest Hills yesterday, as Guillermo Vilas beat Jimmy Connors in four thrilling sets for the men's single title at the United States Open tennis championships.

The scores were 2–6, 6–3, 7©, 6__, and the 3-hour–16–minute match can stand by itself alongside the other treasures that graced the center court at the West Side Tennis Club.

In taking the $33,000 first prize, from a total purse of $462,420, the 25-year-old Vilas extended his amazing summer winning streaks to 39 matches and 46 on clay or Har-Tru surfaces. He also appeared to assure being named the world's No. 1 player for the year on the men's pro tour.

A More Disciplined Vilas

Vilas did so the hard way, dethroning a determined defending champion who felt that he owned a piece of the concrete horseshoe, and continually coming back just when it seemed as if he might be counted out.

But then this was a tougher, more disciplined player than the cerebral artist who was knocked out in straight sets by Connors in the semifinals here last year.

"His biggest improvement was his mental attitude," said Ion Tiriac, the intense Rumanian, who sat at courtside in a black leather jacket and counseled his charge during the match. "He can concentrate. He believes in himself. He didn't choke."

Vilas lost the first set and was a point from 1-5 in the third and down 2 set points serving at 4-5, 15-40. Not until he nailed the 25-year-old Connors with some winning shots in a third-set tiebreaker, taking the 12-point playoff,

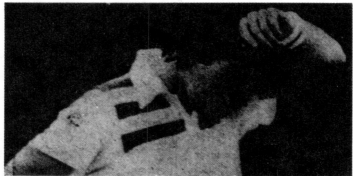

The New York Times/Barton Silverman

Jimmy Connors pausing to wipe his brow in match against Guillermo Vilas

7-4, did the Argentine left-hander finally seem in command.

The match had all the dramatic ingredients of a heavyweight title fight, even a bomb scare earlier in the day and a protest demonstration against South Africa outside the gates of the club. And there was the rivalry of the two "cornermen," Tiriac and Pancho Segura, who were seated in different corners at the north end of the court.

The final mob scene at center court, with Vilas riding on the shoulders of joyous supporters, followed a confusing last point. And then there was Connors, brushing through the madness and ducking a last news conference, but not before he made a vulgar reference to the crowd and added, "I'm going

to live in Monaco."

Connors, who finished as runner-up to Bjorn Borg at Wimbledon earlier this summer, rushed through the first set in 38 minutes by dominating the rallies and moving Vilas from corner to corner with strong, deep ground strokes. And now the crowd of 12,644 began to sense a repetition of last year's straight-set rout.

The Champion Struts

Connors acted the part of the champion who thought he could put away the challenger at any moment. Beating Vilas to the punch with put-away volleys, Connors cockily stood at the net and stared almost condescendingly at his rival. The psych was on.

But, while Connors strutted, Vilas turned his back and began his own

handiwork. He changed the pace on his backhands, mixing slices with top-spin drives; went from a spin first serve to a hard, flat first delivery, and began attacking the net.

All were elements that Tiriac had stressed in attempting to turn Vilas from a clay-court player into a complete professional.

Vilas began to make his points in the second set, as Connors powered forehands into the net with increasing regularity and Vilas forgot about the swirling wind that had carried his top-spin balls into the seats earlier in the match.

The third set was reminiscent, especially for its drama, of last year's Connors-Borg final, except that Connors lost the tiebreaker instead of winning it.

Vilas saved his greatest heroics for the 10th game, saving 2 set points from 15-40. An ace and a backhand down the line that Connors misvolleyed brought the game to deuce. Connors then overhit two forehands.

Vilas never trailed in the tiebreaker, as Connors netted a forehand on the first point, one of 64 unforced errors by Connors off the forehand. Although he is a great player, Connors remains vulnerable on short forehand approach shots, primarily because of his desire to chase the knockout punch regardless of the circumstances.

Connors was never in the fourth set, frustrated by his forehand errors and Vilas's passing shots, which came from all angles and delighted the crowd.

"The only time I was nervous was when I led 5-love in the last set, and 40-love," Vilas said. "Until then I had not thought about the tournament.

Then I started thinking about my match with Orantes a few years ago, where I had match point and lost after a 5-love lead. It made me nervous, and I had to jump around."

The final point will be discussed long after the tournament has taken up residence at Flushing Meadow Park next year.

Connors drove a forehand down the line, the side linesman appeared to hesitate on the call, and Connors turned and walked toward the baseline, thinking the shot had been good.

But Tiriac, seated on the same side as the linesman, suddenly stood up and protested, and the linesman then signaled the shot wide. Before the umpire could announce "game, set, match," and with Connors's back still turned, fans poured onto the court.

Asked afterward to cite the single most important element in the match, Vilas replied, "Tiriac." Perhaps more than anything else, the presence of the redoubtable Tiriac at courtside is the psychological stimulus that has brought Vilas seven straight tournament titles and his new status as a champion. Tiriac, a fierce competitor, has become the alter ego.

"I wanted to be No. 1 in the world," Vilas said. He is, and enjoying it.

"I'm very happy with myself," he teased. "I'm a very good friend of mine."

Even before Connors and Vilas took the court for their match, there was activity inside and outside the stadium.

The top-seeded women's doubles team of Betty Stove and Martina Navratilova, beaten in the final at Wimbledon, won the $13,125 top prize yesterday with a 6-1, 7-6 victory over Dr. Renee Richards and Bettyann Stuart.

Miss Stove then returned with Frew McMillan, and they took the mixed doubles crown (worth $6,500), 6-2, 3-6, 6-3, from Vitas Gerulaitis and Billie Jean King.

The mixed doubles produced some of the tournament's most interesting matches. Both semifinals had been decided in three sets, and the lively exchanges at the net seemed more entertaining for spectators than some of the dull, baseline rallies during singles matches.

The second bomb scare of the tournament proved harmless, as was the first, after members of the police bomb squad had been called because of what was described as a "suspicious-looking package" in the women's locker room.

The package turned out to hold packets of mail. A telephoned bomb threat on opening day had proved a hoax.

Further, security personnel received a report yesterday of a man carrying a gun in the marquee. But a search failed to turn up any gun.

Outside the entrance to the club, about 200 demonstrators passed out leaflets and protested the presence of South African players in the tournament and the "relationships" between the United States Tennis Association and South Africa.

The protest had been organized by the American Coordinating Committee for Equality in Sport and Society, a coalition of national civil rights, religious, political and sports organizations.

The demonstrators chanted: "Sports yes; apartheid, no; tennis with South Africa's got to go!" They waved signs and heard several speakers, including Arthur Ashe, the black tennis professional, condemn South Africa's apartheid policy.

"I just wish there were 10,000 people out here," Ashe told the group, whose chants could barely be heard inside the concrete horseshoe.

Before addressing the protesters, Ashe had held an impromptu news session. South Africa should withdraw or be thrown out of the Davis Cup, because its presence "has reduced the competition by one-half and has done more harm than good," said Ashe, the first champion of the United States Open. "They've made the competition ridiculous."

September 12, 1977

South Africa Barred From 2 Tennis Cups

MONTE CARLO, April 16 (AP)—The committee of management of the International Tennis Federation expelled South Africa from the Davis Cup and Federation Cup competition today.

The three tennis bodies of South Africa—one white, one black, and one multiracial—were given until next Feb. 1 to form a new nonracial organization for administering the game.

David Gray, secretary of the I.T.F., said, "If they have not reached agreement by that time we will send a committee of inquiry to look into the reasons why."

The predominantly white South African Tennis Union, which is recognized by the I.T.F., will continue to be recognized until the new body is formed.

That means South African players may continue to compete as individuals on the tournament circuit.

But South Africa will be barred from next year's Davis Cup competition and next year's competition, and the 1978 women's Federation Cup, which is scheduled for Australia in December.

Philippe Chatrier, president of the I.T.F., headed a four-man inquiry commission on a visit to South Africa early this year. The committee of management spent five hours today considering the commission's report.

"We feel this will be a test of everyone's sincerity," Gray said. "We are asking the whites to sacrifice a year of Davis Cup play, and we are asking the nonwhites to give up an important card in their bid to control the game in South Africa."

Protests over South Africa's racial policies have played havoc with the Davis Cup for years. Certain countries consistently have refused to play against South Africa.

In 1974, South Africa won the trophy for the first time. But it had two walkovers—first because Argentina boycotted a match and then in the final when India refused to play.

South Africa was expelled from the Olympic Games in 1970, and of the 26 international federations that control Olympic sports, only 10 still recognize South Africa.

April 17, 1978

CBS: No Tennis Deceit

By NEIL AMDUR
Special to The New York Times

WASHINGTON, Nov. 3—Officials of CBS Sports acknowledged today "sloppy" performance in the publicity and advertising of the "Heavyweight Championship of Tennis" series, but denied any attempt to deceive the public during telecasts of the controversial "winner-take-all" matches.

Robert Wussler, president of CBS Sports, told members of the House Communications subcommittee that the network was not proud of its record in the series and had recognized its "wrongdoing" in promoting the matches as "winner-take-all" when players had received specific guarantees whether they won or lost.

Jimmy Connors, who was involved in all four matches, was guaranteed $500,000 and Ilie Nastase received $150,000 in the most recent match last March in Puerto Rico. Rod Laver, John Newcombe and Manuel Orantes also played in the series, which began in 1975.

"We never attempted to deceive the public," Wussler said, repeating these words on several occasions under intense questioning by committee members and Harry M. (Chip) Shooshan 3d, the chief counsel.

A staff report to the 14 committee members, six of whom attended today's hearing, had suggested that "in view of the facts which were in the possession of responsible CBS officials and the failure of those officials to take timely action to disclose those facts, CBS had sought to mislead the public."

In his introductory remarks, Shooshan stressed that the integrity of the matches were not in question, but rather "the way in which the matches were promoted."

"This incident more than anything else has provoked these hearings," Representative W. Henson Moore, Republican of Louisiana, said referring to the subcommittee's two-day probe into the relationship between television and sports pursuant to revisions in the Communications Act of 1934.

The CBS behavior throughout the series, and its belated on-the-air disclaimer last May that the matches were not winner-take-all, "almost amounts to fraud," Moore said.

Wussler Takes Blame

Representative Louis Frey Jr., Republican of Florida, termed the failure of network executives to sense what was happening around them, "an infectious virus."

Wussler, who recently returned to sports after serving as president of the network, said he took the "ultimate responsibility" for what he termed "errors of omission." But he insisted that "sloppiness should not be confused with an effort to deceive the public," and said the network had expanded its manpower in sports and instituted strict new corporate procedures to avoid such problems in the future.

All contracts for shows will be screened in advance by executive producers, with producers, directors and announcers being informed about specific clauses related to the promotion and production of the event, Wussler said.

These assurances seemed to satisfy most members of the subcommittee, who saw the CBS action as a result of Congressional concern and its four-month inquiry into events surrounding the matches. But the network still may be cited by the Federal Communications Commission for several violations of the Communications Act.

November 4, 1977

Miss Navratilova Rallies to Take Wimbledon Crown

Chris Evert Loses Final By 2-6, 6-4, 7-5

By NEIL AMDUR
Special to The New York Times

WIMBLEDON, England, July 7 — Martina Navratilova, who left her parents and homeland three years ago in pursuit of freedom, won the women's singles title at Wimbledon today in a courageous three-set comeback victory over Chris Evert.

In a match filled with the same drama that accompanied Virginia Wade's triumph during last year's centennial championships, the 21-year-old Miss Navratilova rebounded from the loss of the first set and deficits of 2-4 and 4-5 in the third for a 2-6, 6-4, 7-5 victory.

As a final backhand volley landed for a winner on the soft grass court of the stately All England Lawn Tennis Club, Miss Navratilova could hardly believe that she had won the crown she said she had thought about since she was a schoolgirl in Czechoslovakia. She raised her arms triumphantly, put her hands to her face and shook her head in disbelief as tears welled in her eyes.

Miss Navratilova's defection to the United States during the United States Open championships three years ago created an international stir. She has not seen her mother, father or sister since but said she repeatedly thought of them during today's 1-hour-43-minute match, and was saddened not to be able to share the joy with them.

Trip to Top Often Lonely

In some respects, today's match typified the highs and lows that have followed Miss Navratilova on her financially rewarding, but often lonely and sometimes frustrating trip to the top. Strong in spirit, Miss Navratilova always believed in herself, as she did during today's final. But until she pulled her imposing physical tools and sensitive psyche together early in the second set, after embarrassingly swinging and missing at an overhead in the second game, it appeared that the top-seeded Miss Evert might repeat her singles titles of 1974 and 1976.

The missed overhead, or "whiff ball," as Miss Navratilova later described it, seemed to wake her up, even though she lost serve from deuce. After managing less than 50 percent on her first serves in the opening set, an important element in her attacking left-handed game, she improved to 64 percent over the last two sets. Miss Navratilova also began paying more attention to the ball instead of allowing emotion to slip-slide her shots off the court.

It was as if someone had put a magic wand in her hand, Miss Navratilova recalled later.

This fact was not lost on Miss Evert, who had been beaten by Miss Navratilova, 6-4, 4-6, 9-7, two weeks ago in the final of a women's tournament at Eastbourne. Even when Miss Evert broke at love for 4-2 in the final set with consecutive service-return winners and a backhand cross-court placement, Miss Navratilova did not panic, something she might have done several years ago.

"I had my chances, especially when I was 4-2 in the third," Miss Evert recalled, of a service game she lost at 15, on two forehand volley winners and a net-cord placement by Miss Navratilova. "! was too anxious."

Perhaps, or it may have a case of Miss Navratilova simply craving a title more than Miss Evert, who, at 23, has achieved everything in the sport.

Serving at 4-5, when she might have been most vulnerable, Miss Navratilova seemed to draw courage from adversity. She powered in four first serves and held at love, then Miss Evert committed four unforced errors to drop service at 15 for 6-5. With the match in her grasp, Miss Navratilova won a crucial first point when Miss Evert drove a backhand service return long. Three more solid first serves, and the match was over at love.

"I could do nothing with her serve," Miss Evert said. "When I did have the chances, maybe I tried too hard for it."

So Many Emotions

Miss Navratilova, seeded second in the draw, collected the equivalent of $32,000 for her victory and raised her earnings for the year to more than $285,000. But as she kissed the silver gilt salver she had won and held it aloft before the Duchess of Kent and the capacity crowd of 14,000, the money was as secondary as Miss Wade's achievement before Queen Elizabeth II last year, with joyous spectators chanting "for she's a jolly good fellow."

"I feel like there's so many emotions I don't know what to feel first," Miss Navratilova said.

Some spectators had been there before. In 1954, another self-exiled tennis player from Czechoslovakia, Jaroslav Drobny, won the men's singles title at Wimbledon over Ken Rosewall at the age of 32. Drobny had left Czechoslovakia in 1948, lived for a time in Egypt and now is a British subject.

Asked after the match whether the title represented a victory for Czechoslovakia or the United States, where she now has a home, Miss Navratilova said, "It's more for Czechoslovakia. I always will be a Czech down in my heart. I hope the Czech people will be proud of me."

Miss Navratilova, who dominated the women's indoor tour this year during the four-month absence of Miss Evert, survived a series of interesting tests en route to her first international singles title. She was extended to three sets by Barbara Jordan in the third round, beat Tracy Austin, 6-2, 6-3, in the round of 16 and eliminated Evonne Goolagong, 2-6, 6-4, 6-4, in a tight semifinal on the center court.

Miss Evert earned $15,000 as a Wimbledon runner-up for the second time. But at another level, the Floridian may be reaching a significant crossroads in her competitive career.

Reid-Turnbull Gain Final

"I realize if I want to be No. 1," she said afterward, "I'm probably going to have to want it more." The desire was there today, Miss Evert said, but the intensity was lacking.

Intensity flowed in the women's doubles final where Kerry Reid and Wendy Turnbull of Australia played off two match points in a second-set tiebreaker and went on to defeat Mima Jausovec of Yugoslavia and Virginia Ruzici of Rumania, 4-6, 9-8, 6-3.

The second-set tiebreaker went to 10-8 before the Australians prevailed.

Tomorrow there should be more drama when Bjorn Borg faces Jimmy Connors in a rematch of last year's five-set men's singles final, which Borg won. A victory by the 22-year-old Swede would put him into the record-book alongside Fred Perry of Britain as the first player to win three consecutive men's singles crowns.

Drama also will unfold in the mixed doubles final, where Mrs. Billie Jean King will seek a record 20th Wimbledon title. Mrs. King and her partner, Ray Ruffels, reached the final by beating Allan Stone and Dianne Fromholtz, 6-3, 6-4, today.

There will be a surprise team in the men's doubles final, John McEnroe of Douglaston, Queens, and Peter Fleming of Chatham, N.J. The pair upset the second-seeded duo of Wojtek Fibak and Tom Okker, 1-6, 6-3, 9-7, 6-4, and will play the world's top doubles team, Bob Hewitt and Frew McMillan, in tomorrow's final.

July 8, 1978

Borg Overcomes Connors For 3d Wimbledon Crown

By NEIL AMDUR
Special to The New York Times

WIMBLEDON, England, July 8 — Bjorn Borg looked invincible today in a 6-2, 6-2, 6-3 rout of Jimmy Connors for his third consecutive Wimbledon singles title. Perhaps it is time to find a spot for the 22-year-old Swede among the best tennis players ever.

Fred Perry, who won his third straight Wimbledon crown 42 years ago, was the first person after Connors to shake Borg's hand at center court after the 1-hour-48-minute execution. Later, at a news conference, the 69-year-old Perry put Borg in a class with Jack Kramer, Lew Hoad, Pancho Gonzales and Ellsworth Vines. That is top-10 company on any list.

"Everything went Borg's way today," Perry said. "If he had fallen out of a 45-story window in a New York skyscraper, he would have gone staight up."

Rises to the Challenge

Even Lennart Bergelin, Borg's long-time coach, could hardly restrain himself. Borg has played better in "a few little matches," Bergelin said, "but this is the best big match he ever played."

The bigger the challenge, the better he responds has become the essence of Borg. He crushed Guillermo Vilas, 6-1, 6-1, 6-3, on clay, which is slower than the grass here, in the French open final last month. And here he won his last four matches in straight sets.

Borg's run clearly has carried him past Connors as the sport's dominant player. After having held a physical and mental grip over his younger rival for several years, the 25-year-old Connors now has lost five of the last six matches in their rivalry and has won only 11 games in the last six sets.

Once it was Connors throwing the aggressive punches and boring in for the killing volleys, with Borg counterpunching from the backcourt. Today Borg was serving so strongly that he broke strings on two racquets and had one racquet fly out of his hand.

But that was about the only time he lost control, even though he acknowledged afterward that "when I saw a good chance to win it, I got tight."

In less than five years on the international scene, Borg has won three Wimbledons, three French opens, two Italian opens and the World Championship of Tennis title.

This season he has swept 40 consecutive singles matches, having been last beaten in March in Miami by Tom Gullikson. His victories at Paris and here gave him two legs on the the Grand Slam, a feat last achieved by Rod Laver in 1969 and considered almost unattainable under present competitive conditions

"Now I have a very good chance," Borg said, looking toward the other two legs of the Slam — the United States Open in September and the Australian open in December.

Both players were physically fit for the final, in contrast to last year when Connors played with a fractured right thumb (Borg won in five sets) and their Grand Prix Masters final at Madison Square Garden in January, when Borg was weak with a virus (Connors won in three sets). However, their mental attitudes differed. In that aspect Borg rivals Laver and Kramer for toughness and temperament. He had termed the match the biggest of his career — "absolutely, for sure" — and he played that way.

Connors, an even-money choice among British bookmakers, would not say he was in a daze but admitted afterward, "Mentally, I never got into the match."

Serve Improved Greatly

One reason was Borg's serve. In two years he has improved it from a rifle to a cannon. Although Connors has the best service return in the game, he seemed powerless against Borg's delivery, the power and effect of which could be measured statistically. Borg got in 49 of 88 first serves, a respectable 56 percent He had five aces, six service winners and induced 13 return errors. Thus, 24 of the 88 points in the match were decided on Borg's serve.

The improvement has come from several factors — physical maturity, confidence, concentration. But mostly it has come from minor technical adjustments and long hours of practice.

"You have to throw the ball high so the motion is slower, so you have time to say 1,2," Bergelin said, explaining how he had refined Borg's rhythm and motion. "You have to take it easy, not force it. You must be relaxed on the mental side. He was doing that very well in the last two matches."

Connors knew he did not serve well. "It took a day off," he quipped, alluding to his delivery. His inability to make Borg respect his serve left the second-seeded American in trouble from the start.

Holds in Opening Game

In the opening game he held from 30-40, then broke Borg for 2-0. But Borg was so relaxed and confident that "I felt I could break him every time." For a time he did, for 1-2, 3-2 and on a game-ending double fault for 5-2.

Connors again held in the opening game of the the second set, but was broken from 40-30 in the third. The key game, which provided an example of Borg's serving, was the fourth. Connors held triple break point at 0-40 and could have got back to 2-all. But he netted a backhand return, Borg put away a smash to 30-40 and then hit a service winner with such force that Connors's attempted forehand return flew 20 feet straight up. That made it deuce.

"To beat Jimmy, you have to serve well," Borg said. "Today I was serving well."

Borg netted an overhead, giving Connors a fourth break point. But he angled a backhand drop volley, got the ad on Connors's netted backhand and then nullified one of Connors's infrequent net rushes with a backhand cross-court pass.

In retrospect, Connors said, perhaps he should have been more aggressive "instead of pooping the ball." But Borg never allowed him to find a groove as he changed the pace of rallies, rushed the net off sliced backhand cross-court shots to Connors's forehand and returned serve almost flawlessly.

Borg made only four service-return errors in the match. He forced Connors to dig out low-bouncing balls on the soft grass of the All England Lawn Tennis Club. With Connors serving at 3-5, 30-all, Borg rushed the net and reached match point on a backhand drop volley. Then Connors stroked a backhand volley over the baseline, and it was over.

Borg dropped his racquet and fell to his knees, overwhelmed more by the occasion than the $34,000 first prize.

"I think it was probably one of my best matches," he said.

Acceptance of Borg's greatness has come grudgingly in a sport in which tradition and classic strokes are cherished like good wine. He has brought a different taste to the game, with his unorthodox stroke production — a looping, topspin forehand and two-handed backhand and impenetrable mental armor.

He represents the future of the sport rather the past. "Borg is just so good that there's no reason why he can't become one of the all-time greats, if he isn't already," Billie Jean King said.

Borg has grown a beard for each of the last three Wimbledons. Perry had wanted him to shave it off because he said it didn't make Borg look good. Borg agreed to shave the beard tonight, but only for a razor-blade commercial, and after he had joined Perry in the record books.

July 9, 1978

TENNIS is an outdoor or indoor game, played on a rectangular court by two persons (singles) or by four persons (doubles), who use rackets to hit a ball back and forth across a net. The object is to score points by striking the ball in such a way that an opponent cannot return it successfully. The game originated in England and was first played on grass. It was called *lawn tennis* to distinguish it from *court tennis,* the ancient parent game. Today, however, the game is referred to as tennis.

Tennis is popular among persons of all ages, both male and female. When played solely for recreation, the game attracts millions of participants. Only a few hundred players enter international tournaments, most of whom are professionals who compete for prize money. Governing all play are the rules established by the International Lawn Tennis Federation (ILTF), founded in 1913. The federation embraces more than 70 national organizations, among them the U.S. Lawn Tennis Association (USLTA).

The four major championships on the international circuit are the British, Australian, French, and the United States, together known as the Big Four. Other important tournaments include the Italian, West German, and South African. The premier title is the British, popularly called Wimbledon. The richest is the U.S. Open, held at Flushing, N.Y., offering more than $150,000 in prize money.

The most coveted team trophy in men's international play is the International Lawn Tennis Challenge Trophy donated in 1900 by an American, Dwight F. Davis, and known as the Davis Cup. More than 50 countries, organized by geographical zones, enter the annual competition. Since its inception, only four countries have ever won the trophy—Australia and the United States, which have dominated play, and Britain and France.

In 1963, in observance of its 50th anniversary, the ILTF inaugurated the Federation Cup for the world women's team championship. More than 20 countries compete for the trophy. British and American women's teams play annually for the Wightman Cup. Hazel Hotchkiss Wightman of California presented the cup to the USLTA in 1919; competition began in 1923.

The National Lawn Tennis Hall of Fame and Tennis Museum opened in Newport, R.I., in 1954. Distinguished players and officials are selected for membership in the Hall of Fame on the basis of sportsmanship, skill, and contributions to the game.

The Court and Equipment. The court measures 78 feet (23.77 meters) long at the *sidelines* and, for the singles game, 27 feet (8.2 meters) wide at the *base lines.* For doubles, the court is made 9 feet (2.7 meters) wider by extending the base lines 4½ feet (1.37 meters) in each direction. The extensions, enclosed by added sidelines, are called *alleys.*

A net parallel to the base lines divides the court at the center. The net, which is of natural or synthetic cord, is strung between two posts. It is 3 feet (0.91 meter) high at the center and 3½ feet (about 1 meter) at the sideline posts. On either side of the net, 21 feet (6.4 meters) from it and parallel to it, are the *service lines.* A *center line* between the service lines and parallel to the sidelines creates two service courts, each 13½ feet (about 4 meters) wide. These service courts are used in serving for both singles and doubles.

Any of several surfaces may be used on the court, including grass, clay, cement, wood, and synthetic fibers. The size, shape, and markings, however, are standard.

The ball is a cloth-covered rubber sphere that is white or yellow in color, approximately 2½ inches (6.35 cm) in diameter and 2 ounces (56.69 grams) in weight. It is pressurized so that it will bounce at least 53 inches (134.62 cm) and not more than 58 inches (147.32 cm) when dropped 100 inches (254 cm) onto a concrete base. The livelier, high-pressure ball is more common in the United States than in other countries, favoring the hard-driving "power game." The lower pressure ball is easier to control, and an exchange back and forth over the net usually lasts longer. This applies especially to a clay surface, which is generally considered "slow" because the ball takes a higher, more leisurely bounce. Grass is considered a "fast" surface because the ball takes a low, uncertain, and skidding bounce.

Traditionally the leading titles—Wimbledon, United States, and Australia—have been contested on grass. The grass court is being replaced in the United States by synthetic turf. The French championship is considered the world's foremost clay-court event, with the Italian and West German championships gaining stature. The South African championship is played on a slow cement, although cement is usually a fast surface. The top indoor events in the United States are conducted on a variety of synthetic surfaces, fast and slow.

Rackets of laminated wood predominate as the implement for striking the ball. Steel, aluminum, fiber glass, and plastic are also used for racket material. There are no limitations on racket size or weight. However, the weight usually averages between 13 and 15 ounces (368.5—425 grams), and the length is about 28 inches (71 cm). An open oval frame, or head, is attached to a straight handle, which measures about 4½ inches in circumference at the grip. The frame, about 9 inches (22.8 cm) wide, is crossed horizontally and vertically with gut or nylon strings.

Scoring. Units of scoring are points, games, sets, and matches. Scoring is the same in singles and in doubles. A player or team scores a *point* when the opposition fails to return the ball properly. A side must score at least four points to win a *game*. The first point made is called *15;* the second, *30;* the third, *40;* and the fourth, *game*. If both sides score 3 points—that is, if the score is 40—40, or 40 all—it is a *deuce,* or tie, game. To win a deuce game, one side must score two consecutive points from deuce. The first point is called *advantage,* or *ad*. If the player holding advantage wins the next point, he wins the game. Otherwise, the score reverts to deuce. The term *love* means zero. Thus a score of 30—love is 30—0.

The side winning six games wins a *set*. If each side wins five games—that is, if the score is 5 all—it is a deuce set, which can be won only by the player or team that wins two games in a row. The deuce principle may result in prolonged matches.

A *match* consists of winning two of three sets (women and men) or three of five sets (men only). The most famous comeback on record is that of Henri Cochet of France, who defeated Bill Tilden of the United States at Wimbledon in 1927. Although Cochet trailed, seemingly hopelessly, by two sets and by 1—5 in the third, he won the match 2—6, 4—6, 7—5, 6—4, 6—3.

The longest singles match was played in Warsaw in 1966 in the King's Cup tournament. A total of 126 games were played before Roger Taylor of Britain defeated Wieslaw Gasiorek of Poland 27—29, 31—29, 6—4. In a doubles match in the Newport (R.I.) Casino Invitation in 1967, Richard Leach and Richard Dell defeated Leonard Schloss and Thomas Mozur 3—6, 49—47, 22—20, a total of 147 games.

To avoid such tennis marathons and to permit a match to be completed within a predictable amount of time, a sudden-death tie-breaker system augmented the traditional tennis scoring in 1970. With the tie-breaker method, if a set reaches 6 all in games, the players alternate serves in a best-of-nine points sequence. For example, the first server (A) serves points 1 and 2. The second server (B) serves points 3 and 4. A serves points 5 and 6, and B serves points 7, 8, and 9, if necessary. The first player to score five points in the playoff wins the set or match. The set is scored 7—6.

In 1958, James Van Alen of the United States, the inventor of the sudden-death tie-breaker system, introduced the Van Alen Streamlined Scoring System (VASSS), which uses single points. The first player to reach 31 points wins the set, and the 31-point set must be won by at least two points. Serve changes every five points. Another feature of VASSS is No-ad, eliminating deuce. The first player to win four points wins a game. The first to win six games wins a set, unless games are 5 all. In this case a sudden-death tie-breaker is played.

Play Procedures. Before a match the choice of sides on the court and the right to serve or receive service are decided by toss of a coin. The server begins play for the first point of a game from behind the base line in the right half of the court. He tosses the ball into the air and hits it with the racket diagonally across the net into the right service court of his opponent. If he drives the ball into the net, or if the ball goes beyond the receiver's service court, it is a *fault,* and he must serve again. The server can also commit a fault by touching the base line or any part of his court with his feet while serving. He has two serves to begin the point. If he faults both times he commits a *double fault* and loses the point. A served ball that strikes the top of the net and drops into the receiver's service court is a *let ball*. A let does not count, and the server gets another try. After the serve, a ball that touches the net and lands fair is a *net-cord ball* and remains in play. A good serve that the receiver cannot hit with his racket is called an *ace*.

Once the first point is made, the server delivers the ball for the second point from behind the base line in the left half of the court and to the left service court of the receiver. Services in succeeding points are alternated behind the halves of the base line. After each game, the contestants alternate the service. Players change sides of the court after odd-numbered games beginning with game one.

The receiver must return a served ball on the first bounce. Then an exchange, or *rally,* continues until a player either wins

the point outright by striking a ball that the opponent is unable to return or loses the point by an *error*—for example, missing the ball, stroking the ball into the net, or sending the ball out of bounds. During a rally for a point, players may strike the ball before it bounces (on the *volley*), or on its first bounce. The player who permits a ball to bounce twice loses the point.

Doubles play is similar to singles, but partners must alternate in serving complete games when it is their team's turn to serve. Partners receive the service alternately throughout each game. During a rally, either member of the team may make a return.

Fundamentals of Play. There are five basic tennis strokes: the *service,* an overhead stroke, used to begin play for a point; the forehand and backhand *drives,* strokes made after the ball bounces; the *volley,* a short stroke made before the ball touches the ground; and the *smash,* a hard overhead stroke. (A *lob* is a ball lofted high.) How a player holds the racket to make these strokes is an individual matter. He must find the most comfortable and effective position for the hand.

Of the three types of grips—Eastern, Continental, and Western—the Eastern is the norm from which most players make slight adjustments and adaptations in playing the ball. The forehand grip is taken by standing the racket on the edge of the frame and then "shaking hands" with it. As the fingers close around the handle, the "V" formed by the fingers and thumb rests over the plane of the handle, which is a continuation of the frame. The line of the arm, wrist, and racket is straight. For the Eastern backhand grip, the handle is held with the back of the hand uppermost and the knuckle of the first finger directly on top of the handle. The thumb may extend up the handle as a brace. Forehand and backhand shots are made on different faces of the racket. In the course of play, a person makes a quick change from the forehand to the backhand grip by turning the hand slightly counterclockwise.

The Continental grip is halfway between the Eastern forehand and backhand. The "V" formed by the thumb joining the hand rests directly on the top of the handle. A player makes the forehand and backhand shots on opposite sides of the racket face but does not change his grip.

To take the Western grip a player places the racket with its face parallel to the ground and then drops his hand on top of the handle. For the forehand drive the hand is almost underneath the handle. The same racket face is used for the forehand and the backhand strokes. With the Western grip, it is difficult to handle low bouncing balls. This grip puts strain on the wrist and it is seldom used. Bill Johnston, U.S. title holder in 1915 and 1919 and a member of the Davis Cup team, was an exponent of the Western grip.

A beginning player should try to hit the ball *flat,* that is, his racket at impact should meet the ball squarely. The flatter the hit the greater the ball's speed through the air and the swifter its bounce. Knowledge of the effects of *spin* on the ball helps a player's overall game. Spin means control. The more spin on the ball the less pace. Hitting over the top of the ball imparts top spin, which tends to make the ball drop and bounce high, and an opponent has trouble volleying it. To *slice* the ball, the player passes the racket under the ball. A slice results in a low bounce. With a *chop,* the ball receives its rotation from a downward glancing blow from the racket. The backspin or underspin thus imparted causes the ball to bounce abruptly and low, with no speed.

The Service. The Eastern backhand grip is the one most often used in the service. To serve, the player stands perpendicular to the net, with his front shoulder in line with the spot where he wants the ball to land. For a flat service, he tosses the ball well above his head and slightly in advance of it. He swings the racket back, up, and forward and meets the ball over the head squarely, as he transfers the weight to the ball of his front foot. He hits the ball down into the opponent's court from the highest point of the raised racket. After contact with the ball, the player continues the swing in a follow-through down and across the body. It is advisable to stand about six inches behind the base line in serving to avoid stepping on the line. This breach of the rules is called a *foot fault*.

Players usually impart spin to the service, and the Continental grip is popular for those who impart top spin or slice the ball. A right-handed player tosses the ball up and over his left shoulder and then imparts top spin by hitting over the ball. The ball will bounce high and to the right of the server. To cause the ball to skid off to the opponent's right, he slices the ball after tossing it slightly to his right.

Forehand and Backhand Drives. For the forehand and backhand strokes, a level swing with the arm fully extended at the moment of impact is the ideal for which to strive. In the forehand, the palm (fore) of the racket hand leads in the direction in which the hand is moving. With the backhand, the racket strikes the ball with the back of the hand leading. Both strokes begin with the body perpendicular to the net.

A right-handed player hits a forehand by pivoting on his right foot and pointing his left shoulder toward the ball. As his body turns, he carries his racket back to the right on a line with the flight of the oncoming ball. He keeps his knees bent and, if playing a low ball, bends them even more to permit a level swing. A ball coming over the net high probably will bounce high. If it just clears the net the bounce may be low. As he swings the racket forward to meet the ball, the player transfers the body weight from the rear to the front foot. After the hit, the follow-through carries the racket in the direction the ball has taken. On a flat drive, the racket movement ends in front of the body. On a forehand with topspin, the racket head ends toward the far shoulder.

The principles of the backhand stroke are the same as for the forehand. However, the position of the feet and hitting arm and the body movement are reversed. The right-hander keeps the right shoulder facing the net from the backswing until the start of the follow-through. The techniques discussed should be reversed for a left-handed player.

The Volley and Smash. The *volley* is made facing the net. Using a short backswing, the player punches the ball with the racket instead of swinging at it. The *smash* is made with the body sideways to the net. The player hits the ball overhead with much the same motion as for the serve. The smash is often used to return a lobbed ball. With a particularly high lob, a player may let the ball bounce before he makes the smash.

Bibliography

Barbaby, John M., *Racket Work: The Key to Tennis* (Rockleigh, N.J., 1969).

Brady, Maurice, *Lawn Tennis Encyclopedia* (New York 1969).

Davidson, Owen, and Jones, C.J., *The Great Ones* (London 1970).

Gensemer, Robert E., *Tennis* (Philadelphia 1969).

Grimsley, Will, *Tennis: Its History, People and Events* (Englewood Cliffs, N.J., 1971).

King, Billie Jean, and Chapin, Kim, *Tennis to Win* (New York 1970).

Lardner, Rex, *Complete Beginners' Guide to Tennis* (New York 1967).

Laver, Rodney, and Collins, Bud, *The Education of a Tennis Player* (New York 1971).

Pollard, Jack, *Lawn Tennis the Australian Way* (London 1964).

Talbert, William F., and Old, Bruce S., *Game of Doubles in Tennis,* 3d ed. (Philadelphia 1968).

Talbert, William F., and Old, Bruce S., *Game of Singles in Tennis* (Philadelphia 1962).

United States Lawn Tennis Association, *The Official Yearbook and Tennis Guide* (New York, current edition).

BRITISH (Wimbledon) CHAMPIONS

Men's Singles

1877	Spencer W. Gore
1878	P. Frank Hadow
1879–80	J. T. Hartley
1881–86	William Renshaw
1887	Herbert F. Lawford
1888	Ernest Renshaw
1889	William Renshaw
1890	Willoughby J. Hamilton
1891–92	Wilfred Baddeley
1893–94	Joshua L. Pim
1895	Wilfred Baddeley
1896	Harold S. Mahony
1897–1900	Reginald Doherty
1901	Arthur W. Gore
1902–06	Hugh L. Doherty
1907	Norman Brookes (Austr.)
1908–09	Arthur W. Gore
1910–13	Anthony F. Wilding (N.Z.)
1914	Norman Brookes (Austr.)
1915–1918	No competition
1919	Gerald Patterson (Austr.)
1920–21	William T. Tilden (U.S.)
1922	Gerald Patterson (Austr.)
1923	William Johnston (U.S.)
1924	Jean Borotra (Fr.)
1925	René Lacoste (Fr.)
1926	Jean Borotra (Fr.)
1927	Henri Cochet (Fr.)
1928	René Lacoste (Fr.)
1929	Henri Cochet (Fr.)
1930	William T. Tilden (U.S.)
1931	Sidney B. Wood (U.S.)
1932	Ellsworth Vines (U.S.)
1933	John Crawford (Austr.)
1934–36	Fred J. Perry
1937–38	J. Donald Budge (U.S.)
1939	Robert L. Riggs (U.S.)
1940–45	No competition
1946	Yvon Petra (Fr.)
1947	John A. Kramer (U.S.)
1948	Robert Falkenburg (U.S.)
1949	Fred R. Schroeder (U.S.)
1950	J. Edward Patty (U.S.)
1951	Richard Savitt (U.S.)
1952	Frank Sedgman (Austr.)
1953	E. Victor Seixas (U.S.)
1954	Jaroslav Drobny (Czech.)
1955	Tony Trabert (U.S.)
1956–57	Lewis Hoad (Austr.)
1958	Ashley Cooper (Austr.)
1959	Alejandro Olmedo (Peru)
1960	Neale Fraser (Austr.)
1961–62	Rodney Laver (Austr.)
1963	Charles McKinley (U.S.)
1964–65	Roy Emerson (Austr.)
1966	Manuel Santana (Spain)
1967	John Newcombe (Austr.)
1968–69	Rodney Laver (Austr.)
1970	John Newcombe (Austr.)
1971	John Newcombe (Austr.)
1972	Stan Smith (U.S.)
1973	Jan Kodes (Czech.)
1974	Jimmy Connors (U.S.)
1975	Arthur Ashe (U.S.)
1976	Bjorn Borg (Sweden)
1977	Bjorn Borg)Sweden)
1978	Bjorn Borg (Sweden)
1979	Bjorn Borg (Sweden)

Women's Singles

1884–85	Maud Watson
1886	Blanche Bingley
1887–88	Lottie Dod
1889	Blanche Bingley Hillyard
1890	L. Rice
1891–92	Lottie Dod
1894	Blanche Bingley Hillyard
1895–96	Charlotte Cooper
1897	Blanche Bingley Hillyard
1898	Charlotte Cooper
1899–1900	Blanche B. Hillyard
1901	Charlotte Cooper Sterry
1902	M. E. Robb
1903–04	Dorothy K. Douglass
1905	May G. Sutton (U.S.)
1906	Dorothy K. Douglass
1907	May G. Sutton (U.S.)
1908	Charlotte Cooper Sterry
1909	Dorothea P. Boothby
1910–11	Dorothy D. Chambers
1912	Ethel W. Larcombe
1913–14	Dorothy D. Chambers
1915–1918	No competition
1919–23	Suzanne Lenglen (Fr.)
1924	Kathleen McKane
1925	Suzanne Lenglen (Fr.)
1926	Kathleen McKane Godfree
1927–29	Helen N. Wills (U.S.)
1930	Helen Wills Moody (U.S.)
1931	Cecil Aussem (Ger.)
1932–33	Helen Wills Moody (U.S.)
1934	Dorothy E. Round
1935	Helen Wills Moody (U.S.)
1936	Helen H. Jacobs (U.S.)
1937	Dorothy E. Round
1938	Helen Wills Moody (U.S.)
1939	Alice Marble (U.S.)
1940–1945	No competition
1946	Pauline Betz (U.S.)
1947	Margaret Osborne (U.S.)
1948–50	Louise Brough (U.S.)
1951	Doris J. Hart (U.S.)
1952–54	Maureen Connolly (U.S.)
1955	Louise Brough (U.S.)
1956	Shirley J. Fry (U.S.)
1957–58	Althea Gibson (U.S.)
1959–60	Maria Bueno (Brazil)
1961	Angela Mortimer
1962	Karen H. Susman (U.S.)
1963	Margaret Smith (Austr.)
1964	Maria Bueno (Brazil)
1965	Margaret Smith (Austr.)
1966–68	Billie Jean King (U.S.)
1969	Ann Haydon Jones
1970	Margaret S. Court (Austr.)
1971	Evonne Goolagong (Austr.)
1972–73	Billie Jean King (U.S.)
1974	Chris Evert (U.S.)
1975	Billie Jean King (U.S.)
1976	Chris Evert (U.S.)
1977	Virginia Wade
1978	Martina Navratilova (U.S.)
1979	Martina Navratilova (U.S.)

U.S. OPEN CHAMPIONS

Men's Singles

1881–87	Richard D. Sears
1888–89	Henry W. Slocum
1890–92	Oliver S. Campbell
1893–94	Robert D. Wrenn
1895	Fred H. Hovey
1896–97	Robert D. Wrenn
1898–1900	Malcolm Whitman
1901–02	William A. Larned
1903	Hugh L. Doherty (U.K.)
1904	Holcombe Ward
1905	Beals C. Wright
1906	William J. Clothier
1907–11	William A. Larned
1912–13	Maurice E. McLoughlin
1914	R. Norris Williams
1915	William Johnston
1916	R. Norris Williams
1917–18	R. Lindley Murray
1919	William Johnston
1920–25	William T. Tilden
1926–27	René Lacoste (Fr.)
1928	Henri Cochet (Fr.)
1929	William T. Tilden
1930	John H. Doeg
1931–32	Ellsworth Vines
1933–34	Fred J. Perry (U.K.)
1935	Wilmer L. Allison
1936	Fred J. Perry (U.K.)
1937–38	J. Donald Budge
1939	Robert L. Riggs
1940	W. Donald McNeill
1941	Robert L. Riggs
1942	Fred R. Schroeder
1943	Joseph R. Hunt
1944–45	Frank A. Parker
1946–47	John A. Kramer
1948–49	Richard A. Gonzales
1950	Arthur D. Larsen
1951–52	Frank Sedgman (Austr.)
1953	Tony Trabert
1954	E. Victor Seixas
1955	Tony Trabert
1956	Kenneth Rosewall (Austr.)

1957	Malcolm Anderson (Austr.)
1958	Ashley Cooper (Austr.)
1959–60	Neale Fraser (Austr.)
1961	Roy Emerson (Austr.)
1962	Rodney Laver (Austr.)
1963	Rafael Osuna (Mexico)
1964	Roy Emerson (Austr.)
1965	Manuel Santana (Spain)
1966	Fred S. Stolle (Austr.)
1967	John Newcombe (Austr.)
1968	Arthur R. Ashe
1969	Rodney Laver (Austr.)
1970	Kenneth Rosewall (Austr.)
1971	Stan Smith
1972	Ilie Nastase (Rum.)
1973	John Newcombe (Austr.)
1974	Jimmy Connors
1975	Manuel Orantes (Spain)
1976	Jimmy Connors
1977	Guillermo Vilas (Argent.)
1978	Jimmy Connors
1979	John MacEnroe

Women's Singles

1887	Ellen F. Hansell
1888–89	Bertha L. Townsend
1890	Ellen C. Roosevelt
1891–92	Mabel E. Cahill
1893	Aline M. Terry
1894	Helen R. Helwig
1895	Juliette P. Atkinson
1896	Elisabeth H. Moore
1897–98	Juliette P. Atkinson
1899	Marion Jones
1900	Myrtle McAteer
1901	Elisabeth H. Moore
1902	Marion Jones
1903	Elisabeth H. Moore
1904	May G. Sutton
1905	Elisabeth H. Moore
1906	Helen Homans

1907	Evelyn Sears
1908	Maud Bargar-Wallach
1909–11	Hazel V. Hotchkiss
1912–14	Mary K. Browne
1915–18	Molla Bjurstedt
1919	Hazel H. Wightman
1920–22	Molla B. Mallory
1923–25	Helen N. Wills
1926	Molla B. Mallory
1927–29	Helen N. Wills
1930	Betty Nuthall (U.K.)
1931	Helen Wills Moody
1932–35	Helen H. Jacobs
1936	Alice Marble
1937	Anita Lizana (Chile)
1938–40	Alice Marble
1941	Sarah Palfrey Cooke
1942–44	Pauline Betz
1945	Sarah Palfrey Cooke
1946	Pauline Betz
1947	Louise Brough
1948–50	Margaret O. duPont
1951–53	Maureen Connolly
1954–55	Doris J. Hart
1956	Shirley J. Fry
1957–58	Althea Gibson
1959	Maria Bueno (Brazil)
1960–61	Darlene R. Hard
1962	Margaret Smith (Austr.)
1963–64	Maria Bueno (Brazil)
1965	Margaret Smith (Austr.)
1966	Maria Bueno (Brazil)
1967	Billie Jean King
1968	Virginia Wade (U.K.)
1969–70	Margaret Smith Court (Austr.)
1971–72	Billie Jean King
1973	Margaret S. Court (Austr.)
1974	Billie Jean King
1975	Chris Evert
1976	Chris Evert
1977	Chris Evert
1978	Chris Evert
1979	Tracy Austin

Davis Cup Challenge Round

Year	Result
1900	United States, 5 British Isles 0
1901	(not played)
1902	United States 3, British Isles 2
1903	British Isles 4, United States 1
1904	British Isles 5, Belgium 0
1905	British Isles 5, United States 0
1906	British Isles 5, United States 0
1907	Australia 3, British Isles 2
1908	Australasia 3, United States 2
1909	Australasia 5, United States 0
1910	(not played)
1911	Australasia 5, United States 0
1912	British Isles 3, Australasia 2
1913	United States 3, British Isles 2
1914	Australasia 3, United States 2
1915–18	(not played)
1919	Australasia 4, British Isles 1
1920	United States 5, Australasia 0
1921	United States 5, Japan 0
1922	United States 4, Australasia 1
1923	United States 4, Australasia 1
1924	United States 5, Australasia 0
1925	United States 5, France 0

1926	United States 4, France 1
1927	France 3, United States 2
1928	France 4, United States 1
1929	France 3, United States 2
1930	France 4, United States 1
1931	France 3, Great Britain 2
1932	France 3, United States 2
1933	Great Britain 3, France 2
1934	Great Britain 4, United States 1
1935	Great Britain 5, United States 0
1936	Great Britain 3, Australia 2
1937	United States 4, Great Britain 1
1938	United States 3, Australia 2
1939	Australia 3, United States 2
1940–45	(not played)
1946	United States 5, Australia 0
1947	United States 4, Australia 1
1948	United States 5, Australia 0
1949	United States 4, Australia 1
1950	Australia 4, United States 1
1951	Australia 3, United States 2
1952	Australia 4, United States 1
1953	Australia 3, United States 2
1954	United States 3, Australia 2

1955	Australia 5, United States 0
1956	Australia 5, United States 0
1957	Australia 3, United States 2
1958	United States 3, Australia 2
1959	Australia 3, United States 2
1960	Australia 4, Italy 1
1961	Australia 5, Italy 0
1962	Australia 5, Mexico 0
1963	United States 3, Australia 2
1964	Australia 3, United States 2
1965	Australia 4, Spain 1
1966	Australia 4, India 1
1967	Australia 4, Spain 1
1968	United States 4, Australia 1
1969	United States 5, Romania 0
1970	United States 5, W. Germany 0
1971	United States 3, Romania 2
1972	United States 3, Romania 2
1973	Australia 5, United States 0
1974	South Africa (default by India)
1975	Sweden 3, Czech 2
1976	Italy 4, Chile 1
1977	Australia 3, Italy 1
1978	United States 4, Great Britain 1

UPDATE SUPPLEMENT—1988

To accompany and be integrated with
Intermediate Accounting, Second Canadian Edition

Second Canadian Edition

INTERMEDIATE ACCOUNTING

Donald E. Kieso Ph.D., C.P.A.
Northern Illinois University
DeKalb, Illinois

Jerry J. Weygandt Ph.D., C.P.A.
University of Wisconsin
Madison, Wisconsin

V. Bruce Irvine Ph.D., C.M.A., F.S.M.A.C.
University of Saskatchewan
Saskatoon, Saskatchewan

W. Harold Silvester Ph.D., C.A., C.P.A.
University of Saskatchewan
Saskatoon, Saskatchewan

WILEY

John Wiley & Sons Canada Limited

Toronto   New York   Chichester   Brisbane   Singapore

Canadian Cataloguing in Publication Data

Silvester, W. Harold
  Update supplement 1988 t/a Intermediate accounting,
second Canadian edition

Supplement to: Intermediate accounting.
2nd Canadian ed.
ISBN 0-471-79657-3

1. Accounting. I. Title. II. Title: Intermediate
accounting. 2nd Canadian ed.

HF5635.I5732 1988   657'.044   C88-094858-2

TO THE STUDENT

Although your textbook, *Intermediate Accounting*, Second Canadian Edition, by Kieso, Weygandt, Irvine, and Silvester, is only two years old, numerous accounting pronouncements have been issued that render certain coverage incomplete or obsolete. The purpose of the *Update Supplement—1988* is to update your textbook and keep you abreast of the latest developments in financial accounting. The material presented here complies with the latest pronouncements of the Canadian Institute of Chartered Accountants.

TO THE INSTRUCTOR

Update Supplement—1988 to accompany Kieso, Weygandt, Irvine, and Silvester, *Intermediate Accounting*, Second Canadian Edition, exemplifies the commitment of John Wiley & Sons Canada Limited and our authors to provide the finest in educational materials and services to our customers. We have, therefore, provided you and your students with this supplement, free of charge, as part of our ongoing effort to meet this commitment. We invite your comments, queries, and suggestions.

CONTENTS

SIGNIFICANT PRONOUNCEMENTS ISSUED SINCE SEPTEMBER 1985

CICA HANDBOOK REVISIONS

Date Issued	Section No.	Title
Sept. 1985	1540	Statement of Changes in Financial Position
Apr. 1986	3460	Pension Costs and Obligations
Sept. 1986	3400	Revenue
Aug. 1987	3850	Interest Capitalized—Disclosure Considerations
May 1988	4230	Non-Profit Organizations—Specific Items

RELEVANT CICA EXPOSURE DRAFTS

July 1986	Portfolio Investments
Jan. 1987	Future-Oriented Financial Statements
Feb. 1988	Financial Statement Concepts

TOPIC: ACCOUNTING FOR PENSION COSTS

APPLICATION
IN TEXTBOOK: Chapter 21 (substitute this for all of Chapter 21).

SOURCE: "Pension Costs and Obligations," *CICA Handbook*, Section 3460.

21

ACCOUNTING FOR PENSION COSTS

Since the late 1800s, many business organizations have been concerned with providing for the retirement of employees. During recent decades, a marked increase in this concern has resulted in the establishment of private pension plans in most large companies and in medium- and small-sized ones.

The substantial growth of these plans, both in numbers of employees covered and in amounts of retirement benefits, has increased the significance of pension cost in relation to the financial position and the results of operations of many companies. Widely divergent practices in accounting for the cost of pension plans have persisted until recent years. The complex array of social concepts, legal considerations, actuarial techniques, income tax regulations, and varying business philosophies that characterizes the environment in which pension plans have developed is partly responsible for the accounting profession's motivation to standardize practice in this area.

Generally accepted accounting principles for accounting by employers for pension plans are provided in Section 3460 of the *CICA Handbook*. This section was amended in 1986 following publication in 1963 and 1980 of two significant CICA research studies. The first was "Accounting for Costs of Pension Plans" by W. B. Coutts and R. B. Dale-Harris, and the second was "Accounting for Pension Costs and Liabilities" by T. Ross Archibald. The latter study emphasized concerns related to accounting practices in the area of pensions. Many of these concerns were addressed in the 1986 amendments to Section 3460. The material in this chapter presents a discussion of pension plans and the basic procedures for pension accounting recommended in the *CICA Handbook*.

TYPES OF PENSION PLANS

A **pension plan** is an arrangement whereby an employer promises to provide benefits (payments) to employees after they retire. The two most common types of pension arrangements are **defined contribution plans** and **defined benefit plans**.

In a **defined contribution plan**, the employer's contribution to the plan is defined by the terms of the plan; that is, the employer agrees to contribute a certain sum each period based on a formula. This formula might consider such factors as age, length of service, employer's profits, and compensation level. It is important to note that only the employer's contribution is defined; no promise is made concerning the ultimate benefits to be paid out to the employees.

On the other hand, a **defined benefit plan** defines the benefits that the employee will receive at the time of retirement. The formula that is typically used provides for the benefits to be a function of an employee's compensation level when he or she nears retirement and the employee's years of service. For example, a plan may stipulate that upon retirement employees will receive an annual pension equal to two percent of their final annual salary times the number of years of eligible service. In these plans it is necessary to determine what the contribution should be today to meet the pension benefit commitments that will arise at retirement. It is important to recognize that many different contribution approaches could be used to fund (pay for) the pension benefit at the time of retirement. Naturally, regardless of the funding method employed, sufficient funds should be available at retirement to meet the benefits defined by the plan.

Accounting for a defined contribution plan is straightforward. In this type of plan, the benefit of gain or the risk of loss from the assets contributed to the pension plan is borne by the employee. The employer's responsibility is simply to make a contribution each year based on the formula established in the plan. As a result, the employer's obligation is easily determined. It follows that **the amount of the contribution required each period is reported as pension expense**.

Conversely, accounting for a defined benefit plan is complex. Because the benefits are defined in terms of uncertain future variables, an appropriate funding pattern must be established to assure that enough funds will be available at retirement to meet the benefits promised. This funding level depends on a number of factors such as turnover, mortality, length of employee service, compensation levels, discount rates, and interest earnings. Employers are at risk because they must be sure that they make enough contributions to meet the cost of the benefits that are defined in the plan. The expense recognized each period is not necessarily equal to the cash contribution. Similarly, the amount to report as a liability is controversial because the measurement and recognition of the liability relate to unknown future variables.

The most popular type of plan is the defined benefit plan because it provides more protection to the employee. Unfortunately, the accounting issues related to this type of plan are the most difficult. Our discussion in the following sections deals primarily with defined benefit plans.

EMPLOYER VERSUS PLAN ACCOUNTING

The subject of pension accounting may be divided into **accounting for the employer** and **accounting for the pension fund** and treated separately. The company or employer is the organization sponsoring the pension plan; the employer incurs the cost and makes contributions to the pension fund. The fund or plan is the entity that receives the contributions from the employer, administers the pension assets, and makes the benefit payments to the pension recipients (retired employees). The diagram below shows the three distinct entities involved in a pension plan and indicates the flow of cash between them.

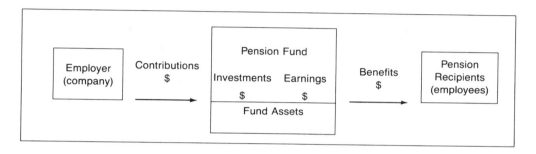

The pension plan above is being **funded**; that is, the employer (company) sets funds aside for future pension benefits by making payments to a funding agency that is responsible for accumulating the assets of the pension fund and for making payments to the recipients as the benefits become due. In an insured plan, the funding agency is an insurance company; in a trust fund plan, the funding agency is a trustee. The process of making the cash payments to a funding agency is called **funding**. Some plans are **unfunded**; that is, the fund is under the control of the company instead of an independent funding agency. In unfunded plans, pension payments to retired employees are made directly by the company as they become due.[1]

Some plans are **contributory**; the employees bear part of the cost of the stated benefits or voluntarily make payments to increase their benefits. Other plans are **noncontributory**, the employer bearing the entire cost. Companies generally design **registered pension plans** in accord with income tax requirements that permit deductibility of the employer's contributions to the pension fund (within certain limits) and tax-free status of the earnings of the pension fund assets.

Because the problems associated with pension plans involve complicated considerations, **actuaries** are engaged to insure that the plan is appropriate for the employee group covered.[2] An actuary's primary purpose is to ensure that the company has established an appropriate funding pattern to meet its pension obligations. This computation entails the development of a set of assumptions and continued monitoring of these assumptions to assure their realism.

---

[1]As indicated above, when used as a verb, **fund** means to pay to a funding agency (as to fund future pension benefits or to fund pension cost). Used as a noun, it refers to assets accumulated in the hands of a funding agency for the purpose of meeting the pension benefits when they become due.

[2]That the general public has little understanding of what an actuary does is illustrated by the following excerpt from *The Wall Street Journal:* "A polling organization once asked the general public what an actuary was and received among its more coherent responses the opinion that it was a place where you put dead actors."

The need for proper administration of and sound accounting for pension funds becomes apparent when one appreciates the absolute as well as the relative size of these funds. For example, the companies listed below recently had pension fund assets and related shareholders' equity as follows:

Company	Size of the Pension Fund	Total Shareholders' Equity
TransCanada Pipelines Ltd.	$ 109,000,000	$ 2,122,300,000
Bell Canada Enterprises Inc.	5,826,000,000	10,962,100,000
Canadian General Electric Company Ltd.	415,371,000	465,581,000

The fund should have a separate legal and accounting identity for which a set of books is maintained and financial statements are prepared. Maintaining books and records and preparing financial statements for the fund, known as ''accounting for employee benefit plans,'' is not the subject of this chapter. This chapter is devoted to the pension accounting and reporting problems of the employer as the sponsor of a pension plan.

THE ACTUARY'S ROLE

One of the actuary's first jobs when a pension plan is being established, or an existing plan is being amended, is to determine the **present value of the prospective benefits** (often referred to as the accrued benefit obligation) that will be paid in the future. That is, the actuary needs to determine the amount of money it would take today to pay for all retirement benefits for both active and retired employees. For example, the following circle indicates the present value of the prospective benefits that will have to be paid to both active and retired employees.

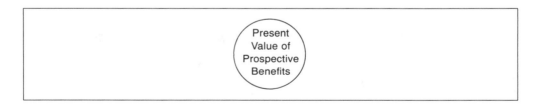

The size of the circle depends upon four factors:

1. **The benefit provisions of the pension plan.** The higher the benefits to be paid to retired employees, the larger the circle.
2. **Characteristics of the employee group.** The older the work force and the closer to retirement, the larger the present value of prospective benefits. Primarily all male employee groups have a lower present value of prospective benefits because their mortality rates are higher than those of females (all other factors equal).
3. **Actuarial assumptions.** Assumptions have to be made for such items as retirement rate, salary amounts, disability rate, and turnover rate. To illustrate, the higher the expected salary level in the future, the higher the present value of the prospective benefits.
4. **Interest rate.** Assumptions must be made regarding the earnings rate on funds invested. The higher the earnings (interest) rate, the less funds that must be contributed to the pension fund to meet benefits payable to retirees (the smaller the circle).

These factors are indicated in the following diagram:

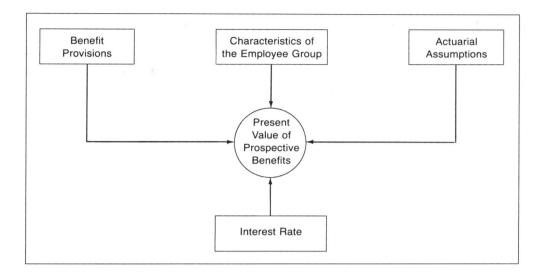

Note that actuaries can, and often do, differ in regard to the assumptions to be used in computing the prospective benefit obligation. For example, an examination of the two circles that follow might indicate that these are different plans. In reality, the two circles represent the same plan but, because the actuary is using different assumptions, the present value of the prospective benefits is larger in the one situation than in the other.

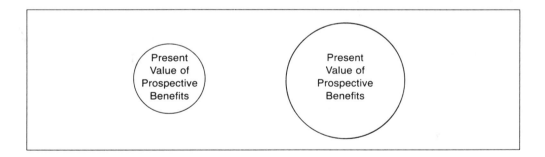

Regardless of the assumptions used by the actuary, the pension plan must have sufficient assets available at the time of the employee's retirement to pay benefits established by the pension plan. If the actuary's assumptions are too liberal or too conservative initially, the contributions by the employer must be adjusted as indicated by actual experiences.

ACTUARIAL FUNDING METHODS

After the actuary has computed the prospective benefit obligation, the next step is to determine how the company should fund the pension plan to insure that this obligation is met.

One option is to fund the obligation immediately. This situation is highly unlikely as most companies would not find immediate funding an efficient use for their liquid resources. As a result, actuaries have devised a number of **actuarial funding methods** (often referred to as actuarial cost methods) to determine the periodic contributions that the employer might make to the pension fund to insure that the funds are available to meet the retirees' claims to benefits. In addition, most provinces have legislation specifying maximum funding periods for certain pension costs.

As an illustration, assume that the benefits to be paid to an employee in five years are $100,000 and that the rate of return earned on assets is assumed to be 10%. What approach might the actuary use to be sure that $100,000 will be available five years from now? One funding method is to compute the amount that would have to be contributed at the end of each year bearing interest at 10% to accumulate a fund of $100,000. The amount to be contributed is $16,379.75, computed as follows:

$$\frac{\text{Amount of an ordinary annuity}}{\text{of 1 for 5 periods at 10\%}} \times \frac{\text{Periodic}}{\text{deposit}} = \$100,000$$

$$6.10510 \times \text{Periodic deposit} = \$100,000$$
$$\text{Periodic deposit} = \$100,000 \div 6.10510$$
$$\text{Periodic deposit} = \$16,379.75$$

Thus, $16,379.75 deposited at the end of each year will provide $100,000 at the end of five years.

Other approaches could be employed to fund these prospective benefits. Some funding approaches lead to lower payments earlier and higher payments later. Others do just the opposite. The selection of the funding pattern is based on a number of considerations. For example, **some companies employ shorter periods in order to maximize tax deductions and build funds for increased benefits. Others choose longer periods in order to retain working capital**. Whatever actuarial funding method is used for funding purposes, enough funds must be on hand to pay retirees in accordance with the plan agreement.

Actuarial funding methods have been used not only to determine the amounts to be funded, but also to measure pension expense. Prior to the recent revision of Section 3460, the provision for pension expense was based on one of several actuarial funding methods. Consistent use of any one of the actuarial funding methods selected was considered to result in a systematic and rational allocation of the total cost of pensions during the employees' years of active service. Furthermore, the use of a common actuarial method by all firms would enhance the comparability of reported pension costs and other information.

ACTUARIAL METHODS—A CLOSER LOOK

As indicated by the previous discussion, actuarial methods are important from two viewpoints. First, they are used to insure that enough funds are on hand at retirement; second, they are used to measure and report pension expense and related liability.

Two general approaches are often considered when an actuarial method is being selected: the cost approach and the benefit approach. **Cost approaches** project an estimated total benefit at retirement and then compute the level cost that will be sufficient, together with interest expected to accumulate at the assumed rate, to provide the total benefits at retirement. (The cost allocated to each period may be level in dollar amount or level as a percentage of salary.) The example used in the previous section illustrates a cost approach that is level in dollar amount ($16,379.75 each year). **Benefit approaches,** on the other hand, determine the amount of pension benefits attributable to employee service to date (earned to date) and then compute the present value of these benefits.

To illustrate the theory underlying the benefit approaches, assume that Royal Ltd. requests that an actuarial study be made of a proposed pension plan.[3] The actuarial firm of Harlowe & Sons is commissioned to provide information on an appropriate funding pattern and the pension expense that Royal Ltd. might incur for a typical employee. The typical employee has the following characteristics:

1. The employee works for three years and then retires.
2. The employee's salary is as follows: 1987, $30,000; 1988, $33,000; 1989, $36,300.
3. The defined benefit formula states that the pension benefit is 1% of final salary for each year of service, payable as a lump sum at retirement.[4]
4. The interest rate (discount rate) is 12%.

From this information, the amount needed to meet the benefits required at the retirement date is $1,089, computed as follows:

Salary at retirement	$36,300
Formula rate	1%
	$ 363
Years of service	3
Benefits required at retirement	$ 1,089

If $1,089 is the amount of the benefits that must be paid at retirement, at what amount should the pension expense and related pension obligation be reported in 1987, 1988, and 1989?

Accumulated Benefits Approach

Two benefit approaches are discussed in this chapter: the accumulated benefits approach and the projected benefits/pro rated on service approach. Under the first approach, a pension expense is computed each period solely on the basis of the plan formula applied to years of service to date and **based on existing salary levels**.

---

[3]The example is adapted from "Employers' Accounting for Pensions and Other Postemployment Benefits," *FASB Discussion Memorandum* (Stamford, Conn.: FASB, 1981), pp. 52–54.

[4]Normally, a lump-sum payment will not be made at the time of retirement. That is, most pension plans provide benefits to the employee on a periodic basis as long as the retiree lives. A lump-sum payment is assumed here to simplify the issue because a number of different periodic payments to retirees can be made equivalent to a lump-sum distribution at retirement.

To illustrate, for 1987 the following computation for Royal Ltd.'s typical employee is as follows:

Accumulated Benefits Approach 1987	Benefits	Expense	Liability
Benefits attributed to date by plan formula (.01 × $30,000 × 1 year)	$300		
Liability at end of 1987 Present value at 12% of $300 payable in 2 years ($300 × .79719)			$239.16
Expense for 1987 Compensation component		$239.16	
Interest component		–0–	
Total		$239.16	

The computation above indicates that the total benefit to be paid to date (December 31, 1987) is $300 based on current salary and years of service. Because this benefit will not have to be paid for two more years, the expense is $239.16—the present value of the $300 payment to be made in two years. The pension obligation is also $239.16 ($300 × .79719).

Note that the 1987 interest component is reported as zero. This component indicates that if the pension cost is not funded fully each period, an adjustment to pension expense is needed. In 1988, the following is reported:

Accumulated Benefits Approach 1988	Benefits	Expense	Liability
Benefits attributed to date by plan formula (.01 × $33,000 × 2 years)	$660		
Liability at end of 1988 Present value at 12% of $660 payable in 1 year ($660 × .89286)			$589.29
Expense for 1988 Compensation component Increase in plan benefit ($660 − $300 = $360) Present value at 12% of $360 payable in 1 year ($360 × .89286)		$321.43	
Interest component Interest on previous year's liability ($239.16 × 12%)		28.70	
Total		$350.13	

In 1988, the pension obligation is adjusted on the basis of the employee's present salary and years of service. The pension expense is computed as the present value of the increase in the present value of plan benefits from 1987 to 1988. That is, in 1988, when a new salary level is achieved, the compensation component of pension expense increases. Note that pension expense is also increased by the interest component on the obligation from 1987. If the obligation is not funded at the end of 1987, then interest expense is incurred, which is considered part of pension expense. The computations for 1989 are as follows:

	Benefits	Expense	Liability
Accumulated Benefits Approach			
1989			
Benefits attributable to date by plan formula (.01 × $36,300 × 3 years)	$1,089		
Liability at end of 1989			
Present value at 12% of $1,089 payable today			$1,089
Expense for 1989			
Compensation component			
Increase in plan benefit			
($1,089 − $660 = $429)			
Present value at 12% of $429 payable today		$429.00	
Interest component			
Interest on previous year's			
liability ($589.29 × 12%)		70.71	
Total		$499.71	

As indicated from this information, the following is reported for Royal Ltd. (assuming the plan was unfunded):

	Royal Ltd. (Unfunded)	
Year	Pension Expense	Pension Liability
1987	$239.16	$ 239.16
1988	350.13	589.29
1989	499.71	1,089.00

Projected Benefits Approach Pro Rated on Services

The **projected benefits approach pro rated on services** (PB/PS) is very similar to the accumulated benefits approach. The major difference is that the accumulated benefits approach assigns expense and computes the obligation on the basis of **current pay**, whereas the projected benefits approach pro rated on services uses the **final pay** as its basis. The projected benefits approach pro rated on services therefore requires an estimate of the total benefits to be paid. Use of this approach means that future salaries must be projected in order to determine funding policy as well as recognition of pension expense and the related obligation. To illustrate this approach, the following computations are made for Royal Ltd. for its typical employee:

Projected Benefits Approach Pro Rated on Services 1987	Benefits	Expense	Liability
Benefits attributed to 1987 ($1,089 ÷ 3 years)	$363		
Liability at end of 1987 Present value at 12% of $363 payable in 2 years ($363 × .79719)			$289.38
Expense for 1987 Compensation component Present value at 12% of $363 payable in 2 years		$289.38	
Interest component		–0–	
Total		$289.38	

The computations are self-explanatory. Note that the benefits are not considered in terms of current benefits but in terms of projected benefits.

In this situation, the plan's benefit formula is used as a basis for measuring how much benefit is earned and therefore how much cost is incurred. The computation for 1988 is shown below:

Projected Benefits Approach Pro Rated on Services 1988	Benefits	Expense	Liability
Benefits attributed to 1988 ($1,089 ÷ 3 years)	$363		
Benefits attributed to date ($363 × 2 years)	$726		
Liability at end of 1988 Present value at 12% of $726 payable in 1 year ($726 × .89286)			$648.22
Expense for 1988 Compensation component Present value at 12% of $363 payable in 1 year ($363 × .89286)		$324.11	
Interest component Interest on previous year's liability ($289.38 × 12%)		34.73	
Total		$358.84	

For 1988, note the interest component that affects pension expense. The computation for 1989 is as follows:

Projected Benefits Approach Pro Rated on Services 1989	Benefits	Expense	Liability
Benefits attributed to 1989 ($1,089 ÷ 3 years)	$363		
Benefits attributed to date ($363 × 3 years)	$1,089		
Liability at end of 1989 Present value at 12% of $1,089 payable today			$1,089
Expense for 1989 Compensation component Present value at 12% of $363 payable today		$363.00	
Interest component Interest on previous year's liability ($648.22 × 12%)*		77.78	
Total		$440.78	

*Adjusted $.01 for rounding

The projected benefits approach pro rated on services is required by Section 3460.28 of the *CICA Handbook*. A comparison between the accumulated benefits approach and the projected benefits approach pro rated on services is as follows:

Year	Accumulated Benefits Approach Pension Expense	Pension Liability	Projected Benefits Approach Pension Expense	Pension Liability
1987	$239.16	$ 239.16	$289.38	$ 289.38
1988	350.13	589.29	358.84	648.22
1989	499.71	1,089.00	440.78	1,089.00

The obligation computed under the accumulated benefits approach is referred to as the **accumulated benefit obligation**. It is the present value of benefits attributed by the pension benefit formula to service before a specified date; it is based on employee service and compensation (if applicable) prior to that date.

The obligation computed under the projected benefits approach pro rated on services is the **projected benefit obligation**. It is the present value as of a certain date of all benefits attributed by the pension benefit formula to employee service rendered to that date. The projected benefit obligation is measured using assumptions as to future compensation levels if the pension benefit formula is based on those future compensation levels. As indicated earlier, the accumulated benefit obligation differs from the projected benefit obligation in that it does not consider future compensation levels. As a result, the obligation under the projected benefits approach pro rated on services will be higher than it would be under the accumulated benefits approach (assuming salary increases).

Plans in which the pension benefit is based on future compensation are often called **pay-related, final-pay, final-average-pay**, or **career-average-pay plans**. For example, the formula used earlier to compute pension benefits is an example of a final-pay plan in that the benefit formula bases benefits on the employee's compensation for a specified number of years near the end of the employee's service period. It should be noted that certain pension plans such as **non-pay-related** or **flat-benefit plans** are not based on future compensation levels. (A flat-benefit plan pays a fixed amount per year of service, such as $200 per year of service.) In a non-pay-related or flat-benefit plan, the accumulated benefit obligation and the projected benefit obligation are the same.

In summary, the two actuarial methods used to assign pension costs and measure the pension obligation are:

1. **Accumulated benefit obligation**, which is the present value of benefits to date based on current salary levels.
2. **Projected benefit obligation**, which is the present value of benefits accrued to date based on future salary levels.[5]

ACCOUNTING ISSUES

Up to this point, we have shown how a pension plan operates. As indicated, the prospective benefits to be paid present or expected retirees is a function of many factors. After the prospective benefit obligation is determined, the actuary determines how this obligation can be funded. Numerous actuarial funding methods can be used; the final selection depends upon the company's preferences. Some companies fund higher amounts earlier, whereas others choose a method that will require higher contributions later.

Now that the basic operations of a pension plan are understood, the next question is "How do we account for the costs, assets, and liabilities associated with these plans?" In accounting for pensions, three major issues are involved:

1. How should the cost of the pension plan be allocated to the proper accounting periods?
2. How should the assets and obligations arising from a pension plan be measured and reported?
3. How should the status and effects of the pension plan be disclosed in the financial statements and related notes?

PENSION EXPENSE

Until the mid-1960s, with few exceptions, companies applied the **cash basis** of accounting to pension plans by recognizing the amount paid in a particular accounting period for pension benefits as the pension expense for the period. However, the amount paid or funded in a fiscal period is dependent upon financial management and may be discretionary. For example, funding may be based on the availability of cash, the level of earnings, or other factors unrelated to proper measurement of pension expense. While alternative funding methods are appropriate for cash

---

[5]When the term present value of benefits is used throughout this chapter, it really means the actuarial present value of benefits. Actuarial present value is the amount payable adjusted to reflect the time value of money and the probability of payment (by means of decrements for events such as death, disability, withdrawals, or retirement) between the present date and the expected date of payment. For simplicity, the term present value will be used in this discussion instead of actuarial present value.

management purposes, the amount funded should not be used to determine the amount of the periodic pension expense.[6]

There is broad agreement now that pension cost should be accounted for on the **accrual basis**. Most accountants and an increasing number of business managers recognize that **accounting for pension plans requires measurement of the cost and its identification with the appropriate time periods**, which involves application of accrual, deferral, and estimation concepts in the same manner that they are applied in the measurement and the time-period identification of other costs and expenses. The determination of pension cost, however, is extremely complicated because it is a function of the following factors:

Service Cost. As indicated earlier, a pension arrangement is generally viewed as a promise by the employer to provide an employee's pension in return for services provided by the employee. In this view, a pension is viewed as a form of **deferred compensation** that will be paid to the employee upon retirement. It follows that the cost of the pension accrues over the period that the employee provides services to the employer. This component of pension expense is often referred to as the **service cost** component or **normal cost** component.

Interest. Because a pension is a deferred compensation arrangement, this element of wages is deferred; therefore, a liability results. In effect, the employee provides a service and the company incurs a liability. Because the liability is not paid until maturity, it is measured on a discounted basis. Each year interest accrues on the pension obligation. While some argue that this interest is actually a cost of financing, it is treated as an **addition** to pension expense.

Past Service Cost. Plan initiation or amendment often includes provisions to increase benefits for service provided in prior years. For example, an employer may amend a final-pay plan. As a result of this amendment, credit may be provided for past service. Because plan amendments are granted with the expectation that the employer will realize economic benefits in future periods, the cost of providing these retroactive benefits is generally considered to be allocated to pension expense in the future.

Expected Return on Plan Assets. The employer may discharge its liability for deferred wages by funding the liability as it occurs. In this case, the assets contributed to the fund and interest thereon should be sufficient to pay the pension claimants. The amount of interest expected to be earned on fund assets (expected return of plan assets) is a **reduction** of the periodic pension expense. In a fully funded plan, interest on the pension obligation would be exactly offset by the expected return on plan assets. If, however, as a result of estimates that have been inaccurate or a funding method that does not keep the fund assets equal to the pension obligation, interest on the obligation will not equal the expected return on plan assets. In these situations, pension expense will be increased (reduced) by the excess (deficiency) of interest over expected return.

Experience Gains and Losses. Experience gains and losses arise from two sources: (1) projected obligations that do not materialize and, consequently, do not agree with the obligation determined using year-end assumptions, and (2) when the expected return on plan assets is not equal to the actual return accomplished. As indicated earlier, a set of assumptions is used to estimate the pension obligation and the fund balance. If these assumptions are proven to be inaccurate by later events such as changes in service lives, adjustments are needed. That is, the experience gains and losses that develop as a result of the difference between actual and expected experience must be accounted for.

---

[6]For example, two once-common funding methods, **pay-as-you-go** (recognize pension costs only when benefits are paid directly to the retired employee) and **terminal funding** (recognize pension costs when annuity is purchased or contribution is made to the trust for retired employees), are no longer considered acceptable. They are cash-basis oriented and do not recognize pension costs prior to the retirement of employees.

In summary, then, the components of pension expense and their effect are as follows:

Service cost (increases pension expense).
Interest (increases pension expense).
Expected return on plan assets (decreases pension expense).
Past service cost (generally increases pension expense).
Experience gains and losses (increases and decreases pension expense).

Each of these factors is discussed in more detail in the following sections.

Service Cost

What appropriate method should be used to assign the cost of deferred compensation associated with a pension plan to accounting periods? Historically, accounting for this service cost component has been based on actuarial funding methods that were developed for funding purposes. Although many argue that the means of funding a plan should not dictate how pension cost should be charged to expense, for all practical purposes, an actuarial funding method invariably was used as a basis to determine expense recognition.

In Section 3460 of the *CICA Handbook*, the Accounting Standards Committee indicated that the service cost component recognized in a period **should be determined as the actuarial present value of benefits attributed by the pension benefit formula to employee service during that period**. According to this view, only the benefit approaches discussed earlier should be considered as a basis for assigning pension cost to an accounting period. The Committee's position is understandable in that accounting should look to the terms of the agreement as a basis for recording expenses and obligations. The plan's benefit formula provides a measure of how much benefit is earned and, therefore, how much cost is incurred in each individual period.

The Committee also stated that the usefulness of pension information could be improved if the present range of methods of allocating pension cost were narrowed. The Committee noted that the use of a single pension accounting approach would improve comparability and understandability of financial reporting even if it were determined that no one approach provided a better measure than the alternatives. The question then is the following: Which of the benefit approaches best meets the objective of reporting benefits owed to date?

The Committee concluded that **future compensation levels had to be considered in measuring the present obligation and periodic pension expense if the plan benefit formula incorporated them.** In other words, the present obligation resulting from a promise to pay a benefit of 1% of an employee's **final pay** is different than an employer's promise to pay 1% of **current pay**. To ignore this fact would be to ignore an important aspect of pension expense.

As a result, **the Committee indicated that the projected benefits method pro rated on services should be used for pension benefit formulas that define benefits for all years of service**. As indicated earlier, this method incorporates the final pay in determining pension expense and the related pension liability. If the pension benefit formula does not reflect the substance of the arrangement, then specific rules must be followed that are beyond the scope of this discussion.

Some object to this determination, on the basis that a company should have more freedom to select an expense recognition pattern. Others believe that incorporating future salary increases into current pension expense is accounting for events that have not happened yet. They argue that if the plan were terminated today, only liabilities for benefits earned by service to date would have to be paid. Nevertheless, the Committee indicated that the projected benefit obligation provides a more realistic measure on a going-concern basis of the employer's obligation under the plan.

Interest

The second component of pension expense is interest. As indicated earlier, a pension is a deferred compensation arrangement under which this element of wages is deferred and an obligation is created. Because the obligation is not paid until maturity, it is measured on a discounted basis and accrues interest due to the passage of time over the life of the employee. The interest component for the period is computed on the projected benefit obligation outstanding during the period. For example, in the illustrations of the projected benefits approach pro rated on services on pages 988–989, the interest cost component of pension expense is $34.73 for 1988 and $77.78 for 1989.

How is the interest rate determined? The Committee stated that the assumed discount rate should **reflect management's best estimates**. In determining these rates, it would be appropriate for management to look to available information about rates implicit in current prices of annuity contracts that could be used to effect settlement of the obligation. (Under an annuity contract, an insurance company unconditionally guarantees to provide specific pension benefits to specific individuals in return for a fixed consideration or premium.) Other rates of return on high-quality, fixed-income investments might also be employed.

The interest component is an extremely important part of pension expense. If a company uses a high interest rate to discount its projected benefits, the projected benefit obligation will be small. Thus, the pension plan may appear overfunded when it is not; or, if too low an interest rate is used, it may appear underfunded when it is not.

The *Handbook* **requires companies to select their assumptions regarding the interest rate explicitly**. That is, the interest rate assumption used should represent the best estimate of the plan's expected experience with respect to interest rates. In the past, some companies used an interest rate that did not reflect current market conditions. They used a lower rate, arguing that other assumptions counterbalanced the low interest rate used. In other words, some companies used an **implicit approach**, which means essentially using two or more assumptions that do not individually represent the best estimate of what will happen, but their aggregate effect will be the same as if explicit assumptions were used. The profession, however, believes that explicitly selecting the interest rate in realistic terms and using other assumptions consistent with the selection of a realistic rate will be more useful to financial statement readers. To emphasize why this is true, one only has to look at the wide variances of interest rates that have been used by corporations. For example, in one recent year, the interest rates used by a number of large companies varied by as much as 9.5 points. It is obvious that some companies were using an explicit rate and others an implicit rate, which leads to difficulty in evaluating the overall soundness of a pension plan.

Expected Return on Plan Assets

A third component of pension expense is the expected return earned on plan assets. This is referred to variously as the expected return on plan assets, expected asset return rate, and expected asset earnings rate. This rate is multiplied by the plan assets (defined below) to arrive at the expected return on plan assets. This component will be referred to as the expected return and homework problems should be worked accordingly.

Plan assets for purposes of applying the rate of return are usually shares, bonds, and other investments such as real estate that have been segregated and restricted to provide for pension claims. Plan assets include contributions made by the employer and contributions made by employees when a contributory plan of some type is involved. Plan assets cannot normally be withdrawn from the plan. Pension assets that are still under the control of the company are not considered plan assets. That is, if the company may use these assets as it desires, the company has not funded the pension plan. Pension assets must be segregated in a trust or effectively restricted to be considered plan assets. Receivables from the employer should not be considered plan assets for purposes of applying interest because the employer has not provided the funds on which to earn interest.

A final question relates to how plan assets should be valued. Some argue that **plan assets should be measured at their fair value**. Fair value (market value) is defined as the amount that the plan could reasonably expect to receive for its assets in a current sale between a willing buyer and seller. Thus, a forced liquidation value would not be considered an appropriate measure of fair value. For many investments for which an active market exists, the market price is considered to represent fair value. If no market is available, similar types of assets selling in an active market should be used. Where a market price is not available, the present value of estimated future cash flows may be used. Plan assets used in the plan operations, such as buildings, equipment, and furniture, would be measured at cost less depreciation or amortization.

Others disagree with measuring plan assets at fair value only at a certain date for purposes of determining the expected return on plan assets. They note that fair value can change dramatically from day to day based on factors that might in the long run offset one another. Some type of moving average to dampen or smooth out random fluctuations in fair values would be more appropriate. A major concern with the use of fair value is that it may lead to increased volatility related to pension expense and therefore to reported income.

Although the Committee believes that the use of **market values** at the reporting date is appropriate, it also permits companies to use an asset value that reflects an **average of fair values over a period of time**. When a moving average of asset values is used, the term should not exceed five years and the underlying assumptions used should be consistent with those used by the actuary in determining the value of accrued benefits. Since market values may not be available for some assets in the pension fund, other valuation methods such as **appraisals** and **discounted present values** may be used. Since a variety of valuation methods may be used and each method reflects either market or an approximation of market values, the phrase ''**market-related values**'' is used to denote any one of the above methods. The method used by a company should be consistent from period to period.

Past Service Cost

When a defined benefit plan is either initiated (plan adoption) or amended, credit is often given to employees for years of service provided before the date of initiation or amendment. As a result of this change, both the accumulated benefit obligation and the projected benefit obligation are usually greater than before. In many cases, the increase in the accumulated or projected benefit obligation is substantial.

One question that arises is whether an expense and related liability for these **past service costs** (often referred to as **retroactive benefits**) should be fully reported at the time a plan is initiated or is amended to increase benefits. Since it is not likely that an employer would provide credit for past years of service unless it expected a future benefit, **the retroactive benefits should not be recognized entirely as an expense in the year of amendment but should be recognized during the service periods of those employees who are expected to receive benefits under the plan.**

The cost of the retroactive benefits is the increase in the projected benefit obligation at the date of the amendment. In assigning the cost of these retroactive benefits, one approach is to assign an equal amount to each future period of service of employee group active at the date of amendment. It is recognized that it is difficult to determine the number of periods benefited by a retroactive plan amendment. However, the criterion of basing amortization on the expected future service life of the employee group active at the time of the plan amendment is reasonable.

Some argue that a declining amortization charge is a suitable method of assigning past service costs to the appropriate accounting periods. Some of the employees who are granted retroactive benefits are likely to leave or retire each year. Consequently, the amount of employee services to be received will also decline. Therefore, higher costs should be allocated to the earlier years.

Determination of proportion of cost to be assigned to each year would be quite speculative and could prove to be inaccurate. The straight-line approach (assigning an equal amount to each year of expected future service), on the other hand, is simple to apply. Since most companies are likely to use the straight-line amortization method for past service costs, homework problems should be solved using the straight-line method.

To illustrate the amortization of past service cost under the straight-line approach, assume that Soft-White Ltd. has a defined benefit pension plan covering its 90 employees. In its negotiations with its employees, Soft-White agrees to change its pension formula from 1% to 2% of the last three years of pay multiplied by the number of years of service on January 1, 1989. As a result, assume that the projected benefit obligation increased by $900,000. This amount should be amortized over the expected average remaining service life (EARSL) of the employee group benefiting from the plan amendment. To compute the expected average remaining service life, it is first necessary to compute the expected number of employee-years of service. This computation is illustrated in the following schedule.

Individuals	Expected Departures[a]	Years of Service[b]
A1-A9	9	9
B1-B9	9	18
C1-C9	9	27
D1-D9	9	36
E1-E9	9	45
F1-F9	9	54
G1-G9	9	63
H1-H9	9	72
I1-I9	9	81
J1-J9	9	90
	90	495[c]

[a] The number of employees expected to depart in the year shown.
[b] The total years of service at January 1, 1987, from the group of employees expected to depart in the year shown.
[c] This amount is the total expected future years of service. The total expected future years of service can also be computed by the following formula:

$$\frac{N(N + 1)}{2} \times P = \text{Total Expected Future Years of Service,}$$

where N = the number of years over which services will be performed and P = population decrements each year.

The computation of the expected average remaining service life is, therefore, as follows:

$$\frac{\text{Total Expected Future Years of Service}}{\text{Number of Employees}} = \frac{\text{Average Remaining}}{\text{Service Period}}$$

$$\frac{495}{90} = 5.5 \text{ years}$$

The straight-line periodic amortization amount would be $163,636.36 ($900,000 ÷ 5.5). Note that the $900,000 projected benefit obligation is **not** recorded as a liability. Therefore, the entry to record the periodic amortization (usually combined with the entry to record the year's pension expense) and the funding payment (assumed to be $200,000) would be as follows:

Pension Expense	163,636.36	
Deferred Pension Cost	36,363.64	
Cash		200,000.00

Note that employees hired after the date of amendment are not considered in the computation. A plan amendment can reduce, rather than increase, the projected benefit obligation. Such an amount would be amortized in the same manner as increases in the projected benefit obligation.

Experience Gains and Losses

As discussed earlier, actuaries deal with several uncertainties in estimating the cost of a pension plan. In tentatively resolving these uncertainties, actuaries make assumptions. Assumptions, for example, usually have to be made about such items as the interest rate, mortality rate, retirement rate, turnover rate, disability rate, and salary amounts. Seldom does actual experience coincide with estimated results. Consequently, **adjustments may need to be made to reflect (1) deviations between estimated conditions and actual experience and (2) revisions in the underlying assumptions**. These adjustments are referred to as "experience gains and losses." If the experience is favourable (actual earnings rate exceeds the projected earnings rate) or if the new assumptions are more optimistic, the adjustments that result are gains; if experience has been unfavourable (i.e., salary rates of employees are higher than projected salary rates) or if the new assumptions are less optimistic, the adjustments are losses. The net effect of the gains and losses determined in a particular valuation period is dealt with as a single amount.

Once the gains and losses have been identified and measured, the problem becomes one of determining how they should affect the computation of pension expense. The profession requires that these gains and losses be amortized over an "appropriate" period of time, which is generally the expected average remaining service life of the employee group.

To illustrate how experience gains or losses affect pension expense, assume the same information that was used by Soft-White Ltd. to compute amortization of past service cost (see page 995).

Experience gains and losses are generally amortized in the current period only if, as of the **beginning of the year**, there is an unamortized gain or loss. That is, if no unamortized gain or loss existed at the beginning of the period, there usually will be no recognition of gains or losses in the current period. This delay in recognition is acceptable because the gains and losses are long-term in nature and it is more convenient to begin amortization in the fiscal period following their occurrence.

To illustrate the amortization of gains and losses, assume the following additional information for Soft-White Ltd.:

Soft-White Ltd.
Calculation of Net Experience Losses (Gains)

Fund Assets

	1987	1988	1989
Fund assets (first of year)	$2,190,000	$2,850,000	$3,795,000
Expected return on fund assets	219,000	285,000	379,500
Funding contributions (end of year)	590,000	625,000	648,000
Projected asset value	2,999,000	3,760,000	4,822,500
Market-related asset value	2,850,000	3,795,000	4,950,000
Experience loss (gain)	$ 149,000	$ (35,000)	$ (127,500)

Pension Obligation

	1987	1988	1989
Pension obligation (first of year)	$2,190,000	$2,950,000	$3,800,000
Past service cost (plan amendment)	–0–	–0–	900,000
Interest (10%)	219,000	295,000	470,000
Accrual for service (at end of year)	590,000	625,000	648,000
Expected obligation	2,999,000	3,870,000	5,818,000
Year-end actual	2,950,000	3,800,000	5,990,000
Experience gain (loss)	$ 49,000	$ 70,000	$ (172,000)

Net Experience Loss (Gain)

	1987	1988	1989
Fund assets	$149,000	$ (35,000)	$(127,500)
Pension obligation	(49,000)	(70,000)	172,000
Net experience loss (gain)	$100,000	$(105,000)	$ 44,500

If the expected average remaining service life is 5.5 years, the schedule to amortize the loss is as follows:

Soft-White Ltd.
Amortization of Experience Loss (Gain)

	1987	1988	1989
Opening balance	$ –0–	$100,000	$(23,182)
Experience loss (gain)	100,000	(105,000)	44,500
Amortization of 1987 loss*		(18,182)	(18,182)
Amortization of 1988 gain**			19,090
Closing balance	$100,000	$(23,182)	$ 22,226

*$100,000 ÷ 5.5
**($105,000) ÷ 5.5

As indicated from the schedule, the loss recognized in 1988 increased pension expense by $18,182. This amount is small in comparison with the total loss of $100,000. The net amount (gain) of the 1989 amortization would be $908 [($100,000 ÷ 5.5) + (−$105,000 ÷ 5.5)]. Note that it has been assumed that the expected average remaining service life remained constant (5.5 years). In practice, the expected average remaining service life may change from year to year.

PENSION LIABILITIES

The question of pension liabilities is very controversial. Some believe that the unfunded projected benefit obligation should be recognized as a liability. Others argue that the unfunded accumulated benefit obligation is more reliable and represents the amount that firms would be required to pay if making immediate settlement. The profession in the United States has adopted a modified version of this approach.

Finally, there is substantial support for the argument that pension benefit obligations are too difficult to measure with sufficient accruacy to warrant any liability recognition. The accounting profession in Canada has adopted the latter approach. No pension liability is recognized as such. However, the cumulative difference between the amounts included in pension expense and the amounts contributed to the fund is recorded as either a deferral or an accrual. That is, if the cumulative amount of pension expense exceeds the cumulative amounts funded, an "accrued pension cost" account is established. On the other hand, if the funding amount exceeds the amount expensed, a "deferred pension cost" account is used to balance the entries. The use of these accounts is illustrated in the following section.

ILLUSTRATIVE ACCOUNTING ENTRIES

To illustrate the accounting entries that result under a defined benefit plan, assume that on January 1, 1988, Hadley Ltd. adopts a defined benefit pension plan. No retroactive benefits are provided for existing employees. The plan is noncontributory. A bank is engaged as trustee for the pension fund. An actuarial consulting firm recommends a 10% interest rate as appropriate to settle any projected benefit obligation. The expected return on plan assets is also 10%. No gains and losses have occurred. Funding payments are made to the bank at the end of the year. The accrued benefits pro rated on services results in a service cost component of pension expense of $100,000 for 1988 and of $110,000 for 1989.

Case A—Pension Expense and Pension Funding the Same

Management decides to fund the pension plan at exactly the same amount at which it records the pension expense. That is, management decides to use the projected benefits approach pro rated on services for funding and to comply with Section 3460 to measure pension expense. In order to simplify the calculations, it is assumed that pension costs accrue at year end and that funding payments are also made at the end of each year.

The components of pension expense for 1988 are provided below:

Service cost	$100,000
Interest on projected benefit obligation ($0 × 10%)	–0–
Expected return on plan assets ($0 × 10%)	–0–
Pension expense	$100,000

As a result, the following entries are made in 1988:

Pension Expense	100,000	
Cash		100,000

In 1988, the beginning balances of both the projected benefit obligation and the plan assets were zero. As a result, no interest is incurred on the pension obligation and there is no expected return on plan assets during 1988. In addition, there are no gains or losses or prior service cost.

The components of pension expense for 1989 are provided below:

Service cost	$110,000
Interest on projected benefit obligation ($100,000 × 10%)	10,000
Expected return on plan assets ($100,000 × 10%)	(10,000)
Pension expense	$110,000

In 1989, the entry to record pension expense is as follows:

Pension Expense	110,000	
Cash		110,000

As indicated earlier, a pension fund is established and maintained for the purpose of accumulating the amounts necessary to pay retirement benefits as they become due. The primary source of pension funds is, of course, the periodic contributions of the employer. Another source of funds assumed in determining the amount of the employer's contributions and expense is the earnings on the pension fund assets.

Case B—Pension Expense Higher than Pension Funding

Assume the same facts as those above, except that management decides to fund a lesser amount in the earlier years of the pension plan. The funding pattern is $90,000 for 1988 and $95,000 for 1989.

In this situation, the pension plan is considered underfunded; that is, the employer chooses to fund the plan at an amount less than the $100,000 incurred amount. As a result, an accrual for pension cost is reported. This amount is reported in the liabilities section of the balance sheet. We use one general account, Accrued/Deferred Pension Cost, to account for the difference between the amount expensed and the amount funded. If this account has a credit balance, it is identified as accrual; if it has a debit balance, it is an asset called deferred pension cost. The computation for pension expense for 1988 is provided below:

Service cost	$100,000
Interest on projected benefit obligation ($0 × 10%)	–0–
Expected return on plan assets ($0 × 10%)	–0–
Pension expense	$100,000

The entry to record pension expense in 1988 is as follows:

Pension Expense	100,000	
Cash		90,000
Accrued/Deferred Pension Cost		10,000

In 1989, because the employer underfunds the pension plan, earnings do not materialize in an amount actuarially assumed to meet the projected benefit obligation. The computation of the pension expense for 1989 is as follows:

Service cost	$110,000
Interest on projected benefit obligation ($100,000 × 10%)	10,000
Expected return on plan assets ($90,000 × 10%)	(9,000)
Pension expense	$111,000

The pension expense is recorded as follows:

Pension Expense	111,000	
Cash		95,000
Accrued/Deferred Pension Cost		16,000

Note that the balance in the projected benefit obligation (all other factors held constant) at the end of 1989 is $220,000 ($100,000 + $110,000 + $10,000); the balance in the pension plan asset fund (all other factors held constant) is $194,000 ($90,000 + $95,000 + $9,000). In addition, at the end of 1989, accrued pension cost of $26,000 is reported in the liabilities section of Hadley Ltd.'s balance sheet.

Case C—Pension Expense Lower than Pension Funding

Assume that management decides to fund the plan in 1988 at $120,000 and in 1989 at $130,000.
    The computation for pension expense for 1988 is as follows:

Service cost	$100,000
Interest on projected benefit obligation ($0 × 10%)	–0–
Expected return on plan assets ($0 × 10%)	–0–
Pension expense	$100,000

The entry to record pension expense in 1988 is as follows:

Accrued/Deferred Pension Cost	20,000	
Pension Expense	100,000	
Cash		120,000

The prepaid pension cost is classified as a deferred charge in the balance sheet. The computation of the pension expense in 1989 is as follows:

Service cost	$110,000
Interest on projected benefit obligation ($100,000 × 10%)	10,000
Expected return on plan assets ($120,000 × 10%)	(12,000)
Pension expense	$108,000

In 1989, the pension expense is recorded as follows:

Accrued/Deferred Pension Cost	22,000	
Pension Expense	108,000	
Cash		130,000

In this case, because funding exceeds the pension expense, the pension fund assets are greater than the projected benefit obligation. As a result, pension expense is decreased because the expected return on assets is higher than the interest incurred on the projected benefit obligation.

The unrecognized balance of the projected benefit obligation (all other factors held constant) at the end of 1989 is $220,000 ($100,000 + $110,000 + $10,000); the unrecognized balance in the pension plan assets (all other factors held constant) is $262,000 ($120,000 + $130,000 + $12,000); the recognized deferred pension cost in the amount of $42,000 ($20,000 + $22,000) is reported in the asset section of Hadley's balance sheet.

Case D—Amendment to the Existing Plan

Assume that Hadley Ltd. amends its pension plan at the beginning of 1989 and gives retroactive benefits to current employees for one year of past service. These retroactive benefits increase the projected benefit obligation from $100,000 to $180,000. At the time of the plan amendment, the market-related asset value of fund assets was $120,000. The past service cost is amortized over an expected average remaining service life of 20 years. Funding will be accomplished by making 20 annual payments of $9,400 at the end of each year. The service cost component for 1989 is $140,000 and is funded in that amount.

The computation to determine pension expense for 1989 is as follows:

Service cost	$140,000
Interest on projected benefit obligation ($180,000 × 10%)	18,000
Expected return on plan assets ($120,000 × 10%)	(12,000)
Amortization of unrecognized past service cost ($80,000 × 5%)	4,000
Pension expense	$150,000

The entry to record pension expense in 1989 is as follows:

Pension Expense	150,000	
Accrued/Deferred Pension Cost		600
Cash		149,400*

*$140,000 + $9,400

Assuming that pension benefits accrue at the end of the year and that funding payments are made at year end, the expected balance of the projected benefit obligation (all other factors held constant) at the end of 1989 is $338,000 ($180,000 + $140,000 + $18,000). Plan assets will have an expected balance of $281,400 (all other factors held constant) at the end of 1989. This is computed as follows:

Beginning balance	$120,000
Expected return on plan assets ($120,000 × 10%)	12,000
Service cost funding	140,000
Past service cost funding	9,400
Expected balance of plan assets	$281,400

In this case, it is sometimes difficult to understand what is being amortized because the past service cost to be amortized is unrecorded; that is, no recognized asset or liability was increased when the projected benefit obligation increased as a result of the plan amendment.

TRANSITION—A SPECIAL IMPLEMENTATION PROBLEM

Because the amendments to Section 3460 involved such significant changes in pension reporting, the Accounting Standards Committee decided to delay their adoption so that companies could adjust to the new reporting system. As a result, companies on a calendar-year reporting basis did not have to follow the requirements until 1988.

When companies changed over to the new reporting system, an important factor to be considered was the transition amount that would occur. That is the excess of the projected benefit obligation over the fair value of the pension plan assets would have to be determined and amortized in the future. This transition amount was amortized over the expected average remaining service life of the employees participating in the plan.

To illustrate, assume that Swingline Ltd. decided to adopt the requirements of Section 3460 in 1988. At the beginning of the year, its projected benefit obligation was $900,000 and the fair value of its pension plan assets was $750,000. Assuming that the expected remaining service life is ten years, the computation of the transition amount is as follows:

Projected benefit obligation	$900,000
Plan assets (at market-related value)	750,000
Unrecognized net obligation (transition amount)	$150,000

This amount is not recorded as a liability. The periodic amortization of the initial unrecognized net liability is included in pension expense.

REPORTING PENSION PLANS IN FINANCIAL STATEMENTS

Within the Financial Statements   As already indicated, if the amount paid (credit to Cash) by the employer to the pension trust is less than the annual provision (debit to Pension Expense), a credit balance accrual in the amount of the difference arises. This accrued pension cost usually appears in the long-term liability section and is described as Accrued Pension Cost.

If the cash paid (amount funded) to the pension trust during the period is greater than the amounts expensed, a deferred charge equal to the difference arises. This deferral should be reported as Deferred Pension Cost in the deferred charges section of the balance sheet.

Under present GAAP, unexpensed past service cost is not reported as a liability. Past service cost, although measured by employee service in years prior to the incurrence of the cost, is considered an expense of periods subsequent to the plan initiation or amendment. Although some argue that unfunded past service cost should be recognized as a liability on the date that the benefits are granted, past service cost is not presently considered to have accounting significance until it is recognized as expense under appropriate accrual accounting.

Within the Footnotes   Because company pension plans are frequently important to an understanding of financial position and results of operations, the following information, if not disclosed in the body of the financial statements, may be disclosed in the notes. These notes are particularly important for pensions because of inherent complexities and compromises that were made in establishing the recognition of financial statement amounts. For defined benefit plans, the *CICA Handbook* requires disclosure of "the actuarial present value of accrued pension benefits attributed to services rendered up to the reporting date and the value of pension fund assets."[7] Companies having defined contribution plans are only required to disclose the amount of the required contribution for the period.[8] Other details may be disclosed at the discretion of management. The following general disclosures and rationale for each is provided to illustrate the information that firms may wish to include in the notes to the financial statements.

1. A general description of the plan including employee groups covered, type of benefit formula, funding policy, type of assets held, and the nature and effect of significant matters affecting comparability of information for all periods presented.
     Rationale   Because the measurement of pension expense is based on the benefit formula, a description of the plan and the benefit formula is useful. Furthermore, disclosure of funding policies and types of assets held helps in determining cash flows and their likelihood, as well as highlighting the difference between cash flow and pension expense. Finally, significant events affecting the plan are noted so that the readers of financial statements can better predict these effects on long-term trends of the plan.
2. Pension expense for the period.
     Rationale   Information about the amount helps users to understand better how pension expense is determined. Thus, reasons for the change in expense from one period to the next are understood better.
3. The value of pension fund assets, the actuarial present value of accumulated pension obligations, and the date of the most recent actuarial valuation.

[7]*CICA Handbook*, Section 3460.60.
[8]*CICA Handbook*, Section 3460.65.

Rationale   The funded status of the plan is of obvious importance. In addition, some believe that the unfunded accumulated benefit obligation is a liability. In this disclosure, a reader can determine this amount.

In summary, mandatory disclosures are minimal when compared to the information that may be useful. One factor that has made pension reporting difficult to understand in the past has been the lack of consistent terminology. Furthermore, a substantial amount of offsetting was done to arrive at pension expense. These required and suggested disclosures should take some of the mystery out of pension reporting, particularly when a large cost or asset has been offset by a revenue or liability to produce small reported net amounts.

COMPREHENSIVE ILLUSTRATION

To illustrate the basic accounting issues related to pensions in a more integrated fashion, assume that Astro-Technology Ltd. has a defined benefit pension plan that covers all of its 100 full-time employees. Prior to January 1, 1988, the cumulative pension expense recognized equalled cumulative contributions. On January 1, 1988, the company decided to adopt the accounting method prescribed in Section 3460 of the *CICA Handbook*. The projected benefit obligation and plan assets were as follows:

Projected benefit obligation	$1,000,000
Plan assets (at market-related value)	900,000
Unrecognized net obligation (transition amount)	$ 100,000

Consultation with Astro-Technology's actuaries elicits the following information:

1. Under the projected benefits approach pro rated on services, the service cost component of pension expense is $300,000 for 1988.
2. The funding pattern selected requires a contribution of $334,000 to be made to the pension fund in 1988.
3. The interest rate used by the actuary is 9% and the expected rate of return on fund assets is 9%.
4. Five percent of the 100 employees are expected to leave (either retire or quit) in each of the next 20 years.   EARSL = 20×21 × 0.05 ÷2 = 10.5 yrs
5. Funding payments are made at the end of each year and pension benefits are assumed to accrue at year end.
6. Other relevant information as of December 31, 1988 is as follows:

Market-related asset value	$1,275,000
Projected benefit obligation	$1,385,000

Computation of Pension Expense

To compute the amount to be reported as pension expense in 1988, the company must determine five components. These are (1) service cost, (2) interest on accumulated benefit obligation, (3) expected return on plan assets, (4) amortization of experience gains and losses, and (5) amortization of the transition amount.

Determining three of these components for 1988 is relatively straightforward. The amounts are as follows:

Service cost (given)	$300,000
Interest on projected benefit obligation ($1,000,000 × 9%)	90,000
Expected return on plan assets ($900,000 × 9%)	(81,000)
Amortization of experience gain or loss	–0–

As indicated earlier, the service cost component under the projected benefits approach pro rated on services is $300,000. Interest is computed on the beginning balance of the projected benefit obligation. The expected rate of return (9%) on plan assets is multiplied by the beginning market-related asset value to provide the expected return on plan assets. Since the provisions of the *Handbook*, Section 3460, are being applied for the first time, there are no experience gains or losses at the beginning of 1988.

The computation of the final component of pension expense for 1988 is amortization of the transition amount. Given that the company has 100 employees who are expected to receive benefits under the plan, and 5% are expected to depart or retire each year, the number of employee-years of service is computed as follows:

Year	Expected Departures[a]	Years of Service[b]
1988	5	5
1989	5	10
1990	5	15
1991	5	20
1992	5	25
1993	5	30
1994	5	35
1995	5	40
1996	5	45
1997	5	50
1998	5	55
1999	5	60
2000	5	65
2001	5	70
2002	5	75
2003	5	80
2004	5	85
2005	5	90
2006	5	95
2007	5	100
	100	1,050[c]

[a]The number of the original 100 employees expected to depart in the year shown.

[b]The total years of service at January 1, 1988, from the group of employees expected to depart in the year shown.

[c]The total expected future years of service. The total expected years of service can also be computed by the following formula:

$$\frac{N(N + 1)}{2} \times P = \text{Total Expected Future Years of Service,}$$

where N = the number of years over which services will be performed and P = population decrements each year.

The computation of the expected average remaining service life is follows:

$$\frac{\text{Total Expected Future Years of Service}}{\text{Number of Employees}} = \frac{\text{Average Remaining}}{\text{Service Period}}$$

$$\frac{1,050}{100} = 10.5 \text{ years}$$

The amortization of the transition amount is therefore computed as follows:

$$\frac{\text{Orginal Transition Amount}}{\text{Average Remaining Service Period}} = \frac{\text{Amortization of Transition}}{\text{Amount}}$$

$$\frac{\$100,000}{10.5} = \$9,524$$

As indicated, Astro-Technology amortizes $9,524 of the $100,000 transition amount to expense. The computation of pension expense for 1988 is as follows:

Astro-Technology Ltd. Computation of Pension Expense—1988	
Service cost (given)	$300,000
Interest on projected benefit obligation ($1,000,000 × 9%)	90,000
Expected return on plan assets ($900,000 × 9%)	(81,000)
Amortization of experience gain or loss	–0–
Amortization of transition amount	9,524
Pension expense	$318,524

The entry to record pension expense and the funding payment for 1988 is as follows:

Pension Expense	318,524	
Accrued/Deferred Pension Cost	15,476	
Cash		334,000

Financial Statement Presentations—1988

The deferred pension cost of $15,476 would be reported on the balance sheet for Astro-Technology at the end of 1988. This would appear as follows:

Astro-Technology Ltd. BALANCE SHEET As of December 31, 1988 (Pension Information Only)	
Assets	
Intangible assets	
Deferred pension cost	$15,476

The 1988 pension expense of $318,524 would be reported in the income statement under an appropriate title.

The note disclosure in the 1988 financial statements for Astro-Technology would be as follows:

NOTE TO THE FINANCIAL STATEMENTS

Note I.   The company has a pension plan covering substantially all of its employees. The plan is contributory and provides pension benefits that are based on the employee's length of service and compensation during the three years before retirement.

Actuarial reports prepared during 1988 were based on projections of employees' compensation levels at the time of retirement. The present value of the benefits accrued and the market value of the assets available to provide these benefits as of December 31 are as follows:

Accrued pension benefits	$1,385,000
Pension fund assets	1,275,000

The 1988 pension expense of $318,524 includes the amortization of experience gains and losses and a transition amount. These amounts are being amortized on a straight-line basis over 10½ years.

The cumulative difference between the amounts expensed and the funding contribution has been reflected in the balance sheet as a long-term deferral. The amount recorded in 1988 is $15,476.

Subsequent Periods

To illustrate the proper accounting for Astro-Technology for 1989 and 1990, assume the following:

Astro-Technology Ltd.
Computation of Pension Expense
Fund Assets

	1988	1989	1990
Fund assets (first of year)	$ 900,000	$1,275,000	$1,754,000
Expected return on fund assets	81,000	114,750	157,860
Funding contributions (end of year)	334,000	347,000	351,000
Projected asset value	1,315,000	1,736,750	2,262,860
Market-related asset value	1,275,000	1,754,000	2,242,000
Experience loss (gain)	$ 40,000	$ (17,250)	$ 20,860

Pension Obligation

	1988	1989	1990
Pension obligation (first of year)	$1,000,000	$1,385,000	$1,842,000
Past service cost (at first of year)			150,000
Interest	90,000	124,650	165,780
Accrual for service (at end of year)	300,000	315,000	325,000
Expected obligation	1,390,000	1,824,650	2,482,780
Year-end actual	1,385,000	1,842,000	2,490,000
Experience gain (loss)	$ 5,000	$ (17,350)	$ (7,220)

Net Experience Loss (Gain)			
	1988	1989	1990
Opening balance—loss (gain)	$ -0-	$35,000	$31,416
Experience loss (gain) this year	35,000	100	28,080
Amortization of 1988 gain (loss)		(3,684)	(3,684)
Amortization of 1989 gain (loss)			(12)
Closing balance	$35,000	$31,416	$55,800

Pension Expense			
	1988	1989	1990
Accrual for service	$300,000	$315,000	$325,000
Interest	90,000	124,650	165,780
Expected return on plan assets	(81,000)	(114,750)	(157,860)
Amortization of experience loss (gain)	-0-	3,684	3,696
Amortization of transition amount	9,524	9,524	9,524
Amortization of past service			17,647
Total pension expense	318,524	338,108	363,787
Less: Amount funded	334,000	347,000	351,000
Accrued (deferred) pension cost	$ (15,476)	$ (8,892)	$ 12,787

Pension Entries—1989

The 1988 net experience gain ($35,000) would be amortized commencing in 1989 over the expected average remaining service life of the employee group (9.5 years). The entry to record the 1989 pension expense and funding would be as follows:

```
Pension Expense                              338,108
Accrued/Deferred Pension Cost                  8,892
   Cash                                                   347,000
      (To record pension expense and funding)
```

The balance sheet and income statement for 1989 for Astro-Technology would be as follows:

Balance Sheet	
Assets	
Intangible assets—deferred pension cost	$24,368
Income Statement	
Pension expense	$338,108

Pension Entries—1990

On January 1, 1990, the company amended the pension plan and granted credit to qualifying employees for prior services. Actuaries estimated the present value of these additional benefits to be $150,000. This amount is amortized over the expected average remaining service life (8.5 years) of the employee group beginning in 1990. The journal entries to record pension information for 1990 are as follows:

Pension Expense	363,787	
Accrued/Deferred Pension Cost		12,787
Cash		351,000
(To record pension expense and funding)		

The balance sheet and income statement for Astro-Technology for 1990 are as follows:

Balance Sheet	
Assets	
Deferred pension cost	$11,581
Income Statement	
Pension expense	$363,787

MULTIEMPLOYER PLANS

Multiemployer pension plans are plans sponsored by two or more different employers. They are often negotiated as part of labour union contracts in trucking, coal mining, construction, and entertainment industries. Although a multiemployer plan may have the characteristics of a defined benefit plan, each employer participating in the plan may not have access to the necessary actuarial amounts. In these cases, the employer would account for the pension plan as if it were a defined contribution plan.

PENSION TERMINATIONS

One politician has recently noted that "employers are simply treating their employee pension plans like company piggy banks, to be raided at will." What this person was referring to is the practice by some companies that have pension plan assets in excess of projected benefit obligations of paying off the obligation and pocketing the difference. Generally, provincial laws prevent companies from recapturing excess assets unless they pay participants what is owed to them and then terminate the plan. As a result, companies sometimes buy annuities to pay off the pension claimants and use the excess funds for other corporate purposes.[9]

The accounting issue that arises from these terminations is whether a gain should be recognized by the corporation when these assets revert back to the company. This issue is complex because, in some cases, a new defined benefit plan is started after the old one has been eliminated. Therefore, some contend that there has been no change in substance, but one in form.

The profession requires recognition in earnings of a net gain or loss when the employer settles or curtails a pension obligation either by lump-sum cash payments to participants or by purchase of annuity contracts. In other words, gains or losses arising as a result of plan settlements or curtailments are recognized immediately as unusual or extraordinary items.

---

[9]A real question exists as to whose money it is; that is, some argue that the excess funds are for the employees, not for the employer. In addition, given that the funds have been reverting to the employer, critics charge that cost-of-living increases and the possibility of other increased benefits in the future will be reduced, because companies will be reluctant to use those excess funds to pay for such increases.

POSTEMPLOYMENT BENEFITS

As well as pensions, postemployment benefits can include all forms of benefits, such as health insurance, life insurance, and disability benefits, provided to a former employee. Although these benefits have generally been charged on a pay-as-you-go basis, some argue that they are similar to pensions and should be accrued and funded prior to the time the employee retires. Because of the escalating costs of such benefits to retirees, these expenditures can be substantial.

All postemployment benefits other than pensions should be treated as contingencies. That is, they should be accrued and reported as a liability if likely to occur and reasonably estimable. If the benefits are material but not reasonably estimable, then disclosure in the notes to the financial statements is required. However, if the amount is immaterial, no disclosure is required.

TERMINATION BENEFITS PAID TO EMPLOYEES

It is not unusual for an employer to offer for a short period of time special benefits to its employees to induce termination or early retirement. These special termination or early retirement benefits can take the form of lump-sum payments, periodic future payments, or both. The payments may be made directly from the employer's assets, an existing pension fund, a new employee benefit plan, or a combination thereof. Some accountants believe that the cost of such special termination benefits should be recognized as an expense of future periods, whereas others believe that the costs of those benefits should be expensed immediately.

A recordable liability exists if the following two conditions are met:

1. The employee(s) accept the offer.
2. The amount can be reasonably estimated.

Included in the amount recognized should be (1) any lump-sum cash payments, (2) the present value of any expected future payments, and (3) if reliably measurable, the effect of the special termination benefit offer on previously accrued pension expense.

CONCLUDING OBSERVATION

The Accounting Standards Committee in its revision of Section 3460 has attempted to clarify many of the accounting issues that confused those who wished to understand the implications of a company's pension plans. Critics still argue, however, that much remains to be done. One issue in particular relates to the delayed recognition of certain events. The delayed recognition feature adopted by the Committee means that changes in pension plan obligations (such as for plan amendments) and changes in the value of plan assets are not recognized immediately but are systematically incorporated over subsequent periods. The Committee recognizes this problem, noting that the delayed recognition feature for certain events excludes the most current and most relevant information from the balance sheet. However, as indicated, it is possible to find information about the excess of plan assets over the projected benefit obligation and vice versa in the notes to the financial statements.

KEY POINTS

1. A pension plan is an arrangement whereby an employer promises income benefits for employees after they retire. Two common types are defined contribution plans and defined benefit plans. Defined benefit plans provide the most difficulty from an accounting standpoint.

2. An actuary's primary purpose is to ensure that the company has established an appropriate funding pattern. Actuaries have devised a number of actuarial funding methods to determine the periodic contributions that the employers might make to the pension fund to ensure that funds are available to meet the retirees' claim to benefits. Two general approaches considered when selecting an actuarial funding method are the cost approach and the benefit approach.

3. Two actuarial funding methods that follow the benefit approach are the accumulated benefits approach and the projected benefits approach pro rated on services. The major difference between the two approaches is that the accumulated benefits approach assigns expense and computes the obligation on the basis of current pay, whereas the projected benefits approach pro rated on services uses the final pay as its basis.

4. Three major accounting issues related to pensions are: (1) How should the cost of the pension plan be allocated to the proper accounting periods? (2) How should the assets and obligations arising from a pension plan be measured and reported? (3) How should the status of the pension plan be disclosed in the financial statements and related notes?

5. Pension cost is a function of six factors: (1) service cost, (2) interest, (3) expected return on plan assets, (4) past service cost, (5) experience gains and losses and amortization of adjustments due to changes in assumptions, and (6) amortization of the transition amount.

6. A standardized method (projected benefits approach pro rated on services) is now used for measuring pension expense. As a result, future compensation levels must be considered in measuring the present obligation and periodic pension expense if the plan benefit formula incorporates these compensation levels.

7. A discount rate (settlement rate) should be used to compute the present value of the projected benefit obligation. A market-related asset value is multiplied by the expected rate of return on plan assets to arrive at the expected return on plan assets for purposes of computing pension expense.

8. At the time of plan change (initiation or amendment of a plan), no liability should be recognized. Nor should retroactive benefits be recognized as pension expense entirely in the period of amendment; instead, they should be recognized during the service period of those employees who are expected to receive benefits under the plan.

9. Gains and losses are adjustments made to reflect (1) deviations between estimated conditions and actual experience and (2) revisions in the underlying assumptions. To eliminate wide fluctuations in pension expense caused by these gains and losses, the profession requires amortization over the estimated remaining service life of the employee group.

10. Usually, an accrued pension cost or deferred pension cost will be reported on the balance sheet when funding is different from the amount of expense recognized.

11. The required disclosures related to defined benefit pension plans are very minimal. These disclosures may provide descriptive information about the plan, the estimated amount of projected benefits, the market-related value of fund assets, the amount of pension expense for the period, and the amount of deferred or accrued pension costs.

QUESTIONS

1. Define a private pension plan. Differentiate between a funded and an unfunded pension plan. How does a contributory pension plan differ from a noncontributory plan?

2. Differentiate between a defined contribution plan and a defined benefit plan. Explain how the employer's obligation differs between the two types of plans.

3. Differentiate between "accounting for the employer" and "accounting for the pension fund."

4. The meaning of the term "fund" depends on the context in which it is used. Explain its meaning when it is used as a noun. Explain its meaning when it is used as a verb.

5. What is the role of an actuary relative to pension plans? What are actuarial assumptions?

6. Distinguish between level contribution approaches and accrued benefit approaches as used by actuaries in developing actuarial funding methods.

7. Name two accrued benefit approaches and explain how they differ.

8. Explain how the cash basis of accounting for pension plans differs from the accrual basis accounting for pension plans. Why is cash basis accounting generally considered unacceptable for pension plan accounting?

9. Identify the six components that comprise pension expense. Briefly explain the nature of each component.

10. Explain how the pension plan benefit formula affects pension expense for a period.

11. Distinguish between an explicit approach and an implicit approach with regard to assumptions made in determining pension information.

12. What is meant by "past service cost"? When is past service cost recognized as pension expense?

13. What are "experience gains and losses" as related to pension plans?

14. If pension expense recognized in a period exceeds the current amount funded by the employer, what kind of account arises and how should it be reported in the financial statements? If the reverse occurs—that is, current funding by the employer exceeds the amount recognized as pension expense—what kind of account arises and how should it be reported?

15. Morton, Inc. decided to adopt immediately the requirements of Section 3460 of the *CICA Handbook*. At the date of adoption, Morton, Inc.'s plan assets (at market value) were $900,000 and its accrued benefit obligation was $1,000,000. What is the transition amount? Will it cause a decrease or increase in pension expense in the future?

16. At the end of the current period, Warren, Inc. had an accrued benefit obligation of $400,000, pension plan assets (at market-related value) of $300,000, and a balance in deferred pension cost of $35,000. Assuming that Warren, Inc. follows Section 3460, what account(s) and amount(s) will be reported on the company's balance sheet as pension assets or pension liabilities?

17. At the end of the current year, Sport Roe Co. has unrecognized past service cost of $9,000,000. Should the unrecognized past service cost be reported on the balance sheet?

18. Determine the meaning of the following terms:
    (a) Contributory plan.
    (b) Retroactive benefits.
    (c) Final-pay plan.

19. One disclosure required by Section 3460 of the *Handbook* is that "an enterprise should disclose separately the actuarial present value of accrued pension benefits attributed to services rendered up to the reporting date and the value of pension

fund assets." Section 3460 also suggests that companies may wish to disclose additional information such as "description of the plan, pension expense for the period, the amount of deferred charge or accrual for pension costs, the basis of valuing pension fund assets, the salary and interest assumptions." What is the rationale for such disclosure?

20. What is a multiemployer plan? What accounting questions arise when a company is involved with one of these plans?

21. A headline in *The Wall Street Journal* stated that "Firms Increasingly Tap Their Pension Funds to Use Excess Assets." What is the accounting issue related to the use of these "excess assets" by companies?

CASES

C21-1 The following items appear on Trendler, Inc.'s financial statements.
1. Under the caption "Assets":
Deferred pension cost.
2. Under the caption "Liabilities":
Accrued pension cost.
3. On the income statement:
Pension expense

Instructions

With regard to "Pension costs and obligations," explain the significance of each of the items above on corporate financial statements. (Note: All items set forth above are not necessarily to be found on the statements of a single company.)

C21-2 Many business organizations have been concerned with providing for the retirement of employees since the late 1800s. During recent decades, a marked increase in this concern has resulted in the establishment of private pension plans in most large companies and in many medium- and small-sized ones.

The substantial growth of these plans, both in numbers of employees covered and in amounts of retirement benefits, has increased the significance of pension cost in relation to the financial position and results of operations of many companies. In examining the costs of pension plans, a CA encounters certain terms. The elements of pension costs that the terms represent must be dealt with appropriately if generally accepted accounting principles are to be reflected in the financial statements of entities with pension plans.

Instructions

(a) Define a private pension plan. Differentiate between a funded and an unfunded pension plan. How does a contributory pension plan differ from a noncontributory plan?

(b) Differentiate between "accounting for the employer" and "accounting for the pension fund."

(c) Explain the terms "funded" and "pension liability" as they relate to:
1. The pension fund.
2. The employer.

(d) 1. Discuss the theoretical justification for accrual recognition of pension costs.
2. Discuss the relative objectivity of the measurement process of accrual versus cash (pay-as-you-go) accounting for annual pension costs.

(e) Distinguish among the following as they relate to pension plans:
1. Service cost.
2. Past service cost.
3. Actuarial funding methods.

C21-3 Wilson, Inc. is interested in examining the impact of the revised Section 3460 of the *CICA Handbook* entitled "Pension Costs and Obligations." As a consequence, the financial vice-president has instructed you to develop a computer run of pertinent information for management to examine at its next Board of Directors meeting, assuming the company follows the pronouncement starting in 1988. The results of your computer run are as follows for 1987, 1988, and 1989.

Results of Computer Run

Plan Assets and Liabilities	Current Practice	Under Sec. 3460 Requirements	
(as of beginning of year)	1987	1988	1989
Projected benefit obligation	$1,930,000	$1,620,000	$2,300,000
Assets at market value	1,700,000	1,800,000	2,100,000
Components of pension expense (income)			
Service cost	N/A	42,000	43,000
Interest cost	N/A	145,000	184,000
Expected return on assets	N/A	(172,300)	(156,000)
Amortization of transition amount	N/A	(31,000)	(26,000)
Amortization of gains or losses	N/A	–0–	–0–
Pension expense (income)	$ 83,000	$ (16,300)	$ 45,000
Pension expense under old accounting	$ 83,000	$ 89,000	$ 94,000

The president and the vice-president of finance have examined the computer run carefully. They have decided to discuss these figures with you prior to the board meeting because they have some questions regarding the amounts you determined.

Instructions

Answer the following questions.

(a) The president does not understand how the projected benefit obligation for 1988 can decrease from that of 1987. Furthermore, the president thought that Wilson had an underfunded plan in 1987, and now it appears that it has an overfunded plan in 1988. How can this be?

(b) The vice-president notes that in 1988 the company is going to report pension income instead of pension expense. The vice-president simply does not understand how this can happen, when the actual funding in 1988 is $84,000. Explain to the vice-president why this situation has occurred.

(c) The pension expense (income) number does not appear to be consistent from period to period. Under the old accounting, the pension expense was increasing, but in a steady fashion. What is happening in this situation?

(d) Both executives do not understand what is meant by "amortization of the transition amount." Explain this amortization to them.

(e) The vice-president of finance indicates that the company has never reported any asset or liability related to pensions on its balance sheet. Will this also be true in 1988 and 1989?

C21-4 Marion Frye, president of Champion Motors, is discussing the possibility of developing a pension plan for its employees with Mark Sullivan, controller, and William Strang, assistant controller. Their conversation is as follows:

MARION FRYE: If we are going to compete with our competitors, we must have a pension plan to attract good talent.

MARK SULLIVAN: I must warn you, Marion, that a pension plan will take a large bite out of our income. The only reason why we have been so profitable is the lack of a pension cost in our income statement. In some of our competitors' cases, pension expense is 30% of pretax income.

WILLIAM STRANG: Why do we have to worry about a pension cost now anyway? Benefits do not vest until after ten years of service. If they do not vest, then we are not liable. We should not have to report an expense until we are legally liable to provide benefits.

MARION FRYE: But, Bill, the employees would want credit for past service with full vesting ten years after starting service, not ten years after the plan. How would we allocate the large past service cost?

WILLIAM STRANG: Well, I believe that the past service cost is a cost of providing a pension plan for employees forever. It is an intangible asset that will not diminish in value because it will increase the morale of our present and future employees and provide us with a competitive edge in acquiring future employees.

MARION FRYE: I hate to disagree, but I believe the past service cost is a benefit only to the present employees. This past service is directly related to the composition of the employee group at the time the plan is initiated and is in no way related to any intangible benefit received by the company because of the plan's existence. Therefore, I propose that the past service cost be amortized over the expected average remaining service life (EARSL) of the existing employee group.

MARK SULLIVAN (Somewhat perturbed): But what about the income statement? You two are arguing theory without consideration of our income figure.

MARION FRYE: Settle down, Mark.

MARK SULLIVAN: Sorry, perhaps Bill's approach to resolving this problem is the best one. I am just not sure.

Instructions

(a) Assuming that Champion Motors establishes a pension plan, how should their liability for pensions be computed in the first year?

(b) How should pension expense be computed each year?

(c) Assuming that the pension fund is set up in a trustee relationship, should the assets of the fund be reported on the books of Champion Motors?

(d) What interest rate factor should be used in the present value computations?

(e) How should experience gains and losses be reported?

C21-5 Mr. Charles Schwabee is an astute investor who studies corporate annual reports very carefully. He prides himself on his understanding of generally accepted accounting principles but is perplexed by an item that appears on the financial statements of Discount House, Inc., a company in which he has a substantial stock investment. The item that caught his attention concerned the company's reporting of pension cost on the comparative income statement below:

	For Year Ended December 31,	
	1989	1988
Net periodic pension expense (income)	$(27,619)	$55,425

The notes to the 1988 annual report indicated that the company's pension plan funding policy was to contribute annually an amount equal to the amount recognized as pension expense. Therefore, in 1988, $55,425 was the company's expense and the amount paid to the pension fund trustee. In reading the notes to the 1989 financial statements, Mr. Schwabee was surprised to learn that the company paid $62,300 to the pension fund trustee, and yet there was no pension expense recognized in 1989; instead, pension income of $27,619 was recognized. Other information disclosed about the pension plan is as follows:

	Dec. 31, 1988	Jan. 1, 1989	Dec. 31, 1989
Projected benefit obligation	$2,585,000	$2,000,000	$2,200,000
Pension assets market value	2,500,000	2,500,000	3,580,000
Interest rate	6%	9%	9%
Expected asset return rate	7%	9%	10%

The company has elected to adopt the requirements of *CICA Handbook*, Section 3460, ''Pension Costs and Obligations,'' effective January 1, 1989. The company has a stable labour force of 100 employees who are all expected to receive future benefits. It is expected that the expected average remaining service life of the employee group is 20 years.

Mr. Schwabee is still confused and has decided to contact a CA to find out more about pension accounting.

Instructions

Answer the following questions raised by Mr. Schwabee:

(a) ''I thought sponsoring a pension plan that provides benefits to employees when they retire was an additional cost of doing business. Aren't pension benefits just a form of deferred compensation that will be paid to employees when they retire? Under accrual accounting, shouldn't the company recognize an expense for these future benefits in the same period as employee services are being performed? How can the company be generating income by promising to pay benefits in the future?''

(b) "If the pension plan is generating income, why did the company pay $62,300 in cash to the pension plan trustee to fund the plan in 1989? Why didn't the company increase my dividends instead? I need it more than the pension plan does."

(c) Prepare a schedule for Mr. Schwabee that indicates how the net periodic pension income was computed.

C21-6 In examining the costs of pension plans, a CA encounters certain terms. The elements of pension costs that the terms represent must be dealt with appropriately if generally accepted accounting principles are to be reflected in the financial statements of entities with pension plans.

Instructions

(a) 1. Discuss the theoretical justification for accrual recognition of pension costs.
2. Discuss the relative objectivity of the measurement process of accrual versus cash (pay-as-you-go) accounting for annual pension costs.

(b) Explain the following terms as they apply to accounting for pension plans:
1. Market-related asset value.
2. Actuarial funding methods.

(c) What information should be disclosed about a company's pension plans in its financial statements and its notes?

(AICPA adapted)

EXERCISES

E21-1 The Bella Pizza Company sponsors a defined pension plan for its employees. The following data relate to the operation of the plan for the year 1989:

1. The actuarial present value of future benefits earned by employees for services rendered in 1989 amounted to $50,000 using the projected benefits approach pro rated on years of service.
2. The company's funding policy requires a contribution to the pension trustee amounting to $135,000 for 1989.
3. As of January 1, 1989, the company had an accrued benefit obligation of $1,000,000. The pension asset market value was also equal to $600,000. The expected return on plan assets and the settlement rate were both 9%.
4. Amortization of unrecognized past service cost was $40,000 in 1989; amortization of unrecognized net gain or loss was not required in 1989.

Instructions

(a) Determine the amounts of the components of pension expense that should be recognized by the company in 1989.

(b) Prepare the journal entries to record pension expense and the employer's contribution to the pension trustee in 1989.

(c) Indicate the amounts that would be reported on the income statement and the balance sheet for the year 1989:

E21-2 The Avanti Bread Company received the following information from its pension plan trustee concerning the operation of the company's defined benefit pension plan for the year ended December 31, 1989:

	January 1, 1989	December 31, 1989
Accrued benefit obligation	$2,000,000	$2,275,000
Market value of pension assets	800,000	1,230,000
Actuarial (gains) losses	–0–	(200,000)

The service cost component of pension expense for employee services rendered in the current year amounted to $75,000 and the amortization of unrecognized past service cost was $115,000. The company's actual funding (contributions) of the plan in 1989 amounted to $250,000. The expected return on plan assets and the interest rate were both 10%.

Instructions

(a) Determine the amounts of the components of pension expense that should be recognized by the company in 1989.

(b) Prepare the journal entries to record pension expense and the employer's contribution to the pension plan in 1989.

(c) Indicate the pension-related amounts that would be reported on the income statement and the balance sheet for the Avanti Bread Company for the year 1989.

E21-3 National Carpet Company has sponsored a noncontributory defined benefit pension plan for its 200 employees since its incorporation in 1981. Employment levels have remained constant and are expected to remain stable in the future. The expected average remaining service life of the employee group is 25 years. All these employees are expected to receive benefits under the plan. On January 1, 1988, the company's actuary has calculated the following: accrued benefit obligation, $3,200,000; market value of pension plan assets, $2,600,000. Because management wishes to report under *CICA Handbook*, Section 3460, requirements in 1988, it desires to know the transition component of pension expense. The company will amortize the transition amount based on the expected average remaining service life of participants.

EARSL=25 yrs

Instructions

(Round to the nearest dollar.)

(a) Calculate the transition amount as of January 1, 1988.

(b) Prepare a schedule that reflects the amount of the unrecognized transition amount to be recognized as a component of pension expense for the years 1988, 1989, and 1990.

(c) What is the balance of the unrecognized transition amount at the end of each of the three years?

E21-4 Tastee Donut Company sponsors a noncontributory defined benefit pension plan for its 50 employees who are represented by the National Bakers Union. On January 1, 1988, the company's actuary determined that the accrued benefit obligation and the pension plan assets (at market-related value) amounted to $1,800,000 and $1,300,000, respectively. The company's labour force has remained constant and is expected to be stable in future years. Retirements and/or terminations of existing employees are based on an expected average remaining service life of 25 years. All these employees are expected to receive benefits under the plan.

During labour negotiations in 1988, Tastee Donut Company agreed to an amendment to the pension plan that would grant retroactive credit for past service rendered by employees in periods prior to the amendment. The amendment increases the unrecognized past service cost on January 1, 1988, the date of the plan amendment, by $200,000.

Instructions

(Round to the nearest dollar.)

(a) Calculate the transition amount on January 1, 1988, assuming that management wishes to report in accordance with the new pension recommendations.

(b) Compute the transition amount amortized as a component of pension expense for the year 1988. What is the balance of the unrecognized transition amount cost at the end of the year?

(c) Prepare a schedule that reflects the amount of unrecognized past service cost and the transition amount amortized as a component of pension expense for the years 1989 and 1990.

(d) Determine the balance of the unrecognized past service cost and the transition amount at December 31, 1990.

E21-5 Zambeel Tool Company sponsors a defined benefit plan for its 100 employees. On January 1, 1988 (date company adopts CICA's amended Section 3460), the company's actuary provided the following information:

Pension plan assets at market-related value	$200,000
Accrued benefit obligation	350,000

The labour force has remained constant over the years and it is expected to remain stable in the future. The expected average remaining service life of the present employees is 20 years. All these employees are expected to receive benefits under the plan. On December 31, 1988, the actuary calculated that the present value of future benefits earned for employee services rendered in the current year amounted to $50,000, the accrued benefit obligation was $450,000, and the market asset value was $260,000. The expected return on plan assets and the discount rate on the accrued benefit obligation were both 10%. There were no actuarial gains or losses that needed to be recognized in 1988. The company's current year's contribution to the pension plan amounted to $65,000.

Instructions

(Round to the nearest dollar.)
(a) Determine the components of pension expense that the company would recognize in 1988.
(b) Prepare the journal entries to record the pension expense and the company's funding of the pension plan in 1988.
(c) Determine the pension liability on the balance sheet for the year ended December 31, 1988.

E21-6 Glamour Fashions, Inc. initiated a noncontributory defined benefit pension plan for its 100 employees on January 1, 1988. Employment levels have remained constant and are expected to be stable in the future. All these employees are expected to receive benefits under the plan. It is calculated that the expected average remaining service life of the employees is 25 years. On December 31, 1988, the company's actuary submitted the following information:

Accrued benefit obligation	$110,000
Employer's funding contribution for 1988	
(made on December 31, 1988)	125,000
Interest rate used in actuarial computations	8%
Expected return on plan assets	8%

During 1989, the company amended the pension plan by granting credit for past services performed prior to January 1, 1989, the date of the plan amendment. The plan amendment increased unrecognized past service cost by $100,000, which is to be amortized based on the expected average remaining service life of the employees. The company's accountants calculated the pension expense that is to be recognized in 1989 at $166,492.

Instructions

(Round to the nearest dollar.)
(a) Calculate the amount of the pension expense to be recognized in 1988. Explain.
(b) Prepare the journal entries to record pension expense and the employer's funding contribution for 1988.
(c) Describe how the company's accountants calculated the $166,492 as the pension expense to be recognized in 1989. Indicate each of the six components that make up the total amount to be recognized.

E21-7 The Blizzard Ice Cream Company obtained the following information from the insurance company that administers the company's employee defined benefit pension plan:

	For Year Ended December 31,		
	1988	1989	1990
Plan assets (at market value)	$300,000	$417,000	$611,000
Pension expense	95,000	128,000	130,000
Employer's funding contribution	110,000	150,000	125,000
Past service cost not yet			
recognized in earnings	553,846	509,538	467,077

Prior to 1988, cumulative pension expense recognized equal cumulative contributions. The company has decided to adopt the recommendations of the *CICA Handbook*, Section 3460, "Pension Costs and Obligations," beginning with the 1988 financial statements.

Instructions
(a) Prepare the journal entries to record pension expense and the employer's funding contribution for the years 1988, 1989, and 1990.
(b) Indicate the pension-related amounts that would be reported on the company's income statement and balance sheet for 1988, 1989, and 1990.

E21-8 The Goodshow Cable TV Company sponsors a defined benefit pension plan for its 50 employees. On January 1, 1988, the company's actuary calculated the following:

Accrued benefit obligation	$1,200,000
Plan assets at market-related value	800,000
Opening net obligation (transition amount)	$ 400,000

The company's labour force is expected to remain stable in the future with an expected average remaining service life of 25 years. All these employees are expected to receive benefits under the plan. The actuary calculated the present value of future benefits attributed to employees' services in the current year to be $65,000. A 10% interest rate (settlement rate) is assumed for the actuarial computations. The expected return on plan assets is 11%. The company's funding contribution to the pension plan for 1988 was $125,000. The status of the pension plan's operations at December 31, 1988, is as follows:

Accrued benefit obligation	$1,310,000
Plan assets at market value	900,000

Instructions
(Round to the nearest dollar.)
(a) Determine the amounts of the components of pension expense that should be recognized by the company in 1988.
(b) Prepare the journal entries to record pension expense and the employer's funding contribution for 1988.
(c) Indicate the pension-related amounts that would be reported on the company's income statement and balance sheet for the year 1988.

E21-9 Presented below is partial information related to the pension fund of Arco Electronics.

Funded Status (end of year)	1988	1989	1990
Plan assets at market value	$1,400,000	$1,700,000	$1,950,000
Accrued benefit obligation	1,600,000	1,910,000	2,500,000
Amounts To Be Recognized			
Pension expense	$ (300,000)	$ (312,000)	$ (350,000)
Contribution	310,000	310,000	320,000

Instructions
(a) What pension-related amounts are reported on the balance sheet of Arco Electronics for 1988, 1989, and 1990?
(b) What are the journal entries made to record pension expense in 1988, 1989, and 1990?

E21-10
The actuary for the pension plan of Doublesweet Gum Company calculated the following net gains and losses:

	Net Gain or Loss
For the Year Ended December 31,	(Gain) or Loss
1988	$250,000
1989	510,000
1999	(180,000)
1991	(300,000)

Other information about the company's pension obligation and plan assets is as follows:

As of January 1,	Accrued Benefit Obligation	Plan Assets at Market Value
1988	$3,500,000	$2,100,000
1989	3,980,000	1,900,000
1990	4,630,000	2,400,000
1991	3,830,000	2,730,000

Doublesweet Gum Company has a stable labour force of 400 employees who are expected to receive benefits. It is anticipated that the expected average remaining service life is 25 years. All these employees are expected to receive benefits under the plan. The company has elected to apply the recommendations of *CICA Handbook*, Section 3460, "Pension Costs and Obligations," beginning in 1988. As a result, the beginning balance of unrecognized net gain or loss is zero on January 1, 1988. (Assume that the EARSL decreases each year.)

Instructions

Prepare a schedule that reflects the amount of experience gain or loss amortized as a component of net periodic pension expense for each of the years 1988, 1989, 1990, and 1991.

E21-11 The Olympic Sports Equipment Company sponsors a defined benefit pension plan for its 500 employees. The company's actuary provided the following information about the plan:

	January 1, 1988	December 31, 1988	December 31, 1989
Accrued benefit obligation	$3,000,000	$3,850,000	$4,600,000
Plan assets at market value	1,900,000	3,100,000	3,800,000
Experience (gain) or loss	–0–	(410,000)	350,000
Discount rate		11%	8%
Expected asset return rate	10%	10%	

The company anticipates that the expected average remaining service life of the employees is 20 years. All these employees are expected to receive benefits under the plan. The service cost component of net periodic pension expense for employee services rendered amounted to $400,000 in 1988 and $475,000 in 1989.

Instructions

(a) Compute the amount of the initial transition amount at January 1, 1988, assuming Olympic wishes to follow *CICA Handbook*, Section 3460, requirements.

(b) Prepare a schedule that reflects the amount of unrecognized past service cost to be amortized as a component of net periodic pension expense for 1988 and 1989.

(c) Prepare a schedule that reflects the amount of unrecognized experience gain or loss to be amortized as a component of net periodic pension expense for 1988 and 1989.

(d) Determine the total amount of net periodic pension expense to be recognized by the company in 1988 and 1989.

E21-12 The Brite-Smile Toothpaste Company initiates a defined benefit pension plan for its 50 employees on January 1, 1988. The insurance company that administers the pension plan provided the following information for the years 1988, 1989, and 1990:

	For Year Ended December 31,		
	1988	1989	1990
Plan assets at market value	$45,000	$110,000	$246,000
Accrued benefit obligation	55,000	190,000	305,000
Employer's funding contribution	45,000	60,000	95,000

The expected return on plan assets was 10% over the three-year period but the interest rate used to discount the company's pension obligation was 13% in 1988 and 8% in 1989. The service cost component of net periodic pension expense amounted to the following: 1988, $55,000; 1989, $85,000; and 1990, $115,000. The company estimates that the expected average remaining service life of the employees is 25 years, and that the company's total employment level will remain constant at 50 employees. All these employees are expected to receive benefits under the plan.

Instructions

(a) Calculate the amount of net periodic pension expense that the company would recognize in 1988, 1989, and 1990.

(b) Prepare the journal entries to record net periodic pension expense and employer's funding contribution for the years 1988, 1989, and 1990.

PROBLEMS

P21-1 Turbo Bicycle Company has sponsored a noncontributory defined benefit pension plan for its employees since 1973. Prior to 1987, cumulative net pension expense recognized equalled cumulative contributions to the plan. Other relevant information about the pension plan on January 1, 1988, is as follows:

1. The company has 200 employees who are expected to receive benefits under the plan. The expected average remaining service life of the employees is 25 years. EARSL The company expects to maintain a stable labour force of 200 employees. All these employees are expected to receive benefits under the plan.

2. The accrued benefit obligation amounted to $5,000,000 and the market-related value of plan assets was $3,000,000.

On December 31, 1988, the accrued benefit obligation was $4,750,000. The market-related value of plan assets was $3,790,000. A 10% interest rate and a 10% expected asset return rate was used in the actuarial present value computations in the pension plan. The present value of benefits attributed by the pension benefit formula to employee service in 1988 amounted to $200,000. The employer's contribution to the plan assets amounted to $575,000 in 1988.

Instructions

(a) Compute the initial unfunded obligation as of January 1, 1988.

(b) Prepare a schedule, based on the expected future years of employee service, showing the transition amount that would be amortized as a component of pension expense for 1988, 1989, and 1990.

(c) Compute pension expense for the year 1988.

(d) Prepare the journal entries required to report the accounting for the company's pension plan for 1988.

P21-2 The Zesta Cola Company sponsors a noncontributory defined benefit pension plan for all of its 500 employees. The expected average remaining service life of the employees is 20 years. All these employees are expected to receive benefits under the plan. Prior to 1988, the year of transition, cumulative pension expense recognized exceeded cumulative contributions by $400,000; this amount appears as an accrued pension cost on the company's balance sheet at December 31, 1987. On January 1, 1988, the following information was obtained from the pension plan's trustee: accrued benefit obligation, $10,000,000; market value of plan assets, $4,500,000. Other pertinent information about the operation of the pension plan for 1988, 1989, and 1990 follows:

	For the Year Ended December 31,		
	1988	1989	1990
Plan assets at market value	$5,800,000	$7,500,000	$8,100,000
Accrued benefit obligation	6,500,000	7,100,000	8,225,000
Pension expense	1,500,000	1,800,000	2,000,000
Employer's contribution	2,100,000	2,000,000	1,550,000

Instructions

(a) Compute the amount to be considered as the transition amount on January 1, 1988.

(b) Prepare a schedule that shows the transition amount to be amortized in 1988, 1989, and 1990. What is the balance of the transition amount at the end of each of the three years?

(c) Prepare the journal entries required to report the company's recording of pension expense, the employer's contribution, and the required pension liability for the years 1988, 1989, and 1990.

(d) Indicate the pension amounts that would appear on the company's balance sheet for each of the three years.

P21-3 The Norris Equipment Company has 300 employees covered by a defined benefit pension plan. The labour force has remained relatively constant over the years and is expected to be stable in the future. The expected average remaining service life of the employees is 20 years. All these employees are expected to receive benefits under the plan. On January 1, 1988, the pension plan trustee indicated that the actuarial present value of the accrued benefit obligation was $9,000,000 and that the market value of plan assets amounted to $5,000,000. In 1989, as a result of labour contract negotiations with the employees' labour union representatives, Norris Equipment Company agreed to an amendment of the pension plan that would grant credit for past services rendered by employees prior to January 1, 1989. The actuarial present value of the increased benefits granted to employees for past services amounted to $2,000,000 on January 1, 1989. The company amortizes unrecognized past service cost over the expected future years of service of participants.

Instructions
(a) Prepare a schedule that reflects the amortization of unrecognized transition amount and the past service cost for the years 1988 and 1989.

(b) What is the total amount of unrecognized transition amount and past service cost at December 31, 1988, and December 31, 1989?

(c) What justification is there for allocating past service cost to future periods?

P21-4 Dan Thompson Piano Company is facing stiff competition from foreign imports. In negotiating a new labour contract with its employees' labour union, the company gained a concession in the labour contract that reduced benefits previously granted for past services. The reduction in the unrecognized past service cost at January 1, 1988, the date of the pension plan amendment, amounted to $2,000,000. In 1987, the year of transition, the company reported pension activities in accordance with CICA Handbook, Section 3460, "Pension Costs and Obligations." On January 1, 1987, the following information was available:

Accrued benefit obligation	$4,000,000
Plan assets at market value	1,500,000
Number of employees	200
Expected average remaining service life	25 years

Employment levels have remained stable in 1987 and 1988 and are expected to remain so in the future. All these employees are expected to receive benefits under the plan.

Instructions
(a) Prepare a schedule that reflects the amount of unrecognized past service cost and the transition amount that would be amortized as a component of pension expense for the years 1987, 1988, and 1989.

(b) What is the total amount of unrecognized past service cost and the total of the unrecognized transition amount at December 31, 1987; December 31, 1988; and December 31, 1989.

P21-5 The Goodview Video Company was incorporated in 1979. On January 1, 1987, the company initiated a noncontributory defined benefit pension plan that grants benefits to its 100 employees for service rendered in years prior to the adoption of the pension plan. The expected average remaining service life of the employees is 25 years. An actuarial consulting firm has indicated that the present value of the accrued benefit obligation on January 1, 1987, was $2,200,000. On December 31, 1987, the following information was provided concerning the pension plan's operations for its first year:

1. Service cost of benefits earned during the year	$ 150,000
2. Employer's contribution for the year (at end of year)	565,000
3. Accrued benefit obligation	2,800,000
4. Plan assets at market value	520,000
5. Expected asset return rate	7%
6. Assumed discount rate	8%

Instructions

(a) What is the amount of the unrecognized transition amount on January 1, 1987, the date the plan was initiated?

(b) Compute the pension expense to be recognized in 1987 and show the individual components making up the pension expense.

(c) Prepare the journal entries required to reflect the accounting for the company's pension plan for the year ending December 31, 1987.

(d) Indicate the amounts that are reported on the income statement and the balance sheet for 1987.

P21-6 The Carasota Record Company has provided a funded defined benefit pension plan for its 200 employees since 1984. The company's balance sheet for the year ended December 31, 1986, reflects an asset of $50,000, which represents the employer's excess cumulative contributions over cumulative pension expense recognized. On January 1, 1987, the accrued benefit obligation was determined by an actuary to be $875,000 and the pension plan assets at market value amounted to $850,000 on that date. The company estimates that the expected average remaining service life of its employees is 20 years. All these employees are expected to receive benefits under the plan. Other relevant information about the operation of the pension plan for 1987, 1988, and 1989 follows:

	For the Year Ended December 31,		
	1987	1988	1989
Pension expense	$ 325,000	$ 390,000	$ 425,000
Employer's contribution	400,000	430,000	480,000
Plan assets at market value	1,100,000	1,500,000	2,200,000
Accrued benefit obligation	1,200,000	1,675,000	2,125,000

Instructions

(a) Compute the amount to be considered as the transition amount on January 1, 1987.

(b) Prepare a schedule that shows the unrecognized transition amount to be amortized (based on the expected future years of service of participants) in 1987, 1988, and 1989. What is the balance of the unrecognized transition amount at the end of each of the three years?

(c) Prepare the journal entries required to reflect the company's recording of pension expense and the employer's contribution for the years 1987, 1988, and 1989.

(d) Indicate the pension amounts that would appear on the company's balance sheet for each of the three years.

P21-7 The Microbyte Computer Company sponsors a noncontributory defined benefit pension plan that covers all 300 of its employees. Employment levels have remained constant and are expected to remain so in the future. It is estimated that the expected average remaining service life of its employees is 25 years. Prior to 1987, cumulative pension expense recognized equalled cumulative funding. On January 1, 1987, the company's insurance company, who is administering the pension plan, determined the following:

Accrued benefit obligation	$3,000,000
Plan assets at market value	2,100,000
Initial unfunded obligation	$ 900,000

The company's funding policy is to contribute annually at a rate of 15% of covered employees' payroll. The insurance company provided the following information at December 31, 1987:

Plan assets at market	$2,424,000
Accrued benefit obligation	2,964,000
Pension benefits earned	125,000
Actuarial gain	200,000
Actuarial discount rate	10%
Expected return on plan assets	10%

The annual payroll of employees covered by the pension plan amounted to $2,500,000 in 1987.

Instructions

(a) Calculate the pension expense to be recognized in 1987 and show the individual components making up the pension expense. The actuarial valuation of plan assets is equal to the market value of plan assets.

(b) Prepare the journal entries required to reflect the company's recording of pension expense and the employer's contribution for 1987.

(c) Prepare a schedule reconciling the funded status of the plan with amounts reported in the company's balance sheet.

21-8   Roseanna Wine Company established a noncontributory defined benefit pension plan for its employees in 1973. On January 1, 1987, there were 100 employees covered under the plan and it is expected that employment levels will remain constant in the future. It is estimated that the expected average remaining service life of the employees is 20 years. On January 1, 1987, the insurance company that administers the pension plan computed the accrued benefit obligation at $6,500,000 and the market value of the pension plan assets at $4,800,000. An assumed discount rate of 8% was used in the actuarial computations. The expected return on plan assets was also 8%. The company's funding policy is to contribute annually 13% of payroll for the covered employees. Additional information at the year end follows:

	For Year Ended December 31,		
	1987	1988	1989
Plan assets at market value	$5,534,000	$6,000,000	$6,935,000
Accrued benefit obligation	6,100,000	6,325,000	6,825,000
Pension expense	497,905	502,875	548,730
Annual employee payroll	3,750,000	4,000,000	4,300,000

Instructions

(a) Prepare the journal entries to record the pension expense and the employer's contribution for funding for 1987, 1988, and 1989.

(b) Prepare a schedule that reflects the components of pension expense recognized in 1987.

(c) Indicate the pension-related amounts reported on the income statement and the balance sheet for 1987, 1988, and 1989.

P21-9   The Maxwell Coffee Company initiated a noncontributory defined benefit pension plan for its 200 employees on January 1, 1987. Employment levels are expected to remain stable and it is estimated that the expected average remaining service life of its employees is 25 years. All these employees are expected to receive benefits under the plan. The pension fund trustee provided the company with the following information on December 31, 1987:

1. Actuarial determined pension expense	$200,000
2. Employer's annual funding contribution (at December 31, 1987)	$210,000
3. Discount rate and expected return on assets	10%

On January 1, 1988, the company amended its pension plan. The amendment increased unrecognized past service cost by $100,000 as a result of granting credit to employees for past services rendered in 1988. On December 31, 1988, the pension fund trustee submitted the following:

1. Plan assets at market value	$535,000
2. Accrued benefit obligation	$650,000

3. Service cost of benefits earned	$325,000
4. Employer contributions to plan	$320,000

Instructions

(a) Compute the amount of pension expense that the company should recognize in 1987.

(b) Prepare the journal entries to record the pension expense and the employer's funding contribution for 1987 and 1988.

(c) Calculate the components of pension expense for 1988.

(d) Indicate the pension-related amounts that would be reported on the income statement and balance sheet for the years ended December 31, 1987, and December 31, 1988.

P21-10 The Comprehensive Book Company provides a noncontributory defined benefit pension plan for its 200 employees. Prior to 1987, the cumulative pension expense recognized equalled cumulative contributions. On January 1, 1987, the company's actuary provided the following information:

Accrued benefit obligation	$5,000,000
Plan assets at market value	3,000,000
Initial unfunded obligation	2,000,000

Other relevant information about the pension plan's operations follows:

	For Year Ended December 31,			
	1987	1988	1989	1990
Plan assets at market value	$3,500,000	$3,900,000	$4,900,000	$5,200,000
Accrued benefit obligation	5,300,000	6,350,000	5,900,000	6,300,000
Pension expense	550,476	634,531	751,966	683,777
Employer's funding	604,800	729,200	885,000	340,900

On January 1, 1988, the company amended its plan in order to grant retroactive credit for past service rendered by employees prior to the amendment. This amendment increased unrecognized past service cost by $500,000. The company's labour force has been stable and it is expected to remain so in the future. It is estimated that the expected average remaining service life of the employees is 20 years. All these employees are expected to receive benefits under the plan.

EARSL = 20 yrs.

A discount rate of 8% was used in the actuarial calculations. An expected asset return rate of 8% was also assumed.

Instructions

(a) Prepare the journal entries to record the pension expense and the employer's funding contribution for the years 1987, 1988, 1989, and 1990.

(b) Prepare a schedule that reflects the amounts of unrecognized past service costs to be amortized each year for 1987, 1988, 1989, and 1990. Indicate the balance of the unrecognized past service cost at the end of each of the four years.

TOPIC: STATEMENT OF CHANGES IN FINANCIAL POSITION

APPLICATION
IN TEXTBOOK: Chapter 24 (substitute this for all of Chapter 24).

SOURCE: "Statement of Changes in Financial Position," *CICA Handbook*, Section 1540.

24

STATEMENT OF CHANGES IN FINANCIAL POSITION

How did Campeau Limited finance the $6.58 billion required to purchase Federated Department Stores Inc.? How did Petro-Canada Ltd. finance the large investment it made to acquire Petrofina Canada? How will deHavilland finance the new Dash 8 aircraft that it is building for the airline industry? How was Sears Industries Inc. able to purchase long-term assets in the same year that it sustained a net loss? How much of the proposed expansion by Marriott Hotels will be financed through the reinvestment of net income? Will a company have a sufficient cash flow to repay its debts? These types of questions are often asked by investors, creditors, and internal management, all of whom are interested in the financial operations of a business enterprise. However, an examination of the balance sheet, income statement, and statement of retained earnings often fails to provide ready answers to questions of this type.

The balance sheet presents the status of the assets and equities as of a specific date; the income statement presents a summary of the nature and results of transactions affecting net income. The statement of retained earnings provides an analysis of changes in retained earnings. These statements present information about the financial activities of an enterprise during the period. As examples, comparative balance sheets help to show what new assets have been acquired or disposed of and what liabilities have been incurred or liquidated. The income statement provides information as to resources provided by operations. The statement of retained earnings provides information as to the resources used to pay dividends. However, none of these statements presents a detailed summary of all the resources provided during the period and the uses to which they were put.

EVOLUTION OF A NEW STATEMENT

A statement specifically designed to furnish this information is issued by all major business enterprises as one of the primary financial statements. This statement, the **Statement of Changes in Financial Position,** is designed to present information on the financing and investing activities of a business enterprise. The evolution of this statement provides an interesting example of how the needs of financial statement users are met.

The statement originated as a simple analysis called the "Where-Got and Where-Gone Statement" that consisted of nothing more than a listing of the increases or decreases in the company's balance sheet items. After some years, the title of this statement was changed to "the funds statement." In 1961, the AICPA, recognizing the significance of this statement, sponsored research in this area that resulted in the publication of *Accounting Research Study No. 2,* entitled " 'Cash Flow' Analysis and the Funds Statement."[1] This study recommended that the funds statement be included in all annual reports to the shareholders and that it be covered by the auditor's opinion.

Prior to 1974 this statement was known as the "Statement of Source and Application of Funds." In 1974 the CICA revised and expanded Section 1540 of the *Handbook* that deals with this statement. In the revision, the statement was given the title "Statement of Changes in Financial Position." The objective of this statement was to provide information as to how the activities of the enterprise have been financed and how its **financial resources** have been used during the period covered by the statement. Accordingly, the statement summarized the sources and uses of funds; namely, details of how funds were acquired by the company (through borrowings, sales of assets, etc.) and how the company used these funds (to retire debt, to purchase assets, etc.). In preparing the statement, companies were permitted to use various definitions of "funds" such as cash, quick assets, or working capital.

In September, 1985, an important revision to Section 1540 was released. In this revision the objective was changed to "provide information about the operating, financing, and investing activities of an enterprise and the effects of those activities on **cash resources**."[2] The change in emphasis from providing information about changes in financial resources to providing information about changes in cash resources has important implications for accountants. Under the new Section, information about inflows and outflows of cash and cash equivalents is required. Although the *Handbook* does not explicitly require all firms to present a statement of changes in financial position with their financial statements, it is required of companies that operate under the jurisdiction of the Canada Business Corporations Act.[3]

---

[1]Perry Mason, " 'Cash Flow' Analysis and the Funds Statement," *Accounting Research Study No. 2* (New York: AICPA, 1961).

[2]*CICA Handbook*, Section 1540, par. 01.

[3]*Financial Reporting in Canada—1987* (Toronto: CICA, 1988), for example, indicates that 299 of the 300 companies presented a statement of changes in financial position in 1986.

REASONS FOR CHANGE TO THE CASH BASIS

Why the sudden change in the financial reporting environment? One major reason is that investors and analysts are concerned that **accrual accounting has become far removed from the underlying cash flows of the enterprise**.[4] They contend that accountants are using too many arbitrary allocation devices (deferred taxes, depreciation, amortization of intangibles, accrual of revenues, etc.) and are therefore computing a net income figure that no longer provides an acceptable indicator of the enterprise's ability to generate cash. Similarly, **because financial statements take no cognizance of inflation, many look for a more concrete standard like cash flow to evaluate operating success or failure**. In addition, others contend that the **working capital concept does not provide as useful information about liquidity and financial flexibility as does the cash basis**. A statement of changes in financial position is useful to management and short-term creditors in **assessing the enterprise's ability to meet cash operating needs**.

PURPOSE OF THE STATEMENT OF CHANGES IN FINANCIAL POSITION

The primary purpose of the **statement of changes in financial position** is to provide information about the cash receipts and cash payments of an entity during a period.[5] A secondary objective is to provide information about the investing and financing activities of the entity during the period. This statement, therefore, summarizes the operating, investing, and financing activities of the business; it provides a detailed summary of the sources of cash during the period and the uses of cash. It thus helps to provide the answers to the questions raised in the previous section. For example, the statement indicates how it is possible to report a net loss and still make a large capital expenditure or pay dividends. Or, it will tell you whether the company issued or retired debt or common shares or both during the period.

The balance sheet, income statement, and retained earnings statement do present some information about the financing and investing activities of an enterprise during a period. For example, comparative balance sheets help to show what assets have been newly acquired or disposed of and what liabilities have been incurred or liquidated. The income statement gives some hint as to the amount of cash and noncash resources generated by operations. And the statement of retained earnings discloses the resources used to pay dividends. But none of these statements presents a detailed summary of all of the cash operating, investing, and financing activities of an entity during the period.

Reporting the net increase or decrease in cash is considered useful because investors, creditors, and other interested parties want to know and can generally comprehend what is happening to a company's most liquid resource—its cash.

A statement of changes in financial position is useful because it provides answers to the following simple but important questions about the enterprise:

---

[4]See "Where's the Cash?" *Forbes* (April 8, 1985), p. 120; three reasons cited for the rising importance of cash flow analysis are: (1) the high and continuing debt levels of many companies, (2) the trend over the past 20 years towards capitalizing and deferring more expenses, and (3) a wave of corporate bankruptcies in the early 1980s.

[5]The basis recommended by *CICA Handbook*, Section 1540, for the statement of changes in financial position is actually "cash and cash equivalents." **Cash equivalents** include cash net of short-term borrowings and temporary investments.

1. Where did the cash come from during the period?
2. What was the cash used for during the period?
3. What was the change in the cash balance during the period?

CLASSIFICATION OF CASH FLOWS

The statement of changes in financial position classifies cash receipts and cash payments attributed to operating, investing, and financing activities. Transactions and events characteristic of each kind of activity are as follows:

1. **Operating activities** involve the cash effects of transactions that enter into the determination of net income, such as cash receipts from sales of goods and services and cash payments for acquisitions of inventory and expenses.
2. **Investing activities** include changes to assets classified as long-term investments and include such transactions as (a) acquiring and disposing of investments and productive long-lived assets, and (b) lending money (other than through trade accounts and notes) and collecting on those loans.
3. **Financing activities** involve liability and owners' equity items and include (a) obtaining cash through the issuance of debt and repaying the amounts borrowed, and (b) obtaining capital from owners and providing them with a return on their investment.

The following schedule lists the typical receipts and payments of a business enterprise that are classified according to operating, investing, and financing activity classifications.

Operating
  Cash inflows
    From sale of goods or services.
    From returns on loans (interest) and on equity securities (dividends).
  Cash outflows
    To suppliers for inventory.
    To employees for services.
    To government for taxes.
    To lenders for interest.
    To others for expenses.
Investing
  Cash inflows
    From sale of property, plant, and equipment.
    From sale of debt or equity securities of **other** entities.
    From collection of principal on loans to **other** entities.
  Cash outflows
    To purchase property, plant, and equipment.
    To purchase debt or equity securities of **other** entities.
    To make loans to **other** entities.
Financing
  Cash inflows
    From sale of **own** equity securities.
    From issuance of debt (bonds and notes).
  Cash outflows
    To shareholders as dividends.*
    To redeem long-term debt or reacquire share capital.

    *Some accountants classify the payment of dividends as an operating activity.

Note that (1) operating activities usually involve income determination (income statement, current asset and current liability) items, (2) investing activities involve cash flows generally resulting from changes in long-term asset items, and (3) financing activities involve cash flows generally resulting from changes in long-term liability and shareholders' equity items.

Some cash flows relating to investing or financing activities are classified as operating activities. For example, receipts of investment income (interest and dividends) and payments of interest to lenders are classified as operating activities.

Conversely, some cash flows relating to operating activities are classified as investing or financing activities. For example, the cash received from the sale of property, plant, and equipment at a gain, although reported in the income statement, is classified as an investing activity, and the effects of the related gain would not be included in net cash flow from operating activities. Likewise, a gain or loss on the payment (extinguishment) of debt would generally be part of the cash outflow related to the repayment of the amount borrowed and therefore is a financing activity.

FORMAT OF THE STATEMENT OF CHANGES IN FINANCIAL POSITION

The three activities discussed in the preceding paragraphs constitute the general format of the statement of changes in financial position. The cash flows from the operating activities section always appear first, followed by the investing activities and the financing activities sections. Also, the individual inflows and outflows from investing and financing activities are reported separately. Thus, the cash outflow from the purchase of property, plant, and equipment is reported separately from the cash inflow from the sale of property, plant, and equipment. Similarly, the cash inflow from the issuance of debt securities is reported separately from the cash outflow from the retirement of debt. Not reporting them separately obscures the investing and financing activities of the enterprise and makes it more difficult to assess future cash flows. The skeleton format of the statement of changes in financial position is:

Company Name
STATEMENT OF CHANGES IN FINANCIAL POSITION
Period Covered

Cash flows from operating activities		
Net income		XXX
Add (deduct) items not affecting cash		
(List of individual items)	XX	XX
Net cash flow from operating activities		XXX
Cash flows from investing activities		
(List of individual inflows and outflows)	XX	
Net cash provided (used) by investing activities		XXX
Cash flows from financing activities		
(List of individual inflows and outflows)	XX	
Net cash provided (used) by financing activities		XXX
Net increase (decrease) in cash		XXX

PREPARATION OF THE STATEMENT

Unlike the other major financial statements, the statement of changes in financial position is not prepared from the adjusted trial balance. The information to prepare this statement usually comes from three sources:

1. **Comparative balance sheets**. Information in these statements indicates the amount of the changes in assets, liabilities, and equities from the beginning to the end of the period.
2. **Current income statement**. Information in this statement helps the preparer determine the amount of cash provided by or used by operations during the period.
3. **Selected transaction data**. Data from the general ledger provides additional detailed information needed to determine how cash was provided or used during the period.

Preparing the statement of changes in financial position from the data sources above involves three major steps:

1. **Determine the change in cash and cash equivalents**. This procedure is straightforward because the difference between the beginning and the ending cash and cash equivalent balances can easily be computed from an examination of the comparative balance sheets.
2. **Determine the net cash flow from operating activities**. This procedure is complex; it involves analyzing not only the current year's income statement but also comparative balance sheets as well as selected transaction data.
3. **Determine cash flows from investing and financing activities**. All other changes in the balance sheet accounts not accounted for in step 2 must be analyzed to determine their effect on cash.

FIRST ILLUSTRATION—1988

To illustrate a statement of changes in financial position, we will use the **first year of operations** for Tax Consultants Ltd. Tax Consultants Ltd. started on January 1, 1988, when it issued 60,000 no-par value common shares for $60,000 cash. The company rented its office space and furniture and equipment and performed tax consulting services throughout the first year. The comparative balance sheets at the beginning and end of the year 1988 appear as follows:

Tax Consultants Ltd. COMPARATIVE BALANCE SHEETS			
Assets	Dec. 31, 1988	Jan. 1, 1988	Change Increase/Decrease
Cash	$49,000	$-0-	$49,000 Increase
Accounts receivable	36,000	-0-	36,000 Increase
Total	$85,000	$-0-	
Liabilities and Shareholders' Equity			
Accounts payable	$ 5,000	$-0-	$ 5,000 Increase
Common shares	60,000	-0-	60,000 Increase
Retained earnings	20,000	-0-	20,000 Increase
Total	$85,000	$-0-	

The income statement and additional information for Tax Consultants Ltd. are as follows:

Tax Consultants Ltd.
INCOME STATEMENT
For the Year Ended December 31, 1988

Revenues	$125,000
Operating expenses	85,000
Income before income taxes	40,000
Income tax expense	6,000
Net income	$ 34,000

Additional information
Examination of selected data indicates that a dividend of $14,000 was paid during the year.

The first step in preparing a statement of changes in financial position is **determining the change in cash**, and this is a simple computation. For example, Tax Consultants Ltd. had no cash on hand at the beginning of the year 1988, but $49,000 was on hand at the end of 1988; thus, the change in cash for 1988 was an increase of $49,000. The other two steps are more complex and involve additional analysis.

Determine Net Cash Flow from Operating Activities

A useful starting point in **determining net cash flow from operating activities** is to understand why net income must be converted. Under generally accepted accounting principles, companies use the accrual basis of accounting. This basis requires that revenue be recorded when earned and that expenses be recorded when incurred. Net income may include credit sales that have not been collected in cash and expenses incurred that may not have been paid in cash. Thus, under the accrual basis of accounting, net income will not indicate the net cash flow from operating activities. To arrive at net cash flow from operating activities, it is necessary to report revenues and expenses on a **cash basis**. This is done by eliminating the effects of income statement transactions that did not result in a corresponding increase or decrease in cash. The relationship between net income and net cash flow from operating activities is graphically depicted as follows:

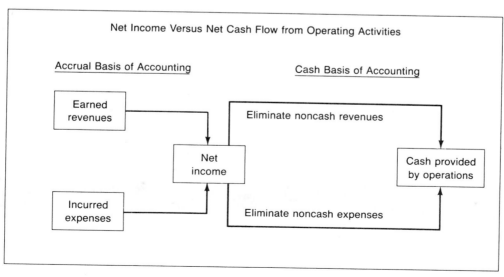

In this chapter, we use the term net income to refer to accrual based net income. The conversion of net income to net cash flow from operating activities may be done through either a direct approach or an indirect approach as explained in the following discussion.

Direct Approach   Under the **direct approach** (or income statement approach), cash revenues and cash expenses are determined. The difference between these two amounts is the net cash flow from operating activities. In other words, the direct approach deducts from cash revenues only those expenses that used cash.

As indicated from the accrual based income statement, Tax Consultants Ltd. reported revenues of $125,000. However, because the company's accounts receivable increased during 1988 by $36,000, only $89,000 ($125,000 − $36,000) in cash was collected on these revenues. Similarly, Tax Consultants Ltd. reported operating expenses of $85,000, but accounts payable increased during the period by $5,000. Assuming that these payables related to operating expenses, cash payments for operating expenses were $80,000 ($85,000 − $5,000). Because no taxes payable exist at the end of the year, the $6,000 income tax expense for 1988 must have been paid in cash during the year. Then the computation of net cash flow from operating activities is as follows:

Direct Approach—Computation of Net Cash Flow from Operating Activities	
Cash collected from revenues	$89,000
Cash payments for expenses	(80,000)
Cash payments for income taxes	(6,000)
Net cash flow from operating activities	$ 3,000

"Net cash flow from operating activities" is the equivalent of cash basis net income.

Indirect Approach   Another approach, referred to as the **indirect approach** (or reconciliation approach), is simply to start with net income and convert it to net cash flow from operating activities. In other words, **the indirect approach adjusts net income for items that affected reported net income but did not affect cash.** That is, noncash charges in the income statement are added back to net income and noncash credits are deducted to compute net cash flow from operating activities. Explanations for the two adjustments to net income in this example, namely, the increases in accounts receivable (net) and accounts payable, are as follows.

Increase in Accounts Receivable. When accounts receivable increase during the year, revenues on an accrual basis are higher than revenues on a cash basis because goods sold on account are reported as revenues. In other words, operations of the period led to increased revenues, but not all of these revenues resulted in an increase in cash. Some of the increase in revenues resulted in an increase in accounts receivable. To convert net income to net cash flow from operating activities, the increase of $36,000 in accounts receivable must be deducted from net income.

Increase in Accounts Payable. When accounts payable increase during the year, expenses on an accrual basis are higher than they are on a cash basis because expenses are incurred for which payment has not taken place. To convert net income to net cash flow from operating activities, the increase of $5,000 in accounts payable must be added to net income.

As a result of the accounts receivable and accounts payable adjustments, net cash flow from operating activities is determined to be $3,000 for the year 1988. This computation is shown as follows:

Indirect Approach—Computation of Net Cash Flow from Operating Activities		
Net income		$34,000
Add (deduct) items not affecting cash		
Increase in accounts receivable	$(36,000)	
Increase in accounts payable	5,000	(31,000)
Net cash flow from operating activities		$ 3,000

Note that net cash flow from operating activities is the same whether the direct or the indirect approach is used.

Determine Cash from Investing and Financing Activities

Once the net cash flow from operating activities is computed, the next step is to determine whether any other changes in balance sheet accounts caused an increase or decrease in cash. For example, an examination of the remaining balance sheet accounts shows that both common shares and retained earnings have increased. The increase in common shares of $60,000 resulted from the issuance of common shares for cash. The issuance of common shares is a receipt of cash from a financing activity and is reported as such in the statement of changes in financial position. The retained earnings increase of $20,000 is caused by two items:

1. Net income of $34,000 increased retained earnings.
2. Dividends declared of $14,000 decreased retained earnings.

Net income has been converted into net cash flow from operating activities as explained above. The additional data indicate that the dividend was paid. Dividend payments may be classified either as an operating activity or as a financing activity. In this and other examples, dividend payments are reported as a cash outflow classified as a financing activity.

Statement of Changes in Financial Position—1988

Having performed the analysis above, we are ready to prepare the statement of changes in financial position. The statement starts with the operating activities section. Either the direct or indirect approach may be used to report net cash flow from operating activities. The indirect approach, which is used more extensively in practice, is used throughout this chapter. (You should use the indirect method in doing homework assignments unless instructed otherwise.)

The statement of changes in financial position for Tax Consultants Ltd. is as follows:

Tax Consultants Ltd.
STATEMENT OF CHANGES IN FINANCIAL POSITION
For the Year Ended December 31, 1988

Cash flows from operating activities		
Net income		$34,000
Add (deduct) items not affecting cash		
Increase in accounts receivable	$(36,000)	
Increase in accounts payable	5,000	(31,000)
Net cash flow from operating activities		3,000
Cash flows from financing activities		
Issuance of common shares	$ 60,000	
Payment of cash dividends	(14,000)	
Cash provided by financing activities		46,000
Net increase in cash		$49,000

As indicated, the increase of $60,000 in common shares results in a cash inflow from a financing activity. The payment of $14,000 in cash dividends is classified as a use of cash from a financing activity. The increase in cash of $49,000 reported in the statement of changes in financial position agrees with the increase of $49,000 shown as the change in the cash account in the comparative balance sheets.

SECOND ILLUSTRATION—1989

Tax Consultants Ltd. continued to grow and prosper during its second year of operations. Land, building, and equipment were purchased, and its revenues and earnings increased substantially over the first year. Presented below is information related to the second year of operations for Tax Consultants Ltd.

Tax Consultants Ltd.
COMPARATIVE BALANCE SHEETS
As at December 31

Assets	1989	1988	Change Increase/Decrease
Cash	$ 37,000	$49,000	$ 12,000 Decrease
Accounts receivable	26,000	36,000	10,000 Decrease
Prepaid expenses	6,000	–0–	6,000 Increase
Land	70,000	–0–	70,000 Increase
Building	200,000	–0–	200,000 Increase
Accumulated depreciation—building	(11,000)	–0–	11,000 Increase
Equipment	68,000	–0–	68,000 Increase
Accumulated depreciation—equipment	(10,000)	–0–	10,000 Increase
Total	$386,000	$85,000	
Liabilities and Shareholders' Equity			
Accounts payable	$ 40,000	$ 5,000	$ 35,000 Increase
Bonds payable	150,000	–0–	150,000 Increase
Common shares	60,000	60,000	–0–
Retained earnings	136,000	20,000	116,000 Increase
Total	$386,000	$85,000	

Tax Consultants Ltd.
INCOME STATEMENT
For the Year Ended December 31, 1989

Revenues		$492,000
Operating expenses (excluding depreciation)	$269,000	
Depreciation expense	21,000	290,000
Income from operations		202,000
Income tax expense		68,000
Net income		$134,000

Additional information
(a) In 1989, the company paid a cash dividend of $18,000.
(b) The company obtained $150,000 cash through the issuance of long-term bonds.
(c) Land, building, and equipment were acquired for cash.

To prepare a statement of changes in financial position from this information, the first step is to **determine the change in cash**. As indicated from the information presented, cash decreased $12,000 ($49,000 − $37,000). The second and third steps are discussed in the next paragraphs.

Determine Net Cash Flow from Operating Activities—Indirect Approach

Using the indirect approach, net income of $134,000 on an accrual basis is adjusted to arrive at net cash flow from operating activities. Explanations for the adjustments to net income are as follows.

Decrease in Accounts Receivable. When accounts receivable decrease during the period, cash collections are higher than revenues reported on an accrual basis. To convert net income to net cash flow from operating activities, the decrease of $10,000 in accounts receivable must be added to net income.

Increase in Prepaid Expenses. When prepaid expenses increase during a period, expenses on an accrual basis income statement are lower than they are on a cash basis income statement. Expenditures (cash payments) have been made in the current period, but expenses (as charges to the income statement) have been deferred to future periods. To convert net income to net cash flow from operating activities, the increase of $6,000 in prepaid expenses must be deducted from net income. An increase in prepaid expenses results in a decrease in cash during the period.

Increase in Accounts Payable. The 1989 increase of $35,000 in accounts payable represents expense items and purchases that have not yet been paid for and, therefore, must be added to net income to convert to net cash flow from operating activities.

Depreciation Expense (Increase in Accumulated Depreciation). The purchase of depreciable assets is shown as a use of cash in the investing section in the year of acquisition. The depreciation expense of $21,000 (also represented by the increase in accumulated depreciation) is a noncash expense on the income statement that is added back to net income in order to arrive at net cash flow from operating activities. The $21,000 is the sum of the depreciation on the building of $11,000 and the depreciation on the equipment of $10,000.

Other charges to expense for a period that do not require the use of cash, such as the amortization of intangible assets and depletion expense, are treated in the same manner as depreciation. Depreciation and similar noncash charges are frequently listed in the statement as the first adjustments to net income.

As a result of the foregoing items, net cash flow from operating activities is $194,000 as computed in the following manner:

Computation of Net Cash Flow from Operating Activities		
Net income		$134,000
Add (deduct) items not affecting cash		
Decrease in accounts receivable	$10,000	
Increase in prepaid expenses	(6,000)	
Increase in accounts payable	35,000	
Depreciation expense	21,000	60,000
Net cash flow from operating activities		$194,000

Determine Cash Flows from Investing and Financing Activities

After you have determined the items affecting net cash flow from operating activities, the next step involves analyzing the remaining changes in balance sheet accounts. Changes in noncurrent asset accounts may result from cash transactions or exchanges involving noncash items. The following transactions are assumed to have involved cash. Noncash transactions are explained later in this chapter.

Increase in Land. As indicated from the change in the Land account, land of $70,000 was purchased during the period. This transaction is an investing activity that is reported as a use of cash.

Increase in Building and Related Accumulated Depreciation. As indicated in the additional data, an office building was acquired using cash of $200,000. This transaction is a cash outflow reported in the investing section. The Accumulated Depreciation account increase of $11,000 is fully explained by the recording of depreciation expense for the period. As indicated earlier, the reported depreciation expense has no effect on cash.

Increase in Equipment and Related Accumulated Depreciation. An increase in equipment of $68,000 resulted because equipment was purchased for cash. This transaction should be reported as an outflow of cash from an investing activity. The increase in Accumulated Depreciation—Equipment was explained by the recording of depreciation expense for the period.

Increase in Bonds Payable. The Bonds Payable account increased $150,000. As indicated from the additional information, cash received from the issuance of these bonds represents an inflow of cash from a financing activity.

Increase in Retained Earnings. Retained earnings increased $116,000 during the year. This increase can be explained by two factors: (1) net income of $134,000 increased retained earnings; (2) dividends of $18,000 decreased retained earnings. The net income is adjusted to net cash flow from operating activities in the operating activities section. Payment of the dividends is a financing activity that involves a cash outflow.

Statement of Changes in Financial Position—1989

Combining the foregoing items, a statement of changes in financial position for

1989 for Tax Consultants Ltd., using the indirect method to compute net cash flow from operating activities, shows the following data:

Tax Consultants Ltd.
STATEMENT OF CHANGES IN FINANCIAL POSITION
For the Year Ended December 31, 1989

Cash flows from operating activities		
Net income		$134,000
Add (deduct) items not affecting cash		
Depreciation expense	$ 21,000	
Decrease in accounts receivable	10,000	
Increase in prepaid expenses	(6,000)	
Increase in accounts payable	35,000	60,000
Net cash flow from operating activities		194,000
Cash flows from investing activities		
Purchase of land	$ (70,000)	
Purchase of building	(200,000)	
Purchase of equipment	(68,000)	
Cash used by investing activities		(338,000)
Cash flows from financing activities		
Issuance of bonds	$150,000	
Payment of cash dividends	(18,000)	
Cash provided by financing activities		132,000
Net decrease in cash		$(12,000)

THIRD ILLUSTRATION

This third illustration covering the 1990 operations of Tax Consultants Ltd. is slightly more complex; it again uses the indirect approach to compute and present net cash flow from operating activities.

Tax Consultants Ltd. experienced continued success in 1990 and expanded its operations to include the sale of selected lines of computer software that are used in tax return preparation and tax planning. Thus, inventory is one of the new assets appearing in its December 31, 1990, balance sheet. The comparative balance sheets, income statement, and selected data for 1990 are as follows:

Tax Consultants Ltd.
COMPARATIVE BALANCE SHEETS
As at December 31

Assets	1990	1989	Change Increase/Decrease
Cash	$ 54,000	$ 37,000	$ 17,000 Increase
Accounts receivable	68,000	26,000	42,000 Increase
Prepaid expenses	4,000	6,000	2,000 Decrease
Inventories	54,000	–0–	54,000 Increase
Land	45,000	70,000	25,000 Decrease
Building	200,000	200,000	–0–
Accumulated depreciation—building	(21,000)	(11,000)	10,000 Increase
Equipment	193,000	68,000	125,000 Increase
Accumulated depreciation—equipment	(28,000)	(10,000)	18,000 Increase
Total	$569,000	$386,000	

Liabilities and Shareholders' Equity			
Accounts payable	$ 33,000	$ 40,000	$ 7,000 Decrease
Bonds payable	110,000	150,000	40,000 Decrease
Common shares	220,000	60,000	160,000 Increase
Retained earnings	206,000	136,000	70,000 Increase
Total	$569,000	$386,000	

Tax Consultants Ltd.
INCOME STATEMENT
For the Year Ended December 31, 1990

Revenues		$890,000
Cost of goods sold	$465,000	
Operating expenses	221,000	
Interest expense	12,000	
Loss on sale of equipment	2,000	700,000
Income from operations		190,000
Income tax expense		65,000
Net income		$125,000

Additional information

(a) Operating expenses include depreciation expense of $33,000 and amortization of prepaid expenses of $2,000.
(b) Land was sold at its book value for cash.
(c) Cash dividends of $55,000 were paid in 1990.
(d) Interest expense of $12,000 was paid in cash.
(e) Equipment with a cost of $166,000 was purchased for cash. Equipment with a cost of $41,000 and a book value of $36,000 was sold for $34,000 cash.
(f) Bonds were redeemed at their book value for cash.
(g) Common shares were issued for cash.

The first step in the preparation of the statement of changes in financial position is to **determine the change in cash**. As is shown in the comparative balance sheets, cash increased $17,000 in 1990. The second and third steps are discussed below.

Determine Net Cash Flow from Operating Activities—Indirect Approach

Explanations for the adjustments to net income of $125,000 are as follows.

Increase in Accounts Receivable. The increase in accounts receivable of $42,000 represents recorded accrual basis revenues in 1990 in excess of cash collections in 1990; therefore, the increase is deducted from net income to convert from the accrual basis to the cash basis.

Increase in Inventories. The increase in inventories of $54,000 represents an operating use of cash. The incremental investment in inventories during the year increases cash cost of goods sold and therefore is deducted from income to convert from the accrual basis to the cash basis. In other words, when inventory purchased exceeds inventory sold during a period, cost of goods sold on an accrual basis is lower than on a cash basis.

Decrease in Prepaid Expenses. The decrease in prepaid expenses of $2,000 represents a charge to the income statement for which there was no cash outflow in the current period. The decrease is added back to net income.

Decrease in Accounts Payable. When accounts payable decrease during the year, cost of goods sold and expenses on a cash basis are higher than they are on an accrual basis because on a cash basis the goods and expenses are recorded as expense when paid. To convert net income to net cash flow from operating activities, the decrease of $7,000 in accounts payable must be deducted from net income.

Depreciation Expense (Increase in Accumulated Depreciation). Accumulated Depreciation—Building increased $10,000 ($21,000 − $11,000). The Building account did not change during the period, which means that $10,000 of depreciation was recorded in 1990.

Accumulated Depreciation—Equipment increased by $18,000 ($28,000 − $10,000) during the year. If Accumulated Depreciation—Equipment was decreased by $5,000 as a result of the sale during the year (cost, $41,000 − book value, $36,000 = $5,000 accumulated depreciation on equipment sold), depreciation for the year is $23,000. The reconciliation of Accumulated Depreciation—Equipment is as follows:

Beginning balance	$10,000
Add depreciation for 1990	23,000
	33,000
Deduct accumulated depreciation on sold equipment	5,000
Ending balance	$28,000

The total depreciation of $33,000 ($10,000 + $23,000) charged to the income statement must be added back to net income in our determination of net cash flow from operating activities.

Loss on Sale of Equipment. Equipment having a cost of $41,000 and a book value of $36,000 was sold for $34,000. As a result, the company reported a loss of $2,000 on the sale of the equipment. To find the proper amount to report as net cash flow from operating activities, it is necessary to add back to net income the loss on the sale of the equipment. The reason is that the loss is a noncash charge to the income statement; it did not reduce cash but it did reduce net income.

From the foregoing items, the operating activities section of the statement of changes in financial position is prepared as follows:

Computation of Net Cash Flow from Operating Activities		
Net income		$125,000
Add (deduct) items not affecting cash		
Depreciation expense	$33,000	
Increase in accounts receivable	(42,000)	
Increase in inventories	(54,000)	
Decrease in prepaid expenses	2,000	
Decrease in accounts payable	(7,000)	
Loss on sale of equipment	2,000	(66,000)
Net cash flow from operating activities		$ 59,000

Determine Cash Flows from Investing and Financing Activities

By analyzing the remaining changes in the balance sheet accounts, cash flows from investing and financing activities can be identified.

Land. Land decreased $25,000 during the period. As indicated from the information presented, land was sold for cash at its book value. This transaction is an investing activity that is reported as a $25,000 source of cash.

Equipment. An analysis of the Equipment account indicates the following:

Beginning balance	$ 68,000
Purchase of equipment	166,000
	234,000
Sale of equipment	41,000
Ending balance	$193,000

As indicated, equipment with a fair value of $166,000 was purchased for cash. This is an investing transaction that is reported as a cash outflow. The sale of the equipment for $34,000 is an investing activity that is reported as a cash inflow.

Bonds Payable. Bonds payable decreased $40,000 during the year. As indicated from the additional information, bonds were redeemed at their book value. This financing transaction used $40,000 cash.

Common Shares. The Common Share account increased $160,000 during the year. As indicated from the additional information, common shares of $160,000 were issued. This is a financing transaction that provided cash of $160,000.

Retained Earnings. Retained earnings changed $70,000 ($206,000 − $136,000) during the year. The $70,000 change in retained earnings is the result of net income of $125,000 from operating activities and the financing activity of paying cash dividends of $55,000. The net income is adjusted to net cash flow in the operating activities section. Payment of the dividends is reported as a financing activity cash outflow.

Preparation of the 1990 Statement (Indirect Approach)

The following statement of changes in financial position is prepared by combining the foregoing items.

Tax Consultants Ltd.
STATEMENT OF CHANGES IN FINANCIAL POSITION
For the Year Ended December 31, 1990

Cash flows from operating activities			
Net income			$125,000
Add (deduct) items not affecting cash			
Depreciation expense		$ 33,000	
Increase in accounts receivable		(42,000)	
Increase in inventories		(54,000)	
Decrease in prepaid expenses		2,000	
Decrease in accounts payable		(7,000)	
Loss on sale of equipment		2,000	(66,000)
Net cash flow from operating activities			59,000
Cash flows from investing activities			
Sale of land		$ 25,000	
Sale of equipment		34,000	
Purchase of equipment		(166,000)	
Cash used by investing activities			(107,000)
Cash flows from financing activities			
Redemption of bonds		$ (40,000)	
Issue of common shares		160,000	
Payment of cash dividends		(55,000)	
Cash provided by financing activities			65,000
Net increase in cash			$ 17,000

SOURCES OF INFORMATION FOR THE STATEMENT OF CHANGES IN FINANCIAL POSITION

These are the important points to remember in the preparation of the statement of changes in financial position.

1. Comparative balance sheets provide the basic information from which the report is prepared. Additional information obtained from analyses of specific accounts is also required.
2. An analysis of the Retained Earnings account is necessary. The net increase or decrease in retained earnings without any explanation is a meaningless amount in the statement, because it might represent the effect of net income, dividends declared, appropriations of retained earnings, and "prior period" adjustments.
3. The statement includes all changes that have passed through cash or have resulted in an increase or decrease in cash.
4. Write-downs, amortization charges, and similar "book" entries, such as depreciation of plant assets, are considered as neither inflows nor outflows of cash because they have no effect on cash. To the extent that they have entered into the determination of net income, however, they must be added back to or subtracted from net income to arrive at net cash flow from operating activities when using the indirect approach.

NET CASH FLOW FROM OPERATING ACTIVITIES— INDIRECT VERSUS DIRECT APPROACH

As we discussed previously, the two different approaches available to adjust income from operations on an accrual basis to net cash flow from operating activities are the indirect (reconciliation) approach and the direct (income statement) approach.

Indirect Approach

For consistency and comparability and because it is the most widely used approach in practice, the indirect approach was used in the illustrations just presented. Net cash flows from operating activities were determined by adding back to or deducting from net income those items that had no effect on cash. The following diagram presents more completely the common types of adjustments that are made to net income to arrive at net cash flow from operating activities.

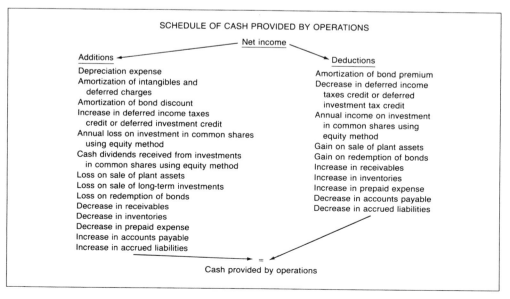

The additions and deductions listed in the preceding diagram reconcile net income to net cash flow from operating activities, illustrating the reason for referring to the indirect approach as the reconciliation approach.

Direct Approach

Under the direct approach the statement of changes in financial position reports net cash flow from operating activities as major classes of operating cash receipts (for example, cash collected from customers, and cash received for interest and dividends) and cash disbursements (for example, cash paid to suppliers for goods, to employees for services, to creditors for interest, and to government for taxes).

The direct approach is illustrated here in more detail to help you understand the difference between accrual based income and net cash flow from operating activities and to illustrate the data needed to apply the direct approach. For example, assume that Farmer Limited has the following selected balance sheet information:

	1988	1987
Cash	$ 54,000	$ 48,000
Receivables	60,000	68,000
Inventory	110,000	112,000
Prepaid expenses	9,000	8,000
Accounts payable	75,000	87,000
Taxes payable	8,000	3,000

Farmer Limited's income statement and additional information are

Sales	$232,000
Cost of goods sold	94,000
Gross profit	138,000
Selling and administrative expenses	70,000
Income before income taxes	68,000
Income tax expense	12,000
Net income	$ 56,000

Additional information
(a) Receivables relate to sales and accounts payable relate to cost of goods sold.
(b) Depreciation of $4,000 and prepaid expenses both relate to selling and administrative expenses.

The adjustments to arrive at net cash flow from operating activities are as follows:

Cash Sales. Sales on an accrual basis are $232,000. If receivables have decreased $8,000 ($68,000 − $60,000) during the year, the cash collections are higher than accrual basis sales. The decrease in receivables must be added to accrual basis sales to determine cash sales as follows:

Sales	$232,000
Add decrease in receivables	8,000
Cash sales	$240,000

Cash Purchases. To find cash purchases, it is first necessary to find purchases for the year. Given that inventory decreased during the year, it means that goods from prior periods were used to increase cost of goods sold. As a result, the decrease in inventory is deducted from cost of goods sold to arrive at purchases. This computation is as follows:

Cost of goods sold	$94,000
Deduct decrease in inventories	(2,000)
Purchases	$92,000

After purchases on an accrual basis are computed, cash purchases are determined by finding the change in accounts payable. Accounts payable has decreased $12,000 ($87,000 − $75,000), which means that more cash was paid this period for goods than is reported under accrual accounting. Cash purchases are therefore determined as follows:

Purchases	$ 92,000
Add decrease in accounts payable	12,000
Cash purchases	$104,000

Cash Selling and Administrative Expense. The selling and administrative expenses are stated at $70,000. Selling and administrative expenses, however, include a noncash charge related to depreciation of $4,000. In addition, prepaid expenses increased $1,000 ($9,000 − $8,000) and therefore this amount must be added to selling and administrative expenses. The computation of cash selling and administrative expenses is as follows:

Selling and administrative expenses	$70,000
Deduct depreciation expense	(4,000)
	66,000
Add increase in prepaid expenses	1,000
Cash selling and administrative expenses	$67,000

Cash Income Taxes. Income taxes on the accrual basis are $12,000. Taxes payable, however, has increased $5,000 ($8,000 − $3,000), which means that a portion of the taxes has not been paid. As a result, income taxes paid are less than income taxes reported on an accrual basis. This computation is as follows:

Income taxes	$12,000
Deduct increase in taxes payable	(5,000)
Cash income tax expense	$7,000

The computations illustrated here are summarized in the following schedule:

Farmer Company
SCHEDULE OF CHANGES FROM THE ACCRUAL
TO THE CASH BASIS INCOME STATEMENT
(Direct Approach)

	Accrual Basis	Adjustment	Add (Subtract)	Cash Basis
Sales	$232,000	+ Decrease in receivables	$ 8,000	$240,000
Cost of goods sold	94,000	− Decrease in inventories	(2,000)	
		+ Decrease in accounts payable	12,000	104,000
Selling and administrative expenses	70,000	− Depreciation expense	(4,000)	
		+ Increase in prepaid expenses	1,000	67,000
Income tax expense	12,000	− Increase in taxes payable	(5,000)	7,000
Total expenses	176,000			178,000
Net income	$ 56,000			$ 62,000

Presentation of the direct approach for reporting net cash flow from operating activities takes the form of a condensed cash basis income statement:

Farmer Company
STATEMENT OF CHANGES IN FINANCIAL POSITION (Partial)
(Direct Approach)

Cash flows from operating activities		
Cash received from customers		$240,000
Cash paid to suppliers	$104,000	
Selling and administrative expenses paid	67,000	
Cash paid for taxes	7,000	
Cash disbursed for operating activities		178,000
Net cash flow from operating activities		$ 62,000

The indirect approach arrives at the same net cash flow from operating activities as is shown in the partial statement for Farmer Limited:

Farmer Company
STATEMENT OF CHANGES IN FINANCIAL POSITION (Partial)
(Indirect Approach)

Cash flows from operating activities		
Net income		$56,000
Add (deduct) items not affecting cash		
Depreciation expense	$ 4,000	
Decrease in receivables	8,000	
Decrease in inventory	2,000	
Increase in prepaid expenses	(1,000)	
Decrease in accounts payable	(12,000)	
Increase in taxes payable	5,000	6,000
Net cash flow from operating activities		$62,000

SPECIAL PROBLEMS IN STATEMENT ANALYSIS

Some of the special problems related to preparing the statement of changes in financial position were discussed in connection with the preceding illustrations. Other problems that arise with some frequency in the preparation of this statement may be categorized as follows:

1. Adjustments similar to depreciation.
2. Accounts receivable (net).
3. Other working capital changes.
4. Net losses.
5. Gains.
6. Stock options.
7. Pensions.
8. Extraordinary items.
9. Significant noncash transactions.

Adjustments Similar to Depreciation

Depreciation expense is the adjustment to net income that is made most commonly to arrive at net cash flow from operating activities. But there are numerous other expense or revenue items that do not affect cash. Examples of expense items that must be added back to net income are the **amortization of intangible assets** such as goodwill and patents, and the **amortization of deferred costs** such as bond issue costs. These charges to expense involve expenditures made in prior periods that are being amortized currently and reduce net income without affecting cash in the current period. Also, **amortization of bond discount or premium** on long-term bonds payable affects the amount of interest expense, but does not affect cash. As a result, amortization of these items should be added back to or subtracted from net income to arrive at net cash flow from operating activities. For example, if the amount of goodwill to be amortized in the current year is $10,000, the journal entry to record this amortization would be:

Amortization Expense	10,000	
Goodwill		10,000

The effect of this entry is to increase expense by $10,000 and decrease goodwill by $10,000. Since the amortization expense of $10,000 was deducted when computing net income but did not require a cash payment in the current year, it must be added to net income in computing the amount of cash provided (used) in operations.

In a similar manner, **changes in the Deferred Income Taxes and Deferred Investment Tax Credit** account balances affect net income but have no effect on cash.

A change related to an investment in common shares when the income or loss is accrued under the equity method is another common adjustment to net income. For example, General Motors Corporation's equity in undistributed earnings of unconsolidated subsidiaries recently increased by approximately $111 million. Such an increase, however, is not represented by a cash inflow; hence, it was deducted from net income to arrive at net cash flow from operating activities. If a company receives a dividend from its equity investee, the cash provided from the dividend is recorded as a reduction of the Investment account; an adjustment to net income is necessary, since the cash dividend received is considered an operating activity cash inflow.

Accounts Receivable (Net)

The Allowance for Doubtful Accounts is a contra account to the current asset, Accounts Receivable. Up to this point, we have assumed that no allowance for doubtful accounts was needed to offset accounts receivable. However, if an allowance for doubtful accounts is needed, how does it affect the determination of net cash flow from operating activities? For example, assume that Redmark Ltd. reports net income of $40,000 and has the following balances related to accounts receivable.

	1990	1989	Change Increase/Decrease
Accounts receivable	$105,000	$90,000	$15,000 Increase
Allowance for doubtful accounts	10,000	4,000	6,000 Increase
Accounts receivable (net)	$ 95,000	$86,000	

The proper reporting treatment using the indirect and direct approach is illustrated in the following sections.

Indirect Approach   An increase in the allowance for doubtful accounts is caused by a charge to bad debts expense and neither provides nor uses cash. Consequently, an increase in the allowance for doubtful accounts should be added back to net income to arrive at net cash flow from operating activities. One method for presenting this information of cash flows is as follows:

Redmark Ltd.
STATEMENT OF CHANGES IN FINANCIAL POSITION (Partial)
For the Year 1990

Cash flows from operating activities		
Net income		$40,000
Add (deduct) items not affecting cash		
Increase in accounts receivable	$(15,000)	
Increase in allowance for doubtful accounts	6,000	(9,000)
		$31,000

Instead of separately analyzing the allowance account, a short-cut approach is to net the allowance balance against the receivable balance and to compare the change in accounts receivable on a net basis. This presentation would be as follows:

Redmark Ltd.
STATEMENT OF CHANGES IN FINANCIAL POSITION (Partial)
For the Year 1990

Cash flows from operating activities	
Net income	$40,000
Add (deduct) items not affecting cash	
Increase in accounts receivable (net)	(9,000)
	$31,000

This short-cut procedure also works if the change in the allowance account was caused by a write-off of accounts receivable. In this case, both the Accounts Receivable and the Allowance for Doubtful Accounts are reduced, and no effect on cash flows occurs. Because of its simplicity, you should use the net approach on your homework assignments.

Direct Approach   If the direct approach is used, the allowance for doubtful accounts should **not** be netted against the accounts receivable. To illustrate, assume that Redmark Ltd.'s net income of $40,000 was comprised of the following items:

Redmark Ltd.
INCOME STATEMENT
For the Year 1990

Sales		$100,000
Expenses:		
Salaries	$46,000	
Utilities	8,000	
Bad debts	6,000	60,000
Net income		$ 40,000

If the $9,000 increase in accounts receivable (net) is deducted from sales for the year, cash sales would be reported at $91,000 ($100,000 − $9,000) and cash payments for operating expenses at $60,000. Both items are misstated because cash sales should be reported at $85,000 ($100,000 − $15,000) and total cash payments for operating expenses should be reported at $54,000 ($60,000 − $6,000). The proper presentation is as follows:

Redmark Ltd.
STATEMENT OF CHANGES IN FINANCIAL POSITION (Partial)
For the Year 1990

Cash flows from operating activities		
Cash received from customers		$85,000
Salaries paid	$46,000	
Utilities paid	8,000	54,000
Net income		$31,000

An added complication develops when accounts receivable are written off. Simply adjusting sales for the change in accounts receivable will not provide the proper amount of cash sales. The reason is that the write-off of the accounts receivable is not a cash collection. Thus an additional adjustment is necessary.

Other Working Capital Changes

Up to this point, all of the changes in working capital items (current asset and current liability items) have been handled as adjustments to net income in determining net cash flow from operating activities. You must be careful, however, because some changes in working capital, although they affect cash, do not affect net income. Generally, these are investing or financing activities of a current nature. For example, the purchase of **short-term investments** (e.g., marketable securities) for $50,000 cash has no effect on net income but it does cause a $50,000 decrease in cash.[6] This transaction is reported as follows:

[6]When the basis of the statement of changes in financial position is cash and cash equivalents and the short-term investment is considered a cash equivalent, then nothing would be reported in the statement because the balance of cash and cash equivalents does not change as a result of the transaction.

Cash flows from investing activities
Purchase of short-term investments $(50,000)

Another example is the issuance of a $10,000 **short-term nontrade note payable** for cash. This change in a working capital item has no effect on income from operations but it increases cash $10,000. It is reported in the statement of changes in financial position as follows:

Cash flows from financing activities
Issuance of short-term note $10,000

Another change in a working capital item that has no effect on income from operations or on cash is a **cash dividend payable**. Although the cash dividends when paid will be reported as a financing activity, the declared but unpaid dividend is not reported on the statement of changes in financial position nor does the payable affect any adjustment of net income.

Net Losses

If an enterprise reports a net loss instead of a net income, the net loss must be adjusted for those items that do not result in a cash inflow or outflow. The net loss after adjusting for the charges or credits not affecting cash may result in a negative or a positive cash flow from operating activities. For example, if the net loss was $50,000 and the total amount of charges to be added back was $60,000, then net cash flow from operating activities is $10,000, as shown in this computation:

Computation of Net Cash Flow from Operating Activities (Cash Inflow)		
Net loss		$(50,000)
Add (deduct) items not affecting cash		
Depreciation of plant assets	$55,000	
Amortization of patents	5,000	60,000
Net cash flow from operating activities		$ 10,000

If the company experiences a net loss of $80,000 and the total amount of the charges to be added back is $25,000, the presentation appears as follows:

Computation of Net Cash Flow from Operating Activities (Cash Outflow)	
Net loss	$(80,000)
Add (deduct) items not affecting cash	
Depreciation of plant assets	25,000
Net cash flow from operating activities	$(55,000)

Although it is not illustrated in this chapter, a negative cash flow may result even if the company reports a net income.

Gains

In the third illustration (1990) of Tax Consultants Ltd., the company experienced a loss of $2,000 from the sale of equipment. This loss was added to net income to compute net cash flow from operating activities because the loss is a noncash charge in the income statement. If a gain from a sale of equipment is experienced, it too requires that net income be adjusted. Because the gain is reported in the statement of changes in financial position as part of the cash proceeds from the sale of equipment under investing activities, the gain is deducted from net income to avoid double counting—once as part of net income and again as part of the cash proceeds from the sale.

Stock Options

If a company has a stock option plan, compensation expense will be recorded during the period(s) in which the employee performs the services. Although Compensation Expense is debited, Shareholders' Equity (the Contributed Surplus Accounts) is credited, with cash being unaffected by the amount of the expense. Therefore, net income has to be increased by the amount of compensation expense in computing net cash flow from operating activities.

Pensions

If a company has an employee pension plan, it is likely that the pension expense recorded during a period will be either higher or lower than the amount of cash funded. In these circumstances, net income must be adjusted by the difference between cash paid and the expense reported in computing net cash flow from operating activities.

Extraordinary Items

The net income amount that begins the operating activities section under the indirect approach and ends the operating activities section under the direct approach **is actually income from operations before extraordinary items**. Cash flows from extraordinary transactions and other events whose effects are included in net income, but which are not related to operations, should be reported either as investing activities or as financing activities, whichever is appropriate. For example, if Tax Consultants Ltd. had extinguished its long-term bond debt of $40,000 by paying bondholders $35,000 in cash, it would have recognized a $3,000 ($5,000 gain less $2,000 of taxes) extraordinary gain. In the statement of changes in financial position, the $3,000 gain would be ignored in the operating activities section. The $37,000 ($35,000 cash paid to bondholders + $2,000 cash paid for taxes) would be reported as a financing activity as follows:

Cash flows from financing activities	
Extraordinary item—extinguishment of debt including extraordinary gain of $3,000	
(net of tax)	($37,000)

In addition, in the operating activities section, net income would be labelled "income before extraordinary item."

Significant Noncash Transactions

Because the statement of changes in financial position only reports the effects of operating, investing, and financing activities in terms of cash flows, some significant noncash transactions and other events that are investing or financing activities could be omitted from the body of the statement. Among the more common of these noncash transactions that should be reported or disclosed in some manner are the following:

1. The acquisition of assets by assuming liabilities (including capital lease obligations) or by the issuance of equity securities.
2. Exchanges of nonmonetary assets.
3. Refinancing of long-term debt.
4. Conversion of debt or preferred shares to common shares.
5. The issuance of equity securities to retire debt.

These transactions are similar to a cash inflow with a simultaneous cash outflow and should be reported in the statement of changes in financial position. If material in amount, they should be shown as financing and investing activities with an appropriate reference to show that they are related.

Certain other significant noncash transactions or other events are generally not reported in conjunction with the statement of changes in financial position. Examples of these types of transactions are **stock dividends, stock splits, and appropriations of retained earnings**. These items represent neither financing nor investing activities. In addition, they do not represent changes in either the resources or obligations of a firm. Consequently, they are not reported in the statement of changes in financial position.

COMPREHENSIVE ILLUSTRATION—USE OF A WORK SHEET

When numerous adjustments are necessary, or other complicating factors are present, **many accountants prefer to use a work sheet to assemble and classify the data that will appear on the statement of changes in financial position**. The work sheet is merely a device that aids in the preparation of the statement; its use is optional. The skeleton format of the work sheet for preparation of the statement of changes in financial position using the indirect approach is shown in the following example.

XYZ Limited
STATEMENT OF CHANGES IN FINANCIAL POSITION
For the Year Ended...

Balance Sheet Accounts	End of Last Year Balances	Reconciling Items Debits	Reconciling Items Credits	End of Current Year Balances
Debit balance accounts	XX	XX	XX	XX
	XX	XX	XX	XX
Totals	XXX			XXX
Credit balance accounts	XX	XX	XX	XX
	XX	XX	XX	XX
Totals	XXX			XXX

Statement of Changes in Financial Position		
Operating activities		
Net income	XX	
Adjustments	XX	XX
Investing activities		
Receipts and payments	XX	XX
Financing activities		
Receipts and payments	XX	XX
Totals	XXX	XXX
Increase (decrease) in cash	(XX)	XX
Totals	XXX	XXX

The following guidelines are important in using a work sheet:

1. In the balance sheet accounts section, accounts with debit balances are listed separately from those with credit balances. This means, for example, that Accumulated Depreciation is listed under credit balances and not as a contra account under debit balances. The beginning and ending balances of each account are entered in the appropriate columns. The transactions that caused the change in the account balance during the year are entered, and each line pertaining to a balance sheet account should balance across. That is, the beginning balance plus or minus the reconciling item(s) must equal the ending balance. When this agreement exists for all balance sheet accounts, all changes in account balances have been reconciled.

2. The bottom portion of the work sheet consists of the operating, investing, and financing activities sections. Accordingly, it provides the information necessary to prepare the formal statement of changes in financial position. Inflows of cash are entered as debits in the reconciling columns and outflows of cash are entered as credits in the reconciling columns. Thus, in this section, the sale of equipment for cash at book value is entered as a debit under inflows of cash from investing activities. Similarly, the purchase of land for cash is entered as a credit under outflows of cash from investing activities.

3. The reconciling items shown in the work sheet are not entered in any journal or posted to any account. They do not represent either adjustments or corrections of the balance sheet accounts. They are used only to facilitate the preparation of the statement of changes in financial position.

Preparation of the Work Sheet

As with work sheets illustrated in earlier chapters, the preparation of this work sheet involves a series of prescribed steps. The steps in this case are three.

1. Enter the balance sheet accounts and their beginning and ending balances in the balance sheet accounts section.

2. Enter the data that explains the changes in the balance sheet accounts (other than cash) and their effects on the statement of changes in financial position in the reconciling columns of the work sheet.

3. Enter the increase or decrease in cash on the cash line and at the bottom of the work sheet. This entry should enable the totals of the reconciling columns to be in agreement.

To illustrate the procedures for the preparation of the work sheet and to illustrate the reporting of some of the special problems discussed in the prior section, the following comprehensive illustration is presented for Satellite Manufacturing Limited. The financial statements and other data related to Satellite Manufacturing Limited are presented with the balance sheet and the statement of income and retained earnings shown on the following pages. Additional explanations related to the preparation of the work sheet are provided throughout the discussion that follows the financial statements.

Satellite Manufacturing Limited
COMPARATIVE BALANCE SHEETS
As at December 31

Assets	1988	1987	Change Incr./Decr.
Cash	$ 59,000	$ 66,000	$ 7,000 Decr.
Accounts receivable (net)	104,000	51,000	53,000 Incr.
Inventories	493,000	341,000	152,000 Incr.
Prepaid expenses	16,500	17,000	500 Decr.
Investments in shares of Porter Co. (equity method)	18,500	15,000	3,500 Incr.
Land	131,500	82,000	49,500 Incr.
Equipment	187,000	142,000	45,000 Incr.
Accumulated depreciation—equipment	(29,000)	(31,000)	2,000 Decr.
Buildings	262,000	262,000	–0–
Accumulated depreciation—buildings	(74,100)	(71,000)	3,100 Incr.
Goodwill	7,600	10,000	2,400 Decr.
Total Assets	$1,176,000	$884,000	

Liabilities			
Accounts payable	$ 132,000	$131,000	$ 1,000 Incr.
Accrued liabilities	43,000	39,000	4,000 Incr.
Income taxes payable	3,000	16,000	13,000 Decr.
Notes payable (long-term)	60,000	–0–	60,000 Incr.
Bonds payable	100,000	100,000	–0–
Premium on bonds payable	7,000	8,000	1,000 Decr.
Deferred income taxes (long-term)	9,000	6,000	3,000 Incr.
Total Liabilities	354,000	300,000	

Shareholders' Equity			
Common shares	247,000	88,000	159,000 Incr.
Retained earnings	592,000	496,000	96,000 Incr.
Treasury shares	(17,000)	–0–	17,000 Incr.
Total Shareholders' Equity	822,000	584,000	
Total Liabilities and Shareholders' Equity	$1,176,000	$884,000	

Satellite Manufacturing Limited
COMBINED STATEMENT OF INCOME AND RETAINED EARNINGS
For the Year Ended 1988

Net sales	$524,500
Other revenue	3,500
Total revenues	$528,000
Expense	
Cost of goods sold	$310,000
Selling and administrative expense	47,000
Other expenses and losses	12,000
Total expenses	$369,000

Income before income tax and extraordinary item	$159,000
Income Tax	
Current	47,000
Deferred	3,000
Income before extraordinary item	$109,000
Gain on expropriation of land (net of tax)	8,000
Net income	$117,000
Retained earnings, January 1	496,000
Less:	
Cash dividends	6,000
Stock dividend	15,000
Retained earnings, December 31	$592,000
Per Share:	
Income before extraordinary items	$1.98
Extraordinary item	0.15
Net income	$2.13

Additional information

(a) Other income of $3,500 represents Satellite's equity share in the net income of Porter Company, an equity investee. Satellite owns 22% of Porter Company.

(b) Land in the amount of $60,000 was purchased through the issuance of a long-term note; in addition, certain parcels of land were expropriated, resulting in an $8,000 gain, net of $2,500 tax.

(c) An analysis of the Equipment account and related accumulated depreciation indicates the following:

	Equipment Dr./(Cr.)	Accum. Dep. Dr./(Cr.)	Gain or Loss
Balance at end of 1987	$142,000	$(31,000)	
Purchase of equipment	53,000		
Sale of equipment	(8,000)	2,500	$1,500L
Depreciation for the period		(11,500)	
Major repair charged to accumulated depreciation		11,000	
Balance at end of 1988	$187,000	$(29,000)	

(d) The change in the Accumulated Depreciation—Buildings, Goodwill, Premium on Bonds Payable, and Deferred Income Tax accounts resulted from income tax accrual, depreciation, and amortization entries.

(e) An analysis of the Common Shares account discloses the following:

	Common Shares
Balance at end of 1987	$ 88,000
Issuance of 2% stock dividend	15,000
Sale of shares for cash	144,000
Balance at end of 1988	$247,000

Analysis of Transactions

The following discussion provides an explanation of the individual adjustments that appear on the work sheet on pages 1141-1142. Because cash is the basis for analysis, the cash account will be reconciled last. Because income is the first item that appears on the statement of changes in financial position, it will be analyzed first.

Change in Retained Earnings   Net income for the period is composed of "income before extraordinary gain" and an "extraordinary gain." Income before the extraordinary item is $109,000 and the extraordinary gain from expropriation of land is $8,000 (net of $2,500 tax). The land had a book value of $10,500. The entry on the work sheet for certain items affecting retained earnings would be as follows:

(1)

Operating—Income before Extraordinary Item	109,000	
Investing—Expropriation of Land (Gain)	8,000	
Retained Earnings		117,000

Income before extraordinary item is reported at the bottom of the work sheet and is the starting point for preparation of the statement of changes in financial position. The expropriation of the land, gain of $8,000 (net of $2,500 tax), is entered separately at the bottom of the work sheet as an investing activity item. The book value ($10,500) part of this extraordinary item transaction is handled separately in preparing the work sheet.

Retained earnings was also affected by a stock dividend and a cash dividend. The retained earnings statement reports a stock dividend of $15,000. The work sheet entry for this transaction is as follows:

(2)

Retained Earnings	15,000	
Common Shares		15,000

The issuance of stock dividends is not a cash operating, investing, or financing item; therefore, **although this transaction is entered on the work sheet for reconciling purposes, it is not reported in the statement of changes in financial position**.

The cash dividend of $6,000 represents a financing activity cash outflow. The following work sheet entry is made:

(3)

Retained Earnings	6,000	
Financing—Cash Dividends		6,000

The beginning and ending balances of retained earnings are reconciled by the entry of the three items above.

Accounts Receivable (Net) The increase in accounts receivable (net) of $53,000 represents revenues that did not result in cash inflows during 1988; as a result, the increase of $53,000 would be deducted from income. The following work sheet entry is made:

(4)

Accounts Receivable (net)	53,000	
Operating—Increase in Accounts Receivable (net)		53,000

Inventories The increase in inventories of $152,000 represents an operating use of cash. The incremental investment in inventories during the year reduces cash without increasing cost of goods sold. The work sheet entry is made as follows:

(5)

Inventories	152,000	
Operating—Increase in Inventories		152,000

Prepaid Expense The decrease in prepaid expenses of $500 represents an expense on the income statement for which there was no cash outflow in the current period; it should be added back to income through the following entry:

(6)

Operating—Decrease in Prepaid Expenses	500	
Prepaid Expenses		500

Investment in Shares of Porter Co. The investment in the common shares of Porter Co. increased $3,500, which reflects Satellite's share of the income earned by its equity investee during the current year. Although revenue, and therefore income per the income statement, was increased $3,500 by the accounting entry that recorded Satellite's share of Porter Co.'s net income, no cash was provided (i.e., no cash dividends were received). The following work sheet entry is made:

(7)

Investment in Shares of Porter Co.	3,500	
Operating—Equity in Earnings of Porter Co.		3,500

Land Land in the amount of $60,000 was purchased through the issuance of a long-term note payable. This transaction did not affect cash, but it is considered a significant noncash investing/financing transaction that should be reported as both an investing and a financing transaction. Two entries are necessary to record this transaction on the work sheet.

(8)

Land	60,000	
Investing—Purchase of Land		60,000
Financing—Issue of Note Payable	60,000	
Note Payable		60,000

In addition to the noncash transaction involving the issuance of a note to purchase land, the Land account was decreased by the expropriation proceedings. The work sheet entry to record the book value portion of this transaction is as follows:

(9)

Investing—Expropriation of Land (Book Value)	10,500	
Land		10,500

The $10,500 of cash provided by expropriation plus the $8,000 gain recorded earlier constitute the total resources of $18,500 related to the expropriation. The Land account balance is now reconciled. Note that entries (1) and (9) are combined on the final statement which shows $18,500 cash received from the expropriation of the land.

Equipment and Accumulated Depreciation An analysis of the Equipment account and its related Accumulated Depreciation account shows that a number of financial transactions have affected these accounts. Equipment in the amount of $53,000 was purchased during the year. The entry to record this transaction on the work sheet is as follows:

(10)

Equipment	53,000	
Investing—Purchase of Equipment		53,000

In addition, equipment with a book value of $5,500 was sold at a loss of $1,500. The entry to record this transaction on the work sheet is as follows:

(11)

Investing—Sale of Equipment	4,000	
Operating—Loss on Sale of Equipment	1,500	
Accumulated Depreciation—Equipment	2,500	
Equipment		8,000

The proceeds from the sale of the equipment provided cash of $4,000. In addition, the loss on the sale of the equipment has reduced the income before extraordinary item, but has not affected cash; therefore, it must be added back to income before extraordinary item to report accurately working capital provided by operations.

Depreciation on the equipment was reported at $11,500 and should be presented on the work sheet in the following manner:

(12)

Operating—Depreciation Expense—Equipment	11,500	
Accumulated Depreciation—Equipment		11,500

The depreciation expense is added back to the income before extraordinary item because it reduced income but did not affect cash.

Finally, a major repair to the equipment in the amount of $11,000 was charged to Accumulated Depreciation—Equipment. Because this expenditure required cash, the following work sheet entry is made:

(13)

Accumulated Depreciation—Equipment	11,000	
Investing—Major Repairs of Equipment		11,000

The balances in the Equipment and related Accumulated Depreciation accounts are reconciled after adjustment for the foregoing items.

Accumulated Depreciation and Amortization of Goodwill   Depreciation expense on the buildings of $3,100 and amortization of goodwill of $2,400 are both expenses in the income statement that reduce net income but did not require a cash outflow in the current period. The following work sheet entry is made:

(14)

Operating—Depreciation Expense—Buildings	3,100	
Operating—Amortization of Goodwill	2,400	
Accumulated Depreciation—Buildings		3,100
Goodwill		2,400

Other Noncash Charges or Credits   An analysis of the remaining accounts indicates that changes in the Accounts Payable, Accrued Liabilities, Income Taxes Payable, Premium on Bonds Payable, and Deferred Income Taxes balances resulted from charges or credits not affecting cash. Each of the these items should be individually analyzed and entered in the work sheet. We have summarized in the following compound entry to the work sheet these noncash, income related items:

(15)

Income Taxes Payable	13,000	
Premium on Bonds Payable	1,000	
Operating—Increase in Accounts Payable	1,000	
Operating—Increase in Accrued Liabilities	4,000	
Operating—Increase in Deferred Income Taxes	3,000	
Operating—Decrease in Income Taxes Payable		13,000
Operating—Amortization of Bond Premium		1,000

Accounts Payable	1,000
Accrued Liabilities	4,000
Deferred Income Taxes	3,000

Common Shares and Related Accounts   A comparison of the common share balances shows that transactions during the year affected these accounts. First, a stock dividend of 2% was issued to shareholders. As indicated in the discussion of work sheet entry (2), no cash was provided or used by the stock dividend transaction. In addition to the shares issued via the stock dividend, Satellite sold common shares at $16 each. The work sheet entry to record this transaction is as follows:

(16)

Financing—Issue of Common Shares	144,000	
Common Shares		144,000

Also, the company purchased its own common shares in the amount of $17,000. The work sheet entry to record this transaction is as follows:

(17)

Treasury Shares	17,000	
Financing—Purchase of Treasury Shares		17,000

Final Reconciling Entry   The final entry to reconcile the change in cash and to balance the work sheet is as follows:

(18)

Decrease in Cash	7,000	
Cash		7,000

The amount is the difference between the beginning of the year and the end of the year cash balance.

Once it has been determined that the differences between the beginning and ending balances per the work sheet columns have been accounted for, the reconciling transactions columns can be totalled, and they should balance. The statement of changes in financial position can be prepared entirely from the items and amounts that appear at the bottom of the work sheet under "Statement of Changes in Financial Position."

Satellite Manufacturing Limited
WORK SHEET FOR PREPARATION OF STATEMENT OF CHANGES IN FINANCIAL POSITION
For the Year Ended 1988

	Balance Dec. 31, 1987	Reconciling Items—1988 Debits		Credits		Balance Dec. 31, 1988
Debits						
Cash	$ 66,000			(18)	$ 7,000	$ 59,000
Accounts receivable (net)	51,000	(4)	$ 53,000			104,000
Inventories	341,000	(5)	152,000			493,000
Prepaid expenses	17,000			(6)	500	16,500
Investment (equity method)	15,000	(7)	3,500			18,500
Land	82,000	(8)	60,000	(9)	10,500	131,500
Equipment	142,000	(10)	53,000	(11)	8,000	187,000
Buildings	262,000					262,000
Goodwill	10,000			(14)	2,400	7,600
Treasury shares	—0—	(17)	17,000			17,000
Total debits	$986,000					$1,296,100

Credits

Accumulated depreciation—		(11)	2,500			
equipment	$ 31,000	(13)	11,000	(12)	11,500	$ 29,000
Accumulated depreciation—						
buildings	71,000			(14)	3,100	74,100
Accounts payable	131,000			(15)	1,000	132,000
Accrued liabilities	39,000			(15)	4,000	43,000
Income taxes payable	16,000	(15)	13,000			3,000
Notes payable (long-term)	–0–			(8)	60,000	60,000
Bonds payable	100,000					100,000
Premium on bonds payable	8,000	(15)	1,000			7,000
Deferred income taxes	6,000			(15)	3,000	9,000
Common shares	88,000			(16)	144,000	
				(2)	15,000	247,000
Retained earnings	496,000	(2)	15,000			
		(3)	6,000	(1)	117,000	592,000
Total credits	$986,000					$1,296,100

Statement of

Changes in Financial Position

Operating activities:					
Income before extraordinary item	(1)	109,000			
Increase in accounts receivable (net)			(4)	53,000	
Increase in inventories			(5)	152,000	
Decrease in prepaid expense	(6)	500			
Equity in earnings of Porter Co.			(7)	3,500	
Loss on sale of equipment	(11)	1,500			
Depr. expense—equipment	(12)	11,500			
Depr. expense—buildings	(14)	3,100			
Amortization of goodwill	(14)	2,400			
Increase in accounts payable	(15)	1,000			
Increase in accrued liabilities	(15)	4,000			
Deferred income taxes	(15)	3,000			
Decrease in income tax payable			(15)	13,000	
Amortization of bond premium			(15)	1,000	
Investing activities:					
Expropriation of land (gain)	(1)	8,000			
Expropriation of land (book value)	(9)	10,500			
Purchase of land through issuance of					
note payable			(8)	60,000	
Purchase of equipment			(10)	53,000	
Sale of equipment	(11)	4,000			
Major repairs of equipment			(13)	11,000	
Financing activities:					
Payment of cash dividend			(3)	6,000	
Issue of common shares	(16)	144,000			
Issuance of note payable to purchase					
land	(8)	60,000			
Purchase of treasury shares			(17)	17,000	
		$749,500		$756,500	
Decrease in cash	(18)	7,000			
Totals		$756,500		$756,500	

Preparation of Statement

Presented below is a formal statement of changes in financial position prepared from the data compiled in the lower portion of the work sheet. This is a cash basis statement presented in three primary sections: operating, financing, and investing.

Satellite Manufacturing Limited
STATEMENT OF CHANGES IN FINANCIAL POSITION
For the Year Ended December 31, 1988

Cash flows from operating activities:		
Income before extraordinary item		$109,000
Add (deduct) items not affecting cash		
Depreciation expense	$ 14,600	
Amortization of goodwill	2,400	
Amortization of bond premium	(1,000)	
Equity in earnings of Porter Co.	(3,500)	
Loss on sale of equipment	1,500	
Increase in deferred income taxes	3,000	
Increase in accounts receivable (net)	(53,000)	
Increase in inventories	(152,000)	
Decrease in prepaid expenses	500	
Increase in accounts payable	1,000	
Increase in accrued liabilities	4,000	
Decrease in income taxes payable	(13,000)	(195,500)
Net cash flow from operating activities		(86,500)
Cash flows from investing activities:		
Extraordinary item—Expropriation of land,		
including extraordinary gain of $8,000		
(net of $2,500 tax)	$ 18,500	
Purchase of land by issuance of note payable	(60,000)	
Purchase of equipment	(53,000)	
Sale of equipment	4,000	
Major repairs of equipment	(11,000)	
Net cash used by investing activities		(101,500)
Cash flows from financing activities:		
Payment of cash dividend	$ (6,000)	
Purchase of treasury shares	(17,000)	
Issue of note to purchase land	60,000	
Issue of common shares	144,000	
Net cash provided by financing activities		181,000
Net decrease in cash		$ (7,000)

USEFULNESS OF THE STATEMENT OF CHANGES IN FINANCIAL POSITION

The information in a statement of changes in financial position should help investors, creditors, and others to assess the following:

1. **The entity's ability to generate future cash flows**. A primary objective of financial reporting is to provide information that makes it possible to predict the amounts, timing, and uncertainty of future cash flows. By examining relationships between items such as net income and net cash flow from operating activities, or net cash flow from operating activities and increases or decreases in cash, predictions of the amount, timing, and uncertainty of future cash flows can be improved.

2. **The entity's ability to pay dividends and meet obligations**. Simply put, if a company does not have adequate cash, employees cannot be paid, debts settled, dividends paid, or equipment acquired. A statement of changes in financial position indicates how cash is used and its sources. Employers, creditors, shareholders, and customers should be particularly interested in this statement, because it alone shows the flows of cash in a business.

3. **The reasons for the difference between net income and net cash flow from operating activities**. The net income number is important, because it provides information on the success or failure of a business enterprise from one period to another. But some are

critical of the accrual basis net income because estimates must be made to arrive at it. As a result, the reliability of the number is often challenged. Such is not the case with cash. Thus, many readers of the financial statement want to know the reasons for the difference between net income and net cash flow from operating activities. Then they can assess for themselves the reliability of the income number.

4. **The cash and noncash investing and financing transactions during the period**. By examining a company's investing activities (purchase and sales of assets other than its products) and its financing transactions (borrowings and repayments of borrowings, investments by owners and distribution to owners), a financial statement reader can better understand why assets and liabilities increased or decreased during the period. For example, the following questions might be answered:

How did cash increase when there was a net loss for the period?
How were the proceeds of the bond issue used?
How was the expansion in the plant and equipment financed?
Why were dividends not increased?
How was the retirement of debt accomplished?
How much money was borrowed during the year?
Is cash flow greater or less than net income?

KEY POINTS

1. The statement of changes in financial position is designed to present information on the operating, financing, and investing activities of a business enterprise.

2. Currently, the CICA Handbook requires that the statement be presented using the cash and cash equivalents basis.

3. Under the cash basis, changes in the cash balances that have occurred during a period of time are summarized and grouped by major activities such as operating, financing, and investing.

4. Significant noncash transactions and other events that did not either provide or use cash but affected the firms capital and asset structure (such as exchanges of shares for assets or exchanges of debt securities for assets) are reported in the statement of changes in financial position.

5. Generally, a work sheet is used to compute and assemble the information for the statement. The work sheet has one column in which the opening balance sheet account balances are listed, a debit and a credit column for reconciling amounts, and a column for ending balance sheet account balances. The portion of the work sheet below the balance sheet accounts is used to summarize resources provided and resources used. The upper portion of the work sheet provides a means of checking to see if opening and ending balances have been properly reconciled while the lower portion provides the data to be used in the formal statement.

6. If the indirect approach is used, items included in the determination of income that did not either provide or use resources in the current year are added to or deducted from net income from operations to arrive at cash provided from operating activity.

7. Under the direct approach, cash revenues and cash expenses are computed directly so that cash provided from revenue earning activities and cash expended for operating purposes may be reported.

8. CICA Handbook, Section 1540, requires the three-section or activity format. The major sections of this format are: (1) operating activities, (2) investing activities, and (3) financing activities.

24A

THE T-ACCOUNT APPROACH TO PREPARATION OF THE STATEMENT OF CHANGES IN FINANCIAL POSITION

Many accountants find the work sheet approach to preparing a statement of changes in financial position time-consuming and cumbersome. In some cases, the detail of a work sheet is not needed and time does not permit for preparation of a work sheet. Therefore, the **T-account approach** to preparing a statement of changes in financial position has been devised. This procedure provides a quick and systematic method of accumulating the appropriate information to be presented in the formal statement of changes in financial position. The T-accounts used in this approach are not part of the general ledger or any other ledger; they are developed only for use in this process.

To illustrate the T-account approach, we will use the information of the Satellite Manufacturing Ltd. example presented in the comprehensive illustration.

T-ACCOUNT ILLUSTRATION

When the T-account approach is employed, the net change in cash for the period is computed by comparing the beginning and ending balances of the cash account. After the net change is computed, a T-account for cash is prepared and the net change in cash is entered at the top of this account on the left if cash increased, and on the right if it decreased (see illustration of T-account on page 1148). The cash

T-account is then structured into six separate classifications: **Increases**—(1) Operating, (2) Investing, and (3) Financing, on the left; and **Decreases**—(4) Operating, (5) Investing, and (6) Financing, on the right. T-accounts are then set up for all noncash items that have had activity during the period, with the net change entered at the top of each account. The objective of the T-account approach is to explain the net change in cash through the various changes that have occurred in the noncash accounts. The cash T-account acts as a summarizing account. Most of the changes in the noncash items are explained through the cash account. Significant financial transactions that did not affect cash are not recorded in the cash account but are entered in their respective noncash accounts for purposes of reconciling the net changes in these accounts.

To illustrate, a complete version of the T-account approach is presented on the following pages.

The following items caused the change in cash. (You should trace each entry to the accounts that are presented following the entries.)

1. Net income for the period, comprised of income before extraordinary item of $109,000 and an extraordinary gain of $8,000 (net of tax), increased retained earnings by $117,000. To avoid the detail of noncash revenues and expenses, we employ a short-cut by starting with income before extraordinary item and then in subsequent entries adjust it to reflect net cash flow from operating activities, exclusive of extraordinary item. In general journal form, the entry to report this increase and the extraordinary item would be:

Cash—Operations	109,000	
Cash—Investing	8,000	
Retained Earnings		117,000

2. The Retained Earnings account also discloses stock dividends of $15,000. Because this transaction does not affect cash and it is not reported in the statement of changes in financial position, the following entry would be made:

Retained Earnings	15,000	
Common Shares		15,000

3. Further analysis of the Retained Earnings account indicates that a cash dividend of $6,000 was declared during the current period. The entry to record the transaction would be:

Retained Earnings	6,000	
Cash—Financing		6,000

Note that the net change in the retained earnings balance of $96,000 is now reconciled. This reconciliation procedure is basic to the T-account approach because it ensures that all appropriate transactions have been considered.

4. The equity in the earnings of Porter Co. must be subtracted from income before extraordinary item because this income item does not increase cash. The journal entry to recognize this equity in the earnings of Porter Co. is as follows:

Investment in Stock of Porter Co.	3,500	
Cash—Operations		3,500

5. A note of $60,000 was issued to purchase land. Although this transaction did not affect cash, it is a significant financial transaction that should be reported. The transaction is therefore assumed both to have increased cash and to have decreased cash in order to report this amount in the cash account. The following entry would be made:

Land	60,000	
Cash—Investing		60,000
Cash—Financing	60,000	
Note Payable		60,000

An alternative to this approach is simply to adjust the Land and Note Payable account, noting that in a formal preparation of a statement of changes in financial position this transaction must be reported.

6. In addition, land with a book value of $10,500 was expropriated. The entry to record this transaction is as follows:

Cash—Investing	10,500	
Land		10,500

Note that adding the $10,500 book value of this expropriation to the $8,000 extraordinary gain net of $2,500 tax determined earlier provides total cash of $18,500 related to the expropriation.

7. Equipment and the related Accumulated Depreciation accounts indicate that a number of financial transactions affected these accounts. The first transaction is the purchase of equipment, which is recorded as follows:

Equipment	53,000	
Cash—Investing		53,000

8. In addition, equipment with a book value of $5,500 was sold at a loss of $1,500. The entry to record this transaction is as follows:

Cash—Investing	4,000	
Cash—Operations	1,500	
Accumulated Depreciation—Equipment	2,500	
Equipment		8,000

Note that the loss on the sale of the equipment has reduced the income before extraordinary item, but has not affected cash. The loss must therefore be added back to income before extraordinary item to report accurately net cash flow from operating activities.

9. Depreciation on the equipment of $11,500 must be recorded as follows:

Cash—Operations	11,500	
Accumulated Depreciation—Equipment		11,500

10. The major repair reduced cash, and so the necessary journal entry is as follows:

Accumulated Depreciation—Equipment	11,000	
Cash—Investing		11,000

The Equipment account and related Accumulated Depreciation account are now reconciled.

11. Analysis of the remaining **noncurrent accounts** indicates changes in Accumulated Depreciation—Buildings, Premium on Bonds Payable, and Deferred Income Taxes that must be accounted for in determining the net cash flow from operating activities. The compound entry to record these transactions is as follows:

Cash—Operations	3,100	
Cash—Operations	2,400	
Cash—Operations	3,000	
Premium on Bonds Payable	1,000	
Accumulated Depreciation—Buildings		3,100
Goodwill		2,400
Deferred Income Taxes		3,000
Cash—Operations		1,000

12. Analysis of the **current accounts** exclusive of cash indicates an increase in Accounts Receivable (net), an increase in Inventories, a decrease in Prepaid Expenses, an increase in Accounts Payable, an increase in Accrued Liabilities, and a decrease in Income Taxes Payable. All of these changes must be accounted for in determining the net cash flows from operating activities. The compound entry to record these changes is as follows:

Cash—Operations	500	
Cash—Operations	1,000	
Cash—Operations	4,000	
Accounts Receivable (net)	53,000	
Inventories	152,000	
Income Taxes Payable	13,000	
Prepaid Expenses		500
Accounts Payable		1,000
Accrued Liabilities		4,000
Cash—Operations		53,000
Cash—Operations		152,000
Cash—Operations		13,000

13. Examination of the Common Shares account indicates that in addition to the stock dividend (transaction 2), common shares were issued at $16 per share. The entry to record this transaction is as follows:

Cash—Financing	144,000	
Common Shares		144,000

14. The company also purchased treasury shares, which is recorded as follows:

Treasury Shares	17,000	
Cash—Financing		17,000

After the entries above are posted to the appropriate accounts, the cash account (shown below) is used as the basis for preparing the statement of changes in financial position. The debit side of the cash account contains the cash provided and the credit side contains the cash used. The difference between the two sides of the cash account should reconcile to the increase or decrease in cash. The completed statement of changes in financial position is presented on page 1143.

Cash

Increases			Decreases		
			Net change		7,000
Operating Activities:			**Operating Activities:**		
1.	Income before extraordinary item	109,000	4.	Equity in earnings of Porter Co.	3,500
8.	Loss on sale of equipment	1,500	11.	Bond premium amortization	1,000
9.	Depreciation expense	11,500	12.	Accounts receivable (net)	53,000
11.	Depreciation expense	3,100	12.	Inventories	152,000
11.	Goodwill amortization	2,400	12.	Income taxes payable	13,000
11.	Deferred income taxes	3,000			222,500
12.	Prepaid expenses	500			
12.	Accounts payable	1,000			
12.	Accrued liabilities	4,000			
		136,000			
Investing Activities:			**Investing Activities:**		
1.	Expropriation of land	8,000	5.	Purchase of land through	
6.	Expropriation of land	10,500		issuance of note	60,000
8.	Sale of equipment	4,000	7.	Purchase of equipment	53,000
		22,500	10.	Major repair of equipment	11,000
					124,000
Financing Activities:			**Financing Activities:**		
5.	Issue of note to purchase land	60,000	3.	Cash dividends paid	6,000
13.	Issue of common shares	144,000	14.	Purchase of treasury shares	17,000
		204,000			23,000

Accounts Receivable (net)

Net change	53,000		
12. Increase	53,000		

Inventories

Net change	152,000		
12. Increase	152,000		

Prepaid Expenses

		Net Change	500
		12. Decrease	500

Investment in Shares of Porter Co. (equity method)

Net change	3,500		
4. Equity in earnings	3,500		

Land

Net change	49,500		
5. Purchase of land	60,000	6. Expropriation	10,500

Equipment

Net change	45,000		
7. Purchase	53,000	8. Sale of equipment	8,000

Accumulated Depreciation—Equipment

Net change	2,000		
8. Sale of equipment	2,500	9. Depreciation expense	11,500
10. Major repair	11,000		

Accumulated Depreciation—Buildings

		Net change	3,100
		11. Depreciation expense	3,100

Goodwill

		Net change	2,400
		11. Amortization of goodwill	2,400

Accounts Payable

		Net change	1,000
		12. Increase	1,000

Accrued Liabilities

		Net Change	4,000
		12. Increase	4,000

Income Taxes Payable

Net change	13,000		
12. Decrease	13,000		

Notes Payable

		Net Change	60,000
		5. Issuance of note	60,000

Premium on Bonds Payable

Net change	1,000		
11. Bond premium amortization	1,000		

Deferred Income Taxes

		Net change	3,000
		11. Increase	3.000

Common Shares

		Net Change	159,000
		2. Stock dividend	15,000
		13. Issue of common shares	144,000

Retained Earnings

Net Change	96,000		
2. Stock dividend	15,000	1. Net income	117,000
3. Cash dividend	6,000		

Treasury Shares

Net change	17,000		
14. Purchase of treasury shares	17,000		

SUMMARY OF T-ACCOUNT APPROACH

Short-cut approaches are often used with the T-account approach. For example, the journal entries may not be prepared because the transactions are obvious. Also, only the noncash T-accounts that have a number of changes, such as Equipment, Accumulated Depreciation—Equipment, and Retained Earnings, need to be presented in T-account form. Other more obvious changes in noncash items can simply be determined by examining the comparative balance sheets and other related data. The T-account approach provides certain advantages over the work sheet method in that (1) a statement usually can be prepared much faster using the T-account method and (2) the use of the T-account method helps in understanding the relationship between cash and noncash items. Conversely, the work sheet on highly complex problems provides a more orderly and systematic approach to preparing the statement of changes in financial position. In addition, in practice the work sheet is used extensively to ensure that all items are properly accounted for.

The following steps are used in the T-account approach:

1. Determine the increase or decrease in cash for the year.
2. Post the increase or decrease to the cash T-account and establish six classifications within this account: Increases—Operating, Investing, and Financing, and Decreases—Operating, Investing, and Financing.
3. Determine the increase or decrease in each noncash account. Accounts that have no change can be ignored unless two transactions have occurred in the same account of the same amount, which is highly unlikely. A short-cut approach is to prepare T-accounts only for noncash accounts that have a number of transactions. All other changes can be immediately posted to the cash account after examining the additional information related to the changes in the balance sheet for a period.
4. Reconstruct entries in noncash accounts and post them to the noncash account affected.
5. Using the postings from the cash T-account, prepare the formal statement of changes in financial position.

QUESTIONS

1. Why has the statement of changes in financial position become a popular financial statement?
2. What is the purpose of the statement of changes in financial position? What information does it provide?
3. Differentiate between investing activities, financing activities, and operating activities.
4. What are the major sources of cash (inflows) in a statement of changes in financial position? What are the major uses (outflows) of cash?
5. Unlike the other major financial statements, the statement of changes in financial position is not prepared from the adjusted trial balance. From what sources does the information to prepare this statement come and what information does each source provide?
6. Why is it necessary to convert accrual based net income to a cash basis when preparing a statement of changes in financial position?
7. Differentiate between the direct approach and the indirect approach by discussing each method.
8. Prateep Company reported net income of $3.5 million in 1988. Depreciation for the year was $520,000, accounts receivable increased $350,000, and accounts payable increased $400,000. Compute net cash flow from operating activities using the indirect approach.

9. JoEllen King Inc. reported sales on an accrual basis of $100,000. If accounts receivable increased $30,000, and the allowance for doubtful accounts increased $12,000 after a write-off of $7,000, compute cash sales.

10. Your roommate is puzzled. During the last year, the company in which he/she is a shareholder reported a net loss of $654,127, and yet its cash increased $324,585 during the same period of time. Explain to your roommate how this situation could occur.

11. The board of directors of Dougman Corp. declared cash dividends of $260,000 during the current year. If dividends payable was $82,000 at the beginning of the year and $70,000 at the end of the year, how much cash was paid in dividends during the year?

12. Char-Lee Inc. reported sales of $2 million for 1988. Accounts receivable decreased $300,000 and accounts payable increased $200,000. Compute cash sales assuming that the receivable and payable transactions related to operations.

13. The net income for Kapco Company for 1988 was $320,000. During 1988, depreciation on plant assets was $90,000, amortization of goodwill was $40,000, and the company incurred a loss on sale of plant assets of $15,000. Compute net cash flow from operating activities.

14. Each of the following items must be considered in preparing a statement of changes in financial position for Jan Way Inc. for the year ended December 31, 1988. For each item state where it is to be shown in the statement, if at all.
    (a) Plant assets that had cost $20,000 6½ years before and were being depreciated on a straight-line basis over ten years with no estimated scrap value were sold for $6,000.
    (b) During the year 10,000 common shares were issued for $40 a share.
    (c) Uncollectible accounts receivable in the amount of $22,000 were written off against the Allowance for Doubtful Accounts.
    (d) The company sustained a net loss for the year of $50,000. Depreciation amounted to $22,000 and a gain of $7,000 was realized on the sale of equity securities (noncurrent) for $38,000 cash.

15. Classify the following items as (1) operating—add to net income, (2) operating —deduct from net income, (3) investing, (4) financing, or (5) significant noncash investing and financing activities.
    (a) Purchase of equipment.
    (b) Redemption of bonds.
    (c) Sale of building.
    (d) Depreciation.
    (e) Exchange of equipment for furniture.
    (f) Issuance of shares.
    (g) Amortization of intangible assets.
    (h) Purchase of treasury stock.
    (i) Issuance of bonds for land.
    (j) Payment of dividends.
    (k) Increase in interest receivable on notes receivable.
    (l) Pension expense exceeds amount funded.

16. Julie Countryman and Heather Remmers were discussing the presentation format of the statement of changes in financial position of Gary Grandgeorge Co. The amount of $200,000 appeared under the section headed "Investing Activities" as a purchase of land and a similar amount appeared under "Financing Activities" as an issuance of shares for land. Give three other examples of significant noncash transactions that would be reported in the statement of changes in financial position.

17. During 1988, John Clyde Smith Company redeemed $2,000,000 of bonds payable for $1,700,000 cash. Indicate how the transaction would be reported on a statement of changes in financial position, if at all.

18. What are some of the arguments in favour of using the indirect (reconciliation approach) as opposed to the direct approach for reporting a statement of changes in financial position?

19. Why is it desirable to use a work sheet when preparing a statement of changes in financial position? Is a work sheet required to prepare a statement of changes in financial position?

20. Of what use is the statement of changes in financial position?

CASES

C24-1 LaGrange Company is a young and growing producer of electronic measuring instruments and technical equipment. You have been retained by LaGrange to advise it in the preparation of a statement of changes in financial position using the indirect approach. For the fiscal year ended October 31, 1988, you have obtained the following information concerning certain events and transactions of LaGrange.

1. The amount of reported earnings for the fiscal year was $800,000, which included a deduction for an extraordinary loss of $83,000 (see item 5 below).
2. Depreciation expense of $350,000 was included in the earnings statement.
3. Uncollectible accounts receivable of $38,000 were written off against the allowance for doubtful accounts. Also, $45,000 of bad debts expense was included in determining income for the fiscal year, and the same amount was added to the allowance for doubtful accounts.
4. A gain of $5,200 was realized on the sale of a machine; it originally cost $75,000, of which $30,000 was undepreciated on the date of sale.
5. On April 1, 1988, lightning caused an uninsured inventory loss of $83,000 ($170,000 loss, less reduction in income taxes of $87,000). This extraordinary loss was included in determining income as indicated in 1 above.
6. On July 3, 1988, building and land were purchased for $600,000; LeGrange gave a payment $75,000 cash, $200,000 market value of its unissued common shares, and a $325,000 mortgage.
7. On August 3, 1988, $750,000 face value of LaGrange's 10% convertible debentures were converted into no-par value common shares. The bonds were originally issued at face value.

Instructions

Explain whether each of the seven numbered items above is a source or use of cash and explain how it should be disclosed in LaGrange's statement of changes in financial position for the fiscal year ended October 31, 1988. If any item is neither a source nor a use of cash, explain why it is not and indicate the disclosure, if any, that should be made of the item in LaGrange's statement of changes in financial position for the fiscal year ended October 31, 1988.

C24-2 June Yang and Fran Adams are examining the following statement of changes in financial position for Schewe's Clothing store's first year of operations.

Schewe's Clothing Store
STATEMENT OF CHANGES IN FINANCIAL POSITION
For the year ended January 31, 1988

Sources of cash	
From sales of merchandise	$350,000
From sale of share capital	440,000
From sale of investment	80,000
From depreciation	70,000
From issuance of note for truck	20,000
From interest on investments	8,000
Total sources of cash	968,000
Uses of cash	
For purchase of fixtures and equipment	340,000
For merchandise purchased for resale	250,000
For operating expenses (including depreciation)	160,000
For purchase of investment	85,000
For purchase of truck by issuance of note	20,000
For purchase of treasury stock	10,000
For interest on note	3,000
Total uses of cash	868,000
Net increase in cash	$100,000

June claims that Schewe's statement of changes in financial position is an excellent portrayal of a superb first year with cash increasing $100,000. Fran replies that it was not a superb year, that the year was an operating failure, that the statement was incorrectly presented, and that $100,000 is not the actual increase in cash.

Instructions

(a) With whom do you agree, June or Fran? Explain your position.

(b) Using data provided, prepare a statement of changes in financial position in proper form. The only noncash items in the income statement are depreciation and the loss from the sale of the investment.

C24-3 Each of the following items must be considered in preparing a statement of changes in financial position for Wisner Fashions Inc. for the year ended December 31, 1988.

1. Fixed assets that had cost $10,000 6½ years before and were being depreciated on a 10-year basis, with no estimated scrap value, were sold for $3,125.

2. During the year, goodwill of $10,000 was completely written off to expense.

3. During the year, 500 common shares were issued for $31 a share.

4. The company sustained a net loss for the year of $2,100. Depreciation amounted to $900 and patent amortization was $400.

5. An appropriation for contingencies in the amount of $80,000 was created by a charge against Retained Earnings.

6. Uncollectible accounts receivable in the amount of $2,000 were written off against the Allowance for Doubtful Accounts.

7. Investments that cost $12,000 when purchased four years earlier were sold for $11,000. The loss was considered ordinary.

8. Bonds payable with a par value of $24,000 on which there was an unamortized bond premium of $1,800 were redeemed at 102. The gain was credited to income.

Instructions

For each item, state where it is to be shown in the statement and then illustrate how you would present the necessary information, including the amount. Consider each item to be independent of the others. Assume that correct entries were made for all transactions as they took place.

C24-4 The following statement was prepared by Leitzen Corporation's accountant:

Leitzen Corporation
STATEMENT OF SOURCES AND APPLICATION OF CASH
For the Year Ended September 30, 1988

Sources of cash	
Net income	$ 72,000
Depreciation and depletion	61,000
Increase in long-term debt	189,000
Common shares issued under employee option plans	16,000
Changes in current receivables and inventories, less	
current liabilities (excluding current maturities of long-term debt)	14,000
	$352,000
Application of cash	
Cash dividends	$ 44,000
Expenditure for property, plant, and equipment	224,000
Investments and other uses	20,000
Change in cash	64,000
	$352,000

The following additional information relating to Leitzen Corporation is available for the year ended September 30, 1988:

1. The corporation received $16,000 in cash from its employee stock option plans, and wage and salary expense attributable to the option plans was an additional $22,000.

2.
Expenditures for property, plant, and equipment	$242,000
Proceeds from retirements of property, plant, and equipment	18,000
Net expenditures	$224,000

3. A stock dividend of 10,000 common shares was distributed to common shareholders on April 1, 1988, when the per-share market price was $7.

4. On July 4, 1988, when its market price was $6 per share, 16,000 Leitzen Corporation common shares were issued in exchange for 4,000 preferred shares.

5.
Depreciation expense	$58,000
Depletion expense	3,000
	$61,000

6.
Increase in long-term debt	$610,000
Retirement of debt	421,000
Net increase	$189,000

Instructions

(a) In general, what are the objectives of a statement of the type shown above for the Leitzen Corporation? Explain.

(b) Identify the weaknesses in the form or format of the Leitzen Corporation's statement of changes in financial position without reference to the additional information.

(c) For each of the six items of additional information for the statement of changes in financial position indicate the preferable treatment and explain why the suggested treatment is preferable.

(AICPA adapted)

EXERCISES

E24-1 Condensed financial data of Leslie Graham Company for 1987 and 1988 are presented below.

Leslie Graham Company
COMPARATIVE BALANCE SHEET DATA
As of December 31, 1987 and 1988

	1987	1988
Cash	$1,150	$1,800
Receivables	1,300	1,750
Inventory	1,900	1,600
Plant assets	1,700	1,900
Accumulated depreciation	(1,150)	(1,200)
Long-term investments	1,400	1,300
	$6,300	$7,150
Accounts payable	$900	$1,200
Accrued liabilities	300	200
Bonds payable	1,500	1,400
Capital shares	1,700	1,900
Retained earnings	1,900	2,450
	$6,300	$7,150

Leslie Graham Company
INCOME STATEMENT
For the Year Ended December 31, 1988

Sales		$6,900
Cost of goods sold		4,700
Gross margin		2,200
Operating expenses:		
Selling expense	$450	
Administrative expense	650	
Depreciation expense	50	1,150
Net income		1,050
Cash dividends		500
Income retained in business		$ 550

Additional information:
There were no gains or losses in any noncurrent transactions during 1988.

Instructions

(a) Prepare a statement of changes in financial position using the indirect approach.
(b) Prepare a statement of changes in financial position using the direct approach.

E24-2 Condensed financial data of Pockets Company for the years ended December 31, 1987, and December 31, 1988, are presented below.

Pockets Company
COMPARATIVE POSITION STATEMENT DATA
As of December 31, 1987 and 1988

	1987	1988
Cash	$ 38,400	$160,800
Receivables	49,000	123,200
Inventories	61,900	112,500
Investments	97,000	90,000
Plant assets	212,500	240,000
	$458,800	$726,500
Accounts payable	$ 67,300	$100,000
Mortgage payable	74,900	50,000
Accumulated depreciation	52,000	30,000
Common shares	131,100	175,000
Retained earnings	133,500	371,500
	$458,800	$726,500

Pockets Company
INCOME STATEMENT
For the Year Ended December 31, 1988

Sales	$440,000	
Interest and other revenue	20,000	$460,000
Less:		
Cost of goods sold	130,000	
Selling and administrative expenses	10,000	
Depreciation	42,000	
Income taxes	5,000	
Interest charges	3,000	
Loss on sale of plant assets	12,000	202,000
Net income		258,000
Cash dividends		20,000
Income retained in business		$238,000

Additional information:
New plant assets costing $105,000 were purchased during the year. Investments were sold at book value.

Instructions

(a) Prepare a statement of changes in financial position using the indirect approach.
(b) Prepare a statement of changes in financial position using the direct approach.

E24-3 Comparative adjusted trial balances for Mary Kanable Company are presented below.

Mary Kanable Company
ADJUSTED TRIAL BALANCE

	Dec. 31, 1987		Dec. 31, 1988	
	Dr.	Cr.	Dr.	Cr.
Cash	$ 5,400		$ 9,100	
Marketable securities	20,000		23,000	
Receivables (net)	60,000		75,400	
Inventories	64,000		65,400	
Delivery equipment	29,000		40,500	
Accumulated depreciation—delivery equipment		$ 17,000		$21,000
Machinery	14,500		16,000	
Accumulated depreciation—machinery		8,500		12,500
Building	55,000		55,000	
Accumulated depreciation—building		7,000		15,000
Land	15,000		15,000	
Accounts payable		47,500		43,000
Accrued expenses		8,000		9,500
Long-term notes payable		11,000		5,000
Bonds payable		50,000		50,000
Common shares		65,000		65,000
Retained earnings		38,000		48,900
Sales		294,900		351,500
Cost of goods sold	220,000		245,000	
Operating expenses	48,000		61,000	
Income taxes	16,000		16,000	
	$546,900	$546,900	$621,400	$621,400

Instructions

Using the information above, prepare a statement of changes in financial position (indirect approach).

E24-4 Don and Diana are equal partners in the Whitehorse Restaurant. Don withdraws from the partnership at the end of 1988, terminating the partnership. Below you are given comparative financial data and other pertinent information.

	Dec. 31, 1987	Dec. 31, 1988	Increase or (Decrease)
Cash	$ 5,700	$ 7,400	$1,700
Receivables	7,800	11,400	3,600
Allowance for doubtful accounts	(900)	(1,000)	(100)
Marketable securities	5,600	5,600	—
Prepaid expenses	1,300	1,100	(200)
Land	10,000	10,000	—
Building and equipment	31,600	35,600	4,000
Accumulated depreciation	(3,700)	(5,300)	(1,600)
	$57,400	$64,800	

Accounts payable	$ 3,000	$ 2,200	$ (800)
Notes payable (short-term)	1,700	1,000	(700)
Accrued expenses	1,500	1,800	300
Mortgage payable	21,500	20,000	(1,500)
Don, capital	17,400	24,600	7,200
Diana, capital	12,300	15,200	2,900
	$57,400	$64,800	

1. Equipment was purchased for $4,000 in 1988.
2. At the time of the termination, Don makes withdrawals totalling $2,600; Diana has withdrawn $5,400.

Instructions

Prepare a statement of changes in financial position (indirect approach) for the year 1988.

E24-5   Presented below are data taken from the records of Jill Hankin Company.

	December 31, 1987	December 31, 1988
Cash	$ 8,000	$ 15,000
Current assets other than cash	55,000	85,000
Long-term investments	58,000	10,000
Plant assets	215,000	366,000
	$336,000	$476,000
Accumulated depreciation	$ 40,000	$ 20,000
Current liabilities	22,000	35,000
Bonds payable	–0–	80,000
Share capital	254,000	254,000
Donated capital	–0–	31,000
Retained earnings	20,000	56,000
	$336,000	$476,000

1. Securities carried at a cost of $48,000 on December 31, 1987, were sold in 1988 for $39,000. The loss (not extraordinary) was incorrectly charged directly to Retained Earnings.
2. Plant assets that cost $50,000 and were 80% depreciated were sold during 1988 for $8,000. The loss (not extraordinary) was incorrectly charged directly to Retained Earnings.
3. Net income as reported on the income statement for the year was $57,000.
4. Dividends paid amounted to $10,000.
5. Depreciation charged for the year was $20,000.
6. Land was donated to Jill Hankins Company by the city. The land was worth $31,000. (Assume credit to Donated Capital is correct.)

Instructions

Prepare a statement of changes in financial position for the year 1988 (indirect method).

E24-6   Comparative balance sheets at December 31, 1987 and 1988, for Rick's Pottery are presented below.

	1987	1988
Cash	$ 48,000	$ 70,000
Receivables	66,000	60,000
Inventory	112,000	100,000

Prepaid expenses	8,000	9,000
Plant assets	240,000	312,000
Accumulated depreciation	(41,000)	(66,000)
Patents	40,000	30,000
	$473,000	$515,000
Accounts payable	$105,000	$ 85,000
Accrued liabilities	63,000	68,000
Mortgage payable	70,000	-0-
Preferred shares	-0-	125,000
Common shares	200,000	200,000
Retained earnings	35,000	37,000
	$473,000	$515,000

1. The only entries in the Retained Earnings account are for dividends paid in the amount of $20,000 and for the net income for the year.

2. The income statement statement for 1988 is as follows:

Sales	$124,000
Cost of sales	94,000
Gross profit	30,000
Operating expenses	8,000
Net income	$ 22,000

3. The only entry in the Accumulated Depreciation account is the depreciation expense for the period. Depreciation and patent amortization are included in cost of sales in the income statement.

Instructions

From the information above, prepare a statement of changes in financial position: (a) Use the indirect approach. (b) Use the direct approach.

E24-7 Chari Sorenson, Inc. had the following condensed balance sheet at the end of operations for 1987.

Chari Sorenson, Inc.
BALANCE SHEET
December 31, 1987

Cash	$ 8,500	Current liabilities	$ 15,000
Current assets other than cash	29,000	Long-term notes payable	25,500
Investments	20,000	Bonds payable	25,000
Plant assets (net)	67,500	Share capital	75,000
Land	40,000	Retained earnings	24,500
	$165,000		$165,000

During 1988 the following occurred:

1. A tract of land was purchased for $4,450.
2. Bonds payable in the amount of $6,000 were retired at par.
3. An additional $10,000 in share capital was issued.
4. Dividends totalling $9,375 were paid to shareholders.
5. Net income for 1988 was $35,250 after allowing depreciation of $11,250.
6. Land was purchased through the issuance of $22,500 in bonds.
7. Chari Sorenson, Inc. sold part of its investment portfolio for $12,875. This transaction resulted in a gain of $875 for the firm. The company often sells and buys securities of this nature.
8. Both current assets (other than cash) and current liabilities remained at the same amount.

Instructions

(a) Prepare a statement of changes in financial position for 1988.

(b) Prepare the condensed balance sheet for Chari Sorenson, Inc. as it would appear at December 31, 1988.

E24-8   The accounts below appear in the ledger of Linda Leise Company.

	Retained Earnings	Dr.	Cr.	Bal.
Jan. 1, 1988	Credit Balance			$42,000
Aug. 15	Dividends (Cash)	$18,000		24,000
Dec. 31	Net Income for 1988		$12,000	36,000

	Machinery	Dr.	Cr.	Bal.
Jan. 1, 1988	Debit Balance			$140,000
Aug. 3	Purchase of Machinery	$62,000		202,000
Sept. 10	Cost of Machinery Constructed	48,000		250,000
Nov. 15	Machinery Sold		$56,000	194,000

	Accumulated Depreciation—Machinery	Dr.	Cr.	Bal.
Jan. 1, 1988	Credit Balance			$84,000
Apr. 8	Extraordinary Repairs	$21,000		63,000
Nov. 15	Accum. Depreciation on Machinery Sold	25,200		37,800
Dec. 31	Depreciation for 1988		$16,800	54,600

Instructions

From the information given, prepare entries in journal form for all adjustments that should be made on a work sheet for a statement of changes in financial position. The loss on sale of equipment (Nov. 15) was $14,800.

E24-9

1. Convertible bonds payable of a par value of $250,000 were exchanged for unissued no-par value common shares. The market price of the bonds was par and the price of the common shares was $250,000.

2. The net income for the year was $60,000.

3. Depreciation charged on the building was $24,000.

4. Organization costs in the amount of $10,000 were written off during the year as a charge to expense.

5. Some old office equipment was traded in on the purchase of some dissimilar office equipment and the following entry was made:

Office Equipment	5,000	
Accumulated Depreciation—Office Equipment	3,000	
Office Equipment		4,000
Cash		3,400
Gain on Disposal of Plant Assets		600

The Gain on Disposal of Plant Assets was credited to current operations as ordinary income.

6. Dividends in the amount of $18,000 were declared. They are payable in January of next year.

7. The Appropriations for Bonded Indebtedness in the amount of $400,000 was returned to Retained Earnings during the year, because the bonds were retired during the year.

Instructions

Show by journal entries the adjustments that would be made on a work sheet for a statement of changes in financial position.

E24-10 Below is the comparative balance sheet for Charlie Doss Corporation.

	Dec. 31, 1987	Dec. 31, 1988
Cash	$ 20,000	$ 16,500
Short-term investments	20,000	25,000
Accounts receivable	45,000	43,000
Allowance for doubtful accounts	(2,000)	(1,800)
Prepaid expenses	2,500	4,200
Inventories	65,000	81,500
Land	50,000	50,000
Buildings	73,500	125,000
Accumulated depreciation—buildings	(23,000)	(30,000)
Equipment	47,000	53,000
Accumulated depreciation—equipment	(16,500)	(19,000)
Delivery equipment	39,000	39,000
Accumulated depreciation—delivery equipment	(20,500)	(22,000)
Patents	–0–	15,000
	$300,000	$379,400
Accounts payable	$ 16,000	$ 26,000
Short-term notes payable	6,000	4,000
Accrued payables	5,000	3,000
Mortgage payable	53,000	73,000
Bonds payable	62,500	50,000
Capital shares	106,000	150,000
Retained earnings	51,500	73,400
	$300,000	$379,400

Dividends in the amount of $10,000 were declared and paid in 1988.

Instructions

From this information, prepare a work sheet for a statement of changes in financial position. Make reasonable assumptions as appropriate.

E24-11 Presented below is information related to Vern Hasse, Inc. for the years 1987 and 1988 to aid in preparing a statement of changes in financial position.

Vern Hasse, Inc.
COMPARATIVE BALANCE SHEETS
As at December 31

Assets	1988	1987
Current assets:		
Cash	$ 128,000	$ 100,000
Marketable securities	160,000	–0–
Accounts receivable—net	415,000	320,000
Merchandise inventory	305,000	210,000
Prepaid expenses	50,000	25,000
	1,058,000	655,000
Property, plant, and equipment	749,000	440,000
Less accumulated depreciation	55,000	25,000
	694,000	415,000
	$1,752,000	$1,070,000

Equities

Current liabilities:

Accounts payable	$ 424,000	$ 340,000
Accrued expenses	70,000	65,000
Dividends payable	30,000	–0–
	524,000	405,000
Notes payable—due 1991	245,000	–0–
Shareholders' equity:		
Common shares	600,000	500,000
Retained earnings	383,000	165,000
	$1,752,000	$1,070,000

Vern Hasse, Inc.
INCOME STATEMENTS
For the Years Ended December 31, 1988 and 1987

	1988	1987
Net sales—including service charges	$2,840,000	$2,000,000
Cost of goods sold	1,950,000	1,600,000
Gross profit	890,000	400,000
Expenses (including income taxes)	500,000	260,000
Net income	$ 390,000	$ 140,000

Additional information available included the following:

All accounts receivable and accounts payable relate to trade merchandise. Cash discounts are not allowed to customers but a service charge is added to an account for late payment. Accounts payable are recorded net and always are paid to take all of the discount allowed. The Allowance for Doubtful Accounts at the end of 1988 was the same as at the end of 1987; no receivables were charged against the allowance during 1988.

The proceeds from the note payable were used to finance a new store building. Common shares were issued to provide additional working capital.

Instructions

Compute the following for the year 1988:
(a) Cash collected from accounts receivable, assuming that all sales are on account.
(b) Cash payments made on accounts payable to suppliers, assuming that all purchases of inventory are on account.
(c) Cash dividend payments.
(d) Cash receipts that were not provided by operations.
(e) Cash payments for assets that were not reflected in operations.

E24-12 Joseph McCormick Co. has recently decided to go public and has hired you as the independent CA. One statement that the enterprise is anxious to have prepared is a statement of changes in financial position. Financial statements of Joseph McCormick Co. for 1987 and 1988 are provided below.

Joseph McCormick Co.
COMPARATIVE BALANCE SHEETS
As at December 31

	1987		1988	
Cash		$ 13,000		$ 25,000
Accounts receivable		14,000		29,000
Inventory		35,000		26,000
Property, plant, and equipment	$78,000		$60,000	
Less accumulated depreciation	(24,000)	54,000	(20,000)	40,000
		$116,000		$120,000
Accounts payable		$23,000		$34,000
Short-term notes payable		30,000		25,000
Bonds payable		33,000		37,000
Common shares		14,000		6,000
Retained earnings		16,000		18,000
		$116,000		$120,000

Joseph McCormick Co.
INCOME STATEMENT
For the Year Ended December 31, 1988

Sales		$220,000
Cost of sales		180,000
Gross profit		40,000
Selling expenses	$18,000	
Administrative expenses	6,000	
		24,000
Income from operations		16,000
Interest expense		5,000
Income before taxes		11,000
Income taxes		2,000
Net income		$ 9,000

The following additional data were provided:

1. Dividends for the year 1988 were $3,500.
2. During the year equipment was sold for $8,500. This equipment cost $18,000 originally and had a book value of $12,000 at the time of sale. The loss on sale was incorrectly charged to retained earnings.
3. All depreciation expense is in the selling expense category.

Instructions

Prepare a statement of changes in financial position using (a) the indirect approach and (b) the direct approach. All sales and purchases are on account.

E24-13 Clarence Hankes Co. reported $145,000 of net income for 1988. The accountant, in preparing the statement of changes in financial position, noted several items that might affect cash flows from operating activities. These items are listed below:

1. During 1988, Hankes purchased 100 treasury shares at a cost of $20 per share. These shares were then resold at $25 per share.

2. During 1988, Hankes sold 100 shares of IBM common at $200 per share. The acquisition cost of these shares was $150 per share. This investment was shown on Hankes' December 31, 1987, balance sheet as a current asset at cost.

3. During 1988, Hankes changed from the straight-line method to the double-declining balance method of depreciation for its machinery. The debit to the Retained Earnings account was $13,500 net of tax.

4. During 1988, Hankes revised its estimate for bad debts. Before 1988, Hankes' bad debts expense was 1% of its net sales. In 1988, this percentage was increased to 2%. Net sales for 1988 were $500,000.

5. During 1988, Hankes issued 500 of its no-par common shares for a patent. The market value of the shares on the date of the transaction was $23 per share.

6. Depreciation expense for 1988 is $38,000.

7. Hankes Co. holds 40% of the Seabrook Company's common shares as a long-term investment. Seabrook Company reported $26,000 of net income for 1988.

8. Seabrook Company paid a total of $2,000 of cash dividends in 1988.

9. A comparison of Hankes' December 31, 1987, and December 31, 1988, balance sheets indicates that the credit balance in Deferred Income Taxes (classified as a long-term liability) decreased $4,000.

10. During 1988, Hankes declared a 10% stock dividend. One thousand no-par value common shares were distributed. The market price at date of issuance was $20 per share.

Instructions

Prepare a schedule that shows net cash flow from operating activities.

E24-14 Dawn Long Company has not yet prepared a formal statement of changes in financial position for the 1988 fiscal year. Comparative statements of financial position as of December 31, 1987 and 1988, and a statement of income and retained earnings for the year ended December 31, 1988, are presented below.

Dawn Long Company
STATEMENT OF INCOME AND RETAINED EARNINGS
For the Year Ended December 31, 1988
($000 Omitted)

Sales		$3,760
Expenses		
Cost of goods sold	$1,100	
Salaries and benefits	725	
Heat, light, and power	75	
Depreciation	80	
Property taxes	18	
Patent amortization	25	
Miscellaneous expense	10	
Interest	30	2,063
Income before income taxes		1,697
Income taxes		849
Net income		848
Retained earnings—Jan. 1, 1988		310
		1,158
Stock dividend declared and issued		600
Retained earnings—Dec. 31, 1988		$ 558

Dawn Long Company
COMPARATIVE STATEMENTS OF FINANCIAL POSITION
December 31
($000 omitted)

Assets	1987	1988	
Current assets			
Cash	$ 100	$ 383	233
Treasury bills	50	–0–	
Accounts receivable	500	740	(240)
Inventory	560	720	(160)
Total current assets	1,210	1,843	
Long-term assets			
Land	70	150	(80)
Buildings and equipment	600	940	(340)
Accumulated depreciation	(120)	(200)	80
Patents (less amortization)	130	105	25
Total long-term assets	680	995	
Total assets	$1,890	$2,838	
Liabilities and Shareholders' Equity			
Current liabilities			
Accounts payable	$340	$420	80
Taxes payable	20	40	20
Notes payable	320	320	
Total current liabilities	680	780	
Term notes payable—due 1993	200	200	
Total liabilities	880	980	
Shareholders' equity			
Common shares	700	1,300	
Retained earnings	310	558	
Total shareholders' equity	1,010	1,858	
Total liabilities and shareholders' equity	$1,890	$2,838	

Instructions

Prepare a statement of changes in financial position that reconciles the changes in cash balance. Use the direct approach. Changes in accounts receivable relate to sales and cost of sales. Taxes payable relates only to income taxes.

(CMA adapted)

PROBLEMS

P24-1 The manager of Curt Dittmer Limited has reviewed the annual financial statements for the year 1988 and is unable to determine from a reading of the balance sheet the reasons for the cash flows during the year. You are given the following comparative balance sheet information of Curt Dittmer Limited.

	Dec. 31/88	Dec. 31/87	Increase or (Decrease)
Land	$ 138,000	$ 218,000	$ (80,000)
Machinery	470,000	200,000	270,000
Tools	40,000	70,000	(30,000)
Bond investment	20,000	15,000	5,000
Inventories	172,000	207,000	(35,000)
Goodwill	–0–	14,000	(14,000)
Buildings	810,000	550,000	260,000

Accounts receivable	292,000	92,000	200,000
Notes receivable—trade	96,000	176,000	(80,000)
Cash in bank	–0–	8,000	(8,000)
Cash on hand	7,000	1,000	6,000
Unexpired insurance—machinery	700	1,400	(700)
Unamortized bond discount	2,000	2,500	(500)
	$2,047,700	$1,554,900	$ 492,800
Share capital	$ 900,000	$ 400,000	$ 500,000
Bonds payable	160,000	130,000	30,000
Accounts payable	63,500	38,800	24,700
Notes payable—trade	7,000	10,000	(3,000)
Accrued interest	9,000	6,000	3,000
Accrued taxes	4,000	3,000	1,000
Allowance for doubtful accounts	4,700	2,300	2,400
Accumulated depreciation	300,400	181,000	119,400
Retained earnings	599,100	783,800	(184,700)
	$2,047,700	$1,554,900	$ 492,800

You are advised that the following transactions took place during the year:

1. The income statement for the year 1988 was:

Sales (net)		$1,276,300
Operating charges:		
Material and supplies	$250,000	
Direct labour	210,000	
Manufacturing overhead	181,500	
Depreciation	158,900	
Selling expenses	295,000	
General expenses	230,000	
Interest expense (net)	15,000	
Unusual items:		
Write-off of goodwill	14,000	
Write-off of land	80,000	
Loss on machinery	6,600	1,441,000
Net loss		$ (164,700)

2. A 5% cash dividend was declared and paid on the outstanding shares at January 1, 1988.
3. There were no purchases or sales of tools. The cost of tools used is in depreciation.
4. Common shares were issued during the year at $90.
5. Old machinery that cost $16,100 was scrapped and written off the books. Accumulated depreciation on such equipment was $9,500.

Instructions

(a) Prepare a statement of changes in financial position. Use the indirect approach. All sales and purchases of inventory are made on account.

P24-2 The balance sheet of Red River Limited at December 31, 1987, is as follows:

Red River Limited
BALANCE SHEET
December 31, 1987

Cash	$ 189,000
Receivables	258,000
Inventories	174,000
Prepaid expenses	28,000
Total current assets	649,000

Investments (long-term)			102,000 (102)
Land		$45,000	
Buildings	$570,000		
Less accumulated depreciation	110,000	460,000	
Equipment	385,000		
Less accumulated depreciation	180,000	205,000	710,000
Patents			122,000
			$1,583,000
Accounts payable			$ 60,000
Notes payable			120,000
Taxes payable			188,000
Total current liabilities			368,000
Bonds payable			500,000
Preferred shares		$400,000	
Common shares		300,000	
Retained earnings		15,000	715,000
			$1,583,000

Red River Limited's management predicts the following transactions for the coming year:

Sales (accrual basis)	$4,840,000
Payments for salaries, purchases, interest, taxes, etc. (cash basis)	4,520,000
Decrease in prepaid expenses	5,500
Increase in receivables	110,000
Increase in inventories	35,000
Depreciation:	
Buildings	55,000
Equipment	80,000
Patent amortization	11,000
Increase in accounts payable	22,000
Increase in taxes payable	90,000
Reduction in bonds payable	500,000
Sales of investments (all those held Dec. 31/87)	110,000
Issuance of common shares	100,000

Instructions

(a) Prepare a balance sheet as it will appear December 31, 1988, if all the anticipated transactions work out as expected.

(b) Prepare a statement of changes in financial position for 1988, assuming that the expected 1988 transactions are all completed. Use the indirect approach.

(c) Compute net cash flow from operating activities, using the direct approach.

P24-3 The following financial data were furnished to you by Digby Limited:

1. A six-months note payable for $55,000 was issued toward the purchase of new equipment.
2. The long-term note payable requires the payment of $20,000 per year plus interest until paid.
3. Treasury shares were sold for $4,500 more than cost.
4. All dividends were paid by cash.
5. All purchases and sales were on account.
6. The sinking fund will be used to retire the long-term bonds.
7. Equipment with an original cost of $54,000 was sold for $32,000.

8. Selling and General Expenses includes the following expenses:

Expired Insurance	$ 4,000
Building depreciation	10,000
Equipment depreciation	15,500
Bad debts expense	10,000
Interest expense	18,000

Digby Limited
COMPARATIVE TRIAL BALANCES
At Beginning and End of Fiscal Year Ended October 31, 1988

	October 31, 1988	Increase	Decrease	November 1, 1987
Cash	$ 333,500	$218,300		$115,200
Accounts receivable	146,000	46,000		100,000
Inventories	291,000		$ 9,000	300,000
Unexpired insurance	7,000	3,000		4,000
Long-term investments at cost	10,000	30,000		40,000
Sinking fund	90,000	10,000		80,000
Land and building	195,000			195,000
Equipment	215,000	95,000		120,000
Discount on bonds payable	8,400		2,400	10,800
Treasury stock at cost	5,100		4,900	10,000
Cost of goods sold	420,000			
Selling and general expense	153,000			
Income tax	31,000			
Loss on sale of equipment	12,000			
Capital gains tax	3,000			
Total debits	$1,920,000			$975,000
Allowance for doubtful accounts	$ 10,000	$ 5,000		$ 5,000
Accumulated depreciation— building	30,000	10,000		20,000
Accumulated depreciation— equipment	33,000	5,500		27,500
Accounts payable	50,000		$35,000	85,000
Notes payable—current	75,000	55,000		20,000
Accrued expenses payable	20,000	5,000		15,000
Taxes payable	33,000	23,000		10,000
Unearned revenue	3,000		12,000	15,000
Note payable—long-term	40,000		20,000	60,000
Bonds payable—long-term	250,000			250,000
Share capital—common	401,000	125,500		275,500
Appropriation for sinking fund	90,000	10,000		80,000
Unappropriated retained earnings	90,000		22,000	112,000
Sales	753,000			
Gain on sale of investments (ordinary)	42,000			
Total credits	$1,920,000			$975,000

Instructions

(a) Prepare schedules computing

    1. Collections of accounts receivable.

    2. Payments of accounts payable.

(b) Prepare a statement of changes in financial position for Digby Limited. Use the indirect approach.

(c)   Prepare a cash flow from operating activities section using the direct approach.

(AICPA adapted)

P24-4   Presented below are the balance sheets of Farrell Limited as of December 31, 1988 and 1987, and the statement of income and retained earnings for the year ended December 31, 1988.

Farrell Limited
COMPARATIVE BALANCE SHEETS
As at December 31

	Dec. 31/88	Dec. 31/87	Increase or (Decrease)
Assets			
Cash	$ 275,000	$ 180,000	$ 95,000
Accounts receivable, net	295,000	305,000	(10,000)
Inventories	549,000	431,000	118,000
Investment in Hall, Ltd. at equity	73,000	60,000	13,000
Land	350,000	200,000	150,000
Plant and equipment	624,000	606,000	18,000
Less accumulated depreciation	(139,000)	(107,000)	(32,000)
Goodwill	16,000	20,000	(4,000)
Total assets	$2,043,000	$1,695,000	$348,000
Liabilities and Shareholders' Equity			
Accounts payable and accrued expenses	$ 604,000	$ 563,000	$ 41,000
Notes payable, long-term	150,000	–0–	150,000
Bonds payable	160,000	210,000	(50,000)
Deferred income taxes	41,000	30,000	11,000
Share capital	656,000	575,000	81,000
Retained earnings	432,000	334,000	98,000
Treasury shares, at cost	–0–	(17,000)	(17,000)
Total liabilities and shareholders' equity	$2,043,000	$1,695,000	$348,000

Farrell Limited
STATEMENT OF INCOME AND RETAINED EARNINGS
For the Year Ended December 31, 1988

Net sales		$1,950,000
Operating expenses:		
Cost of sales	$1,150,000	
Selling and administrative expenses	505,000	
Depreciation	53,000	1,708,000
Operating income		242,000
Other (income) expenses:		
Interest expense	$ 15,000	
Equity in net income of Hall, Ltd.	(13,000)	
Loss on sale of equipment	5,000	
Amortization of goodwill	4,000	11,000
Income before income taxes		231,000
Income taxes:		
Current	$ 79,000	
Deferred	11,000	90,000
Net income		141,000
Retained earnings, January 1, 1988		334,000
		475,000
Cash dividends, paid August 14, 1988		43,000
Retained earnings, January 1, 1988		$432,000

Additional information:

1. On January 2, 1988, Farrell sold equipment costing $45,000, with a book value of $24,000, for $19,000 cash.
2. On April 1, 1988, Farrell issued 1,000 common shares for $23,000 cash.
3. On May 15, 1988, Farrell sold all its treasury shares for $25,000 cash.
4. On June 1, 1988, individuals holding $50,000 face value of Farrell's bonds exercised their conversion privilege. Each of the 50 bonds was converted into 40 common shares.
5. On July 4, 1988, Farrell purchased equipment for $63,000 cash.
6. On December 31, 1988, land with a fair value of $150,000 was purchased through the issuance of a long-term note in the amount of $150,000. The note bears interest at the rate of 15% and is due on December 31, 1993.
7. Deferred income taxes represent timing differences relating to the use of straight-line depreciation for financial statement reporting and CCA for income tax reporting.

Instructions

Prepare a statement of changes in financial position for Farrell Limited, using the indirect approach.

P24-5   The comparative balance sheets for Lester F. Ltd. show the following information:

	December 31, 1988	December 31, 1987
Cash	$ 38,500	$13,000
Accounts receivable	12,250	10,000
Inventory	12,000	9,000
Investments	–0–	3,000
Building	–0–	29,750
Equipment	40,000	20,000
Patent	5,000	6,250
Totals	$107,750	$91,000
Allowance for doubtful accounts	$ 3,000	$ 4,500
Accumulated depreciation on equipment	2,000	4,500
Accumulated depreciation on building	–0–	6,000
Accounts payable	5,000	3,000
Dividends payable	–0–	6,000
Notes payable, short-term (nontrade)	3,000	4,000
Long-term notes payable	31,000	25,000
Common shares	43,000	33,000
Retained earnings	20,750	5,000
	$107,750	$91,000

Additional data related to 1988 are as follows:

1. Equipment that had cost $11,000 and was 30% depreciated at time of disposal was sold for $2,500 (net of tax).
2. $10,000 of the long-term note payable was paid by issuing common shares.
3. The only cash dividends paid were $6,000.
4. On January 1, 1988, the building was completely destroyed by a flood. Insurance proceeds on the building were $29,750 (net of tax).
5. Investments (long-term) were sold at $3,700 (net of tax) above their cost. The company has made similar sales and investments in the past.
6. Cash of $15,000 was paid for the acquisition of equipment.
7. A long-term note for $16,000 was issued for the acquisition of equipment.

Instructions

Prepare a statement of changes in financial position. Flood damage is unusual and infrequent in that part of the country.

(AICPA adapted)

P24-6 Reed McKnight Limited has prepared its financial statements for the year ended December 31, 1988, and for the three months ended March 31, 1989. You have been asked to prepare a statement of changes in financial position for the three months ended March 31, 1989. The company's balance sheet data at December 31, 1988, and March 31, 1989, and its income statement data for the three months ended March 31, 1989, follow. You have previously satisfied yourself as to the correctness of the amounts presented.

	Balance Sheet	
	December 31, 1988	March 31, 1989
Cash	$ 24,400	$103,320
Marketable investments	17,600	7,300
Accounts receivable, net	24,620	63,142
Inventory	29,590	88,004
Total current assets	96,210	261,766
Land	41,300	28,700
Building	250,000	250,000
Equipment	–0–	42,000
Accumulated depreciation	(15,000)	(17,750)
Investment in 30%-owned company	60,920	82,480
Other assets	24,300	24,300
Total	$457,730	$671,496
Accounts payable	$ 21,220	$ 16,000
Income taxes payable	–0–	95,037
Total current liabilities	21,220	111,037
Other liabilities	186,000	186,000
Bonds payable	45,000	115,000
Discount on bonds payable	(2,400)	(2,000)
Deferred income taxes	5,610	846
Preferred shares	30,000	–0–
Common shares	80,000	110,000
Retained earnings	92,300	150,613
Total	$457,730	$671,496

	Income Statement Data for the Three Months Ended March 31, 1989
Sales	$352,071
Gain on sale of marketable investments	3,400
Equity in earnings of 30%-owned company	21,560
Gain on expropriation of land (extraordinary)	20,400
	397,431
Cost of sales	138,407
General and administrative expenses	22,010
Depreciation	2,750
Interest expense	1,150
Income taxes	99,801
	264,118
Net income	$133,313

Your discussion with the company's controller and a review of the financial records have revealed the following information:

1. On January 8, 1989, the company sold marketable securities for cash.
2. The company's preferred shares are convertible into common at a rate of one share of preferred for two shares of common.
3. On January 17, 1989, three acres of land were expropriated. An award of $33,000 in cash was received on March 22, 1989. Purchase of additional land as a replacement is not contemplated by the company. (Treated as a capital gain for tax purposes.)

4. On March 25, 1989, the company purchased equipment for cash.
5. On March 29, 1989, bonds payable were issued by the company at par for cash.
6. The company's tax rate is 45% for regular income and 20% for capital gains.
7. The company declared and paid a dividend of $75,000 during the first quarter.

Instructions

Prepare in good form a statement of changes in financial position for Reed McKnight Limited for the three months ended March 31, 1989 (indirect approach).

(AICPA adapted)

P24-7 You have completed the field work in connection with your audit of Webster Limited for the year ended December 31, 1988. The following schedule shows the balance sheet accounts at the beginning and end of the year.

	Dec. 31, 1988	Dec. 31, 1987	Increase or (Decrease)
Cash	$ 267,900	$ 298,000	$ (30,100)
Accounts receivable	741,700	610,000	131,700
Inventory	691,700	660,000	146,424
Prepaid expenses	12,000	8,000	4,000
Investment in subsidiary	110,500	—	110,500
Cash surrender value of life insurance	2,304	1,800	504
Machinery	187,000	190,000	(3,000)
Buildings	535,200	407,900	127,300
Land	52,500	52,500	—
Patents	69,000	64,000	5,000
Goodwill	40,000	50,000	(10,000)
Bond discount and expense	4,502	—	4,502
	$2,522,030	$2,035,200	$486,830
Accrued taxes payable	$ 95,250	$ 79,600	$ 15,650
Accounts payable	299,280	280,000	19,280
Dividends payable	70,000	—	70,000
Bonds payable—8%	125,000	—	125,000
Bonds payable—12%	—	100,000	(100,000)
Allowance for doubtful accounts	35,300	40,000	(4,700)
Accumulated depreciation—building	424,000	400,000	24,000
Accumulated depreciation—machinery	173,000	130,000	43,000
Premium on bonds payable	—	2,400	(2,400)
Capital shares—no par	1,280,200	1,453,200	(173,000)
Appropriation for plant expansion	10,000	—	10,000
Retained earnings—unappropriated	10,000	(450,000)	460,000
	$2,522,030	$2,035,200	$486,830

STATEMENT OF RETAINED EARNINGS

Jan. 1, 1988	Balance (deficit)	$(450,000)
Mar. 31, 1988	Net income for first quarter of 1988	25,000
Apr. 1, 1988	Transfer from common shares	425,000
	Balance	–0–
Dec. 31, 1988	Net income for last three quarters of 1988	90,000
	Dividend declared—payable January 20, 1989	(70,000)
	Appropriation for plant expansion	(10,000)
	Balance	$ 10,000

Your working papers contain the following information:

1. On April 1, 1988, the existing deficit was written off against share capital created by reducing the stated value of the no-par stock.

2. On November 1, 1988, 29,600 no-par shares were sold for $252,000.

3. A patent was purchased for $15,000.

4. During the year, machinery that had a cost basis of $16,400 and on which there was accumulated depreciation of $5,200 was sold for $7,000. No other plant assets were sold during the year.

5. The 12%, 20-year bonds were dated and issued on January 2, 1976. Interest was payable on June 30 and December 31. They were sold originally at 106. These bonds were retired at 101 (net of tax) plus accrued interest on March 31, 1988.

6. The 8%, 40-year bonds were dated January 1, 1988, and were sold on March 31 at 98 plus accrued interest. Interest is payable semiannually on June 30 and December 31. Expense of issuance was $839.

7. Webster Limited acquired 70% control in the Subsidiary Company on January 2, 1988, for $100,000. The income statement of the Subsidiary Company for 1988 shows a net income of $15,000.

8. Extraordinary repairs to buildings of $7,200 were charged to Accumulated Depreciation—Building.

Instructions

From the information above prepare a statement of changes in financial position. A work sheet is not necessary, but the principal computations should be supported by schedules or skeleton ledger accounts.